GREAT
POWERS

ALSO BY THOMAS P. M. BARNETT

Romanian and East German Policies in the Third World
The Pentagon's New Map
Blueprint for Action

GREAT
POWERS

America and the World
After Bush

———◆———

THOMAS P. M. BARNETT

G. P. PUTNAM'S SONS

New York

PUTNAM

G. P. PUTNAM'S SONS
Publishers Since 1838
Published by the Penguin Group
Penguin Group (USA) Inc., 375 Hudson Street, New York, New York 10014, USA • Penguin Group
(Canada), 90 Eglinton Avenue East, Suite 700, Toronto, Ontario M4P 2Y3, Canada
(a division of Pearson Canada Inc.) • Penguin Books Ltd, 80 Strand, London WC2R 0RL,
England • Penguin Ireland, 25 St Stephen's Green, Dublin 2, Ireland (a division of Penguin Books Ltd) •
Penguin Group (Australia), 250 Camberwell Road, Camberwell, Victoria 3124, Australia
(a division of Pearson Australia Group Pty Ltd) • Penguin Books India Pvt Ltd,
11 Community Centre, Panchsheel Park, New Delhi–110 017, India • Penguin Group (NZ),
67 Apollo Drive, Rosedale, North Shore 0632, New Zealand (a division of
Pearson New Zealand Ltd) • Penguin Books (South Africa) (Pty) Ltd, 24 Sturdee Avenue,
Rosebank, Johannesburg 2196, South Africa

Penguin Books Ltd, Registered Offices: 80 Strand, London WC2R 0RL, England

Library of Congress Cataloging-in-Publication Data

Barnett, Thomas P. M.
Great powers : America and the world after Bush / Thomas P. M. Barnett.
p.   cm.
Includes bibliographical references and index.
ISBN 978-0-399-15537-6
1. United States—Foreign relations—21st century. 2. United States—Foreign relations—2001– .
3. World politics—1989– . 4. United States—Military policy. 5. Great powers. 6. Strategy.
7. Progressivism (United States politics). 8. United States—Foreign relations—Philosophy.
9. Bush, George W. (George Walker), 1946– —Political and social views.
10. Cheney, Richard B.—Political and social views. I. Title.
E895.B38   2009   2008046360
973.93—dc22

Printed in the United States of America
1   3   5   7   9   10   8   6   4   2

BOOK DESIGN BY AMANDA DEWEY

A lonely sail is flashing white
Amidst the blue mist of the sea!
What does it seek in foreign lands?
What did it leave behind at home?

Waves heave, wind whistles,
The mast, it bends and creaks . . .
Alas, it seeks not happiness
Nor happiness does it escape!

Below, a current azure bright,
Above, a golden ray of sun . . .
Rebellious, it seeks out a storm
As if in storms it could find peace!

—MIKHAIL LERMONTOV, "The Sail" (1832)

Contents

———◄••►———

THE SHAPE OF THINGS TO COME

L ately, we are being told that this is no longer our world. America is in decline, and the rest of the world has caught up to us. Wars may be won, but the peace belongs to others—we just have to get used to it.

And it is true that in the tumultuous times since 9/11 sent our world spinning that much faster, America has searched for a grand strategic vision to animate our spirit and guide our actions, and it has failed. When we should have inspired hope, we have stoked fears, and where we should have built bridges, we have erected walls.

So I won't tell you the critics are wrong—just that their own vision is too limited. This *is still* America's world, and if we have the will to step up to the plate, we can make things right—right now.

America's journey back to where we once belonged begins with one simple realization: This is a world of our making. Neither accident nor providence, this "flat world" is fundamentally our design—a template of networks spreading, economies integrating, and states uniting. It's so damn competitive merely because that's our natural habitat; we don't know how to make it any other way.

In this world we find no strangers, just younger versions of ourselves, who are prone to all the same sins and manias we once suffered, even as they teach us magnificent new ways to improve our lives and secure our tightly shared future. We must neither fear nor dismiss them, but encourage their pursuit of happiness, and in doing so, we'll find their main goal is one very familiar to us—the attainment of a middle-class existence.

This looming achievement will put the planet under great duress in coming decades, much as it once did these United States. For this path to remain sustainable, compromises must be made and great technologies found. Some may see only billions of mouths to be fed, but in reality it is billions of minds to be harnessed. The one resource we will never deplete is our collective imagination.

But imagination requires confidence, which both spreads and dissipates with the velocity of a virus. Here America plays a special historical role, not as the only great power—because there are so many great powers at work in this complex world—but as the power with the greatest opportunity either to extend or to sabotage globalization's stunning advance around the planet.

We are modern globalization's source code—its DNA. As the world's oldest and most successful multinational economic and political union, we remain the planet's most communicable ideology—its most potent insurgency. Those thirteen colonies may have begun—quite implausibly— as the world's original anti-imperialist league, but our international liberal trade order now encompasses the vast majority of the planet's population.

If we own up to our past, we can command our future. We can realign ourselves immediately to a world transforming. Some will see great compromise on this path, but it is really great consistency. America's grand experiment has always balanced the needs of the many against the needs of the few—or the one. Our main challenge today—indeed, our main opportunity—is not those superempowered *few* seeking to do us harm but those unprecedented *many* seeking to do us one better.

Yes, we have displayed the temerity to bring the mountain to Mohammed, extending our American System–cum–globalization to the most traditional civilizations still thinly connected to its networks, and we have triggered great friction with the power of that force. But in obsessing over that friction, we have lost all perspective on the forces we have created— the great powers unleashed.

The terrorist attacks of 9/11 challenged America to redefine the international security system. It was a challenge that the Bush-Cheney administration took up with a vengeance, sensing in that moment a chance to reposition both the presidency and the United States in terms of leadership—even primacy. In this bold quest, the White House's sins of omission and commission were many. Recounting the most grievous ones (Chapter 1, "The Seven Deadly Sins of Bush-Cheney") is essential to America's successful reengagement with a world left more unnerved by our government's counterterrorism strategy than it was ever perturbed by actual terrorists. But our recovery doesn't stop there. Fences need mending and relationships require repair. We'll cover that gamut in Chapter 2, "A Twelve-Step Recovery Program for American Grand Strategy."

Before we can go on to explore the handful of major but necessary realignments that lie ahead, a bit of history is in order—specifically, American history. Citizens of this great country need to better understand its seminal role in constructing our current world, an environment that quite frankly too many of us today find frighteningly alien, when it is—pure and simple—the result of a conscious grand strategy pursued from the earliest days of our republic right through Bush's decision to invade Iraq. And so, in Chapter 3, we'll speak of great men and great powers and how each shaped the American trajectory and its impact on world history.

Then we come to the hard part: recognizing where and how America lost its way in the years since 9/11. Since we're talking about a world transforming in a dual sense, both from an American-engineered globalization process (ongoing) and Bush-Cheney's decision to launch a "global war" (we'll see where that takes America next), we need to approach this complex issue from a variety of storytelling angles—*Rashomon* style. So in Chapters 4 through 8, we'll explore what I have come to realize are the five essential realignments to be made in America's grand strategy going forward. We'll start with economics, then expand into diplomacy and security, before branching out further into global networks and all the larger global equations (e.g., our planet's increasingly fragile environment, heightened spirituality and religious identity, rising immigration rates) that must likewise inform America's strategic realignment following Bush.*

---

*See also the short glossary of terms at the back of the book.

The next few years will constitute the first true test of globalization. As our globalized system continues processing its worst financial crisis ever, President Barack Obama encounters an international order suffering more deep-seated strain than at any time since the Great Depression. If there was any remaining doubt that the world's great powers either all swim or all sink together in this interconnected global economy, then this recent contagion has erased it. Globalization is no longer a national choice but a global condition, and at this seminal moment in history it demands from its creator renewed—and renewing—leadership. President Obama's opportunity to—as he has so often put it—"turn the page" could not be greater, for history rarely offers such made-to-order turning points.

The United States isn't coming to a bad end but a good beginning—our American System successfully projected upon the world. Our Rome wasn't built in a day but constructed over many decades of struggle, our governing rules subject to constant revision and improvement. "These truths" may have seemed "self-evident" from the start, but self-actualized they were not. That the same is now true for this globalization-of-our-making should not cause us despair. We have been down this path before, taming both a wilderness and the market forces we later unleashed upon its settled lands. We are simply blessed today by a global economy whose expansion has already surpassed all past hopes and dreams for a connected, superempowered world. So many frontiers, so little time.

Let us begin this journey of integration, not with a vague sense of foreboding but with a firm grasp of the possibilities. America has done a world of good to get humanity to the point where wars are disappearing and networks are proliferating. Where we need to take it next is well within our grasp. As long as we can remember what got us here, trust me, we'll recognize the shape of things to come.

One

———◼️◆◼️———

THE SEVEN DEADLY SINS
OF BUSH-CHENEY

It is tempting to write off the entire Bush-Cheney administration as one long unilateral deviation from the emerging global norm of multi-lateral cooperation, perhaps one even so great as to create a counter-norm by which rising great powers go their own way in response. But this view simultaneously gives the administration too little credit and too much blame.

Clearly, 9/11 exposed America's vulnerabilities in this network age and thus triggered a mad rush of new rules to fill in those gaps. For steering this effort, Bush-Cheney deserve some real credit. Their many new rules said, in effect, "Going forward, this is the new minimum security standard for remaining connected to the global economy—meet it or else!" As the world's sole superpower and primary defender of our international liberal trade order, the United States needed to put forth that standard, if only to immediately restore some confidence to the international system. Did Bush-Cheney overreach in many of their proposed new rules? You bet. But in our system, we expect the executive branch to overdo it in response to crisis and the judiciary to trim back those excesses slowly over time. As for the international overreach, well, that's pretty much the subject of this book; suffice it to say that in a "flat world," great-power balancing can come in many forms, with only the most un-imaginative among us expecting it to appear solely as a military buildup.

Having triggered this global counterreaction, we find that our natural instinct now is to return sheepishly to the bosom of the Old Core West, believing that step will restore the fabled alliance and make it once again powerful enough to both continue this long war against violent extrem-ism and meet the rising challenge of Eastern autocracies (read, Russia and China). This would be a double mistake, for Donald Rumsfeld's much-vilified notion of a "new" and "old" Europe contained an essential truth: Those states that most recently joined our international liberal trade or-der are logically more willing to defend it. They're also far more likely to be less democratic, however, given their historical trajectory, than the demographically older and more mature market economies of the West. So when Bush-Cheney made democratization a key pillar of their long-war approach, it effectively put America at odds with many of the New Core great powers (again, Russia and China) that would otherwise natu-rally be drawn to our military cause.

Thus it makes little sense to toss out Bush-Cheney's "baby" (the long war) with the "bathwater" (the premature fixation on democratization), for the former connects us logically with today's new great powers (China, Russia, India) while the latter binds us rather restrictively to last century's quorum of aging, democratic great powers (Western Europe, Industrial-ized Asia). So credit Bush-Cheney on their strategic instincts while con-demning their execution, but do not, on that basis, suddenly abandon our historic role as globalization's primary defender. It may be wrong to de-scribe this long struggle as a "global war," but there remains a global peace (the international liberal trade order) worth preserving.

While some experts believe America should start from scratch in re-casting—or merely accepting—some new global order, presumably one that pits "good guys" against "bad" or recognizes the onset of competing "empires," we need to recognize how the choices we've made over the past eight years shifted the global landscape in ways that simply cannot be reversed with a new American president or even new American poli-cies. Our unilateral "bender" forced a number of rising great powers to rise even faster, accelerating their natural trajectory out of the fear that an

America unchallenged was an America unhinged. Our improved behavior in the coming months and years will not erase their rise. Indeed, it will probably accelerate it, further narrowing our window for strategic rapprochement (rising powers are not, as a rule, great bargainers).

So like it or not, the Bush-Cheney era has forged a lasting international legacy that cannot be reversed even as it must be redirected. We have inadvertently raised the price of cooperation from those new great powers upon which our future grand strategy must ultimately depend. Bush-Cheney did not kill the Western alliance, but it did leave America with little choice now but to seek new alliance with the rising great powers of our age. The alternative is to retain all our old Cold War enemies (e.g., Russia, China) in addition to all our new post-9/11 foes—an unsustainable pathway.

The Bush-Cheney administration came into power seeking to realign the strategic relationships among the great powers: whipping NATO *into shape;* putting rising China, India, and Russia *in their place;* and reasserting American leadership. The irony, of course, is that the now infamous neocons achieved the exact opposite across the board. Russia's pounding of Georgia in the summer of 2008 gave us a glimpse of that unwelcome future; exercising its own perceived right for unilateral military action following 9/11, America's modeled behavior inevitably spawns the worst sort of imitation. The chickens have indeed come home to roost.

BUT FIRST, THE VIRTUES WORTH CITING

As many historians have already buried these would-be Caesars, let me now take a moment to praise them before casting seven stones with great deliberation.

A key attribute of America's sole military superpower status is that by maintaining our conventional Leviathan, we've so raised the "barrier to entry" into the market of great-power war that even having nuclear weapons doesn't really qualify a state anymore. Americans would do well to remember what a huge gift to humanity that force represents. We were told by international affairs "realists" at the Cold War's end that America would not be allowed to continue owning the world's largest gun, that other great powers would necessarily balance us symmetrically by creating one of their own. This has not happened and isn't close to happening anywhere, not even with "rising China," whose military buildup specifically targets *our* ability to target *their* ability to target *Taiwan's* ability to defend itself.

Say that fast five times in a row!

My point is this: The continued de facto worldwide moratorium on preparation for straight-up, great-power-on-great-power war is a monumentally positive influence on human history. This is why it is so crucial that we shut down the remaining Sino–American scenarios for potentially direct confrontations (ditto for Russia), because as long as both sides allow their militaries to be shaped by such myopic scenarios, precious resources will be wasted that could be put to better use elsewhere in a complementary fashion.

The Bush administration's two terms overlapped extensively with the almost eight-year reign of Taipei's provocatively nationalistic Democratic Progressive Party government of President Chen Shui-bian. To mince no words, the Bush-Cheney team handled the entire situation with great restraint and wisdom. The same can largely be said about handling China's "rise" in general, including refusing to go off the deep end in response to various missteps and gaffes by Beijing (e.g., the satellite shoot-down test, the occasional spy scandal, refusing U.S. Navy ships safe harbor in a storm, the Tibet/Olympic torch protests). Instead, what we got from a Bush administration that came into power clearly itching for confrontation with China (remember the E-P3 plane incident in April 2001) was a calm, steady hand at the wheel of our bilateral relations, best exemplified by Henry Paulson's stint as secretary of treasury, Robert Zoellick's tenure as deputy secretary of state, the successive commands of admirals William Fallon and Timothy Keating at Pacific Command, and Assistant Secretary of State Chris Hill's supremely patient efforts at "cat herding" the six-party talks on North Korea.

The lack of a serious U.S.–China confrontation in the years since 9/11 is the most important dog that did not bark during the Bush-Cheney administration. In the grand sweep of history, this is arguably George W. Bush's greatest legacy: the encouragement of China to become a legitimate "stakeholder" in global security—Zoellick's term. This sort of effort at grooming a great power for a greater role in international affairs is a careful balancing act, and the Bush team sounded most of the right notes, from reassuring nervous allies in Asia, to avoiding the temptation of trade retaliation while simultaneously pressuring Beijing for more economic liberalization, to drawing China into the dynamics of great-power negotiation over compelling regional issues like the nuclear programs in North Korea and Iran. We can always complain that Bush-Cheney didn't do more to solidify what was the most important bilateral relationship of the twenty-first century, but we cannot fault them for any lasting mistakes, and that alone is quite impressive. Indeed, history will be likely to judge this success as greater than the Bush administration's failures in Iraq.

To a lesser degree, the same can be said of Bush-Cheney's handling of Vladimir Putin's consolidation of power in Russia and that country's re-emergence as a player to be reckoned with in international affairs. Yes, many lament Moscow's slide toward authoritarianism, decrying the "loss" of democracy that never really existed in the first place, but the key thing to remember in the rise of the so-called "security guys" (*siloviki*) is that it has eliminated Western—and Eastern—fears of Russia's imminent collapse and all the security burdens such an event could have foisted upon outside powers. Plus, any careful reading of Russian history will tell you that Moscow's periodic depressive phases can—and should—last only so long, so a subsequent manic recovery was preordained. But just as important, it was both inevitable and good that Putin's crowd arrested Russia's long and pitiful downward spiral as a failed great power, because Moscow's resurgence forces everybody to bring something closer to their "A" game when we butt heads over Eastern Europe, the Balkans, the Caucasus, and Central Asia. Real power vacuums are almost never adequately or intelligently filled, so better to let whatever power shifts must come do so at a gradual pace, allowing the targeted parties the time and confidence to play all ambitious external powers off one another. The strategic danger here arises when small states like Georgia (which started the conflict, mind you) are allowed to unilaterally declare war between Russia and the West, but here even we must acknowledge Bush-Cheney's sensible restraint. Without it, we'd face a plethora of small-state nationalist leaders "auditioning" for the historic role of Archduke Ferdinand—unwitting trigger of World War I. That's a casting call better skipped.

While Bush-Cheney achieved only modest results in global trade policy, locking in several important bilateral free-trade agreements, they also steered the nation through plenty of rough waters without ever succumbing to congressional or popular pressures for trade protectionism. Moreover, the Bush White House made a good fight of trying to reduce America's disastrously unfair agricultural subsidies as part of the World Trade Organization's Doha Development Round negotiations, a stance that looks increasingly ridiculous—in addition to immoral—with global agricultural prices rising so high. If we factor in Bush's dramatic increase of funding for global HIV prevention, as well as his creation of the innovative Millennium Challenge Corporation to encourage developing economies toward foreign direct investment-threshold status, then it's fair to say that, outside of its failed reconstruction efforts in Afghanistan and Iraq, this administration has displayed real strategic imagination regarding development issues. In this regard, I would also consider Bush-Cheney's long-standing opposition to the Kyoto Treaty on global warming to have had a beneficial effect. How so? It delayed its effective ratification until such time as the world came to realize the sheer folly of excluding rising China and India from its ranks of the constrained.

Finally, I still admire George W. Bush's display of audacity and hope in launching his Big Bang strategy upon the Persian Gulf. There's no question in my mind that, no matter the weak rationales offered (or the slick sales job), Saddam Hussein was a horrific dictator whose time had come. That Bush-Cheney were able to pin that tail on the 9/11 donkey didn't bother me in the least, for democracies such as our own always have to make it personal before we can launch a war of choice. That Iraq became a *cause célèbre* for the region's radical jihadists likewise caused me no regret, because no matter what we did following 9/11, al Qaeda would have located some justifying cause somewhere in our actions. So if a center of gravity was to be had, better it be located over there than over here, and better that it involved our professional warriors instead of our untrained civilians. Most shocking perhaps, even the cynical realist in me has to admit that while an Iraq postwar done right would have had a revolutionary effect on the region, an Iraq postwar done wrong has had much the same effect—namely, making it impossible for the region to ever go back to what it once was. By locking America into real, long-term ownership of strategic security in the Gulf, Bush-Cheney transformed our dedication to maintaining an open door to that region's energy into a commitment to bodyguard globalization's ongoing transformation of those traditional societies.

To some, that historical process will always smack of "globalization at the barrel of a gun," but to me, the genuine realist recognizes the fact that whenever globalization creeps in, it is always the most ambitious and most talented that step forward to cut their own deals (like the Kurds in Iraq), triggering social tumult and ethnic divisions and even political fragmentation as a result. As I will argue later on, globalization will remap the Gap (my term for globalization's poorly integrated regions), forcing new political configurations that repair the many wrong divisions left behind by Europe's colonial cartographers. This wave of disintegrating integration is beyond anyone's control at this point, for it is fueled by the demands for a better life of 3 billion–plus new capitalists around our planet—arguably the greatest collective power the world will endure across this century. Simply put, these once-and-future consumers will not be denied, only placated. So what George W. Bush's Big Bang amounted to was an attempt, however unconscious, to step in front of that historical tsunami and ride it toward lasting political change for the better. In the end, I believe history will vindicate Bush's audacity in this regard, however poor his follow-up execution proved to be. As Fareed Zakaria notes in his book *The Post-American World*, what is stunning to anyone visiting the Middle East today is *not* how much Iraq has destabilized the region but how stable and thriving the region is *despite* Iraq's violence.

Bush-Cheney also deserve plenty of credit for leaving Iraq far more stable at the end of their second term compared with where it stood in 2005–6. The call on the surge wasn't easy but needed to be made. Harder still was sticking with that tough choice during the initial ramp-up in U.S. casualties. While the surge was years late in coming and wasn't accompanied by a similar diplomatic surge (as called for by the Iraq Study Group), it did finally reduce the overall violence, meaning Bush-Cheney's strategic patience—always a question mark for U.S. administrations—clearly paid off.

History will inevitably record that it was better for America to have made this strategic commitment than any other great power, and better for us to force this fight with the radical Salafi jihadists *now* before some eventual success on their part fostered a mad dash among economically vulnerable external great powers to salvage the situation. Needing to be "cruel to be kind, in the right measure" is an occupational hazard of owning the world's largest gun. Bush-Cheney understood that, even if their many cardinal sins condemned their immediate efforts in this long war against violent extremists.

NOW FOR THE SINS

Lust, Leading to the Quest for Primacy

The Bush administration's allegedly secret plan for world domination was nothing more than a 1992 Pentagon policy white paper produced by then Undersecretary of Defense for Policy Paul Wolfowitz. In this document, known as the Defense Planning Guidance, or DPG, Wolfowitz and his aide, Lewis Libby, issued a rather full-throated policy version of the "reconstitution" pillar already in vogue in force-structure planning circles ("force structure" referring to the mix of troops and hardware in the force). The reconstitution argument stated that the U.S. military must retain sufficient industrial base capacity (e.g., infrastructure and factories capable of generating large, Cold War–style platforms such as long-range bombers, aircraft carriers, tanks), along with a reasonably—and gradually— downsized existing force (a process known informally as the "Powell downward glidepath," for then Chairman of the Joint Chiefs of Staff Colin Powell), to hedge against the possible resurgence of a post–Soviet Russian threat. Wolfowitz's articulated grand strategy, immediately dubbed the Wolfowitz Doctrine, argued for a long-term lock-in against any possible emergent superpower-like military threat, to include the use of preemptive war and unilateralism when required.

At the time, I can tell you, few in the national security community took the secret planning guidance to be anything more than a Cold Warrior's fantasy of making permanent what Charles Krauthammer had described as America's "unipolar moment" of the early 1990s. If anything, the conventional wisdom stuck to the realists' track of assuming a balancing function was inevitable, and since Japan's "rising sun" served as that era's favorite bogeyman inside the community (sad, I know), the DPG's focus on military balancing struck many as painfully unimaginative in its assumption that the only counter to America's dominance would be symmetrically mounted by future adversaries—in other words, *they* would build a military force like ours and confront us primarily on that basis. In truth, most farsighted defense analysts found the notion of maintaining America's geopolitical primacy through military domination rather orthogonal to the real tasks at hand: managing a messy world, which at that time was experiencing a historic tide of civil strife and ethnic violence, stemming largely from the Soviet bloc's collapse. In sum, Wolfowitz's vision struck us as oddly detached from global affairs, even mildly isolationist.

But the primacy argument did fit well with what became the Powell Doctrine of limiting America's involvement in messy, long-term interventions. In effect, it offered the "then" corollary to the Powell Doctrine's "if" assertion: *If* we avoided Vietnam-like quagmires, *then* we'd be better able to keep our powder dry and our technology high for the looming near-peer competitor to come. When Wolfowitz and Libby returned to power with the Bush-Cheney administration in 2001, the preferred near-peer target of the Wolfowitz Doctrine was clearly China. But after 9/11 forced a strategic redirect toward Southwest Asia, Wolfowitz's previously voiced concerns (going back to his "Team B" days as a critic of détente in the mid-seventies) about a great power targeting the Persian Gulf for domination found fresh impetus in the administration's declaration of a "global war on terror." When Bush-Cheney proposed a policy of preemptive war as part of the mix, for all practical purposes declaring Iraq the next front in a sequential conflict, it appeared to many observers at the time—both inside (I was working in the Office of the Secretary of Defense) and outside of government—that the Wolfowitz Doctrine had met its historic moment.

Once revealed in its apparent ambition in the 2002–3 run-up to the Iraq invasion, the Wolfowitz-cum-Bush Doctrine, when linked to the administration's early tendency toward treaty breaking and go-it-alone-ism in international bodies, raised fears, both at home and abroad, that Bush-Cheney were exploiting the long war against violent extremism to further an agenda of America's global military hegemony. The Bush White House did plenty to exacerbate that concern when, in late 2001, it announced that it would withdraw the United States from the Anti-Ballistic Missile Treaty concluded with the Soviet Union in 1972, the *first time ever* that America had disavowed a major arms agreement. While claiming this was necessary to deal with mounting missile threats from regional rogues like Iran and North Korea, many arms experts considered the need for ballistic missile defense against such powers to be a poor excuse for withdrawing from the treaty. Why? Deterring such attack from smaller powers is seen as a relatively straightforward affair, and if the fear is that such rogues will transfer nuclear technology to terrorist groups, then the notion of terrorists delivering such an attack using medium-range or long-range missiles seems far-fetched. A better route would be to smuggle such a device into the United States for later detonation—perhaps inside one of the many bales of marijuana that so regularly traverse our less-than-secure borders.

The Bush administration's 2006 decision to push for the construction of missile defense sites in Eastern Europe (a deal later secured immediately following Russia's August 2008 invasion of Georgia), allegedly to protect the region from Iran's missiles, only confirmed more suspicions among the missile defense program's many vociferous critics that Bush-Cheney were indeed seeking a clear-cut strategic advantage not merely against regional rogues but against potential great-power competitors like Russia, which has consistently and vehemently contested missile defense, and China, which has long complained over a similar Bush-Cheney joint military program with Japan to protect that nation—allegedly—from North Korean missiles alone. In effect, both Moscow and Beijing suspect the Bush administration is trying to erect close-in strategic missile defense capabilities against their own nuclear arsenals, raising the unholy specter of America trying to eliminate its vulnerability not just to terrorist strikes but to the very logic of mutually assured destruction itself, thus calling into question the entire stability of nuclear deterrence as a strategic bulwark against great-power war. It is this kind of behavior that got us Russia threatening to target our missile defense sites and China staging a showy shoot-down of its own satellite—clear signaling that neither state will let America permanently tilt the correlation of strategic forces in its favor. Can we achieve such a permanent tilt in this manner? Not really. But quite frankly, that only makes our behavior seem all the more provocative—as in, What else do the Americans have up their sleeves?

Here's how we tie this sin back to failures in America's grand strategy since 9/11: In its continued if fanciful lust for geopolitical primacy, Bush-Cheney had created an untenable long-term burden. Not merely content to add our new enemies in this long war against violent extremism, Bush-Cheney chose to keep our old Cold War targets (Russia, China) on our strategic radar screen, not only denying us effective partnership with these rising powers but also encouraging their strategies of obstructionism. Oddly enough, after all this strategic disingenuousness, the Bush administration was confounded by Russia's and China's reluctance to crack down hard on either Iran or North Korea regarding their nuclear programs!

To remain "fit," in the parlance of American strategist Colonel John Boyd, our nation's grand strategy needs to attract more allies than it repulses. Bush-Cheney's none-too-subtle lust for primacy effectively sabotaged that fundamental goal by stating to the world that America wants to have its cake (the long war) and eat it too (global primacy). That approach simply won't fly in the age of globalization: America can't take on both its friction (a terror-based global insurgency) and its force (rising great powers). For if we do, we'll lose the one thing that truly allows us to play military Leviathan on behalf of globalization's Functioning Core: the ability to access regional crises with our forces without having that act alone constitute an additional crisis. Think about that for a moment, because it's an amazing writ that America should not trash in some quixotic bid to impede—or worse, *repeat*—history.

Anger, Leading to the Demonization of Enemies
America was naturally in an angry mood after 9/11, and the do-whatever-it-takes-to-protect-us atmosphere that prevailed during those days fed into the Bush administration's own take-no-prisoners-and-offer-no-

compromises style of ruling from the Republican base. This internalized anger ("They hate us, so why not hate them back?") saps our virtue in ways almost too numerous to count.

First, it forces us to focus on bad outcomes to be prevented rather than good ones to be promoted, because in our demonizing of enemies we set the bar on good outcomes far too high. Now, it's not only that democracy must prevail (and fast, mister!) but that *secular* democracy must prevail, otherwise we're offering our enemies at best a partial victory in any vaguely Islamist government we let come to power and at worst a political back door for future radicalization. We presume that *they* must be adapted to our form of government and not our government adapted to *their* ways! In my mind, America should be dedicated to the goal of encouraging secular democracy around the world, but committed to forcing its appearance nowhere. Democracy is a dish best served cold.

And when we obsess over the friction (political radicalization), we tend to underestimate, as well as make too little effort to facilitate, globalization's larger forces (e.g., the Middle East's growing financial connectivity with the global economy), preferring to economically isolate our enemies rather than let others—obviously less trustworthy than ourselves for wanting trade and investment connectivity in the first place—step into that void, generating potential political leverage down the road. So if Iran is a member of the "axis of evil," then any economic connectivity with Iran sought by Russia, India, and China is also inherently evil—no matter what their trade requirements may be (like India and China having their energy demand double in the next generation). What does that get us downstream? A demonized Iran with its finger on the bomb and the only leverage we possess is secondhand, through actors we've long chided for such connectivity in the first place. In short, we need to place more faith in markets and realize that there are many possible paths to political pluralism (especially in a Middle Eastern regime where political leaders are actually voted out of office on a regular basis).

The demonization of enemies lends itself to the hyping of victories, like toppling Saddam's regime while letting the first few months of the postwar reconstruction pass unnoticed in the celebration, or our subsequent fixation on Saddam's capture and trial while the insurgency blossomed into a full-fledged civil war. It also leads us down the path of emotional investment in our enemies' propaganda, allowing them to drive our responses to their latest "outrage." It encourages such outrages because our enemies justifiably feel empowered by them, like al-Zarqawi's many atrocities in Iraq or Ahmadinejad's calculated inflammatory rhetoric. Cede these "demons" enough of your anger and they'll get to time your missile strikes at *their* convenience while you play the part of Pavlov's jerk. And when we match such fiery rhetoric? Well, that gets you statements like "dead or alive" and "axis of evil," and those declarations often come back to haunt you when the time for deal-making arrives—as it always does.

Globalization is all about connectivity, and connectivity comes as a result of deals made—not broken. When Bush-Cheney indulged our demonizing tendencies (doesn't America always go to war against evil?), we at once gave them frightening writ to walk away from past deals that might limit our ability to battle evil (like the ABM Treaty) and to turn down whatever new offers came down the pike from the evildoers themselves (like Iran's early offers to help us against both the Taliban and Saddam, its two worst regional enemies at the time). Over time, that attitude not only limits our potential pool of allies but raises the price for co-opting current foes as well. Demonization also encourages our general intransigence against socializing any one problem, because in seeking to spread the pain we must inevitably deal with actors we consider evil, like Iran on the question of postwar Iraq. Thus demonization denies our ability to regionalize what must be regionalized and globalize what must be globalized, because when you take on evil, you simply don't want to risk your enemy escaping through the deal-making of others. Extend that more broadly and you can see why, although Bush often liked to compare himself to Harry Truman, he made no attempts to match that president's record for establishing new international organizations in response to a dramatically changed security environment and the prospect of persistent conflict with a global foe.

The most mindless form of demonization across the Bush-Cheney years was the White House's tendency to conflate radical Shia entities with radical Sunni ones, as if distinguishing between the two had no tacti-

cal value. The hubris on that one was simply too monumental to calculate, but alas, several of Bush's neocons (most notably, Wolfowitz and
Undersecretary of Defense for Policy Douglas Feith) had, in their youth,
so internalized the historical lessons of Germany's Nazi period that Shia
Iran and Sunni al Qaeda were casually lumped together in the same de-
monic stew of "Islamofascism." The nonnegotiability of such charges was
arguably the prime reason why Bush-Cheney never yielded to the many
calls for some sort of regional security dialogue on Iraq, preferring the bilateral, shuttle-style diplomacy that kept America's talking points on the
evening news but relegated our secretaries of state to playing a manipulative version of "telephone" as they hopped from capital to capital. Yes, this
process kept us in control, but it also kept us tied down in a diplomatic
quagmire of our own making.

Bush-Cheney's demonization of our enemies also yielded the bitter
fruit of intense anti-Americanism not merely throughout the Middle East
but to a frightening degree throughout the world. In the summer of 2007
I traveled to Australia to speak at a regional meeting of the World Economic Forum populated primarily by senior officials of the Australian
government. Figuring I couldn't find, even at this late date, a more conge-
nial audience for my message of how to fix America's institutional approaches to the long war, I nonetheless ran into more anti-American
sentiment there than I have subsequently met, several times, in the Middle East! What that told me was this: It's one thing to disappoint those
whom you've often disappointed, but quite another to disappoint your
closest friends.

But we did worse than disappoint our closest friends; we tainted them
with our own shame through the atrocities that we, in our confident righ-
teousness, committed against the demons of our naming. By giving in to
the demands of so many pundits and strategists that we "see our enemies
for who they are," the Bush administration created the Manichaean atmosphere that encouraged the torture of prisoners in facilities like Abu
Ghraib, thus turbocharging the region's already profound instinct to assume that America's "evil" knows no bounds and thus deserves no boundaries in reply. This is where indulging our anger creates deadly friction for
our troops. In *Fiasco: The American Military Adventure in Iraq*, Thomas
Ricks's masterful account of America's difficult occupation of Iraq, there

are two quotes from U.S. military personnel that sum up this danger. The first comes from a young Marine who, upon seeing the first news descriptions of the scandal, complained to his general that "some assholes have just lost the war for us." James Mattis, that Marine general, would state a year later that "when you lose the moral high ground, you lose it all."

Greed, Leading to the Concentration of War Powers

The Bush administration's connections with the post-Watergate, post-Vietnam administration of Gerald Ford were many, but the two most important ones were Vice President Dick Cheney and Secretary of Defense Donald Rumsfeld, both of whom served in that White House as chief of staff, with Rumsfeld later running the Pentagon for the first time. As Charlie Savage notes in his 2008 book *Takeover: The Return of the Imperial Presidency and the Subversion of American Democracy*, their timing was "terrible," for they had reached the pinnacle of executive power "just as those powers had come under fierce assault." In subsequent years, Cheney would describe the Ford administration as a "low point" of presidential power, and once he had his chance to correct what he characterized as the "unwise compromises" that had weakened the presidency, he set about in 2001 to reverse this longtime "erosion of the powers and the ability of the president of the United States to do his job." What ensued was an unprecedented power grab by the White House, under the excuse that America is not just a nation at war but a nation at war for its very survival.

Here's where we begin to see the interplay of these deadly sins. The lust for primacy requires a strong United States helmed by a supremely empowered president able to forgo reliance on allies unwilling to go all the way. Such a concentration of power is only possible under conditions of war, and not just any war, but one of survival, meaning our enemies can be cast as the most extreme forms of evil. Once these dynamics are set in motion, the president's greed for power should be encouraged to the greatest extent possible, taking advantage of the nation's unleashed anger, for who knows when such conditions will once again arise in a long war against violent extremists? Cast in such a light, none of these acts are perceived by their instigators as cardinal sins but rather as cardinal virtues blessed by historical circumstance: *We are doing what's right and what's good at the only moment when such deeds are permissible.* Little wonder this administration remained in constant political campaign mode throughout its first term.

Of course, all revolutions are justified in this manner by men who perceive their historical vision to be clearer than that of all others in their time. This is how America was born and, on regular occasion, this is how America is renewed. But the greater danger is equally clear. In the pursuit of a critical mass of authority to render great change, these wielders of great power often lose their ability to listen to the criticism of the masses. Their focus on the *one* danger blinds them to all others—again, especially when the justification is national survival. For once that mantra is invoked, all discipline goes out the window and excess becomes the order of the day. Worse, those who argue for such a free hand in the short run, ostensibly to preserve it over the long run, are often forced to extend the sense of emergency *ad infinitum* in a vain attempt to codify its use for those times when emergencies are not easily declared. Since such writ is typically retracted during normal times, those who wish to preserve it inevitably turn to secrecy—that killer of transparency. And once that happens, the vicious cycle is set.

Secrets beget secrets, leaving less and less of the leader's grand strategy transparent to the public, which is increasingly left to its own imagination to fill in the blanks. Over time, after being force-fed slogans that do not inform and explanations whose "truthiness" is subject to easy parody, the public becomes divided between believers and unbelievers, with rationality both despised and in short supply. There is no surer sign of this regression than when "infotainers"—especially comedians—conduct the most gratifying public discourse on current events, for when Jon Stewart and Stephen Colbert are among the most trusted names in broadcast news, America has lost its moral center of gravity and conspiracy theorists rank equally with serious grand strategists in the collective public mind. The result? Even what little grand strategy is actually articulated by the secretive leadership is instinctively dismissed by half the population, making it dead on arrival. As for the rest of the world? Forget about it!

Where this aggressive approach has damaged America's global leadership most has been in the area of international law—specifically, the Bush administration's treatment of suspected terrorists. Here again, Bush-Cheney tried to have their cake (insisting America is at war) and eat it too (declaring our enemies to be "unlawful combatants" and therefore undeserving of international legal protections historically afforded prisoners of war). Meanwhile, the condemnations have continuously rolled in from all corners of the globe regarding a host of questionable American practices either pioneered or resurrected by the Bush administration: the suspension of habeas corpus; the holding of ghost detainees who disappeared into the paperwork; the ordering of "extraordinary renditions," by which suspects are deposited with allies who have long histories of torture; and the extraction of confessions by methods right out of the Spanish Inquisition (as well as U.S. military counterinsurgency operations in the Philippines more than a century ago). Thus, in far too many ways, the Bush administration purposefully kept America mired in its post-9/11, Jack Bauer phase of busting heads and torturing bad guys to get the truth. Until we move beyond that us-against-the-world mindset, we'll never achieve the us-plus-the-world cooperation—much less competency—to effectively police our common enemies. Our anger never quite sated means that our grand strategy's higher aspirations will never be fully stated by leaders more interested in preserving their power than in defeating our enemies.

Pride, Leading to Avoidable Postwar Failures

Already in print are numerous highly praised journalistic accounts of how the Bush administration systematically thwarted attempts throughout the U.S. government to plan adequately for the postwar occupation of Iraq, even going so far as to ignore—and in a few key instances squelch—the plethora of warnings from across the national security establishment of what would inevitably follow (e.g., looting, insurgency, ethnic cleansing, the attraction of jihadists from abroad, soft partition). In his 2008 political memoir, the much-vilified Douglas Feith makes a convincing case for a more nuanced diagnosis: The Bush administration's interagency process, by law managed through the National Security Council in the person of the president's national security adviser (then Condoleezza Rice), was dysfunctional in the extreme, largely because of Rice's personal management style. Having learned the role as a prized protégée of national security adviser Brent Scowcroft during the earlier presidency of George H. W. Bush, Rice had a strong preference for preventing State–Defense policy clashes from reaching the president, and this was the main problem (Scowcroft had managed the NSC in this manner out of deference to the senior Bush's distaste for such open conflict during the Reagan administration). By purposefully crafting policy compromises that combined clearly contradictory stances, Rice often presented to President Bush, for his approval, "decisions" so middling in content and so muddled in potential execution that all the major players seated at the policy table were able to walk away from these exercises convinced they could go their own bureaucratic way.

The result, at least to anyone familiar with the turf-conscious workings of executive branch departments, was painfully predictable: a near-total lack of interagency coordination among departments whose competing agendas often worked—sometimes stunningly so—at cross-purposes to one another. The main beneficiary of such confusion, even as implied by Feith's often self-serving account, would appear to have been Vice President Cheney's office, which, by all accounts, *did* play an unprecedented, behind-the-scenes role in quietly shooting down policies (and policymakers) it did not approve of (more on that point later) and orchestrated much of the administration's—in the words of former press secretary Scott McClellan—"truth shading" sales job to Congress and the American public on the decision to invade Iraq (a show of propaganda force later matched by the Pentagon's clever marshaling of retired flag officers for mass media appearances in which they blessed the administration's apparent progress in stabilizing Iraq in the early postwar months).

Tragically, virtually all of what subsequently transpired in Iraq was preventable, because policymakers and experts had significant recent historical experience from which to draw, as did the military in charge. Besides our previous experience in Iraq itself (the temporary occupation of Kurdish Iraq and the humanitarian operations there following Desert Storm), there were similar nation-building and postconflict relief efforts in Haiti, Somalia, Bosnia, Kosovo, and Afghanistan. It was therefore inexcusable that anyone involved in planning and executing Saddam's toppling should have been under the delusion that our responsibility ended with mere liberation.

Some, like onetime neoconservative Francis Fukuyama, excuse the neocons' false assumptions of a "cakewalk" on their bad reading of history, specifically the ease with which Eastern Europe threw off Soviet-style tyranny at the end of the Cold War. Other examples cited as influencing their thinking include Israel's invasion of southern Lebanon in 1982 (where liberators were indeed welcomed by local Shia with flowers), Kurdish and Shia resistance to Saddam's rule following the first Gulf war, and the ease with which the Taliban were ejected from Afghanistan as a result of our coordinated efforts with Northern Alliance forces. Then there is the deeply conflicted role of the Iraqi expatriates who were more than willing to see our decisive victory followed up by an incoherent occupation, because it fit with their own particular plans for Kurdish separatism, Shia domination, and dreams of personal rule. Nor should we be surprised that the most prominent Shia "external," Ahmed Chalabi, was in cahoots with Tehran, feeding them intelligence and acting as their influencer in our decision-making. To expect Iran not to have a postwar plan for their next-door neighbor was idealistic in the extreme. Our real shame should come in realizing, however, that Tehran's plans were more comprehensive and realistic than our own.

While stipulating all these causes, I don't believe, in the end, that Bush-Cheney or the neocons were under any serious illusions about how hard the occupation would be. They simply chose to ignore the responsibility for the reasons already cited: America's primacy must be preserved, presidential prerogatives must be protected, and any accommodation of evil must be avoided at all costs. As Thomas Ricks observes, "What Bush did was tear down the goalposts at halftime in the game." So no, Bush-Cheney would not be submitting their Big Bang strategy for UN approval, nor would they share control of the occupation with other great powers. The White House would deny effective interagency cooperation between Defense and State by favoring the former's penchant for "overwhelming force" (the Powell Doctrine) at the expense of the latter's argument for overwhelming responsibility (Colin Powell again, this time with his "Pottery Barn rule," which says, "If you break it, you own it"). Simply put, it's not a quagmire if you refuse responsibility. More cynically, it's not Vietnam if your ultimate goal was to exploit our failures in postwar Iraq as a springboard to follow-on war with Iran—arguably the Cheney "doctrine" all along.

Here's where the administration's assumptions reached dizzying heights: The war would be waged so decisively by our "transformed," high-tech force that reconstruction would be simplified to the point of handing over the reins of power to Chalabi and the "externals" in a political "shock therapy" married to an economic equivalent by which rapid-fire flows of foreign direct investment, in addition to jump-started oil revenue, would rescue the Iraqi economy from its decades of abuse (e.g., war, state control) and neglect (isolation, sanctions). Unlike the "incompetent" Clinton administration, Bush-Cheney would not be reduced to consulting opinion polls, placating allies, or submitting itself to a long-term babysitting job, for all of those "gives" represented failure—failure to lead decisively.

Did the Bush administration, in its extreme pride, have any difficulty locating military leadership that met its biases? Absolutely not. As I stated earlier, previewing Ricks's analysis, our post–Vietnam generation leadership took great pride in fielding a "first-half team," believing the "second half" lay beyond their logical purview. So Rumsfeld was right when he responded to complaining troops in Kuwait one afternoon in late 2004 that "you go to war with the Army you have" and not "the Army you might want or wish to have at a later time." The army we took to Iraq was the army that the Army itself had wanted to use there, the one it had been buying and building for the previous thirty years, ignoring the mountain of operational experience accumulated since Vietnam. Colin Powell might have switched sides to the State Department, but his ethos lived on in his beloved military: *We do war. We don't do windows. Tell me which smoking holes you want and which bodies need snatching, and then tell me when I get to go home.*

To say then that Bush-Cheney and the neocons abandoned the principles of realism is incorrect. They stuck to the narrow principles all right, but in their pride they vastly expanded the acceptable parameters: They would wage war with little responsibility for the peace, for their true goals (primacy and prerogative) brooked no such obligation.

Envy, Leading to the Misguided Redirect on Iran

Americans, in their natural state of ideological skepticism, love to debase our victories—military or otherwise—with the observation "We may have fought X, but Y won the war." So America fought the Nazis only to have the Soviets win World War II. We fought the Soviets only to have the Taliban win Afghanistan. Most recently, we toppled Saddam only to have the Iranians win Iraq. To some, these realizations say, "Be careful with whom you align," but to me they say, "Co-opt whom you must to win wars, but be realistic about what comes next."

The Bush administration was supremely unrealistic about what came next in the Persian Gulf following our takedown of Saddam. As Vali Nasr argues in his brilliant 2006 book, *The Shia Revival*, what came next was completely predictable. When Bush-Cheney created the first Arab Shiite state in Iraq, they naturally unleashed a pent-up demand among the region's long-suppressed Shia for more political power, in turn re-elevating Shiite Iran back to the role of regional kingpin, a position it had not truly enjoyed since the earliest days of the Islamic revolution there. Naturally, the Bush administration seemed aghast at this turn of events. Expecting some Iraqi version of Thomas Jefferson–cum–Ahmed Chalabi, instead we got Grand Ayatollah Ali al-Sistani, a Nelson Mandela–like figure for Iraqi Shia whose veto power over every political solution we proposed was substantial. Born in Iran, Sistani speaks Arabic with a pronounced Persian accent, which naturally stokes fears of undue Iranian influence. But in truth, Tehran's mullahs have more to fear from Sistani's "quietism" philosophy, or the notion that religion is best practiced when it is removed from politics. Over time, a Shia-dominated Iraq that nonetheless grants significant autonomy to its Sunni minorities in the west and north (the non-Arab Kurds) could well play Poland to Iran's Russia—that is, it could serve as the cultural conduit for liberalizing norms.

But that scenario requires that the United States acquiesce to the inescapable logic of Iran becoming a major sponsor of Iraq's recovery, or at least that of its Shiite portion. Much as Turkey has—despite its separatist fears—quietly eased itself into becoming the external sponsor of the Kurdish region's economic boom (with $10 billion in foreign direct investment), and spunky Jordan aspires to the same for the western Sunni provinces, Iran is the logical regional integrator of Shia Iraq, and thus the main beneficiary of its liberation from Saddam Hussein's dictatorship. Given America's long-standing fixation on Iran's nuclear program, as well as Tehran's vigorous support for Hezbollah in southern Lebanon and Hamas in the Palestinian territories, that simply was not an outcome that the Bush administration, in its envy of Iran's improved regional fortunes, could accept.

No, there was never any doubt among Western regional experts that Iran would benefit from America's decisions to topple both the Taliban and Saddam, its two neighboring enemies. But what truly amazes me to this day is that the Bush administration somehow managed to get nothing in return from Tehran for these favors, refusing from the start to acknowledge, much less offer compensation for, Iran's repeated offers of substantive cooperation. Imagine if Franklin Roosevelt had managed our World War II relationship with the Soviet Union in the same manner, when we had bigger fights to wage on Russia's eastern and western borders? Instead of co-opting Iran in these two conflicts, Bush-Cheney chose to continue containing Iran in deference to the wishes of our regional allies, the Saudis and the Israelis, who likewise feared Iran's further rise.

And so, just as Bush's Big Bang strategy was yielding significant fruit all over the region a couple of years into our occupation of Iraq (e.g., the Cedar Revolution in Lebanon and Syria's withdrawal, local elections in Saudi Arabia, early signs of a political thaw in Egypt, the first-ever free elections in Palestine), the White House began its slow but steady drumbeat on possible military strikes against Iran. Just when Bush-Cheney had their wish, and it seemed as though the region's entire chessboard was in play, the administration redirected its entire strategy toward isolating Iran and rolling back its regional influence. By refusing direct bilateral talks until Tehran yielded—unconditionally—on its pursuit of the bomb, Bush-Cheney signaled Iran that it would continue targeting the country for regime change until the Iranians acquired a nuclear deterrent. Talk about a Catch-22! In effect, Bush-Cheney played the role of the cop who orders the suspect to drop his weapon while giving every indication that he plans to fire his own. After all, America's military had just dispatched two neighboring "suspects," so how could we then, in all good conscience, claim to be surprised by Tehran's reach for the bomb?

Consider this more forceful analogy: I walk up to three guys sitting on a park bench and shoot the guy on the right through the forehead. Next I double-tap the one on the left. In the meantime, the fellow in the middle frantically fumbles for his handgun. My question for you is: Is this guy irrational? Or did I make this decision for him?

As for Iran's assumption that getting the bomb will keep it safe from a U.S. invasion designed to topple the regime? Well, on that score the mullahs have only six-plus-decades-and-counting of world history that says they're *exactly correct*. So again, who's being irrational here? Who's being unrealistic? Which side has lost control of its emotions?

Here's the inescapable ground truth: America's choices up to now have led to a region-wide Shia revival that has greatly empowered Iran, which as a result must be accommodated on some level if we're going to stabilize both Iraq and Afghanistan. If we, in our strategic impatience, cannot stand Iran's short-term gains, then we have no business attempting to transform the region. Grand strategy is not about what you can pull off by the end of your administration; it's about how you systematically improve the global security environment for the next administration. By chasing the dream of America's primacy while denying Iran's regional version, Bush-Cheney stalled their own grand strategy of reshaping the Middle East. In the end, Tehran's mullahs get everything Stalin achieved after World War II: the bomb plus hegemonic influence over half the region. What did we get? Too many American soldiers unnecessarily killed.

Sloth, Leading to the U.S. Military Finally Asserting Command

This strategic sin emanated naturally from the first five: The quest for primacy meant Bush-Cheney entered into the occupations of both Afghanistan and Iraq with far too few allies and thus far too few troops. Their conflation of various enemies disallowed the effective regionalization of the solution after their arrogance in war translated into botched postwar execution. When things got bad enough, they located an effective scapegoat in Iran and began a painfully transparent countdown to war, to which Tehran responded by preemptively launching an "all-proxy" war in the region in the late summer of 2006, siccing its minions (Hezbollah, Hamas) against our own (Israel), all the while ratcheting up its mischief in both Iraq and Afghanistan. Meanwhile, as our body count grew higher and the institutional pain in both the Army and the Marine Corps grew too great for their leaders to bear, the Bush administration finally acquiesced and essentially outsourced the Iraq occupation to the generals with the decision to launch the surge in early 2007. What was Bush's war to begin now became General David Petraeus's war to end. For a presidency devoted to expanding its prerogatives, it was a stunning abdication of power engineered behind the scenes, according to Bob Woodward in *The War Within: A Secret White House History, 2006–2008*, by retired Army four-star general Jack Keane, Petraeus's longtime mentor. After Petraeus's historic testimony before Congress in September 2007, Keane told him privately, "What you have is beyond what any other leader has"—an ability to shape public opinion on the war *even more than the President of the United States.*

With Rumsfeld cashiered by the 2006 midterm elections and the Iraq Study Group begging for some regional political dialogue, our military was finally given the go-ahead to embrace a non–kinetically focused and therefore lengthy counterinsurgency strategy of empowering the locals to police their own. This change took many forms, the most important one being that our troops increased their community visibility by getting out of their big, isolating bases and effectively living among the people, like cops on the beat. Coming at the time of the Anbar "awakening," the surge created an immediate breathing space that the Bush administration made little effort to exploit through regional diplomacy, thus effectively acquiescing to Iraq's soft partition into four spheres: Kurdish, Sunni, Shia, and the capital city of Baghdad. With the Kurds essentially autonomous from day one (really, since we started the northern No-Fly Zone more than a decade earlier) and the Sunni tribes effectively "flipped" through a combination of our bribes and their being fed up with al Qaeda's brutality, General Petraeus turned next to quelling intra-Shiite conflict and slowly pacifying a Baghdad already "cleansed" in ethnic terms (hint: the Shia won), while continuing to prosecute al Qaeda's lingering presence in the Sunni north.

That's the CliffsNotes version of the timeline. What's important for this discussion is how long it took the Bush administration to realize the folly of their grand strategic design. Transforming the Middle East was always going to be about connecting it to the world at large, but by demanding virtually unilateral control over the focal points of Afghanistan and Iraq, Bush-Cheney ended up isolating America in both the Persian Gulf and Central Asia more than any potential rivals—including the Iranians. What that forced our military to do was to fight both wars under the worst possible strategic conditions: progressively denuded of allies and increasingly beset by spoilers on all sides, we had simply no military solution to these inherently political problems. A "clear-and-hold" military strategy meant little if the follow-up consisted of sparse aid and virtually no economic reconstruction, two processes that would reach inflection point only if and when solutions were regionalized—admitting that neighboring powers would essentially drive economic integration leading to sustainable political relationships. So yes, Iran wins. So do Turkey and Jordan. Beyond them, so do China and Russia and India. Admit those "losses" and whatever breathing space your counterinsurgency strategy may create will eventually bear some fruit. Deny them and all you accomplish is to delay future civil wars, at the end of which we'll still see the same "winners" collect their "earnings" while we contemplate our deeply sunk costs.

Inevitably as a result of the Bush administration's poor strategic choices, our Army and Marine Corps were forced to climb a steep operational learning curve. Fortunately, the military's tipping point roughly corresponded to the bankrupting of Bush-Cheney's political capital across the summer of 2005 through the fall of 2006, or basically from the debacle of the administration's response to Hurricane Katrina until the Republicans lost both houses of Congress in the midterm elections. So while the Bush White House busied itself in redirecting its strategic attention from Iraq to Iran, the Army and Marines were studiously processing the lessons learned from returning military leaders, exemplified by then Major General David Petraeus's return to command the Army's primary "schoolhouse," the Command and General Staff College in Leavenworth, Kansas, and then Major General James Mattis's return to helm the Marine Corps's primary schoolhouse, the Marine Corps Combat Development

Command in Quantico, Virginia. Together, these two "monks of war," as I dubbed them in an *Esquire* profile, oversaw the creation of the first-ever dual-designated Army–Marine Corps field manual on counterinsurgency operations, published formally in December 2006.

Contrary to the public perception that the new counterinsurgency (COIN) doctrine represents our military's adjustment to the grand strategic vision put forth by Bush-Cheney, it's the exact opposite that's true. For as Sarah Sewall, a Harvard human rights expert who collaborated in the COIN's construction, states, "The field manual implicitly asks Americans to define their aims in the world and accept the compromises they require. COIN will not effectively support a revolutionary grand strategy. Counterinsurgency favors peace over justice. Revolution destabilizes the status quo in the name of justice. They are fundamentally at odds." This is where the rubber of America's grand strategy meets the road of globalization's advance: We can respond to its friction (violent global insurgency) and we can facilitate its force (the integration of emerging economies), but what we cannot do is mandate their combined solution according to our preferred model (liberal democracy). In accepting the benefits of peace over justice, we accept a multiplicity of political outcomes: Sometimes our models will win, and sometimes other models will prevail. Either America submits to the dominant dynamics of this era's aggressively expansive globalization, or we risk derailing the process as a whole. Or to put it another way, if we're willing to go slow on the politics (multiparty democracy) while getting our way on the economics (expanding world middle class), we'll eventually achieve the primacy of our ideals (pursuit of happiness). So America needs to ask itself: Is it more important to make globalization truly global, while retaining great-power peace and defeating whatever antiglobalization insurgencies may appear in the decades ahead? Or do we tether our support for globalization's advance to the up-front demand that the world first resemble us politically?

If you favor the former route, then our military's transformation via Afghanistan and Iraq has not been in vain. Judging by the new "COIN of the realm," our military leaders have finally figured out what Abraham Lincoln once described as the "terrible math" involved in winning long wars such as this one.

But if you favor the latter route, then you have been doubly misled by Bush-Cheney's attempted grand strategy of the last seven years.

Gluttony, Leading to Strategic Overhang Cynically Foisted upon the Next President

Gluttony is perhaps the most self-conscious of sins, because your transgressions become undeniably apparent both to yourself and to others. So it is with grand strategies, where the usual descriptor is "imperial overreach," a phrase that has been bandied about by realist-school academics since the Soviet Union's collapse raised the possibility of its corollary among American strategists.

First, let us examine some facts. U.S. defense spending as a percentage of national GDP is smaller than it's ever been since World War II, falling steadily downward from its high of just over one-third in 1945, dropping to the Korean War figure of 11.7 percent, to Vietnam's 9.8 percent, to the Reagan buildup's 6.0 percent, to the first Gulf war's 4.6 percent, to our current mark hovering in the 4.3–4.4 percent range. Yes, the American military has spread itself out today to more nations than ever in terms of overseas bases and facilities, but in terms of what most Americans recognize as major bases, there our global footprint remains limited to about thirty or so foreign states. In effect, the hundreds of smaller facilities that now connect our forces to several dozen more nations worldwide reflect the same sort of in-neighborhood networking that Petraeus's COIN strategy implemented in Iraq: Professional working relationships are established with local militaries, which in turn allow our small training and liaison units to set up small facilities inside their existing bases. If you use America's military to engage the world primarily in local capacity building, that's what the footprint looks like. Finally, consider this measure of individual burden: In 1968, at the peak of the Vietnam War, approximately one out of every 200 American citizens was in uniform, serving abroad. Today, that burden has dropped to roughly one out of every 800 Americans.

Having said all that, we can see that there are clear limits to how much we can employ U.S. forces abroad in de facto combat zones at high rates of rotation—in other words, keeping them there longer or sending them back there faster and thus more frequently. In a professional military that's at once older, more educated, more married, and more burdened with children than your dad's military once was, "quality-of-life" issues reign paramount for overall service readiness, meaning the capacity to suddenly gear oneself up for a new combat mission. As such, there is a level of effort, or maximum capacity, that our armed forces can sustain for any one period of time. When sizable numbers are involved in two lengthy interventions like Afghanistan and Iraq, our military is essentially tied down on a near-global basis. That means that, at best, we could muster two or three smaller contingency responses elsewhere around the planet, and could respond to a significant combat scenario at first only primarily with naval and Air Force assets. Simply put, America cannot place large numbers of boots on the ground any-where right now, and to do so with any speed would be monumentally difficult.

So if we're going to fault Bush-Cheney on grand strategic terms, we'd need to divide our criticism between the following two points: the op-portunity costs involved and the strategic overhang created. The former refers to crises not responded to during the time frame of our combined Afghanistan-Iraq deployments. This is a tricky thing to measure, because, by many experts' definitions, most of the world's so-called crises are not truly international security crises if the United States military doesn't show up. Instead, they're "hot spots," failed states, chronic wars, "disturb-ing developments," and the like. Genocide is, of course, a special category, which is why great powers argue so interminably about when to actually employ the term. Sudan's Darfur crisis arguably falls into this always disputed category: bad enough to get a few African Union, UN, and even NATO advisers and would-be peacekeepers to show up, but not suf-ficiently important for a decisive military response by America. Here's a simple rule of thumb: If nobody's shooting except for the bad guys, it's not a real crisis, because if you want the good guys to shoot back, that happens only when the Americans show up. I'll skip boring you with a long list of actual events, like Darfur, where American forces could have made a difference. The simple reality is, the Bush administra-tion chose Afghanistan and Iraq, ceding the rest of the planet—or less hyperbolically stated, the rest of what I call the Non-Integrated Gap—to the tender mercies of whoever bothers to show up when the shooting starts.

If opportunity costs are an inherently slippery way of measuring the strategic sin of gluttony, then downstream overhang is less so, and by that I mean—in effect—how long it would take successive administrations to "burn off" the "weight" of long-pursued interventions with deeply sunk costs. How long have Bush-Cheney tied down U.S. military forces in Afghanistan and Iraq so as to make impossible any serious redirect to other regions in the event of a crisis truly perceived as such by Washington? Possible examples would be a major intervention into collapsing North Korea, the always available Iran scenario, the possibility of China's invasion of Taiwan, and Russia's next adventure. Most immediately, a major intervention into northwest Pakistan commands significant attention. Given that all of these scenarios are brewing at something above room temperature right now, we can approximate our strategic overhang by sensing how "soft power" oriented—or diplomatic—America's attempts have been to manage these situations under Bush-Cheney. In that regard, I would have to say that all but the Iranian situation elicited rather accommodating stances by the United States: China's Taiwan-focused military buildup saw us chastising Chen Shu-bian's Taipei for dangerous provocations; North Korea's testing of a nuclear device was rewarded by our offering to negotiate a peace treaty to end the Korean War; Pervez Musharraf's temporary use of emergency rule in Pakistan won him an influx of military support against the Taliban threat in his northwest territories; Putin's crackdown in Georgia won Mikheil Saakashvili humanitarian aid and little else; and, as for Iran . . . well, it seems well on its way to ruling out regime change by generating a sloppy, asymmetrical form of near-nuclear deterrence—namely, given our current tie-down, America can't stop Tehran from getting nuclear unless we go nuclear first, as conventional air strikes against Iran's deep underground facilities would accomplish a delay but not a firm denial of what seems inevitable now.

On that scale, then, it would seem that our current strategic overhang led the Bush administration, in its last years, to sue for peace everywhere except Afghanistan and Iraq. Will the situation get any better anytime soon for our incoming president? Unlikely. Even with a strategic withdrawal from one or both situations, the institutional "healing time" involved for the Army and Marines will be substantial, and it's extremely unlikely that any president would endure that loss of strategic face without respecting that requirement. As for another scenario forcing such an immediate shift, there I think you'd have to consult the Bush-Cheney second-term record, cited in the preceding paragraph, to recognize just how hard that would be. Does this overhang prevent the sort of air-delivered strikes so favored by the Clinton administration over the 1990s? Absolutely not. You name the country and America's airpower could deliver a major-league hurt within days, if not hours. The problem is, of course, that in most plausible scenarios there's little to actually target, meaning we end up lobbing a few cruise missiles and calling it a day—or more to the point, a 24-hour news cycle. But as Clinton was routinely derided throughout his years for employing such "pinprick" responses, don't expect that tactic to scratch too many strategic itches in the years ahead.

Here we finally get to the meat of the matter: By consuming so much of America's military force during these seven long years of nonstop, high-tempo, high-rotation action, the Bush administration basically condemned its successor to what will probably be an additional seven lean years of military operations. Whether it's simply winding down Afghanistan and/or Iraq and "replenishing the force," or shifting dollars from operations and maintenance funds to cover a plethora of Cold War "programs of record" (weapons systems and major platforms) that the Bush administration has refused to scale back (even as it gobbled up relatively huge—as in $100 billion plus—supplemental defense spending bills every year since 2001), the next administration has been handed a veritable train wreck in terms of future budgetary crises. Something will have to give. If that "something" is not an improved situation in Afghanistan and Iraq, then you can pretty much forget about any significant U.S. military interventions anywhere else. But even if it is, we're still probably looking at four to eight very lean years (and if you've already spotted the corollary in federal budget deficit spending, then go to the head of the class!).

What does that mean for the next president? It means ingenuity and inventiveness will be at a premium, because our incoming president's grand strategy is necessarily one of realigning America's trajectory to that of a world being transformed by the simultaneous rise of numerous great powers.

There will be no more swimming against the tide.

Two

A TWELVE-STEP RECOVERY
PROGRAM FOR AMERICAN
GRAND STRATEGY

Now that we know the sins, there must be penance. If not for Bush and Cheney, then it must come for America.

Here, I'll describe the basic steps we Americans need to take to regain some control over our destiny and realign our as yet unstated grand strategy to a world transforming at incredible speed. And taking these steps isn't merely about our reasserting our virtue. Because there's even more at stake than our salvation. A world that rapidly doubles its middle-class ranks in a generation's time is either going to become very content or very conflicted, and no nation can do more to ensure either outcome than America.

For the past eight years, America has remained somewhat trapped in angry isolation, cherishing its fears and nurturing its resentments. But we need to stop looking for security at the bottom of the bottle labeled "Shoot First" unilateralism, because we will never find it there, certainly not in this world of rising connectivity and interdependency. We instinctively reached for that empowering brew after 9/11, and our state of strategic intoxication since then has left a trail of tears—among our warriors and their families, among the recipients of our violent outbreaks, among a world's population that suspects—and hopes—that we're capable of so much more self-control. It has also isolated us from the society of fellow states and caused us to doubt our exceptional role in world history. No one on this planet who wants a better tomorrow welcomes this sad state of affairs.

We need to recognize our past mistakes and strengths if we're going to recapture some grand strategic momentum and once again start paddling faster than globalization's surging current. There is a new world still out there, awaiting some great nation's discovery and description. It's a world in which globalization has been made truly global, according to a system of rules that's both fair and self-sustaining but most of all is empowering to the middle, to individuals, and to the self-made. That is a world of unlimited creativity, energy, and ingenuity, and we as its dominant species need to get there fast.

The world desperately wants America back. In the best tradition of self-help programs, here are the twelve steps to get back to where we once belonged.

1. ADMIT THAT WE AMERICANS ARE POWERLESS OVER GLOBALIZATION.

Today's globalization is the Pandora's Box we opened long ago; it's past the point where we—or really *anybody*—can claim to be in charge. If globalization comes with rules but not a ruler, then it is those rules we must collectively manage better, not just in their constant extension to new territories and domains, but also in their constant improvement and progressive deconflicting.

We Americans survey the hypercompetitive global landscape with its cheap labor and trade protectionism, and we call these practices "un-American," when of course they're the most American things in the world—in their good time. So how do we keep ourselves competitive in this globalization of our making, realizing we're playing against "younger" versions of ourselves in many instances? And how do we simultaneously muster the will and the resources to play the vital role of bodyguard that we have long assumed in friction-filled locales distant from our shores?

We do what any general contractor does: We hire out the lower-end jobs to the most competent, entry-level providers and we keep the top-of-the-pyramid work for ourselves. We stop trying to pretend we can do it all by ourselves and thus get to call all the shots. We admit that the rising complexity of all this connectivity means we're but one seat at a very large table of rule-proposers and rule-deciders. But it's a key seat because our node is the terminus for a lot of consumption in this global economy and the starting point for a lot of innovation. Remember that as we move ahead: In a global economy, demand determines power far more than supply. We're also first among equals because our financial networks process risk with speed and daring (i.e., the booms) and a brutal honesty (read, the busts) that's the envy of the world. (Yeah, I said it.)

What we absolutely should not do is what our nativist instincts tell us to do: throw up walls. Every generation of immigrants that's ever come to America has quickly tried to slam the door shut behind it. Every generation of industry titans that's ever conquered America's markets has demanded shelter from the storms of global competition. Every well-established religion wants its faith and community protected from the dilution and damnation that come from too much intermingling with a desperate, grubby world. As Theodore Roosevelt would have surely argued, it's been our democratic rejection of exclusionary thinking and complete lack of inbreeding that have kept America strong—culturally, technologically, politically, militarily, you name it.

So we Americans need to embrace Thomas Friedman's "hot, flat, and crowded" global future for what it really is: a chance to evolve into something even better, and then take everything we've learned along the way and sell it around the planet at suitably discounted prices. That includes our best rules for managing all this complexity, because those rules not only will constitute the new definition of security in the twenty-first century, but also will remain one of America's best exports and a principal means for shaping international order.

There's much left for us to do in building out this American System on a global scale, so grab your tool of choice and let's get started.

2. COME TO BELIEVE THAT ONLY A BIPARTISANSHIP FAR GREATER THAN THAT DISPLAYED BY OUR NATIONAL LEADERS CAN RESTORE SANITY TO AMERICA'S FOREIGN AFFAIRS.

Modern American political history, meaning since the start of the twentieth century, has veered from periods of great partisanship to periods of great compromise.

The period of extreme partisanship that we've just lived through is not new; we endured something quite like it from Teddy Roosevelt right through Franklin D. Roosevelt's first term, an age dominated by partisan armies, commanding majorities, and a high degree of party discipline. The resulting political environment nonetheless saw huge bursts of legislative creativity, especially with TR, with Woodrow Wilson, and early in FDR's presidency. As Ronald Brownstein notes in *The Second Civil War,* the country was "deeply divided but not closely divided" in those first decades of modern America. When one side won, it won big, and thus ruled "big." As the country moved deeper into the Great Depression, however, it entered into a bipartisan age that stressed negotiation and compromise, by Brownstein's measure the longest such period in American history. In an age of great conflict and harsh ideological choices, America "was closely but not deeply divided": Everyone basically wanted the same general outcomes, and so cross-party dominance, so to speak, was the order of the day. That age of bargaining yielded, starting with the Kennedy administration, to an atmosphere of greater partisanship due to the controversies of the civil rights movement, the Vietnam War, the Watergate scandal, and the subsequent rise of the "Reagan Republicans." Our current period of hyperpartisanship can be said to have arrived when the GOP finally won control of the House of Representatives in 1994, after four decades of minority status. Since that time we've seen party discipline reach stunning heights in a Boomer-dominated political landscape that finds America both deeply and closely divided, meaning Democrats and Republicans don't agree on much, but neither commands a serious majority. This era came to an end with the election of 2008.

In my opinion, the Boomer generation represents one of the weakest cohorts of politicians America has ever produced. Like most revolutionary generations, the Boomers were frustrated by the lack of the political change they effected in their youth, so the bulk of their talent and ambition thereupon went into the private sector. This dynamic is common to many revolutionary generations throughout history: Thwarted on the political front, they turn to the far less restricted domains of business and technology in an attempt to change their world from another angle. The result is typically a huge burst of creativity and entrepreneurship. We saw this in Europe after the failed revolutions of 1848, in the United States following the Civil War, and in today's China after Tiananmen Square. The serious talent simply skips a political process it considers "low" and "demeaning" and instead chooses the real "business" of social and economic progress, believing that "what's good for my company/industry is good for my country!" If I were to compare the Boomers as a political generation to one from America's past, it would be to the last quarter of the nineteenth century, or roughly from 1870 to 1900. The reason why that comparison will strike so many of you as obscure is that most Americans can't name any presidents or prominent politicians from that age, but know well the industrial and financial titans such as Andrew Carnegie, J. P. Morgan, and John D. Rockefeller. Decades from now the key names most Americans will remember from our age will be Bill Gates, Warren Buffett, and Rupert Murdoch (yes, he's a Yank now, too), while virtually all our politicians will slip into well-deserved obscurity.

That may seem a harsh judgment, but let me explain why I think it's so crucial for America's grand strategy going forward that we as a nation move beyond the political rule of the Boomers. Morris Massey, an expert on conflict between generations, pioneered the argument that states, "What you are is where you were when . . . ," meaning all of us reach a point in life where we discover a world larger than ourselves. At that juncture, we become cognizant of the morals we've developed across our early years, and those morals—or worldview—tend to persist across our adult years. For most people, that fateful transition occurs in the teenage years, which explains our tendency to stick with the popular music of those years throughout adulthood. Admit it. You stayed cool enough across your twenties and maybe you faked it deep into your thirties, but then you woke up in your forties and realized you absolutely hated your kids' music! It happens to everyone.

So Massey's basic point is that our worldview is essentially formed by the time we hit college. Everything that came before is considered normal, and much of what comes after is viewed as just plain weird. Given enough grounding by parents and religion, most people hold on to their "normal" as they grow older, taking in stride the increasingly "weird," but eventually succumbing to nostalgia for the "good old days." One trick I've learned as a foreign policy strategist is that whenever I encounter somebody with a clear position on something, I simply check how that issue was playing out back when this person was a teenager. It usually matches up quite well. Let me give you an example: Talk to anybody about China today and you'll typically encounter first impressions formed in adolescence. For those who came of age in the 1950s (think Korean War), China remains an aggressive Communist regime that cannot be trusted, no matter how many stripes that tiger changes. Fast-forward to the 1960s crowd and you'll find a lot of China-coming-apart-at-the-seams arguments, meaning the country's rapid rise is likely to trigger its internal collapse. Coming of age in the 1960s meant your dominant impressions of China consisted of widespread famine ("Eat your dinner! Kids in China are starving!") and the temporary insanity of Mao's Cultural Revolution.

It's really only when you start bumping into children of the 1970s like me (born 1962) that you tend to find a more benign view of China's rise. Why? Our China has always been opening up to the outside world, starting with Richard Nixon's historic trip in 1972.

So it's no surprise that my generation is the first to be so open to strategic partnership with China in global affairs. To us, that seems "normal" enough.

After World War II, American politics was dominated by the "greatest generation" for four decades (1952–1992, from Eisenhower through Bush the Elder). Following that long reign, the presidency basically skipped the fifties generation (e.g., Mondale, Dukakis) and moved right into the 1960s Boomers (first Clinton, then Bush the Younger). So with regard to China, we've basically moved beyond the reflexive hostility of the early Cold War crowd and into the persistent suspicions of aging Boomers who still largely favor "containing" China and hedging against its rise. Looking back over the past two Boomer presidencies, we see them chock-full of that sixties mindset, and that's just not good enough given our current strategic situation—namely, too many new enemies and too few new friends. Iraq is not Vietnam, and the long war against extremism is not a rerun of the Cold War against Communism. It's time for our debates on national security strategy to draw upon a worldview shaped more by the 1970s—an understanding of international affairs better in line with today's globalization paradigm (e.g., have/have-not conflicts, oil price shocks, transnational terrorism, global environmentalism).

Boomer politicians obviously care about these issues. I'm just saying that how they frame possible solutions is reflected—and too often restricted—by "where they were when . . ."

That's why the candidacy of Barack Obama (born 1961) hit so many national chords in 2008. His vision of a post-Boomer bipartisanship made instinctive sense to a lot of Americans, especially young Americans, who felt that sixteen years of Boomer rule has seen this nation argue incessantly over several weeks of a fetus's life and the last couple of minutes of a person's death and barely touched upon a host of huge issues lying in between those extremes. The same can be said of our foreign policy: It's either "Shoot all the bad guys" or "We want democracies now," when most of the world is struggling with tough issues between that baseline security goal and that top-line political achievement. Now it's President Obama's chance to change all that.

In short, being closely divided is fine, but being deeply divided is not. As long as we lack any comprehensive middle-class consensus on issues like globalization and overseas military interventions, we'll have a hard time defining, much less sticking to, a feasible grand strategy. Why? We'll continue to treat globalization as a zero-sum game in which the rise of a global middle class threatens our way of life, and that attitude will simply place us on the wrong side of progress—even history.

3. MAKE THE DECISION TO COORDINATE ALL ELEMENTS OF AMERICA'S NATIONAL POWER ACCORDING TO A GRAND STRATEGY THAT WE HAVE COLLECTIVELY DEFINED.

The Bush administration actually did a great job of boosting the profile and volume of foreign aid within the so-called DIME package (standing for diplomacy, information, military, economic) of U.S. government assets. It increased the total amount of U.S. foreign aid by almost one-third in its first two years and elevated the flow to sub-Saharan Africa to its highest level ever, including boosting the U.S. government's spending on HIV-AIDS by a tremendous amount. Bush may not have engaged the world in the "kinder, gentler" manner of his father or felt Africa's pain as empathetically as Bill Clinton, but the man did put some serious money where his mouth was on the subject of relieving human suffering and promoting economic development.

Having done all that, the Bush administration disappointingly continued down the path of further embedding the U.S. Agency for International Development within the dysfunctional State Department, where USAID was cast as State's "implementation arm." While it is technically an independent agency, the truth remains that USAID lacks any serious voice or coordinating power in the U.S. foreign policy apparatus, leading such prominent think tanks as the Brookings Institution and the Center for Strategic and International Studies to jointly recommend a cabinet-level Department of Global Development to "realize the president's vision of elevating development as a third pillar alongside diplomacy and defense." For now, despite such high-level recommendations (matching my own recommendation in *Blueprint for Action* four years ago), the structure of America's foreign aid program continues to mark us as uncoordinated and therefore unstrategic in our approach. With a current portfolio of dozens of separate programs spread across seven federal departments, USAID, the Millennium Challenge Corporation, and eleven other significant government agencies, we mirror the bureaucratically diffuse approach of Germany and Japan, two governments we purposefully restructured following WWII to have a modest foreign policy agenda. Instead, it is obvious that we ought to use a more logical model: Great Britain's Department for International Development. The Bush administration missed a golden opportunity to create my "Department of Everything Else" in response to the widely perceived failures of our postwar reconstruction efforts in Afghanistan and Iraq. Then again, people don't like to admit it when they screw up royally—least of all politicians.

If foreign aid was suitably upgraded under Bush, most experts argue that the State Department, especially in its public diplomacy (i.e., the "hearts and minds" information-dissemination programs like the old Radio Free Europe), remains significantly underresourced. Let me offer a different take. I view the State Department as largely playing the role of "good cop" across the Core, or those nations already enjoying significant levels of connectivity to the global economy, and the Defense Department as fundamentally playing the role of "bad cop" inside the Gap, where globalization's frontier-integration projects are located. Seeing them as such, I'm less interested in "supersizing" State, as one blue-ribbon government commission put it, to make it more capable inside the Gap than I am in seeing foreign aid in general elevated to the level of a cabinet department.

So where do I argue a shifting of funds should occur?

In general, I am skeptical of any suggested increase in "strategic communications" by the U.S. government. In a connected world, I don't see a big requirement for U.S.-sponsored mass media projects. Plus, if Americans don't trust our government's propaganda today, why should anybody else? If we're talking better security for America's information networks, through which all these hearts and minds can allegedly be won (or just detected and kept under surveillance), then that's different. But frankly, I don't see the government taking the financial and technological lead on network security, but rather the private sector, which the public distrusts slightly less when it comes to their freedom of communication (another Bush-Cheney legacy). As for the intelligence component (e.g., analysis, spying, technical snooping), of course I'm all for reform within the intelligence community. Who isn't? And yet, in an increasingly open-source world, I don't advocate shifting more government money in that direction—save for more language training—because I remain highly pessimistic that the spy agencies, be they dominated by analysts or machines, can sufficiently overcome their collective cult of dysfunctional secrecy to outperform mass media journalism, the emerging blogosphere, and the Internet in general as a source for "centralized intelligence." I want an intelligence community that's far more open to interacting with the world at large, not one given more snooping technology, because its biggest problems lie in *not knowing* what it does not know. Rather than "boil the ocean" by trying to make sense of the entire Internet every night, we need an intelligence community that masters searching more than sheer processing.

Where I do see the need to shift resources is within the military itself. While the Department of Defense has certainly spent a lot of supplemental funds (i.e., episodic funding by Congress for actual operations) on what I call System Administrator–oriented operations (e.g., postwar/

disaster reconstruction and stabilization operations and counterinsurgency campaigns) inside Afghanistan and Iraq, in terms of dedicated annual budget, it continues to buy for the "big war" Leviathan force (more Navy and Air Force) while starving the "small wars" SysAdmin force (more Army and Marines). The vast majority of long-term spending (R&D, acquisition) remains focused on big platforms (ships, aircraft, Army's Future Combat System) designed to fight more traditionally arrayed opponents in conventional warfare, while glaring needs inside the ground services tend to go unaddressed (e.g., more special operations/unconventional capabilities in general, dramatically increasing the size of the Marine Corps and Army, creating a special military advisory/training corps), resulting in the Army and Marines trying to fund as much of these requirements on the bureaucratic sly, using O&M (operations and maintenance) funds or the congressional supplementals. This has to end. We can't keep funding one force (the Leviathan) while working the other force (SysAdmin) to death. When almost 90 percent of your officers say the war in Iraq has stretched the U.S. military dangerously thin, they're talking people first, equipment second, and platforms third. And when over 90 percent of your casualties in Iraq and Afghanistan occur *after* the wars of liberation, the national security community simply isn't doing its job, which is preparing for, and achieving, victory at a reasonable cost in treasure—and blood.

There will be a significant push within the next administration's defense posture to "get back to basics" and "heal the force" after Afghanistan and Iraq. To the extent that this becomes a bureaucratic cover for going back to old spending habits (Thanks a billion, Mr. Putin!), America will simply be setting itself up for more failure down the road inside the Gap. Worse, if the United States were to somehow signal to the rest of the world's great powers that big-war spending is the way to go, we would almost force them to emulate our bad choices in force-structure planning. How does that matter? China's future military requirements aren't being met by the People's Liberation Army's acquisition focus on Taiwan, nor does India prepare its military for its future overseas responsibilities by continuing to focus on Kashmir. Already, we see what damage such a big-war focus has done to Pakistan's military capabilities to deal with its northwest territories: All that American military aid over the years has been spent building up a force more appropriate to fighting India than for taming its Federally Administered Tribal Areas. Now, as the real push comes to shove over the rising operational capabilities of the Taliban and al Qaeda inside northwest Pakistan, America finds itself having to recast the Pakistan military's force structure, raising the obvious question, Why wasn't Islamabad spending all those billions in American military aid for these purposes the whole time?

There are a lot of U.S. Marine and Army officers asking the same questions about the Pentagon's spending priorities back home.

4. MAKE A SEARCHING AND FEARLESS MORAL INVENTORY OF THE "GLOBAL WAR ON TERROR."

In a nutshell: The good news is that we have killed or captured a good portion of al Qaeda's senior brain trust, meaning the generational cohort of leaders who built up the transnational network to the operational peak reached on 9/11. As a result, al Qaeda's network is a lot more diffuse and dispersed, with the surviving leadership's role trimmed back largely to inspirational guidance from above on strategy and tactics. Yes, al Qaeda now takes credit for virtually every terrorist act across the globe, but as worldwide revolutionary movements go, this one is relatively contained, in geographic terms, and thus successful only in terms of generating local stalemates against intervening external powers. Most crucial is that al Qaeda's brutal tactics have cost it popular support throughout the Islamic world. The bad news is that while al Qaeda's operational reach may now be effectively limited to the same territory (Southwest Asia and extending to adjacent areas) as were the classic Middle Eastern terrorist groups of the 1970s and 1980s, that just means America's efforts to date have made us safer at the expense of allies in Europe, Asia, and Africa. By turning back the clock while making no strategic headway, the Bush administration merely engineered a back-to-the-future operational stalemate at an unsustainably high cost, effectively isolating America from the world in the process. The pessimist in me says we've reached a strategic cul-de-sac.

Thus, seven years into this long war against violent extremists, we measure our progress and naturally feel depressed: enemies proliferating, friends disappearing, and the front seemingly limitless. So stipulated—regarding the war. And yet this war's worldwide impact pales in comparison with ongoing changes triggered by globalization. We need to remember that larger context if we're ever going to recognize this struggle's successful conclusion. Remember, the Cold War didn't end with World War III but with 3 billion new capitalists joining the global economy. We were never ahead in that war, either, but clearly we triumphed in everything else.

As globalization expands, it naturally invades those regions most disconnected from its influences to date. In effect, this struggle marches backward in time as we quell civil strife and battle violent extremists in increasingly primitive locations. So don't expect less violence as globalization permeates the Middle East and Africa. Entrenched elites and cultural fundamentalists will resist globalization's democratizing effects, especially when it comes to the rights and prerogatives of women. Globalization brings networks. Networks are gender-neutral. Provide such connectivity to a traditional society and you'll turn it upside down by empowering women disproportionately to men. Put most crudely, this long war will see us liberating females through economic connectivity while killing off self-righteous young men standing in the way. Why do fundamentalists deny real education to young girls? Because that's where all this "trouble" starts. No modern economy has ever developed without first liberating its women with expanded economic opportunity, then social change (often related to birth control, best accomplished with a paycheck), and finally political participation.

We've got to get better at defining both enemies and allies in this long war. We instinctively interpret any religious awakening as a sign of increasing fundamentalism, when more times than not it's an attempt to reconcile tradition with modernity. Unlike fundamentalists who advocate disconnectedness from the "corrupt" world, evangelicals of all faiths work to connect populations across borders, generating self-help networks and empowering individuals relative to elites. According to experts who track such trends, evangelism is exploding around this planet while fundamentalism is declining. Missionary activity, for example, has never been higher globally, signaling this century will be far more religious than the last. Having said that, we must carefully disaggregate our perception of the Islamic threat: Not every Muslim is an Islamist is a fundamentalist is a jihadist. Many Muslims thrive in market democracies, not just in the West but in South and East Asia, where their largest populations are found.

More specifically, Islamists want governments in predominantly Muslim countries to reflect Muslim values, just as America's government reflects our predominantly Judeo-Christian roots. But wanting that doesn't automatically make you a fundamentalist who demands civilizational apartheid from the West, nor does it commit you to violence toward such ends. If the Islamic Middle East is truly to embrace globalization, then we must respect the many compromises that faith will demand in return. The problem of threatened cultural identity cannot be allowed to overwhelm the profound benefit of economic connection, especially in the short term.

Both al Qaeda and the West's antiglobalism fanatics are operating under the pathetic delusion that this era's version of globalization is an elitist ideology to be defeated instead of a profound force driven by individual ambition that's been unleashed upon the world by the collapse of socialism in the East. Judging the long war strictly as war will always yield a depressing verdict. So don't expect the killing to stop anytime soon, because the greater the force (globalization's spread), the hotter the friction (terror-based resistance). Thus, judging this ongoing struggle within the context of globalization's progressive advance across the world provides useful perspective, as well as confidence that we stand on the right side of history.

So how do we realistically define victory? Most people think it's killing terrorists and incapacitating their networks, but to me it's less about "draining the swamp" than about filling that space with something better. The opposite of war isn't peace, it's creation. Thus, the only "exit strategy" I recognize is local job creation. Headlines will frequently proclaim the "failure" of our military strategy against al Qaeda. Don't be disheartened by that judgment. It may be true, but it is completely irrelevant.

In operational terms, the entire history of al Qaeda, which emerged from Islamic resistance to the Soviet occupation of Afghanistan in the 1980s, has been one of moving from one center of gravity to the next. Not welcome in Saudi Arabia following the Soviet withdrawal, al Qaeda was effectively stood up in its modern form in Sudan in the mid-1990s. Driven out by the Sudanese government in 1996, al Qaeda returned to Afghanistan, later to be evicted by the U.S.-led invasion following 9/11. To no one's surprise, al Qaeda next slipped into Pakistan's ungoverned northwest tribal areas, reconstituting itself there, along with the ousted Taliban.

If al Qaeda must resort to hiding in one of the most off-grid locations on the planet, I would call that a success. If a Web-enabled al Qaeda can effectively coordinate terrorist attacks in the West from there, then—again—we're back to the pre-9/11 standoff. That means America and the world remain highly incentivized to continue tightening up security practices, but since this is highly desirable for all sorts of reasons relating to globalization's rapid expansion, al Qaeda's historical function here is both useful and invariable—its continued efforts simply force more resiliency from us. Then again, so do tainted Chinese products, avian flu, global warming, high oil prices, and financial market crashes. Al Qaeda may grab headlines occasionally, but in global terms its impact rarely rises above the white noise generated by globalization's skyrocketing transaction rate and its associated mishaps.

Al Qaeda clearly profited from Iraq's dissolution as a unitary state, but quite frankly al Qaeda will always have some *cause célèbre*. As a fundamentalist movement combating globalization's creeping embrace of its sacred places, it will always have "infidels" worth driving out. Nothing short of complete civilizational apartheid will ever satisfy al Qaeda's agenda, and even that would simply expand its geographic ambition. So if al Qaeda's resurgence is hardly remarkable, and its temporary ideological profiteering in Iraq was simply a function of President Bush's Big Bang strategy, then neither outcome adds up to a loss in this long war, even as neither points out the path to victory. As America's combat role in Iraq inevitably winds down, our definition of progress must inevitably broaden beyond simply "killing weeds" to "growing some lawn." As the guy who cuts my grass likes to say, you can't do both at the same time.

And the lawn is growing. Foreign direct investment flows to the Middle East and North Africa have quadrupled since 2000. Thanks to Asia's growing energy thirst, higher oil prices provided the initial trigger, but what's truly important this time around is that the region's oil-rich economies are choosing to invest in energy-poor neighbors, such as Morocco and Egypt, in desperate need of outside capital. Instead of governments leading the way, this time it's private investors. Instead of white elephants, this time we're seeing bold forays into all sorts of infrastructure and networks that link this region more effectively to the global economy. For now, it remains primarily the elites who benefit, with the big question being how much of this expanded economic opportunity in the coming years will make it to the masses, for there lies the youth bulge that Arab governments must manage lest idle hands be seduced by radical ideologies.

My point is this: In security terms, it's always going to feel like we're "losing" this war or—at best—achieving an operational stalemate. The real victory won't come on any battlefield, however, but rather in boardrooms. In the end, we can't kill bad guys faster than our enemies can grow them. Instead, we must offer them a more attractive recruitment package.

Progress isn't about less violence, it's about speeding the killing to its logical conclusion in any one battlefield to shift the fight to its next logical stand. After the Middle East, the next theater of combat lies to the south, meaning the war's geography shifts to sub-Saharan Africa in coming decades. Americans are routinely accused of lacking strategic patience. We want our wars finished by the next major holiday or certainly by the next election. Given that mindset, we're forced to subsist on current events for encouragement—as in, "Which famous al Qaeda figure did we kill this week?" But if you admit this is going to be a long struggle, you look for trends and not individual events to drive your strategic calculations. Ultimately, we're trying to connect the Middle East to the global economy on the basis of something besides oil, turning all those idle young males into jobholders instead of bomb-throwers. Meanwhile, the radical Salafi jihadists seek to disconnect the region from what they see as the corrupting—and growing—influence of globalization.

Here's the most important news in terms of America's grand strategy: Time is on our side.

Consider the demographics. The Middle East is overwhelmingly young, with roughly two-thirds of its population under thirty. As a result, a huge youth bulge is working its way through these traditional societies, creating immense strains on modest educational systems and setting up authoritarian governments for persistently high levels of unemployment—a great mix for revolutionary change throughout history. After a baby boom, there's typically a baby bust, and sure enough, fertility rates have dropped dramatically across much of the Middle East. That demographic inevitability yields the following positive trend: The Middle East will "middle-age" over the next quarter-century. Revolutions are a young

man's game, so Osama bin Laden has barely a generation to achieve his
dream of civilizational apartheid. Because if he can't, we'll be looking at
a very different Middle East come 2025. And we'd better, because, as
far-sighted demographers point out, a subsequent "echo boom" (i.e., a
follow-on smaller youth bulge begotten by today's version) will emerge
in most Arab states later that decade, meaning time is on our side—but
not forever.

Three external trends will also fuel this transformation, each producing a profound blowback to the region. The first will arise in North America, and it will involve Islam's religious reformation at the hands of women
and young people within its ranks. Unlike in Europe, our Muslim immigrants are not socially and economically ghettoized, so it's not surprising
that Muslim women, once exposed to our gender equality, have begun
agitating for a greater role in the practice of their faith. The same goes for
Islamic youth who brazenly split the difference between Sunni and Shia
by dubbing themselves "sushi"—a religious mash-up certain to infuriate
their parents.

The second blowback will come from Europe, and it will involve Islam's political reformation. Islamist parties will eventually emerge
throughout Europe, inevitably mainstreaming themselves in the electoral
process in much the same way that Marxist parties did during the Cold
War. It sounds inconceivable, but it will be a very good thing because it
will reduce the socioeconomic isolation of Muslim communities there.
Europe either draws Muslims into the political process or resigns itself to
watching numerous reruns of 2005's Paris riots. Turkey's the "lead goose"
in this formation, and its innovative political accommodations of Islamist
impulses remain impressive, along with its courage in contextualizing
Muhammad's many teachings within the framework of modern life.

The third blowback will come from Asia, and it will involve Islam's
economic reformation. The lead geese here will be Singapore, Indonesia,
and especially Malaysia, where leaders are handcrafting a market-friendly
and democracy-tolerant form of Islamic civilization. These Islamic states
give proof to the lie that their religion lacks the genetic makeup to embrace globalization's demands for economic and political freedom—or
even religious tolerance.

Add it all up and you quickly realize that our victory isn't defined as hunting down and killing every Islamic terrorist but simply not allowing their murderous tactics to poison these much-needed reformation trends within globalizing Islam. With time, such trends will push the Middle East to age out of its current political and economic stagnation. History says that as long as your population is overwhelmingly young, democracy is a hard proposition to achieve, but a quick tour of the planet also shows us that older nations are invariably associated with more democratic political systems. So yes, there will be many more Osama bin Ladens seeking to hold off these historical tides. But so long as America remains operationally vigilant and tactically agile, this long war will continue to unfold to our strategic advantage.

5. ADMIT TO THE WORLD AND TO OURSELVES THE EXACT NATURE OF OUR MISTAKES IN IRAQ AND AFGHANISTAN.

First, I'll stipulate that I don't consider the invasion of Iraq to have been an unnecessary diversion in the long war.

The global jihadist movement chooses its fronts in this asymmetrical struggle, as does America. These targets don't match up very well, but that's because each side is fighting a very different war. The jihadists seek to hijack predominantly Muslim countries out of globalization, thus eliminating any risk of "Westoxification." In response, President Bush toppled the worst dictator in the Middle East in the hope that the subsequent tumult would trigger significant change throughout the region, which it has—both good and bad. We endeavor to connect Islam to the globalizing world, while al Qaeda promises permanent civilizational apartheid. Only one of those outcomes brings lasting peace. For that reason alone, simply overthrowing the much-hated Taliban wasn't enough. Al Qaeda's leadership is forced to hide in off-grid locations like the Afghanistan-Pakistan border, but its dream of totalitarian empire centers on the Middle East. By toppling Saddam, Bush brought this fight home where it belongs—the Persian Gulf. If the United States had concentrated solely on isolated Afghanistan, both the central front and the *cause célèbre* would have simply been located in a state with no strategic significance to either side, playing into al Qaeda's hands. The more you focus on Afghanistan, the more you're sucked into the far bigger problem next door called Pakistan. Tempting, I know. But if we couldn't handle 25 million Iraqis, what makes you think we'd do better with 172 million Pakistanis? It was better to throw down our gauntlet in Iraq, because there we got Iran, Jordan, Syria, Lebanon, Israel and Palestine, Saudi Arabia, and even Egypt spinning in response. Scary, yes, but in terms of grand strategy, far more profound.

Must we stipulate that the Bush administration "sold" the war under false pretenses? Clearly, the White House exerted significant pressure throughout the government to use intelligence—however scant and faulty—to link Saddam's regime to weapons of mass destruction. Like the crooked cop who shouts out, "He's got a gun!" just before plugging a suspect about whom he knows otherwise, it's tempting for Americans to disown the entire enterprise, especially because what Bush-Cheney truly lied about was the inevitable length and inherent difficulty of our resulting stay. But that was the intrinsic mistrust of the American people that the Bush administration consistently displayed. It was assumed that we couldn't handle the truth.

Do we stipulate that the Bush administration magnificently screwed up the reconstruction of postwar Iraq? Hard not to. I've got a whole bookshelf of award-winning journalistic accounts on that score. But far worse than that, the Bush administration wasted the Big Bang's momentum by rerunning the weapons-of-mass-destruction drama with Iran. This revealed the neocons' stunning lack of strategic imagination, their tactical myopia hobbling those regional dynamics before they could pick up speed.

What wasn't inevitable—and thus remains unforgivable—in this storyline was the amount of casualties we've suffered along the way, but let's be honest with ourselves here, because the Bush administration was by no means solely to blame, even if it deserves the lion's share. America's political system and defense-industrial complex were fundamentally incapable of adjusting to this long war against violent extremism absent the sort of undeniable failure represented by our postwar mismanagement of Iraq. Failure is a harsh but excellent teacher. Long addicted to the Powell Doctrine's central tenet of avoiding another Vietnam at all costs, we went into Iraq with the force we'd been building for the previous quarter-century. That military didn't do postwars; it didn't plan for them or equip for them or even have a credible doctrine for them. Rather, America was led by political masters who openly disdained such things.

What did that legacy cost us? Arguably as many as 3,000 American lives, or roughly what we lost on 9/11. Our military conducted a brilliant war in Iraq to topple Saddam's regime, losing less than 140 troops over two months. From May 2003 through March 2004, our average postwar monthly casualty totals dropped from roughly 70 to just over 40, a decrease of almost 40 percent. Those eleven months constituted the lost year in our postwar response. For roughly the next three and a half years (!) we averaged approximately 75 deaths per month, until the surge, combined with the Anbar "awakening," brought those numbers down. By not mounting a serious postconflict stabilization-and-reconstruction effort and refusing the advice of many military officers to abandon the big-base operational mentality and get our troops out among the people (the COIN strategy *finally* adopted), the Bush administration essentially let the postwar lapse back into war-level casualty rates. Does that make the neocons war criminals? No. Unfortunately it just marks them as amazingly incompetent strategists.

Now imagine the army we should have surged the moment Saddam's statues fell: our troops riding in mine-resistant ambush-protected (MRAP) vehicles, trained and operating according to our new counterinsurgency doctrine, and led by officers prepared for a long, hard postwar slog instead of an easy, light-up-your-victory-cigar endstate.

If all that force accomplished had been to keep its casualties from rising from that initial postwar average, we would have suffered at least a thousand fewer deaths. If we had attracted enough coalition forces to field a peacekeeping force on a par with those generated by NATO for Bosnia and Kosovo, or roughly two dozen troops per 1,000 local citizens, history says we could have reduced our casualty rates far more significantly. Approximately 85 percent of America's cumulative casualties—or roughly 3,500 of the more than 4,100 lost by the fall of 2008—have come since that first, "lost" postwar year passed. It's little wonder that our army's younger officers are demanding systemic change.

As for Iraq itself, we've collectively entered a strategic space where it's possible to chart real progress across three mini-states surrounding a politically dysfunctional but reasonably stable capital. Now, instead of trying to rebuild Iraq as a unified whole, we face the more manageable challenges of connecting the Kurds, the Shia, and the Sunni—in that order—

to the global economy and then to each other, on more equal terms. It'll be mostly oil at first, but at least they've all got some. The long-successful Kurds now become nation-building role models for the Sunni, whose tribes have given up trying to recapture Baghdad or regain their former dominance. Their tactical alliances with the American military in 2007 thus served two rather expedient purposes: driving out the hated and ultraviolent al Qaeda and protecting the Sunni from Shia militias and a Shia-dominated central government. America's surge-extended force then focused in 2008 on driving out the remnants of al Qaeda in the north and reducing Iran's clandestine military efforts among the Shia, where from the start Tehran cleverly backed all horses in the race.

Iran naturally wants to fuel Iraq-wide pressure to reduce America's continued military presence, because the sooner the Americans draw down, the better Iran's chances to further expand its influence, which is growing by leaps and bounds. Plus, a staunchly anti-American stance in Iraq dovetails nicely with the regime's pursuit of nuclear weapons to deter U.S. military intervention aimed at regime change, as well as its overall regional strategy of combining anti-Americanism with anti-Israeli fervor in a united Islamic front. Iran pushes the ideal of a united anti-American/anti-Israeli Islamic front for the same reasons its Shia protégé in Lebanon, Hezbollah, makes common cause with Palestinian Hamas against Israel: It masks a reach for power by the historically oppressed Shia across a region long dominated by Sunni autocracies. By toppling Iraq's Sunni dictator, Saddam Hussein, and setting in motion the region's first Arab Shia-dominated state, the Bush administration unwittingly revived Persian Iran's revolutionary ambitions, which now must be quelled along with Iraqi Shiite ambitions to dominate Iraq.

Where our military's counterinsurgency strategy succeeded best was in taking what seemed like an accumulating Iraq conflict and morphing it into a sequential conflict: Where previously our troops were facing al Qaeda *plus* Sunni insurgents *plus* Shia militias *plus* Iran, by the end of 2008 our agenda appeared largely reduced to just some Shia militias *plus* Iran. By flipping the Sunni tribes against al Qaeda, our forces effectively moved on to the next challenge. Can we backslide on that progress? You bet. This babysitting job is nowhere near to being done. But the Anbar "awakening"—as long as it holds—does represent an incredibly important tipping point when it comes to U.S. domestic support for our continued operations. As long as our forces seem to be moving sequentially from one challenge to the next, as they did in the Balkans across the 1990s, the American public will sense just enough progress to stomach our losses in this far costlier effort. Then there's the larger question of whether Washington can stomach Iran's increasing influence throughout the Shia and Kurdish portions of Iraq.

Thus, the great temptation in the months and years ahead will be to dip into military strikes against Iran under the dual premises of reducing its meddling in Iraq and setting back its efforts toward achieving nuclear capability. Plenty of political leaders fancy this route, especially if it's limited to air strikes alone, so don't assume the danger disappears once Bush left office. While this approach would clearly satisfy our allies in Israel and Saudi Arabia, it will likewise push Tehran into an all-out effort at sabotaging our maturing victory in Kurdistan and our nascent success among the Sunni—not to mention yet again turning Hezbollah and Hamas loose against Israel. Unfortunately, a better, more patient approach would be to let our forces continue to make their careful efforts among Iraq's Shia while the incoming administration focuses mightily on boosting Kurdistan's continued economic emergence and jump-starting reconstruction and recovery in southern Iraq. If the stability holds, and that's a big but worthy *if*, the best course going forward would be to lock in what security gains we can in Iraq before conflating that conflict with another involving Iran. After so many U.S. casualties, the American people deserve nothing less from a new president than an Iraq postwar finally done right.

6. WE ARE ENTIRELY READY TO WORK WITH THE INTERNATIONAL COMMUNITY TO REMOVE THESE DEFECTS OF WARTIME INJUSTICE.

More than seven years after 9/11, the United States still struggles to create an alternative judicial system to prosecute terrorists for war crimes as "unlawful enemy combatants." Over and over, the United States Supreme Court does not quite approve. Meanwhile, the International Criminal Court (ICC), set up in 2002 to adjudicate such individuals for crimes against humanity, continues to grow in stature, competency, and—most important—actual cases. So the question begs: Why must America construct its own war-crimes court when the world seems content with the ICC?

America's relationship with the ICC is strained at best, as the U.S. government has systematically strong-armed roughly a hundred nations into signing bilateral immunity treaties that render us exempt from its prosecution. We worry that American troops and even government officials will be subject to war-crimes accusations following future military interventions. That's not an unreasonable fear, so I've long supported these "interventionary prenups," as I like to call them. There's little incentive in serving as the world's marshal if rounding up the bad guys gets you in legal trouble on a regular basis.

But having achieved such blanket immunity from the vast majority of states likely to be on the receiving end of a U.S. military intervention, why should America remain so aloof from the ICC? After all, the court's purview truly extends only to lawless or rogue states that refuse, or are unable, to police their own. So far, all of the ICC's cases have involved the very same states from which America has obtained or sought ICC immunity (by the way, virtually all these countries are found in my Non-Integrated Gap, to no surprise). The Bush administration's stubborn stance, continued from the Clinton years, retarded the development of global case law concerning the terrorists, warlords, and dictators whom America routinely targets in this long war against violent extremism. Not surprisingly, our go-it-alone strategy undercuts our moral authority around the world. I mean, if our own judicial system can't stomach much of this, how can we expect to win any hearts and minds abroad by mimicking the human rights abuses of the very same authoritarian regimes (e.g., Saudi Arabia, Egypt) targeted by our lawless enemies, the Salafi jihadists?

The ICC, which was set up as a permanent version of the UN-sponsored International Criminal Tribunal for the former Yugoslavia, is—in many fine ways—a logical descendant of the American-designed Nuremberg war-crimes court constituted after World War II to try Nazi officials (nod to FDR's Atlantic Charter). With more than a hundred signatory states, the ICC possesses a well-credentialed system for adjudicating and imprisoning these bad actors. What the ICC critically lacks is a credible mechanism for snatching these criminals and hauling them before the court once they've been indicted. Good example: The ICC has indicted Sudanese government officials of war crimes concerning the government-sanctioned ethnic cleansing in Darfur. The problem is, zero arrests so far. By definition, all the ICC's indicted war criminals remain beyond the reach of accepted law, hiding out either in failed states or behind rogue dictatorships. Oddly enough, the United States possesses just such a mechanism in our armed forces, whose global reach allows us to snatch and grab these bad actors with relative impunity, only then to shunt them into our highly controversial alternative military judicial system.

You don't have to be a grand strategist to see where I'm going with this: Once America gets the ICC comfortable enough with its unique "marshaling" capability, there's no reason why this new class of combatants shouldn't be prosecuted in this setting. Indeed, figuring out how to stitch these two systems together is only logical and inevitable.

We've got to rejoin the civilized world on this one.

7. HUMBLY ASK THE INCOMING PRESIDENT TO REVERSE AMERICA'S RECENT UNILATERALISM.

As someone who worked extensively throughout the national security community across the Bush administration, both inside and outside government, I am deeply struck by how the world has basically returned to its pre-9/11 correlation of forces, like a cosmic clock being reset. It's almost as if the sum total effect of the second Bush term was an attempt to repair the damage caused by the first—*mea minima culpa.*

The Bush team's policy reversals of the last two years amounted to a stunning repudiation of the first six years of George W. Bush's presidency—Mr. Hyde subsumed within Dr. Jekyll. Where allies were previously disrespected, at the end they were viewed as essential. Where diplomacy was long eschewed, it was finally pursued with vigor. After six long years of trying to run the entire government from his base, George W. Bush finally attempted, in his final two years, to lead the entire nation. Bush's political opponents rightfully detected weakness and regret and a last-ditch attempt to salvage legacy, while supporters pointed to a self-professed dissident leader extending a freedom agenda in his final months. Both perspectives held much truth, and therein lies an inescapable reality for the incoming president: Bush and Cheney consumed every last ounce of unilateralism afforded us by the world's sympathy over 9/11. Simply put, that well is dry.

They say time heals all wounds. Similarly, it muddles all doctrines. When Bush entered office, transnational terrorism seemed dangerous but manageable—an "over there" challenge. Fast-forward to 2009 and tell me what's different, other than your approach to air travel. Yes, we now know that a 9/11 is eminently possible, and we're keenly aware of its likely engineers and where they now reside—one apartment over in northwest Pakistan. When they pull off the next one, probably in Europe, we'll collectively head to roughly the same spot to roust them out again. Meanwhile, we'll make reasonable efforts to bolster networks against their threats, both here and there, but the world must go on. Terrorists monopolized America's attention for a while, but this happened nowhere else, either because other regions were used to such travails or because bigger things were happening.

At the beginning of 2001, we sensed that the Middle East was broken, with little chance of peace. Iraq and Iran were clearly dangerous, but both were considered manageable through a mix of economic and military efforts. No doubt we have many more boots on the ground today, and our cumulative sacrifice in blood and treasure is alarmingly large, but back then the Persian Gulf was seen as something primarily left to the U.S. military to handle, and so it is again today. Bush's preemptive war became General David Petraeus's counterinsurgency becomes Central Command's enduring challenge, along with Afghanistan and—suddenly in late 2007—Pakistan. If, in 2001, I described a Pentagon dreaming of brilliant, high-tech war with rising China but operationally engrossed by a messy, unstable, low-tech security landscape, today you'd find all the same bureaucratic tensions, exponentially expanded and increasingly fueled by a young generation of ground officers bristling for institutional reform.

The Bush administration entered office complaining that scant attention was being paid to the big pieces of international security, like Russia, China, Europe, and India. Then 9/11, triggering a fit of unilateralist pique, pushed all those great-power concerns aside as we targeted failed states and rogue regimes. Again, fast-forward to today and watch our new president focus—yet again!—on how those big pieces help us manage the little ones (sometimes not bothering to garner international permission before-hand, like Russia's recent beatdown of Georgia). It turns out that you'd better ask the neighbors before you start draining the swamp—or assassi-nating people inside their borders.

Was it enough, in the end, for Bush's second administration to repair, to some extent, the damage to America's global standing created by his first? Yes and no. The reason I supported John Kerry in 2004 was that I felt the Bush team, while being more than up to the necessary task of reset-ting the rules in the wake of 9/11, was distinctly incapable of subsequently gaining much buy-in from the rest of the world. Generating such buy-in always involves trade-offs: Winning most means compromising some. I remain convinced that a Kerry administration would have propelled America far faster toward that inevitable adjustment, the very same re-alignment the Bush White House was finally forced to undertake, in part because the U.S. electorate turned on it and in part because the disrespect shown America by tinhorn dictators the world over simply got too em-barrassing for the neocons to suffer.

So what's been lost? Merely time and opportunity, our two most precious assets in grand strategy.

Our new president has to adjust to this enduring truth: Globali-zation—just like these United States—is all about connectivity, and con-nectivity is all about deal-making, not deal-breaking. Sometimes, as in 1776 and 1945, America is called upon to break some old rules while making up some new ones; 2001 was such a year. But a rule set whose adhering popu-lation consists of America and America alone does not constitute an ad-vance in our grand strategy but an abdication of our global leadership.

8. MAKE A LIST OF ALL THE GREAT POWERS WHOSE NATIONAL INTERESTS WE HAVE HARMED, AND BECOME WILLING TO MAKE CONCESSIONS TO THEM ALL.

Vice President Dick Cheney stated that the long war against radical Islamic extremism would "occupy our successors for two or three or four administrations to come." He was right. But the Bush administration's re-fusal to launch a regional security dialogue in the Middle East was dead wrong. When we don't give all interested parties—both internally and externally—a chance to steer strategic outcomes, we simply invite their counterproductive meddling.

The Bush administration's Big Bang strategy was designed to shake up the Middle East and set in motion transformational change. Done well (the hope going in) or done badly (today's inescapable reality), change is still clearly unfolding. But it's arrogance of the worst sort to expect the world's other great powers to blindly follow America's lead in the numerous resulting scenarios—for example, Iraq's breakup, Iran versus Saudi Arabia in the Gulf, Iran versus Israel on nukes, Syria and Iran versus Israel in Lebanon/Palestine. America's strategic relationships encompass only a fraction of the chessboard currently in play. We have serious influence with Egypt, Saudi Arabia, Israel, Jordan, and—now—Iraq. But our European allies clearly take the lead in Syria, Iran, Lebanon, and Turkey, whereas Russia is the primary political actor throughout Central Asia and the Caucasus—its so-called near abroad. China's growing economic network connects it to Pakistan, a longtime ally, and Iran, its new best friend on energy. It's also rapidly becoming, along with Turkey, a leading economic actor across the "Stans." Finally, there are India's long-standing ties with Iran and the Gulf States, plus Japan's rather extreme dependence on the region's energy.

A regional security dialogue that involves both internal and interested external players is the obvious alternative to the Bush administration's dangerous attempt to enlarge our Iraq problem to include Syria and Iran. It should be modeled on the same "linkages" approach Henry Kissinger employed decades ago in the Cold War in Europe. In 1975, America helped create the Organization for Security and Co-operation in Europe (OSCE), which in the years since has become the "primary instrument for early warning, conflict prevention, crisis management, and postconflict rehabilitation" for its fifty-six member states stretching from Vancouver to Vladivostok. For the first twenty years of its existence, the OSCE was merely a conference where direct adversaries and interested third parties met continuously on issues such as human rights, political reform, and security confidence-building measures.

How important was the OSCE to the Cold War's peaceful denouement? Without it, it's hard to imagine figures like Poland's Lech Walesa or the Czech Republic's Václav Havel rising to the forefront of revolutionary political change, eventually becoming inaugural presidents of their countries' post-Soviet governments. It's also hard imagining the relatively successful processing of the breakup of the former Yugoslavia. Chortle if you must, but the Dayton Peace Accords ten years later look pretty good compared with Iraq. I know some history books say it all came down to Reagan, Pope John Paul II, and Star Wars, but the locals actually involved in the Cold War's dismantling routinely cite a host of smaller, nonheadline issues that got hammered out—month after month and year after year—in the OSCE. Granted, it's boring stuff compared with decapitating air strikes, but it's how the lasting victories are actually secured.

Right now there's nothing in the Middle East that compares to the OSCE (forget about the Arab League), and as the Iraq Study Group, headed by Reagan's old "left" hand, James Baker, argued, there should be. Yes, it would mean Washington couldn't call all the shots, but frankly, it's hard to argue that that would be a bad thing given our recent record. In its absence, expect more Russian complaints and meddling by the day. Also expect China to expand its own regional security policy, selectively favoring certain local dictators over our own. And by all means, feel free to call that kettle black, for what it's worth. Meanwhile, Europe drags its heels on anything that enables another America-instigated war, and regional powers Iran, Israel, and Saudi Arabia wage pointless proxy struggles with one another, begetting nothing but more instability and death. The saddest thing about the antiwar chant of "Blood for oil" is that it's mostly our blood and somebody else's—as in, Asia's—oil. That glaring strategic imbalance will only grow in coming years, making any unilateral approach to "fixing" the Middle East all the more untenable.

George W. Bush was right to lay a Big Bang on the Middle East's calcified political landscape, but it's now clear to everyone concerned that this long war is not ours alone to wage. That inescapable truth awaits the next two or three or four administrations, making it a clear focus of any grand strategy America tries to pursue.

9. MAKE DIRECT OVERTURES TO VIOLENT NONSTATE ACTORS WHENEVER POSSIBLE, EXCEPT WHEN DOING SO WOULD DAMAGE EXISTING ALLIANCES.

Inside the national security community there is the widespread assumption that all new technologies favor our superempowered enemies overwhelmingly over ourselves, leaving them to serve as the fountainhead of real innovation while we're allegedly always in a defensive, reactive crouch. (I know, it sounds almost too stupid to write.) While it is true that criminals and other informal-economy types tend to exploit new communications technologies faster than business or the general population (i.e., the first *anything* usually involves pornography), there is no lasting or pervasive advantage that accrues to nefarious nonstate actors over time, as history demonstrates decade after decade. The "Wild West" stays wild for only so long.

In obvious contrast to this notion is the bias that says all new technologies favor those seeking systematic control over others—the Orwellian perspective. The reality, of course, is that each new wave of technological advance creates more freedom for individuals, not less, and more systematic capacity for self-governance and resilience, not less. Still, this worst-case bias within the national security community is quite pervasive, speaking to that cohort's innate tendency to focus on dangers instead of opportunities.

More broadly, there is the sad tendency inside the Beltway to believe Washington runs America, and the Defense Department is the only truly capable change agent inside the United States goverment, ergo the Defense Department can be used to change the world, using the Trojan Horse of "interagency." If that sounds like the neocon worldview that served us so badly in postwar Iraq, then you're paying attention.

In my opinion, America should view the spread of networks through globalization's advance as an opportunity—not a danger. The more our networks extend, the greater the transparency for our intelligence community, the more the private sector becomes the pervasive and less resisted agent of rule-set enforcement, and the more resilient communities can become—both inside globalization's Core and throughout its Gap regions. Competition is nothing; co-optation and coevolution are everything. In the information technology sector, where I'm a senior executive,

I can tell you, every player my company encounters ends up being simultaneously a client, a distributor, a supplier, a competitor, and an ally.

There is the human assumption that familiarity breeds trust and that connectivity—especially trade connectivity—breeds peace. Over the long haul, this is clearly the case in international affairs. But in the short term, especially under conditions of globalization's rapid advance, the usual reaction from all sides is heightened nationalism. Moreover, when there is heightened connectivity between societies of different levels of modernity, we tend to see a rise in spirituality in the less advanced society as individuals there reach for religion as a way to maintain collective cultural identities that face transformation, and even extinction, because of the exposure to outside, foreign influences—globalization's most threatening dynamic.

In the cyberworld, this dynamic speaks to the Balkanization scenario, which, to some, signals a chaotic fragmentation that subverts the Internet's promise of creating a global culture or village. But to others, this dynamic merely signals that the Internet will largely conform to the real world's cultural contours—at least in the foreseeable future. It also signals that the resulting cybersphere will more likely resemble the sloppy, cultural mash-up that is the United States than any clearly demarcated civilizations—again recognizing the rising Asian quotient to that global mix. So think more *Blade Runner* than *Mayberry R.F.D.*, but keep in mind the globalization of hip-hop.

Dealing with nonstate actors isn't about diminishing their demand for superempowerment but meeting it. The unreasonable ambition of the national security community with regard to moving as far "left of boom" as possible (i.e., preventing the bomb by preventing the bomber) stems from the belief that even if root causes cannot be addressed, effective therapy can somehow be administered through "strategic communications." Two varieties are found: (1) the Oprah-like "If they only knew us better, they'd like us more" approach, and (2) the "We'll *dis*inform them to death" approach. Neither is very realistic, given the tendency of believers of all stripes to self-select their sources of news and information. In other words, pissed-off individuals look for rationalizations on the Web, not conversions. Underlying these approaches is the notion that if demand can be turned off, then the pool of potential violent nonstate actors can be reduced to those already lost to an aggressive stance—in effect, the at-risk population is depopulated.

The problem with this mindset, besides that tendency toward self-selection, is that it seeks to reduce the demands of targeted individuals instead of simply meeting them—for instance, promoting secularism over religiosity when the former denies the search for reinforcing cultural identity and the latter enables it. Until, for example, it becomes clear to an individual that his religious identity can be maintained under the new conditions of heightened connectivity with the outside world, any communications pushing the desirability of religious freedom comes off as a none-too-subtle assault on existing local tradition—as in, "Let my version of non-/religion enter into your culture and compete with yours—or else!"

To truly reduce the pool of potentially violent nonstate actors is to meet their demands for identity-protecting cultural "tariffs," not refuse them. If we expect these traditional cultures to let globalization in, then such generational trade-offs are inevitable. In the end, only the locals can ostracize violent nonstate actors, meaning nonstate actors are the best at flipping other nonstate actors—potential or realized. This is especially true when it comes to young people and even more true for this current generation raised under conditions of hyperconnectivity. In general, young people respond to peer pressure better than authority figures, and authenticity here cannot be spoofed.

10. CONTINUE TO REVIEW OUR GOAL OF ACCELERATED DEMOCRATIZATION AND, WHEN WE ARE WRONG IN OUR STRATEGIC APPROACH, PROMPTLY ADMIT IT.

An old friend explains the difference between dedication and commitment this way: The chicken is dedicated to your breakfast, but the pig is committed. Think about that wide chasm and you'll come to understand how America's grand strategy got so confused under the Bush administration: We committed ourselves to specific outcomes where we should have remained dedicated to broader goals. America should be dedicated to the goal of encouraging democracy around the world, but committed to forcing its appearance nowhere.

It was perfectly fine to topple the right dictator (Saddam Hussein) under the right circumstances ("indicted" by the UN Security Council more than a dozen times), but wrong to commit to Iraq's rapid transition to democracy—an unrealistic goal. The more we remain committed to Iraq's premature democracy, the longer this struggle appears to be America's to prolong or end. But this is an illusion. Iraq's multiple struggles— both violent and merely political—are not ours to win or lose. We've run into levels of commitment on virtually all sides that we're unwilling to match. We conflated the American public's dedication with the Bush administration's commitments—two very different things. The way ahead seems clear enough: Settle for what we can get now and remain dedicated to improving the situation over time. What can we get? First, we've launched a successful Kurdish nation, into which America should logically send some of its forces as a long-term stabilizing presence—just as we did in Kuwait. Second, we're stuck with a long-term Sunni–Shiite tension that either goes dormant because Iraq's neighbors commit themselves to squelching it, or extends itself *ad infinitum* because Saudi Arabia and Iran are both committed to ruling the Gulf now that America is clearly overextended and far too isolated.

The Bush administration's unwavering commitments elsewhere in the region complicated our seemingly intractable position in Iraq. Bush-Cheney remained unblinking in their commitment to Israel, the region's only true democracy, but only marginally dedicated to a peaceful solution between Israel and Palestine. The Bush administration's commitment to Israel naturally translated into further commitment: stopping Tehran's reach for the bomb. America may be dedicated to stopping the spread of nuclear weapons, but we're committed to stopping only certain states from obtaining them. Israel, the world's most powerful undeclared nuclear state, possesses at least two hundred warheads, in addition to a conventional military significantly superior to Iran's. Thanks to our enduring commitment, Israel could easily wipe Iran off the map—today. And yet there is serious talk still throughout Washington about our inevitable war with Iran. Ask yourself whose interests are advanced by such commitment. American? Israeli? Saudi? Remember this: When we go to war, our home front is dedicated but our troops are committed.

Those who make the case for pushing democracy at all costs often point out that terrorists are a function of politics, not economics. As many experts point out, most terrorists who ply their craft in our neck of the woods are middle-class and well educated. Princeton economist Alan Krueger, whose 2007 book *What Makes a Terrorist: Economics and the Roots of Terrorism* explored this subject, employs a lot of historical data to show that when it comes to reducing the pool of terrorists, there's no clear link between reducing poverty or raising educational levels and that end goal. So what makes terrorists? Krueger's data say most arise in states that suppress civil liberties and deny political rights. In short, dictatorships spawn terrorists, because wherever "nonviolent means of protest are curtailed, malcontents appear to be more likely to turn to terrorist tactics." That answer provides a motive and posits that an absence of opportunity drives some toward violence, but here is where things become complex.

Truly strong dictatorships tend not to suffer domestic terrorists, simply because they suppress civil liberties so effectively. These regimes may frequently sponsor terrorists abroad, but that's an easily explained tactic: Weaker states employ terrorists in asymmetrical warfare against stronger foes, while stronger ones may sponsor terrorists to avoid direct warfare with similar opponents. When it comes to domestic terrorism, it's the weaker authoritarian regimes that both spawn terrorists and have a hard time controlling them. In those situations, potential terrorists are afforded just enough economic opportunity to make them dangerous—namely, access to financial, communication, and travel networks that facilitate their tactics. Authoritarian regimes can also push these troublemakers abroad, and therein lies our main interest in this long war. But since almost 90 percent of attacks occur in the terrorist's country of origin, 9/11-like strikes remain statistically rare, meaning the average American is far more likely to be killed by lightning than by al Qaeda.

Shifting gears, you might argue that since most predominantly Muslim countries feature authoritarian regimes, Islam itself is the real culprit. I don't know about you, but asking Muslim societies to become less Muslim strikes me as a nonstarter in a world where globalization's systematic advance naturally triggers a revival of religious fervor and cultural identity. But even if we—for the sake of argument—accept that causal link, we're still left with the question of how to increase civil liberty within the political system, and here's where Krueger's argument that economics doesn't have any direct impact leaves me unsatisfied. If you want to increase civil liberties, then you must increase the size of the middle class, because, historically speaking, nothing predicts the rise of democracy better than a growing (and aging) middle class.

Indeed, numerous studies today note the same correlation: The bigger the middle class's share of national income, the greater that country's civil liberties. In contrast, oligarchic capitalism, or economies in which a small elite controls the vast majority of the wealth, trend overwhelmingly toward authoritarianism—the oil-rich Middle East particularly.

How do you create a middle class? You raise income broadly by fostering individual economic freedom and women's rights, and seeking sufficiently deep economic connectivity with the outside world so those empowered entrepreneurs can access new sources of capital and technology. If you attempt to short-circuit that historical evolution by imposing democracy upon too small an economic base, you'll end up with what Fareed Zakaria calls an illiberal democracy, or elections in which radical extremists prevail.

This long war requires serious grand strategy, not seductive shortcuts. The United States should be in the business of applying both its hard-power and soft-power assets toward the same grand strategic end: globalization made truly global. Feed stomachs and wallets first, *then* hearts and minds will follow. In this change process, globalization is both contagion and cure, acting as a volatile accelerant of freedom's expansion around the world.

11. SEEK TO CREATE STRATEGIC ALLIANCES WITH RISING POWERS THROUGH DIPLOMATIC LINKAGES AND MILITARY-TO-MILITARY COOPERATION.

For America to win a long war against violent extremism, we must effectively integrate the one-third of humanity whose noses remain pressed to the glass, wondering when they'll be invited to the global economic party. That process is labor-intensive, whether it's postconflict stabilization and reconstruction in failed states or infrastructure development and market creation in developing economies. Americans price out far too high, whether we're talking the political costs of our soldiers or our private contractors' wages. Yes, we must be significantly involved, but it's not going to be Americans—much less Europeans—who do the heavy lifting.

No, it's going to be those longtime frontier laborers of the global economy, the Chinese and the Indians. But these rising powers need our help, too. As both become increasingly dependent on resources drawn from unstable regions, Beijing and New Delhi must continue leveraging U.S. military power. Otherwise, they'll be left unduly subsidizing weak or corrupt regimes, with their economic connectivity put at risk by local warlords, chronic insurgencies, and violent extremists bent on driving out globalization's networks. If America can't afford to maintain global security on its own, and these rising pillars of the global economy can't afford to replace our effort, then strategic alliance makes eminent sense. Put our nations together, and the global economy cannot be hijacked by shared enemies; but put them at odds, and we could easily destroy globalization much as we did in the 1930s.

Still, here's the question I often face: Why doesn't America choose India over China for this alliance? India is already a democracy, while China is expected to remain authoritarian for quite some time. I certainly don't argue against strategic alliance with India. I'd like it as soon as possible, but I nonetheless prioritize China for several reasons. First, a great portion of our national security establishment wants desperately to cast China as our inevitable long-term threat (now along with a resurgent Russia). Why? It allows it to buy and maintain a huge, high-tech military force for large-scale wars. Second, by keeping China our preferred threat, we deny ourselves access to its significant military manpower and growing budget. With Europe and Japan both aging dramatically and Beijing's strategic interests in unstable regions skyrocketing, this makes no sense. Third, if we capture China in strategic alliance, we'll get India in the bargain. But if we try it the other way around, we'll probably ruin our chances with Beijing, whose leaders fear an encirclement strategy by Washington with India as its key western pillar. Better to lock in China as soon as possible as the land-power anchor of an East Asian NATO. The sooner we achieve that, along with Korea's reunification, the sooner we can draw down our military in the region and better employ them in hotter spots around the world.

A smart America co-opts China's rise just as Britain shaped ours a century ago. Instead of containing China, we should steer its rise to suit our strategic purposes. And what China must do is what America did back then: build its military and rebrand it as a force for global stability. In grand strategic terms, China's embryonic military dialogue with the

United States should be viewed as anything but adequate. Rather than continuing to size our conventional forces implicitly with China's residual "threat" in mind, our military commands around the world should rapidly and dramatically expand their military-to-military cooperation with the People's Liberation Army—not because we "trust" China or because we "fear" it but simply because America cannot hope to govern the emerging global security environment on its own.

12. HAVING HAD A STRATEGIC AWAKENING AS THE RESULT OF THESE STEPS, AMERICA MUST TRY TO SELL THIS GRAND STRATEGY TO THE WORLD, AND PRACTICE THESE PRINCIPLES IN ALL ITS EFFORTS TO SHRINK THE GAP AND MAKE GLOBALIZATION TRULY GLOBAL.

The ancient Greek poet Archilochus opined, "The fox knows many things, but the hedgehog knows one big thing." Let me submit that we just lived through eight years of the decidedly hedgehog presidency of George W. Bush, whose strategic failures must logically be remedied by a new American grand strategy of "many things" instead of the "one big thing" called terrorism.

Americans generally prefer leaders to be steadfast and armed with a readily identifiable worldview. To have a mind subject to periodic change is considered weak and irresolute. We often label these individuals flip-floppers, liars, and—worst of all—politicians, when "lifelong learners" and "deal-makers" are equally applicable. Our democracy regularly requires painful compromises to balance the extremes against the large, mushy middle that encompasses most American voters. After all, this republic is ruled by the majority, which sometimes craves the hedgehog's unwavering consistency (e.g., Abraham Lincoln, Henry Clay) and at other times welcomes the fox's intellectual agility (Alexander Hamilton, Theodore Roosevelt).

During the 1930s Great Depression, Americans trusted the preeminent presidential fox, Franklin Roosevelt, to navigate those shoals and the subsequent world war. Taking many of his cues from his ultrafox mentor, Woodrow Wilson, Roosevelt aimed for nothing less than reshaping the world order in America's image. When FDR passed, history offered us a true hedgehog in Harry Truman, to whom George W. Bush deserves comparison. Faced with a dangerously fluid global security environment,

Harry "gave 'em hell" in the form of a military-industrial complex and the containment strategy, defining our Cold War vision for decades to come. A war-weary America turned next to hedgehog Dwight Eisenhower, hoping his steadying hand would calm our increasingly volatile confrontations with the Soviets. The result was both comforting and suffocating: our "happy days" stability and slow-but-steadily-improving race relations came at the price of McCarthyism and father-knows-best gender conformity.

A trio of fox presidents defined the tumultuous 1960s. It started with John Kennedy's cacophony of bold visions (e.g., space race, foreign aid, irregular warfare), grew with Lyndon Johnson's legislative genius (civil rights, Medicare, voting rights), and culminated in Richard Nixon's stunningly ambitious diplomatic schemes. Linking all three in failure, however, was the intractable Vietnam conflict and the social unrest it eventually triggered back home. Following Nixon's frightening self-destruction through the Watergate scandal, Americans selected three consecutive hedgehog presidents to achieve—across a long historical arc—a resurrection of America's self-confidence and character. Gerald Ford afforded us "a time to heal," while Jimmy Carter restored morality to our national politics and foreign policy. But it was Ronald Reagan, a quintessential hedgehog, who most shaped the global superpower that emerged—seemingly unscathed—from the Cold War. His turbocharged defense buildup begat the awesome conventional warfighting capacity we possess today—the Leviathan ensuring peace among great powers. Most important, Reagan restored America's belief in its inherent goodness and its duty to combat evil in this world.

The Cold War's end demanded a new strategic nimbleness from presidents free of that era's ideological rigidity. We got that agility in global security affairs from George H. W. Bush's pragmatic administration and in global economic affairs from Bill Clinton's free-trade evangelism. After the dizzying ride of the go-go nineties, George W. Bush pulled off the electoral miracle that was the 2000 election, promising more humility in our foreign policy. At least, that was the theory going in. To that end, the inexperienced former governor was provided several steadying hands from previous Republican administrations (e.g., Cheney, Rumsfeld, Powell, Rice). But when 9/11 intervened, Americans discovered George

Bush—so long incurious about global affairs—to be the most myopically hedgehog president in modern times, a man whose entire legacy will be defined by his decision to invade Iraq and occupy it badly.

Now, as the Obama administration settles in, let me offer this advice: Seek out foxes and avoid hedgehogs. Don't listen to leaders who tell you our recent election boiled down to one thing and one thing alone. While that approach made sense for some time following 9/11, America has clearly moved past that historical inflection point. We need to grant our new president the opportunity to supply more than one answer to every question; he must have a toolkit that is as diverse as America's middle-class ideology must remain flexible. We need a deal-maker, a compromiser, and a closer. We need someone able to finish what others cannot, and start that which others dare not.

We need leaders who know many things, because we've had enough of those who know only one big thing.

Three

THE AMERICAN TRAJECTORY
Of Great Men and Great Powers

No outcome under the sun is certain. In America's short history, there have never been inevitable outcomes. Uniting these states took great work by great men with great vision.

As a relatively young country, we Americans spend little time remembering our history. That tendency gives us a bit of myopia when it comes to judging the political evolution of other countries. We simply cannot understand why everyone shouldn't be able to quickly put together a democracy like our own. As we scan the horizon looking for the future, and as we regard the development of men and nations on distant shores, and as the American System spreads across the world through the revolutionary force known as globalization, we would do well to remember how we ourselves became a great power in the first place, and that the process wasn't at all pretty. American liberal democracy did not spring whole from the head of Zeus.

The harsh truth is that most developing countries that embrace markets and globalization do so as single-party states. Sure, many feature a marginal opposition party, just as the Harlem Globetrotters always play the Washington Generals, but they're still single-party states. Mexico was like this for decades, as were South Korea and Japan.

Once economic development matured enough, a real balance took hold, and power started shifting back and forth between parties. Malaysia heads for the same tipping point today.

Americans, especially experts and politicians, typically view these regimes with a certain disdain, wondering how a public can put up with a manipulative political system where elites decide who runs for high office and only a tiny fraction of the population has any real influence. We demand more competition, more suffrage, and freer elections—now!

But take a trip back with me to the beginnings of our own country, and let me try to convince you that America needs to summon more patience with such developments, because we often demand of others what we certainly didn't have ourselves as we struggled to our feet as a nation.

Remember this: Our country was born of revolution, including a nasty guerrilla war waged by a ragtag collection of militias against the most powerful military in the world at that time. We fought dirty, even launching a surprise attack during a religious holiday. We mercilessly persecuted fellow citizens who sided with the occupational authority. The enemy branded our military leader a terrorist. In fact, its parliament was the first in history to use such terminology to describe our violent attacks against its commerce. And true to our violent extremism, we "elected" this rebel military leader our first president in 1789. I use the word "elected" loosely, because he essentially ran unopposed—by design.

Less than 2 percent of our country's population was actually able to cast votes, as roughly half of the states chose electors in their legislatures— rich landowning patricians selecting one of their own. This rebel leader ran unopposed again for reelection three years later in 1792.

When the general finally stepped down in 1797, an outcome by no means certain, he was replaced by another revolutionary leader—an unlovable enforcer to whom the revolutionary elite had delegated a number of unsavory jobs over the years. Like the general, this radical lawyer wasn't associated with an organized party as such. His revolutionary credentials were beyond reproach.

Our third president, one of the world's most notorious radical ideologues, ushered in a period of single-party rule in 1800. During that election, only six of sixteen states actually allowed the "people"—white men who met certain qualifications—to vote in the presidential race. Certain racial groups were denied the right to vote, as were women.

This one-party rule, subsequently dubbed the Era of Good Feelings, extended almost a quarter-century, getting so stale at one point that an incumbent president ran unopposed.

Finally, a whopping forty-eight years after we issued our famous Declaration of Independence declaring all men equal, we conducted a presidential election in which three-quarters of the states let their citizens vote directly for electors.

Four years later, in 1828, America finally saw an "outsider," meaning someone not from the first revolutionary generation or its immediate progeny, win the White House. Naturally, he was another war hero, who, over his eight years in office, brutalized his political opponents so much that they mockingly dubbed him "King Andrew."

The "king" then displayed the Putinesque temerity to handpick his successor, earning him the equivalent of a "third term."

This was the first half-century of American political history.

It took us 89 years to free the slaves and 189 years to guarantee African-Americans the right to vote.

Women waited 144 years before earning suffrage.

If a mature, multiparty democracy was so darn easy, everybody would have one.

IN ORDER TO FORM A MORE PERFECT GLOBALIZATION . . .

There are four fundamental reasons why American grand strategy matters more right now than any other nation's grand strategy.

The first is that the American example is the source code for this era's version of globalization, which superseded the colonial model of world integration after its collapse as a result of the massive continental civil war that ran from 1914 to 1945. These United States represent the oldest and most successful multinational economic, political, and security union on the planet, a collection of states whose integration has been so successful and so deep that we forget the fantastic journey that brought us to this present state of being. We should not forget it, because it is our essential gift to world history, currently finding its replication—finally—in the European context from which we sprang. The success of that model, the European Union, has made it the second great source code for the future of globalization. By both improving upon and falling short of the original, it provides the world a much-needed contrast and range of choices. It also lightens America's load in shrinking the Gap.

The second reason is that America currently serves as the sole historical bridge between settled Europe's postmilitary, postnationalistic achievement of stable identity and rising Asia's premilitary, prenationalistic pursuit of the same. In other words, while Europe has evolved past the great sources of twentieth-century conflict (militarism, nationalism, ideologies in general), Asia's emerging powers—except for Japan—are rapidly approaching these historical phases, largely clinging to the hope that comprehensive marketization of their economies alone will so integrate their societies with the larger world as to render these traps obsolete. The trade-off, however, is substantial for the planet as a whole, because in so rapidly integrating with the global economy, Asian nations have turbocharged globalization's dynamics to the point of resurrecting fears of zero-sum competitions among great powers for resources, markets, and military allies in the decades ahead. They've resurrected the specter of empires. Having avoided that historical path through our pursuit of an "empire of ideals," America remains at once militarily empowered and still ideologically committed enough to use that power in defense of the global system we did so much to create. Europe is no longer able to play that muscular role, and Asia—save Putin—seeks to avoid the temptations associated with it.

Thus, by occupying the military role of global Leviathan, America frees Europe to pursue the further evolution of its multinational union that currently abuts several troubled zones desperately in need of such integration—North Africa, the Middle East, the Caucasus and the Balkans—while likewise providing security coverage for Asia's far cruder extensions of economic networks in many of these same trouble zones, plus a significant number of others (e.g., Central Asia, Southeast Asia, sub-Saharan Africa, and Andean South America). The trick, of course, is calibrating America's grand strategy as a whole, and particularly its use of that unequaled military power, to these seemingly competitive but actually overwhelmingly complementary dynamics of global integration. Pursued too unilaterally or recklessly, America's use of force in managing globalization's further expansion can easily trigger conflicting responses from Europe and/or Asia, with the most likely outcome being an East–West standoff painfully reminiscent of the Cold War. If use of force is pursued too "humbly" or with too much deference, today's emerging powers might feel compelled to replicate the sort of self-destructive foreign policy practices once employed by past colonial powers—a zero-sum mindset the planet can ill afford in the decades ahead.

Third, America's ability to maintain its status as global military Leviathan is far from assured absent a clear grand strategy that articulates the rationale for such a role. That articulation is what sustains the American public's support for the regular employment of that force, while dispelling the fears of the rest of the world regarding the use of military might that is often seen as arbitrary or self-aggrandizing. The sweet spot to be targeted is thus a vision that says to both Americans and the rest of the world: These are the mutually agreed-upon conditions under which U.S. military forces are deployed to improve the global security environment. Does this give the world a say in how we use military force? Yes. But it defines more the "ceiling," or those lines we will not cross, than the "floor," the minimum effort we are compelled to make. Frankly, America's fears have always tended more toward the higher boundaries (Have we gone too far?) than the lower ones (Should we be doing more?), given our overall wealth, geographic security, and sense of duty to others. And so we desire constraints on our tendency to go overboard, just as the world does. If reasonably achieved, such a grand strategy both preserves and sanctifies our status as sole global military superpower.

Finally, America's grand strategy matters most right now primarily because it is so off-kilter from globalization's current trajectory. We're fighting a "global war" that no one else on the globe seems to recognize, against enemies whose power we consistently exaggerate to the point of provoking disbelief among even our closest allies. America seems paranoid and belligerent at exactly the historical moment when the world is going our way. And when that exemplar, sporting the world's biggest gun, seems so disturbed about global trends, it sows the seeds of uncertainty across the international system by suggesting that we don't have a clue about what lies ahead. Neither Europe nor Asia can fill this vision void, because while each can offer models (Europe's integration of states, China's national development, Russia's petrocracy), none other than the United States of America can offer a trusted mechanism for eliminating the risk of debilitating conflict—however scaled. The price of war determines all other prices in the global marketplace. Either America backs those "securities" or they will be subject to wild fluctuation.

BORN IN THE USA

In this chapter, we will journey through America's two great historical arcs: the creation, transformation, and taming of the United States from 1776 to the start of the twentieth century; and the subsequent projection of that "states uniting" model upon the global landscape, beginning with the administration of Theodore Roosevelt, whose presidency marked the great tipping point between the two eras. In the first arc, we'll see an American System proposed by our revolution and increasingly imposed across a continent's wilderness, tested by the scourge of civil war and transformed by the process of frontier integration, and then finally shamed by its cruel excesses and tamed by a progressive spirit that marked our true flowering as a nation. Once defined, *this* United States proposed, with utmost sincerity, a similar solution for the world as a whole, defensively imposing such structure on part of it only after a period of unprecedented global strife, then to have that model immediately tested by its ideological opposite—the Soviets' empire of force. Meeting that challenge, and better yet, ultimately co-opting it, the American System of states—uniting in increasingly freer markets, integrating trade and production, explicit collective security, and improved network transparency—found its historic moment at the Cold War's end. This "end" of the Old World's history saw the exuberant resumption of the New World's destiny as source code for freedom's viral advance around the planet, even as that code remains largely "uncracked" by today's grand strategists and unarticulated by a succession of post–Cold War presidents.

But just as assuredly, the tsunami of integration that is globalization generated many new forms of upheaval and even more forms of local modification, triggering great unease in its modern originator and protective Leviathan. Why? Because this United States failed to recognize its own history in these integrating processes—these states uniting—and thus, in its fears and impatience, began to describe the emerging system it had unleashed as "unmanageable" and "chaotic," constituting a threat to our future. And when that threat was made manifest on 9/11, our search for a new destiny began, albeit one immediately and instinctively defined in the most selfish and zero-sum terms: securing the homeland from the chaos of globalization's many untamed frontiers. To their credit, other poles (the EU, China, Russia, India, Brazil) have since stood up to balance our mania, and it is now our challenge to realign our sense of historical purpose with their mix of needs and knowledge, for in our combined assets we locate more than enough resources to master the global challenges that lie ahead. Our American System, tested and transformed by the Cold War into a global platform that we now share with the world, subsequently enters into the same "shaming and taming" period that once marked our own graduation from nearly unsalvageable union to rising world power. Only this time the stakes are not merely our nation's health but the survival of the world.

Having successfully replicated the economic construct of our American System among the vast majority of the world's population, we are now faced with the long-term challenge of replicating its political constructs—its laws, its institutions, its culture and associated freedoms of religion, speech, and leadership choice—not merely *within* nations but *across* the international system as a whole (and yes, that does mean our global leadership is likewise anything but assured).

This is the world we have created. These are the forces we have unleashed.

Once we bullied, cajoled, and convinced a majority of the planet to embrace our economic model, we set in motion—through the extreme resource demands it has generated and will continue to generate—the historical process by which some version of democracy would emerge worldwide. For only through the flowering of such political openness will all that popular demand be accommodated. Our planet's ecological limits will simply not tolerate any alternative for long, no matter how virulent the *ism*. As we know so well, that journey from economic interdependence (that which says we must share to get collectively rich) to political interdependence (the Golden Rule) is fraught with danger. We know where this global journey must lead because we have surmounted these challenges, however imperfectly, in these United States, where our democracy of "tribes"—at times constituted as states and sections, mobs and majorities, trusts and self-made men, cultures and factions, special interests and economic classes, movements and rebellions—has slowly but surely negotiated the needs of the many against the needs of the few.

THE AMERICAN SYSTEM, PROPOSED AND IMPOSED

If America is indeed the source code for this era's globalization, then we can with great certainty locate America's kernel code, or its core operating system, within Britain's political evolution of the seventeenth and eighteenth centuries, highlighted by the Glorious Revolution of 1688, which established both the rule of parliament over the crown and the political rights of citizens vis-à-vis their government in a Bill of Rights. As Walter Russell Mead correctly notes:

> As the heir to centuries of Anglo-Saxon politics the United States supports, however inconsistently, a political and social philosophy based on free choice and private property, tolerance among religions found in Protestant Christian values, and the idea that individuals—including women—have inalienable and equal rights which states must observe and protect.

That freedom from interference "from above," when combined with the European Enlightenment's radical notion of individual improvement "from below," or the idea that economic growth and social progress improve human morality, yields the essential equation of American democracy: Self-rule, however flawed, is progressive rule because of the social and economic talent that is unleashed for the benefit of society, including the systematic improvement of both leadership and laws. Our political development is therefore intimately intertwined with our sense of economic achievement and self-improvement—the pursuit of happiness subject to constant reinvention.

In construct, then, America was built for speed, for the cutting edge, and for both producing and attracting ambition. Our promise is of equal opportunity, not equal outcome. And so, in our supreme optimism, we are the perpetual start-up company of nations, built around ideals that assume an unlimited market for personal growth. So give us your square pegs, your chronically dissatisfied, your insufferable oddballs yearning to try something different, because here, with the most minimal liability we can collectively stomach, we'll give you that chance to fail repeatedly until you strike your version of gold. In a country where truths are self-evident, anybody can come up with evidence of a better way, because, in the end and from our very beginning, America's political model revolves around the social and economic goals of constant, individual-led improvement.

But the success of our bizarre revolution-from-below was far from assured in its early days. In a time of "great upheaval" that historian Jay Winik argues "gave birth to the modern world," America was but one of three age-defining experiments in political liberalization, the other two being the bloody and chaotic French Revolution and Catherine the Great's ambitious reforms in Imperial Russia. Neither ended well, and if not for George Washington's unprecedented decisions, first to *willingly* surrender his sword to Congress in 1783 as the commander of a victorious revolutionary army and then in 1797 to *voluntarily* step down from near-sovereign power after seven years as our president, who can say how our experiment in self-rule would have turned out?

As Winik describes our infancy, "America was born as an artificial series of states, woven together with the string of precariously negotiated compacts and agreements, charters and covenants." We had no natural borders, save for that created by the Atlantic Ocean, and the 1783 treaty that ended our revolutionary war against England codified the expansionistic claims of several of America's free and sovereign states to the lands of the trans-Appalachian West, putting them in potential conflict with one another, as well as with Britain, France, and Spain for future control of the continent. Befitting their individual ambitions and mutual suspicions, each independent state maintained its own army and navy. Our vaunted Constitution, written in 1787 and put into effect two years later, contained so many tortured compromises between the Federalists and the proponents of states' rights (the Anti-Federalists), including the poison pill of slavery, that the words "nation" and "national" never even made it into the signed document.

And what did our first decade of official existence bring? There was an undeclared quasi-war with France that triggered, in a spasm of fear, the Alien and Sedition Acts of 1798—John Adams presaging Dick Cheney. There were also three significant insurrections, including one—the Whiskey Rebellion, peaking in 1794—that forced, for the first and only time in American history, a sitting president (Washington, naturally) to assume actual field command of U.S. military forces. Meanwhile, our ships came under such casual assault across the world's oceans that at one point roughly one-fifth of the federal budget went to paying Barbary Coast pirate kings ransom for cargo and personnel captured. Amazingly, with all that going on, there wasn't a single slave rebellion. Those would come later.

Despite its internal divisions and inherent weakness, this young nation put aside all logical fears of becoming, as Washington feared, the "sport of European politics," and instead concentrated all its energies on rapid expansion westward. As Robert Kagan writes in *Dangerous Nation*, "inducements to expansionism were embedded in the new republic's legal and institutional structures," meaning that "American settlers venturing to the frontier carried their rights and their political influence with them." The Northwest Ordinance of 1787 was the road map, less a foreign policy than simply the continued exploitation of an inviting geography. The same private initiative that drove the original colonies' success made Americans the most invasive of species. This "guest worker" would one day show up in your territory and not leave your lands until they were his. Once his numbers were great enough, his portable rights suddenly became your insoluble problem and his new nation's new *cause célèbre*. Early Americans were the economic jihadists of their age, with their "caliphate" incomplete until they had reached the Pacific shore, driving off or killing any who stood in their way and calling upon their government's "revolutionary guards," or state militias, as their bodyguards.

Although early Americans saw nothing revolutionary in their philosophy of work as self-improvement, especially working the land, its impact on Native Americans was clearly catastrophic. They were simply swept aside by the Americans' superior numbers and willingness to use force to protect their new holdings. As Kagan notes, by imposing "one set of values upon a people with a very different conception of human nature and social order," American settlers were effectively pioneering globalization—the cross-cultural engulfing of traditional societies by American-style market economics—as in, *Whatever your old values were, this is how property and goods and services will now be valued and traded.* As today, the rationale is always brutally competitive: If I can create more value than you, then why shouldn't I be allowed to dominate this market for the larger good? To the extent that many Americans today find themselves on the receiving end of such cruel logic (e.g., the "China price," sovereign wealth funds), that chicken has finally come home to roost.

In forging this ambitious course, America was likewise pioneering the art of separatism prompted by a propitious exposure to the global economy—another invention that now circles back to haunt us. As we have already seen with modern globalization and will continue to witness in the decades ahead, once transnational connectivity takes root across a political entity easily divided by geography or ethnicity or socioeconomic status, it is always the most ambitious portion that inevitably seeks political divorce in order to cut a better economic deal with the outside world. Examples are Slovenia in the former Yugoslav Republic and the Kurds in what will someday be the former or federated Iraq. In colonial America, the proximate trigger for such revolution was the British crown's illegitimate taxes, but the ultimate rationale was that the colonies simply felt they could do better on their own and that Britain was holding them back from their natural potential to dominate the continent, regardless of the geopolitical grief it might cause distant London with Europe's other colonial powers. As such, George Washington's retiring admonition to avoid "foreign entanglements" spoke less to avoiding meddling in European affairs than to concentrating all attention on America's westward advance at the expense of those same European powers. We didn't revolt from Britain to become something unlike it but ultimately to grow beyond it in strength and world influence. Not surprisingly, our great divorce from Britain lasted until British needs for protective alliance against Germany early in the twentieth century made a new arrangement possible and necessary. Only then did the "special relationship" take root. Before that, America was at once dependent on British investment and resentful of British power and prestige—a situation the United States would experience from the other side with many countries in the twentieth century.

Intimidated by the loss of Britain's protection on the high seas and subject to its economic sanctions, America had the grand strategic goal from the start, as Kagan notes, to become a "great world power" by establishing an inland empire. On this point, all our Founding Fathers were in clear agreement. The real question, however, was the best method for achieving that power, and here is where the matter of grand strategy actually shaped the future course of American politics by ultimately encouraging the rise of competing political parties, each centered on a particular answer to the question, How best to make America a world power? This development was neither preordained nor desired by the Founding Fathers, virtually all of whom feared divisive "factions" as a source of internal weakness leading to failed statehood that would invite foreign meddling. Indeed, Washington himself foresaw the possibility of secessions and civil strife as a result of political parties, believing they were inimical to the long-term health of the nation.

On the one side stood the Federalists, led by Alexander Hamilton, an entirely self-invented individual whose Dickensian childhood in the West Indies taught him much about the value of commerce and available finance and the dangers of relying primarily on agricultural commodities for export earnings. The Federalists believed in a strong central government and focused their sights on commercial expansionism. On the other side stood an evolving cast of characters: first the Anti-Federalists, concentrated primarily in the South, where states' rights would remain a battle cry for decades, over time to be embodied in Thomas Jefferson and his leadership of the republican faction (the forerunner of Andrew Jackson's Democratic Party) that clashed with Hamilton, hurling the slander at him that, through his proposed strong central government, he sought to replicate aspects of the British monarchy in the New World. Jefferson believed America's future development should remain more agriculturally based, fearing that the rise of too much industry would generate the many social ills seen in industrializing England.

Yet Jefferson too was an avowed expansionist. It's just that he, like most "states' rights" elements from the South, defined their expansionism first and foremost as the acquisition of land—meaning more farmland. In

Jefferson's dream of America, the reach of the central government would have been limited (e.g., a small committee would manage affairs in peacetime, with Congress seeing only episodic sessions), cities would remain of modest size, farmer-citizens would rule largely from below, and our country would become an agricultural superpower in the mode of today's Brazil. Indeed, Jefferson would have found much to praise in Brazil's current role as leader of emerging markets in globalization. If Hamilton took his cues largely from urbanizing, industrializing Britain, then Jefferson's ideal (based on his time there as ambassador) was rural, republican France. How reasonable was this view? You have to remember that throughout the first half of the nineteenth century, Europe viewed America, 95 percent of whose population at that time was involved in agriculture, almost exclusively as a source of staple commodities. Indeed, beaver pelts were the signature export through the 1830s, giving American explorers their primary motivation to map the Western wilderness. Later, as cotton became king, America would dominate that global market at a level that today's OPEC could never dream of achieving in oil.

Hamilton, in contrast, saw our agricultural exports and dependence on raw materials as a prescription for permanent underdevelopment. Indeed, America's living standards in the first quarter of the nineteenth century compare nicely to your average Third World economy today. Hamilton had no desire to see America in a state of permanent anger against the Great Satan of his day, Britain, or locked into a long-term dependent trade relationship with the advancing economies of the age, held back by the scourge of slavery. If, in looking deep into the future, Hamilton could have named the country plight to be avoided, he might have easily selected today's Iran as his nightmare: pointlessly revolutionary and anti-imperialist, with a leadership fixated and provocatively hostile to past colonial rulers, commercially and financially retarded, dominated by religious and cultural zealots who limit trade ties with the outside world and keep economic development largely centered on natural resources— in short, a country operating far below its natural potential for power and influence.

Hamilton had argued from the beginning that unless a strong central government was created, America would be permanently subject to the dangers of secession, breakup into smaller confederacies, and even civil war, with each possibility affording opportunity for Europe's meddling powers to divide and conquer these disunited states. In his mind, unless an organizing principle of economic-development-leading-to-world-power were enunciated and pursued, America would dissolve into pieces for all the same reasons that the colonies first sought independence from Britain: States or sections would simply decide to follow their own vision of development (with slavery a crucial delineator) and, believing a better deal could be cut with the global economy, would go their own way.

Hamilton's grand strategy was actually a catch-up strategy, in many ways the first great rapid-development strategy of the modern world. Today we view such strategies primarily through the lens of the socialist experiments of the twentieth century: Stalin's forced industrialization and collectivization of agriculture, Mao's insane "great leap forward," and so on. But Hamilton's was the first great expression of a market-based "great leap forward," and in his precocious brilliance, he laid it all out, at age thirty-six, in his 1791 "Report on Manufactures" as our nation's first secretary of the treasury. This document is reasonably described as the world's first grand strategic description of what we today know as globalization, originally defined within the American context: a superstate directing the development of a common, continental-sized market. It was the first clear articulation of the American ambition to global power.

The plan featured aggressive state intervention in the economy's development. It would select which industries should be developed first and then encourage their rise through protective tariffs and favorable credit. Following Washington's lead, Hamilton believed first attention should be given to industries that provided America capacity to build its own military armaments. Moreover, industrial espionage was to be encouraged and sanctioned by the government. Once such thievery was achieved, Hamilton directed the U.S. government to issue patents. As biographer Ron Chernow writes, "Building upon this precedent, Hamilton put the full authority of the Treasury behind the piracy of British trade secrets."

But even more crucial than such initial industrial planning, protectionism, and espionage, Hamilton's vision of an American System centered on the state's active role in financing "internal improvements," with a special focus on roads and canals and other modes of public infrastructure, the avowed goal being, in Chernow's words, "to meld America's scattered regional markets into a single unified whole." By arguing for this course, Hamilton laid out a truly grand strategy for a young nation, one that can only be viewed, from the perspective of that age and America's meager government, as insanely ambitious. But in this precocious description of multinational union leading to global economic power, we can locate the very same prime directives that later animated the rise of the European Union and today's China, right down to the need for the government to closely inspect its products for compliance with regulations specifically designed to advance the nation's industrial prowess.

Hamilton's "Report on Manufactures" was clearly ahead of its time. Chernow calls him "a messenger from a future that we now inhabit." But Hamilton was far more than a prophet. As Winik notes:

> Hamilton's fingerprints are on every facet of modern American life: the Constitution, the *Federalist Papers* (which he wrote the bulk of), a strong presidency, an independent judiciary, a powerful federal government, big cities, capital markets, Wall Street, the legal profession, the newspaper profession (he started the *New York Post*), a vigorous military, and remarkably, that is not an exhaustive list.

Indeed, for Hamilton likewise created the Customs Service and the U.S. Coast Guard during his initial stint as secretary of the treasury, and launched the original Bank of the United States, the forerunner of today's Federal Reserve System. But it is true that Hamilton's vision of an American System would not enjoy its realization until the decades immediately following America's Civil War.

The great bridge between Hamilton's original articulation of an American grand strategy to achieve global power and its true flowering in the Second Industrial Revolution of the late nineteenth century can be found in the long political career of Kentucky's Henry Clay. A committed Jefferson Republican from the day he first arrived in Washington in 1807 and the acknowledged leader of the Whigs at the time of his death in 1852, Clay played, across four decades of national statesmanship, the role of tireless champion of what he first dubbed "an American System" that would allow its citizens, in their economic integration of not just the

United States but over time possibly the entire Western Hemisphere, to "become real and true Americans." Clay followed Hamilton's plan to the best of his considerable ability as the "great compromiser" of his age, serving consecutively as the first dominant speaker of the House of Representatives (he engineered the Missouri Compromise of 1820), then as John Quincy Adams's secretary of state, next as Andrew Jackson's main political foil, and finally as the Senate's "great pacificator," whose 1850 "great compromise" staved off Civil War for another decade. It is argued by some historians that if Clay, a perpetual candidate for the presidency, had won the office in 1844 instead of James K. Polk, not only would there have been no Mexican War but possibly the Civil War itself might have been averted.

Clay's primary scheme to implement "internal improvements" was to use high tariffs to protect nascent industries and develop what he called "the home market," while promoting the sale of public lands and using the proceeds as the basis for funding roads and canals. An unrepentant economic nationalist, Clay effectively played Hamilton to Andrew Jackson's Jefferson, battling "King Andrew the First" over high tariffs, the second chartered Bank of the United States, and Jackson's preference for infrastructure development that favored agricultural exports over industrial goods—in effect, *external* improvements. Still, much as Hamilton pushed Jefferson toward significant infrastructure development, Clay's persistence likewise helped to steer Jackson's two administrations (1829–1837) toward a rough tripling of federal expenditures for infrastructure in a frenzy of spending that would not be surpassed until the late 1850s. Clay's Whigs were the essential modernizers of antebellum America, and railroads, encouraged through state and local public-private partnerships, became their primary instrument for knitting America together east to west, just as canals and turnpikes had been in the decades before. Jackson, as historian Daniel Walker Howe notes, entered Washington for his inauguration in a carriage but left the town eight years later on a train.

Howe argues that Clay expanded Hamilton's original vision of the American System from one of mere national development to a sense of hemispheric dominion and direct resistance to Britain's growing domination of the global economy. In that sense, Clay gave fuller voice to America's emergent grand strategy of not just surpassing Britain in power but ultimately replacing it as the grand arbiter of international commerce. This was Hamilton's ambition from the start, for as early as 1774 he predicted that "in fifty or sixty years, America will be in no need of protection from Great Britain," for "she will then be able to protect herself, both at home and abroad." That day was indeed coming, but not before America would finally collapse in an unprecedented spasm of violence over the issue of slavery. After that crucible, America would need a new generation of grand strategists to realize the dream of a United States that stretched from the Atlantic to the Pacific.

THE AMERICAN SYSTEM, TESTED AND TRANSFORMED

It is interesting to note that virtually all America's grand strategists–cum–politicians were natural outsiders or, in the American vernacular, "men of the West." But in a political system whose underlying ethos constantly spoke to westward expansion, this only makes sense, for Americans have always been frontiersmen of sorts, it's just that the frontiers have changed with time from the wilderness to untamed technologies and markets. Where the cutting edge of Kentucky once produced Henry Clay and then, farther westward, Illinois tempered his onetime acolyte Abraham Lincoln for greatness, future American generations would likewise see great leaders arise from across the plains and then finally spring with regularity from the Pacific coastal state of California, where today Silicon Valley continues to sharpen our competitive blade.

America of the mid–nineteenth century was a country out of sync with itself. Driven westward at a hurtling speed over the first half-century, it had increased its geographic size several times over from its original thirteen-colony spread. In this blindingly ambitious dash, America's economic acquisitiveness knew few bounds and respected few political boundaries, and not surprisingly, when such a gap opens up between economic connectivity and the political rule sets by which such dominion is determined, much violence ensues. If the first arc of America's continental ascendancy was driven by economics, then its second was riven with war, as America, which found its house divided between an industrializing North and an agriculture-bound South, would end up fighting its first true war of globalization within its own tenuous boundaries.

America the experiment was looking mighty shaky as it finally moved beyond its original revolutionary generation. For all practical purposes, you could describe America as a single-party state characterized by, as Howe calls it, "nonparty politics," for its first five decades, until Andrew Jackson, our first "Western" president, rode into power in 1828. Jackson ascended to the presidency on the back of America's first true political party, the Democrats, ushering in an age of raucous and mean-spirited mobocracy that witnessed: the onset of the "spoils system" of political patronage; government-sanctioned extension of slavery into what was then the American "southwest" of Alabama and Mississippi; and an accompanying policy of rapid and wholesale ethnic "cleansing" of Native American tribes located therein, to include the final liquidation of the first of America's many "Tibets"—the Seminole nation of Florida. As Howe writes:

> Our own age finds the limitations on the democracy of that period glaring: the enslavement of African Americans, the abuse of Native Americans, the exclusion of women and most nonwhites from the suffrage and equality before the law. The Jacksonian movement in politics, although it took the name of the Democratic Party, fought so hard in favor of slavery and white supremacy, and opposed the inclusion of nonwhites and women within the American civil polity so resolutely, that it makes the term "Jacksonian Democracy" all the more inappropriate as a characterization of the years between 1815 and 1848.

It is surprising that the word "nationalism" first appears in America's political lexicon only during the 1830s, for there was plenty of evidence of its popular existence following the defeat of the British in the War of 1812. But as Howe argues, for nationalism to achieve real meaning, there needed to be firm evidence that the nation was truly coming together in economic terms, and the one development that signaled that possibility more than any other was the building of the Erie Canal—"the first step in the transportation revolution that would turn an aggregate of local economies into a nationwide market economy." The canal also catapulted its oceanfront terminus, New York City, into the forefront of national and international commerce and finance, almost as if "New York had redrawn the economic map of the United States and put itself at the center."

But another reason nationalism became a more prominent national characteristic in the 1830s was that America finally had a hero in the White House whose fame was not tied to the Revolution but to an episode in the nation's subsequent history—Jackson's defeat of the British at the Battle of New Orleans in 1815. Jackson's victory had stirred the nation's heart like nothing before, not simply because it erased the humiliation of the capital city's sacking and the burning of the new executive mansion, but more so because vanquishing Britain once and for all effectively banished the nation's fear of reenslavement at the hands of its former colonial master. The son had finally been freed from the grasp of the father and was now his own man, far more sure of himself and feeling his vigor and confidence grow with every passing year. Old Hickory, with his unapologetically authoritarian manner, signaled by his unyielding concentration of presidential power that America was now led by a new father.

"King Andrew" was, in many ways, the classic "great man" of an emerging regional power, and his style of rule reminds us that leaders of countries enjoying such a trajectory often come off as unrepentant thugs to allies and enemies alike. Jackson's leadership, upon close examination, is more than a bit reminiscent of the sort of heavy-handed and corrupt political practices of Russia's *siloviki*, or "security guys," under Vladimir Putin. I do not consider this a wild comparison, for Putin, like Jackson, made his initial marks in national security, ruled autocratically with a tendency toward political vendetta against his enemies and economic largesse dispensed to his cronies, cracked down viciously on secessionist sentiment whenever and wherever it cropped up, and made no secret of his desire to catapult his nation toward global greatness on the basis of its most precious natural resources (slave-raised cotton for Jackson, state-owned energy for Putin). Like Putin, Jackson deeply—and personally—disliked the era's dominant great power. Finally, Jackson granted himself a "third term" by appointing his successor, Martin Van Buren, in much the same way Putin selected his own colorless protégé-cum-replacement, Dmitry Medvedev.

Jackson's age likewise saw plenty of social unrest and spiritual awakening. America endured its first great wave of immigration in this period, with the influx of Irish Catholics being particularly disturbing to the dominant Protestant denominations of the age, so much so that public education was pioneered in an attempt to dilute the impact of this new, Roman Catholic minority, which was viewed as essentially nonwhite. The incoming Irish were simultaneously the Muslims and Mexicans of their day: generating irrational social fear with their exclusionary, religious-based schools and being shunted into the "3D" jobs of the economy—dirty, dangerous, and difficult—which in turn allowed them to send substantial amounts of remittances back to their distressed homeland, dwarfing the official humanitarian aid offered by Britain during the Great Potato Famine of the 1840s.

America's Second Awakening in religious fervor, fueled in part, and ironically enough, by New England choosing to disestablish state religions, set in motion an expansion of evangelical missionary activity across both America and the world at large, reaching all the way to the original promised lands of the Middle East. It also triggered, by forcing religious denominations to compete for believers on their own, a tremendous influx of faith-based group involvement in the social issues of the day, first and foremost among these being the abolition movement. This rise in social awareness coincided with the first great instances of slave rebellion, highlighted by the Nat Turner–led insurrection of 1831 and the famous case of the slave-ship revolt in 1839, which led prominent abolitionist John Quincy Adams to defend the *Amistad*'s rebel leader in court. Quincy Adams, by the way, introduced in Congress the first official call for secession from the Union on the basis of the evil of slavery, when in 1842 he presented a petition from the citizens of Haverhill, Massachusetts, asking that their city be allowed to leave the United States and thus end their unwanted association with the abominable practice.

America was most assuredly splitting into two opposing camps, even two opposing nations with competing foreign policies. As Robert Kagan argues, the South was becoming "increasingly despotic, and not only toward slaves and free blacks." As a result, "antislavery agitators, when they were not hanged, were tortured, tarred and feathered, and driven from southern towns," which, in turn, only increased the North's mirror-imaged paranoia that the South "aimed to destroy the North's free-labor civilization." What had been the United States' unitary focus on westward expansion in decades past now became, thanks to its codification in the Missouri Compromise of 1820, an avowed competition between North and South to see which could pile up the most states—free or slave. As the South increasingly dreamed of erecting a social firewall—in effect creating civilizational apartheid—between itself and the North, the lure of "tropical empire" beckoned in the Caribbean, a proxy war inevitably erupted in the border territories of Kansas-Nebraska, and America was agitated toward war with Mexico, culminating in 1845 with the capture and incorporation of the biggest slave state yet—Texas.

In effect, the outlines of a Cold War were emerging between a North hell-bent on containing—perchance even rolling back—the scourge of cotton-driven slavery and a South vocally and violently committed to rapid westward and southward expansionism. But in a similar sense, America was enduring internally the sort of war of identity that marks our current struggle with Islamic radicalism in the Middle East. The American South was the Saudi Arabia of its day: taking in "guest workers" and pumping out the cotton with an attitude of "Don't bother us about what goes on down on the plantation, because as long as the cotton stays cheap and plentiful, then, buddy, that's none of your damn business! For this is our way of life." The South's corollary of exported troublemakers were the sort of adventurers and slavery jihadists who were more than happy to stir up trouble and even terrorist violence in the name of spreading their self-evident truth that some men are equal but that others—skin-tone infidels, if you will—are subhumans to be regarded only as property, and with God's blessing. By the time the Fugitive Slave Act of 1850 essentially condoned a government-sponsored rendition program of returning escaping slaves to their masters, the South had become, as Kagan puts it, a "rogue state" increasingly isolated within an emerging global antislavery crusade.

From Jackson's election in 1828 until Lincoln's shocking rise to the presidency in 1860, the South had effectively achieved political "safe harbor." But with Honest Abe's stunning victory, the Whigs' grand strategy of consummating America's potential as a global power was reborn in the newly formed Republican Party, the main stalwarts of which all made it into Lincoln's original cabinet, including the party's original standard-bearer, William Seward, as Lincoln's secretary of state. Lincoln and Seward, Kagan notes, "had remained consistent supporters of the American System throughout the Jacksonian era, favoring federal support for internal improvements and a strong federal bank." Lincoln himself, who idolized fellow Kentuckian Henry Clay as a "beau ideal of a statesman," openly bragged, during his early stint as an Illinois state legislator, that he aimed to become "the DeWitt Clinton of Illinois," proposing an "Illinois System" of canals and roads that he hoped would transform that prairie state as Clinton's visionary leadership had built New York into the Empire State with the construction of the Erie Canal. Lincoln's grand plans came to nothing, thanks to the national economic crisis of 1837, but when later granted the extraordinary powers of a wartime president, he would take up those plans on a continental scale.

Lincoln believed deeply in the essential equation of American democracy, seeing its truest test in its ability to "elevate the condition of men." In this manner, historian Doris Kearns Goodwin links Lincoln, Seward, Treasury Secretary Salmon Chase, and Attorney General Edward Bates, "a team of rivals" for the Republican presidential nomination in 1860, to a new generation of Americans eager to leave behind the eighteenth century and its ills—specifically slavery. Seeing their nation, as a young Lincoln once put it, "in the peaceful possession of the fairest portion of the earth," and believing, as Goodwin notes, that "the only barriers to success" found therein "were discipline and the extent of one's talents," this generation of Americans born to the Union were driven by a supercharged zeal to propel it beyond its status as a unique political experiment into the full realization of its potential as the Western Hemisphere's undisputed giant.

Of course, Lincoln's very election, leading to the secession of a slew of Southern states that immediately reformed themselves into a confederacy committed to remaining forever independent, constituted the single greatest crisis the still young nation had ever known. The first order of business was salvaging the Union through war. Faced with fielding a "B team" effort because so many of the country's best flag officers had stuck with their native South, including General Robert E. Lee, to whom Lincoln had initially offered command of the federal forces, the new president was forced to run through numerous lesser talents before finally locating the primary architects of his victory, Ulysses S. Grant and William Sherman, two previously undistinguished prewar officers who rose to the rank of general, and proved capable of the impossible task of not merely defending the North but of subjugating the South.

Beyond that, the primary strategic challenge of the war lay in the ability of Lincoln and Seward to forestall any entry by European powers in support of the Confederacy, whose economy Union naval forces slowly strangled with a very effective blockade. To this task, Seward brought a naïve bravado, immediately suggesting to the new president that the best way to reunify the country would be to preemptively declare war on Spain and France while threatening the same to Britain and Russia if they did not immediately back down from their meddlesome threats. Lincoln wisely tempered Seward's zeal to expand the conflict across the ocean, and, as Goodwin notes, "history would later give Secretary of State Seward high marks for his role in preventing Britain and France from intervening in the war."

Stipulating those two successes, as desperately tenuous as the odds may have seemed through the war's first several years, let me now argue specifically where Lincoln's genius as a grand strategist was revealed.

First was Lincoln's bold decision to transform an initially limited war of reunification into a total war of transformation by making public his planned Emancipation Proclamation in September 1862, when victory was far from certain. Indeed, Seward displayed his own substantial wisdom in talking Lincoln out of his original desire to announce the proclamation in the sullen July days following General George McClellan's disastrous Peninsula Campaign, instead holding off until the Union's victory at Antietam two months later. What Lincoln risked by this declaration was the fate of the entire Union, because Southerners most certainly knew then that defeat would mean total social and economic revolution in their homelands, and therefore they would be emboldened to fight on with the desperation of one who has everything to lose. Seward himself feared that an ensuing race war inside the South would so damage its long-term ability to produce cotton that Britain and France might feel forced to intervene. But Lincoln, Goodwin writes, "intuitively understood that once the Union truly committed itself to emancipation, the masses in Europe, who regarded slavery as an evil demanding eradication, would not be easily maneuvered into supporting the South."

As many would later argue, Lincoln's real genius here lay in understanding the commitment to total victory that the proclamation would elicit from a Northern population now deeply engaged in a war that many felt Washington was waging too feebly. In effect, the gloves would come off now, the generals able to master the "terrible math" would be elevated to positions of commanding leadership, and the war would henceforth be waged with a clearer understanding of its strategy of attrition against an enemy that had just seen—based on nothing more than a piece of paper—more than one-third of its population transformed into the North's "fifth column."

But to me, Lincoln's genius for grand strategy was equally demonstrated in the way he front-loaded the Union's overall postwar recovery, not in a South he planned to reconstruct, but in a West slated for rapid and comprehensive integration. Whereas Lincoln planned the gentlest possible reintegration of the South, arguing in advance that any Confederate state that could muster 10 percent of its population toward taking a new oath of loyalty to the Union be admitted basically "as is," when it came to the West he engineered nothing less than its systematic economic transformation and de facto political integration in a quarter-century's time. Within twenty-five years of the Civil War's end, there would be no unassigned federal lands west of the Mississippi, and what little remained of the Native American tribes of the Great Plains, the Southwest, and the coastal Pacific would all be confined to geographically isolated and undesirable land. In sovereign terms, America already possessed virtually all the lands that would eventually make up the contiguous United States, but in actuality, the vast majority of the territory was unclaimed and undeveloped. All of that would change in a mere two and a half decades, in great part because of a series of laws engineered by Lincoln that deeply incentivized private individuals and businesses to flood the Western territories in search of more than just California's gold.

Amazingly, from today's perspective, all five of these historic bills were passed in a single congress—the 37th, which ran from March 1861 through March 1863, encompassing Lincoln's first two years in office. How was this possible? With only twenty-five member states, the smaller

Congress featured strong Republican majorities in both houses, meaning the wartime president and commander in chief could basically pass any bill he wanted, which Lincoln of course did.

Perhaps the most important bill was the Homestead Act, which, as Carl Sandburg described, gave a free farm to "any man who wanted to put a plough to unbroken soil." He did not even have to be a citizen but could be a brand-new immigrant who had but to express a desire to become a citizen eventually, and who could manage the $10 fee. The only restrictions were put on those who had ever borne arms against the United States, meaning Confederate soldiers. After the war, Union soldiers could count their time in service against the residency requirements. On the far side of those meager requirements stood title to 160 acres. As a wartime measure, this was beyond brilliant, for not only did it immediately attract tens of thousands of British, Irish, German, and Scandinavian immigrants to the American West ("What a good new country where they give away farms!"), but it also boosted the nation's food supply while a significant portion of its normal agricultural workforce was otherwise employed. Between 1862 and 1890, the U.S. added 32 million people to its population. One out of every sixteen of those people settled on farms through the Homestead Act. According to the U.S. Archives, "By 1934, over 1.6 million homestead applications were processed and more than 270 million acres—10 percent of all U.S. lands—passed into the hands of individuals."

The rest of Lincoln's legislative agenda included: the Pacific Railroad Act, which quickly led to the first transcontinental railroad line; the Morrill Act, which provided public lands for land-grant colleges; the Legal Tender Bill, which created the first, single paper currency the United States had ever enjoyed, known as "greenbacks" (at the time, over 8,000 different types of banknotes circulated in the economy), and allowed the federal government to raise, in conjunction with a second National Bank Act, $450 million of wartime finance through the issuance of Treasury bonds; and finally, an omnibus tax act that both established the forerunner of today's Internal Revenue Service and, for the first time in American history, taxed the incomes of individual Americans (a practice to be permanently instituted in 1913).

As historian Heather Cox Richardson argues in *West from Appomattox*, postwar "reconstruction" was truly less about rebuilding the South than about knitting together the North, South, and—most important—the West into a coherent national whole for the very first time. To accomplish that, the country needed a coherent national identity, something that unified its citizens' collective pursuit of individual happiness across a collection of far-flung regions and "sections."

In Richardson's view, it was during that process of political unification that the integration of the trans-Mississippi West gave birth to the nation's emerging "middle-class ideology," a decidedly American worldview that divided people into two groups: so-called hardworking types that made up the vast middle and nefarious "special interests"—both rich and poor—that inhabited society's margins. That admittedly expansive self-declaration of middle-class status (admit it, don't *most* Americans still think of themselves as middle-class?) went on to define the stable center of U.S. politics across the twentieth century. Its erosion—both perceived and real—in the face of globalization's many and growing competitive pressures over the past couple of decades should naturally concern us, because if anybody's going to sabotage the emergence of a stabilizing global middle class, it'll be a United States acting out of a fear that says our middle class must perish to accommodate what Fareed Zakaria calls the "rise of the rest."

Only Dr. Frankenstein can kill this monster—or meet its voracious demands by structuring a suitably resilient international system.

So as we think about grand strategy, it's crucial that we better understand how America built that middle-class ideology and, in doing so, formed the bulk of Americanism or the American national identity, something we still take for granted today. It's crucial not just so America can realign itself ideologically with a world transforming today, but because mastering those dynamics of rapid integration is essential to forging a national grand strategy for effectively doing the same across the Non-Integrated Gap in the decades ahead, something with which the West in general has been struggling since the end of the Cold War. Like many thinkers at the end of the American Civil War, we made the assumption at the end of the Cold War that reconstructing the defeated East was our main task, when in reality, as we've since discovered, both the great challenge and the great opportunity of our age come in integrating what we used to call the Third World and what I now identify as the Gap. It is in that integration process, much as it was for post–Civil War America in the American West, that we locate the global identity—the global middle-class ideology—that will define this globalization process for the rest of this century. That global middle-class person, in aggregate, will reshape the planet with his pursuit of happiness across this century. There is no stopping this demand, only shaping it.

A tough challenge, to be sure, but the *best* one we could face right now.

But most important to remember is this: *We've done this before, so now's not the time to go all wobbly.*

Yes, in this process of global integration there will be insurgencies galore. There were plenty that raged on in the American South and parts of the West for decades after the Civil War, and as today, the lines between legitimate activists and "dangerous agitators" and simple criminals were often blurred. Back then, in our fears, we reached for many of the same options that we employ today: long-term occupational forces to settle down the "badlands," private security corporations whose scary agents operate outside the law, ethnic enclaves that are part sanctuary and part prison, squatters' rights finally recognized with land titles, individual ambition finally addressed with installment plans and micro-loans, sweetheart deals given to big corporations so they'll move in and build transportation and communications infrastructure (sometimes under fire, so we'll offer them military bodyguards, too), first-time voting for previously disenfranchised populations, special treatment for various utopian religions that demand separation from an "evil world," universal education that actually includes women as much as men, retailers that master the art of selling to poor people the things that everybody deserves to have, new state governments created seemingly out of thin air, making sure the farmer and the cowboy will be friends, electrification for all, and a chicken in every pot!

Lincoln and Seward were real grand strategists because they recognized that when frontiers are closed, ambition is shut down, and when people cannot connect to their dreams, no amount of freedom or material goods or rule of law will forge a stable national identity. America had just fought a war of identity, very similar to the conflicts we now engage in across our world, and the only way you win a war of identity is to forge a transcendent synthesis of the conflicting worldviews. For Lincoln, simply imposing the North's worldview on the South was no answer. No, the American System, in finally coming to fruition, offered the only way ahead: a Western, middle-class, frontier-integrating identity. Lincoln's genius is found in his continued recognition, streaming back through Clay and Hamilton, of the identity-forging power of purposeful nation-building, and if the West represented his last great option, then the West it would be.

THE AMERICAN SYSTEM MATURED, THEN EXTRAPOLATED

Americans tend to forget just how young our country is, but I can, for example, run through our entire nation's history by looking back just six generations into my family's past. Joseph Barnett (born 1754) saw thirteen colonies form a new nation, and then grow to twenty-six states total, before he died in 1838. His son Andrew (born 1797) witnessed eighteen states join the Union, only to see it rip apart just as he passed in 1862. Then came Jared (1831–1911), who, across his tumultuous eight decades, watched nine new states join, eleven of them leave in a huff (only to be forcibly readmitted), and then another thirteen added! Jared's boy Harry (1864–1948) had his national flag go from thirty-five stars to forty-eight. My grandfather, J.E. (1896–1983), got five new stars, and his only son, my dad, John (1922–2004), saw just two new states—Alaska and Hawaii.

What about me, born in 1962? Bupkes! So far.

But hold that thought for now, because I'd like to give you another example of what a small world it really is here in America by showing you how I'm linked, by six degrees of separation, to a Founding Father, John Adams: (1) As a young Marine officer in World War I, my grandfather (who loved to tell me these stories when I was a kid) got to meet a lot of famous Americans through his cousin, General George Barnett. (2) As commandant of the Marines, General Barnett had long-standing relationships with President Woodrow Wilson and former presidents William Taft and Theodore Roosevelt. (3) Roosevelt's first secretary of state was John Hay. (4) As a young man, Hay served as personal secretary to President

Abraham Lincoln. (5) Lincoln, with his idol Henry Clay, served in the U.S. Congress alongside ex-president John Quincy Adams, with Clay holding Old Man Eloquent's hand on his deathbed and Lincoln helping to organize his state funeral. (6) Quincy Adams was the son of John Adams, signer of the Declaration of Independence and our nation's second president.

My point is this: If you think American foreign policy is dominated today by a small network of policymakers and strategic thinkers (say, a thousand or so individuals), then you have to realize how much smaller and more durable that network was throughout most of our nation's history. Indeed, until we reach the rise of the military-industrial complex in World War II, you can track most of America's grand strategic thinking through a couple of dozen individuals at most. One of those individuals is John Hay, who links our storyline from Lincoln all the way through Teddy Roosevelt.

If you view the American Civil War the way Robert Kagan does, as the "second American Revolution," then you can sort of cast John Hay as an American Zhou Enlai, the famously taciturn but strategically minded minister of China's foreign affairs from the end of its Communist revolution (1949) through the opening to America in the early 1970s. Hay didn't hold the top diplomatic job anywhere near as long as Zhou, but as one of America's longest-serving senior diplomats, he has a legacy that clearly links Lincoln's American System writ large to Roosevelt's writ *even*-large-*r* version. After his wartime service to Lincoln and a stint in the upper echelons of the Union Army, Hay went into the diplomatic service and represented America for years in Europe, moving from Paris to Vienna and Madrid and finally reaching the rank of ambassador to the Court of St. James in 1897. A year later President William McKinley made Hay his secretary of state, a job he held under McKinley's successor, Roosevelt, until his death in 1905.

Before TR started meddling in Asian wars, it was John Hay who formulated and announced America's Open Door policy regarding China, and before Teddy got to stick his shovel in Panama's isthmus, it was John Hay who concluded three treaties with Panama, Colombia, and Great Britain to smooth the way. In all, Hay concluded fifty treaties across his seven years as secretary, an amazing total indicative of America's sudden and vigorous entry onto the world stage at the beginning of the twentieth century.

It's hard for Americans to remember a time when our country wasn't deeply engaged in global affairs, but again, I only have to go back as far as my grandparents' childhoods to locate an upstart United States just beginning to demand a seat at the table of great powers. Much like China and India today, the America of that era had already come to the conclusion that its exploding economic and network connectivity with the outside world had far outpaced its diplomatic and military capacity to defend its expanding national interests. While populists and progressives alike took turns at taming America's rough-and-tumble capitalism, America's leading strategic thinkers, like Admiral Alfred Thayer Mahan, looked ahead to a day when the United States would need a bigger "stick."

The World's Columbian Exposition of 1893, also known as the Chicago World's Fair, constituted America's coming-out party as an aspiring world power (not unlike what the 2008 Beijing Olympics did for China). It was at this historic event that a University of Wisconsin professor, Frederick Jackson Turner, delivered one of the great lectures of American history. His "frontier thesis" traced American exceptionalism, even the very definition of American identity, to the historical process of westward expansion, beginning with the original colonies and culminating in the "closing" identified in the 1890 census that revealed—for the first time ever—the lack of unassigned land in the West. This verdict was both revelatory (This is why we're different from Europeans!) and distressing (How will our character change if we have no new frontiers to conquer?). There was a profound economic dimension as well: With immigrants once again pouring in, how would American workers rise above the limits of wage labor if there was no more open land offering them refuge and freedom?

Part of the answer was clearly continuous technological advancement. Before the American Civil War, the leading American industries were cotton textiles, lumber, boots, and shoes—the very profile of a low-end emerging economy. After the war, machinery manufacturing rapidly became our number-one export, followed by iron and steel—the profile of a rapidly maturing economy. Railroad companies dominated the economic and social landscape: telling us what time it was (railroad standard time), creating corporate behemoths through vertical integration, scheduling both our booms and our busts, and determining even where we should live (railroads were laid between towns in the East, but it was the other way around in the West). Leap ahead to our current information revolution and you can easily insert into a similar description of modern life things like "Internet time," Microsoft and Google, the tech boom and the tech crash, and telecommuting from home. My point again is that we've done it all before.

But the post–Civil War long boom—punctuated by nasty busts, mind you—was also a clear tipping point in our journey from states uniting to *the* United States. In the metaphors Thomas Friedman uses to explain modern globalization, America was leaving behind the "olive tree" world that focused on blood ties, the land, and sectionalism, and began moving toward modernity, or the "Lexus" world of increasingly high-tech production and international commerce. As historian Edmund Morris notes, "America was no longer a patchwork of small self-sufficient communities," but "a great grid of monopolistic cities doing concentrated business with one another: steel cities and rubber cities, cities of salt and cloth and corn and copper." The United States was the rising China of the age, zooming up to and—in many categories—zooming past our model, Great Britain. If you think Americans use Chinese products to the exclusion of all else now, the same realization was dawning on the British regarding America at the beginning of the twentieth century. Consider this account from Morris:

> Current advertisements in British magazines gave the impression that the typical Englishman woke to the ring of an Ingersoll alarm, shaved with a Gillette razor, combed his hair with Vaseline tonic, buttoned his Arrow shirt, hurried downstairs for Quaker Oats, California figs, and Maxwell House coffee, commuted in a Westinghouse tram (body by Fisher), rose to his office in an Otis elevator, and worked all day with his Waterman pen under the efficient glare of Edison light bulbs.

As China today markets tequila to Mexico (!), back then America was managing the equally inconceivable, coal-to-Newcastle feat of exporting beer to Germany! America could consume only a fraction of what it produced, meaning the rest had to be exported, resulting in a trade surplus and an inflow of foreign direct investment that left Wall Street awash in capital, much the way Shanghai's stock market finds itself so popular among international investors today. If Americans today fear that China, with its $2 trillion reserve, could buy our economy tomorrow, back then steel magnate Andrew Carnegie "calculated that America could afford to buy the entire United Kingdom, and settle Britain's national debt in the bargain." What the world's economies feared most back then was the all-powerful "American price," much as so many U.S. manufacturers today fear the seemingly bottomless "China price."

But as with China today, the ease with which America conquered foreign markets and expanded commercially (the Hamiltonian dream) hid a lot of rising problems at home in a capitalism that seemed at once unforgivably cruel, hopelessly unequal, and increasingly unmanageable. If that is globalization's nightmare image today, with China serving as poster boy for all that's out of control, then America served the same function in that earlier globalization age. But unlike China today, which feels little responsibility for fixing a global economic model that it had no real hand in shaping, the United States would eventually come to the conclusion that reformation of the European-style, imperial model of glo-colonialization, if you will, was both inevitable and much needed. But before America could display such ambition for "big" foreign policy, it would need, as Robert Kagan notes, a "big" government to manage it, and that big government would arise first in response to the dire challenges of the American Civil War, but next in response to the moral challenges of taming America's too-brutal markets in the latter decades of the nineteenth century.

See if any of this rings a bell with regard to today's globalization and its many discontents.

Already in the 1870s, America began to see a wave of corporate and political scandals, including many that connected those two communities in a web of seamy corruption. Like China and Russia today, America back then had a hard time separating business and politics, as congressmen were easily bought and sold by "gilded age" private-sector behemoths helmed by lavishly compensated executives. Workers were feeling increasingly alienated from the upper class. Before the Civil War, America's nonagricultural workers identified themselves by the section of the country where they lived, in part because they worked for smaller, regional companies, and usually knew their companies' owners personally. After the Civil War, all that began to change: Workers identified themselves more as an economic class, labored for national companies, and never met their companies' owners face-to-face. Before the Civil War, public corporations needed to cite some public good to justify their formation. After the war, private ambition was enough. Despite the incredible rise of disposable income and mass consumerism in the 1880s, this decade was viewed as "hard times" for most Americans in an economy where inequality among households was greater than it's been at any other time in our nation's history.

There was also a growing sense that manipulators of all sorts were keeping the average worker down by restricting the supply of money (backed by limited gold supplies), fixing laws to benefit certain companies, and monopolizing markets to charge usury rates. "Dangerous" ideas about trade unionism were filtering in from Europe, where, in 1871, the Paris Commune briefly institutionalized the notion of worker control of the economy. Cities were becoming overly crowded, unmanageable, and downright deadly to their inhabitants. In the 1880s, it was common for one-quarter of American babies born in urban metropolises to die before reaching the age of one. Only half made it to the age of five. Not surprisingly, hard times amid apparent plenty created angry people, and so America entered into a rather harsh, populist phase that extended into the mid-1890s. As many laborers saw their incomes flatten, the public turned increasingly antiblack, anti-immigrant, antibusiness, and antipolitics. Jim Crow laws proliferated in the South, along with lynchings, while Eastern European immigrants in northern cities were increasingly greeted with more open hostility and job discrimination. Popular demand was growing for trust-busting, improving public health and working conditions, cleaning up disorganized and corrupt elections, and reforming and professionalizing government service. The crystallizing moment? In 1881, a deranged man, angry over being denied a government job, gunned down President John Garfield. For the second time in sixteen years, an American president had been murdered by one of his fellow citizens.

Into this increasingly violent fray stepped a man too good to be true: Theodore Roosevelt. Born of a Northern father and a Southern mother three years before the Civil War, Roosevelt would barely survive the fragile health of his childhood and, upon suffering the deaths of his mother and first wife on the same night, would retreat into America's baddest frontier lands and, in that healing place, transform himself into the quintessential Western man—the rough-and-tough cowboy. At a time when the world's growing complexity seemed to know no bounds, Roosevelt's capacity for self-education seemed equally limitless. He was master of numerous foreign languages and the author of dozens of scholarly books. His stunning rise through state and national political circles across the 1880s and 1890s made his ascendancy to the White House in 1901, after yet another presidential assassination, almost anticlimactic. Roosevelt the progressive crusader had already led reform efforts at virtually every level of American government, from the lowest post office and most dingy police station to, as assistant secretary of the Navy, the grand strategic aspirations of global seapower. He also organized and presided over the world's first environmental organization and led what can be legitimately described as a special operations unit into battle. It was almost as if America's destiny in the first decade of the twentieth century had manifested itself, in all its glories and contradictions, inside a single man. When TR was sworn into office, he was arguably the most broadly accomplished and experienced individual ever to serve as president. He was also the youngest. Neither feat has since been replicated.

Roosevelt transformed the office in a way no other president had since Andrew Jackson. "Theodore the Sudden" would launch a massive legal assault against the business "combinations" of the day, filing forty-four pioneering lawsuits that ultimately led to his "busting" of more than three dozen trusts in industries such as railroads, banking, and oil. His handpicked successor, William Taft, would go on to disassemble more than twice that. Between them, they regraded America's corporate landscape through these revolutionary executive-branch interventions into private business. But Roosevelt's meddling streak exhibited itself in many

other ways, likewise establishing stunning precedents. His personal intervention into a threatened coal strike in 1902 averted a national emergency, and his personal diplomacy in negotiating an end to the 1905
Russo-Japanese War won him a Nobel Peace Prize, the first ever awarded
to an American and the only one ever granted to a sitting president. Roosevelt appointed the first Jew to a cabinet-level office and hosted the first
African-American in the White House—Booker T. Washington. Among
his many legislative accomplishments were the Meat Inspection Act and
the Pure Food and Drug Act.

Roosevelt's most farsighted accomplishments had to do with elevating a budding, grassroots conservation movement in America into the political mainstream. The first president to raise environmental issues, he
doubled the number of national parks to ten, exploited the just-passed
Antiquities Act to designate the Grand Canyon and fifteen other natural
sites as National Monuments, started the National Forest Service and established fifteen new national forests, created the forerunner of the National Wildlife Refuge System by designating sixteen federal bird refuges,
and initiated twenty federal irrigation projects under the National Recla-
mation Act that he signed into law. In all, Roosevelt set aside more park-
land and preserves than all his predecessors combined. The sum total
rivals the land transfer triggered by the Homestead Act and is equal to
7 percent of the entire U.S. territory, meaning TR created almost as much
public land as Honest Abe gave away.

Despite all those domestic accomplishments that did much to house-
break American capitalism, Roosevelt's greatest accomplishment, from
our perspective here, came in effectively pivoting America's ambition for
system creation from the continental scale to that of the Western hemisphere and beyond. Despite his reputation as a "cowboy" president and
international gunslinger, he started no wars, and if not for the ongoing
U.S. military occupation of the Philippines, begun under his predecessor
McKinley, TR would have suffered no military combat casualties across
his seven-plus years as president. In Roosevelt's own opinion, his greatest
foreign policy accomplishment came in concluding the treaty with newly
independent Panama that allowed American construction and leased
ownership of the Panama Canal, in effect giving the growing U.S. Navy
the capacity to move ships far more quickly between America's coasts.

While that strategic capacity never proved decisive in either of the twentieth century's world wars, the United States did consider the canal a strategic enough asset to deploy almost 70,000 troops to defend it in WWII, and the canal's impact on maritime commerce was profound across the twentieth century.

Roosevelt's desire to extend the logic of the American System hemispherically was equal parts offensive and defensive. The offensive impulse was internal. Following Frederick Jackson Turner's notion that the "closed frontier" represented a stagnating threat to the further development of American character, Roosevelt, who spoke publicly with ease of the "wealthy criminal class" and the divide between "haves and have-nots," evinced similar fears of a "stationary state" that, if boxed in by circumstances, would become hypercompetitive and consume itself to the point where the only alternative to chaos would be authoritarianism.

The defensive impulse was external: Roosevelt saw, as he put it, a present where "the globe's waste spaces are being settled and seeded." If America was going to retain enough competitive space in the global landscape, it would have to move fast. That "new and dark power" within American society, which threatened its competitive landscape and thus spoiled its social environment, found its global corollary in Eurasia's colonial empires—the trusts and combinations of the imperial age. If anything, TR was a committed anti-imperialist who wanted to keep the competitive environment as natural as possible. When a younger Teddy declared to a military audience in 1883 his dream "to see the day when not a foot of American soil will be held by any European power," he was rather expansively suggesting that the same benefits of liberty afforded to citizens of the United States should be made available to all *Americans*— north and south.

Roosevelt's Fair Deal, thus translated to the rest of the Western Hemisphere, presages his young cousin's attempt, four decades later, to extrapolate his own New Deal logic throughout the world. Far from being what most people understand as "imperial" ambition, this was an instinct for System Administration that must be taken at face value. TR's "Roosevelt Corollary" to the Monroe Doctrine simply extended America's guarantee of protection from the baseline of military protection from foreign domination to economic protection from foreign domination. Is that not what the International Monetary Fund has sought to accomplish over the past several decades? Buying the "little guy" economic breathing space during periods of great economic duress? In this light, is it not fair to view the "dollar diplomacy" of TR's successor, William Taft, as simply extending the same "rescue package" logic of the Fed's "open-market operations" (pioneered, by the way, by Alexander Hamilton) but on a hemispheric scale? In other words, these were baby steps toward the international liberal trade order we later imposed, not rote imitations of European colonialism.

Outside of the Western Hemisphere, Roosevelt's instinct was, in John Hay's phrase, to maintain an "open door." In that way, TR's attempts to keep Asia in play presaged our successful efforts during the Cold War to both establish and defend market beachheads in places like Japan and South Korea, paving the way for capitalism's ultimate and pervasive triumph throughout the region. It's interesting to note, especially now that we find ourselves making similar efforts throughout a poorly marketized Middle East, just who popularized the open door as a strategic concept—Alfred Mahan (who also popularized the term "Middle East"). Mahan's notion of sea commerce "pressure points" nicely predicts the ship-rotational "hubs" that the U.S. Navy, once it achieved its two-ocean fleet during World War II, actively maintained throughout most of the Cold War. By progressively extending that "cop on the beat" naval presence across the world's oceans, America's military assumed the same function as Britain's had in the previous era of glo-colonialization: keeping sea lanes open for everyone's trade. When President Jimmy Carter finally extended that promise into the Persian Gulf with his Carter Doctrine (the promise to prevent any outside great power from dominating the region militarily), he simply made universal the Monroe Doctrine/Open Door, resulting in our blood now being spilled to preserve the world's stable access to the region's energy. The best proof of our good intentions? America consumes about one-tenth of the Persian Gulf's oil; the rest goes elsewhere.

If anything, Roosevelt's global ambitions were wildly premature. As the saying goes, America in that era—much like China today—was all hat and no cattle. Then again, as Iraq proves today, the definition of "cattle" changes with time. In Roosevelt's time, though, the definition was clear:

seapower. While America was decades away from achieving Mahan's naval force-structure requirements, that didn't stop TR from projecting a show of force such as the world had never before seen mounted by a Western Hemispheric power: the Great White Fleet's globe-circling tour from December 1907 through February 1909, when those sixteen great battleships came home to mark Roosevelt's farewell from office. As he himself declared, "I could not ask a finer concluding scene for my administrations."

Roosevelt was a depressed, volatile ex-president who almost immediately grew unhappy with his handpicked successor's performance and ran against him in the 1912 election as a third-party (Progressive) candidate, finishing a distant second to the Democrats' Woodrow Wilson, who had once described TR as "the most dangerous man of the age." In terms of TR's legacy as a grand strategist, it is arguably more illuminating to track the seeds of his long-term influence on the "speak softly" side of his most famous foreign policy formulation, not simply because it would be a long time before America truly wielded a "big stick," but also because Roosevelt's focus on dampening self-destructive competition through the extension of new, protective rule sets nicely rounds out a global extrapolation of his Fair Deal philosophy. Plus, quite frankly, given his seven years of starting no wars but rather ending them or preventing new ones, I have to agree with Edmund Morris's verdict that Roosevelt's surest legacy was proving that "it is the *availability* of raw power, not the use of it, that makes for effective diplomacy."

If John Hay connects Theodore Roosevelt back to America's bloody Civil War, then his onetime secretary of war and then Secretary of State (replacing the deceased Hay) Elihu Root logically connects him forward to America's twentieth-century championing of good global governance (e.g., post-WWI League of Nations, post-WWII United Nations). I don't pretend that Roosevelt was anything but an ardent nationalist, but rather suggest that, much as he did in his stated position on the League of Nations (he called it "an addition to" American power but not "a substitute for" a strong America), he positively viewed such international forums as rule-set adjudicators that kept the game fair. As such, it's most worthy to celebrate Root's long list of career achievements, including extensively reforming the U.S. Army into its modern institutional form as secretary of war and so championing the cause of international arbitration during his subsequent stint as Roosevelt's secretary of state that he became the second American, following TR himself, to be awarded the Nobel Prize for Peace. Root also helped launch the Carnegie Endowment for International Peace and the Council on Foreign Relations and served on a commission of jurists that established the League of Nations' Permanent Court of International Justice.

Theodore Roosevelt's presidency marks the great tipping point between America-the-potential and America-the-power. His success in creating a "fair-play" competitive landscape inside the United States, leveraging the middle-class ideology born of the nation's post–Civil War reconstruction and westward tilt, emboldened him to project that most American model onto a global environment still dominated by Eurasian imperial projects. As such, Roosevelt's grand strategic instincts were roughly a half-century ahead of their time, for Eurasia's imperial powers would have to destroy one another, and the uncompetitive model of globalization they had erected, before TR's global dream would once again be chased by another president named Roosevelt.

A GLOBAL AMERICAN SYSTEM,
AN AMERICAN CENTURY

As we move deeper into the twentieth century, we leave behind an America that did whatever it had to do on its continent and then across its hemisphere to preserve its sense of limitless opportunity, and meet an America that sensed its grand experiment could not survive globally unless certain threats were addressed. Gone were the territorial designs, but the economic demands for free access and fair play continued unabated, just levied with far less hypocrisy as we began to lower our own protectionist stance, which had nurtured Clay's "home market" throughout the nineteenth century. This push was not "messianic" or the product of American exceptionalism. Rather, it was our natural instinct for survival, born of decades of frontier integration. We Americans can't help being who we are—the original castoffs who inevitably return to homelands intent on spreading our definition of happiness pursued. We don't, in our historical insouciance, project our globalization model upon the world out of hubris or sheer ambition. Like any revolutionary regime, we see our ideals as universal and needing to be spread. But given our geographic isolation and our natural impulse to always seek freedom from authority, we need to feel cornered by history before we'll strike out. We need to feel the walls closing in before taking action because we fear opportunities lost more than responsibilities undertaken.

Growing our peculiar version of "states-uniting" globalization in the historic shadow of the Eurasian imperial model of glo-colonialization, we were noticed by other great powers and somewhat feared for our meteoric rise. The world was not quite sure what to make of an imperial power that eschewed traditional colonies and instead trumpeted the spread of its laws and argued that others should adjust to these principles by arbitration—as though lawyers could manage a great power's rise! Remember that when today's neocon hardliners dismiss all talk of negotiation as "appeasement."

Nonetheless, as the Eurasian imperial powers found themselves inexorably drawn into conflict, it quickly became clear that America's path would consist of more than just pushing legalisms on the international order; in the decline of the Old World imperial order, America would step into the role of global balancer and decisive swing vote in times of great conflict. Worse for the Old World, the price of our involvement would be their acceptance of our globalization model of free trade, free markets, collective security, and transparency. Oh, and democracy where it could be managed or at least reasonably faked.

With the collapse of the Old World globalization order, there stood only two alternatives: America's free markets versus the Soviets' planned markets. Since the latter always required far more resources to impose and maintain control, and because it trapped ambition and talent instead of unleashing those creative spirits, the outcome of the resulting world-wide struggle was never really in doubt—just occasionally threatened by the illogic of great-power war in a nuclear age.

But what was always in doubt, across the first half of the twentieth century, was whether America would transform itself sufficiently at home. Would we become a mature model of multinational economic and political union? And could we project that model on the international stage?

The imperial model of globalization-through-colonization was limiting for reasons that are obvious; eventually all the world's "waste spaces" would be conquered and the competing "mini-world" economies would be forced into violent conflict as they bumped up against one another, fighting over resources in a zero-sum manner. Unlike America's domestic economy in the late nineteenth century, no global version of trust-busting would be required. The two world wars would accomplish that feat quite nicely, fatally wounding all of Eurasia's great empires. But the great antithesis to this exploitation-from-above model was also brewing in its shadow: the Left's answer of class dictatorship-from-below, found first in Lenin's Bolshevik Revolution and later extended over the bulk of Eurasia by the combined terror of Stalin and Mao. Theodore Roosevelt had feared that an America left ungovernable by untamed capitalism might head down a similar path, and so he did his best to defuse the "stationary state" conditions he feared could enable the Left's radicalization here. But after America had tamed its own capitalism, the question remained, Could it export that middle-class progressivism to the world amid all these brewing great-power conflicts, or were those titanic clashes inevitable?

The answer is, America tried and failed following the First World War, and in that failure we withdrew from the world, yielding the initiative to others. Eventually, others filled the void, but instead of America's model of self-rule from the middle it was fascism's dictatorship from the right.

Why did we fail?

On one level, Europe's centuries-in-the-making imperial model of globalization, especially once its implied challenge was picked up by competitors in the East (Russia, Japan), was simply too pervasive and too entrenched for America's rather idealistic counternarrative to dislodge it. Vladimir Lenin's corollary to Karl Marx's diagnosis was essentially correct: European-style predatory capitalism could stave off its demise at home by extending its life span through overseas empires that shifted unfair exploitation to distant populations, but eventually those empires would bump up against one another on a global scale, resulting in global war. America's alternative model of tamed competition at home (TR's "fair deal") extrapolated to fair competition abroad (Hay's "open door") was simply too far ahead of its time in its embrace of postnationalist, secularist, non-zero-sum progressivism. Neither Europe nor Asia could aspire to such modern logic, because neither region had been forced to engineer a synthetic identity such as America had been forced to achieve. Our mid-nineteenth-century Civil War and the subsequent integration of the Western frontier would yield that synthesis. Europe's violent internal struggle would continue for a century longer, extinguishing itself only in a post–WWII final treaty known as détente. Asia's own version of wars of identity would likewise continue through Mao's Cultural Revolution and the conflicts of Southeast Asia, achieving stability only after Deng Xiaoping's development model, which mirrored America's own "peacefully rising" period of the late nineteenth century, was put in place across China's vast population, triggering the regional economic integration process we now witness. Simply put, America had to wait for the rest of the world's great powers to come to the same self-evident truths about life, liberty, and the pursuit of happiness that we had radically proposed in the late eighteenth century and had largely—but not completely—achieved by the start of the twentieth century.

America simply didn't have the Leviathan-like capabilities necessary to impose its globalization model upon the world until World War II forced such developments. Mahan's dream of a two-ocean navy would not be fulfilled until then, nor Dwight Eisenhower's nightmare of a permanent military-industrial complex. Then again, America wasn't doing the world much of a favor in the early twentieth century—any more than China is today—by merely "speaking softly" and carrying a "big stick" whose reach was regional at best. For the United States to impose its model of interstate political and economic relations globally would require a military Leviathan, and such a military was simply impossible to achieve absent the rise of a strong federal government back home. While the Civil War certainly accelerated that development, as did Theodore Roosevelt's presidency, it would take the twin challenges of the Great Depression and World War II to make America's federal government truly strong enough to raise and maintain a global military Leviathan capable of (1) standing up to the Soviet threat, and, upon waiting it out, (2) providing the muscle to ensure globalization's rapid advance both eastward and southward over the past quarter-century.

That testing and that transformation of our global system is the story of the second half of the twentieth century. The story of the first half of the twentieth century is one of America's *proposing* that global model following World War I (Woodrow Wilson) and then, following that failure, finally *imposing* that model on as much of the world as we could readily control following World War II (Franklin Roosevelt's "New Deal for the world" yielding to the near-term requirements of Harry Truman's containment of the Soviet threat). In this first half of the twentieth century, then, America would learn a series of profound lessons, using them to effectively rebrand our nation from its previous role as mere shining example to that of architect of a global environment we came to recognize as defining our national interest. During that time, those various "stationary states," whose lineup would change over the decades as we successfully co-opted them, would birth a sequence of *isms* that we've spent the last century battling: Europe's fascism, Eurasia's Communism, and now Islam's terrible twins of rancid authoritarianism and violent radicalism.

The basic outline of this historic journey can be summed up as follows: Europe's imperial powers go to war with one another, beginning in 1914; after various surging tides favoring one side or the other, America enters the war in 1917 and, by surging huge numbers of troops across the summer, proves decisive in favor of Great Britain and France; after allied Russia dissolves into revolution and as Germany's surrender looms imminent, President Woodrow Wilson proposes 14 Points to guide the subsequent peace talks, with roughly half addressing specific national claims and the other half proposing a new international order, including a "general association of nations" (later to become a League of Nations) for arbitrating disputes and processing demands for national self-determination within crumbling empires. The subsequent negotiations at Versailles end the following summer with England and France imposing a very harsh peace upon Germany, including unbearably heavy economic reparations. In the process: Wilson's 14 Points largely go by the wayside, even though the resulting League of Nations represents a significant step forward; Wilson returns to an American public not given to embracing the responsibilities of enforced collective security implied by membership in the League, and the treaty is twice rejected by the U.S. Senate; while America progressively withdraws from the global scene to concentrate on domestic developments, the global economy suffers increasing volatility until a great stock market crash in 1929 sends all advanced powers into a frightening tailspin that is further exacerbated by their self-destructive policies of trade protectionism in subsequent years. And by 1933, the fascist Nazi party has gained control of enfeebled, chaotic Germany, and the long march to World War II in Europe begins, with Imperial Japan playing a similarly disruptive and aggressive role in East Asia. The lineup of forces in this resumed conflict is very similar to the first conflagration, with America once again joining in midstream and this time proving decisive in both the European and Asian theaters. Learning multiple lessons from WWI, America proactively shapes the postwar settlement, generating a host of international institutions (e.g., United Nations, World Bank, International Monetary Fund, North Atlantic Treaty Organization) and resource flows (e.g., Marshall Plan, Truman Doctrine, Berlin Airlift, postwar rehabilitations of German and Japan), many of which prove critical in generating and maintaining a Western identity in the follow-on Cold War against the Soviet Union and the bloc of states it dominates and/or supports as a result of WWII and subsequent revolutionary developments in Asia (e.g., Chinese Revolution, Korean War, Vietnam Conflict).

In homage to Wilson, I offer Barnett's 14 Points to remember from this journey, all of which are elemental to America's becoming a great power in the last century, and foundational to grand strategy today.

1. MAKE SURE YOU CAN ACCESS THE CRISIS WITHOUT ADDING TO THE CRISIS.

The first thing to recognize is that America had begun an effective rebranding of its military long before its entry into the First World War put us in the position of proposing a new global order based on the American historical orientation. There is a great lesson in this process, because absent that effective rebranding, starting roughly in 1880 with the building up of America's naval forces and extending through our war with Spain and subsequent quasi-imperialist experiences in the Philippines and the Caribbean (subtext: start easy and work your way up), America would have had neither the ambition nor the wherewithal to have engaged that distant conflict to Great Britain's advantage. And absent that slow, painful learning process on Great Britain's part (in effect, "Who's your daddy now?"), it's not clear that London would have been strategic enough the second time around in WWII to have so singularly sought America's alliance, even to the point of sacrificing its imperial economic order in the process (Churchill's agonizing choice). My point in mentioning this is: Absent that realization among grand strategic thinkers like Theodore Roosevelt and Alfred Mahan, America would not have made the long-term effort to effectively position itself for the opportunities and challenges that inevitably lay ahead. They knew, in effect, that America would be forced by events to project its model of globalization upon the world in order to continue flourishing, accepting what obligations came its way as a result.

Simply put, the nonstationary state could not abide a stationary system.

I mean "inevitably" in the following sense: America's strategic thinkers of the 1880s could see how our nation's economic and network connectivity with the global economy was expanding far beyond our diplomatic and military capabilities to defend it, and realizing that this capabilities gap constituted its own strategic threat to our growing national interest, they decided to gradually eliminate it through (a) a buildup of such needed capabilities, (b) a progressive willingness to employ those burgeoning capabilities, and (c) a grand strategic vision that justified both. At first, the grand strategy came in pieces: the "open door," the Great White Fleet, a focus on arbitrationism (negotiating and enforcing rules), and so on. It took the crystallizing experience of World War I to force a more coherent expression—namely, Wilson's 14 Points, which projected an American-inspired constellation of global governing principles and institutions to modulate future imperial clashes over trade and territory and to process future claims for national self-determination within that crumbling imperial order.

It's important to remember this journey, because today we're watching similarly rising powers, such as China and India, propose their own, internally driven expressions of such grand strategies to justify their own instinctive buildup of capabilities—especially naval capabilities. Then there's a similarly resurgent Russia that again lays claim to its historical spheres of influence, intimidating its targets in the manner it knows best—tanks and rockets. For now, those grand strategies are rather incoherent and poorly articulated, meaning we can let current events fill in those blanks (e.g., letting third parties declare *our* wars against *their* preferred targets) or we can seek out alliances with these powers in such a way as to force a synthesis between their strategies and our own. If we do it well, we won't face a crucible, such as a global conflict, that forces our pained accommodation of their "reasonable" demands, much as Great Britain was forced to accept ours following WWII. Then again, given the experience to date in our self-declared "global war on terror," there's good reason to believe that, in today's interdependent environment, something far less obvious than global war might do the trick—to wit, our strategic tie-down in Iraq and Afghanistan. Perhaps any "new global order" won't arrive in the form of new international institutions but simply sovereign wealth funds' acquiring our economic assets in some sort of superpower "estate auction." Bottom line: We need to be working on our strategic protégés now as opposed to waiting on events, because the earlier you engage, the lower the price.

And yes, their price is a function of their confidence, just as it was with us roughly a century ago.

The most important reason America should want to rebrand rising powers like China and India (and to a lesser extent the demographically moribund Russia) as globally accepted interventionary forces is that getting them to the war ensures they'll be interested—and credentialized—for the postwar. This is something America discovered in the Versailles talks after WWI: Because we hadn't played militarily in the Middle East, whenever that subject came up Wilson was effectively excluded from the debate. A century later, we're still haunted by that reality in terms of the "badly drawn" states that emerged from that postwar process. That doesn't always mean you can fix things simply by being at the table. It means that unless you're at the table, there's no chance of making your voice heard.

2. FIGURE OUT YOUR ACTUAL ECONOMIC LEVERAGE GOING IN AND MAKE IT CLEAR IN NEGOTIATIONS.

Wilson arrived at Versailles in 1918 believing he had his European allies over a barrel because of their growing dependence on American agriculture and financial capital. It would, as Wilson confided to an aide, "force them to our way of thinking." Over the long haul, as the influential British economist and policymaker John Maynard Keynes would argue, Wilson was correct on finance but less so on agriculture, because America's domestic demands were rapidly rising. But the war didn't drag on long enough to maximize America's financial hold over the Europeans, who were willing to spend the money we lent them in American markets during the war (as we demanded), but then abruptly started canceling contracts as soon as peace talks were slated, immediately curtailing America's wartime boom and thus diminishing Wilson's capital. Certain realities should have driven this home to Wilson, such as our military's dependence on Britain's diminished but still sizable merchant fleet to return our troops home (our planned merchant fleet was just beginning to be built). As historian Kendrick Clements notes in his biography of Wilson, "Despite the extraordinary reversal of roles between creditor and debtor that had taken place during the war, the United States was caught up in a web of interdependence and was less dominant than its leaders imagined."

Fast-forward to Franklin Roosevelt's historic decision to launch, in response to Winston Churchill's 1940 request, the Lend-Lease Program, by which substantial amounts of war matériel were lent to the British in return for nominal basing rights in the Western Hemisphere. Lend-Lease was designed, as historian Elizabeth Borgwardt states, "as a lawyerly end-run around the entrenched culture of the Neutrality Act of 1935," which an isolationist Congress had passed, along with three expansive renewals in subsequent years, to prevent FDR from embroiling America in yet another costly European world war. Robert Skidelsky, British biographer of Keynes, describes Lend-Lease as "the most adventurous political coup of Roosevelt's presidency" precisely because it broke from the American tradition of wartime loans made strictly on business terms, something America did right through WWI. As President Calvin Coolidge coldly replied in response to European pleas to help them out with their American bank creditors following that war, "We hired them the money, didn't we?"

By making such concessionary loans, FDR did two things: (1) he established the precedent that made the later Marshall Plan possible; and (2) he so indebted the British to U.S. economic aid that during subsequent negotiations on a postwar liberal trade order, Roosevelt's administration was able to hold the British to their promise, made in Article 7 of the Lend-Lease agreement, to end their system of imperial trade preferences and submit to the Bretton Woods Agreements—the "real price" of Lend-Lease.

As we look back from today's perspective, it's interesting to note how private-sector loans and harsh economic reparations defined WWI, while WWII is best known for Lend-Lease and the Marshall Plan. As for today's "global war on terrorism"? So far we can cite higher oil prices and an unprecedented amount of government postwar reconstruction contracts granted to private contractors, but no overarching economic agenda proposed or implemented by the Bush administration, which, like the Wilson administration, seemed to overestimate our home market's power to "force them to our way of thinking"—to wit, Bush's admonition to citizens to keep shopping despite the war on terror. But as we're already seeing with the rise of a global middle class, flush with insatiable desires and enough disposable income to warrant market respect, America no longer wields the same immense—if passive—demand power within globalization.

3. BUILD YOUR DOMESTIC CONSTITUENCY FROM THE START AND KEEP IT BIPARTISAN.

Wilson, whose 1885 scholarly book *Congressional Government* set the standard for describing, as Clements termed it, "the American political system not as it was supposed to function but as it actually worked," was enormously successful in pushing his progressive domestic agenda through Congress in his first term, despite the highly partisan nature of that age. Nonetheless, Wilson totally blew his chances of gaining Senate acceptance for the League of Nations charter. By taking no senators along to the Versailles talks, much less any prominent Republicans, Wilson alienated the very body he needed to institutionalize his dreams for a liberal postwar order. This was not a singular mistake. Rather, it followed Wilson's pattern of managing America's participation in the war in a highly unilateral fashion, not even including any military officers in his war council. It also reflected Wilson's personality: Despite the obvious social demands of the office, he was distinctly uncomfortable at White House social events and thus sought to limit their number to an absolute minimum. In short,

Dr. Wilson didn't make or offer house calls on rival politicians, thus depriving his administration of their lubricating effect.

But it was more than that with Wilson, who, as a true academic genius, had an ego to match. As Clements argues, "He wanted to be remembered as the author of a new international structure that could abolish war" and felt that "he alone had a clear vision" of what that structure needed to be. As for his assumption that he could cajole Europe's leaders into accepting a new global order that would accommodate the growing revolutionary impulse of national self-determination, well, they would just have to be made to see the logic of it all. After all, when Wilson landed in France in 1918, he was arguably the most popular leader in the world. If Wilson's arrogance and ambition blinded him during this crucial period, the danger was apparent to others. As Walter Lippmann, a future influential columnist and then assistant secretary of war, penned six months prior in an internal memo concerning Wilson's plans for the Middle East, America was liable "to win a war and lose the peace" unless the president's rhetoric was quickly reconciled with the reality that, as one academic involved in the U.S. government's secret planning for the region's postwar structure put it, most of Wilson's European counterparts at Versailles viewed it as the "great loot of the war." In the end, Arabs who believed Wilson's 14 Points had promised them freedom were sorely disappointed by the colonial mandates produced by the Versailles Treaty.

Franklin Roosevelt would likewise be blamed for disappointing postwar outcomes, particularly in his apparent accession, at the infamous Yalta Conference of February 1945, to Soviet demands for political hegemony over Poland and the rest of Eastern Europe. Given the military facts on the ground at that time, Roosevelt had little choice, in my opinion, especially since he was eager to gain Russia's entry into our Pacific War, which, at that time, appeared as though it could drag on for a significant amount of time and at great human cost. Nonetheless, it was exactly that sort of balancing between external goals and internal cost considerations that made FDR's management of the war so impressive. For it was the mix of relatively low American casualties, significant wartime economic advance, and the unprecedented exposure of millions of Americans to a larger world (almost 10 percent of all Americans served abroad in the military) that enabled such a strong postwar public consensus to emerge concerning the need for the nation to stay globally engaged, as well as establish and join permanent international organizations designed to prevent future wars.

Beyond the strategic choices made, Roosevelt was simply a master at shaping public opinion through his frequent "fireside chats" with America, as well as a slick political manipulator of his political opposition through his consistent willingness to "reach across the aisle" for bipartisan support. Once the war began, FDR also benefited greatly from the public's strong historical awareness of the mistakes made by politicians following WWI. Senator Arthur Vandenberg, for example, an ardent isolationist prior to WWII, came to realize during the course of the war how history seemed to vindicate Woodrow Wilson and vilify his main Republican opponent in the Senate, Henry Cabot Lodge.

As for the Bush administration since 9/11, it was not known for generating any long-term bipartisan support for its "global war on terror"—just the opposite. With the political parties so clearly divided over Iraq, it's fair to say that congressional oversight of the Bush administration's wartime policies was highly restricted by Republican fear that any damaging information provided would lead to Democrats seeking to derail the war effort. This partisan rationale led congressional Republicans to go easy on the Bush administration while encouraging the White House to become even more secretive as the extreme partisanship wore on. Unlike Harry Truman's administration, which clearly benefited from the general bipartisanship generated by the previous war, as well as its tendency to discourage strong ideological stances on the part of politicians, Bush's post-9/11 "honeymoon" was relatively short, both domestically and internationally, as so far the "global war on terror" has created no identifiable *zeitgeist* that politicians have been able to harness for bipartisanship. Indeed, to the extent one has been created, it has been limited overwhelmingly to military personnel who've served in Iraq and Afghanistan. Over time, as many of these military leaders transition to postcareer prominence in the political realm, this situation is likely to improve.

4. BE REALISTIC ABOUT WHAT YOU CAN ACHIEVE BY INTERVENING.

Being a national security novice and not given to seeking out military advice, Wilson tended to misjudge what the application of military force overseas could generate in political leverage. In other military interventions, such as sending U.S. Marines to Siberia following the Russian Revolution, he clearly underestimated the local hostility engendered and overestimated what U.S. forces could achieve. Wilson's first-term effort to conclude a Pan-American nonaggression treaty that would "serve as a model for the European Nations when peace is at last brought about" died in large part because America's previous and ongoing military interventions in the Caribbean and Mexico engendered significant fear in Latin America that such a treaty would simply condone more such interventions in the future. For Wilson thereupon to demand Europe's colonial powers display a more hands-off attitude toward the Middle East naturally came off as somewhat hypocritical. When a rising economic power like America looked upon a "level playing field," it saw unlimited opportunity, while competing states naturally feared they'd be shut out and local ones feared they'd be competitively bulldozed. Transpose this perspective to China today in its relations with Latin America and sub-Saharan Africa and you'll spot many of the same fears among both local governments and external great powers. It's easy to push a "consultative" model of political interactions when you know your overwhelming economic competitiveness will grant you sufficient leverage over lesser powers. When military power is used in such situations, it naturally comes off as overkill, thus yielding more local resistance and less leverage than anticipated.

In the Second World War, America's rude awakening to the Soviet Union's postwar intentions was coterminous with Harry Truman's trial-by-fire adjustment to the office of the presidency following FDR's death in the spring of 1945. In FDR's final address to Congress in March of that year, he laid down a rather impossible challenge when he said, "Twenty-five years ago, American fighting men looked to the statesmen of the world to finish the world of peace for which they fought and suffered. We failed—we failed them then. We cannot fail them again, and expect the world to survive again." FDR had made his pact with the devil (Stalin) much in the same way Churchill had with the Americans: buying victory in the war by accepting a less-than-desirable peace. For Churchill, it was the loss of his empire's preferential trading system, which meant he traded Great Britain's empire for his civilization's ultimate survival. For FDR, leveraging the Soviet Union's manpower to bleed Nazi Germany allowed him to navigate history's bloodiest conflict at a stunningly low per capita casualty rate (actually, the lowest in the war among all participants). FDR's grand strategic brilliance lay primarily in these two accomplishments: giving his successor the chance to dramatically spread our model of a liberal trade order and the legal arbitration of interstate disputes (perfected at home, now projecting abroad), while leaving him not only an America that was financially and economically strong but a public that remained overwhelmingly open to the notion of the responsibilities of global leadership.

Truman's brilliance revealed itself in the execution of that dream, curtailing its aspects as required by the immediate Soviet threat of continental aggression across Eurasia. Despite his lack of foreign policy experience (he later admitted he had been an "innocent idealist" when he first met Stalin at the Potsdam Conference), but clearly buttressed by his own combat military experience in WWI, Truman executed a series of very difficult calls across the first twenty-seven months of his presidency, including the first and only use of nuclear weapons (trading that horrific precedent against the likelihood of increasing America's total wartime casualties by 50 percent in any attempt to subdue Japan's homeland), the formulation of the Truman Doctrine (picking up bankrupted Britain's security-assistance role in Greece and Turkey), proposing and getting congressional approval for the Marshall Plan, and launching the Berlin Airlift. All these decisions represented severe contingency responses that emphasized America's continuing exceptional role as guarantor of freedom, peace, and fair trade while accepting the emerging reality that our definition of that "free world" was rapidly shrinking, meaning we'd be able to protect only ourselves and the rest of what came to be known during the Cold War as the "West." In 1950, that West constituted roughly a quarter of the world's population, whereas already one-third of humanity was trapped behind the Iron Curtain, leaving about 40 percent of the planet up for grabs, especially after Europe's remaining colonial empires fell apart across the next quarter-century.

In retrospect, this was a stunning comedown from our immediate postwar expectations: Instead of saving the entire world, we secured a mere quarter while "losing" substantially more to our rising rival in the

East. But the next steps were relatively simple enough: contain our rivals while replicating our model to the greatest extent possible in the areas we had secured, and give as much attention as we could to replicating our-selves in the remaining ideological "waste spaces" that came to be known, alternatively, as the Third World or the Non-Aligned Movement. In many ways, this is the same sort of realism we need to apply today: locking in political and security alliances with those new adherents to our globaliza-tion order (especially rising Asia) while doing our best to replicate our models inside the Gap.

5. NO POLITICAL SOLUTIONS FOR ECONOMIC PROBLEMS.

Reflecting our "special relationship" with Great Britain across this time period, much of the grand strategic logic animating our effort to project the American System upon the global stage following World War II emanated from a British economist. John Maynard Keynes, whose "spend to save" logic launched a global economic revolution in govern-ment interventionary policies in the decades following the 1936 publica-tion of his seminal textbook, *The General Theory of Employment, Interest, and Money*, had his first and primary influence as a grand strategist (or what he called a "master economist") in his short 1919 treatise (*The Eco-nomic Consequences of the Peace*) condemning the Treaty of Versailles, in whose negotiations he participated as a representative of the British Trea-sury. In this amazingly prescient book, Keynes not only correctly foresaw how Versailles's harsh peace would fail and ultimately unleash a German "vengeance" that he dared to predict "will not limp," he likewise under-scored how a Europe already deeply dependent on a global economy (and America in particular) could no longer operate in a mode of interstate war while holding on to a standard of living it could only maintain through continuing to interweave its national economies with one another and the larger world outside. In short, "Europe before the war" had so cast its eco-nomic lot with the dynamics of regional interdependence and global eco-nomic trade that destruction of one of its main components (here Germany) preordained both destruction of the regional whole and great havoc inflicted upon global order.

To prevent such an outcome, or basically the descent toward global chaos embodied in the economic nationalism of the Great Depression, the commensurate triumph of fascism in Europe, and the unleashing of the most destructive war in human history, Keynes made a series of extraordinarily bold proposals. These proposals, none of which found sufficient execution after WWI, all found their way into being in the American-imposed international order following WWII—including the United Nations; the Bretton Woods Agreements creating an International Monetary Fund, World Bank, and General Agreement on Tariffs and Trade (forerunner of the World Trade Organization); the Marshall Plan from America; the long-term logic for a "free-trade union" to unite Europe (foreshadowing the EU); and even the requirement to contain the Communist political threat from the East while promoting a détente-like policy of increasing economic trade. In less than thirty pages of text (Chapter VII: "Remedies"), Keynes projects a long-term solution set that accurately predicts the next seven decades of European history, his key insight being that economic security is the *sine qua non* of a stable peace. In my opinion, this short book is the most compelling example of sound grand strategy ever put into print. It is also arguably the best single expression of the economic logic behind America's unstated grand strategy throughout its history. By sticking with his "It's the economy, stupid!" bias, Keynes articulates, really for the first time in history, not merely a theory of peace through trade, but a grand strategic vision for engineering trade for stability.

If you want to win a global war on terror through nonkinetics, there is no better blueprint, because engineering trade for stability is the essential guiding principle of our country's entire development as a nation-state and its rise to global power. The idealism of the Wilsonian impulse notwithstanding, it's the economic pragmatism of the Keynesian revolution, later embodied in FDR's New Deal package and subsequently projected upon—admittedly just—the West that makes modern (as in, American-style) globalization possible. That's not to say American-style globalization is the only answer worth pursuing as we move forward, because it can't be. It's just reminding us of our seminal role in shaping the world we live in today. Again, globalization is not some unfamiliar monster, even if it often appears that we are Frankenstein to its unintentional creation.

Wendell Willkie, Republican nominee for the presidency in the 1940

election, wrote a runaway bestseller in 1943 titled *One World*, in which he argued that the Versailles Treaty hadn't worked to keep the European peace because it did not "sufficiently seek solution to the economic problems of the world. Its attempts to solve the world's problems were primarily political. But political internationalism without economic internationalism is a house built upon sand." By the early 1940s, this essentially Keynesian view was becoming accepted wisdom, primarily because the Great Depression of the 1930s *plus* the resumption of world war drove home to most Americans the new reality that their personal freedom stemmed primarily from their economic security—long taken for granted—and that their economic security could be greatly threatened even if their physical security could be maintained.

As Keynes had previously recognized in WWI-era Europe, the Americans of this era were getting the first great glimpse of the complex interdependency of a then globalizing American economy that today sits so enmeshed in a global economy of our making that we do not recognize its profound revolutionary impact around the planet. Back then, the revolutionary impact of our growing economic and security connectivity with the outside world was felt more at home than abroad: By finally embracing global leadership we were forced to—really for the first time in our history—define Americanism completely, including, over the next quarter-century, finally resolving most of the residual institutional racism in our society as a result of greater international scrutiny. As we now watch globalization make similar demands on traditional societies regarding religious freedom and the rights of minorities and women, the continuing revolutionary impact of our system-creating efforts—first at home and then globally—must be kept in mind. Why? Because we still have that tendency, so much displayed by the Bush administration, to demand immediate political solutions to long-term economic problems.

6. STATE YOUR POSITIVE GOALS AS EARLY AS POSSIBLE.

Here, Wilson was hamstrung by his election promises to keep America out of Europe's war, especially after he won reelection in 1916 by a narrow margin. Once into the fight, however, Wilson expressed his idealism in the most ambitious form in his declaration of war on Germany:

The world must be made safe for democracy. Its peace must be planted upon the tested foundations of political liberty. We have no selfish ends to serve. We desire no conquest, no dominion. We seek no indemnities for ourselves, no material compensation for the sacrifices we shall freely make. We are but one of the champions of the rights of mankind. We shall be satisfied when those rights have been made as secure as the faith and the freedom of nations can make them.

What's interesting about these goals, per Keynes's harsh criticism of Wilson's conduct at the Versailles Treaty negotiations, is their intense political focus. Wilson yielded on war reparations and colonial-style mandates for the Middle East and Africa because he felt that creating the political construct of the League of Nations was more important—more crucial to building a stable peace.

The contrast with Franklin Roosevelt is not as stunning as you might expect, for FDR considered himself a true Wilsonian, having served in his cabinet as an assistant secretary of the Navy. On timing, however, FDR was far more aggressive, preemptively declaring America's war aims in his joint statement, with Great Britain's Winston Churchill, of the Atlantic Charter in August 1941, more than three months prior to Japan's attack on Pearl Harbor. Reflecting the New Deal experience, FDR's Atlantic Charter basically expanded his Four Freedoms construct (speech, religion, from want, and from fear) to encompass the larger world. As Elizabeth Borgwardt argues, "Just because the New Deal had expanded the idea of 'security' to encompass economic and social security did not mean that the concept was now confined to these domestic dimensions," especially as many Americans "anticipated widespread unemployment and even chaos in the conflict's wake." Thus, "it seemed only natural that the New Deal's sweeping institutional approaches to intractable problems would be translated to the international level by Roosevelt administration planners." This "integrated vision of social and economic rights," as Borgwardt describes it, actually made the Atlantic Charter's promise of future stability more individually oriented than state-focused, in effect making the declaration the first great expression of human rights in the modern world—a modern declaration of *individual* independence.

In the end, FDR sought basically the same package of political rights (e.g., national self-determination) and legal arbitration (a global governance body and international court) that Wilson did. But what he added to the mix, and what really sold an American public that had just experienced the Great Depression, was the promise of an international liberal trade order that was effectively institutionalized. Wilson made similar noises about free trade (point 3), but then let that element of his agenda be largely defined in terms of war reparations. George Bush, one could say, played more of a Wilsonian hand in his "war on terror," stressing a world made safe for democracy but largely missing the chance to define—as FDR did in a nod to Theodore—a more middle-class ideology of economic security. As such, Bush was rightfully accused of sharing Wilson's ambition and myopia when it comes to grand strategy.

7. PLAN FOR THE POSTWAR RIGHT FROM THE START.

This may seem obvious from today's perspective, but it certainly wasn't to Wilson's administration during World War I. Almost purposefully playing behind the curve, Wilson spent his first three years in office assuring the American public he'd keep them out of Europe's war ("too proud to fight" was how he initially responded to Germany's sinking of the ocean liner *Lusitania*), only to whip that same public into anti-German and antisocialist frenzy once America entered the conflict in 1917, employing a massive propaganda effort through the government-sponsored Committee on Public Information and encouraging private vigilante groups of the American Protective League. Having made virtually no prewar attempt at economic mobilization, in part out of the fear of triggering wartime loyalties among an American population in which one out of six were foreign-born and overwhelmingly of European stock, Wilson thereupon aggressively stoked government-sponsored zealotry against any group or individual failing to meet the new standard of "100% Americanism." Not surprisingly, this flood of chauvinism wasn't easy to stem once the Armistice of 1918 arrived, complicating Wilson's subsequent attempts to sell the American public on membership in the League of Nations and the global responsibilities it implied. That's not to say Wilson's government did not engage in postwar planning prior to the war's end, because it did in the form of "The Inquiry," a group of about 150 aca-

demics and experts who met for months in New York's American Geo-
graphical Society building. This group's research definitely shaped many
of Wilson's 14 Points, the vast majority of which, unfortunately, came to
naught.

American planning for WWII's postwar actually began before our entry into the war, and it was overwhelmingly economic in its perspective,
as evidenced by FDR's Lend-Lease program and the Article 7 obligation
forced upon Great Britain, as well as Secretary of State Cordell Hull's
consistent prewar push for a liberal trade order. After an abortive attempt
to launch a government-wide postwar planning effort in 1940, Hull's
State Department began planning for real in 1941, engaging, among so
many "technicians," a young official by the name of Dean Acheson, who,
over the course of the next several years, would play a key role in either
planning or selling virtually every aspect of the proposed international
order, only to shift from articulation to execution as Truman's secretary of
state from 1949 to 1953. From conceptualization through precedent-
setting implementation, Acheson is arguably the most consistently seminal figure among the so-called "wise men" who guided America's postwar
planning and execution. In one form or another, Acheson worked it all:
the postwar implications of Lend-Lease (conversing with Keynes himself), the United Nations Relief and Rehabilitation Agency (UNRRA),
the Food and Agricultural Organization (FAO), the Bretton Woods Agreements, the United Nations (writing Truman's speech for the inaugural
San Francisco meeting and guiding the Senate's ratification for State), the
H-bomb program, the Truman Doctrine and the Marshall Plan, the National Security Council's creation and its historic policy document (NSC-
68) setting up the Defense Department and Central Intelligence Agency,
the NATO treaty, right on through the conduct of the Korean War—the
first great conflict of the Cold War. His Pulitzer Prize–winning 1970 autobiography said it all, for Acheson was indeed "present at the creation."

What Acheson's career progression represented was America's instinctive reach to own the postwar order as much as—or more than—it
tried to dominate the war's conduct. In that instinctive ambition, not
much has changed, the big difference between now and then being the
talent pool the U.S. government could bring to bear and the confidence it
had on the subject of nation-building.

8. RECOGNIZE THAT YOUR RECENT EXPERIENCES
DETERMINE YOUR USABLE SKILLS.

WWI-era America wasn't ready for any proactive postwar reconstruction role in Europe or really anywhere else; its government lacked the institutions, the people, and the experience. Most of all, it lacked the idea of such work because similar domestic efforts had only begun inside of America since the advent of the progressive era in the mid-1890s. The pre-Keynesian American presidency prior to the Great Depression likewise lacked an overarching mandate for such broad economic stewardship.

The Great Depression, of course, changed all that, empowering FDR's administration to become, as Keynes put it, the "economic laboratory of the world." Keynes himself was fascinated by Roosevelt, who, on the basis of one brief face-to-face encounter, appeared to return the compliment to the man whose theories would encapsulate much of FDR's own instinct that America needed to "spend to save" itself from the clutches of the Great Depression's monetary trap. As my own Depression-era mother always describes the times, "Everybody wanted work, but nobody had any money." Many economic historians have argued that FDR's New Deal did little on its own to lift America out of depression, because that hard time was not simply limited to the U.S. economy but rather reflected a global capitalist crisis extended—seemingly *ad infinitum*—by the trade protectionism to which so many governments resorted across the 1930s. FDR could reverse that policy tide at home, but he couldn't force larger architectural changes on international trade—until WWII gave him the opportunity.

Almost immediately once the war started, the nation's best and brightest, an entire generation of New Dealers with years of experience in economic-stimulus packaging, institution-building, and state-building in general, were put to work thinking ahead about how the New Deal could be translated into a new international economic order. Paramount in their thinking, as Keynes's biographer Robert Skidelsky notes, was "one overriding aim: to do better than last time." As policymakers on both sides of the Atlantic knew, America was—in Skidelsky's description—the "great unknown" in this equation, having chosen withdrawal after the last world war. As long as Roosevelt remained in power, America's commitment to follow through seemed clear. Sensing that FDR did not have long to live, the Democratic Party experienced a tremendous struggle leading up to the 1944 convention to determine who would serve as vice president. Because there were many prominent New Dealers in the mix, the selection of Harry Truman was hailed as "the Missouri Compromise." With no foreign policy experience to claim and a tainted association with one of the era's most infamous power brokers, the legendary Tom Pendergast, this "failed haberdasher" (referring to a business co-owned by Truman that went bankrupt in the post-WWI bust) struck many Americans as an obscure choice. Even FDR admitted as late as July 1944, "I hardly know Truman."

But here are the two key connections that explain FDR's choice in the end: (1) as Truman himself was to brag, "I was a New Dealer from the start"; and (2) Truman was a popular and trusted member of the Senate, the key decision-making body for the cluster of treaties FDR had envisaged getting passed to cement his postwar economic and security order. Truman's initial instincts in this regard seemed to bear out FDR's wisdom. When stunned by his new responsibilities and the fact that FDR made no effort whatsoever to prepare him (he confessed to the press that he felt "like the moon, the stars, and all the planets had fallen on me"), Truman made a surprise visit to Congress on his first day after being sworn in. The symbolism was not missed among his former colleagues. As journalist Allen Drury noted, "Characteristically, he came to them. He did not, this first time, ask them to come to him." If that first impression endeared him to the Hill, his first postwar message to Congress five months later confirmed his commitment to FDR's New Deal philosophy, as he asked for a stunning package of new federal spending for domestic stimulus programs and extension of his war-powers control over the economy. This single request, coming in the highly charged political atmosphere where, as Truman biographer David McCullough notes, "prophecies of economic doom had become commonplace," was greater than any FDR himself had attempted "at one sitting," complained the House minority leader.

Over time, Truman's New Deal instinct to "spend to save" proved out. Upon surviving those initial, scary postwar months that saw nationwide strikes, rising Soviet aggression in Europe, and Great Britain's economic collapse, Truman's willingness to spend both at home and abroad (the Marshall Plan) won him a narrow reelection in 1948. As McCullough writes of his subsequent inauguration, "No president in history had ever taken office at a time of such prosperity and power." And what did Truman do with that power? McCullough notes of his inaugural address, "The speech was devoted exclusively to foreign policy. Though a major statement of American aspirations, its focus was the world—the 'peace of the world,' 'world recovery,' 'people all over the world.' " Truman's four-point program emphasized the following: (1) America's continued support for the United Nations—FDR's great legacy; (2) continued funding of the Marshall Plan, logically extending FDR's Lend-Lease philosophy; (3) the administration's commitment to join what would eventually become NATO, cementing the transatlantic security bond that Roosevelt had built; and (4) Truman's famous "Point Four" proposal to share American scientific knowledge with the world—in effect, a global stimulus package leveraging America's tremendous scientific gains from the war.

The *Washington Post* headline said it all: "Truman Proposes 'Fair Deal' Plan for the World," and the *New York Times* compared Truman at once to FDR, Woodrow Wilson, Theodore Roosevelt, and Abraham Lincoln!

9. ONCE THE WAR IS WON, THE ONLY ALTERNATIVE TO WITHDRAWAL OR DOMINATION IS TRANSFORMATION.

After achieving decisive victory in war, a dominant world power faces one of three choices, according to political scientist John Ikenberry: It can withdraw from the field, it can dominate the resulting environment "as is," or it can seek to transform that strategic landscape "into a durable order that commands the allegiance of other states within the order." Woodrow Wilson knew, as Franklin Roosevelt himself later argued, that "the colonial system means war," and thus he sought to end that system. He was not successful primarily because America had not amassed sufficient Leviathan-like power to force such change upon Eurasia's imperial order. His League of Nations plan twice defeated in the Senate, Wilson served out his second term an invalid, weakened from strokes brought on by his exhausting attempts to rally public support for the treaty. His replacement, elected in 1920, was Republican Warren G. Harding, who promised a return to "normalcy," withdrawing America from world power.

Roosevelt, by contrast, clearly sought to transform the system rather than dominate it (Stalin's choice). Stalin clearly recognized Roosevelt's planned new world order for what it was: a political revolution in interstate trade, and thus chose to remain outside its economic purview. This made possible America's Cold War policy of containment by forcing an unpalatable choice upon Stalin, who simply couldn't stomach the transparency demanded as the price for membership (indeed, it's why Stalin turned down Marshall Plan aid). If FDR hadn't sought such system transformation, containment would have lacked its technological "stick" and détente would have lacked its trade "carrot." Because FDR demanded, and won, Britain's commitment to end its imperial trade preferences, the world's largest colonial empire was sent into inevitable collapse, eventually taking that of France and other European powers with it in a stunningly rapid period of decolonization, in effect birthing the so-called Third World that would later serve as playing field for superpower rivalry in the Cold War. You may view all these outcomes as suboptimal, and indeed they were. But they were the next logical iteration, given the circumstances presented by World War II. In short, FDR played the best hand possible, transforming the international system as much as America could manage at that time and generating all the positive system dynamics that favored the West throughout the Cold War. And that's all any good grand strategy delivers—the next, best possible iteration.

To the extent that George Bush sought system transformation with his "global war on terror" and focus on democratization, he came closer to repeating Wilson's sins than seeking FDR's salvation. Viewing baseline security (terrorism prevention) and top-line political freedom (democracy) as the two extremes of Maslow's hierarchy of needs, Bush neglected the vast middle that concerns meeting economic needs and progress through individual self-improvement—that essential definition of American democracy. That's too bad, because the global economy is presently witnessing an explosion in its middle class; thus any American grand strategy that does not speak to that perspective—engaging that middle-class ideology—is doomed to have limited worldwide appeal.

A more critical appreciation of Bush, à la Ikenberry, says he sought domination and, in his failure, achieved a strong American impulse toward withdrawal.

10. SOCIALIZE THE PROBLEM, INSTITUTIONALIZE THE SOLUTION.

The key is to institutionalize the postwar order in sustainable, mutually reinforcing packages: not just the politics (League of Nations–cum–United Nations), and not just the law (Permanent Court of International Justice–cum–World Court), but also the economics (Bretton Woods institutions). The last piece was clearly missing in Wilson's post-WWI package; it was clearly the revolutionary centerpiece of FDR's New Deal–gone–global, post-WWII package. That Bretton Woods package (International Monetary Fund, World Bank, General Agreement on Tariffs and Trade) has proven—despite what its critics claim—to be fairly flexible. The IMF began life as the stabilizer of global currencies, and once that function fell by the wayside with Richard Nixon's decision to abandon the gold standard in 1971, it transformed itself into the lender of last resort, and increasingly in recent years, the processor of sovereign bankruptcy (e.g., Russia, Argentina). The World Bank's lending focus has shifted greatly over the years, marking it as either responsive to new trends or a development fad chaser—depending on your point of view. GATT, of course, underwent the most profound transformation, in further institutionalizing itself in the World Trade Organization in 1995. In sum, the legacy of Bretton Woods is an undeniably positive one, if for no other reason than that its institutions promoted the spread of economic best practices throughout the global economy over time—in effect, credentializing its expansion with new and improved rules.

The spread of these best practices represents the ultimate triumph of American capitalism and makes possible the effective replication of the American System of rapid economic development: to first include internal integration (infrastructure development) coupled with a high degree of trade protectionism, and later to expand toward external integration based on the efficiencies afforded by the "open door" philosophy of unhindered trade. When we say globalization integrates trade while disintegrating production chains, we're essentially describing the trade/development aspects of the American System—a sort of "Build it (your national economy) and they (other nations) will trade." As with all things American, it is inherently focused on self-improvement, but tempered with the understanding that progress is not a zero-sum game.

Here again, the Bush administration failed us in its narrowing of America's cooperation with international institutions like the United Nations and the International Criminal Court—although its efforts on the WTO's Doha Development Round were laudably correct and vigorous, especially on the issue of trying to reduce agricultural subsidies among the world's richest economies. Alas, not every leader possesses cat-herding skills, the most essential skill of global trade-pact negotiators, and Bush-Cheney possessed fewer than most.

11. EXPECT A CHALLENGE TO YOUR BEST-LAID PLANS.

All success attracts critics, and all power attracts challengers. Sometimes it's personal, like Henry Cabot Lodge's animus toward Woodrow Wilson, while other times it's structural. America's unprecedented prosperity and power at the end of the Second World War naturally generated hostility from the other great remaining pole in the international order. To our great good fortune, that challenger was unable, in ideological terms, and unwilling, in its cultural paranoia, to engage American power where it mattered most—building a successful global economy.

Here we must judge the Truman administration in a very favorable light. When presented with rising Soviet intransigence and hostility in Europe, Truman met every challenge with a strong response that suggested both the capacity for sustainability and the commitment for endurance: the Truman Doctrine, the Marshall Plan, the Berlin Airlift, the creation of NATO, and the significant military response to the Korean War. Better yet, the Truman administration gave strategic voice to this pattern of responses, taking its cues from George Kennan's "Long Telegram" and later "X" article ("The Sources of Soviet Conduct"), and codifying that approach in NSC-68's creation of the Cold War national security architecture that remains, unfortunately, largely unchanged to this day. Kennan's approach to the Soviets had the blessing of simplicity: behavior modification. By making clear to the Soviets what behavior we would allow and that which we would actively target, we created a basic Cold War rule set, or what Dean Acheson called a "corpus diplomaticum" that would guide subsequent presidential administrations, starting with Truman's second term.

Did Soviet aggression and the resulting Cold War put many of FDR's dreams for a liberal postwar economic order on hold? Yes and no. Yes in the sense that containment's military component overshadowed everything else in our subsequent foreign policy, to Kennan's eternal regret, but no in the sense that that economic order not only successfully emerged but also grew in strength beyond all expectations. By the early 1980s, just as the Soviet Union began its long series of withdrawals from Third World adventurism and China embraced market reforms, the economic bloc of the West, Roosevelt's ultimate legacy, controlled roughly two-thirds of the global economy's wealth and productive capacity on a population base of not much more than 10 percent of humanity. Again, if Roosevelt had not created that liberal economic order, then Truman's subsequent initiation of the containment grand strategy would have gone nowhere over the long run.

12. SELLING GRAND STRATEGY IS ONE THING, EXECUTING IT IS QUITE ANOTHER.

Clearly, Wilson failed badly in the selling aspect, so the question of execution never really arose regarding the League of Nations and the post-WWI international order. America went its way, as did Germany and Soviet Russia, and the rematch was unfortunately set for a generation later.

If grand strategy can be said to be a trinity of word, prophet, and deliverer, then we can delineate Roosevelt's solution set like this: word (*The Economic Consequences of the Peace*), prophet (John Maynard Keynes), and deliverer (Franklin Delano Roosevelt in his "fireside chat" personages known as "Dr. New Deal" and "Dr. Win-the-War"). Keynes, arguably the one true grand strategist of the twentieth century (besides FDR himself), because he understood conflict within the context of the economic *everything else* (as I like to call it), forecast the entire post-WWII package from the perspective of 1919. Of course, he issued that list of remedies in the hope of preventing WWII and not merely improving it vis-à-vis the First World War. He also issued it within the implied context of sustaining Great Britain's hold on its international empire, which, of course, in its ultimate logic it could not do. As such, Keynesianism needed an American deliverer, and Keynes himself basically anointed Roosevelt for that role as international exemplar and experimenter without peer. As stated above, this grand strategy was enormously successful and, in Marxian terms, provided the economic base upon which the additional grand strategy of containment could rest its superstructure of military strength, technological superiority, and sustained superpower rivalry. If the full fruits of this grand strategy were hidden from our full appreciation until the Soviet bloc's collapse, then that only reminds us that good things come to those who wait—or better yet, persevere.

Shifting from base to superstructure, here we find the quintessential model for articulating, selling, and implementing a grand strategy. Here word ("Long Telegram," "X" article) and prophet (Kennan and Clark Clifford in the background, George Marshall and Dean Acheson in the foreground) find their moments primarily in the first Truman administration, with deliverers (Paul Nitze's translation into NSC-68, Acheson's implementation as secretary of state, General Douglas MacArthur's scary turn in Korea and Truman's ultimate decision to sack him) finding their moments more in Truman's second administration. In short, necessary hearts were won in the first administration (e.g., the "sell" to Senate Republicans led by Arthur Vandenberg and Robert Taft), and great minds executed in the second. As Acheson himself put it in his memoirs, "In the first period, the main lines of policy were set and begun; in the second, they were put into full effect amid the smoke and confusion of battle."

Were there mistakes in translation? According to Kennan himself, there were plenty, but primarily in the overmilitarization of the containment strategy, which he viewed primarily in terms of political resistance to the spread of Soviet influence. Like Acheson, Kennan feared European weakness more than Soviet strength. Also, like any good grand strategist, Kennan was infinitely patient, preferring to "give the hand of time a chance to work." For remember, Kennan's primary observation was that the Soviet system was economically uncompetitive, meaning, given enough time, it would collapse under the weight of systemic, internal contradictions.

Of course, the old saw about "mistakes were made" is easier to stomach with the distance of time. Having grown up during the Vietnam War, I remember the nation's great sense of strategic unease back then—this sense that we no longer knew what we were doing but rather were doing what we'd always done simply because we could see no alternative. Here, the narrow orthodoxy of Nitze's translation is somewhat to blame, but that translation unfolds in great deference to the exigencies of the time: the need to "scare the hell out of the country," as Acheson famously put it to Truman; the subsequent "red scare"; deep social fears about the likelihood of global nuclear war; the perceived domino effect triggered by the "loss" of China to Communism; and so on. While the strategist in me deplores the myopia we developed as a result, the grand strategist in me discounts—quite cruelly—the associated cost. In large part, America was killing both people *and* time in Southeast Asia, waiting for the "rot" to set in on the Soviet system while innovation and self-improvement continued in the American System. To the extent our myopia encouraged a similar mindset among the Soviets, then we only sped up their economic demise.

The net impact, though, on the global "correlation of forces" between socialism and capitalism was nil. On that basis alone Vietnam was a pointless exercise, because, as later events showed, the expansion of socialism into Southeast Asia hardly represented a victory for the "monolithic" Soviet bloc. If anything, it simply expanded the field of Sino-Soviet competition and antagonism, the end result being that Soviet satellites there effectively boxed in China, not that much containment was actually required. But again, this only points out how, in the long run, this effort was equally pointless for the Soviet side. No permanent advantage was granted to, or ceded by, either side in the superpower rivalry. Viewed from today's perspective, in which a capitalist domino sequence seems to be unfolding (i.e., Southeast Asia marketizes so as not to fall too far behind dynamo and new regional economic hegemon China), the only clear winner in the process would seem to be the Chinese capitalist "running dog"—an unlimited irony indeed!

13. IF YOU WANT TO MAKE IT STICK,
THEN THE BOYS ARE NEVER COMING HOME.

One of the main reasons Wilson couldn't make his vision work in the aftermath of World War I was that America at the time had no stomach for keeping troops abroad for any length of time beyond what was absolutely necessary to win the war. The slogan of the Marine Corps of that age, "first to fight," was quickly translated into *first to leave* once the shooting stopped, our exodus being so rapid that we had to prevail upon the British merchant fleet to make it happen. In that context, America's demands for a new postwar international order lacked any long-term promise of commensurate enforcement, an effective strategic withdrawal made all too clear by our unwillingness to join the League of Nations.

The same impulse to "bring the boys home" was seen after World War II, and it was indulged with near-equal fervor. U.S. troop strength stood at roughly 12 million at the end of the war, but by the middle of 1947, we had fewer than 2 million men in uniform, resulting in an American military largely unprepared for the ramping up of Cold War tensions with the Soviet Union, much less the rapid response to North Korea's invasion of South Korea in 1950.

What largely defined America's status as a military superpower across the Cold War decades was our willingness, on average, to post about a quarter of our military manpower overseas on a rotational basis, including a steady core of about 300,000 troops in Europe at all times. The total worldwide number of troops varied over time, with two add-on bulges associated with the Korean (500,000) and Vietnam (700,000) conflicts. With the end of the Cold War, the drawdown of American troops in Europe was dramatic, declining to approximately 100,000, or roughly similar to what we've maintained in Asia before and since Vietnam. The highest concentration of American troops today is in the Middle East, where approximately 200,000 total troops are regularly rotated, a certain small percentage serving aboard ships. With the surging of U.S. troops to the region since 2003, the overall total of U.S. troops serving abroad returns to the Cold War levels of the post-Vietnam period (400,000), reversing the trend of the 1990s, when we averaged something closer to 200,000 (split roughly between Europe and Asia).

My point is this: Once Truman committed us to the Cold War, America entered into an era in which the boys never really came home. Despite the illusion of the 1990s, demand around the world remains substantial for our Leviathan service, although in reality the vast majority of our operations—as during the Cold War—remain on the SysAdmin side of the ledger (e.g., crisis response, disaster relief, counterinsurgency, state-building, military-to-military training). Are we going to have troops in the Middle East for decades, just as we did in Europe and Asia? Yes. The real questions we face today involve the mix: How much Leviathan versus SysAdmin capabilities? What geographic spread? How much do we rely on other nations' forces (as with the U.S. Navy's notion of a "1,000-ship navy" that's only one-fifth us and four-fifths the rest of the world)? These are serious questions of grand strategy, reflecting our need to tie off the remnants of the Cold War as quickly as possible if we're going to adjust ourselves to the challenges of today.

Our military today is roughly one-third smaller in personnel than it was at Cold War's end, so maintaining 400,000 troops abroad, operating at a fairly high tempo, is burning out the force. It's simply unsustainable. What we could sustain is more like 250,000 to 300,000 abroad, or at least 100,000 less than today. There are two ways to achieve that: (1) draw down our troop levels in Asia and Europe (harder in the latter, because it's the launching point for rotations in southwest Asia) or (2) get more friends. This is why I focus on the North Korean scenario: I want us to be able to reduce our troops in Asia once Korea is reunified and I want that process to unfold in such a way that China's massive military (followed by India's) is brought into my grand strategic fold. Think the origins of the Cold War don't matter? They haunt us still.

14. NUKES KILLED GREAT-POWER WAR.

One last point reminds us how the first conflicts in a long war can set the tone for the rest that follow, something we see today in how Iraq and Afghanistan are triggering profound changes in our military.

As WWII came to a close, Soviet troops ended up occupying the northern half of Korea as part of Stalin's reward for joining American efforts against the Japanese in the Asian theater. The Soviets routed Japanese forces on Asia's mainland (e.g., Manchuria), exploiting the opportunity to grab geographic buffers. As a result, Korea ended up being divided much as Germany had been in Europe: The Allies drew a line that later became a source of tension between the Americans and the Soviets, who set up mirror images of themselves in the two resulting governments.

When North Korean troops poured over the border into South Korea in June 1950, it came as a stunning surprise to the Truman administration, which scrambled to respond militarily. Taking advantage of the Soviet Union's decision to abstain from participating in the UN Security Council vote (Stalin had personally preapproved North Korea's invasion but could have vetoed any UNSC decision to respond), Secretary of State Dean Acheson engineered the first-ever UN-sanctioned coalition war. As a result of this "police action," Truman's preferred euphemism, U.S. troops were sent overseas to a major war for the first time in our nation's history without Congress making an official declaration of war.

This was a huge turning point in U.S. history: From that day forward the United States would engage in overseas wars primarily to address the structure and stability of the global security order—a tremendous expansion of our definition of national interest. None of these conflicts has ever triggered a declaration of war by Congress, meaning we effectively altered our Constitution as part of a grand strategy we've since employed. By doing so, we shifted the function of war in U.S. grand strategy from survival to shaping; wars were no longer fought to ensure our immediate survival but to shape the global security environment, meaning since 1950 we've engaged solely in wars of discipline and not survival. Wars of survival are, by definition, unlimited or total wars—as in, you do anything to survive, including the use of nuclear weapons. Wars of discipline are limited, meaning you don't go all the way with everything you've got.

The Korean War was the great tipping point in this regard, and Truman's decision not to go all the way with nukes when the tide turned against us was a seminal moment in U.S. grand strategy. You have to remember: This was the only man in human history ever to order the use of nuclear weapons. But he was also the American leader who first realized the limits of great-power war in the nuclear age, and in that moment, whether he realized it or not, Truman effectively killed great-power war. International-relations experts like to date the end of great-power war in 1945, a year marked by the cessation of WWII and the invention and first use of nuclear weapons. But in truth, great-power war died as a concept in April 1951, when Truman relieved General Douglas MacArthur as the commander of U.S. forces in Korea. MacArthur, a living legend and five-star General of the Army, opposed Truman's decision to wage a limited war in Korea, preferring to take the fight directly to North Korea's main manpower patron, the People's Republic of China. Had America done so, World War III could have easily resulted, as the Soviet Union would have been forced to come to China's aid, possibly employing—eventually—its own recently developed nuclear weapons. All of this, of course, is historical conjecture.

What is not historical conjecture is that Truman's decision to fire the popular MacArthur was an act of great political courage. Gallup polls at the time indicated that roughly 70 percent of Americans sided with the legendary general, who many political experts expected would run for and win the presidency in 1952. Instead, another popular WWII five-star general won the presidency—Dwight D. Eisenhower. Ike did take up MacArthur's bold suggestion to threaten the use of nuclear weapons as a means to force a settlement in Korea. There is much historical debate as to how effective this threat was. Later historical evidence makes clear that the Soviets had no capacity for delivering nuclear weapons anywhere in East Asia, much less direct them toward the United States itself, whereas we did have the capacity to deliver them where we wanted. But for our purposes here, we can stipulate its effectiveness, because Ike's threatened use of nukes did not supersede Truman's concept of limited war but rather reinforced it. By threatening the use of nukes, Eisenhower signaled to the socialist-bloc powers America's recognition of the upper reaches of "limited war," a strategic concept that helped birth, after several other moments of mutual recognition (the most famous being the Cuban Missile Crisis of 1962), the notion of mutually assured destruction as the cornerstone of strategic stability in the nuclear age.

Truman, in historical terms, is really Theodore Roosevelt realized: a stick that was big enough so that America's voice was heard the world over. Truman embodied everything that TR was reaching for in his original definitions of American power employed on the global stage: might that buttresses right but does not define it, and power whose main utility is the threat of use that effectively enforces global norms favoring the spread of American influence. That Truman both used and refused nuclear weapons as a tool of war only signals his tipping-point function in American history: our awesome, world-destroying power revealed, it was immediately shelved.

This half-century journey from TR to Truman constitutes America's realization as global Leviathan, a status that would remain subject to testing and ultimate transformation across the Cold War decades to follow. But it's crucial to our understanding of American grand strategy today to realize that this power to shape the global environment—this awesome responsibility of deciding when and where war is allowed around the planet—is *not* something that dropped into our lap suddenly when the Berlin Wall collapsed or when the World Trade Center's twin towers fell. Rather, it was something America's leaders dreamed about from the very beginnings of this grand experiment in multinational union, and something our nation began actively pursuing more than a century ago.

Simply put, America's discipline has ensured the world's survival—time and time again. This is why American grand strategy matters most.

THE GLOBAL AMERICAN SYSTEM
BECOMES GLOBALIZATION

Histories of the Cold War invariably bury the lead by emphasizing nuclear brinksmanship and arms races and proxy wars in distant locales. While all such events captured headlines, the real story of the Cold War is that military strength, as always, bought time for economic superiority to wield its magic—the essence of the containment grand strategy. By salvaging and rehabbing what we could of Europe and helping Japan transform itself in a similar direction, America laid down its global system marker. The West then essentially dared the Soviets to do better in their own, mini–world economy.

The outcome was never really in doubt. Central planning can drive an economy through its early, extensive period of growth, picking industries to expand and mandating infrastructure development, but once the challenge of intensive growth is engaged, meaning not just adding in more inputs (labor, capital, resources) but using them more efficiently, central planning becomes more hindrance than help. The market's "hidden hand" guides intensive growth so much more effectively, allowing the "wisdom of crowds" (e.g., consumers, shareholders, angel investors, venture capitalists, and leveraged-buyout firms) to pick winners and dismember losers on a continuing basis. The Soviets had a bunch of guys sitting around a table in Moscow trying to figure this all out. Guess which side processed the tough questions faster?

History bears out this judgment: As soon as the Soviet economy moved past its extensive-phase recovery from WWII, the resulting, reasonably mature economy almost immediately began slowing down in growth, beginning in the early 1960s. Experiments were tried and "storming" efforts made toward certain technological advances (primarily in the military realm), but a growth gap inevitably opened up, then grew wider even across the West's difficult economic period of the 1970s, and finally became indisputably evident within the Soviet system by the early 1980s, when the technocrats of Mikhail Gorbachev's generation began showing up and quietly asking harder questions.

In a strategic sense, the primary job of U.S. national security was to make sure the West stayed secure across this time frame, picking up no unbearable burdens while encouraging the Soviets to do just the opposite. Both tasks proved very difficult for America's attention-deficit strategists, as evidenced by our going off the deep end on Vietnam and agonizing unduly each time the Soviets picked up another satellite ("Country X has been lost!") that ultimately either drained their resources or sapped the bloc's meager sense of ideological unity. Throughout the Cold War, we tended to discount our economic strength and vastly overestimate Soviet prowess in both economics and defense, our national security establishment tending to worst-case all possibilities and swallow Soviet propaganda far too uncritically. You could blame this on the incredibly high stakes involved (i.e., global nuclear war), but truth be told, it's an endemic analytical problem that continues to this day, based in large part on the nature of people who select such career paths and the painfully isolated intellectual lives they lead (seriously, go talk among yourselves—for several decades!). We also allowed ourselves, as Kennan himself was to complain, to be abused financially by our own rather untrustworthy "allies" in many instances. As our standards for admittance were low (bare minimum: your leader can't show up atop Lenin's Mausoleum in Moscow for the May Day parade), it didn't take much to qualify for Washington's anti-Communist economic or military aid.

My fundamental point is that our grand strategic task in the Cold War was not the military defeat of the Soviet Union but rather its economic defeat, letting that "base" victory destroy its ideological and political "superstructure"—a glorious process of disintegration triggered unintentionally by Gorbachev. That is the primary victory we claim in the Cold War, but it is also the most limited one. The far more complete victory, in terms of our grand strategy of first proving and then expanding our American System model on a global basis, came in opening up China and facilitating its co-optation to market economics. That victory completely overshadows the collapse of the Soviet bloc, which in many ways signaled the "end of history" only in Eurasia by finally discrediting the Left's attempt at a catch-up economic development strategy based on class dictatorship. China's embrace of markets was far more important because it validated early America's neither-Right-nor-Left-but-rather-middle (as in middle-class) strategy of national economic development, which emphasizes a high degree of economic liberty conferred on individuals while allowing, in its extensive phase of growth, a healthy amount of state involvement in developing industry sectors and critical infrastructure plus an avowed policy of trade protectionism.

Does China follow our prescription as we might write it today? Certainly not. It currently follows the prescription we wrote for ourselves across the nineteenth century, with no apologies to anyone and a clear sense of chauvinism directed toward then dominant Great Britain. Are many of our criticisms of China's economic path thus hypocritical? Yes, they are. Should we nonetheless press China on its lack of political liberty, much as Britain long shamed us on the question of slavery? You bet. But of course a certain patience is also called for, because there should be no desire on our part to reverse this greatest victory of the Cold War by insisting on premature political change that would destabilize China's chaotically advancing market economy. Frankly, that's the job of individual Chinese to pursue, with their capacity for pressuring the Chinese Communist Party on the pace of reform. I mean, that's how it happened in America, right? Every political advance we made came when individuals, suitably empowered by economic advance (meaning they had money and a willingness to use it), simply grew fed up with the system as it was and demanded—*en masse* or per special interest—something better.

The key thing for us to remember in this historical jaunt is that by enabling China's embrace of markets, we transformed our American System–cum–globalization model from a rather limited experiment (the West) to a truly global phenomenon. Adding China, all by itself, effectively tipped our model of globalization into majority status, meaning more than half the world was now involved, with China over time pulling India and Russia in similar directions by the combination of its example and sheer economic power. If we had "lost" China at the start of the Cold War, then it was now clearly won, along with serious momentum for a continuing grand strategy of projecting our states-uniting model of economic development upon the world.

By making this argument, I don't seek to completely dismiss the importance of America's superpower rivalry with the Soviet Union as the dominant dynamic of the Cold War period, but rather to put it in its proper place. Successfully containing the Soviet threat effectively closed the door on the twentieth century's long spasm of system-level violence and great-power war. This is a huge accomplishment but essentially a backward-looking one. Co-opting China toward market economics opened the door on the twenty-first century and showed what the goal of our grand strategy must become: completing the construction of a globally integrated economy. Our American System model remains the same: Over time, economies integrate and states unite.

Of course, in retrospect all this seems easy. But the outcome of the Cold War seemed anything but inevitable at the time. If anything, the experience of the first half of the twentieth century seemed to confirm just the opposite: The West and the Soviet bloc were slated, as Stalin himself predicted, to fight another world war within a generation's time. Nuclear weapons would shape that conflict, many thought, but certainly not obviate it. Thus, the journey of mutual discovery that America undertook with the Soviet Union on the question of nuclear weapons was necessary to concluding the Cold War as a transition phase for transforming the American-cum-Western experiment in economic integration into a truly global phenomenon. So long as the world remained trapped in the dynamic of superpower rivalry, too much of the planet would remain off-limits. The man who would change all that, Richard Nixon, thus becomes central to our story.

The actual journey was far shorter than most historians recognize—a mere two decades. Picking up the thread of the story with Eisenhower's threatened use of nuclear weapons in 1953 to force an end to the Korean conflict, we can make two decade-long leaps to conclude the essential narrative.

The first leap takes us to the Cuban Missile Crisis of 1962. Like virtually all Soviet brinksmanship in the Cold War, the Cuban crisis had a distinct tie-in to events in Europe—specifically, West Germany/Berlin. Whenever the Soviets, who were beyond paranoid in fearing a resurgent German threat, felt even the slightest inkling of revived danger or Western intransigence on the subject, they usually acted out somewhere else. In this instance, as eminent Soviet foreign policy expert Adam Ulam argued, the Soviets were fishing for a trigger that might, in a *quid pro quo* fashion, force young President John F. Kennedy's hand on a number of pressing international issues, including the ongoing but contentious negotiations for a German peace treaty that would settle the status of Berlin, where the Soviets had installed their infamous wall the previous year. This scary strategic standoff had two lasting effects: (1) the Soviets drove home to the American public the notion of rough parity, saying in effect, "We're confident enough to try to park some missiles off your coast"; and (2) a somewhat shaken American national security establishment, in the personage of Secretary of Defense Robert McNamara, subsequently moved in the direction of elevating the embryonic concept of mutually assured destruction to the level of a permanent cornerstone of U.S. strategic nuclear planning, in effect saying, "We'll aim for this minimum standard of security but logically no higher."

This was a huge development for America and the world. By coming to the conclusion that nuclear weapons are good primarily for *having* and not *using*, we essentially codified Truman's original instincts in the Korean War: All great-power war in the age of nuclear weapons is by definition limited war. While Truman had come to that conclusion in 1951, the U.S. national security establishment had not—witness Ike's secretary of state John Foster Dulles's toying with the notion of "massive retaliation" as an essential instrument in America's brinksmanship toolkit in the mid-1950s. Because the Soviets appeared to be taking their usual route to brute, numerical superiority across the middle to late 1950s, when the United States first feared a "bomber gap" and then a "missile gap," the decision to put our strategic faith in a secure second-strike capability was a bold move. What MAD basically said was this: "No matter how much you hit me in your first missile strike, I'll have enough second-strike capability to lay your entire country to waste, thus our mutual destruction is assured as long as I maintain a sufficient counterstrike capability." The subtext for the Soviets was "Your attempt to reach numerical superiority is useless. You may, for example, catch a lot of my ground-based missiles in their silos, but you can't possibly intercept all my bombers or target my unlocatable submarines and stop them from striking back."

Of course, it wasn't enough for just the United States to understand and adhere to the notions of MAD; we also had to convince the Soviets of this same logic. This effort took years, finally culminating in the signing of the first Strategic Arms Limitation Talks (SALT) treaty, as well as the Anti-Ballistic Missile Treaty, in May 1972 at the first of three historic summits between Richard Nixon and Soviet president Leonid Brezhnev. By agreeing for the first time ever to limit the nature of its ideological death match with capitalism, the international Communist movement, as Ulam states, "was finished." Yes, there would be future double crosses and spy scandals and proxy wars in the Third World, but none of these events changed the essential correlation of strategic forces—until Reagan threatened to do so with Star Wars in the early 1980s.

But by then, the essential die was cast for the Soviet experiment. Emboldened by détente and America's apparent weakness (e.g., Watergate, Vietnam), the Soviets would make one, last-gasp attempt to spread their brand of Marxism-Leninism in the Third World. While that effort elicited frantic fears in Washington of an "arc of crisis" and a new Communist domino effect in Southwest Asia and sub-Saharan Africa, all that effort really brought Moscow were additional burdens of empire on top of what it already bore in Eastern Europe. Eventually, even the Soviet Politburo's hardliners realized this danger, thanks in part to the Reagan Doctrine's support of rebel movements targeting their client states (particularly the mujahideen in Afghanistan), and thus the Soviets began trimming back their imperial ambitions, triggering a long withdrawal from the world that extended across the entirety of the 1980s and ended only with the Soviet Union's very dissolution in 1991.

There is much debate, naturally, as to the essential reasons why the Soviet bloc eventually disintegrated. My argument is a simple one: The Soviet Union was always going to fail eventually for economic reasons. The only question for grand strategy was, How could America get the Soviets to that point of realization in the safest and quickest fashion? Nixon and Kissinger safeguarded the process, and Reagan accelerated it.

Nixon entered the presidency with a set of unusual handicaps. First, he was effectively the first Republican president in thirty-six years, discounting the nonpartisan Eisenhower. Plus, he was the first president in more than a century to enter office with the opposition party controlling both houses of Congress. Worst, of course, was the strategic corner into which America had already painted itself on Vietnam across the previous two administrations. Read the White House memoirs of both Nixon and Kissinger and you'll see the vast bulk of the pages consumed by Vietnam, arguably only the sixth most important foreign policy legacy of their combined efforts, trailing the settlement of postwar Europe, détente with the Soviets, the codification of MAD in treaties, the opening to China, and taking America off the gold standard. Those were all system-level changes, whereas Vietnam's impact, as far as America was concerned, was largely internal, including the rapid rise and fall of the so-called imperial presidency.

Nixon was intent from the start on creating some strategic wiggle room, believing that America's foreign policy had been, as he put it, "held hostage, first under Kennedy to the Cold War and then under Johnson to the Vietnam war." Seeking out Kissinger's service as national security adviser because of their similar takes on balance-of-power politics and their complete lack of interest in global economics, Nixon took an approach to the presidency that was the opposite of Truman's, compromising on domestic policies while fighting damn near everybody on foreign policy. This was an inevitable tack, given Nixon's ambition to reorder the structure of great-power relations while trying to end an unwinnable and overwhelmingly unpopular overseas war.

Like Nixon, Kissinger was wholly unsatisfied with the way U.S.–Soviet relations had been previously managed, comparing the relationship to "two heavily armed blind men feeling their way around a room, each believing himself in mortal peril from the other whom he assumes to have perfect vision." Not given, as he put it, to the "myth of inexorable Soviet advance carefully orchestrated by some superplanners," Kissinger wanted to end the pendulum-swinging pattern of past diplomacy that saw America veering regularly from "sentimental conciliation" to "liturgical belligerence." With Nixon, he would establish concreteness, restraint, and linkage as the principles for engagement. Linkage, in Nixon's mind, was most important, "since U.S.–Soviet interests as the world's two competing nuclear superpowers were so widespread and overlapping, it was unrealistic to separate or compartmentalize areas of concern."

Seeking to free up American foreign policy would be a difficult trick. Nixon believed the first order of business was to tie off the loose ends of postwar Europe, because until the Soviets were made confident on the German question, getting their help on any other issue was highly unlikely. But as Kissinger points out, any move to engineer a more permanent settlement there raised magnificent fears among our European allies that some sort of "super Yalta" would be arranged by the superpowers alone. As initial overtures to the Soviets on a grand bargain showed them to be unrealistically demanding (they wanted a European settlement and dialogue, arms agreements, and an anti-Chinese alliance *all* on their terms before a summit was possible), Nixon decided to pursue the China option, a direction he'd been signaling going all the way back to a 1967 *Foreign Affairs* article tellingly titled "Asia After Viet Nam." In the piece he stated that America "simply cannot afford to leave China forever outside the family of nations, there to nurture its fantasies, cherish its hates and threaten its neighbors." He put it more expansively in his 1969 inaugural address, where he stated that "we seek an open world—open to ideas, open to the exchange of goods and people—a world in which no people, great or small, will live in angry isolation."

The Chinese leadership, and particularly Mao himself, picked up these cues and thus began a long diplomatic dance, largely through third parties, that finally resulted three years later in the Chinese offering to host Kissinger in Beijing for secret talks designed to craft a joint communiqué that would serve as diplomatic cornerstone for a first summit. Once Nixon publicly announced the trip and communiqué, it had the desired effect on the Soviets, who became, as Kissinger noted, "suddenly anxious to create the impression that more serious business could be accomplished in Moscow than in Peking." As Brezhnev later quipped, Nixon went "to Peking for banquets but to Moscow to do business." But the simple reality was that China and the United States actually had little business to do other than to end the diplomatic void that separated them.

China had no interest in helping America achieve anything in Vietnam except its rapid departure, and sought out U.S. recognition simply to escape the international isolation it had imposed on itself through the Cultural Revolution, an isolation that Mao now feared left China open to military invasion from the Soviet Union, with whom it had been openly feuding for years. If unfriendly countries surrounded China, Mao reasoned, it would be better to have a distant, powerful friend in the United States, or at least a nonenemy. China was playing its "American card" as much as Nixon and Kissinger were playing their "China card." In seeing it as a straight-up trade that bought both sides some breathing space against a common enemy, Mao ended any White House hopes for a Chinese diplomatic rescue on Vietnam. Nonetheless, Nixon and Kissinger got more than enough, in the end, to justify their daring move, which was sure to anger a lot of conservatives back home. They had ended the bipolar order and, by doing so, had bought the Nixon administration a degree of flexibility that it immediately put to use vis-à-vis the Soviets.

Détente with the Soviets in Europe did much more than just settle the question of Germany and the nuclear arms race. Through the Helsinki Accords later crafted under Kissinger's State Department in the Ford administration, détente reintroduced FDR's Atlantic Charter concept of human rights as being applicable, in Elizabeth Borgwardt's description, "within as well as across national borders." As historian John Lewis Gaddis argues, the Helsinki Accords came back to haunt the Brezhnev regime in future years by making Soviet repression of political rights, both at home and in Eastern Europe, subject to the West's diplomatic review, in effect providing dissidents throughout their system an external patron, an independent international body specifically empowered to investigate such matters with Moscow's official sanction. It is impossible to describe the subsequent success of the political dissidence movement inside the Soviet bloc, and especially Eastern Europe, without reference to the "Helsinki movement" and the Organization for Security and Co-operation in Europe, the standing regional conference created by the accords.

Far more damaging for Moscow's Communist leadership were the economic connections with the West triggered by détente. By opening itself up to trade, the USSR's fake economy was ultimately undermined by the dollar's infiltration: Its "hard," or convertible, value in black markets revealed to all, but especially its own citizens, the illogic of the Kremlin's central planning and pretend pricing. In short, Nixon and Kissinger revealed this "emperor had no clothes." By introducing foreign goods with actual values attached and encouraging the Soviets to sell their energy resources on the international market, Western trade poisoned the entire Soviet production chain by suggesting that the vast bulk of its output arrived with little appreciable market value. As long as the Soviet economy remained virtually isolated from free markets, the illusion of productivity was maintained. But once it was connected to the real world, Soviet consumers began to opt out of the dysfunctional Soviet system in increasing numbers, instead availing themselves of desired goods via a black market whose pervasiveness was matched only by its sophistication. Moreover, by the time Mikhail Gorbachev and his fellow reformist technocrats started arriving on the scene in the early 1980s, the government had already become somewhat addicted to the hard-currency foreign revenues obtained through oil exports. After the United States negotiated with the Saudis to lower oil prices, the Soviet economy hit the wall, just as Reagan raised the specter of a costly arms race.

Did Star Wars break the Soviet bank and thus collapse the system later in the decade? The Soviet economy was broken long before the Strategic Defense Initiative (SDI) appeared on the scene, although Reagan's promise to render Soviet nuclear missiles irrelevant did freak out the Soviet leadership to a certain extent. In the past, they had seen American technology pull off difficult stunts far faster than they could (e.g., the race to the moon), so as much as they might doubt SDI's feasibility, they couldn't quite be sure the Americans wouldn't develop something just good enough to make them dangerous. In that sense, as Ulam noted, SDI was a wonderful psychological weapon. But here's my superseding point: Without Nixon's détente, that price tag would have remained incalculable and therefore economically meaningless. Moreover, without the Helsinki movement engineered by Kissinger, there would have been no regional diplomatic top-cover for the dissidence movement to simultaneously emerge. Reagan's sense of timing and theater were brilliant, but Star Wars and demands to "tear down that wall" were not enough. The Soviet leadership needed to know they could no longer pretend to pay while workers pretended to labor, and Soviet bloc populations needed to realize they could stop pretending to respect the authority of leaders who had long since given up any pretense of totalitarian rule.

Nixon's détente created that context by making clear, to Soviet bloc leaders and citizens alike, just how hollow their system was. In the end, the only rationale holding the bloc together was the lie that said, despite its economic backwardness and political crudeness, at least "the little guy" had it better in the East than in the far crueler and more rapacious West. Reagan, with his unaffected, "morning in America" optimism, denied them even that. Worse, after his near-death experience at the hands of a would-be assassin, Reagan, with wife Nancy's strong encouragement, began reconsidering his embryonic legacy, which in the 1982–83 time frame consisted primarily of resurrecting Cold War dynamics with the Soviets to no apparent end. Once Gorbachev had received an ideological seal of approval from Reagan's trusted mentor, Margaret Thatcher, Reagan moved with the strange urgency of a man who seemed to know his physical capital would evaporate far faster than his political capital. Making spur-of-the-moment offers that frightened his advisers, like having both superpowers get rid of all their nuclear weapons, Reagan preemptively did to Gorbachev what the Soviets' top Americanologist, Georgi Arbatov, later claimed Gorby would do to us: Reagan denied Gorbachev's reformists a reason not to move ahead with their system-tinkering plans—he denied them an enemy.

It's important to realize just how different Soviet leadership had become under Gorbachev. Brezhnev's crew was made up of mostly party hacks and ideologues whose main personal attribute was a survivor's instinct. They had grown up amid Stalin's many insane purges, survived the Great Patriotic War, in which more than one out of every eight of their countrymen died, and once in top power slots, had displayed a strange mix of calculating aggression abroad and comfortable corruption at home. By the early 1980s they were a collection of old men who could barely understand the world around them, even as they suspected it was passing them by. They wanted recognition of their sacrifices and achievements, and Nixon gave them that. And once they had finished with their midlife fantasy of guiding socialist revolutions in the world's most backward states, they realized they were spent as a leadership force and handed the reins of power over to Gorbachev and his crew of industrially trained technocrats.

Gorbachev wasted little time in trying to revive public spirit with his campaigns of *perestroika* (restructuring) and *glasnost* (openness), but both had arrived about a generation too late. The middle class Gorbachev had hoped to ignite had already made its peace with the system's failings, preferring its black markets to his red reforms. Too well conditioned by Brezhnev's reign to be happy with what they already had, they welcomed the *glasnost* but passed on the *perestroika*. I spent a summer living in the Soviet Union in 1985, just as Gorbachev's reign began, and I can remember thinking to myself then just how screwed this new leadership already was. Everybody I met had his or her entire existence already worked out according to every workaround you could imagine. There was the official Soviet reality, where nothing of value was created, and there was the *na levo*, or life "on the left," where anything was available on the black market and thus all basic needs were already being met—despite the decrepit system. When Gorbachev appealed to his generation to help him pick up the pieces, they looked at him dumbfounded, like he was from another planet. (Fast-forward to Mahmoud Ahmadinejad's Iran and we basically witness the same dialogue of the deaf, presaging his likely defeat in 2009.)

There was simply no choir left to hear Gorbachev's plaintive preaching. Instead, as subsequent events proved, there were a host of nations, both inside the Soviet Union and across Eastern Europe, that were eager to explore just how fake this empire really was. In his idealism, Gorbachev mistook their warm welcomes as expressions of support for his vision of restructuring the Soviet bloc and making it competitive against the West, when in reality they simply saw him as Margaret Thatcher did—somebody they "could do business with." The problem was, the only business they were interested in pursuing was an immediate divorce. They wanted out. They wanted a better deal with the world. They simply didn't want to live here anymore. When the Berlin Wall fell in 1989 and the Soviet Union dissolved in 1991, in neither case was it really a revolution. There were no opposition parties to speak of, but merely a zoo full of animals that simply wanted out.

As soon as the inmates started running the asylum, the first order of business was simple: In Eastern Europe it was called "seek integration with the West as fast as possible and along as many lines as possible." In the Caucasus and Central Asia, there's been more slippage toward the "olive tree" past than the "Lexus" future, but neither set of packages has proved to be America's problem in a post–Cold War world. Instead, Russia has its definition of a near abroad, with its main problem being that so do China, Iran, and Turkey. But taken as a whole and judged from today's perspective, this process of dissolving the Soviet empire has gone incredibly well and with few serious hitches. If you had told this Sovietologist back in his late 1980s grad school days that we could fast-forward to a future where the EU was successfully integrating former Warsaw Pact states and where Chinese economic interests were penetrating Central Asia, and that the biggest problems we'd face along the way were a minor conflagration in the Balkans, the usual Russian nastiness in the Caucasus, and resurgent nationalism and authoritarian rule in Moscow, I would have considered you fantastically optimistic—perhaps even under the influence. This is not a case of being careful what you wish for. This is a case of being grateful for what history has dropped into America's lap. This is the next best iteration. This is as good as it gets when our grand strategy works: Not everybody suddenly morphing into carbon copies of America, but huge chunks of humanity being returned to play and slowly integrated by various knockoffs of the American System.

I know a lot of Americans are uncomfortable with this outcome. When George H. W. Bush declared his "new world order" in 1990, resurrecting that phrase directly from Woodrow Wilson, it carried that air of "Finally, America's going to get the world it deserves after all our long struggles!" But of course that was a wildly premature and, quite frankly, immature way of viewing things, as Robert Kagan succinctly argues in his 2008 book *The Return of History and the End of Dreams*. What America had been given was a vast new swath of humanity to integrate into our American System–cum–globalization model. It was like we'd just made the "Eurasian Purchase" of 1991 on behalf of the global economy and, instead of recognizing the tasks of integration and state-building that lay ahead, we simply wanted to be able to fast-forward to the good part—you know, where rule of law worked everywhere and everybody's economy and political system looked just like our own. Certainly there'd be no "Injuns" or insurrections or roving criminal gangs or bomb-tossing radicals or civil wars or ethnic cleansing to deal with, right? I mean, if everybody really wants the same things we want for our families, can't we just skip all that bad stuff that we know from American history is a complete waste of time and effort and—you know—make the right package happen right from the start? Isn't there some sort of shortcut everybody can take? Can't we just use some sort of "shock therapy" or "big bang" that'll rejigger the whole thing all at once? And when do we get to bring the boys home, by the way?

Now I hope you're beginning to see why I bothered telling you all this.

We're at a stage in history that's the best iteration yet of the American System projected upon the global stage. These are the best sort of problems to be dealing with: not global nuclear Armageddon, not great-power war, not fascism or Communism or any other perversion of markets—just a lot of economic frontiers to integrate, new allies to mentor, bad actors to track down and kill without remorse, networks to make more resilient, social movements and religious awakenings to harness for their natural progressive tendencies, and an environment that needs equal parts taming and conserving. Hamilton and Clay confronted much the same set of challenges. So did Lincoln and Seward in their time. Theodore Roosevelt tackled most of this work with his bare hands—often before breakfast! His successors, Wilson and FDR, made their ambitious pitches following two global conflicts they helped guide to the best possible conclusions, considering what America could muster in will and capabilities at the time. Truman had to withstand the capitalist system's once-and-future blowback—Communism, setting up the original string of forts that would protect our new Western settlements against the worst trust we'd ever have to bust. But we persevered, with Nixon eventually setting up, and Reagan knocking down, the last serious in-house challenger we'll ever meet. Most important, Nixon's gambit toward China opened a door that Deng Xiaoping, Mao's successor, widened dramatically and permanently, thus ensuring globalization's dominance.

None of this was accidental. And yes, all of it was by design—our design. That design is not—by definition of its global spread—unique to America, even though it took Americans, those most synthetic of God's political creatures, to create it, nurture its spread, and, when required, defend it with arms. That design unfolded as a quintessential American grand strategy, however unconsciously followed at times by leaders who knew instinctively what it meant to be Americans, even if they didn't always know what America meant to the world. This grand strategy resides in America's DNA. We can no more be separated from its impulse for economic expansionism than we can shut off our instincts to resist tyranny in all forms. Americans have always posed this challenge to the world: We simply must *be*. We simply must be allowed to grow and self-improve. We simply must be given the freedom necessary for those tasks. We simply must be granted enough competitive space to pursue our happiness. We simply must be expected to remake as much of the world as is necessary to ensure all these possibilities.

Yes, there are new barbarians at new gates, but the frontier is more distant than ever, and most of humanity is now inside the fence, working security and not defense, raising incomes, not revolutions.

And no, they don't all look like us today, but working together we'll all end up looking like what America needs to become *someday*. To accomplish that, we simply need to recognize that this American experiment has become bigger than just these fifty states united; it's become a globalization that integrates economies and states just as we once integrated economies and states. And since it's become more powerful than we ever imagined it could, we'll need to adapt ourselves to globalization more than even we, its originators, can adapt it to our perceived needs for stability. Theodore Roosevelt's cautions against the dangers of the stationary state still ring true: There is no path but forward, there is no choice but to make globalization truly global, there is no state of being more stable than America's continued state of *becoming*.

Four

———✦———

THE ECONOMIC
REALIGNMENT

Racing to the Bottom of the Pyramid

The United States has been the demand center—meaning the biggest single source of demand—in the global economy for so long that we can't remember what it was like when that wasn't true. And yet it is rapidly becoming true that global corporations view the United States as just another market among many, as the global middle class expands dramatically and rising great powers such as India and China become competing demand poles and—in certain sectors such as infrastructure development—collectively eclipse America as *the* new global demand center. What's it like to be the global demand center? The world revolves around *your* needs, *your* desires, and *your* ambitions. *You* get to set a lot of the new rules that naturally emerge from all this heightened economic connectivity and transaction rates, because the most important power in the global system resides with you—not the suppliers but the *consumers*. That's what it's been like to be the Boomer generation in the U.S. economy for the past several decades—*you're* the center of all economic attention. But just as the Boomers inevitably cede their demand dominance to their demographic successors, the Millennials, so too does America cede its demand dominance to the rising great powers of our age—the price of our success in projecting the American System globally.

Naturally, such a shift is somewhat scary for our nation, having grown so used to our rules holding sway in international forums by dint of our incredible demand power. We sense both a zero-sum loss of our agenda-setting power *and* a new discipline being forced upon us by the highly competitive landscape of this "flat world"—for example, sovereign wealth funds that snatch up our ailing firms (a bruise to our national ego) and the rise of the euro as an alternative global reserve currency (meaning our easy-credit, spendthrift days have ended). But here's where we need to remember our strengths: We've been mastering this "new" globalization phenomenon of economies integrating and states uniting for quite some time. Think of all the economic and political and security rule sets that the United States had to build up over the decades to handle the massive amount of daily transactions between these fifty members: all the travelers, cargo movement, service traffic, communications, cross-border investment flows, interstate contracts, and so on. That's one-quarter of the world's economy packaged into a single nation-state that the twenty-seven econo-mies of the European Union struggle mightily to replicate today.

If our fifty members and the District of Columbia were ranked as in-dividual nation-states in the global economy, this is the equivalent lineup we'd field: France (CA), Canada (TX), South Korea (FL), Mexico (IL), Russia (NJ), Australia (OH), Brazil (NY), Netherlands (PA), Switzerland (GA), Sweden (NC), Belgium (MA), Turkey (WA), Austria (VA), Saudi Arabia (TN), Poland (MO), Indonesia (LA), Norway (MN), Denmark (IN), Greece (CT), Argentina (MI), Ireland (NV), South Africa (WI), Thailand (AZ), Finland (CO), Iran (AL), Hong Kong (MD), Portugal (KY), Venezuela (IA), Malaysia (KS), Pakistan (AR), Israel (OR), Singa-pore (SC), Czech Republic (NE), Hungary (NM), Chile (MS), New Zea-land (DC), Philippines (OK), Algeria (WV), Nigeria (HI), Ukraine (ID), Romania (DE), Peru (UT), Bangladesh (NH), Morocco (ME), Vietnam (RI), Croatia (SD), Tunisia (MT), Ecuador (ND), Belarus (AK), Domini-can Republic (VT), and Uzbekistan (WY). Any superstate that can stitch together all that economic power into a single overarching rule set must know a thing or two about unleashing the cumulative creative power of its people. Those fifty-one nation-states listed above encompass a global population pool of over 2 billion people, and yet somehow our national population of just over 300 million manages to match their combined economic power!

What does that fact tell us about our strengths today? America arose as a global power thanks to its ability to knit together its states: interstate trade integration through the disintegration and geographic distribution of production chains, with transportation infrastructure—sometimes literally—paving the way for national firms with national platforms (i.e., networks) that peddle nationally branded products. The American System is now being replicated on the global stage in basically the same manner: integrating trade by disintegrating production, thus making possible global firms with global platforms for globally branded products. So if this is a "flat world," it's certainly a familiar one—at least to us Americans. As we grew, America's greatest challenge came in improving the rule sets that bound together our constituent states. The same is true for globalization today. My point is this: When it comes to wringing out competitive efficiencies through improved rules (e.g., laws, regulations, procedures, industry best practices, rules of thumb), nobody's done it—or does it—better than America. If we can remember that one thing from our history, we'll be fine.

When 9/11 struck, America, feeling proprietary about the international liberal trade order we created and nurtured into global dominance, naturally felt the need to propose all manner of new rules. But in our haste to demonstrate their effectiveness to the world, we not only botched their initial employment in many instances (Afghanistan and Iraq being preeminent), we scared off many old allies and alienated much of the rest of the world in the process. Meanwhile, globalization's nosebleed trajectory continued unabated, even as America routinely blew its whistle to interrupt game play after every post-9/11 international crisis to announce our latest new rule set for global order. Sometimes our new rules were ignored and other times they met opting-out responses—such as "We'll take our business/tourism/IPOs elsewhere!" Other times, rising great powers simply proposed their own, competing rule sets. For example, while America got fixated on "transforming" the Middle East, the EU focused on eastward expansion, Russia concentrated on extending pipelines in all directions (save north), and China cast its nets pretty much over the rest of the developing world, with India in hot pursuit. Inevitably, America's new definition of post-9/11 "normal" put us increasingly at odds with significant global trends, many of which seemed to accelerate just as we Americans, whose trade-liberalization schemes sent this whole world spinning, began plaintively asking globalization to slow down so that we might regain our strategic balance, feeling—as we were—both subpar and "subprime."

Not surprisingly, much of the world has stopped listening to America over the past few years. Bush-Cheney's push for primacy achieved its desired effect but on an unintentional scale: Most of the world's nations neither fear nor respect America as they once did. As such, we face a series of difficult realignments across all major elements of our grand strategy.

So here's how I'll organize these five "realignment" chapters (economic, diplomatic, security, networks, and strategic social issues), each time taking you through the same seven-step recalibration process designed to reposition the United States along a grand strategic trajectory that makes more sense for the global challenges that lie ahead:

1. *The undeniable strategic trajectory.* First, in each domain, I'll cite what I think is the most important long-term global trend concerning an American grand strategy of making globalization truly global in a post–9/11 world.

2. *America's global system perturbed.* Then I'll explore a serious recent disruption that prompted either new thinking on our part or a retrenchment from our grand strategic vision.

3. *The new rules that emerge.* Next, I'll give you a sense of the new rules that apparently emerged out of that disruption, either from America itself or in partial reaction to—even rejection of— American policies.

4. *The resulting "new normal."* Subsequent to those new rules, I'll outline the "new normal" into which we started slowly settling as the Bush years wound down.

5. *Meanwhile, the global accelerant* . . . Jumping back outside the United States, I'll detail how the trend I spotted in #1 actually hit an inflection point while America was heading off on its own toward its "new normal."

6. *Our inescapable realignment.* Which gets me to the major realignment America needs to make to bring it back in line with the world of our creating.

7. *The better normal America must seek.* Finally, I'll lay out what I think is that next, best iteration of American grand strategy for each particular domain, meaning the downstream global developments we want to be crafting over the next five to ten years.

In each of these chapters, then, my goal is to make clear to you how the United States has run itself off the rails of its natural grand strategy and how we can get back on track.

So let's get started with the domain that drives all others—economics.

THE UNDENIABLE TRAJECTORY:
DENG CHOSE WISELY

When President Richard Nixon reopened diplomatic ties with Mao Zedong's Communist China in 1972, he enabled the most profound global economic dynamic of the last half-century: China's historic re-emergence as a worldwide market force. After constituting roughly one-third of global GDP just as America was starting its climb in the early 1800s, China experienced its "century of humiliation" at the hands of foreign colonial powers that manhandled its economy without ever truly conquering it as a nation. Today's China ranks a G-8 slot (#4, actually) in GDP and trails only the United States when "parity purchasing power" is factored in. China won't overtake America in sheer economic weight anytime soon, but even having to discount that possibility tells you how rapid China's rise has been. Whether you realize it or not, nothing shapes your world today *more* than China's economic growth, and nothing will shape our planet's future more—for good or ill—than China's ongoing trajectory. China's decision to rejoin the world constituted globalization's tipping point, meaning—absent global war—there's no turning back now.

If Nixon opened the door, then Deng Xiaoping, Mao's ultimate successor, led one-fifth of humanity through it. Unlike the Soviet Union's last leader, Mikhail Gorbachev, Deng chose wisely: By tackling economic freedom *before* political liberalization, Deng kept China stable during its tenuous first years of market reform. Deng's dream for China in 1979 would have struck Alexander Hamilton as a mirror image of his own for America in 1789: As historian Michael Marti puts it, "Deng's desire was to create an economic system that would allow China to become a rich and powerful nation by the middle of the twenty-first century." To do so, Deng would have to politically defeat another "immortal" of the Chinese Communist Party, Chen Yun, who correctly feared that Deng's path would dramatically emphasize industry over rural development and lead to a huge rise in Western—and particularly American—cultural influences that would encourage factionalism within the party and among the people. In many ways, Chen's fears for a China that embraced Deng's ambitious agenda mirrored Thomas Jefferson's fears were America to follow the aggressive plan set out by Alexander Hamilton. Both Chen and Jefferson had great trepidation that their countries would abandon their agricultural center of gravity and quickly assume the have-versus-have-not, highly urbanized social structure of their economic model—Britain in the case of America, and the United States in the case of China. Whatever you can say about Mao's bizarre economic campaigns, he did create a society that was quite egalitarian in its lack of development and widespread poverty.

Although Deng is correctly labeled an autocrat, ordering—along with Chen—the bloody suppression of the Tiananmen Square democracy protests in 1989, he's also correctly identified as a modernizer who unleashed a generation's immense creativity. Many from that ambitious generation will tell you that, before Tiananmen, they felt freedom was "90 percent political and 10 percent economic," but after Deng's crackdown, they concluded—somewhat harshly—that real freedom was "90 percent economic and 10 percent political." In other words, they decided that markets were the first, best instruments for generating positive change in

China. Deng's objectives have roughly been met to date: to quadruple China's meager per capita income of roughly $250 in 1981 to approximately $1,000 by the century's end, and then quadruple it again by 2050, something China is well on its way to achieving, having already doubled to more than $2,000 per capita today. Deng's ultimate dream, as Marti notes, was that "China would become the center of an East Asian trading bloc similar to the European Community or the North American Free Trade Area," in effect echoing Henry Clay's lofty vision for America by placing China at the center of a continental system modeled on itself—a Chinese system for an Asian union.

Following the Tiananmen Massacre, Deng and his grand strategy came under attack by the conservative left wing of the party, but in turn that "Soviet faction" suffered its own loss of face when the Union of Soviet Socialist Republics itself dissolved at the end of 1991. Embarking on his historic "southern tour" in 1992, Deng rallied his two great power bases: the People's Liberation Army and provincial officials. Striking back at his opponents, Deng commandeered the Fourteenth Party Congress to reshuffle the Politburo in his favor, installing his followers as the next generation to lead the nation. A "grand compromise" was struck inside the party: Deng won military support for further market reforms as long as a lid was kept on political change, and the army was afforded enough budget to modernize. The party would remain supreme, but state involvement in the economy would shrink, and private business would be encouraged along with investment from, and trade with, the outside world. By engineering the acceleration of market reforms, Deng sought to take advantage of the strategic pause generated by the Cold War's end. As Marti writes, "With a weak Russia to the north, an American withdrawal from the western Pacific, and the willingness and availability of foreign capital to invest in China, Deng argued that it was now or never. Reform and opening must be pushed to the limit."

Much as the U.S. military now plays bodyguard to globalization and once did the same for America's westward expansion across the nineteenth century, Deng enlisted the PLA to play "protector and escort" to China's economic modernization, the goal of which would become the party's basic line, replacing class conflict. Externally, China would adopt a foreign policy of avoiding dangerous entanglements, much as George

Washington had advocated for a young America upon his retirement. No foreign crises or international issues would be allowed to interrupt China's focus on internal economic development, which would center on urbanization, industrialization, attracting foreign capital and maximizing export earnings, and significant trade protectionism to nurture the home market and home companies that would someday dominate global markets. Again, this is basically the American System of the early 1800s, right down to the dominance of a single-party elite and a strong aversion to political factionalism. Even China's infrastructural build-out mirrors our own: first make "external improvements" to link coastal regions to foreign markets, then tax the booming coastal regions to finance internal improvements that reach increasingly inward and westward.

China has experienced incredible economic growth ever since, increasing its GDP annually by almost 10 percent—as fast as you dare expand. But China is also nowhere near becoming a democracy, and that dubious achievement both scares and excites nations around the world, because it suggests that you can rapidly embrace globalization, achieve great income growth, and remain a single-party state. And that's the China model. But here's where the China System must likewise mirror the American System: The bulk of China's population, as well as most of its abject poverty, lies in its interior west. Those underdeveloped provinces represent the caboose on this train, and no matter how fast the train's engine may pull, the booming coastal provinces cannot embrace globalization without pulling the rural poor along for the ride; otherwise the train will break apart, just as China has many times in its history.

THE AMERICAN SYSTEM PERTURBED: 3 BILLION NEW CAPITALISTS REGISTER THEIR DEMAND

China's embrace of markets created the dynamic core of the roughly 3 billion new capitalists who joined globalization over the past quarter-century, expanding the global economy roughly fivefold in terms of population encompassed. This group includes the other members of the "BRIC" quartet (Brazil, Russia, and India), plus all the smaller emerging markets located east and south. As an explosive expansion of the global economy, this influx of new players mirrors America's westward growth across the

1800s, including the immense challenge of making a previously small, in-family rule set (the reconstructed Union for post–Civil War America, the West today) now suddenly—in historical terms—embrace a far wider economic frontier, in this case replete with dozens of emerging markets whose idiosyncratic mix of political rule sets differs greatly, in most instances, from our own—so many Deadwoods, so little time.

This is the preeminent challenge of our age: the sustainable harmonization of these different models of capitalism, or the integration of mature, high-trust environments (the Old Core West) with immature, lower-trust environments (the New Core East/South and Gap). As global trade continues to grow in volume and complexity, globalization's Functioning Core is likely to veer back and forth between, on the one hand, the temptation of populism and economic nationalism during times of economic turbulence (e.g., America from 1875 to 1895) and, on the other hand, progressive collective efforts to tame global market fluctuations and their resulting cruelty (resembling more America from 1895 to 1917). Because these competing models represent countries at different stages of development, America is often put in the ironic position of arguing for policy changes—such as the reduction of tariffs and allowing currencies to float—that we embraced only after becoming a supremely competitive global economic power. This is ironic indeed, because we often end up scolding younger versions of ourselves, instructing them to do as we say and not as we once did.

Mostly, what these 3 billion new capitalists did was simply insert themselves and their cheaper inputs (human labor, natural resources, industrial capital) into the West's existing buyer chains (the Wal-Marts of the world) and producer chains (the Toyotas of the world). Again, globalization tends to integrate trade by disintegrating production. Globalization spreads various segments of production and assembly across those economies that offer the cheapest labor for each particular stage. China has deftly inserted itself into a long list of these chains, becoming the final assembler of note in toys, cell phones, CD players, computers, and auto parts—and just about everything else. By doing so, China has consolidated much of Asia's previous trade surpluses with America into its own burgeoning bilateral trade with the United States. So when you hear about America's huge trade deficit with China, bear in mind that it's the same huge trade deficit we've long had with Asia as a whole.

Also be aware that this figure hides a lot of complexity. Foreign corporations control the majority of this production for export (approximately two-thirds). American companies in particular dominate China's U.S.-export sector, meaning it's basically our companies renting Chinese labor and keeping much of the profit. The Chinese export that sells for hundreds of dollars in America nets only tens of dollars for the Chinese economy. That's how Wal-Mart, the single biggest recipient of Chinese goods in the world (indeed, if Wal-Mart was a state, it would constitute China's fourth-largest export market), keeps its prices so low. So if you think Western companies are exploiting cheap Chinese labor, then understand that you're a prime beneficiary. But it's not just the West. Taiwan, for example, dominates certain information-technology hardware sectors, such as motherboards for computers. Ten years ago, most of that manufacturing happened in Taiwan itself. Now, thanks to significant flows of foreign direct investment (FDI) from Taiwan to China, much of that production occurs on the mainland, with Taiwanese companies controlling the great majority of China's hardware IT exports. China may someday seek to invade Taiwan militarily, but Taiwan has already successfully invaded the mainland economically.

Naturally, China's deep penetration of the U.S. market has raised product-safety issues. Any economy that is growing as fast as China's cuts plenty of corners—welcome to *The Jungle*! But realize that China learns by scandals, just as America did over the past century. Frankly, the best crises are the ones you actually hear about, because that means the international press got ahold of them, and those already affected or at risk will get the information they need to protect themselves. Once the problem is tracked back to China, Beijing is put on public notice that whatever laxness exists simply cannot be tolerated anymore, accompanied with threats of quarantine, bans on exports, cessation of investment flows, and so on. A generation ago, such threats would have elicited yawns from China's ruling elite, but now, with the Communist Party's legitimacy riding on economic expansion, they're taken with the utmost seriousness. In short, China's government is starting to act more like a business that recognizes that its reputation is often its most important asset, because flat-world competition means that today's mistake allows somebody else to steal your customers by the start of business tomorrow.

China's skyrocketing demand for all manner of natural resources, in conjunction with India's rising demand for foreign energy sources, is altering global commodity and energy markets in ways both profound and perverse. China's explosive economic growth forces it to suck in resources from all over the world. Oil imports have increased more than sevenfold since 1995, making China the second-biggest importer of oil in the world, after the United States. China's imports of timber have jumped more than twelvefold over the same time period, meaning certain countries, like neighboring Myanmar, are deforesting themselves at a rapid pace to feed the Chinese economy. Even in coal, which China has plenty of, imports increased fifteenfold from 2001 to 2006. Most global commodity price indices have more than tripled since the late 1990s, and China is the major reason why. (Ditto for when prices drop.)

As a longtime China-watcher, James Kynge notes in his recent book *China Shakes the World*, "China's endowments are deeply lopsided," meaning it tries to act like a "body" economy even though it does not possess the natural resources of one. Blessed with too many people, China is short on just about everything else: arable land, water, energy, and raw materials of all sorts. Thus, the only way China manages to serve as globalization's "manufacturing floor" is to become a leading global importer of virtually any commodity you can name, from cement and copper to oil and gas. You can easily see the environmental danger: Consumer America doesn't care where it gets its cheap products from and manufacturer China doesn't care about who supplies the raw materials. When the resulting environmental degradation from illegal logging helps foster political instability, like a military junta cracking down in Myanmar, everybody in the chain points at everybody else as the villain.

But here's where the political rubber meets the economic road: America's insatiable demand for low-cost Chinese goods drives China's insatiable demand for resources, which in turn drives Beijing to actively court pariah states and "rogue regimes" while the West tries to isolate the same regimes through economic sanctions. Take, for instance, China's relationship with Iran: While American diplomats work night and day to levy even harsher sanctions to slow down Tehran's reach for the bomb, China quietly edges out Japan as Iran's major energy investor, sweetening the deal by reselling it some of that fabulous high-tech military hardware the Chinese military imports from Israel, a portion of which then invariably turns up in southern Lebanon in the hands of Hezbollah as it faces Israeli forces. Talk about a global supply chain! On the face of it, Beijing's embrace of rogue Tehran constitutes obstructionism on China's part, as if it's trying to prevent the global community from cracking down on bad behavior. But the inescapable truth is that China's scramble to find resources means it has to cut deals with anybody, no matter how disreputable their record. So while Sudan's government engages in what many Western states consider "ethnic cleansing" and genocide in its Darfur region, China is more than happy to invest heavily in Sudan's oil industry while supplying the Sudanese government with weapons. Do that long enough and you'll have Hollywood stars decrying your coming-out party as the "genocide Olympics."

But the longer-term danger is this: China, and to a lesser extent India, is becoming awfully dependent on a lot of unstable countries without having the global military footprint of a great power—you know, like somebody building a very large house made of straw nowhere near a fire station. When bad things happen—like, say, that one afternoon nine Chinese oil workers were killed by rebels in eastern Ethiopia—China can't respond like a military power you should fear, because it needs that oil. Once that reality sinks in with local bad actors, expect them to start squeezing Beijing for their own slice of protection money. You know that Thomas Friedman bit about America funding both sides of the "war on terror"? Well, this is how that sort of thing starts. Today, China might get along simply by buying off every dictator it can. But that won't work in a future world defined by hyperconnectivity, where every customer and shareholder can witness the human implications of China's deal-making. Nor will it work in a future world defined by hyperinterdependency, a world China is creating whether it realizes it or not.

In many ways, China is following the classic path of Western economies by moving up the production ladder from commodities to labor-intensive manufactures to higher-tech manufactures and finally to the service sector and intellectual property. India, on the other hand, is leapfrogging right up to the service and IP sectors without really going through any widespread industrialization. According to longtime observer Edward Luce, within India's total labor pool of about 500 million potential workers, only about 10 percent find jobs in the formal sector, the rest making do in agriculture and India's vast informal sector of temp jobs, like driving an unlicensed taxi. Of those roughly 35 to 40 million workers in the formal sector, about half work for the government and the rest work in the private sector. Of those 15 to 20 million in the private sector, about half (7 to 10 million) work in manufacturing and roughly one-tenth (1 to 2 million) work in India's booming service sector. By comparison, China has over 100 million people working in its formal manufacturing sector.

So you'd have to say that Deng also chose wisely by first marketizing China's agricultural sector and, through boosting production there, triggering the rural-to-urban movement of labor that made China's rapid industrialization possible. By staying attached to its Gandhian ideal of the village as the center of national identity, India takes the slower Jeffersonian route, befitting its democratic tradition, while China embraces the more vigorous, Hamiltonian path of directing rapid national economic development from above. Although India may be more like America in its messy democracy and competitive religious landscape, China is far closer to America in terms of its socioeconomic development.

Impossible, you say! Ruled by Communists, China's civilization bears no resemblance to our own! But China's true Communist period was just three decades out of a 5,000-year history, the rest of which featured a natural tendency toward markets in general (the Chinese are inveterate gamblers, for example) and past periods of serious global trade connectivity (recall the Silk Road of yore). Add in the strong focus on family ties and a deep spiritual history that has long featured calm competition among various faiths and we're not exactly talking about some brother from another planet. So forget trying to figure out today's China through its recent history. Instead, simply stipulate that China's last extended period of civil strife (1927–76)—which did not spin to a complete stop until the murderous Mao Zedong departed—deposited China somewhere in the historical vicinity of "rising America" circa 1880, meaning Deng's China is only about thirty years old. Once you realize that, depending on where you go around China, you can locate yourself somewhere in the last 125 years of America's own ascendancy.

Foreign policy–wise, you're looking at a mild-mannered Teddy Roosevelt: China still prefers to speak softly, but it carries a pretty big stick, with which it mostly threatens small island nations off its coast (bully!). The nation is likewise undergoing a construction and investment boom that's right out of 1920s America, and frankly, that should give pause to anyone concerned with global economic instability. China's banking and financial industries are about as regulated as ours were prior to the Crash of 1929. But there's no sign of a slowdown. Shanghai already has twice as many skyscrapers as New York—4,000—and plans another thousand.

Check out China's space program, which just put its first man in orbit. Beijing now speaks openly of repeating our 1960s quest for the moon. Groovy! When the Chinese pull off that miracle, their space program will only be about a decade behind our own, which seems perpetually stuck in the 1970s, thanks to the breakthrough technology (still!) called the Space Shuttle. As for the Chinese military's demonstrated shoot-down of their own space satellite, that just says China's mode of signaling its desire for arms control is also right out of our 1960s.

There's also a sexual revolution brewing inside China, where urban professionals are taking one great leap forward from *Father Knows Best* to *Sex and the City*. This revolution won't be televised, but it's being compulsively blogged. When the Chinese celebrate the Lunar New Year nowadays, more than 10 billion text messages rocket around China's wireless networks—the biggest in the world. As the writer and political scientist Ian Bremmer says, imagine a rerun of the Tiananmen crisis today, with today's level of interpersonal connectivity, not to mention all those camera phones!

In terms of corruption, Beijing remains stuck somewhere prior to our Progressive Era of the late nineteenth century, and that's not good. China's political system needs to be able to process all this social and economic pressure with more flexibility. Citizens are simply growing angrier and more demanding with each passing year, and it's not just peasants staging tens of thousands of violent protests annually, but an emerging middle class increasingly protesting government decisions on issues like where to locate the next commuter rail line connecting downtown Shanghai to the suburbs. The Sichuan earthquake of 2008 ignited plenty of social rage in this regard, triggering a domestic reform impulse that the Communist Party scrambled to accommodate. Again, this process should strike Americans as eminently familiar: Show me any section in the U.S. legal code and I'll show you some preceding historical tragedy that (1) mobilized the national government to prove its responsiveness to popular anger and (2) triggered a "suddenly" imperative set of new regulations.

China's legal system also needs to clean up its act, because the more China's economy opens up, the more the global business community is going to demand greater transparency and better avenues for legal redress. A couple of decades ago, China's courts handled several hundred thousand cases a year. Today that demand is running at more than 5 million cases a year. Corruption already consumes upward of 5 percent of China's gross domestic product. In a hypercompetitive world, such inefficiency eventually can cost a single-party state its popular legitimacy. The 2008 Beijing Olympics was an inadvertent milestone in this regard, pushing Beijing's rulers to crack down on the piracy of video coverage they had sold to foreign broadcasters. You want a responsible "stakeholder"? Put some foreign shareholders on the case!

Still, these are all better problems for China to have today than the ones they faced during Mao's Cultural Revolution. In thirty-five years, China has gone from the world's political basket case to the world's economic powerhouse, matching America's stunning recovery from the Civil War to the start of Theodore Roosevelt's administration. Ronald Reagan, Margaret Thatcher, and Pope John Paul II all stand tall in the Western tale of "How the Cold War Was Won," but the truth is, thanks to Richard Nixon, Deng Xiaoping's decision to reform China is more important by far. As sociologist Juan Enriquez writes of Deng, "No other world leader, ever, has gotten so many people out of poverty as quickly." But the diminutive Deng did more than that, standing head and shoulders above a battered Chinese party leadership that overwhelmingly wanted nothing more than the *status quo ante* Maoism: He said simply, "To get rich is glorious," and at that moment our current world, in all its promise and peril, was born.

Now, whether or not America prefers today's global problems to what came earlier, we have little choice but to become complicit in these 3 billion new capitalists' quest for a good life. We built this liberal trade order and they came—*en masse!* Much as America's unbridled capitalism was in danger of permanently trashing our environment a century ago, triggering the first great political responses from Theodore Roosevelt, the clock is ticking on the world's collective response to the planetary dangers triggered by globalization's seemingly insatiable demands.

As always, it's not when you fail that's scary, but when you succeed.

THE NEW RULES: CHINA BREAKS THE MOLD OR MERELY RECASTS IT?

Western powers today fear that China's stunning rise signals a real challenge to the notion that economic growth triggers democracy. While I understand such fears, let me tell you why they're unfounded: China's economy increasingly mirrors our own.

As business academics William Baumol, Robert Litan, and Carl Schramm argue in their 2007 book *Good Capitalism, Bad Capitalism*, there are basically four types of capitalism operating today. First, there's the family-style oligarchic capitalism found throughout much of Latin America, Africa, the Middle East, and Central Asia. In these low-trust social environments, blood ties trump contracts for getting business done. Second, there is state-guided capitalism that features heavy government protection of national flagship companies that seek to dominate home markets while fueling export-driven growth. In decades past, this was the type of capitalism employed by Japan and South Korea during their rise. Today, we're talking ascending powers like China and Russia. Third is the big-firm capitalism that marked America's corporate heyday of the mid-twentieth century and now characterizes Europe and Japan. These are mature markets, where major players dominate most industries, giving the economy a lot of stability even as these larger entities don't adapt themselves quickly to new markets, while labor tends to be rigid.

Finally, there's the wide-open entrepreneurial capitalism that America always strives for, but which waxes and wanes through our history. For example, most big firms that dominated our economy in recent decades actually began as far smaller start-ups around the start of the twentieth century, when America's regional markets were being knit together into a larger whole that rewarded economies of scale. An entrepreneurial economy features lots of small firms constantly generating new products and technologies. Globally, the purest examples of highly entrepreneurial economies tend to be small "island" economies like Israel and Taiwan, nations for whom an almost nonstop "go global" strategy is the only way to achieve economies of scale in their high-technology products. Both are tumultuously democratic.

In their book, Baumol et al. argue that the current U.S. economy has located its happy historical medium: leading industries dominated by big firms, but continuously invigorated by small, entrepreneurial start-ups that are regularly gobbled up by the big firms once their innovations mature. Good examples can be found in the information technology and pharmaceutical sectors, where a handful of giants represent the vast majority of go-to-market outcomes for start-up firms. The authors single out this mixed model as any nation's best choice for sustained "smart" growth through continuous innovation, meaning America is basically there in terms of market evolution. Is democracy required for this premium category? Entrepreneurs tend to be notoriously independent characters. If you don't give them the freedom they need, they tend to leave.

What does this tell us about China's "challenge"? Here's where I think we locate an underlying theory of market evolution lurking behind these categories (as in, from oligarchic to state-directed to big firm to entrepreneurial), for China's rise has actually mirrored the American model more than we realize. Because China started with a dominant state-run sector and refused to bite the bullet of shock therapy, its leaders adopted a strategy of gradually cannibalizing the economy by encouraging the development of big firms, rising from either the growing private-sector or state-owned entities, whose funding is obtained largely from government-controlled banks. Here's the key part: These big firms are augmented by a growing constellation of private-sector entrepreneurial firms, who get their investment funds from foreign sources. Provincial governments, municipal governments, and individuals can launch these firms.

Thus, China's strategy seems clear enough: "Let the seedlings of new enterprise grow while tending to the forest of the existing [state entities], with the hope that the new ventures eventually will become more important to the economy than the [state outfits]." As Baumol and his colleagues argue, "This is exactly what has happened, apparently with great success." The state-firm share of the national economy has dropped from virtually 100 percent in the early 1980s to approximately one-third of China's gross domestic product today. Point being, China's model of development constitutes more an endorsement of American-style capitalism than an improvement on it—much less a rejection of it. This strategy of "incremental change, or entrepreneurial capitalism at the margin," allows China to gradually shift its economy toward the U.S. blend of big firms surrounded by entrepreneurial small firms.

What comes next? More and more freedom, if China hopes to hold on to those entrepreneurs.

And when should we really get scared? As Fareed Zakaria notes in *The Post-American World*, the historical threshold for democracies lies somewhere between $5,000 and $10,000 per capita annual income. As China's income still stands well below that range and won't reach it for another two decades or more, "it cannot be argued that the country has defied this trend." In other words, stay tuned and stay patient.

THE NEW NORMAL:
DEFAULTING TO THE BEIJING CONSENSUS

Neo-Marxists have long argued that America represents capitalism's last stand, historically speaking, having artificially benefited from the collapse of Europe and Japan's imperial systems and turned itself into a Keynesian military superpower financed by budget deficits over the course of the Cold War. As for Reagan's revival? That was mere market sophistry, as Wall Street constantly comes up with new ways to float debt. Money markets thus become the "final refuge" of our bankrupt capitalist system. Annoyingly enough, whenever there's a true imbalance in the system, such as the dominant reserve currency, the U.S. dollar, being out of whack from its perceived true value, those damned capitalist giants get together and make some accord to correct the situation, putting off capitalism's "death throes" for another global boom or two.

Curses!

Thus the Plaza Accord of 1985 (also known as the Baker Plan, for then U.S. Secretary of Treasury James Baker), which allowed the overvalued dollar to slowly deflate, set off America's manufacturing recovery, triggering in turn a revival of the American economy and a global boom that lasted many years. When that accord had finally run out of steam (or punished Japan sufficiently for having the temerity to be "rising," as the neo-Marxists contend), a subsequent "reverse Plaza Accord" similarly rescued Japan's depressed yen, thus reviving its crisis-ridden manufacturing sector somewhat and facilitating yet more global boom. That accord in turn released a flood of Asian and European money into U.S. stock markets, eventually helping to trigger the Tech Crash of 2000, which in turn revealed the corporate malfeasance of Enron, WorldCom, and others, and somehow, after America put in place a slew of new rules, the global boom continued. Now America reruns the entire drama of the 1980s all over again, as the overvalued dollar's inevitable drop triggers the subprime housing crisis (or vice versa). Once again, our leftist critics agree, "imperial" America is slated for the dustbin of history! Toss in the imperial overreach on Afghanistan and Iraq and this turkey is cooked . . . except those damned sovereign wealth funds kept showing up to rescue Wall Street, pumping tons of cash into the system! Was it enough in the end? No, but recognizing the global economy's survival instinct here is instructive.

It's almost as if America, which is clearly now too large and too far gone for the IMF to save it, somehow knew in advance that it needed to create a global liberal trade order in which, somewhere beyond the foreseeable future, those very same "oppressed" economies, which had long suffered America's privileged domination of global markets, would somehow decide that it's in their own interest to rescue this financial "monstrosity" before its collapse destroys them all! How can this be?

The global economy today represents decades of effort by America in an unstated grand strategy of replicating the wonderfully distributed American System of development and finance on the global stage. Since Nixon took us off the gold standard in 1971, America has basically walked the high wire as the global reserve currency—with no apparent net. Our economic preeminence was such that we could manage that trick and free our system—and thus the global economy—from the artificial growth limitations of remaining somehow proportional to the stock of gold. The dollar thus stopped representing some commodity's value and started representing the world's "full faith and credit" in the American System, which, in its modern form, has the world's only financial markets that directly connect savers with entrepreneurs needing investment. In the rest of the world, commercial banks largely fulfill that function, creating a cautious intermediary in the process. With the American System—for better *and* worse—it's something far closer to peer-to-peer lending, a socialization of investment risk that's necessarily more subject to collective euphoria even as it taps the wisdom of crowds. Judging by the rise of P2P activity on the Internet, I expect to see more of this in coming years. In fact, the hot new item in foreign aid is P2P systems like Kiva.org, where individuals in advanced countries can pool together money for loans to people living in less developed Gap countries ("You need a micro-loan. Well, here's my micro-savings!"). I encourage my blog readers in this way, hosting a mini-portal to Kiva on my weblog (www.thomaspmbarnett.com/weblog).

Yes, it's correct to view Wall Street's September 2008 near-collapse as a firm reminder that improved risk management techniques go hand in hand with risky innovation, but if anyone thinks that investment banking will disappear as a financial function in either the U.S. or the global economy as a result of this latest, quite nasty correction, they're dreaming. Financial system perturbations are part and parcel of globalization's current expansion and maturation, just as they were with America's similar consolidation period of the late nineteenth century. It is a truism of market economics that there is no creation that is not simultaneously destructive. Indeed, rather than a narrowing of investment capital choices, globalization seems to be triggering the opposite—its democratization, with so-called angel investors becoming the superempowered individuals of our financial age.

As senior managing director of a rapidly growing high-tech company that was—until quite recently—overwhelmingly dependent on angel investors, I can readily attest to the joys of last-second financial liquidity ("You'll *get* your paycheck!"). When ordinary individuals accumulate wealth and can invest as they please, good things happen to ambitious entrepreneurs and their start-ups. Call it the wisdom of greedy crowds. The same principle holds for the global economy, especially when some market or currency is seriously out of whack, like the dollar was until recently. Thus our pain equals somebody else's buying opportunity. More generally, when the system is flush with cash and bursting with investors properly incentivized to spread it around, globalization tends to accelerate. When money is tight, that's historically when trade protectionism kicks in, along with anti-immigrant sentiment. So here's the thing the neo-Marxists never get: Rising income is a gift that keeps on giving, primarily because investment risk is more easily discounted. The more money I've got, the greater my appetite for risky business. Good things may come to those who wait, but even greater sums accrue to aggressive investors.

In many ways, sovereign wealth funds, globalization's new buzz phrase for state-controlled investment entities armed with significant pools of currency reserves, represent P2P loans within the global economy ("You got a major bank that's hurting? I've got all these billions sitting around needing some useful investment!"). These reserves are accumulated through trade surpluses: goods and services in the case of Asian economies, energy exports for Russia and Persian Gulf states. Naturally, the rise of SWFs has many in the West concerned.

It's one thing to practice state-guided or oligarchic capitalism in your own backyard, but it's quite another to use the proceeds for state-directed investments in my free-market economy. First, there's the simple matter of fair competition. When China sets aside some fraction of its roughly $2 trillion in U.S. currency reserves for overseas investment by a government-sponsored entity, it instantly creates a financial King Kong able to place frighteningly large bets. That brings us to a second concern: the competency of those making the bets. Just because formerly Communist China and Russia have come into a lot of cash recently doesn't make them Wall Street wizards. SWFs could just end up flooding global financial hubs with lots of foolish, impatient money that creates more trouble than it's worth. Finally, there's the fear that SWFs will be manipulated by their source governments to further those states' national interests in ways that harm our own, such as gaining controlling shares of strategic sectors like energy, infrastructure, or national security.

In China's case, this is a classic example of one-thing-leads-to-another amid globalization's rapid advance. Remember the currency crises of the 1990s, like the Asian Flu of 1997 or when Russia suffered sovereign bankruptcy in 1998? Well, a lot of emerging markets took a very important lesson from those events: You can never have enough foreign reserves on hand to defend yourself from a run on your national currency. But strangely enough, it turns out that you can. When China, for example, stockpiled foreign reserves—primarily American dollars—over the subsequent decade, it amassed holdings far beyond any perceivable requirement for defending its economy from outside speculation. As confidence grew and oil prices rose, governments like China inevitably grew dissatisfied with the low returns they could obtain from safe U.S. Treasury bills. Then there was the additional pressure of watching the dollar fall and seeing the value of their reserves decline as a result.

Since emerging economies typically face demographic pressures over the long haul, as urbanization and industrialization inevitably reduce fertility and thus rapidly age their populations, there is the added urgency to generate higher yields from these reserves to finance rapid economic advance while the worker-to-retiree ratio remains strong. This is especially true for China, which has hundreds of millions still living below the poverty line just as its elder population is set to skyrocket over a generation's time, as well as the Middle East, which needs to generate about 100 million jobs over the next two decades to absorb all those workers coming into the mix. So what began for some as a much-needed fix for the 1990s version of globalization is quickly becoming a powerful new tool for extending its march in coming years—like it or not. In my mind, SWFs are a great development, because they keep money on the table, and when money's on the table, globalization tends to expand into riskier markets.

Will there be busts along with booms? Most definitely, and each round of instability will generate new global rule sets to regulate the behavior of sovereign wealth funds, along with the proliferating universe of investing instruments. But logically over time, the greatest pressure to tame these behemoths will arise from inside the source countries themselves, as ordinary citizens demand greater accountability and transparency from these state-directed funds. Managers of sovereign wealth funds will learn with time that hell hath no fury like a pensioner scammed or a young professional denied a career. One of the reasons resource-rich oligarchic regimes can maintain their grip on power is that they don't need to tax their own people, thus denying citizens the natural desire to oversee how their money is publicly spent. To the extent that the rise of SWFs encourages the equivalent of shareholder interest in such countries (as during last year's financial crash), it is a welcome development.

Americans feel down right now, distrusting globalization—our historical gift to the world—more than ever. Instead of feeling that it's our universe to master with ease, we increasingly feel like we're just one large competitor among many—you know, like we need to pick ourselves up, dust ourselves off, and get competitive all over again. But that's hard to do, and so, in our popular imagination, we prefer to spot looming catastrophes around every corner, with each new sci-fi movie seemingly resulting in New York City's destruction. But citing bigger disasters, like global warming, as an excuse for somehow pulling back from the global economy is deeply misguided. Globalization has simply gotten too big for America to get angry and pick up its ball and go home, because if we do, the game will simply be played more dangerously without us. In that way, globalization is a lot like global warming: There's no stopping it, only adapting ourselves to its forces and seeking to mitigate its worst effects slowly over time.

Contrary to the predictions of the neo-Marxists, we enjoy a wonderfully resilient global economy that's processed numerous financial panics (e.g., Asian flu, Internet bubble) and significant slowdowns by major players (Japan, Europe) over the past two decades while consistently growing. As a result, poverty has been dramatically reduced around the planet and we've got twice as many fast-growing economies right now as we did during the go-go eighties and nineties. Yes, it stings having Arab sovereign wealth funds vying to bail out Wall Street firms in the subprime crisis, but as a method of reinjecting liquidity and confidence into our markets, it sure beat U.S. government–sponsored bailouts in terms of cost and embarrassment. Anyway, by entering at bargain prices (not in 2007, mind you, but *after* the crash), these oil-rich regimes are simply doing what we've long advised: diversifying holdings and connecting their economies more broadly to globalization. It sure beats the alternative of white-elephant projects or military buildups.

Not surprisingly, given Wall Street's latest meltdown, Americans are polling glum, even if the rest of the world isn't. Global opinion trends over the past half-decade portray a rising tide of human happiness among nations that have opened up to globalization and thus enjoyed increasing per capita income. Across the Islamic world, we also see a broad decline in popular support for terrorism and, in particular, al Qaeda's brutality. We're losing old allies over Iraq, but Osama bin Laden is losing the future.

As for recent fears that China will soon rule the world, go slow on that one. The World Bank recently recalculated the purchasing power of China's economy and found it to be about 40 percent smaller than we imagined. China won't be overtaking the U.S. economy anytime soon, if ever. Moreover, while we may fret over Beijing's dollar reserves, you have to remember that China's rapid industrialization has been built on a very shaky environmental and demographic foundation, meaning most of the economy's vast liabilities have been pushed into the future on a scale that makes our Social Security overhang look modest by comparison. China will grow old before it gets rich, and it'll become increasingly unhealthy before it superfunds its environmental cleanup.

Rather than complain about rising multipolarity in our global financial order, like the rise of the euro as an alternative reserve currency, why not be grateful that the enterprise no longer depends solely on the spendthrift American consumer? Frankly, we all knew we were living beyond our collective means these past few years, and deep down, we were hoping somebody would apply some discipline to this unsustainable dynamic. Given that our political system didn't seem up to the task, I say thank God for those whiz kids on Wall Street—you know, the ones who seem to come up with some new, dazzlingly complex risk-management scheme every ten years or so, like junk bonds in the 1980s or the rise of financial derivatives in the 1990s. I'm not being facetious. It's that type of edgy innovation that keeps the United States the most competitive economy in the world, triggering not just our booms but also the necessary corrections—to wit, our pressing need for a global Securities & Exchange Commission. If Wall Street's recent series of financial crises proved one thing, it's that globalization's interdependency has reached the point where the forces of both contagion and correction have gone global, meaning there is no such thing as significant "decoupling," nor the unique discrediting of any economic model. We all feel one another's pain now because we all seek to mitigate collective risks—globalization as one giant credit-default-swapping network. So for all of you who've long dreamed of the day when America wouldn't have to run the world by itself, the good news is, that day has come.

Tougher times are ahead, but we mustn't get vindictive. Sovereign wealth funds represent one chance to do so, as do attempts by foreign state-owned firms to buy American companies (e.g., China National Off-shore Oil Corporation trying to buy Unocal, only to be scared off by a congressional uproar) or to win choice operating contracts (Dubai Ports World, similarly rejected). Having said all that, there's no good reason for Western democracies not to continue pestering state-guided capitalist economies for more transparency in their legislative, executive, and judicial decision-making systems, in addition to their financial markets and whatever sovereign wealth funds they operate. God knows, they'll press us right back. Such prodding is in the best interest of everybody, especially if the lack of transparency encourages trade-protectionist sentiments within our more open political systems.

Deep down, what I think really galls us is this sense that authoritarian capitalism (state-guided like China, oligarchic like the oil-rich Persian Gulf states) is somehow eating our lunch, thanks in no small part recently to higher oil prices and our unquenchable thirst for low-cost imports. The so-called Washington Consensus of the 1990s was really nothing more than a polling of economic experts, in which they were asked, in effect, to describe the most important characteristics of the American economic system as a guide for emerging economies that naturally wanted to emulate our success of that era. It was a great guide for managing the American System at its full maturity, but not surprisingly, given the snapshot nature of the list, it's a rotten guide for managing a less diverse and less networked economy just trying to catch up. The China model is a better guide for closing the Gap. It accurately captures the Hamilton-Clay consensus of early-1800s America even as it needs to move—quickly—into the vicinity of Roosevelt-Taft-Wilson progressivism. Not surprisingly, what would be good for China right now—along with much

of Wall Street—would also be good for the global economy. All are in dire need of a "shaming and taming" period akin to America's Progressive Era.

In many ways, then, the so-called Beijing Consensus attached to China's model is nothing more than the Communist Party's soft-pedaled translation of Theodore Roosevelt's "big stick" in national security policy and a nakedly self-serving version of TR's and Root's arbitrationism in diplomacy, as reflected in China's never-ending "consultative" approach. In its intense fear that national growth will be hemmed in by a lack of access to raw materials, China refuses to take any definitive stands on the many bad practices of its Gap trading partners. They merely "consult" ("And how does that make you feel, Mr. Mugabe?") and leave it to the Americans to try to round up a coalition of the willing to deal with the problem they desperately hope won't interrupt whatsoever the flow of raw materials and energy. In effect, the Beijing Consensus amounts to China saying, "I'm with stupid!" To which I say, "Welcome to the club."

But more to the point, the Beijing Consensus is simply China's admission that their leaders don't feel that it's in their best interests to get out ahead of any inevitable enforcement of global norms. Better to let those crazy Americans get bogged down in their "global war on terror," leaving China a long list of rogues whose natural resources they can access with less competition from the West. If TR played peacemaker among Europe's aggressive imperial powers, then China does the same today—just with a cynical ineptness bordering on immorality—between globalization's Leviathan and its many potential targets.

Some globalization experts, such as Parag Khanna in his 2008 book *The Second World*, argue that Beijing's consultative style represents a distinct third-pole perspective that contrasts with America's coalitional approach and the European Union's consensus-style rule. It does in a tactical sense but not in terms of an alternative grand strategy for the poorly integrated Gap. To the extent that China rests the future security of its globalization-dependent economy on the assumption that America will always be there to bail it out of any truly scary situation and that anything less scary can be handled with consultations and bribery, it is merely free-riding on America's military footprint and exploiting the liberal trade order that we set in motion. The more successful it becomes, the more it will need help in managing the unstable regions of the world upon which it is increasingly dependent. Europe has no real ambitions there; it merely absorbs adjacent states out of the fear that keeping them on the outside looking in is more dangerous. This is nothing more than my "shrink the Gap" strategy pursued on a regional basis. I applaud the logic and the willingness to employ it, but I realize that Europe's perspective does not stretch much beyond the Mediterranean littoral. As for America, we have specific progress in mind for the Gap. In general, this is not where our economy is going to make most of its money in coming decades. But we do want these Gap countries reasonably absorbed into larger economic and security schemes, logically clustered around the largest, most stable economies in any given region, so that they're no longer a source of mass violence (largely perpetrated internally) or transnational terrorism (especially any terrorists capable of bringing their game to the Core).

So in the end, the Beijing Consensus is nothing more than a grand strategy placeholder for the Chinese. It works for countries that reject the implausible economic demands of the Washington Consensus and it's a comforting alternative to America's myopic focus on terrorism. China's leaders know their economic model is not easily replicated, primarily because China itself blocks much entry into globalization's low-end manufacturing right now, and they know they're quite a way from fielding a military capable of defending their global economic footprint. So for now, Beijing bides its time by avoiding any more global responsibility than it can manage, but it hardly wishes for America's collapse as either its crucial trade partner or the ultimate guarantor of global security.

In a grand strategic sense, we again see the essential mismatch: Europe is willing to shrink the Gap, but only on its borders; China must deal with the Gap economically, but refuses any responsibility on security or good governance (as if it could teach that); and so America, which would much prefer to merely teach good governance to the Gap and link such change to improved economic policies (the essence of the Millennium Challenge Account's vision for change), gets stuck holding the bag on mass violence, terror, and rogue regimes inside the Gap's many hot spots. Having so long shaped this global order, we simply feel an overriding responsibility to keep it relatively stable, and since neither Europe nor China aspires to become the Gap's Leviathan, they're more than happy to finance our playing that role. They just want more of a say in that decision-making process after eight years of "Bring it on!" "Who's next?" and "Are you looking at me? *Because I'm the only military superpower on the planet!*"

Bottom line: When your grand strategy seems to consist of Hollywood swagger and B-movie revenge plots, don't be surprised—much less offended—that alternatives are suggested by concerned bystanders. Worse, expect self-serving copycats to emerge over time, offering their own twisted version of "justice" (Thank you for your contribution to global security, Mr. Putin!).

THE GLOBAL ACCELERANT: RUSHING TO SETTLE FRONTIERS

On this one point, the neo-Marxists are absolutely right: For capitalism to succeed, it needs to replicate itself elsewhere. But here's where Marx and Lenin and everyone that's followed them since get it wrong: Capitalism is not a zero-sum game, or even one of perpetually diminishing returns. Human ingenuity is limitless, so the upper bounds of economic development are constantly expanding, but only in those economies where entrepreneurialism is given free rein.

Europe, or more to the point, Great Britain (with an important assist from the Dutch in New Amsterdam–cum–New York), successfully replicated its capitalism primarily in those colonies where serious resettlement of populations occurred, meaning essentially "greenfield operations" like Canada, the United States, Australia, and New Zealand. In these sparsely populated wildernesses, the same social trust and institutions that drove Europe's own rise as a mini–world globalization in the seventeenth and eighteenth centuries were effectively transplanted, with the resulting economic progress and demographic growth essentially dooming the indigenous populations to assimilation or death. Elsewhere around the planet (Latin America, Africa, the Middle East, much of Asia), European colonies made little effort at real replication and instead co-opted select elites into forging bilateral economic ties that facilitated the uncompetitive movement of raw materials from the periphery (colonies) back to Europe. As such, it's no surprise that most of these surviving states maintain an oligarchic form of capitalism, because that's what Europe's colonial powers left behind, often killing off indigenous forms of free markets. As such, colonialism was doomed to ultimate failure, leaving behind a disastrous legacy that we will continue to manage for decades to come.

If Great Britain had not achieved such spectacular success, principally in the North American experiment that begat the American System in its full glory, it's hard to say just how badly Europe's civil wars of the first half of the twentieth century could have turned out. As such, America's system, once projected upon the world's stage, got its first great chance at replication as the result of wars engaged in Asia—namely, against the Japanese in WWII and Korea immediately following. By successfully replicating capitalism within Japan and South Korea, America proved the transferability of the model.

I don't want to make too much of this transfer in a nation-building sense, but more in a system-enabling sense. If America hadn't grown its liberal mini–world trade order in the West across the Cold War, and played de facto Leviathan in the Pacific (including the unsuccessful Vietnam War), it gets hard to imagine how Asia's "tiger" economies could have peacefully emerged. The same can be said for Western Europe during the Cold War. If America had not been committed to both fostering a Western liberal trade order and shielding NATO's member states from Soviet aggression or threats, it's hard to see how the EU could have arisen, much less been so quick to act in response to the Soviet collapse in integrating Eastern Europe. These are enormous peace dividends that arguably include the end of great-power war across the entire Eurasian landscape—a stunning achievement with credit extending across ten American presidencies, from FDR to George H. W. Bush.

If we recognize the limits of the EU's grand strategic ambition as the reunification of all of the Mediterranean littoral (the Caucasus likely being a bridge too far), which, quite frankly, is all we can ask of them, then the real grand strategic question for America is, Who logically leads the rest of the Gap's economic integration into the Core? I say "economic" because in a security sense, no nation other than the United States has any hope of fulfilling the Leviathan role anytime soon.

Looking back over the spread of modern capitalism, we see a European "mini-world" globalization that replicates itself successfully only within the so-called Anglosphere colonies, which in turn successfully replicate themselves, primarily as a result of America's global leadership role, in East Asia, with Japan playing the role of "lead goose," succeeded over time by South Korea and Singapore, and now collectively superseded by China, which pulls in lagging India by example. It is in Asia now where the global economy's newest consumer markets are being rapidly integrated through industrialization and urbanization and deep embedding within global producer chains.

Now, unsurprisingly, it's rising Asia that leads the world in concluding free-trade agreements (FTAs) with the world at large, indicating that this region is the primary driver of globalization's networking function. There are roughly 300 FTAs in the world today, and approximately 120 of them have been negotiated in the Asia-Pacific region since 2002. The United States is moving up to a dozen FTAs, while the EU is closing in on two dozen. China has proposed or is currently negotiating upward of 30 FTAs.

The countries of Asia, as globalization's current big "savers," likewise seek to diversify their holdings by buying American companies and putting their money into American financial networks (stocks and bonds), while simultaneously boosting their investments in those Gap regions (Andean Latin America, sub-Saharan Africa, Southeast and Central Asia) that invariably become their main sources for energy and raw materials but also their inevitable targets for market replication—in other words, the same way America replicated its market dynamic in Asia and before that Europe replicated its market dynamic in North America. In this manner, Asia both integrates itself "upward" into America's financial networks the same way American savers did with European financial markets in the late nineteenth century *and* extends our model of globalization "downward" into those regions still left poorly connected to the global economy; Asia serves as bridge-builder in the twenty-first century in the same way that America did in the twentieth century.

So yes, expect Asia, and China in particular, to buy up a lot of American companies in the next couple of decades, but also expect high-saving

Asians to allow America's Boomers to cash out of the American System in their old age, just as we helped Europe age gracefully before.

But here's where we get into the demographic clock on Asia, and—again—China in particular. By pursuing the one-child policy and basically wiping a slice of their potential population off the books (it is estimated that a population roughly the size of the U.S. population—300-plus million people—were simply never born), China set in motion a demographic wave that currently places them in a sweet spot that they must continue exploiting for all it's worth. Right now, China's got few kids and few old people, so just about everybody's working. But as that leading wedge of the currently vast working population starts edging into its retirement years, China's elder population will explode. By most calculations, China has already passed or is passing the 10 percent mark in terms of elders over age sixty-five. That cohort will rapidly balloon to the "Florida mark" of 20 percent within roughly a generation's time—faster than any nation has ever aged in human history. By 2030, China will have an elderly population roughly the size of the United States, meaning, in my opinion, that China is more likely to pass us in age before ever possibly passing us in overall economic strength.

What's it like for a nation to get old before it gets rich? No one knows, because it's never really happened before, so the process will inevitably redefine the world's understanding of how you care for a nation's elders on a tight budget. But also realize how this demographic time bomb greatly incentivizes China to move as quickly up the production ladder as possible, meaning they need to push off their lower-end, manpower-intensive industries elsewhere. Obviously, China's going to want to shunt some of that production westward, inside China, and a certain portion will need to go locally, within Asia, to keep neighbors happy. But it's just as likely that Beijing will be forced by its growing reliance on African and Latin American natural resources to accommodate local demands that China not just reap their resources and sell to their markets but produce locally as well. Toyota and Honda were forced down this path in America, and it worked out well for them, putting them on the road to becoming what IBM chairman Sam Palmisano calls "globally integrated enterprises" that source local, build local, and sell local.

Then again, that's going to be the primary role for China and Asia on a lot of economic questions: showing the rest of the world how to make markets work under less than advantageous conditions—meaning resource-constrained. That's why I view rising Asia as America's primary strategic asset when it comes to shrinking the Gap economically. If you tell me defense budgets are rising there, I say great, let's access them. If you tell me that Asian religious missionaries are flowing into the Gap in record numbers, I say great, let's facilitate that process the best we can. If you tell me Chinese farmers, shut out of opportunity back home, are heading to Africa in an unprecedented wave, I say great, let's help those foreign homesteaders trigger the same positive development effects there that European homesteaders once helped trigger in America.

Finally, if you tell me the global economy is void of profit opportunities in its mature markets and that its emerging markets are taking in all they can handle, and that therefore we're watching both Western hedge funds and Eastern sovereign wealth funds move into the less developed Gap economies, then I say we've got all the evidence we need to declare that the race is on to see which external players can integrate these economies into globalization's networks faster. That's a near-peer competition that I think America should gladly wage with China.

So can greed save Africa, as one *BusinessWeek* story asked a while back? Only if it's African entrepreneurial greed properly incentivized and channeled. Because if it's just America pushing new security rule sets, China simply seeking raw materials, and investors everywhere looking for the newest "frontier market" (the emerging buzz phrase), then we're arguably looking at no better outcome than the European colonial powers achieved previously. A gold rush mentality is fine, so long as the infrastructure built up—both "hard" connectivity and "soft" institutions—increases Africans' long-term resilience as well as their short-term profits. But it also doesn't make much sense for American politicians to start lamenting China's economic "penetration" of Africa, even when authoritarian states with poor human rights records are involved, because China's growing economic connectivity becomes an asset to be leveraged, not discouraged, and nothing pushes the human rights agenda better than a rising middle class, something Africa needs desperately. Plus, the more China pumps in Chinese nationals, the more China gets on the hook for protecting their rights and property, not because America says so but because those nationals' relatives back in China are making themselves known and pressing their demands upon China's Ministry of Foreign Affairs. In short, anything that increases China's exposure as a rising great power forces it to develop a foreign policy more in line with ours. If we do it well, we help Beijing explore what it means to be a responsible great power on globalization's frontiers.

For now, there seems to be a critical-mass interest in Africa that is primarily economic, not merely humanitarian or relief-oriented, and that's crucial. What we know historically about official developmental aid, or foreign aid, is that it works best in substantial bursts that generate some liftoff but then are reduced in volume, yielding to market-based activities. In many ways, aid is like oil in its detrimental long-term impact: It ruins the incentive structure in the private sector (How does a local farmer compete with free or highly subsidized food provided by outsiders?) while detaching the government from its natural "shareholders," or taxpayers. If the government doesn't need your money, *it won't listen to you.* So as soon as foreign aid constitutes more than about 15 percent of any developing economy's GDP, you've probably poisoned the economic well the same way oil does. Economist Paul Collier, for example, estimates that 40 percent of military spending in Africa is made possible by official developmental aid flows, and that many military coups are nothing more than periodic "profit-taking" exercises.

As far as where to direct what aid the West offers, most experts come down on the side of improving governance, while others, like Columbia University's Jeffrey Sachs, argue that there is a clear and widespread health crisis that ultimately keeps far too much of the potential working population offline, and thus a "big push" of aid that specifically targets those issues is most warranted. Frankly, I don't like to choose between the two, so I advocate whatever "big push" Western governments can manage on health-related aid, so long as money goes directly to the caregiving organizations themselves or, better yet, gets distributed in the same manner as school vouchers are supposed to work in the United States—directly provided to consumers whose subsequent demand for services should create local (or imported) private-sector capacity instead of a temporary influx of foreign aid health workers. Longtime aid expert William Easterly notes that while it's tempting to impose our definitions of who should live and who should die (i.e., mandating certain relatively expensive AIDS treatment options), the logic of individual empowerment says we should leave such difficult choices up to Africans themselves.

As for appropriately screening governments regarding political and policy reforms, which is basically the philosophy of the Bush administration's innovative Millennium Challenge Account, I see that as both appropriate and good when it comes to anything above and beyond temporary humanitarian relief and sustained targeting of the health care sector. As Francis Fukuyama has argued, even if the MCA never gave out any money or if the money it did distribute was badly spent, *just* getting Gap governments to consider policy threshold standards and move in that direction is, in and of itself, a wonderfully positive incentive—in effect saying, *Change in this manner and you'll become that much more likely to attract foreign direct investment.*

What we don't want to assume is that any one mix of policies or political models will work across Africa as a whole. As Easterly notes, China once had all the same problems that Africa suffers today: warlords, civil conflict, unending war, corruption, tyrants, and an imperviousness to past Western efforts to shape events there. And how did China pull itself together economically? Not by following the Washington Consensus of the 1990s, I would argue, but according to a game plan only nineteenth-century American leaders would recognize as fair and just. Plus, as far as Deng's successful experiment went, it was strictly bottom-up in nature: starting with peasants and then moving up into local and provincial governments. Deng, as Easterly describes him, was a natural "searcher" instead of a "planner." As Deng's famous maxim put it, "It doesn't matter whether the cat is black or white, as long as it catches mice." Most of what ends up working in Africa will probably come as a surprise, just as it did in China.

The simplest definition of good government, as Easterly points out, is one that gets the pothole fixed in front of your house. Create the environment in which squeaky wheels are unreasonable enough to ask for grease and you've got the makings of a bottom-up democracy where politicians, just like businessmen, are rewarded for local knowledge and local effectiveness in meeting demands.

So if we look at Jeffrey Sachs's list of missing capital in underdeveloped nations, it would seem to me that the best way to take advantage of globalization's current surge is to follow Sachs's advice to focus on a direct aid push regarding human health issues while letting a Millennium Challenge Account approach push governments on reform, rewarding them with development dollars specifically focused on encouraging a business climate of trust (e.g., property and contract laws). Let our military in-region focus its activities on increasing the professionalism of national armies, and let globalization's big push from the East work the infrastructure and knowledge realms (tech transfer and best practices, primarily). Let the business capital (including the 40 percent of African financial capital currently held overseas for safekeeping) flow according to its own logic, but facilitate P2P programs like Kiva. As for public institutions, nongovernmental organizations are best at building other NGOs, but since less than half of their funding comes from governments, I'd encourage more corporate involvement there and concentrate classic official development aid on the health and humanitarian-relief (postconflict, postdisaster) sectors. In general, I'd get intervening governments out of the business of building anything that requires an operating budget, because if the locals or the private sector can't build it, they'll be unlikely to maintain it.

Again, the overarching goal in all of this is to engender a climate of business trust. The reason so many businesses inside Gap nations are limited by family size is the low trust climate. When you can't tell much about potential counterparties in any deal, you tend to stick with those you know and cash-and-carry with everybody else. Easterly calls this phenomenon a "flea market" economy, but it's a truism for any frontier environment. One useful way to bridge this trust gap, oddly enough, is to invite in as many clannish outsiders as possible. The Chinese are—yet again—the classic example here. The more Chinese your developing economy lets in, the more trade you'll see develop with other countries that also feature a high Chinese population density, including, of course, China itself. This is the so-called bamboo network.

Last, there's a demographic frontier that typically needs settling in most postcolonial developing economies. Most Western businessmen will tell you that when dealing with China, you need to reach down past the generation of businessmen who were raised under Communism and work instead with the generation that has never known the premarket system. Economist George Ayittey makes similar arguments concerning Africa's "hippo" and "cheetah" generations. "Hippo" refers to the first postcolonial generations who've wasted the past several decades trying to prove modernity could be grafted onto a "dysfunctional" peasant-based economy that Ayittey argues wasn't broken until they taxed it to death and ruined the local democratic traditions of the village and the political-economic role of the chiefs, whose main job was the allocation of land. The "cheetah" generation, as Ayittey describes it, represents Africa's new hope:

> They do not relate to the old colonialist paradigm, the slave trade, nor Africa's post-colonial nationalist leaders. . . . The cheetahs know that many current leaders are hopelessly corrupt, and that their governments are ridiculously rotten and commit flagrant human rights violations. They brook no nonsense about corruption, inefficiency, ineptitude, incompetence, or buffoonery. They understand and stress transparency, accountability, human rights, and good governance. They do not have the stomach for colonial-era politics. In fact, they were not even born in that era. As such, they do not make excuses for or seek to explain away government failures in terms of colonialism and the slave trade. Unencumbered by the old shibboleths over colonialism, imperialism, and other external adversaries, they can analyze issues with remarkable clarity and objectivity.

Circling back to my original point of locating bodies and knowledge in the natural frontier-integrators of our age: Being so removed from those experiences, historically speaking, the average Western businessman will walk around Africa noting the bad infrastructure, the weak governments, the harsh soil and climate, and so on, and he'll see a tough place to do business. But put your average Chinese or Indian entrepreneur in that same picture and he sees a business climate not that different from the one he's already mastered back home. So if push comes to shove and the choice is a Western nonprofit organization or a greedy Chinese business, I'll go with the latter every time, trusting the Africans to look out for themselves.

America's grand strategy of shrinking the Gap and making globalization truly global should be about nothing more than encouraging and facilitating New Core Asia's natural desire to replicate itself inside developing economies. So yes, press China over Darfur, but make sure China stays in Sudan—unless you want that fake state to be America's problem alone.

THE INESCAPABLE REALIGNMENT: REMAPPING FAKE STATES

Since I've already displayed the gall to combine Jeffrey Sachs's pro-aid thinking with William Easterly's famous skepticism, let me now try to tie Easterly's thinking on "artificial states" with economist Paul Collier's work on the "bottom billion," or the roughly one billion Gap residents who are falling ever farther behind as globalization seems to be connecting everyone else. This bottom billion must command our attention, because the states where they live represent much of the workload that America and its allies will face in the coming decades.

Easterly's research on artificial states, first published in 2006, finds that postcolonial states with more straight-line borders experience less political stability and economic success than postcolonial states with squiggly natural borders. If your country's borders are squiggly lines on the map, it's probably because they conform to some natural geographic delineator, or perhaps past wars bent them according to tribal boundaries. Conversely, if your borders are straight, some colonial power probably drew them. The colonial power's reasons were typically nefarious: dividing ethnic groups to create permanently unhappy minority groups in fake states ruled by competing tribes. The resulting regimes were thus kept weak by their inability to effectively control their own national territory, leaving them dependent on their colonial patrons. The Middle East, anchored by fake state Iraq (Kurds, Shia, Sunni slapped together by the

Brits), is just the tip of this iceberg. Soviet dictator Joseph Stalin did a similar number on Central Asia, creating five states that all ended up with substantial minorities linking them to neighboring states: Kazakhstan was tied to Russia; Turkmenistan, Tajikistan, and Kyrgyzstan were made forever vulnerable to Uzbekistan's revanchist dreams.

Taken together with Collier's bottom billion, or that share of the global economy that did not take off with the rest in rising connectivity over the past two decades, we find ourselves deep inside that part of the world that I call the Non-Integrated Gap. While the rising demands of the 3 billion new capitalists seem to have fostered all sorts of positive economic opportunity across the periphery regions of the Gap, these are the truly "trapped" populations.

Collier says that fifty-eight countries make up the bottom billion, whose populations, as a result of divergence from emerging economies, now earn a mere one-fifth in income compared with those recent globalizers. Most are located in the interior of Africa and Central Asia. As such, virtually all can be considered the victims of colonial mapmakers, for none of the states in which they reside can be considered real or natural. Indeed, Collier argues that there is simply no logical reason why there should be any landlocked African nations. Only one percent of the Functioning Core's population suffers the odd combination of being landlocked and resource-poor, whereas almost one-third of Africa endures this illogical fate: "Another way of saying this is that other than in Africa, areas that are far from the coast and don't have resources simply don't become countries."

As the former director of research for the World Bank puts it:

> The countries now at the bottom are distinctive not just in being the poorest but also in having failed to grow. They are not following the development path of most other nations; they are adrift. . . . Many of these countries are not just falling behind, they are falling apart.

Why should we care?

As Easterly pointed out in his magnificent book *The White Man's*

Burden, former colonies that score high on partitioned peoples consistently score low on things like democracy, government services, rule of law, lack of corruption, infant longevity, literacy, and clean water. Check enough of those unsavory boxes, and you are a failed state. Such states are easy prey for transnational terrorist groups. Good example? Check out al Qaeda's permanent addresses over the years: Sudan, Afghanistan, and Pakistan. The first is ripe to split into its northern and southern halves (with western Sudan suffering genocide amid militia warfare), while the latter pair is linked by yet another British border that no local tribes recognize, much less respect. Then there's Africa, where America is setting up its new regional combatant command. According to Easterly's research, 80 percent of its borders correspond unnaturally to latitudinal and longitudinal lines, as if some colonial master took a ruler to a map. Sadly, Africa's record on ethnic violence in the post–Cold War era is all too familiar.

Now that they're past the period in which outside superpowers fought proxy wars through client states, those fake states are free to fight among themselves in nearly infinite combinations. The result? A Holocaust's worth of violent deaths, most of them in interior, landlocked Africa. Now, this horrible truth has certainly never stirred us to action in the past. These were just a lot of dark-skinned people dying in a galaxy far, far away . . . until 9/11 reminded us that such distant pain can be transmitted across the global body politic by those still willing to fight and kill and die to preserve their cherished identities in the face of this historic process we call globalization.

Here's the inescapable reality I think we need to get our arms around as a nation: The United States, as long as it remains a global military superpower, is going to be drawn into a lot of these fake states over the next couple of decades as globalization continues its astonishingly rapid advance. For whenever the global economy effectively penetrates these straight-line borders, somebody on the inside wants the equivalent of a national divorce, or worse, wants back payments from some neighbors who they think have been stealing them blind over the years (usually because the former colonial power decided to give them land belonging to somebody else). Those who make the first move are typically the most ambitious and capable: Examples are the Slovenes and Croatians in now defunct Yugoslavia, the Kurds in increasingly federated Iraq, or province Santa Cruz's threatened departure from Bolivia. Other times the dispossessed simply rise up in spontaneous mass violence in response to the right kind of political trigger, as in Kenya's disputed 2007 election (where every tribe seemed to turn on the dominant Kikuyu) or Rwanda's 1994 genocidal fit of rage (Hutu on Tutsi), whose origins can arguably be traced all the way back to the Versailles Treaty of 1919, in which the Belgians took custody from Germany and thereupon placed the minority Tutsi in privileged control.

So what should our goals be? First, as needed, the world's great powers must collectively intervene militarily to prevent or tamp down ethnic conflict. Second, we should make comprehensive efforts to stabilize the affected regions economically, providing what quick connectivity we can to the global economy. If applied prophylactically, either approach can preempt mass violence, as dozens of British marines courageously proved in Sierra Leone in 1999. Third, we must steer all players toward the long-term goal of political reintegration once economic stabilization takes root. Done well, borders need not change even as national economies are comprehensively recast. None of this will come easily or quickly. Indeed, we are looking at the work of one or more generations. But this burden, which will be borne by powers both East and West, is inescapable.

Let me remind you that America has some experience in this regard. Whenever I make this explanation in my brief, I use a slide that builds the map of the contiguous forty-eight states progressively, at first showing the original thirteen colonies, which are half squiggly-lined (the Atlantic coast) but a bit straight-lined here and there, especially in New England. These horizontal straight lines were drawn by European crowns, starting at the coast and simply moving westward, with no regard for who might be living there. Naturally, that led to some mass violence down the road. Then I show the audience the trans-Appalachian west, a historical term denoting the then frontier states between the original thirteen and the Mississippi River. These are far more squiggly-lined primarily on the basis of two major rivers, the Mississippi and the Ohio. The main exception is the exceptionally straight-lined Tennessee, which was broken off from North Carolina's original westward claim. Then I show the trans-

Mississippi Western states, most of which came into being after the American Civil War. Check out a map sometime, because it's a stunning change from what came before. All the Western states are incredibly straight-lined. Did any of these lines correspond to the Native Americans living there? Absolutely not. Those lines were drawn in Washington, and—again—periodic mass violence ensued. My point is this: The faster America grew, the straighter the lines became and the more violence ensued from stubborn, indigenous insurgencies, whose warriors ended up suffering mass extermination in some instances but more often suffered mass relocations to the worst bits of remaining real estate Washington could find, which currently constitute over 500 independent nations *inside* these United States. So don't tell me we don't know how to do ethnic sanctuaries or that we can't imagine what brings a society to the point of ethnic cleansing.

Look deep into our own history and you will find every evil and every virtue currently on display in globalization, *because everything I needed to know about globalization I learned in American history.*

My argument is that when the economies of Easterly's fake states open themselves up to globalization's scary makeover, there's also the great chance they'll succumb to its disintegrating impulses. And the greatest conundrum comes in realizing that the bottom billion, once well exposed to globalization, are likely to face just such centrifugal forces, and that the most likely agent of such connectivity, China, presently has a profound aversion to all the *isms* likely to unfold: extremism, terrorism, separatism (the founding "fears" of China's Shanghai Cooperation Organisation in Central Asia, a region full of fake states and bottom-billion dwellers). If there is one area where U.S.–Chinese strategic dialogue should concentrate intensely, it is on this difficult point. Otherwise, we're likely to find ourselves at loggerheads with the Chinese over such failed/ failing states, even as we agree on the collective security dangers such countries pose. The answer is simple: The United States and China need to target the bottom billion for preemptive nation-building and "external" improvements that better link them to globalization's networks.

Such a grand strategic approach would logically include somehow binding these landlocked states into economic "corridor" packages that link them to coastal states. In Central Asia, this means a corridor that connects the region both westward, through the Black Sea (thus countering Russia in the Caucasus), and southward, through Afghanistan and Pakistan to the Indian Ocean (along with India's booming middle class). In Africa, we're talking about radial-style corridors that connect landlocked countries to the major ports. In combination, then, such a grand strategic vision would kill two birds with one stone: connecting the bottom billion while improving the security situation in the two great regions into which the radical Islamic impulse spreads from its center of gravity in the Middle East.

But here are three inescapable realities Americans must face: (1) globalization will continue to fracture fake states and thus birth new, weak ones; (2) the most likely agents of globalization's connectivity will come from the East, not the West; and (3) our grand strategy needs to consist of getting in front of these powerful forces—not to stem their impact but to shape the ultimate outcomes.

Or we can hope that Brad and Angelina adopt the entire Gap on their own.

THE BETTER NORMAL: RACING TO THE BOTTOM OF THE PYRAMID

Globalization is often described as a "race to the bottom"—as in, to the lowest price or the least protection for workers and the environment. All of these statements are both relevant and untrue. They're untrue because there's a clear correlation between high levels of globalization connectivity and high wages, good regulatory regimes, and better protection of the environment, as well as an undeniable correlation between low connectivity and the worst abuses in each case. What globalization tends to do upon arrival is temporarily make a bad situation somewhat worse, followed by recovery. Why? Once the chimera of zero-sum development is discarded, the locals realize quickly how improving their rules and husbanding their resources will pay off handsomely in income growth. But that only says that the contact phase of globalization's deep penetration is incredibly crucial to alerting the culture to the true possibilities at hand—other than redistribution, separatism, and payback for past inter-tribal abuse. It also says to America that our partnership with Asia's agents of globalizing connectivity is paramount to any grand strategy of making globalization truly global in a manner that's beneficial to the overall security order and sustainable in an environmental sense.

One of the best thinkers along these lines is University of Michigan economist C. K. Prahalad, whom I had the pleasure of meeting at a Pentagon-sponsored workshop of experts who had come to together to discuss ideas of postconflict development tasks a few years back. Prahalad's description in *The Fortune at the Bottom of the Pyramid* is fascinating on many levels. First, he alerts us to the growing reality that most Core corporations cannot eke out that much more profit in increasingly saturated home markets, and instead need to consider the "fortune" of disposable income that's being amassed at lower socioeconomic levels, inside both New Core emerging markets and Gap developing economies, thanks to globalization's advance.

Second, Prahalad reminds us that this is really a back-to-the-future outcome for most Old Core corporations, who long ago were themselves start-ups during similar socioeconomic conditions (i.e., frontier-integration periods inside their own economies, like the settling of the American West) and grew *primarily* because they were innovative at selling to the bottom of the pyramid, meaning low-income-to-lower-middle-class families who needed great value for their money and couldn't afford your standard large purchase. An example the professor likes to use in his talks is the Singer sewing machine company. Back when it began, the company faced the problem of trying to sell a valuable machine to people who couldn't afford it outright. Selling to the top of the pyramid, or rich people, made little sense, because they used tailors. So how to get a do-it-yourself machine in the hands of people who truly needed it? The equivalent of a reverse micro-loan otherwise known as the installment plan. How to get the product in front of "media-dark" populations? That's called the door-to-door or traveling salesman.

Third and most important to American grand strategy is that selling to the bottom of the pyramid is a highly effective means of generating middle-class growth (in effect, changing the pyramid to a diamond) and thus a key component to facilitating democracy inside the Gap. By tapping into this "latent market for goods and services," we trigger individual-level demands for improved "transaction governance capacity" by the state. You want better national governmental institutions? Make local governments *demand* it. You want better local government? Trigger economic transaction rates among the populace, who in turn *demand* it. In short, good governments are not *imposed* from above but *demanded* from below. Despite the many myths of how our country and its political system were constructed one afternoon in Philadelphia and designed near-perfectly from the start, this is essentially how our American System was built over the decades: economic transactions *demanding* more powerful and more efficient government. This long-term process was typically sped up during times of war (the Civil War and especially World War II) and national crisis (Great Depression, early Cold War, the sixties), but at its core *always* remained a *demand* and not a *supply* function. We got bigger and better government when we needed it and trimmed it back when we needed that as well.

Finally, and most important to the long-term health of the planet, which is the ultimate target of our grand strategy of shrinking the Gap, Prahalad shows us that relearning how to sell to the bottom of the pyramid is an innovation booster that can shape more environmentally sustainable development. Why? The bottom of the pyramid is highly resource-conserving in outlook, given the limits of its purchasing power, so we're talking small-units packaging with limited materials employed in both manufacturing and packaging. The bottom of the pyramid needs things that are incredibly robust and durable, given that most live in a "hostile-infrastructure" environment—the essence of the economic frontier setting. Items also need to be highly affordable, accessible for purchase, and available for on-the-spot buying in small numbers. Ask yourself, Where can an American buy a single beer or a single cigarette? Typically, the only places are bodegas or convenience stores that service low-income neighborhoods. Well, most of the Gap's bottom-of-the-pyramid market lives on such "single-serve sachets"—for example, that's how most shampoo is sold in India. It's a low-margin, high-volume, and high-return-on-capital business environment. To master it, you'll be forced into innovation. One example Prahalad cites in his book: In Latin America, most mothers don't want to use more than two diapers a day for babies, meaning manufacturers that want to succeed in that market need to create cheap but highly absorbent diapers. Can that innovation be put to good use not just across the Gap but the world over? Absolutely. As Prahalad sums up:

> Innovation in bottom of the pyramid markets can reverse the flow of concepts, ideas and methods. Therefore, for a multinational corporation that aims to stay ahead of the curve, experimenting in bottom of the pyramid markets is increasingly critical.

Some Core marketers retain the vestiges of this logic: McDonald's, Wal-Mart, and Home Depot all specialize in selling to the bottom of our pyramid, or people willing to bus their own restaurant tables, find rock-bottom prices, or repair their own homes. When such corporations enter bottom-of-the-pyramid environments inside the Gap, they initially adjust themselves to local tastes and customs in order to gain access, but then start forcing the locals to adapt themselves to the firm's core operating principles, thus increasing local competition and, yes, wiping out local businesses that could only remain competitive if the environment remained closed. But the reason such firms can succeed in the Gap the same way they succeed in the Core is that they offer real value to people on tighter budgets, their underlying bottom-of-the-pyramid logic being "I'd rather make a little money on lots of sales than more money on far fewer sales, because if I can't, this huge potential market remains closed to me."

Again, in terms of shrinking the Gap, this logic is monumentally empowering to the billions of people trapped in informal economic settings where contracts are never signed, land is never titled, and dreams are rarely fulfilled. By creating such economic connectivity and thus opportunity, identity is generated on a demand basis: "This is who I am and this is what I want." If you want globalization to empower and provide identity and not just challenge its traditional definitions, there's no better way than to put hard-earned money in people's hands and give them the economic freedom to choose how they spend it. That's why income growth is so crucial, because it's the wellspring for all market opportunity.

Moreover, the historical opportunity here is immense. We will add about one billion people to the planet's population in the next dozen years, but the ranks of the middle class will grow at nearly twice that rate, or between 1.5 to 2 billion people, roughly doubling the middle class's percentage share of the world population. Shaping that middle-class identity and associated ideology, much as the American System managed to accomplish during our own frontier-integrating age, is how we trigger both the progressivism and the environmental awareness that marked Theodore Roosevelt's age in the United States. That's our grand strategic target for the planet: making people rich enough to care.

The good news is that Asia's emerging pillars, especially China and India, are already moving in the direction of viewing the Gap, and particularly Africa, as targets for their market replication and extension. According to a new World Bank study titled *Africa's Silk Road*, here's how it works in a nutshell: Globalization integrates trade among countries by disintegrating production chains and dispersing them across economies. As such, multinational corporations account for roughly two-thirds of global trade, and half of that share is actually intra-industry or intra-corporate transactions. Such traffic is called "network trade." As rising Asia increasingly looks to Africa for resources, there's also a natural tendency to want to shift production facilities there for three potential outcomes: producing and selling to local markets, home markets, and advanced third-party markets, i.e., the West.

Right now, most of what chain connectivity is brewing inside Africa is of the buyer-chain variety, with Wal-Mart as a logical template. Buyer chains feature a focus on consumer products with retailers, branded marketers, and branded manufacturers playing the central role. These "buyer-driven networks" tap into Africa's cheap labor pool by concentrated purchasing of labor-intensive, low-end goods. The bigger opportunity here is to migrate African economies into producer-driven networks, where a major manufacturer like Toyota is more the model. Producer chains feature multinational corporations with strong vertical integration in capital- and technology-intensive industries looking for cheaper inputs and further opportunity to disperse production in the most cost-efficient and resilient fashion. The fact that Indian and Chinese companies are already looking at Africa along these lines is hugely positive.

Yes, in the grand scheme of things, these Asian investment flows are currently small, but they're rising dramatically and they're quickly becoming "about far more than resources," as the report notes. China and India have become global leaders in forging "bilateral investment treaties" with other developing economies, and wherever their investments go, there follow three important and positive trends: (1) more trade with Asia; (2) more internal competition within the target economy; and (3) more trade connectivity between the targeted economy and the rest of the global economy. The big holdup is, in many ways, the poor and complex regulation of the investment climate in Africa. Simply put, there's a "spaghetti bowl" of overlapping free-trade areas. American efforts in the region should logically pursue simplification of this investment landscape wherever possible, facilitating India's and China's deeper penetration, along with any American companies prepared to play this game. This is a complete win-win in grand strategic terms. Instead of pretending that weak African economies can scale the development mountain on their own, we hitch their future to rising India and China, who in turn link African workers to their firms, then to our firms, and finally to everybody's markets.

You want to "drain the swamp" preemptively and foreclose opportunities for terrorists in the backwaters of the earth? This is how it's done, this is where it will be done, and this is whom we need to help. The average Muslim living inside the Gap earns about one-half the average global income. That simply does not spell victory. In a world where network connectivity determines wealth, America's grand strategy seems abundantly clear, especially when military interventions are involved: Whatever we do and wherever we do it, *leave the place more connected than we found it, because jobs are the only exit strategy.* World trade has more than tripled since the mid-1980s and FDI flows have increased more than tenfold, but America continues to act, in grand strategic terms, as though terrorism is a supply-side problem best addressed by capturing and/or disrupting terrorist networks, when in reality it's a demand function linked to globalization's rapid advance around the planet. America's problems with Native American "insurgents" in its West were not a function of their supply but our national demand for frontier integration. The same is true with violent extremists today. The answer isn't simply to hunt them down and kill them, although we'll do plenty of that and should. The answer is to align ourselves with this tsunami of demand for frontier integration and ride it on through its inevitable conclusion.

If you really want to win this long war, then do whatever it takes to make globalization go faster.

Five

THE DIPLOMATIC
REALIGNMENT
Rebranding the Team of Rivals

E very functioning state pursues some form of grand strategy, either
purposeful or accidental. Sometimes a leader will seek to sell a national strategy to the public, hoping to garner popular support. Other
times he will keep it secret, because he can or because he must. In ages
past, one leader might encompass this whole process. In today's modern
government, the norm is for hundreds and even thousands of key people
to be involved, for change to be incremental and spread over years, and
for significant disjuncture to occur only with shifts in top political leadership. The modern grand strategist therefore aims to forge a lasting chain
from analysis synthesized to vision spread to values embedded to leadership executed. A grand strategy is not an "elevator speech." It cannot be
slipped in like a password. Its *why* must be inculcated in younger minds
so that when they become older hands, these leaders know which levers
of power to pull—and when.

So when I speak in this book of affecting significant and lasting change
in America's grand strategy, or its diplomatic approach to shaping this age
of globalization, understand that I target not merely one administration

or one party or one generation of leaders, but this nation's sense of historical purpose—its political soul. America's grand strategy must reflect our
complex internal makeup as a people, but likewise our magnificent impact upon the world since our beginning as a nation. It must at once incorporate our imagined identity (we are the most synthetic of political
creatures) and the world's emerging ambitions, which we have enabled
through our stewardship of global affairs. This challenge properly met, we
bequeath unto our children a most wonderful world; the challenge abandoned, we condemn them to a fate of dead-ended dreams and open-
ended conflicts.

Grand strategy is like imagining the chess game from start to finish,
except that, in today's world of rapidly spreading globalization, it's never
quite clear how many players are involved at any one moment or which
pieces they actually control. It may seem as though there are no rules, but
that means it's important to make explicit our definition of the rules and
realize that playing consists largely of making our rule set seem attractive
to others, regardless of how the game unfolds. This game-within-the-
game resembles the highly iterative process of generating our own grand
strategy. As Parag Khanna argues in *The Second World*, the line distinguishing geopolitics (the relationship between power and space) and globalization (the global economy's expanding connectivity) has been
effectively erased. Therefore, my nation's grand strategy—and therefore
its diplomacy—is mostly about trying to shape every other state's grand
strategy more than they shape mine. What was once highly hierarchical is
now far more peer-to-peer in dynamics, thanks to globalization's stunning
advance. In a frontier-integrating age, you're either the integrator or the
integrated.

That's not to suggest that any American citizen should simply wait for
Washington to get this right. Frankly, everyone and anyone who wants to
make a difference should just go ahead and get his or her own foreign
policy and stop waiting on change from above. It's a perfectly American
thing to do.

THE UNDENIABLE TRAJECTORY:
THE "GLOBAL WAR ON TERROR"

America's current definition of grand strategy seems to be working the shoulders of globalization's bell curve: obsessing over terrorists on one end and democracy on the other. In combination, these two foci amount to American myopia on the Middle East, where democracy is unlikely to be forthcoming anytime soon and where terrorism, the tactic of the weak, is likely to continue for quite some time, given the durability of authoritarian rule there and the global economy's continued dependence on the region's energy flows. As such, it is a grand strategy destined to be a long and frustrating slog, generating magnificent friction and pushing America into morally questionable situations.

And this seems to be the main problem in current American grand strategy—its unreasonable expectations for immediate success (democracy) and its tendency to treat terrorism as a supply-side problem. If we admit that we cannot kill them faster than our enemies can recruit them, and that there is growing demand, as Ian Bremmer argues, for terrorism in too many parts of the Islamic world, where these angry young men "have little hope of lawfully altering their fates," then we're forced to move beyond the knee-jerk kinetics to address seriously the underlying demand for personal liberty. America can, by its own lack of historical awareness, pretend the political freedom as exemplified in a mature democracy is the first best answer, but in today's world we're largely alone in that assumption. If we weren't, China's development model wouldn't be so attractive and Vladimir Putin wouldn't be so popular. Plus, if we weren't so forgetful of our own national history, we would better recognize how many decades it took us to achieve the sort of inclusive, multiparty democracy we now enjoy, which, even by the kindest reading of American politics, *did not appear until half a century after our own revolution, and even then purposefully excluded women and sanctioned slavery.*

Yes, we can most definitely say we know better now, but it gets awfully hard to expect others to make that journey overnight, especially when we ask them to adjust their culture and even their observance of religious faith to accommodate diversity forced upon them by globalization's creeping embrace. If, in our patience, we are able to place more

faith in economic liberty through marketization and admit (as it has been
proven throughout our own history) that political liberalization *never* occurs in a sustainable fashion *absent rising incomes,* and that increasing income in this world is virtually impossible without connecting to the
global economy, then we will finally begin to recognize our liberal international trade order for what it truly represents—a global revolution in
the most fundamental sense.

But more important, we will begin to realize that our myopic fixation
on terrorism and democracy risks short-circuiting those carefully laid
plans, as well as possibly negating the decades of effort—in both blood
and treasure—that the United States has expended to bring our American System–cum–globalization to these world-spanning heights. And we
risk it all just because we can't have it all *right now.*

Today, America sees a very different world from that seen by the rest
of the planet: We want it instantly tidied up with no terrorists and no autocrats and no environmental damage—a grand strategy predicated on
some notion of perfection. Meanwhile, that young, ambitious non-
Western chunk of humanity focuses on an entirely different agenda—a
grand strategy that entails getting ahead at all costs. As a result, when our
leaders speak to the world, they are not heard. That's a big problem, not
so much because America is the only nation capable of leading as because
the world is a more uncertain and less secure place when we are perceived as having lost our way. Our "go-go" economic philosophy has long
been countered, as well it should have been, by Europe's "go-slow" focus
on successfully integrating its poorer neighbors. The world is a better
place for having that debate as long as both sides admit there's something
to learn from the other. But today, too much of the world seems to view
our "go-go" as having gotten up and gone off the deep end in the service
of extreme, self-serving goals, and unsustainable consumption.

That's not to condemn emerging markets for wanting all the same
things we enjoy. Heck, we talked them into going down this path in the
first place! Rather, it's just pointing out how much all that non-Western
economic activity is reshaping our world, because that's where we find
the truly inescapable challenges—and opportunities—of our age. But instead of looking those challenges—especially the cumulative environmental ones—straight in the face, we obsess over (1) global terror, the

vast majority of which never comes close to touching American lives;
(2) democracy in the shallowest form of free elections and little else;
and (3) worst of all, nuclear weapons—a bogeyman without parallel in
our minds.

In the summer of 2007, on a remote Australian island near the Great
Barrier Reef, I had the privilege of spending time "on the beach"—so to
speak—with Nobel economics laureate Thomas Schelling, whose thinking on nuclear deterrence shaped the international security environment
we enjoy today. Expecting to find the wizened strategist downcast on the
subject of nuclear proliferation (has it not always been *increasing?*), I instead found an outlook as optimistic as my own. Speaking to a World
Economic Forum retreat, Schelling admonished everyone to remember
just how effectively nuclear deterrence has worked over the past six decades. No state, he noted, that has developed nuclear weapons has ever
been attacked by another state. Moreover, no state armed with nuclear
weapons has ever attacked another state similarly armed.

Think about that for a minute.

America, the first state with nuclear weapons, is the only one ever to
use them: twice on Japan to end World War II. Justified? As the child of a
World War II Navy veteran who would have participated in America's inevitable invasion of the Japanese mainland, I'll pass on that one.

But what has the world witnessed since that initial demonstration effect? America, as Schelling noted, could have employed nuclear weapons
in its subsequent wars but did not. Nor did the Soviets. Because of the
equalizing threat of mutually assured destruction, these devices cannot
win wars but only prevent them. The same logic has held all these decades for powers as diverse as the United Kingdom, France, China, India,
Pakistan, and Israel, with North Korea stepping up to the plate and Iran
on deck. Somehow, despite all the irrationalities ascribed to each new
member, the logic of nuclear deterrence holds fast.

Will anything change when Iran's Shia bomb squares off against Pakistan's Sunni bomb or Israel's Jewish bomb? Objectively no, although in
its numerical infancy, Tehran's initial nuclear capability will make a tempting target for a nervous Tel Aviv and a trigger-happy Washington. Since
conventional invasion is hard to imagine following America's difficulties
in far smaller Iraq, and because conventional bombing alone can't rid Iran

of its nuclear capabilities, both Israel and the U.S. face an equally unthinkable choice: going nuclear to prevent Iran's nuclear capability. That gets us back to Schelling's basic point: get a nuke and permanently rule out invasion. Whether we care to admit it or not, Iran has already achieved a sloppy, asymmetrical form of deterrence. Tehran doesn't need to field nuclear weapons to maintain this deterrence. Like Japan, it can simply stop its nuclear efforts at a point from which weaponization can be achieved within a short time frame—a "break this glass in the event of imminent threat" capability. Our intelligence community's November 2007 estimate indicated that Iran was aiming for just such a carefully triangulated position: developing the "gunpowder" (enriched uranium) and clearly possessing the "gun" (ballistic missiles), but refusing—since 2003, as indicated in the report—to take the final step of building the "bullets."

So what does Iran's fairly clever positioning on this explosive issue mean for the world? I have little doubt, as long as America keeps up its diplomatic pressure on Iran and consistently states "all options are on the table," that Iran will continue moving toward an A-to-Z nuclear capability. Expect those additional reports to keep filtering in about Iran's "secret program" on this or that link in the chain. In the end, they'll all be true. But here's the larger point: In combination with its growing energy connectivity eastward, Tehran is making a backdoor bid for being considered "in the club" of great powers for whom great-power-on-great-power war is no longer an option. I believe, given Asia's rising energy requirements, that Iran has effectively succeeded in this quest, whether or not we choose to recognize it. But I believe that admitting Iran into these ranks will be a good thing. Again, remember the history cited by Schelling: Soviet nukes balanced American nukes, and those powers never dared to wage war with each other, despite all the early loose talk about wiping each other off the map. The same was true for China versus the USSR, America versus China, China versus India, India versus Pakistan, and the French versus the Brits.

Okay, I included that last one just to be comprehensive.

But the history is undeniable: Highly unstable two-state standoffs were—in each instance—stabilized, no matter the nature of the "ancient hatreds" or the incendiary rhetoric flowing from leaders.

Would a nuclear Iran pass a weapon to terrorists? For most people, that's the big question. The history on proliferation says that undeclared states are your problem, not recognized ones, which, in effect, got what they wanted from other great powers—recognition of fellow great-power status, which rules out invasive war by others. Once achieved, that status isn't simply handed over to one's nonstate minions to do with as they please. Moreover, when you want to point fingers on secretive sharing, the culprits have all been undeclared (e.g., Pakistan and North Korea with others, Israel and South Africa with each other). On the contrary, there's solid logic that says a recognized nuclear Iran would necessarily become more careful in its support for violent nonstate actors in the region. Why? Any hint of technology transfer could quickly force Tel Aviv into a preemptive nuclear strike of its own against Iran, not just with American backing but very probably with American nuclear participation. So if Iran wants in the "big boy" club, I say, pull it all the way in. There are few better ways to sober up a failed revolution.

Yes, Israel remains the big wild card in this unavoidable scenario pathway. But if Israel acts preemptively, let's be clear that it would essentially be acting to protect its long-standing regional monopoly on weapons of mass destruction. That monopoly hasn't kept Israel safe from conventional military attack; Israel's military superiority does that. It also hasn't prevented terrorism, even though Israel maintains a world-class defensive capacity there, too. All Tel Aviv's WMD monopoly generates is diplomatic opportunity: As soon as somebody else in the region gets a few nukes to challenge Israel's roughly two hundred warheads, the world's great powers will collectively force direct negotiations leading to—at least—a bilateral strategic arms treaty between the two states.

Why? The world's great powers will find the tenuous standoff too much to bear, not just in the West but far more in the East, which relies on Persian Gulf energy too much to suffer such strategic uncertainty. What would such urgency get us? It would get us Iran having to recognize Israel to achieve its primary goal in pursuing a nuclear capacity—namely, America's promise not to engage in forcible regime change in Tehran. Since that goal will effectively be achieved by Tehran's looming nuclear capacity anyway, then we're heading into a different dynamic: simultaneously creating a stable nuclear standoff between Israel and Iran, a dyad that quickly becomes a triad if Saudi Arabia decides that Arab Sunnis need their own nuclear champion to balance the Persian Shia. Let's not forget regional great power Turkey either.

For many regional and nuclear experts, such developments would constitute an almost unthinkably unstable strategic situation, but again, the only way to stabilize such a situation would be to force a trilateral or even regional security scheme that acknowledges each state's nuclear weapons explicitly and links those capabilities to one another through the condition of mutually assured destruction. Thus, pursued intelligently by outside great powers, Iran's reach for the bomb could end up being the event that makes real peace in the Middle East truly possible.

As for the notion that such thinking will only lead to every great-power wannabe around the planet wanting nukes, I've been hearing since I was a little boy that the world is only a few years away from two to three dozen nuclear states. Decade after decade passes and we're still under one dozen. That's what America's grand strategic patience on nuclear weapons has achieved: the end of great-power war at the cost of a stunningly slow proliferation of the technology, which has, in standoff after standoff, reproven its strategic worth. If only we were as patient with the long-term effects of a liberal international trading order.

THE AMERICAN SYSTEM PERTURBED: THE BIG BANG LAUNCHED

Of the dozens of reasons offered by the Bush administration for toppling Saddam, the one that most attracted my attention as a grand strategist was the notion of shaking up the chessboard of the Middle East by toppling its worst dictator. It was, to put it lightly, a very daring approach by anyone's standards, but one buttressed by the cynic's knowledge that whether we succeeded or not in Iraq, the region would be forever changed by the sheer connectivity triggered by such a massive intervention. But because the Bush administration was purposefully uninterested in attracting sufficient allied support (the primacy instinct), its primary public arguments centered on the twin possibilities that Saddam Hussein's regime was both close to achieving some semblance of a nuclear threat and had sufficient ties to al Qaeda to suggest that a transfer could someday be made. When such accusations later proved spurious, the botched postwar execution—which if done well would have discouraged the subsequent debate all together—naturally triggered the counteraccusation that "Bush lied, thousands died." So instead of keeping the focus on a brutal, mass-murdering dictator's justified demise, Iraq—and by extension its people—was recast as the "innocent victim" of an unjustified American invasion.

Worse, because of the deep and close political divide back home, President Bush was loath to admit his postwar mistakes in Iraq, and almost as soon as he won reelection in 2004, he began to slowly build a strikingly similar case against Iran. Once Mahmoud Ahmadinejad was elected president and began shooting off his mouth very cleverly in this direction, the die was cast and America would take its eye off the ball in both Iraq and Afghanistan. In this manner, the entire promise of extending the Big Bang beyond Iraq, which at several points in 2005 looked entirely possible given all the positive political events going on in the region, was sacrificed to the extremely myopic security fixation on nukes plus terror—the strategic sales job that would not end. This was a poor choice in grand strategy, because what Iran represents in the region is more promise than peril, when all factors are objectively weighed and America stops surrendering its entire strategic flexibility to that dynamic duo of threats. As long as Pavlov's dog keeps salivating on cue, more and more troublemakers are going to keep ringing that bell.

According to two former National Security Council officials, Flynt Leverett and Hillary Mann, who worked the region in the years surrounding the Big Bang, the Bush administration went out of its way to discount any help Iran offered in the region, ostensibly to foreclose any possible rapprochement. Right up to when she joined Condoleezza Rice's National Security Council a few weeks following 9/11, Hillary Mann had conducted secret negotiations with an Iranian diplomat at the United Nations. This diplomat had signaled Tehran's willingness to "cooperate unconditionally" with America's impending retaliation against Iran's neighbor to the east, Afghanistan's ruling Taliban, whom the Iranians despised almost as much as their immediate neighbor to the west—Saddam Hussein. Mann saw it as an offer that "could have changed the world."

Flynt Leverett, sitting high up in the State Department at the time, saw similar offers coming across his desk from longtime enemies Syria, Libya, and Sudan.

Were these rogue regimes looking to advance American interests? *Are you kidding?* Just like Iran, these states were hoping to take advantage of the suddenly changed strategic circumstances to come in from the cold and rehabilitate their relations with an angry America, something only Libya later achieved by surrendering its nuke program.

As part of the Big Bang strategy, Iran's offer of unconditional cooperation could have been put to magnificent use in Afghanistan and Iraq—not to mention the Israeli-Palestinian conflict. But the White House decided to pass on Iran's offer, citing what became known as the Hadley Rules, so named for then Deputy Director of the National Security Council Stephen Hadley. From a December 2001 memo stating the administration's approach: "If a state like Syria or Iran offers specific assistance, we will take it without offering anything in return. We will accept it without strings or promises. We won't try to build on it." This is, of course, a ridiculous proposition, and ignores the fundamental truth in diplomacy that linkages are good. Tehran subsequently—and quite rationally—accelerated its pursuit of the bomb as protection from anticipated U.S. invasion. You could say that, as in the case of Stalin's USSR, America's conflict with Iran was inevitable, so better to pursue it sooner than later. I would reply that in strategizing war and peace, timing and sequence are everything.

Bush's push to isolate Iran was consistently undermined by Russia's desire to maintain its status as Iran's main supplier of nuclear energy infrastructure, as well as India's and China's growing thirst for Iranian oil and gas. All three naturally fear being denied such access to a post–regime change Iran, just as they were initially with Iraq. Ironically enough, thanks to our poorly run postwar there, Iran, Turkey, China, and Russia now appear to be cleaning up when it comes to winning Iraqi government reconstruction contracts (with China winning the first major oil deal), indicating that they were our silent partners all along, despite their unwillingness to support America's decision to go in, and despite Washington's attempts to keep them out of the postwar rebuilding process as much as possible by favoring American firms. Simply put, the Baghdad central government is trying to diversify its nation-building team, something we should have sought from the start and certainly can't blame the Iraqis for engineering today.

The Bush administration blew it by refusing to strike while Iran's iron was hot. Negotiating with the mullahs doesn't mean simply making demands and expecting utter capitulation. It means that we'd get some of what we want, but we'd likewise need to give Tehran some of what it wants and is already achieving, thanks to a Shia revival—significant regional influence. The alternative is that Iran achieves the same rough level of regional influence and owes us nothing in return. Worse, Iran achieves this position and is hostile to our interests, and generates violence to veto America's efforts at stabilizing several ongoing regional crises. So how to engage such a confident enemy? How did the United States pull off such a mix of engagement and containment with Leonid Brezhnev's superconfident USSR in the early 1970s? And look what that got us a mere generation later.

If America wants to encourage democratization in the region, we have to recognize the inescapable reality that half of the Persian Gulf's population is Shia, and that, outside of Iran, Shia have historically played the role of the repressed minority/majority in country after country. If we pursue a "one man, one vote" policy (long allowed by Tehran's theocrats, mind you) in the region, we will have to figure out how to co-opt Iran as some sort of regional pillar—plain and simple. This is not a fantastic scenario, for as Middle East expert Vali Nasr points out, many American perceptions of Iran remain hopelessly outdated. Yes, in the 1980s it was the Shia that represented the radical elements of Islam and the Sunni regimes that epitomized stability, but today that situation is largely reversed: Now it's the Sunni groups, including al Qaeda, that constitute the bulk of the region's radicalism and intolerant fundamentalism (much of it bankrolled by the House of Saud), and it is Iran that is far more open to tolerating the regional balance of power, which, thanks to our creation of modern Islam's first Arab Shia state in Iraq, inevitably turns in its favor.

Frankly, when I see a country with that sort of strategic confidence, that's not when I try to get the regime to back down on the basis of military threats that everyone knows I will have a hard time delivering on. No, that's when I remember that Nixon went to China in 1972, and that's when I start looking for a grown-up of similar symbolic stature to engage Iran in direct talks (following all the necessary preliminaries, of course). As Beijing did then, Tehran now shows the classic signs of a revolution that is completely spent, with no victories to show after decades of trying to export revolution: a tired authoritarian regime looking to end its isolation, consolidate its regional influence, and remove the threat of outside invasion; a population that's overwhelmingly pro-American in orientation despite decades of indoctrination to the contrary; and shared enemies (namely, radical Sunni Islamic transnational terrorist networks) in regions of shared concern (e.g., the Persian Gulf, Central and South Asia). When Tehran's hardliners employ extreme anti-Israeli and anti-American rhetoric and threats, they're looking to consolidate their power internally and hold off a conservative-but-pragmatic wing, as well as the reformist wing that seeks a more normal relationship with the outside world. By continuing to play into the radicals' hands, Washington effectively denies itself the one regional ally most inclined to acquiesce to our long-term goals of triggering widespread political pluralism in the region. Why? Because Shia will be empowered as a result of this process.

As always, can we trust the Iranians to be anything but Iranian? First, don't buy into the notion that Iranians and Israelis are natural enemies. Before the 1979 revolution, after which Ayatollah Khomeini sought to rally a pan-Islamic banner in opposition to Israel and the United States, Iran never really had a sustained period of anti-Semitism. Indeed, Iranians, as Shia, have more in common with Jews than they do with much of the Sunni world, being, as the Jews were in Europe, longtime sufferers of discrimination. Second, despite the obvious control exerted over the political system by the ruling mullahs, Iran is the one country in the region where political leaders are actually voted out of power peacefully and allowed to retire or even continue political life. Considering that across the rest of the region the usual retirement package is death or violent overthrow, Iran is about as good as it gets—for now. Finally, as we're already managing a two-country intervention in the region, let me submit that Iran is not the third country (smack dab in the middle, mind you) we should want to add to the mix, especially when America's ongoing efforts in Afghanistan have already drawn us into the far larger problem set called Pakistan (172 million to Iran's 66 million).

Again, timing and sequencing matter, as does strategic patience. This is not a point in our grand-strategy storyline where we should all of a sudden go wobbly over Iran, hysterically inflating its threat to Hitlerian or Soviet proportions. Nor do we need a Maginot Line of missile defense in East Central Europe (another Bush-Cheney beauty). We never offered Western Europe a zero-deductible strategic defense policy during the Cold War, and we shouldn't be talked into one for Israel today. By not letting America paint itself into any strategic corners over the combined bogeymen of nukes and terrorists—two potentially intertwined issues that we successfully processed at much higher risk levels with the Soviets decades ago—we get a whole lot more realistic about what our power can achieve in this world of our making.

THE NEW RULES: FROM INDISPENSABLE SUPERPOWER TO INSOLVENT LEVIATHAN

Madeleine Albright, secretary of state to Bill Clinton, liked to describe America as "the indispensable nation." She was right. Without the prospect of American military force—the only military that can be projected to distant regions and sustained there—most attempts by the international community to stem endemic conflicts go absolutely nowhere. The post–Cold War period has so far been much bloodier than it needed to be, reflecting our learning curve on the question "How much is just enough to manage this world being transformed by globalization?" The administration of George H. W. Bush declared a "new world order" that was based on little more than temporary Soviet acquiescence to American global leadership during clearly defined military crises. Bill Clinton spoke of "enlargement," which meant we'd lead NATO's effort in the Balkans but shy away from anything having to do with expansive military operations in Gap regions. And so Central Africa burned very brightly across his eight years, swallowing up the equivalent of a Holocaust in victims. Where Clinton tried to do too little, Richard Haass asserts, George W. Bush tried to do too much, proving that "in the end, the United States does not need the world's permission to act, but it does need the world's support to succeed."

Part of the problem was the Bush administration's desire, as Haass wrote in *The Opportunity*, to take advantage of the chance to "define an era" that was already favorably tilted in our direction: our liberal trade order triumphant, the global economy humming, no great ideological fault lines or overt great-power rivalries, a U.S. defense budget that remained overwhelmingly focused outside of our hemisphere, and our most profound advantage still in place—the ability to access military crises distant from our shores without the world's considering that to be an additional crisis. Think about that last point for a second, because no other great power enjoys that luxury: the ability to finance a Leviathan force and use it with the tolerance of the international community. If we were to endure a true balance-of-power world, in which several great powers simultaneously pursued vigorous arms races and proxy wars throughout the Gap, not only would that drain our resources, it would sabotage any hope of an American grand strategy that consolidated, and made truly global, our American System–cum–globalization model of a liberal trade order. Some defense hawks will tell you that these dynamics already exist—witness China's military buildup and Russia's invasion of Georgia. I will tell you these sightings are but the tip of a far larger iceberg still—thankfully—submerged within globalization's pacifying interdependency. Most people (and experts) have no idea how much more costly such balancing could really become.

Naturally, our current difficulties at home and in Southwest Asia have pushed many American experts and politicians to call for a grand strategy of detachment, which is arguably the worst possible proposal ever made in the entire history of American foreign policy. The dream, of course, is of energy independence—a chimera of a strategic goal that makes zero sense. Why America, right at the dawning of the most intensely integrating period our model of globalization has ever seen, considers autarky on energy to be an ideal is truly bizarre. It is, in fact, nothing but escapism, and in that perhaps it is an understandable product of our Middle East problem thus far this century. But guess what? The Middle East with no oil would still be a disaster at managing globalization. The Middle East without Israel would still be a disaster at globalization. The Middle East without a single U.S. military boot on the ground would still be a disaster at globalization. Wish away enough reasons for Western interventions and you turn the Middle East into Central Africa. Absolve the West's sense of strategic responsibility through energy autarky and you simply invite the energy-dependent East to meddle in our place. But forget all that natural escapism and hold on to this one thought: An America that integrates with the global economy on everything but energy will also probably torpedo globalization. Why? Because such a selfish goal would encourage great powers toward trade protectionism of the sort unseen for decades, and that would set the stage for a fearsome age. So, by all means, diversify America's energy sources and innovate at high speed, but please, no fantasy of "independence."

Yes, it's fun to watch the Lou Dobbs types rant about unfair trade, but we don't have to imagine what the combined upshot of protectionist measures would produce in the global economy. We ran that experiment to ground in the 1930s, and once global trade, capital flows, and immigration started plummeting, the political movement that took greatest advantage was the fascists. Just applying such containment to the Middle East's currently narrow participation in the global economy would only boost demand inside the Muslim and Arab worlds for more radicalism in the face of heightened authoritarianism. As Ian Bremmer wisely observes, "Left to their own devices, a few who are excluded from globalization's benefits will turn to the only widely practiced methods of leveling the playing field available to them: insurgency and terror."

That's why the uncomfortable truth we face in this long struggle, something that will remain at the heart of any grand strategy we pursue to make globalization truly global, is that America will not leave the Middle East militarily until the Middle East joins the world in a comprehensive fashion. We cannot run away from this fight or the integration process that will ultimately overwhelm it. All we can really do is socialize the problem.

Here's why we need to socialize this problem now, and by that I mean encourage not just NATO's military efforts in the region, such as they are, but likewise attract—yes, I said *attract*—Eastern military powers into the mix, and as quickly as possible. Within a decade's time, all the remaining major war scenarios for the United States will be gone. When that happens, there will be significant domestic pressure to lower overall defense spending, especially on the wildly expensive, big-ticket items that define the Leviathan force's major capabilities. Within a decade's time, it'll be far harder to imagine a U.S.–China war over Taiwan (just see what the Kuomintang have accomplished since their return to power on the island), and there's very little likelihood that North Korea will still exist as a separate entity (Beijing has made the decision to slowly pull the plug). Finally, Iran's achievement of a nuclear capability will eliminate any potential for a U.S.-led "hard-kill" regime change operation there.

Those are the surviving big-war scenarios that the Pentagon uses to justify its Leviathan force, and all three will evaporate well before 2020, meaning America's military-industrial complex will be reduced within a decade's time to justifying its Leviathan *primarily* in terms of potential resource wars waged in Gap regions against other great powers. This is a Cold War storyline sure to gain favor in coming years, even as it completely ignores the reality of existing economic interdependence among the world's great powers—namely, the world is no longer divided up into competing "mini-me" global economies hermetically sealed off from one another. The financial contagion of 2008 proved that.

So the grand strategic choices are relatively clear: (1) we accept the limits of our Leviathan (both operational and financial) and stay militarily connected to the Persian Gulf by encouraging an increased regional presence by Asian military powers (e.g., India, China); (2) we disengage unilaterally in the pursuit of "energy autarky"; or (3) in continuing to play regional Leviathan on our own and refusing to socialize the problem over time, we're forced to disengage "multilaterally" down the road when those same Asian military powers feel compelled to show up and challenge our alleged control of the situation. I feel confident in saying that the liberal international trade order would not survive the second and third scenarios, leaving us truly with just one choice for an American grand strategy that seeks to complete the global project begun decades ago by the so-called greatest generation.

Why am I so adamant that America will be unable to maintain regional stability in the Persian Gulf without dramatically ramping up military cooperation with rising China and India? Right now, the United

States takes only about 10 percent of the Persian Gulf's total oil exports. That share will not rise over the next two decades, according to long-range forecasts by the U.S. Department of Energy. The Gulf's share of America's total oil imports is less than 20 percent today and should remain under 20 percent in 2030. That means that only one out of five barrels we import comes from the Persian Gulf and only one out of every ten barrels of oil that the Gulf exports comes to the United States. In contrast, Asia takes about half of the Persian Gulf's oil exports today and will probably account for a 60 percent share in 2030, or roughly six times the flow to the United States. The Gulf accounts for over 60 percent of Asia's imports today, and that percentage will likewise remain steady in the future, even as China's dependence continues to grow rapidly.

I personally don't find it strange that China is looking for landline connections to the Persian Gulf or endeavoring to create a "string of pearls" chain of naval facilities between itself and the Straits of Hormuz. If I expected to be taking upward of twice as many barrels of oil (approaching 6 million) each day out of the Persian Gulf region as the United States (3.5 million) in 2030, I surely wouldn't leave that growing vulnerability to America's good graces, either. But at the same time, with China's drive to secure access to Persian Gulf oil, we can expect the Pentagon to move consistently in the direction of increasingly justifying its big-war force on China's rise as a presumed near-peer competitor and the clear and present danger it presents. While this thinking makes almost no sense on either strategic or economic grounds, it is nonetheless natural.

During the Reagan administration, the Pentagon began producing an annual report on the Soviet Red Army (*Soviet Military Power*) to justify its massive defense buildup—the biggest peacetime increase ever. The series ended, after eleven volumes, along with the Soviet Union in 1991. In 1997, the U.S. Congress mandated that a similar report be prepared each year on the Chinese military (*Selected Military Capabilities of the People's Republic of China*). The thirteenth volume comes out later this year. The strategic horizon for the report is instructed to be the following:

> The report shall address the current and probable future course of military-technological development on the People's Liberation Army and the tenets and probable development of Chinese grand

strategy, security strategy, and military strategy, and of the military organizations and operational concepts, through the next 20 years.

The U.S. Congress does not mandate a similar report on any other military in the world (but don't be shocked if we soon get a new series on Russia). Last year's volume noted that "improvements in China's strategic capabilities have implications beyond the Asia-Pacific region" and that the lack of transparency regarding Chinese intentions "will naturally and understandably lead to hedging against the unknown" by the international community. Care to guess who constitutes the "international community" on this one? Because if you can't, let me introduce you to 535 prime suspects, the vast majority of whom have a major Defense Department "program of record" in their home state or congressional district.

Okay, that's a bit harsh. The truth is that several Asian countries (e.g., South Korea, Japan, Taiwan, Australia, India) also produce similar reports on Chinese defense spending. Why? Because China goes out of its way to hide what it procures and then slyly trots out its big-ticket items every so often to pointedly give our satellites a few snapshots. We have it within our power to alter this dynamic, but for now, it is simply too useful to too many members of the military-industrial complex on our side. Much as in the case of Iran, so long as we don't link our demand for their transparency to some larger understanding of what they shouldn't fear from us, we're unlikely to change this situation. But remember this: We choose to force this military balancing dynamic on others—yet another example of why America's grand strategy matters more than any other great power's.

Beyond the Taiwan question for China, which has obviously driven much of its acquisitions up to now, the 2008 report also noted that China is currently the third-largest oil importer in the world and that its car population is expected to increase more than tenfold by the year 2030. I don't know about you, but with almost two decades of professional service in this business, I would say the intentions behind China's naval buildup are transparent. To argue objectively on the facts of future international oil flows, it is America's huge military buildup in the Gulf of the last few years that seems suspiciously illogical.

Ah, but America loves its bogeymen, and we love to tether our force-acquisition policies to them, because the bogeyman that lives long and prospers is an ideal target against which to scale our ever-growing defense budget.

Still, simply swapping in the Chinese because we no longer have the Soviets is not grand strategy but rather something more akin to a jobs bill—nice (home-district) work if you can get it. But it's not a stretch to say that this kind of stubborn, strategic bias is killing our military personnel in Iraq and Afghanistan today by default. When you insist on buying one military (the Leviathan) while constantly operating another (the Sys-Admin), personnel are most definitely going to be needlessly sacrificed in a long war. I find that sort of thinking strategically unsound, and I believe the associated greed to be morally indefensible. I prefer America's natural greed for market domination—along with everybody else's—be more suitably incentivized for this frontier-integrating age.

THE NEW NORMAL: AMERICA THE CONTAINED

Once Hurricane Katrina prematurely triggered the postpresidency of George W. Bush in the summer of 2005, America found itself subject to a universe of players all seeking to contain its use of power internationally. Some were internal, like a U.S. military that became increasingly and openly critical of Bush administration decision-making and an intelligence community whose November 2007 National Intelligence Estimate on Iran—which significantly downplayed the threat—constituted a mini-revolt within national security establishment ranks. The White House, thus challenged openly, took the highly unusual step of removing Admiral William J. Fallon from command of Central Command in early 2008 following an *Esquire* article by yours truly that detailed his long-standing—and highly public—opposition to military strikes on Iran. According to Bob Woodward's *War Within*, Fallon and President Bush had locked horns from the start over the admiral's contrary desire to "get engaged with these guys" somehow. This time "Truman" removed "MacArthur" because the latter *resisted* adding a third country to the war. But most such resistance across Bush's second term was external, such as a growing chorus of small- and medium-sized rogues whose leadership (the classic here being Venezuela's Hugo Chávez) began insulting the United States openly in international forums like the United Nations, where White House attempts to further isolate Iran economically were likewise frustrated by a mini-bloc of rising powers determined to rein in our "global war." Naturally, the Bush administration covered this diminution of our international standing the best it could, discovering the concept of diplomacy very late in the second term after the November 2006 midterm elections confirmed the White House's growing irrelevance. (As soon as your president starts boasting to the press that he's still relevant, his presidency is basically finished.) With our secretary of state reduced to trotting around the world delivering talking point after talking point, America effectively yielded its global leadership for the first time since the end of the Carter administration—our "humbler" foreign policy finally achieved.

The good news, of course, is that America's new president will face a world eager to herald our return. Our new commander in chief is looking at 50 percent being taken off the top in terms of other leaders' price tags for renewed friendship and alliance. No surprise there, as the world greatly fears for its future whenever America is perceived to have gone off on an ideological bender. Nonetheless, President Obama is looking at a serious task: getting other powers to recognize that we now realize the limits of our power. If that realization cannot be demonstrated, or if the Obama administration somehow fails at signaling such awareness (the temptation to circle the West's wagons here is great), then America will most definitely be looking at (1) a continuing effort by many of our true allies to dissuade us from further overextension, and (2) increasingly open displays by rising powers of their willingness to seek one another's solidarity on security issues while pointedly excluding the United States.

If we remain on this ill-advised course, then the most likely greatpower flash point for the United States in coming years will be either China or Russia, with the latter vaulting now into the lead thanks to its invasion of Georgia. Neither represents a systemic threat, because each supports globalization's advance, and so regards the world's dangers much as we do. But it's also clear that while the rest of the world fears globalization primarily in terms of a perceived extension of U.S. soft power, in America we now essentially view globalization in terms of a perceived extension of Chinese soft power, much as Europe fears Russia's growing domination of its energy markets. But since China's soft sell will only grow more oblique in its application over time (i.e., they continue to "hit 'em where we ain't"), Russia, under Putin's continued stewardship, is more likely to become the East's de facto standard-bearer in any future attempts to contain a United States that refuses to mend its ways, much the way Brazil and India, with great diplomatic skill, manage to represent the Gap's economic interests in global forums.

If the Obama administration does not seek a more discreet and less martial tack with the world, then engaging Russia negatively on this score will be a big mistake—the ultimate diversion in this long war. I realize the temptation here is great for many—and overwhelming for some—following Russia's conflict with Georgia. But here's where we misdiagnose Russia's grand strategy: Its move on Georgia was less an attempt to redefine intra-Core security (i.e., Georgia's ill-fated attempt to join NATO) than to make clear its strategic ambition to reintegrate the Caucasus into its economic orbit (i.e., the question of who controls the pipelines—thus the energy flow—from East to West). In effect, Russia's historically inevitable resurgence has progressed to the point where Moscow's bosses now feel empowered enough to launch their own "transformations" of neighboring Gap regions. Again, where did they learn such strategic chutzpah? From America—of course. Contrary to neocon imagination, the terrorist strikes of 9/11 did not grant the United States a permanent—much less exclusive—global concession on identifying and punishing "rogues."

As with so many emerging powers that are experiencing a rise in nationalism as they engage the world more deeply, Russia's heightened chauvinism is both natural and unstoppable, for it signals a growing national pride that should be shaped and not merely opposed. In general, rising nationalism reflects simple pride in one's own economic advance. When countries get wealthier, most of them also become more nationalistic, which in turn is often historically related to increased rule of law and decreased corruption (clearly not yet the case in energy-rich Russia). The rising nationalism created by globalization's spread, hardly a uniform menace that needs be stamped out, should be viewed by America as sim-

ply the collective pursuit by a society of a firm identity amid all this growing connectivity, much like growing religiosity. A country with a rising
income and a firm national identity should be far easier to cut deals with
than one whose income remains flat or declines and whose people seek
refuge in some combination of religious and ethnic identity. In short, the
more nationalistic a country becomes in response to globalization's many
promises and perils, the more likely it is to remain a real state not subject
to remapping by the global economy's progressive penetration. As Gustavo de las Casas has argued, "In a world where war is expensive, borders
are largely settled, and the actions of nations are usually tied to some
moral code," today's rising nationalism "often leads citizens to look inward
and focus their energies on bettering their countries."

Quite frankly, a good expression of such rising nationalism is found in
Russia under Putin. There, as longtime observer Dmitri Trenin argues, we
see, virtually for the first time in recorded history, a Russian state that's
both nationalistic and nonexpansionistic, even as it has long sought clear
spheres of influence in its so-called near abroad (i.e., former Soviet republics it now views as its last buffer against an expanding NATO/EU). Truly
postimperial for the first time in centuries, the current "Russia Inc." mindset of the leadership projects a decidedly "In capital we trust" nonideology
that should strike most Americans as reminiscent of our own, post–Civil
War economic brutalism, including our open bullying of small neighboring states. And like America in that period of history, Russian society today has seen social trust replaced with widespread cynicism, even as
collective economic fortunes have risen. Values are viewed as unimportant,
the crude but accurate assumption being that private and corporate interests control most political decisions. In a Dickensian world where dog-eat-
dog competition reigns and "homo economicus" is considered the most
evolved state of being, Russians today sense little difference between their
universe and the larger globalization process at work around the world. In
that way, you could describe Russia as possibly the most well-adjusted
great power out there, its lack of illusions being one of its greatest strengths.
As Trenin puts it, Russian leaders "enjoy being an energy power" and essentially view the world's governments as all being equally imperfect and
therefore separated primarily by the power they wield.

In many ways, Russia today embodies both Karl Marx's description of bureaucratic capitalism (i.e., big business *is* the state), as well as Theodore Roosevelt's fears concerning a "stationary state" in which ruthless competition within the economy is tempered primarily by the rise of authoritarianism in politics and the dominance of markets by giant trusts to which the government is beholden. Russian leaders view a harshly competitive global landscape with equanimity, their sense of expansionism—much like Roosevelt's—limited to market domination. In that sense, Russia today is incredibly transparent in its desires and tactics: What the state wants is what Russian business wants—like no competing Western pipelines in the Caucasus. Russian society is likewise becoming ever more familiar to America. With its crude individualism and crass materialism, it grows more American and less European with each passing year.

In its foreign policy, Russia represents a crudely utilitarian partner for an American grand strategy of pushing globalization's advance: Willing to use force in international crises, but exceedingly businesslike—sometimes to a brutal fault—in its economic diplomacy, it views any state as both partner and competitor. With a complete lack of emotion, Moscow pragmatically sees America for what it truly is right now: militarily overextended, financially overdrawn, and ideologically overwrought. As such, we make an easy target for domestic propaganda about a cruel world that Moscow must engage with equal cruelty, but even that anti-Americanism is largely for show, as America has long polled better in Russia than in most European nations. Even after its conflict with Georgia, Moscow wonders openly why Washington would choose Tblisi's manic nationalism over its cool Machiavellianism. In the end, Putin & Co. see the same multipolar world that Washington, in its recent failures, has finally come to recognize, and welcomes it for the opportunities to make Russia once again powerfully relevant in global affairs. Since we need that as well, Russia's renewed willingness to exercise force should be managed with great pragmatism on our side—much like the way Theodore Roosevelt managed the rising Japan and Germany of his day—because trying to influence Russia's internal developments through a renewed Cold War stance will simply play into the hands of al Qaeda by dividing the Core against itself.

In the coming years, the United States is going to bump up against plenty of younger versions of itself, like Russia. If we're lucky, the Putin-esque "supercorporation" package will become a familiar one: a rising power joining the global economy on its own nationalistic terms, headed up by a heavy-handed, rather clannish business elite that is more techno-cratic than ideological in outlook, and whose aim is to maximize the economy's international leverage and network connectivity based on the country's most strategic assets. Simply put, these are economic rivals we should naturally want on our team: They are not interested in challenging the dominant liberal trade order but merely exploiting its opportunities for maximum selfish benefit. More important, they view globalization as vital enough to their continued growth in wealth and power that they are willing to defend it.

In harshly realistic terms, I'm hard-pressed to describe a better Russia for our grand strategic purposes right now: a brutally ambitious builder of economic empire that's willing to crush obstacles in its path. I mean, haven't we long complained that none of our allies want to go anywhere and kill anybody? So now that Russia proves itself up to the game, we im-mediately toss it out of all our great-power clubs? But none of that will register with a Washington hell-bent on defining our current age as a "global war of survival" or a bloc-defined clash between democracies and autocracies. Potentially useful allies like Russia aren't interested in any of that because they see it as our transparent attempt to limit their global economic power while maximizing our own.

And they're right.

THE GLOBAL ACCELERANT:
SOFT-POWER BALANCING

Even as many emerging powers are starting to "feel their oats" in sharp contrast to America's growing world-weariness, few are willing to engage in anything but the most passive-aggressive containment strategies with regard to our self-declared "global war," the best examples being the col-lective efforts of the Shanghai Cooperation Organisation to slowly shrink our military footprint in Central Asia. In effect, most of the world logi-cally expects we'll eventually run out of money and come to define these threats in less earth-shattering terms, or maybe some new global crisis will catch our attention and we'll redirect ourselves (Thanks, Wall Street!). Plus, with the amount of anti-Americanism in the world as of late, it is getting harder and harder for the United States to access crises without the locals' seeing that as more additive than subtractive, the assumption being that once we show up, we'll decide to label someone an enemy of global order and then the shooting will start. The longer the world maintains that impression of us, the more it'll be happy to see our continued tie-down in Southwest Asia extended.

On some level, the high-consumption approach of the Bush administration preordained this outcome. By using up the force, piling up unprecedented budget deficits, and spending virtually all of the political goodwill extended to us after 9/11, it effectively condemned the next president to one of two pathways: (1) staying the course in Iraq segueing to Afghanistan/Pakistan, which extends our strategic myopia and draws down our national power for another half-decade or longer; or (2) a period of relative quietude during which we endeavor to unwind both our strategic tie-down and our financial crisis by reengaging the world with a new brand of global leadership. My fear is that the first path effectively rules out the second, because by the time we come to our senses, too many opportunities and rising powers would have passed us by.

This is the true ideological threat posed by China: the continued diminution of our national brand and our historical association with this liberal trade order. Our disavowing that historical parentage effectively cedes globalization's future to the China model—a painfully limited alternative. But in the absence of America's sustained leadership, emerging powers will inevitably begin emulating China's mercantilist mindset on trade, mimicking its growing fears of resource dependency, which it defines in very mid-twentieth-century terms (i.e., I have to own the barrel *in the ground*, as well as the grain *in the soil*). Once such self-fulfilling prophecies are launched from enough players (e.g., Saudi Arabia already mimics China's push to buy up arable land abroad), America's big-war national security community will feel justified in pushing a mirror-imaging strategic mindset, and soon enough we'll all be off to many races—for

Africa's raw materials, for Arctic energy, for South America's farms, for whatever resource we deem panic-worthy. In that pathway, the only surfeit we'll enjoy is unlimited numbers of Chicken Littles—academic chin-pullers and their Greek chorus in the blogosphere dispensing predictions of "perpetual war."

This would be a crying shame, given the progressive upgrading of leadership we'll definitely see in both Washington and Beijing over the next decade, as the Boomers depart from top political ranks here and the fifth and sixth generations of Chinese leadership begin asserting themselves over there. In both instances, we'll see emerging elites with a far greater understanding of globalization's inherent complexity and rising interdependency. But that's what makes the next ten years so incredibly important: Unless the United States can begin articulating a grand strategic vision within which emerging powers like Russia and China can logically locate themselves, we're likely to find ourselves increasingly downgrading our own perceived global reach. What was once a liberal trade order that opened doors the world over to American business, and has allowed the U.S. military to access crises virtually the world over, will inevitably suffer partition as competing rule sets, offered in contrast to our manic focus on terrorism and WMD, fence off regions of the world from our influence. This is the essential forecast of Parag Khanna in *The Second World:* America largely contained to the Western Hemisphere, Europe owning the Mediterranean littoral Roman-style, and China's soft-power networks managing Asia and the rest. (Khanna discounts Russia as a dominant power.) Like most big-picture books published at the end of the Bush administration, Khanna's extrapolates America's exceedingly narrow, post-9/11 grand strategy *ad infinitum.* Such is the state of our grand-strategy debate.

The problem is, of course, that we have little historical basis upon which to forecast a global future that features the sole military superpower allowing rising economic pillars to continue free-riding on its military efforts long enough for them to construct viable hemispheric security regimes on their own, replete with their own military capacity to play Leviathan. Given Europe's past negative experiences, Russia's demographic decline, and China's complete lack of experience in this regard, it gets hard to generate plausible global scenarios where globalization's burgeoning network trade does not force a similar "chain reaction"—if you will—upon the security realm. I mean, why would the global economy embrace such production-chain connectivity only to parcel out the associated security responsibilities on a regional or even hemispheric basis? Surely the global business community will eschew such inefficient partitioning, making it hard for business-sensitive elites to move down this pathway without suffering a profound loss of competitiveness in a flat world. Putin, for example, must keep Russia's oligarchs happy, lest they, like a disgruntled board of directors, dump their company's CEO in search of better returns on investment.

Ah, but what if the main character in this drama, the United States, is actually the one great power within which leadership and political power is wielded by an elite with a drastically poor understanding of global economics, one given to populist tendencies and ideological slants reflecting its career status as lifelong politicos with little to no entrepreneurial experience? Granted, the EU's insular technocracy could probably give our Boomers a run for their (tax) money in this regard, but isn't it amazing to think that the oldest players in this globalization game, Europe and America, are arguably the least pragmatic (in a business sense) and the most ideological (in a political sense) with regard to the game's long-term management? And that the former socialists—like India, Russia, and China—are actually more in tune with globalization's evolution right now?

If so, Joshua Kurlantzick's recent book *Charm Offensive: How China's Soft Power Is Transforming the World* is a valuable rendering of the current counternarrative being offered by Beijing regarding globalization's advance into Gap regions. As he puts it, "In a short period of time, China appears to have created a systematic, coherent soft power strategy, and a set of soft power tools to implement that strategy." Of course, a similar description could have been given to American efforts, starting with William McKinley's administration through that of Woodrow Wilson's first five years, including the naval buildup, the focus on conflict mediation, the use of "dollar diplomacy" to smooth market entry, the open-door policy, and so on. As the new power on the block, we enjoyed the same honeymoon period then that Kurlantzick describes China as exploiting today.

The self-limiting aspect of this process, however, is that "with great power comes great responsibility," with most of that responsibility defined by your nation's business interests and expatriates abroad. The more you connect, the more those elements of your own network begin making demands, something the Chinese Ministry of Foreign Affairs, according to senior State Department officials involved in these high-level talks, now routinely quizzes its American counterparts about in terms of best practices and basic coping strategies. In short, the more successful you are in spreading your national brand, the more you're required to protect it— and money doesn't always talk loud enough.

Still, China's "charm offensive" tells us what's selling best right now in the shadow of our myopic grand strategy of "kicking asses and taking names": a willingness to join multilateral institutions, support for peacekeeping under UN auspices, doing whatever it takes to power economic growth in developing regions, and mediating other countries' conflicts while espousing noninterference and persistent struggle against terrorism, extremism, and separatism. If that doesn't sound like an ideal "good cop" counterpart to what we've been doing for the last eight years, I don't know what does. The downside is, as Kurlantzick points out, China's growing tendency to export its domestic problems, like poor environmental practices, political repression and censorship, and weak regulatory standards in general. Plus, with such a strong noninterference focus, China is naturally most welcome among the world's many rogue regimes and small economies that undoubtedly hope that China's economic domination will somehow improve upon the past versions offered by European colonial powers and "ugly Americans," despite Beijing's avowedly mercantilist mindset (dream on, I say). Still, there's no denying that Chinese companies, having first grown adept at navigating China's developing economy, bring a set of business skills logically more appropriate to the task of replicating capitalism in Gap economies.

Naturally, as Kurlantzick points out, the local backlash on China's economic expansionism is just beginning. In this regard, China's insistence that its foreign policy goal is to extend economic ties without attached political or security demands is as naïve as America's claims were more than a century ago. Eventually, you end up having to use that big stick now and then, especially since trade ties create political ties and po-litical ties typically engender shared security interests. If, in previous glo-balization eras, trade followed the flag, nowadays it's more the other way around, as China will inevitably discover.

This is what I tell Chinese long-range planners and policy analysts whenever I sit down with them in Beijing: "Your problem is not unlike what America faced in the last years of the nineteenth century. We began to realize that our economic and network connectivity with the outside world was ballooning, but our political-military capacity to do anything about it lagged far behind. That growing gap *was* our security problem—plain and simple. Eventually, our enemies both large and small would have discovered ways to exploit it, meaning we needed to close that gap either on our own or in alliance with others. But either way, we needed to mount a catch-up strategy on security that would synch up with our growing success in the economic realm."

If China can continue free-riding on the global security system main-tained by America's military forces, this gap might never be revealed—much less become crucial. But consider: Globalization's advance, currently identical in the minds of many with becoming more Western, especially American, will soon enough start being identified with becoming more Asian, especially Chinese. As that inevitability unfolds, China will then find itself targeted the way America is today by those who violently op-pose globalization. Extremists, seeking civilizational apartheid, or separa-tion from a "corrupt, materialistic world," will attack Chinese influence just as they today seek to limit Westernization. Eventually, their familiar-ity with China will breed contempt and the honeymoon period will end. In that future, a China that cannot adequately defend its economic inter-ests globally in a manner similar to that of America—and, to a lesser ex-tent, Europe through NATO—will represent a serious source of global instability. China will either be forced to retreat from the world or—in addition to paying protection money in all directions on the ground—rely on others to defend its overseas interests, neither being a path we should welcome for all the reasons America itself would find such a situation unbearable.

Thus, in my mind, trying to cast China's "charm offensive" as generat-ing a new model for controlling the international system is a stretch.

China is basically playing the "good cop" working his own beat opposite that of the "bad cop," leveraging the latter's "badass" reputation. To the extent China succeeds at this, there's little harm, even as there are likely to be many "fouls" in terms of corrupt business practices. Indeed, it can be argued that China plays the implicit role of America's "limited-liability" or "silent" partner throughout much of the Gap, inherently limiting our strategic liability in those off-grid locations unlikely to elicit a security response from us, even under conditions of extreme and widespread violence. Sudan offers a good example of this: We don't want to go there, and neither does China in a security sense (although it is inevitably being forced to), but as long as China's investments continue generating a boom in parts of the country, our liability is somewhat reduced. Not a great system, but it beats having no economic connectivity whatsoever.

The trick for the United States is to figure out how to harness China's expanding economic presence across the Gap in a more explicit good cop, bad cop routine. Because what we've got right now is (1) a seemingly unprincipled Leviathan that, not caring in any way whatsoever about global law, roams the planet at will, shooting up bad neighborhoods and leaving them perhaps more safe but definitely less connected than it found them, and (2) a seemingly unprincipled SysAdmin that, not caring whatsoever about human rights, roams the planet at will, building up infrastructure in bad neighborhoods and leaving them definitely more connected but perhaps more corrupt than it found them.

Put these two characters together and we've got ourselves a full-service superpower far more capable of shrinking the Gap.

THE INESCAPABLE REALIGNMENT:
REBRANDING A TEAM OF RIVALS

For years I have said, in response to questions about the differences in working with the executive branch during the Clinton and the George W. Bush eras, that each administration fielded strong but unbalanced teams—Clinton doing better on economics and Bush better on security. Clinton ignored a lot of global security while helping to spread globalization with a speed that can legitimately be described as radical/reckless, and Bush is rightly accused of just the opposite. If we put these two strengths together, we'll end up with the foreign policy this country needs: clearly focused on expanding the global economy but aggressive in addressing the security situations that naturally arise as a result. As the two administrations have amply demonstrated, there is little use in getting out way ahead on one element and hoping the other will catch up in its own time. The results in each instance are simply too destabilizing.

But just as clearly, it seems to me, the time has passed when America can, by itself, account for such balance on an international scale. We need, then, to build a team of rivals who can cover our weaknesses as we cover theirs. When Doris Kearns Goodwin described the personal skills that Abraham Lincoln brought to the presidency in 1861, she captured much of what's missing in American grand strategy today:

> This, then, is a story of Lincoln's political genius revealed through his extraordinary array of personal qualities that enabled him to form friendships with men who had previously opposed him; to repair injured feelings that, left untended, might have escalated into permanent hostility; to assume responsibility for the failures of subordinates; to share credit with ease; and to learn from mistakes. . . . His success in dealing with the strong egos of the men in his cabinet suggests that in the hands of a truly great politician the qualities we generally associated with decency and morality—kindness, sensitivity, compassion, honesty, and empathy—can also be impressive political resources.

If I were to put America's recent grand strategy on the couch, I could come up with no better diagnosis or prescription. We don't need primacy to prove our importance or secure our future; that perceived need has been overtaken by the success we've experienced in spreading our American System–cum–globalization around the planet. But we do face the great possibility that this house will once again be divided against itself, primarily because we have been unable to deal with countries that have previously opposed us, sensing in their lack of political similarity (and by extension their diplomacy) an intention to oppose us on security, when a more empathetic reading of today's highly competitive economic landscape yields a less harsh judgment of their motives. Indeed, if we were truly honest with ourselves, we would see ourselves—younger, more desperate, more ambitious—in these emerging powers and put aside our ego to accommodate theirs. In that sense, we don't need to feel their pain but recognize their ambition.

Again, some will say we must stick with those friends we know—to wit, Robert Kagan's "league of democracies" argument, which inadvertently dismisses his previous claim that Europe and America see the world differently. But frankly, we'll be waiting for those Godots forever. By rescuing Germany and Japan following WWII and remaking them in our image, we created friends out of enemies, building lasting alliances in the process. But we also freed Europe and Industrialized Asia to evolve in ways both wonderful and alien to our thinking, and detrimental to our global responsibilities. Trying to turn back the clock on these allies will be a fruitless effort, especially since the regional integration tasks they—and only they—must address are intimidating, whether it's Europe's need to reach out to Muslims both at home and around the Mediterranean littoral, or Industrialized Asia's task of shaping a regional security environment that, for the first time in history, must accommodate both a strong Japan *and* a strong China. America has long engaged regions diplomatically by focusing our attention on lesser powers made nervous by larger neighbors. Now we need to focus on emerging powers made nervous by a global order they feel no longer addresses their core concerns. We need to make them co-drivers in this globalization process, and not merely keep them passengers. We need to expand our definition of "team" to accommodate these obvious economic rivals.

So it's not a "league of democracies" that's called for right now but a league of capitalist powers committed to making capitalism, expressed in the American System–cum–globalization, truly and finally workable on a worldwide stage. Having achieved the most difficult part, or waiting out all serious opponents to markets, we now need to make global markets work in a way that keeps them reasonably open to all comers and tolerant of the catch-up strategies many states must employ to protect themselves and their populations in this flat-world competitive landscape.

I see five main reasons why we need to build this team of rivals.

The first is the most obvious: Each time the West squares off against a rogue, we find many of these emerging powers sitting on the wrong side of the negotiating table. Whether it's Iran, Venezuela, North Korea, Myanmar, Zimbabwe, Sudan, or Uzbekistan, it seems that whenever we run into behavior we'd rather not tolerate, there stand several rising powers whose empathy for such tactics seems to know no bounds, even as they themselves, in their growing success, realize their own need to move beyond such behaviors. As such, these great powers can do more for us than simply obstruct our instinct to punish, because serving as back-channel conduits for negotiations simply isn't enough anymore. They must, over time, step into serious mentoring roles that the United States, operating in its "bad cop" Leviathan guise, often cannot and should not embrace. We need to find suitable "Nixons" to journey to all the would-be "Chinas" out there.

Second, these rising pillars give off all the signs of being the right people at the right time. Nayan Chanda's history of globalization throughout the ages, *Bound Together*, provides us the four basic characters in search of an author for their implied grand strategy of spreading globalization: "traders" in the form of financial markets and chain-building enterprises, "adventurers" in the form of bottom-of-the-pyramid-serving firms and resource-capturing multinationals, "preachers" in the form of nongovernmental organizations and private-voluntary organizations, and "warriors" in the form of peacekeepers and private security corporations. In each instance, we're seeing New Core pillars—slowly but surely—step to the forefront of these activities, often in ways that make us uncomfortable but must be inevitably harnessed. Whether it's an Indian industrialist who wants to build and market cheap cars throughout the Gap, or Russia's nuclear industry planning to build a reactor in every regional hot spot, or South Korean missionaries entering today's version of the lion's den, or the People's Liberation Army contradicting the very promise of its name by increasingly playing bodyguard to China's overseas investments, these are profound connecting forces that cannot and will not be denied.

Third, in many instances inside the Gap, these emerging pillars are superseding, as a result of their burgeoning requirements for resources and markets, the role of the West's preferred international financial institutions, such as the IMF and the World Bank. China's soft-loan foreign aid is already eclipsing the World Bank's portfolio in places like Southeast Asia and sub-Saharan Africa and has become highly competitive with U.S. foreign aid even in Latin America—our strategic backyard. As economist Adam Lerrick recently pointed out, "Nations moving up the economic ladder are weakening the [World Bank's] hold." China, Brazil, India, and Russia are funding infrastructure for even the poorest countries, to lock in access to raw materials and export markets. China alone will send $25 billion to Africa over the next three years, 50 percent more than the funds coming from the bank. Bank staffers label these latest lenders "rogue creditors." I call them "adventure capitalists," willing to go where no reputable banker has gone before. But guess what? That's how frontiers are settled. You want it done fast, the way the American West was integrated? Well, you're going to need a lot of "edge" players, or firms willing to take risks others will not, playing by the rules of rough-and-ready capitalism, rules that mature players dare not embrace.

Fourth, all these rising players are thinking—right now—about what it means to become a world power, or in Russia's case, to return to world power. As *Financial Times* Washington bureau chief Edward Luce writes of India, "In recent years it has become commonplace to talk of the country as being on the verge of superpower status." Now is the time for the United States to influence such discussions by making explicit how our grand strategy complements the countries' own. A while back I had the opportunity to have dinner in Beijing with the high-ranking foreign policy expert who produced China Central Television's twelve-part documentary series exploring the history of nine nations that had previously risen to world-power status. His argument was simple: China can no longer ignore the path it's currently taking and must address, on both an elite and a societal level, what it means to be a major world power. Naturally, this official, a longtime observer of America, was most concerned with how Washington would view this emerging debate. Deng had long counseled that China must hide its ambitions so as to avoid triggering a balancing response from others. But that day has passed for China, as it now passes for India, Russia, Brazil, and others. Engaging these governments while their grand strategies are still in their formative phase gives us an opportunity to shape them instead of hedge against them.

Finally, most of these rising powers have militaries that are hopelessly trapped in strategically myopic mindsets that limit their development. China's PLA obsesses primarily over Taiwan. India's military focuses unduly on Pakistan (and vice versa). Russia's strategic vision does not extend beyond its so-called near abroad of Central Asia and the Caucasus. South Korea's military has but one mission: manage North Korea's inevitable collapse. None of these nations can currently step up to the plate, but all will be forced to in coming years. Before long, we'll need them all punching *at* their natural weight.

How did America rebrand its military? We picked our initial targets carefully, like the faltering Spanish in the 1890s, and we waited until we had sufficient naval power-projection capability before we took them on. In the nation-building that ensued (Cuba, Philippines), we learned many hard lessons but stuck with it, moving far up the learning curve on counterinsurgency operations. When Europe went to war in 1914, we bided our time, waiting to see how things would unfold and picking our moment for decisive entry. The end result was stunning: In about four decades we went from nobody to a world military power that could not be ignored, only to thereupon walk away from that role and subsequently be forced to pick it up again—and permanently so—following WWII. Rising powers like India and China don't have four decades to elevate their game, not with their rising dependence on foreign energy sources (and, soon enough, overseas food sources). That's why we need to encourage their rebranding as quickly as possible, so their militaries can likewise access future regional crises without their appearance adding to the tension. They need to become an accepted global brand, just like the U.S. Marines.

Yes, many American national security experts will decry this suggestion as naïve or premature, stating that we must "hedge our bets" in the meantime. But the "meantime" is a lot shorter, in grand strategic terms, than most of them realize. Globalization is rushing into regions previously held off-line from its connectivity, like the Middle East, sub-Saharan Africa, and Central Asia, none of which has the regional security schemes necessary for in-region pillars to manage the inevitable security issues, much less for outside powers to readily access the resulting crises in anything but the most haphazard manner.

We all saw how long it took the "advanced" NATO to deal with the Balkans in the 1990s. Does anyone think the embryonic Shanghai Cooperation Organisation is anywhere near being up to the task of managing something similar in Central Asia, much less next door in Afghanistan/Pakistan, where NATO's identity as an extra-regional force is figuratively coming apart at the seams? When Turkey responds to Russia's invasion of Georgia with a call for a Caucasus Union, Ankara is instinctively reaching for such a rule-setting great-power venue. As for the Middle East, the United States is unable to forge any sort of regional security dialogue, and in Africa, the African Union displays its weakness with every uncredible response it undertakes (e.g., Sudan, Somalia). As one Army War College professor, Colonel Joseph Núñez, has argued, "One NATO is not enough." Indeed, there should be one that corresponds to every American regional combatant command (Latin America, Europe, Middle East, Africa, East Asia), meaning we're at least four short and probably could use two more beyond that (South Asia, Central Asia).

How can we trust these emerging great powers to do the right thing? First, by expecting them to be exactly who they are. Don't expect the Chinese to be anything but Chinese, or the Russians to be anything but Russian, or the Indians to be anything but Indians. Assuming identity of interests, much less world outlooks, simply because such countries join an American-engineered coalition is unrealistic in the extreme. Why? Because there is no reason for any of them to expect the Americans are going to be anything but American—through and through.

But here's the main reason we can trust them over time: The West's "war" against radical Islam is a war of discipline, not survival. There is zero chance that the West will be overcome in this conflict. Indeed, the far more likely outcome is that the Islamic Middle East will devolve into complete and total crisis. However, while radical Islam's global insurgency cannot derail the already rich West, it can cause enough turbulence in the global economy (e.g., a profound disruption of oil production) to effectively stall globalization's advance. In that case, most if not all of the New Core economies face the prospect of persistent decline, leading to fractious domestic political instability. For these states, this long war against radical extremism is a war of survival. Torch globalization tomorrow and

America remains a rich country. So do Europe and Japan. But Russia? China? India? Brazil? These and other emerging economies would be devastated, perhaps derailed as functioning great powers for the foreseeable future.

The longer America insists on holding on to twentieth-century enemies, the harder time we'll have in dealing with twenty-first-century threats and challenges—our implied grand strategy falling increasingly out of sync with the dynamics of this globalization era. Our logical "team of rivals" is staring us in the face, and once assembled, there's no question that our oldest friends will come along for the ride as best they can muster. This isn't about making it a fair contest but about putting together a team that robs our enemies of the opportunity to divide us and, by doing so, delaying the "conquering" that must inevitably happen, not by force but by something far more transformative—the globalization process that sprang naturally from our American System.

THE BETTER NORMAL:
THE SERVICE-ORIENTED ALLIANCE

Those who wage war adapt their strategies to new domains (e.g., terrain or "playing fields") as they are presented throughout history. For example, technological advance created the domain we call the Internet. That domain naturally evolves into a venue for warfare—cyberwar or information operations. As these domains multiply, form follows function: army is complemented by navy, then amphibious forces (Marines), then air forces, and so on. Each added domain allows for new combinations that, in turn, open up avenues for restructuring the force and rethinking its operational ethos. The rise of information technology had, and is continuing to have, such an effect on U.S. military forces, with advocates of "network-centric warfare" arguing that our forces are structured for industrial-era war when they should be optimized for information-age operations. First-generation advocates of such change within any field typically meet huge resistance, for what they propose amounts to grafting new technologies onto old platforms. This resistance ends when subsequent generations emerge: generations that have grown up *inside* this new reality and see its potential in full.

A good example can be seen in architecture in the twentieth century. For ages, humans basically built "crustaceans," or buildings whose structural strength was maintained on the outside. Once forged metals became strong enough to serve as an internal skeleton, the technology of architecture shifted from "crustacean" to "vertebrate." Not surprisingly, the mindset of architects did not keep pace, and so the first skyscrapers to rise up looked very much like the old buildings that previously had been capped at lower heights. It took a new generation of architects to emerge and realize that the shape of buildings could be radically altered to take advantage of these material advances.

As a result of the continuing information revolution, a generation of businessmen and entrepreneurs has arisen to recast the nature of companies. Whereas business has spent the last several decades adapting information technology to existing business structures, now we see business structures adapting themselves to information technology. Service-oriented architecture, or SOA, refers to an architectural design style for creating business services that are independent, reusable, and interoperable, meaning they can be reconfigured at far lower cost than canned software packages and hardwired applications. By adding this interoperable domain on "top" of existing technology platforms and databases, SOA creates a sort of universal translator that allows any portion of a company to interact seamlessly with another portion, or even to outsource necessary functions to other companies altogether. What that means is that today a company can assume almost any distributed form imaginable, concentrating itself in one aspect (say, research and design) and farming out everything else to other firms, or spreading its company assets all over the world to access whatever mix of inputs makes it most efficient (raw materials *here*, technology design *there*, and so on). A simplistic way to express SOA's potential is to say, "If I can do damn near anything over the Internet, my company can assume almost any shape I want."

Being an economic determinist, I'll tell you that technology is shaping business and that business is driving globalization (i.e., integrating trade by disintegrating production), making globalization itself the ultimate service-oriented architecture. That emerging reality will alter politics the world over, making possible political structures no longer tied to territory or citizenship or even shared ethnic identities. We've seen this process unfold many times in the past. World religions, for example, rise in this manner, detaching themselves from land, culture, and race to spread beyond their origins. The most powerful religions, therefore, are the ones *anybody* can join.

The United States itself is the original political SOA. Who can belong to these United States? *Anybody who shows up and gains entry.* There are essentially no citizenship requirements other than mastering a few historical facts and pledging yourself to our relatively wide-open rule set designed to maximize individual economic freedom—basically the Golden Rule politicized (Pass no laws you wouldn't want to obey yourself). Ours is essentially a political structure adapted to individual "applications," otherwise known as citizens, whereas the vast majority of the rest of the world's governments essentially ask their citizens to adapt themselves to the existing political structure—the basic difference between common law and civil law. Compare that flexible design to countries where racial or religious background matters, and you'll spot our structural advantage right away: We can attract talent the world over, and that talent can expect to enjoy the fruits of its labor with minimal restrictions—the pursuit of happiness.

If we view modern globalization in this way, it's little wonder why the world associates it with Americanization, for the former suggests the latter's promise of individual economic empowerment leading to political empowerment. The trick for American grand strategy, however, comes in realizing the natural time lag between economic empowerment and political liberty. Because the United States began as a series of "greenfield operations" (new operations on virgin territory), pursued by those fleeing the lack of economic opportunity and (often) religious rights back home, our citizens' expectations for accompanying political liberty were high from the start. Indeed, in their impatience those expectations triggered our audacious and unprecedented political experiment. If the same were possible the world over, our grand strategy would be simple indeed. Since globalization now reformats some of the oldest civilizations in the world while rapidly penetrating its most unmodern societies, our sense of timing and sequence is of paramount importance—likewise our choice of allies.

Given that globalization is the ultimate service-oriented architecture, it behooves us not to remain wedded only to allies whose political structures match or emulate our own. In general, democracies do not wage war with discipline but rather wage crusades. If anything, the United States needs to surround itself with the most businesslike allies we can find, or those lacking any appreciable ideology save the advance of their economic interests and the resulting growth in national power. We need allies who appreciate our Leviathan power for what it is: not the extension of American empire but the protection of globalization's advancing networks, networks that open doors primarily for *their* market-making opportunities, as it's the economies of rising great powers that gravitate naturally toward bottom-of-the-pyramid salesmanship. I'm not looking to saddle these rising powers with the SysAdmin role of "cleaning up our messes" but to present them with the opportunity to push the envelope of their existing integration efforts while asking them to pay up front for the privilege of early entry.

Again, some readers will bristle at such language. Imagining a conquering international army subduing recalcitrant Gap societies, and pricing out America's botched efforts in Iraq at $3 trillion (the most purposefully expansive, extrapolated tally), they will count up my Gap nations, and assuming all require invasion, will affix a fantastic sum total to this vision. Such calculations are complete nonsense, of course, extrapolating the worst possible execution to date to encompass all potential future cooperation on this score. If that's your definition of progress, then you're wholly out of sync with world history—not to mention human evolution.

The reality is that most of the Gap will be integrated with little to no mass violence, and costs will be borne overwhelmingly by the private sector. This is the history of globalization to date, and assuming any other path requires spurious logic typically rooted in cataclysmic visions—never in shortage—of impending holocausts and Armageddons. What I'm describing here is the Core's collective package—"architected" by services rendered and not according to political ideology or form—for those relatively small number of Gap situations where local friction, if allowed, could well overwhelm globalization's force.

This is not a vision for reformatting cultures that refuse connectivity of their own accord, but history says these tend to be small communities of religious fundamentalists who demand disconnectedness from others as part of their faith. We have these small communities scattered across America, and their presence is easily accommodated. No, this vision speaks to countries in which elites dominate the economy and restrict, largely to preserve their privileged wealth, the masses' ability to connect to the outside world. In countries where the sheer absence of connectivity is the key block, then we're talking the usual constructs of economic aid and targeted private-sector development. In countries where the lack of connectivity is directly linked to the absence of security or the rule of law, then we're talking something in between. But my main point remains: The Leviathan is a big stick rarely employed, even as the SysAdmin function (more civilian than military, more private-sector-funded than public-aid-dominated) will enjoy near-constant use—or better said, will meet near-constant demand for the next two to three decades.

In recruiting those powers currently better suited to the nation-building/economy-connecting role, America does nothing more than rebuild its own tarnished brand by buying start-ups as they appear on the scene—our Leviathan/big-firm approach improved by their SysAdmin/entrepreneurial spirit. In this way, when the charge is leveled that "integrating Africa to the global economy at American prices will bankrupt us all," we can remind critics that Africa's development models are logically located in Asia rather than in North America. Africa will be a knockoff of India, which is a knockoff of China, which is a knockoff of South Korea, which is a knockoff of Singapore, which is a knockoff of Japan, which a half-century ago was developed by us as a knockoff of the United States. Call it globalization's "six degrees of replication."

I'm not going to pretend that I can game this process out to the *nth* degree, but I will suggest the following:

1. America needs to increase dramatically our military-to-military cooperation with all such New Core pillars, especially targeting China, India, Russia, and Brazil—the so-called BRIC quartet—while reaching out aggressively to what Wall Street is now dubbing

the N11 (Next 11): Bangladesh, Egypt, Indonesia (G20 member), Iran, Mexico (G20), Nigeria, Pakistan, Philippines, South Korea (G20), Turkey (G20), and Vietnam.

2. America should be in the business of encouraging security cooperation among any combination of these states—including, most pointedly, the Shanghai Cooperation Organisation, to which America must reach out diplomatically, economically, and militarily. (And let's be clear, when we recently asked for observer status and were turned down, it wasn't America that was rejected but the Bush administration.)

3. In the cases of Central Command (Middle East and Central Asia), Southern Command (Latin American), and the new Africa Command, the United States should aggressively seek out military cooperation with these countries inside the associated regions.

4. To the extent possible, top-level articulation and execution of this American grand strategy should be concentrated at the G8 and G20 great-power forums, with America's number-one task being the expansion of the G8 (meeting at the level of heads of state), including the remaining twelve members (now currently meeting at only the ministerial level), and its number-two task being the expansion of the G20 vision to include security matters in a manner that integrates that discussion with global economic development. And no, it doesn't make sense to toss Russia out of the G8 over Georgia, any more than it would have been justified for other great powers to demand America's removal over Abu Ghraib. When building a world order, you want to keep it easy to join and hard to be tossed out.

5. Six obvious foci for this assembled "team of rivals" are (1) new regulatory oversight of intermarket financial flows; (2) energy, already proposed by China regarding the exploration, production, and protection of new reserves; (3) food, the "oil" of the future

as production patterns change thanks to . . . (4) global warming, which will stress Gap nations by far the most; (5) communicable diseases (ditto); and (6) the security of seaborne commercial traffic, where progress is already being made (more on that in a bit).

America needs to approach this grand strategy with great humility, and by that I mean we need to make sure others get the credit more than we do. Anything less subtle than that and we'll end up creating too much cultural friction with populations whose demand for national pride is rising dramatically. Besides, this approach has the benefit of truthfulness, because globalization will increasingly be dominated by Eastern and Southern cultural influences, the same way several of the world's major religions are currently being tilted in this manner. Accepting such outcomes on a global basis is no harder than what Americans have done instinctively at home across the decades of our society's constant evolution.

In sum, the diplomatic realignment I present here is not an accommodation of America's growing weakness but rather the acceptance of other powers' growing strength. As they have achieved this strength by rising within our liberal trade order, we must process this success with at least as much equanimity as past American grand strategic thinkers applied to previous failures to project our American System abroad.

And no, accepting this pathway does not constitute admission of a "post-American world," in Fareed Zakaria's analysis. It simply marks the accession of many "pre-American" powers into the American System–cum–globalization. No careful observer of America's historical strength in innovative and efficient rule-making can casually dismiss our capacity to further evolve globalization through the biological revolutions currently just beginning to emerge in this century. Mastering our past accomplishments doesn't make rising great powers our superiors but merely our fellow travelers. As always, owning the future is all about shaping the next set of rules in industries not yet discovered, something that requires a huge tolerance for economic—and therefore political—risk. In that competition, I vastly prefer America's chances to those of any other great power on this planet.

As long as we remain the global economy's eminent risk-takers, *there will never be a post-American world*. Just a post-Caucasian one.

Of his cabinet filled with past political rivals, President Lincoln was warned, "They will eat you up."

To this Lincoln replied, "They will be just as likely to eat each other up."

Six

THE SECURITY REALIGNMENT
Rediscovering Diplomacy, Defense,
and Development

A vociferous bureaucratic battle will occur across the first two years of this new administration, one that will greatly determine our military's future capabilities in this long war against violent extremism. On one side will be pitted the big-war crowd (mostly *air-sea* forces), with its emphasis on "resetting" the force following the inevitable drawdown in Iraq. On the other side will stand—ironically enough—those forces (mostly *ground* forces) slated to benefit maximally from any such "healing period." The reset argument rests on one very conspicuous assumption: Iraq was a one-off, not to be repeated and certainly no harbinger of future conflicts. It was, in effect, a second Vietnam, an asymmetrical war that could not be effectively won using conventional military power. To actually succeed in such warfare, you have to make our force increasingly symmetrical to the enemies we face in insurgencies, meaning more focused on generating security, winning hearts and minds, training up foreign militaries, and encouraging economic development. Adapting the U.S. military to these tasks, goes this line of thinking, will thus ruin it for great-power war, something it must remain optimized to wage lest America invite such conflict in decades ahead.

In effect, the big-war crowd asks us to do one of two things: either abandon our historic role as globalization's bodyguard right at the apogee of our system's expansion around the planet, thus ceding leadership to rising great powers in what would inevitably become a decidedly less American and therefore less safe world; or continue trading off hypothetical future casualties from big-war scenarios against current actual casualties from small-war operations, suffering far more of the latter to prevent the possibility of the former. I don't believe our military gets to make that first call; it's simply beyond their pay grade in our civilian-controlled national security establishment. As for the second option, or basically continuing to lowball our SysAdmin effort while overfeeding the Leviathan, I find that both strategically unsound and morally indefensible. As we currently outspend the rest of the planet on defense, we should easily be able to hedge against conventional military threats from other great powers, and as for nuclear war, nothing has changed in that realm besides our provocative insistence on pursuing missile defense in regions neighboring Russia and China.

In the end, the bureaucratic push to reset the force masks the warrior's nostalgia for the simpler wars of the past and industry's greed for the superexpensive weapons systems and platforms associated with such top-line, symmetrical conflicts. It likewise reflects the complete lack of understanding of today's global economics within America's national security community, which casually dreams up fantastic warfighting scenarios that bleed plausibility with each passing year of globalization's advance. Notwithstanding simplistic analogies to pre–World War I Europe's levels of economic integration, the essential truth remains: Nuclear weapons killed great-power war. That means any future resource wars, however implausible, would nonetheless involve our enemies' employing asymmetrical forms of resistance, such as proxy wars. Indeed, if Iraq teaches the world anything, it's that the American military cannot be resisted symmetrically but can be bled asymmetrically.

Listen to Marine Corps general James Mattis, himself a veteran of multiple command tours in Iraq and Afghanistan, decry, already in late 2005, the strategic mindset that suggests:

"Let's hold our breath and get through this, then we get back to proper soldiering by planning for China twenty years from now."

Fuck that. If we fight China in the future, we will also find IEDs and people using the Internet. If we go to Pyongyang and we're fighting there six months from now against a mechanized unit, one hundred thousand Special Forces would be running around doing what they're doing to our rear area now. So guess what? This is the best training ground in the world. For the German troops it was Spain, right? Well, Iraq is ours.

Iraq is ours. Get used to hearing that, because that's the strategic outlook of the generation of Army and Marine Corps officers already forged by the first seven years of this long war against violent extremists. It is not your father's military, because Iraq is not Vietnam.

THE UNDENIABLE TRAJECTORY:
THE MISEDUCATION OF COLIN POWELL

George Kennan, father of America's Cold War grand strategy of containment, spent a year as academic administrator at the National War College in Washington, D.C., following World War II, and the experience unnerved him. The mindset of the officers struck him as wholly incongruous with the challenges of the Cold War that lay ahead—a decades-long war of discipline. As he put it:

> The precedents of our Civil War, of the war with Spain, and of our participation in the two world wars of this century, had created not only in the minds of our soldiers and sailors but in the minds of many of our people an unspoken assumption that the normal objective of warfare was the total destruction of the enemy's ability and will to resist and his unconditional capitulation. The rest, it was always assumed, was easy. This sort of victory placed you in the position to command total obedience on the part of the defeated adversary; it thus opened the way to the unhindered realization of your political objectives, whatever they might be.

The American military has struggled mightily with this mindset ever since, believing that if enough firepower can be employed and sufficient troops put in the field, "real" victory is always at hand. It is the purest expression of an outlook that I've spent my entire career combating: war viewed solely within the context of war.

American military history can be divided into three basic periods since the end of World War II. First there was a three-decade period (1946–75) in which we struggled with the reality of limited war, starting in Korea, and then ultimately came to reject its premise following our failures in Vietnam, despite promising evolutions in the direction of real answers to real problems (the so-called CORDS [Civil Operations, Revolutionary Development Support] program there served as precursor to the Provincial Reconstruction Teams in both Afghanistan and Iraq). Then we spent another three-decade period (1976–2005) retreating—as far as possible—from the Vietnam experience. We professionalized the force (ending the draft) and reembraced an "overwhelming-force" mindset now tailored to smaller wars and interventions, thus accepting the concept of limited war but addressing it through the familiar annihilation-style approach described by Kennan. The third and current transitional period began years into the occupations of Afghanistan and Iraq. In this time frame the Army and Marines are once again moving toward understanding how best to address the challenges of limited war (i.e., effectively placing war within the context of everything else), while the Air Force and Navy continue to straddle these new challenges and their need to justify force-structure requirements with big-war scenarios. If we set aside the larger focus on global war with the Soviets during the Cold War, the more practical question in each historical period remains the same: Are small wars truly different or are they merely a shrunken version of big wars, and do they thus require the same annihilation mentality?

The American military's fix after Vietnam was to say, "A war is a war is a war," and let it go at that. Our military would be used to win wars and nothing else. A critical part of what would become the Reagan Doctrine was that truly limited wars would be effectively outsourced to local "freedom fighters." In assuming this mindset, our military grew distant from its frontier roots and the people and economic activity it once protected on those frontiers. War became detached from society, as did warriors who, in their professional standing, eventually concentrated themselves and their kin in geographic enclaves along America's southern coastlines.

Children followed parents into service, just as in many other professions. A soldier was a soldier until the day he died, a life spent defending the American System but likewise spent apart, because this force was used "over there" to keep bad things "over there." As soon as threats were vanquished, this fearsome beast returned home as quickly as possible and became invisible once again, distributed across its network of military reservations. Done right, our military could remain totally apolitical and robotlike in its efficiency, admired in the abstract but—for the vast majority of Americans—never encountered face-to-face, much like the distant interventions these forces undertook and the rest of us watched on TV.

The terrorist attacks of 9/11 destroyed this artificial wall between the military and society. Suddenly, the military was back in frontier mode— back in "Injun country." The scale was different, but the sense of immediate threat and the need for immediate response were very familiar—almost instinctive. We had been here before and we knew what needed to be done. Wild West imagery resurfaced, along with a dead-or-alive demand for frontier justice. Laws would be put aside for a while, and vengeance would be ours.

The American military that stepped into this maelstrom was *not* a military prepared for a return to frontier-integrating wars—anything but. It was a military of overwhelming force applied to achieve overwhelming victories. There was no "everything else," and if there was, then *somebody else* would have to do it, because that was not what *this* soldier had signed up for and it was certainly not the scenario for which *this* military had long been buying equipment and training. The military needed for post-victory nation-building was *not* the force a generation of senior officers had spent their entire careers reconstructing after the disaster of Vietnam. As far as they were concerned, this was *not* going to be another Lebanon where Marines would be truck-bombed, or another Somalia where U.S. forces would be lured into unwinnable urban shoot-outs, or even another Balkans babysitting job where NATO troops wasted their time DABing ("driving around Bosnia") and doing nothing warriorlike. This war would be fought much like the first Iraq war, where this generation of senior officers felt its first true vindication as professional warriors following Vietnam.

As for what came next, well, that would be easy.

This was the miseducation of an entire generation of military officers, exemplified by everyone's favorite unerring hero, Colin Powell, who, like so many of his contemporaries, deserves our nation's gratitude for rebuilding the U.S. military after Vietnam even if the price was a leadership largely unprepared for what came next—the rough-and-tumble politics of wars fought within the context of everything else. The truth is, most of that generation, like Powell, had retired and were out of the uniform come 9/11. Running the military at that moment was a cohort of their protégés, most of whom thought much the way they did, but some of whom had come to realize that the world had changed and that the future was going to look a whole lot more like Bosnia than the battle for Beijing. Just below that senior leadership was an entirely different generation of officers who came of rank completely in the post-Vietnam military and who had cut their teeth—senior command–wise—in the limited wars and interventions of the 1990s. Instead of viewing the first Iraq war as sheer validation, they saw it as an aberration—a glorious blast from the past that future, smarter opponents wouldn't allow us to repeat in full.

What happened after 9/11 was almost a perfect generational storm: Highly partisan Republican conservatives raised on Reagan's reconstruction of the presidency combined with apolitical senior officers raised on the Powell generation's reconstruction of the military, with only those "soft-on-defense," minority Democrats standing in their way. The choice of instruments was preordained: a "shock and awe" military strike that would trigger—almost magically on its own—a complete political transformation of the Middle East. Little thought would be given to the postwar, because little thought was needed—or so the neocons assumed in their hubris. Dissenting voices were quelled or cowed, and if the military presumed that their icon of "overwhelming force," Colin Powell, would look out for their interests from his new perch as secretary of state, they were sorely disappointed, because, as biographer Karen DeYoung noted, "Powell had not arrived at high office with plans to remake the world; as he himself often pointed out, he was not a grand strategist."

Too bad, because absent a George Marshall–like grand strategist in that seat, the Pentagon's neocons, consistently shielded from reality by the office of Vice President Dick Cheney, ran wild in their exceedingly narrow dreams of transformational warfare. In an age in which globalization's economic forces are reshaping the planet, triggering security threats and political movements galore, these grand tacticians planned to remake—overnight—the world's most rigidly traditional civilization through the use of military force and, as it turned out, military force *alone*. As much as Powell knew the limits of that force, he was unable to dissuade the Bush administration from recklessly employing it, in large part because he—just like the neocons—had neither real-world experience nor practical vision of global change *beyond* military force. It wasn't the lack of local knowledge that doomed this daring enterprise, but the complete lack of any real understanding of the larger economic forces at work in globalization's creeping embrace of the region, as well as of the social blowback that penetration was creating. Instead, the entire equation was reduced to *terrorists* + *dictators* = *WMD*, three entities seemingly subject to the application of military force.

Colin Powell, good soldier that he was, registered his concerns and made his arguments within the administration, and ultimately served as its unwitting point man to win over a reluctant UN Security Council, armed with deeply flawed intelligence about Iraq's alleged attempts to generate weapons of mass destruction and possibly transfer them to transnational terrorists.

Of Vietnam, Colin Powell had once said that "American soldiers answered the call in a war so poorly conceived, conducted and explained by their country's leaders." They would do so again in Iraq in the spring of 2003, but this time the lessons learned inside the military would be different *primarily* because the senior officers who arose in this long war had previously undergone a very different education from the one Powell and his generation had received in Vietnam.

THE AMERICAN SYSTEM PERTURBED: THE LOST YEAR IN IRAQ

The "lost year" in Iraq is defined by most observers as the period running from early May 2003, following President Bush's declaration of "mission accomplished," through the explosion of insurgency violence in Fallujah the following April, following the ambush and gruesome killing of four armed Blackwater contractors operating there. As many experts have argued, none of this was inevitable. The U.S.-dominated Coalition Provisional Authority (CPA), run by Ambassador Paul Bremer (a former assistant to Henry Kissinger), made numerous significant mistakes, including: the immediate disbanding of the Iraqi army and police, thus denying the occupation force a significant source of social control; the expansive de-Baathification of top government and industry leaders (ditto); and the zeroing out of all Iraqi state-run enterprises' savings and debts, which essentially rewarded the most incompetent firms while punishing the most promising—not a great way to jump-start entrepreneurship. The CPA was also guilty of operating in relative isolation from the Iraqi people and their natural leaders (its marginalization of Shia religious leader Ayatollah Sistani and his concerns was stupendously dumb), the U.S. military in country, and even its own political overseers back in Washington, earning the telling sobriquet of "Versailles on the Tigris." Some military officers who interacted with the CPA believed it was so dysfunctional that the U.S. effort would have been more successful without it having been set up.

Back in Washington, the Pentagon's senior civilian leadership went out of its way to freeze out the State Department's postwar planning elements, a great number of which had spent the months leading up to the war generating a thirteen-volume, 2,500-page "Future of Iraq" study that recalled, in its assemblage of relevant facts and policy comprehensiveness (including consideration of the second- and third-order consequences of possible actions), the efforts of Woodrow Wilson's "Inquiry" group during World War I. Under Rumsfeld, the Pentagon likewise ignored numerous preinvasion war-gaming efforts—including those by the military itself—that predicted the vast majority of subsequent problems. None of what came next was a surprise, not even to Secretary Rumsfeld, who routinely wrote his own memos predicting a wide variety of problems, and whose staffers created reams of PowerPoint slides they believed to be far more detailed in their planning. But they weren't. As Thomas Ricks states in *Fiasco*, the resulting disaster "was made possible only through the intellectual acrobatics of simultaneously 'worst-casing' the threat presented by Iraq while 'best-casing' the subsequent cost and difficulty of occupying the country." The classic expression of this mistaken reasoning came in Deputy Secretary of Defense Paul Wolfowitz's stunning dismissal of his own military's estimate that it would actually take *more* troops to secure the country following the conflict than would be required to topple the regime during the war. Not only did this judgment contradict the very real nature of our military's transformation across the 1990s (i.e., underestimating its overmatch against a very weakened Iraqi military), it likewise ignored the extensive experience of U.S. peacekeeping force in the Balkans.

In retrospect, history was a good guide in both the war and the postwar. While Rumsfeld's "transformed" force toppled the regime with roughly half the troops that the Pentagon had used in Desert Storm to eject the Iraqi military from Kuwait and destroy it (240,000 to 250,000 compared with over half a million), it suffered similarly low casualties (139 dead compared with 148 in 1991, and 542 wounded compared with 467) across a similar length of time (a matter of weeks). Part of the invasion force's success came as a result of the Iraqi military's refusal to fight, as Saddam's war plans included the subsequent shift to insurgency tactics against a superior force, meaning one expert's famous prediction that the war would be a "cakewalk" was both accurate and irrelevant. Still, the transformed force performed as advertised, which only made the subsequent long summer pause of U.S. activities in Iraq all the more consequential. As Thomas Ricks argues, the speed of Rumsfeld's transformed force "didn't kill the enemy—it bypassed him." Because the U.S. military focused excessively on the capture of Baghdad, where, presumably, most of the regime's top leaders could be located and captured (the infamous "most wanted" deck of 52 cards), once that objective was taken it "seemed to fall asleep at the wheel."

It was during this summer lull that the tremendous internal political momentum created by Saddam's fall essentially disappeared in a flurry of uncontrolled looting, the disbanding of the government and military, and no clear sense among ordinary Iraqis about what would come next. Meanwhile, as our troops drew down somewhat over the summer of 2003, top commanders were swapped out, and the CPA replaced the original American-led reconstruction entity known as the Office of Reconstruction and Humanitarian Assistance, which never really got off the ground during its brief and troubled existence. As a result, U.S. reconstruction efforts, which were supremely hampered by the summer's looting, didn't really get serious until the fall of 2003, meaning the first half-year of the postwar was basically wasted in our slow transition from liberating force to occupying force. It was almost as if the entire U.S. military on the ground had found itself stunned to realize that it was going to be left holding the bag for the long run. As one soldier who fought in Operation Iraqi Freedom explained to American military historian and strategist Eliot Cohen:

> Well, you know, we went in, and we expected a fight; we got a fight. And then I always expected that I'd look over my shoulder, and there would be battalions of nation-builders from ORHA or someone from the CPA. I kept on looking around, and they didn't show up. Then I realized I'd have to be doing some of that.

As for the postwar, where over 95 percent of American casualties have since come, the Balkans again proved a useful guide. In the Bosnian peacekeeping operation, then Secretary of Defense William Perry used a simple formula to calculate American troop levels relative to the local population. A similar calculation, applied to Iraq, generated the estimate provided to Congress in the spring of 2003 by then Army Chief of Staff General Eric Shinseki, who had himself commanded troops in Bosnia. Shinseki's calculations indicated the United States should field a force in the range of 300,000 to 400,000 personnel, whereas the Pentagon under Rumsfeld had dreams of reducing the invasion force of roughly 240,000 troops to something as small as a 30,000-man occupying force within four months of "victory"! Such plans constituted a complete rejection of the Bosnia and Kosovo peacekeeping models, in which NATO collectively fielded between 20 and 25 troops per 1,000 local population and subsequently suffered virtually no casualties. In Haiti and Somalia we averaged closer to 3 or 4 soldiers per 1,000, with even fewer than that in Afghanistan. For most of the Iraq occupation, U.S. troops registered in the range of 6 or 7 troops per 1,000 local population. Adding in the Iraqi army gets the number up to about 14 per 1,000 by the end of 2006.

Ironically, when U.S. forces surged their numbers in early 2007 and began achieving some success in pacifying the environment, the total number of American-sponsored personnel in Iraq by the fall of that year had roughly achieved Shinseki's preferred target of boots on the ground, with approximately half the total coming in U.S. military troops (168,000) and the other half coming in the form of private-sector contractors (182,000). That's not to pretend that you can simply backfill civilians to achieve the same security effect. My point is this: We naturally ended up paying for the same footprint, given the population-size differential. So when you try to go cheap on government personnel, you simply end up paying high for similar bodies from the private sector. But either way, you're going to pay that piper.

Adding to the overall sloppiness of the postwar effort was the Bush administration's insistence that, as author Rajiv Chandrasekaran put it, "whatever could be outsourced was." This reflected the neocon view that America's participation in the NATO peacekeeping operations in the Balkans had dragged on for far too long and resulted in a dangerous tie-down of U.S. ground forces there, thus the desire to shift the postwar reconstruction dynamics as quickly as possible to private-sector entities. Ironically, the rush to draw down the uniformed presence only ended up extending the stay of the troops, as the deteriorating security situation kept private-sector investors and companies away for the most part, eventually growing so dangerous as to drive off many nongovernmental organizations and the United Nations itself. Over the longer haul, even our military allies began deserting us. Some of these wounds the U.S. military inflicted upon itself by engaging in a series of practices known to constitute poor counterinsurgency operations, such as overemphasizing killing and capturing of the enemy, concentrating forces in large bases, using regular troops in large-scale operations and focusing special operations forces on raids, and allowing relatively open borders. In sum, the more frantically the Bush administration worked to diminish the need for troops, the more it ended up foisting additional aspects of the postwar reconstruction on those very same troops.

The turning point in U.S. military operations in Iraq occurred *after* the "lost year" was allowed to unfold, in the summer of 2004. By this point, anger within the junior officer ranks was just beginning to appear in Internet chat rooms, but more important, a number of crucial milestones had been reached. First, Saddam Hussein had been captured in December

2003, and most of the remaining "deck of cards" had been accounted for. Second, the United States essentially gave up looking for evidence of WMD in Iraq in the spring of 2004. These two events recast the U.S. military's efforts somewhat, allowing for a stronger focus on training the new Iraqi army and police. Third, in a rush to declare "victory"—again prematurely—the Bush administration pressured Bremer's CPA into engineering the handover of political control to the interim Iraqi government in June, following the first national elections there and—more important— five months before the 2004 U.S. presidential elections. This transfer of power left the U.S. military the responsible U.S. government party in country, in tandem with the U.S. ambassador. That's when it really stopped being Bremer's show and started becoming the U.S. military's "war" to own. Fourth, a new wave of officers were beginning their second tours in Iraq, and this time they came armed with a far different set of expectations. Instead of arriving to wage war, they knew full well they'd be knee-deep in postwar stability-and-reconstruction operations, and prepared themselves and their troops better for this inevitability. Finally, some of the most experienced postwar American commanders and junior officers were starting to rotate back to the States, where their presence and new thinking were immediately felt at the major schoolhouses and training centers of the Army and Marine Corps. The students started teaching the instructors about counterinsurgency, and the instructors were listening.

While learning within the Bush administration proceeded at a glacial pace throughout the Iraq occupation, the same could not be said of the U.S. military. The problem, of course, was how long it took a new generation of experienced military commanders, tempered by the crucible of Iraq and Afghanistan, to convince the Bush administration that (1) a full-blown and self-sustaining insurgency had been allowed to erupt, and (2) a dramatically different and purposeful counterinsurgency strategy was needed to combat it. Why did this take so long? As soon as the Bush administration admitted there was a self-sustaining insurgency (something it did only after the 2004 elections), it effectively had to admit that it had bungled the postwar reconstruction and that Iraq's tentative steps toward democracy would not sap the insurgency's strength. But once it admitted that a long-term counterinsurgency strategy was required, it would also have to admit—in a decision that began with an ultra-secret White House "Iraq strategy review" in the summer of 2006—that there was no chance America could achieve anything close to a perceived "victory" in Iraq before the Bush administration came to a close. In the end, that admission of ground truth wouldn't be possible for the White House, as Bob Woodward noted in *The War Within*, until after the November 2006 elections eliminated the political costs associated with coming clean.

THE NEW RULES: FROM THE "MONKS OF WAR," A NEW COIN OF THE REALM

Presidents and secretaries of defense call the big shots, but it is the generals who turn the cranks—and suffer the consequences in terms of personnel lost. If the Bush White House had been slow to learn lessons, reluctant to admit mistakes, and incompetent at adapting to changing realities, those prosecuting the war, those living and dying it, had no such luxury. By the summer of 2004, the overwhelming consensus within the U.S. military was that Afghanistan and Iraq would not be ending anytime soon and that these conflicts would be the first of many in a long struggle that Central Command boss General John Abizaid, who took over from the Baghdad-conquering Tommy Franks in July 2003, had quietly taken to calling the "long war." The grim message was simple: The boys were never coming home.

This shift in grand strategic vision had huge implications for the U.S. military as a whole, but especially for the Army, which had long viewed war as an episodic, high-intensity event followed by a long period of peace, during which the force can recover and regenerate its strength for the next fight—the reset. The long war features no such downtime, nor opponents who array themselves as our Army has for the past century: frontline troops at the ready and reserve units at significantly lower states of readiness—especially in terms of equipment. In the long war, then, the Army faces a dramatically new requirement not unlike that long managed by the U.S. Navy: the ability to keep a significant portion of its force deployed overseas continuously, as opposed to simply garrisoned in places like South Korea or Germany (places to which families could accompany the troops). So when Army chief of staff General Pete Schoomaker took over in the summer of 2003 for Eric Shinseki (who was summarily pushed out by Rumsfeld for his comments on Iraq troop levels), he took Abizaid's concept of the long war to heart and soon set his service on the path of rapidly bringing the entire Army up to frontline status, a move that forced him to reconceive the Army completely as a fighting force.

The Army's active-duty divisions had for a century been structured like mini-armies unto themselves, full of all sorts of combat brigades and specialized support units. The only way to send over competently arrayed troops was to deploy entire divisions at a time, and that simply won't work in a long war. So Schoomaker made a decision—just as the invasion of Iraq was completed—to reformat the entire U.S. Army and its reserve components over the next several years, turning divisions into mere command units and "modularizing" the entire force so that each "brigade combat team" would soon be largely interchangeable with all others, allowing divisions to deploy overseas with mix-and-match brigades, all of which would be self-sustaining combat teams containing all the same supporting units that previously were aggregated only at the division level.

It's hard to overestimate the daring involved in restructuring the Army during significant overseas combat operations, and likewise the revolutionary impact of this historic change. Prior to World War I, the U.S. Army had been organized according to regiments of upward of 5,000 troops each. This was the essential format of the "Army of the West" during America's settling of its trans-Mississippi West, although most operations occurred at the level of far smaller companies (100 to 200 soldiers). In the buildup for World War I, those regiments had been rolled up into large 20,000-man divisions so as to be symmetrically arranged for the type of big-war combat that lay ahead. The U.S. Army kept that division structure through WWII and the Cold War but now was virtualizing it after roughly a century of use, returning to the smaller 4,000-to-5,000-man brigade combat teams that recalled the regiment-size U.S. cavalry of the nineteenth century—Injun Country–sized forces for a return to frontier-integrating wars.

As the war became the occupation, Schoomaker realized something else: The military processed lessons learned from combat experience at an excessively leisurely pace, given the new global security environment.

"Lessons-learned" commands would become a top priority, and three generals, one Marine and two Army, would be brought back from Iraq to teach soldiers what they needed to know to fight wars of the future. In the past, such lessons would prove valuable only to soldiers of the next war; this time, in this long war, casualties would not be marginal, so it would be the goal of these generals to learn these lessons and have them reflected in the training almost on a daily basis. Each of these three generals had already learned his own hard lessons in Iraq. Army general William Wallace conquered Baghdad but likewise oversaw its disastrous looting. David Petraeus worked the sheikhs well enough during his first tour but let a horrifically efficient insurgency build on his watch. Marine general James Mattis didn't lose a sailor or marine during his nation-building stint in the south, only to send a host of marines to their deaths in Fallujah. So all these lessons would be born of failure and all cost blood. As General Mattis likes to say, "Success is a poor teacher."

William "Scotty" Wallace returned from Iraq in the summer of 2003 and took over command of the Combined Arms Center at Fort Leavenworth, Kansas, where he systematized the process of feeding the Army's lessons learned from *ongoing* combat operations into its worldwide collection of training centers. The Army's decision to reform its lessons-learned analysis meant that the combat-training centers would immediately switch from war-gaming against a Soviet-style, tank-heavy "world-class opposition force" to something far more complex, or what the officers now call the Contemporary Operating Environment. Wallace wanted his training simulations to account for the local populations soldiers would encounter; thus role players were added to the training centers by the hundreds to approximate life in Iraqi villages, right down to the call for prayers five times a day.

When Lieutenant General James Mattis returned from Iraq in August 2004 to take over the Marine Corps Combat Development Command in Quantico, Virginia, he initiated a very similar overhaul of how the Marines were collecting and processing lessons learned, pushing his analysts to the point of interviewing wounded Marines right in their beds at Bethesda Naval Hospital, on occasion leading to changes in training that would show up at the Marines' Twentynine Palms combat training center within twenty-four hours. Quantico did have a center for lessons learned before Mattis arrived, but all the data flowed in and not much flowed out. Mattis wanted it flowing out like a river during flood season. If the Marine Corps Center for Lessons Learned learned it, the general wanted it on the unclassified, password-accessed website within hours. Soon after his arrival, close to 90 percent of what the MCCLL reported would appear on the unclassified Marine Corps web. Following his command at Quantico and a brief tour as commander of a Marine Expeditionary Force, Mattis earned his fourth star in late 2007, when President Bush appointed him to lead U.S. Joint Forces Command, the military's preeminent post for guiding the evolution of the future force.

In late 2005, Wallace was elevated to four-star commander of the Army's seniormost schoolhouse command, the Training and Doctrine Command at Fort Monroe, Virginia. His replacement at Leavenworth was arguably—even then—the Army general whose star was rising most rapidly on the basis of his performance in Iraq, Lieutenant General David Petraeus, who led the 101st Airborne Division in northern and central Iraq during the first difficult postwar year and then assumed leadership of the coalition effort to rebuild Iraq's security forces. With his Princeton Ph.D. in international relations and, by that time, already two and a half years in Iraq, Petraeus was the closest thing the Army had to its own Lawrence of Arabia, a comparison that's only grown since Malik Daoud ("King David," as many local Arabs call him) picked up his fourth star and took over command of all U.S. forces in Iraq in early 2007, directing the now-famous "surge" deep into 2008. Petraeus was thereupon tapped by the White House to replace Admiral Fallon as the boss of Central Command, giving him command over both Iraq and Afghanistan.

Mattis served with Wallace and had multiple career overlaps with Petraeus, both in the Pentagon and in Iraq. In the early years of this long war, these generals traded best practices and new technologies like next-door neighbors who've known one another for years, setting in motion a level of Army-Marine cooperation that was unprecedented. I was fortunate to witness this synergy in the fall of 2005, when Petraeus returned from Iraq and took over Leavenworth. The general, who e-mailed me one afternoon to say he was a reader of my weblog (confirming his reputation, much like Mattis, for a voracious and wide-ranging intake of analysis), thereupon invited me to address the student body of the Command and General Staff

College there (an honor I repeated in August 2008 to kick off the school year). Since that invitation came right on the heels of one from Mattis to address the student body of his Marine Corps University in Quantico, I took advantage of the resulting trips to interview both officers (along with Wallace) for a March 2006 *Esquire* article called "The Monks of War."

The timing of the piece couldn't have been better, because it was at the end of 2005 that the two of them, Petraeus and Mattis, had brought together "big-brain" officers from both services to generate what would eventually become the first-ever dual-designated Army/Marine Corps *Counterinsurgency Field Manual.* I distinctly remember my first impressions of the preliminary material, as presented to me in a brief by the study director, Conrad Crane, in November 2005, just a month before the writing team was assembled at Leavenworth. My notes were sprinkled repeatedly with the modifiers "radical" and "stunning," as I struggled to capture just how big a shift this new thinking represented, especially as it was emerging right on the heels of a new Pentagon directive (DoD Directive 3000.05, November 2005) that stated postwar planning for stability-and-reconstruction operations would now have to be pursued by combatant commands in equal measure to their warfighting plans.

At this point in my career, I had spent several years arguing, like some wacked-out John the Baptist in the desert, about the inevitability of a split between the first-half Leviathan force focused on big war and the second-half SysAdmin force focused on all the small but crucial stuff. So the sum total of these changes, coming in rapid fire across 2005, was like manna from heaven to me, including my first interactions with this host of "saviors" in the personages of Schoomaker, Wallace, Mattis, Petraeus, and Colonel John Nagl, whose seminal study of past counterinsurgency campaigns, *Counterinsurgency Lessons from Malaya and Vietnam: Learning to Eat Soup with a Knife,* seemed to channel British colonel T. H. Lawrence (of "Arabia" fame) with the same vigor as many of Petraeus's mantras about counterinsurgency done right. To no one's surprise, Nagl ended up being one of the field manual's primary authors, while much of Petraeus's idiosyncratic translation of Lawrence's "pillars of wisdom" made it into the text as the nine Zen-like "paradoxes of counterinsurgency" (for example, "Some of the best weapons for counterinsurgents do not shoot").

More than three years later it's still hard to overestimate what a paradigm shift all these changes cumulatively represent. Until the Spanish-American War at the end of the nineteenth century, the U.S. Army has been essentially a continental constabulary force that never left home, whereas the Marines were a marginal force with really no significant overseas nation-building/counterinsurgency experience. All that would change over the first half of the twentieth century, setting in motion the rise of the modern version of both services: a Leviathan-like Army and a Marine Corps used primarily for short-term power projection into regional crises. Now the long war was reformatting both services' operational profiles: sucking the Army into a constabulary role it had not embraced in over a century and returning the Marines to nation-building and counterinsurgency operations on a scale recalling their decades serving as "State Department troops" in the Caribbean basin in the early twentieth century. In both cases, we're really talking about rebranding the Army and Marine Corps back in the direction of an operational ethos neither has fully embraced for roughly a century. As such, the new counterinsurgency, or COIN, field manual, in the words of Harvard professor Sarah Sewall (writing in the book's introduction), "challenges much of what is holy about the American way of war." Indeed, as Sewall argues further, "those who fail to see the manual as radical probably don't understand it, or at least understand what it's up against."

What the new COIN field manual is up against—despite its obvious success in Iraq—is half a century of American grand strategic thinking that says our number-one goal as a superpower is to contain or—better yet—prevent the rise of other superpowers, but *not* to manage the global security environment per se. Indeed, much of the military's intransigence about embracing the strategic realities—as I define them—of the post–Cold War era stems from the belief that if America becomes too involved in such small-wars management of the global security order, it will see its forces devolve to the point of inviting the rise of a serious near-peer competitor whose military capability for big war will eventually put our own at unacceptable risk—the essence of the current reset debate, now animated by Russia's conventional crushing of Georgia's military. This is why, in my opinion, our Leviathan's need for the China/Taiwan scenario is ironically self-fulfilling: our military needs China's military to keep getting bigger on the basis of Taiwan, even though China's true strategic risks increasingly overlap with our own as a result of globalization's advance. But if the U.S. national security establishment were to admit that growing coincidence of strategic interests, it would risk losing its primary reason for delaying a deep embrace of the SysAdmin role of managing the global security environment, surrendering to the institutional momentum created by the new COIN field manual, DoD Directive 3000.05, and a host of other recent U.S. military adjustments to the ongoing long war. What do I mean by "deep embrace"? As always, it comes down to *what we buy* more than *how we use it.* Simplest definition? Again, starving the SysAdmin to continue overstuffing the Leviathan with high-tech weaponry and platforms, the vast majority of which will never be effectively exploited in the long war.

What this all says, in the end, is that the Bush administration, in its decisions to invade Afghanistan and Iraq, unwittingly pushed most of the U.S. military to evolve in a manner consistent with Franklin Roosevelt's preferred grand strategy of aggressively expanding American-style capitalism globally in the aftermath of World War II. In a perfect post-WWII "new world order," Soviet Russia would have offered little resistance to FDR's grand scheme. But that's what makes our current global environment so inviting: The clear absence of a competing superpower allows America to optimize its grand strategy, as well as the U.S. military, to this ambitious end—making globalization truly global as quickly as possible. In effect, today we are Theodore Roosevelt's big stick *plus* Franklin Roosevelt's grand vision *minus* Harry Truman's duty to hold off the Soviets. Right now we're living the dream: the power in place, the environment prepared, and nobody of consequence standing in our way. Indeed, on one level we can thank God for providing Osama bin Laden and al Qaeda to sharpen our focus somewhat and provide a measure of urgency.

That's why the most important question today concerning the long war is not "How do you view radical Islam?" but rather "How do you view authoritarian capitalism?" If America's grand strategy cannot move beyond China as its preferred force-optimizing threat (Russia's economic trajectory is far less impressive), it will so retard our military's much-needed evolution toward addressing the long war's many challenges as to make superpower rivalry with China inevitable.

I say again: To the extent America bungles the long war and thus puts globalization at risk, we buy ourselves inevitable conflict with China, presaging America's fall from superpower status.

THE NEW NORMAL: THE LONG (POST)WAR

The first thing Americans need to realize about what comes next is that we've done it plenty of times before, meaning most of our wars have been anything but crusades. As historian Max Boot argued in his book *The Savage Wars of Peace: Small Wars and the Rise of American Power,* there is nothing new to be found in undeclared wars or those without clear exit strategies, wars that were unpopular or lacked a "vital" national interest, much less wars that saw America meddle in the affairs of broken states in the manner of a social worker. The trick in all such interventions is to make sure we detach ourselves from the total-war mentality that democracies typically bring to large-scale conflicts. As soon as "in for a penny" becomes "in for a pound," we find ourselves destroying the village in order to save it. When generals like Petraeus and Mattis talk about those who "get it," this is what they mean: Doing no harm to the people comes before doing—even great—harm to the enemy. Success in small wars is measured by less overall violence, not your casualties relative to your enemy's. Once we lose sight of that larger political and economic context, there's no amount of high technology and firepower that can save us. Revolutionary wars are never won on battlefields but in the hearts and minds of the population. America won its revolution when it declared its independence in 1776; the war, which lasted until 1781, was just about convincing the British. Having said that, history tells us that most insurgencies fail because either local conditions improve or the central authority grants the locals sufficient autonomy. In short, there's more than one way to drain a swamp.

In terms of grand strategy, the trick with small wars is that you're forced to accept higher levels of tactical risk in order to reduce strategic risk. As Sewall argues in her introduction to the *Counterinsurgency Field Manual:* "Getting out and about among the population allows U.S. troops to gather information and more effectively destroy the insurgents. Exercising restraint in applying firepower means fewer enemies to attack your forces. Thus short-term losses can yield success more rapidly and efficiently." I would argue that this explanation constitutes, in a nutshell, the logic of my proposed grand strategy of making globalization truly global: By engaging the forces of disconnectedness inside the Gap, we expose ourselves to more short-term trouble than we'd otherwise have to face in isolation or withdrawal. But there's no more efficient way to achieve our ultimate security than to take advantage of globalization's currently rapid advance, allying us openly with its most prominent agents of change. Our trade-off is admittedly difficult: We sacrifice "force protection" (the safety of our troops) in order to reduce collateral damage. To me, this is the real American way of war, one that connects our actions to our innate spirituality and desire to avoid doing unto others what we would not accept from them. In this way, as Sewall notes, good COIN helps America's warriors find their way back to the Geneva Conventions in this long (post)war.

There is the danger that COIN, in its growing popularity, will suffer the same fate as network-centric warfare: Becoming synonymous with everything, it comes to signify nothing. Counterinsurgency alone will not defeat all terrorist threats or fix all failed states or come anywhere close to comprehensively shrinking the Gap. The dangers of "doctrinal miscegenation," as Sewall puts it, are real. The military loves rank, and so there's the immediate tendency with any popular answer to assume that everything that came before it can be tucked under its umbrella. Still, it's important that COIN does provide doctrinal "cover" for those activities previously relegated to only those operations that involve coalitions or the United Nations, such as nation-building, stability operations, and disaster relief. In that way, COIN provides military rationales that allow us to justify those uses of our forces as being immediately relevant to the larger grand strategy of shrinking the Gap, "draining the swamp," and what have you. All can now be linked to a military strategy that envisions global counterinsurgency operations against a global insurgency.

Again, if we didn't have al Qaeda, it would behoove us to invent it at this time in history, if only to save us from the strategic folly of self-fulfilling prophecies of rising great powers inevitably triggering global conflict. Exploited by the right kind of U.S. leadership, bin Laden and his ilk are history's gift to American grand strategy: the mirror image of a "closer." If you find that imagery disturbing, let me submit that there's hardly anything more meaningful in dying prematurely from violence perpetrated by extremists than there is in dying from disease enabled by economic deprivation. Exposing us somewhat to the former in the service of radically reducing the latter is what I call a victory so subtle that our enemies won't even realize they're losing. Good counterinsurgency is thus ideological inoculation—pure and simple. Sarah Sewall declares that COIN cannot be used to support a revolutionary grand strategy, because it "favors peace over justice." I say, Fine. America's revolutionary grand strategy is globalization itself and globalization thrives on peace while delivering justice first and foremost through income growth, expecting the locals to master the political equations in a direct relationship to their greed for more success. Thus the dynamics of insurgency apply only in specific conditions of critical mass resistance to globalization's penetrating connectivity—specifically, when elites fight to keep it out because it threatens their oligarchic hold over national wealth or when extremists do the same as part of their campaign to achieve dictatorial power.

What I like best about COIN doctrine is that it moves our strategic thinking back to being population-centric. In counterinsurgency, the focus is on the people, because the people are the prize. In an interconnected and interdependent world, made more so each passing year by globalization's advance, force-on-force thinking in security affairs is very dangerous. By force-on-force, I mean the tendency to think it's all about our badasses versus their bad guys: We kill more of them than they kill of ours. The corollary in strategic nuclear warfare is both first strike *and* missile defense, because either way, our promise is that "our missiles will kill your missiles before your missiles can harm us." The intellectual breakthrough afforded by the concept of mutually assured destruction is that it forced both sides to become population-centric and thus do something with nuclear weapons that humans had never done before with any new, more advanced and more powerful weapon—refuse to use them. By refocusing our global counterinsurgency on the people, we reframe the essential competition with this Reagan-like question: "Who's doing more to improve your pursuit of happiness?" If that sounds like bribing our way to victory, well . . . you just might be an American.

Good COIN, persistently pursued, also speaks to the logic of both my Leviathan/SysAdmin split and the need for a department that does "everything else." On the first point, consider this excerpt from David Galula's COIN bible, *Counterinsurgency Warfare: Theory and Practice* (1964):

> *Adaptation of the Armed Forces to Counterinsurgency Warfare:* As long as the insurgent has failed to build a powerful regular army, the counterinsurgent has little use for heavy, sophisticated forces designed for conventional warfare. For his ground forces, he needs infantry and more infantry, highly mobile and lightly armed. . . . For his air force, he wants ground support and observation planes . . . plus short-takeoff transport planes and helicopters, which play a vital role. . . . The navy's mission, if any, is to enforce a blockade. . . . In addition, the counterinsurgent needs an extremely dense signal network. The counterinsurgent, therefore, has to proceed to a first transformation of his existing forces along these lines, notably to convert into infantry units as many unneeded specialized units as possible. The adaptation, however, must go deeper than that. At some point in the counterinsurgency process, the static units . . . will find themselves confronted with a huge variety of nonmilitary tasks which have to be performed in order to get the support of the population, and which can be performed only by military personnel, because of the shortage of reliable civilian political and administrative personnel. . . . Thus, a mimeograph machine may turn out to be more useful than a machine gun, a soldier trained as a pediatrician more important than a mortar expert, cement more wanted than barbed wire, clerks more in demand than riflemen.

Update the technology references and Galula, a French officer writing almost a half-century ago, basically captures all the tension inside the U.S. military today as it struggles with COIN in the long (post)war environments of Afghanistan and Iraq. As Galula avers wryly, "There is room in the armed forces . . . for the cadres who cannot shed their conventional-warfare thinking. They can be assigned to the mobile units" (meaning the Leviathan-like forces that engage boxed-in insurgents in conventional fights whenever possible). In other words, if you're not smart enough to be SysAdmin, don't worry, we can still find a spot for you and your trigger finger.

As for the logic of designating some coordinating agency for all this activity, Sewall admits that the *Counterinsurgency Field Manual* "raises a larger question: if the United States is going to conduct counterinsurgency, will it broaden the associated division of labor and build the necessary civilian capacities?" If not, Sewall seems to suggest, the new COIN doctrine will remain "a moon without a planet to orbit," lacking the "broader strategic framework" that must strike the American public as "compelling."

Here's what I see in all my travels around the U.S. military and national security establishment, to whom I give dozens of speeches each year: agencies and commands across the dial offering up their preferred version of a SysAdmin-style force. The question is, Offering up to whom? The Navy elevates humanitarian assistance and disaster response to a "core mission," a new Army manual declares the mission of stabilizing war-torn nations "equal in importance to defeating adversaries on the battlefield," the Marines repurpose amphibious landing ships for disaster-relief duties, the Air Force designs a bomb to kill people while not harming infrastructure, and Congress wants to create a Civilian Response Corps and stick it in a State Department unable to fill its own quota of personnel in Iraq. Doesn't this all strike you as myriad solutions seeking some institution that will actually *own* the problem?

Meanwhile the burden of duty gets heavier for those who get stuck "holding the dripping bag of manure," as Sewall derisively describes difficult postwar operations. Twenty-something Army and Marine captains are given huge chunks of territory in Iraq and told to "fix it," leading to twenty-one-hour workdays and confessions that "I feel like Dr. Phil with guns." Junior officers are leaving the force in droves, thanks in part to sky-high divorce rates among personnel on deployments that last fifteen months and feature seven-day workweeks. "Unity of command" in (post)war zones comes with its own harsh price, including a lack of recognition. Only five Medals of Honor have been awarded in more than five years of high-tempo operations in Iraq and Afghanistan.

Yes, it's easy to throw your hands up and say, "No more Iraqs." But if we're honest with ourselves about the world we live in, that's not a realistic response. Globalization is coming at these disconnected regions with a power that no military can command, driven by private-sector forces that no government can control. America can withdraw and keep its powder dry for that big war all the world's defense contractors still dream about supplying, but that is a fool's errand.

The new COIN field manual brings our military back to a world it's long ignored. Now if only we can locate enough partners, both in terms of military allies and private-sector entities, to handle the intimidating workload.

THE GLOBAL ACCELERANT: THE PRIVATIZATION OF AMERICAN FOREIGN POLICY

The U.S. government tends to privatize operations whenever the historical tasks at hand outpace the internal resources in hand. War is an obvious example, and the history here is clear: Not only have U.S. government operations vastly—and permanently—increased during significant and long wars, but so has government spending on contractors. Long postwars have also seen the government blur the line between direct hires and contractors, as have periods of intense integration of frontier areas. The Cold War was, in many ways, a decades-long postwar to Europe's long civil war that saw the United States get deeply involved in Western Europe's recovery (Marshall Plan), security (NATO), and finalizing peace-treaty negotiations (the German question that extended into the early 1970s détente process). The private-sector involvement there was enormous: the rise of the industrial side of the military-industrial complex. The other great and long war/postwar combination in American history was the Civil War, which was linked to the South's lengthy, contentious, and violent reconstruction, as well as the stunningly rapid integration of the American West. If World War II's staggering amount of death (concentrated in Europe) created a new sense of American international destiny, that surge merely replicated the profound sense of American national destiny that arose following the Civil War.

What should interest us in considering American grand strategy going forward is how closely integrated the U.S. military became with private-sector interests in these previous extensive postwar experiences, especially in settling the American West after the Civil War. The U.S. Army's bodyguarding role in the West was most explicit, starting with the protection of settler trails and railroad construction corridors, expanding into episodic wars with Native American tribes, and finally settling into the enforcement of the reservation system. Over time, the trans-Mississippi West was divided into Army "departments" that birthed some of the divisions that would later fight in Europe's twentieth-century wars. These departments constituted the U.S. military's original regional combatant commands—continental harbingers of America's post-WWII global command scheme. The Indian agency system, run by civilian supervisors because Congress was uncomfortable with President Ulysses Grant's proposal to have Army officers take charge, eventually outsourced significant portions of its operations to religious charities.

This period constituted the first great expression of the U.S. Army's "system administrator" role in helping to settle and integrate frontier areas, and it employed contractors galore in a variety of key roles, the most famous ones being the scouts with expertise in fighting Native Americans, with Kit Carson as the exemplar. Another classic example was William "Buffalo Bill" Cody, whose career spanned military service in the Civil War, buffalo meat supplier to railroad workers (where he got his nickname), and extensive service as "chief of scouts" for the U.S. 3rd Cavalry during the so-called Plains Wars. More controversial was the Pinkerton Detective Agency, which found its original fame in foiling an assassination attempt on President-Elect Abraham Lincoln. It later became a major contractor to the U.S. Department of Justice, aiding in the detection and suppression of labor unrest in the East, as well as a private military contractor in the American West involved in providing security guards and tracking down criminal elements. U.S. Army personnel themselves often moonlighted in private-sector jobs to augment their meager salaries and simply to fill in downtimes, with land surveying a primary pursuit.

For the U.S. Army, the Indian Wars were a multi-decade affair involving classic counterinsurgency tactics, including many pioneering special operations–style campaigns led by officers such as General George Crook, who famously tangled with the Apache warrior chief Geronimo in the American Southwest. The many conflicts generated more Medal of Honor winners than did every other American war save WWII and the Civil War. As Max Boot observes of America's later, long counterinsurgency campaign in the Philippines, the vast majority of generals (twenty-six of thirty) in that successful postwar occupation had already gained similar experience back home in the Indian Wars. What the American military had first learned at home, it later practiced abroad—the purposeful generation of security in regions on the frontier of advancing economies.

Fast-forward to the Cold War's end and we see America inexorably drawn into the same sort of System Administrator role regarding globalization's rapid advance that our government and army assumed during our nation's rapid surge westward following the Civil War. It's really just a matter of substituting some of the key dynamics. If gold drew America's security umbrella westward in the mid–nineteenth century, oil drew the same umbrella eastward to the Persian Gulf over the past several decades, with supertankers and their well-traveled "sea lines of communication" serving as the railroads of this era. Not surprisingly, given the complexity and geographic reach of these activities, the U.S. national security establishment has turned increasingly to contractors to fill in the blanks of its capabilities and to reduce operating costs.

With each overseas military intervention, then, the role of prominent contractors grew. Kellogg Brown & Root—whose previous incarnation, Brown & Root, built 85 percent of the military infrastructure used by American forces in Vietnam—first achieved significant prominence in the Balkans interventions of the mid-1990s. When you travel to remote U.S. military facilities inside the Gap today, as I have on repeated occasions, you'll find that many of KBR's employees are actually Balkans natives who joined the company during those conflicts. In Iraq, the companies that received the biggest boost were those providing private security guards and military/police training, such as Blackwater, DynCorp, and Triple Canopy. Blackwater's stunning rise from struggling start-up to billion-dollar global enterprise recalls that of the Pinkerton Agency. Having achieved its initial fame by guarding the vulnerable new leaders of countries torn asunder by civil strife (the CPA's Paul Bremer in Iraq, then Afghanistan's Hamid Karzai), Blackwater now aspires to provide intelligence services to governments and private companies alike, along with armed relief services to the international community—founder Erik Prince's dream of fielding a private army to settle Darfur's increasingly lawless situation (a "Janjaweed-Be-Gone" solution, as one Blackwater executive puts it).

As the controversy over Blackwater's role in killing Iraqis (and with it, questions over who is ultimately responsible for governing Blackwater's conduct) demonstrates, there are plenty of new rule sets that need to be constructed for this blending of private and public security elements engaged in frontier-settling activities. But for our purposes, the key thing to keep in mind is that this trend toward outsourcing much of American foreign policy activities is both pervasive and decades in the making, not surprisingly, tracking quite nicely with globalization's rapid expansion around the planet beginning in the late 1970s and early 1980s. Go back to that time period and you'll find the U.S. Agency for International Development recasting itself from being a direct provider of foreign aid to essentially playing the role of pass-through funder of private U.S. development companies. You'll also see the U.S. military letting its first LOG-CAP (Logistics Civil Augmentation Program) omnibus contract in 1985, effectively outsourcing the operation of U.S. military facilities overseas to KBR. By the time we reached the year 2000, more than $200 billion in total U.S. federal contracts was being spent each year outside the United States, and that total has roughly doubled since then. The Defense Department accounts for the bulk of that spending (almost 70 percent), with the departments of State and Homeland Security (combined) representing another 4 to 5 percent.

Back to the arguments of what it takes for America to be successful in waging a global counterinsurgency campaign: If COIN is expensive and long and succeeds primarily in terms of generating local economic growth, doesn't it make sense that we'd see a greater blending of public and private efforts in these frontier economies? Moreover, as Galula noted, insurgencies tend to be cheap to operate and thus extremely fluid in their ability to change tactics. States, by contrast, tend to be rigid in their overall approaches, changing their policies and their spending priorities slowly. By outsourcing more of America's efforts to stabilize Gap regions to private-sector players, the U.S. government is simply tapping the same entrepreneurial pool of talent it previously exploited in taming the American West: people and companies willing to take higher risks in return for higher rewards. Plus, by being more demand-sensitive than governments, private companies seek to turn "early-entry" opportunities into lasting markets that service local needs—the very essence of globalization's networking function.

By casting this long war first and foremost as a *public*-sector venture (*America's* military, *America's* foreign aid, *America's* diplomacy, *America's* strategic communications), the United States excessively narrows its grand strategic vision—not to mention its options. Globalization is *not* a government plot but a planet-spanning force driven primarily by the rising, *private-sector* demands of those 3 billion new capitalists. Americans need to distinguish public-sector *supply* (a response) with private-sector *demand* (the driver), for it's the latter that constitutes the most awesome power within a global economy. We may get bored or tired or angry enough to withdraw from the world, but *those* people will not simply call off globalization to accommodate America's latest populist whim. We may have started this party, but it stopped being ours to organize a long time ago—much less call off.

To be effective, then, America's grand strategy needs to connect its total DIME package—as much as possible—to those tail-end "E" players in the private sector, thus avoiding the self-delusion that globalization expands primarily in response to public-sector supply. This is the grand illusion of our age: the notion that the Gap will be shrunk in direct relation to the Core's public-sector aid or regime-toppling exercises. While it's true that during the Cold War most infrastructure development inside the so-called Third World came as a result of the West's official development aid (a public-sector supply "push" function), the truth today is that the vast majority of infrastructure development ($22 trillion over the next decade alone) inside emerging and developing economies comes as a result of private-sector demand "pull"—those 3 billion new capitalists and all the resources they need to catch up in economic development.

We want to get in front of all that money, then, and not just in front of all the social blowback those aggressive investments trigger. We want to ride globalization's strongest currents, not swim against them in some unilateralist, kinetic fit of pique.

THE INESCAPABLE REALIGNMENT: REBLENDING DIPLOMACY, DEFENSE, AND DEVELOPMENT

President George W. Bush's 2002 National Security Strategy is best known for its enunciation of the military doctrine of preemptive war. More lasting and important was its far more subtle argument that development and diplomacy are the equals of defense when it comes to victory in the long war against violent extremism. Taking that high-level cue, the U.S. Agency for International Development began promoting the so-called 3D approach of blending each element far more synergistically than was being done in either the Afghanistan or the Iraq occupation. Based on my interviews locally for a 2007 *Esquire* story on the rise of U.S. Africa Command, ground zero for this new way of thinking appears to have been the USAID mission in Nairobi, Kenya, one of USAID's larger missions with responsibility for much of the agency's programs across the Horn of Africa.

Of course, USAID wasn't the only government entity calling for such a blend. General James Mattis had been arguing, right from the start of his nation-building exercise with the Marines' 1st Infantry Division in southern Iraq that "jobs, jobs, jobs!" was the primary method of diminishing popular support for an insurgency. The COIN field manual, in arguing for an 80/20 blend of nonkinetics and kinetics, was stealing a line from that great progenitor of twentieth-century "revolutionary war," Mao Zedong, who argued, along with his generals, that successful insurgencies were only 20 percent military in nature and 80 percent political. As such, throughout the Iraq and Afghanistan occupations official Washington has been barraged by blue-ribbon-panel recommendations, op-eds by experts, and calls from the field for some sort of new, blended organizational approach that was not quite State and not quite Defense but somehow made these two antagonistically opposed bureaucracies work with each other seamlessly. While most nongovernmental voices called out for something akin to my proposed Department of Everything Else, government-sponsored "group thinks" favored expanding the State Department, a solution few familiar with that bureaucracy's perfectly preserved nineteenth-century style of operations found acceptable. Both Defense and State have created new senior-level positions to focus on postwar operations, but beyond that, the level of cooperation between the two remains stunningly limited. A good example? In Afghanistan, the United States has sought to hand over coordination of economic and political reconstruction to the United Nations—a sure sign of lack of coordination leading to bureaucratic capitulation.

Again, U.S. history suggests that we've approached this challenge better in the past. By most historians' judgment, the U.S. occupation of the Philippines following the Spanish-American War was quite successful both in terms of waging an effective counterinsurgency and in state-building. To create unity of command and effort, President William McKinley created two successive temporary occupational authorities, the first to deal with the immediate aftermath of the war and a second, led by future president William Howard Taft (who later performed a similar role for President Theodore Roosevelt in Cuba), to oversee the transition from military to civilian rule. General MacArthur's postwar rule in Japan is likewise often cited as an example of successful transition, as is the Allied coalition rule over postwar West Germany. The difference in all these cases would seem to be the underlying logic that everyone involved (both military and civilian) brought to the effort—nation-building was a government-wide effort involving skill sets reasonably transferred from recent American experience back home.

The problem we face today is that America is so far distant—historically speaking—from such nation-building experiences at home that both its leadership and its people have an innate aversion to the concept. What was once viewed as a noble endeavor is now viewed with real distaste, as if it's morally wrong to "impose" a better form of governance upon a society typically lacking a functioning version altogether. The downside, of course, is that we know what the libertarian paradises of the Gap usually produce: widespread violence, disease, and starvation. As soon as America gives up on a country, expect globalization's vultures to start circling.

The reason American politicians resist the notion of embracing these skills to the point of creating a cabinet-level agency is that they, as well as many citizens they represent, fear America will be left with the bulk of the international responsibility, which in turn is then foisted almost solely upon our military. But here's where the "rise of the rest," as Zakaria calls it, works distinctly to our advantage. The reality is that our lack of institutional integrity on this subject makes it harder to attract other nations to our cause, as well as the far more crucial private sector in general. By performing badly, America advertises its incompetence—hardly a turn-on, and by refusing to create a seriously empowered bureaucratic center of gravity, we make it almost impossible for our collective nation-building effort to be approached from outside, a complaint I hear constantly from senior executives of major multinational corporations. The *Counterinsurgency Field Manual*, for example, lists fourteen federal departments or agencies, in addition to the Department of Defense, that are logically considered "key organizations" in any coordinated COIN campaign. Meanwhile, in the field, Provincial Reconstruction Teams attempt to blend all such contributions on the ground. In between, however, a bureaucratic no-man's-land still exists (I'll offer a fix for that in the next chapter).

Legendary baseball manager Casey Stengel once described his job as having to "keep the guys who hate you away from the guys who are undecided." In a nutshell, those are the two very different target populations pursued by Defense (the guys who hate us) and State (the guys who are undecided) in a COIN campaign, the problem being the fundamental lack of coordination—the absence of the manager.

Right now, the U.S. military tries to fill that bureaucratic vacuum to the best of its ability. The reality is, however, that the Pentagon so fears falling into that void, and losing its warfighting *raison d'être* in the process, that innovation in that direction is often squashed as soon as it appears, along with the innovators. This is what Secretary of Defense Robert Gates derisively called "next-war-itis," or the tendency of the big-war crowd to demean attempts to adapt the force to the current "diversionary" struggle, preferring to focus on the sexier, high-tech, conventional wars to come— great-power wars. The training mission is a good example: Colonel John Nagl, a principal author of the new COIN field manual, has long proposed a dedicated Army Advisory Corps (signifying something at least as large as a 20,000-man division) to address the ongoing task of mentoring and building up militaries in failed states. For now, this idea has been rejected by the mainstream Army leadership, which says defensively that such skills will remain a niche within the U.S. military and thus addressable solely by the far smaller special operations community. This is a common bureaucratic tactic among the big-war crowd: pushing off the responsibility of waging a global counterinsurgency to Special Forces. It is, in my mind, at best a highly romanticized reading of the strategic environment that says, "All I need are a few supermen to keep this scary world at bay," and at worst a very self-serving expression of industry greed or military budget territoriality. Interestingly enough, the "direct action," or trigger-puller, community within Special Operations Command (SOCOM) has taken recently to agitating for a dedicated Unconventional Warfare command that would relieve it of this growing responsibility. As far as I'm concerned, when even SOCOM starts asking for its own SysAdmin force, that's a big hint as to where the future lies.

Colonel Nagl, by the way, never made general and now presses his agenda quite ably from a think tank perch in Washington, D.C. Don't be surprised to see him serving as a political appointee someday soon.

In the end, the main obstacle to achieving a serious blending of the three D's will be found inside the military itself, or—more specifically— within the Defense Department's acquisition community. What Dwight Eisenhower once identified as the military-industrial complex remains alive and quite powerful today. In budget cycle after budget cycle, and even in most emergency supplementals, the major "programs of record" have continued to do well throughout this long war. Our troops in the field may go into battle underarmored or forced to buy their preferred personal equipment on their own (waiting forever for reimbursement from the government), but don't expect the fantastically expensive Joint Strike Fighter or the Army's overengineered Future Combat Systems to voluntarily give up much of its funding in response—this on a defense budget that is higher than it has ever been! Thus the conventional wisdom reigns: America must keep all its old, twentieth-century enemies even as it adds all its new twenty-first-century foes.

I've been accused my entire career of trying to "ruin the military," but the truth is, I'm only trying to "ruin" its force structure by improving its operational strength for the tasks I know will dominate our security agenda in the years ahead. Run through the list of insurgent tactics in the COIN field manual and tell me how many major weapons systems you can locate among its challenges: ambushes, assassination, arson, bombing and high explosives, weapons of mass destruction, demonstrations, denial and deception, hijacking and skyjacking, hoaxes, hostage-taking, indirect fire, infiltration and subversion, kidnapping, propaganda, raids or attacks on facilities, sabotage, and seizure. The harsh truth, as Barrett Tillman argues in his book *What We Need: Extravagance and Shortages in America's Military*, is that we need more training, better guns, more maintenance, more linguists, *no* Future Combat System, less Navy power projection but more minesweepers, less stealth aircraft and more electronic countermeasures platforms, more close-air support, a whole lot more helicopters and a lot more unmanned aerial vehicles for real-time surveillance. That is most definitely not the familiar gold mine for today's major U.S. defense contractors, but—quite frankly—if they're not shifting toward becoming tomorrow's leading global *security* contractors, they're lost anyhow.

The good news is this: The deeper we move collectively into this long war, the harder it gets for the acquisition community to remain aloof and unperturbed by the proceedings. Over time, the operational experience builds up, in turn changing tactics, techniques, and procedures, in turn altering training and schoolhouse curricula, in turn unleashing doctrinal shifts and shaping new warfighting scenarios, in turn making it harder and harder for existing programs of record to justify themselves in light of all this change working its way up the bureaucratic food chain.

And when that happens pervasively, then the serious reblending of defense, diplomacy, and development truly begins.

THE BETTER NORMAL: THE COMMAND-AFTER-NEXT

Two realities inform our thinking about what comes next in this long war: (1) Paul Collier's "bottom billion" is clustered mostly in sub-Saharan Africa and Central Asia; and (2) today's radical Salafi jihadist movement is centered in Southwest Asia (from Egypt to Pakistan), a region that effectively links those two impoverished areas. To the extent that we're successful in dislodging al Qaeda from Southwest Asia, the center of gravity is likely to shift to either Central Asia or Africa. If the Shanghai Cooperation Organisation truly represents the will of great powers surrounding Central Asia to keep that region relatively clean of violent extremism, and

I think it does, then the radical Salafist movement, to the degree it either must flee Southwest Asia or attempt to expand its influence from that base, is more likely than not to move into Africa over time. The recent rise of the Salafist Group for Preaching and Combat (GSPC) in North Africa would seem to confirm that judgment. The grand strategic response to that scenario is therefore clear: accelerate Africa's integration into the global economy in a strategic flanking maneuver designed to deny radical Islam's successful penetration there.

Thus, after being ignored since the beginning of time (save for its slaves and its treasure), Africa just got strategically important enough for America to care about. The Bush administration's decision to set up Africa Command is historic, but not for the reasons given or assumed. There aren't enough Islamic terrorists in Africa to stand up a full combatant command. If all we wanted were flies on eyeballs, a small number of special operations trigger-pullers would have sufficed for the foreseeable future. There's oil there, but the United States would get its share whether Africa burns or not, and it's actually fairly quiet right now. The Chinese are arriving *en masse*, typically embedded with regimes we can't stand or can't stand us, like Sudan and Zimbabwe. But the Chinese aren't particularly liked in Africa and seem to have no designs for empire there. Beijing just wants its energy and minerals, and that penetration, such as it is, doesn't warrant Africa Command, either. So, in my mind, America sets up an Africa Command for the same reason people buy real estate—it's a good investment. As the Middle East "middle ages" over the next three decades and Asia's infrastructural build-out is completed, only Africa will remain as a source for both youth-driven revolution and cheap labor and commodities. Toss in global warming and you've got a recipe for the most deprived becoming the most depraved.

America's Central Command set up shop in Djibouti, located right across from Yemen where the Red Sea meets the Gulf of Aden, in May 2003, moving ashore a Marine-led Joint Task Force that had been established six months earlier aboard the command ship *Mount Whitney* to capture and kill al Qaeda fighters fleeing American forces in Afghanistan and Iraq. The task force did register one immediate big hit in November 2002: A top Al Qaeda leader was taken out in Yemen by a Hellfire air-to-ground missile launched from an unmanned Predator drone in a scene right out of the movie *Syriana*. But other than that, the great rush of rats fleeing the sinking ship did not materialize, and so the Marines took up residence in an old French Foreign Legion base located on Djibouti's rocky shore, just outside the capital. Uncomfortable just sitting around, the Marines quickly refashioned the task force with the blessing of General John Abizaid, then head of Central Command, who envisioned Combined Joint Task Force–Horn of Africa (CJTF-HOA) as a strategic inoculant. If the Marines weren't going to get to kill anybody, then they'd train the locals to police the area instead.

But CJTF-HOA, whose area of responsibility stretched from Sudan down to Kenya, soon evolved into something much more: an experiment in applying the 3D approach so clearly lacking in America's recent postwar reconstruction efforts elsewhere. Because the task force didn't own the sovereign space it was operating in, as U.S. forces in Afghanistan and Iraq did, the Marines were forced to work under and through the American ambassadors, their State Department country teams, and the attached U.S. Agency for International Development missions. If little of that cooperation was occurring in Kabul and Baghdad, then maybe Africa would be better suited. CJTF-HOA was implicitly designed to be Washington's bureaucratic *mea culpa* for the Green Zone, a proving ground for the next generation of interagency cooperation that fuels America's eventual victory in the long war. CJTF-HOA became the essential model for AFRICOM, which effectively seeks to replicate its de facto subunified command model (sort of a "mini-me" regional combatant command) in Africa's northern, western, southern, and central regions, corresponding to the African Union's desire to stand up five regional peacekeeping brigades. In effect, AFRICOM will eventually represent a "franchising" of the CJTF-HOA model, complete with its innovative 3D approach.

Thus, Africa Command promises to be everything Central Command has failed to become in its recent interventions. It will be interagency from the ground up. It will be based on interactions with locals first and leaders second. It will engage in preemptive nation-building instead of preemptive regime change. It will "reduce the future battlespace" that America has neither intention nor desire to own. It'll be Iraq done right.

At the end of the day, then, America's strategic interests in Africa, as reflected in AFRICOM, can be summed up thusly: keep civil strife down, build local capacity up, and keep the radical jihadists out. Unstated in that formula for now is the logic of encouraging Asia (and Middle Eastern) firms "in" as a means of plugging African labor into globalization's network trade. If this were all done effectively over the long haul, U.S. military presence and influence in the region would be self-negating: The more successful we are in this strategy, the less influence we have over local African governments. The end goal is simple: not permanent U.S. military bases but African militaries and governments bolstered to the point where continental peacekeeping can be accomplished on the basis of indigenous capacity first, regional cooperation second, and help from external great powers third.

How well will AFRICOM fare? For now it remains an experiment subject to a lot of local suspicions and the usual bureaucratic and budgetary turf battles back in Washington. But it's interesting how—when left to its own devices and located away from the global glare created by U.S. operations in Iraq and Afghanistan—the U.S. military, in the form of CJTF-HOA, basically adopted my Leviathan-SysAdmin split: the joint task force essentially playing SysAdmin with its couple of thousand military trainers, medics, well-diggers, and civil affairs specialists; and CENT-COM's Special Operations Command (SOCCENT) playing occasional Leviathan, such as its short-duration intervention alongside invading Ethiopian troops in Somalia in early 2007 to drive out the radical Council of Islamic Courts (CIC). CJTF-HOA works its many precincts primarily through its system of frontier mini-forts called contingency operating locations (COLs). Operated by KBR civilians, these small bases typically lie inside an existing host-nation military base, such as the COL I visited in Manda Bay, Kenya, in 2007 as part of my reporting for *Esquire*'s story on AFRICOM. Yes, the Manda Bay COL served as a launching point for special operations strikes against Somalia-based al Qaeda and CIC operatives just a few weeks before I got there, but I spent my time trailing a civil affairs Army captain who was checking up on a slew of local capacity-building projects his teams had overseen during the past year. In effect, Manda Bay's handful of civil affairs teams were operating no differently from coalition Provincial Reconstruction Teams in Afghanistan and Iraq; they were, in effect, preconflict PRTs, or the 3D approach applied *before* a regime-toppling or nation-building exercise is required. "Imperialism" to some but nothing more than a pistol-packing Peace Corps to me, because if you want the state-building sans invasion, this is what it looks like—CJTF-HOA growing into AFRICOM.

CJTF-HOA likes to brag that it's never fired a round in anger, and that's true, because it has played the local precinct cop and left it to SOCCENT's SWAT-like forces to pull the triggers as needed. That essential split is being repeated in AFRICOM, where the command has been divided between two deputy commanders: a military officer to run normal military operations (more Leviathan) and a State Department civilian who oversees the "everything else." This is an unprecedented development in the history of U.S. regional combatant commands (thus creating immediate bureaucratic blowback in Washington, where State and USAID fear a militarization of their presence on the continent), but it's one I think we'll see replicated across other commands in coming years. Frankly, you can spot all the same beat cop–versus–SWAT tensions in U.S. military operations in both Afghanistan and Iraq. AFRICOM, in combination with U.S. Southern Command (Latin America), thus represents the sort of 3D template that will eventually remake America's entire military command structure—the essential "cannibalizing agent" triggered by the long war. To that end, SOUTHCOM already moves in the direction of replicating the dual deputy commander structure of AFRICOM.

Yes, America will still need the nineteen-year-old "generation kill" types who can be trained up to do the Leviathan work, but increasingly it will need the older, more experienced type who speaks the local language and works the beat like a regular cop, soaking up "human intelligence" the old-fashioned way—simply chatting up the local citizenry. In short, you can *train* the Leviathan but you need to *educate* the SysAdmin. If all you want to do is kill bad guys, the algorithm for that "kill chain" is relatively simple: a series of steps that get you the desired outcome. That sort of vertical knowledge can be drilled into young recruits: *observe* the environment, *orient* yourself therein, *decide* which steps need be taken against which targets, and then *act* (this is Colonel John Boyd's famous "OODA loop"). But according to the new Army-Marine COIN field manual, the SysAdmin relationship- and network-builder has a tougher row to hoe in terms of successful counterinsurgency: He or she needs to *diagnose* an environment's deficits (e.g., economic, political, security, essential services), *dialogue* with local inhabitants about how to address them, *design* programs, *learn* from their application, and then *redesign* them over and over again until the local capacity has been effectively built up—not a loop to be rushed.

Just as important in all this work is the behavior our troops model for their local counterparts. In Africa, for example, a nation's military has often been a force of repression or great violence against its own people, so professionalizing local militaries becomes a primary goal of COIN or state-building in general. This kind of institutional mentoring takes time—as in, face-to-face time. How do you teach a boy living in a fatherless house to act like a man? You get him a good role model. African militaries need a solid role model, and as imperfect as America's military seems to its critics, it is the gold standard. Plus, it is the only one that actually shows up anywhere inside the Gap in sufficient numbers to make this sort of interaction happen consistently. I say, if you don't want to play "big brother" to the world's militaries, then don't own the world's biggest and best gun, because the rest comes with the territory.

Across the entirety of the Cold War, the United Nations got involved in eighteen peacekeeping operations. Since the Cold War's end, it has accumulated almost four dozen more. That means we've gone from the UN doing a PKO once every two or three years to doing two or three new PKOs every year. Does that sound like a future global security environment that needs a bigger U.S. Leviathan capacity or one that demands something more SysAdmin-like, more in the range of CJTF-HOA and AFRICOM? Because I'll tell you this: Getting China to do more inside the Gap gets a whole lot harder when our main instrument of cooperation is a force largely designed to fight a military like China's. If we want to tap the rising great powers of this age, we need to present them with institutions they can readily access in terms of cooperation. We need new forces and new commands, for new coalitions with new allies, for new types of operations in locales that are historically unknown to us. Or we can simply keep building a Cold War force and wondering why it doesn't perform well in counterinsurgency or state-building and keeps burning itself out trying to adapt itself to these very different tasks.

Everyone always wants a quick fix. We got hit with 9/11 and the quick fix was a new Department of Homeland Security. So sure, after the debacle that was postwar Iraq, it is tempting to reach immediately for some new, cabinet-level department to fix everything that's gone wrong and continues to go wrong. But the far more likely course is this: Left to its own devices, the military experiments with new operating structures in the field (e.g., CJTF-HOA) and then grows those structures upward into new command structures—like AFRICOM. With further experience, those new and different command structures begin to influence older ones, cannibalizing them in their own image. After a while, you've got a profound bureaucratic center of gravity operating out there in all these regional combatant commands, or entities that serve a number of bureaucratic masters (Defense, State, USAID, others) back in Washington. Eventually, those entities will need their own dedicated voice in the corridors of power, and logically their own dedicated source of funding. *That's* when you get a Department of Everything Else: in response to demands from the field to coordinate the huge transaction volume that's *not quite* Defense and *not quite* State and *not quite* USAID but *something quite different altogether.*

Can you mandate such change from above? The example of the Goldwater-Nichols Act of 1986, which radically reblended the military services into a much stronger "unity of command" model, suggests that's possible *within* a single department. The experience of the Department of Homeland Security to date, however, suggests that suddenly kluging together lots of agencies is a bad idea, creating more dysfunction than synergy. So while it's tempting to request some sort of *deus ex machina* to drop out of the theater's upper region and provide a quick and conclusive end to these confused proceedings, the far more likely outcome is that the U.S. military will grow its own SysAdmin solution in places like AFRICOM and the always resource-deprived, and thus inventive, U.S. Southern Command.

Having said all that, and given my druthers, here's how I'd push things along with the AFRICOM experiment: I would definitely franchise the CJTF-HOA structure across the continent, refusing to locate a central headquarters anywhere in Africa. Rather, I'd set it down somewhere in northern Virginia to attract both the necessary civilian talent and to encourage superb interagency development. I would mandate that a retired four-star flag officer (admiral or general) with joint combatant command experience head this "command" (which I would label something less military-sounding) so as to give it a clear civilian head. Then I'd designate as my two deputies a uniformed military officer to work the defense side and a USAID/State official to work the development side. I'd give my retired four-star boss a cabinet-level status (at first just the position, not the command) equivalent to the U.S. ambassador to the United Nations. My cluster of regionally focused combined joint task forces would be set up in a very low-key manner, just like CJTF–Horn of Africa. There would be no "pointy end" on any of those "spears." If kinetics were required, I'd have Special Operations Command run the entire show. Within ten years, these would be my goals: All Defense Department planning for Africa would be based in this blended agency, ditto for State Department diplomatic plans, ditto for USAID development program planning.

In effect, I'd create my interagency process *inside* the command instead of above it in the National Security Council, whose main function, quite frankly, will always remain keeping the president blameless for foreign policy failures. Eventually, Congress would grow so frustrated with its current committee structure that it would need to create a new, 3D-blended committee to conduct a coherent conversation with this entity. As that new conversation unfolded, Congress and the executive branch would come to the same conclusion: What works in Africa should work throughout the Gap. As the Gap shrinks, this Department of Everything Else (obviously given a more bureaucratically appropriate moniker) would evolve into a sort of Department of Network Security for all America's vast globalization connectivity—the equivalent of a Department of Homeland Security *all grown up* or matured beyond its currently myopic fixation on firewalls.

In my mind, Africa and AFRICOM represent the ideal *tabula rasa* for engineering a new type of defense entity that's synergistically blended—from the start—with both diplomacy and developmental aid components. But even more important than that, AFRICOM could serve as the launching point of a new type of security alliance with rising New Core powers such as India and China, neither of whom, like America, comes to Africa with past colonial baggage. It could also pioneer new forms of cooperation with private-sector entities looking to cash in on Africa's rising globalization profile. In short, AFRICOM represents a major opportunity to reset the rules for America's grand strategy. I suppose we could wait for the "threat after next" to pop up and send us scrambling for new answers, or just rerun the Cold War with Russia. But wouldn't it be nice if this time, we started building that "command after next" to shape this potential battlefield so preemptively and so effectively as to rule out the need for old-style interventions by outside powers or—worse—some pathetic rerun of the "race for Africa" among those same powers?

Wouldn't it be nice to own that future instead of replaying the past?

Seven

THE NETWORK REALIGNMENT

The Rise of the
SysAdmin-Industrial Complex

Vint Cerf, a universally acknowledged "father of the Internet," describes the Web in the following manner: "Nobody owns it, everybody uses it, and anybody can add services to it." Since the Internet's spread mirrors the global economy's expansion to a tremendous degree, the same can also be stated about globalization itself. The global economy is the ultimate service-oriented architecture that nobody quite controls even as almost everybody avails himself of its connectivity, adding transactions to its volume every day—mostly good, but some bad, too. So it's a cluster of "frenemies" on top (i.e., rivals who nonetheless collaborate extensively) and all sorts of cats and dogs in a scrum at the pyramid's bottom. Many security experts interpret the current global order in this manner, with some choosing to see "empires" imposed from above, while others are just as certain that they're witnessing uncontrollable "chaos" fomenting down below. In reality, we're all witnessing the rise of a superempowered middle class somewhere in between those two extremes. We just don't yet know how to describe it, much less speak in a language it understands. We only know that it wants . . . *everything!*

THE UNDENIABLE TRAJECTORY:
SUPEREMPOWER ME!

Americans, who are problem-solvers at heart, want answers regarding this clear ambiguity: Is globalization stabilizing or destabilizing? Is it integrating or disintegrating? Does it homogenize or fracture? Is it good or bad? Will we win or lose?

Of course, depending on where you sit, all answers are correct. If you're located in the Core, globalization tends—on average—to stabilize, integrate, and homogenize somewhat. If you're stuck in the Gap, globalization appears to be, at first blush, clearly more destabilizing, disintegrating, and fractious. As for winners and losers, it isn't easy to summarize except to say that globalization superempowers those able to choose their families and locations and networks, while it disempowers those who insist that such interpersonal connectivity is a given and not subject to change. If you can leave your community, marry outside your culture or faith, and choose your profession and your home with great flexibility, globalization is a clear good, because it facilitates such individual-level freedom. But if you cannot do any of those things, because they're beyond your imagination, or transgress your taboos or the code of your tribe, then globalization can hardly seem anything but frightening and revolutionary. So saying yes to globalization is very much like saying yes to emigrating to America: If your reinvention is possible, then your options are many, as are your paths to happiness. Every nation's average citizen does better in America than back home. That's why, of all nations on this planet, America should be least frightened by superempowered individuals (Thomas Friedman's famous term), for we represent their most natural home.

That's another reason I don't worry about the accurate perception that globalization's rapid spread outpaces that of political pluralism—in other words, economic liberty presaging political liberty. As long as any nation allows for increasing economic and network connectivity between its citizenry and the outside world, the long-term effects will always expose the lie that man's path to happiness can be singularly defined. All politics begins with this question: Are man's paths to happiness singular or infinite? If singular, then such order can be imposed from above by an elite. If infinite, then such order can only be granted from below by masses who—through constant negotiation—collectively agree on today's definition of the Golden Rule. Superempowered individuals, by definition, are able to go their own way. For now, the reality is that globalization creates too many superempowered individuals, too many "unreasonable men," and too many Teddy Roosevelts trapped inside too many "stationary states."

What's so scary about globalization today is that it's triggering a global consciousness regarding the possibilities of individual liberty, and in doing so, it places a lot of elites in nondemocratic societies in a tough place. In tandem, they must justify their rule by exploiting globalization's connectivity to raise individual incomes while resisting globalization's cultural "pollution" (i.e., all those dangerous ideas of individual freedom), which only raises individual expectations. In other words, their sell on regime legitimacy becomes, "I'm making this connectivity happen in a way that enriches our nation while protecting all of you from content that will threaten our collective identity." I'm not saying the same isn't true for leaders in democratic nations, just that it's a whole lot easier for them, because, by and large, popular expectations are easier to meet in our type of democracy.

Why? American-style democracies tend to come with a substantial middle class, whose ideology is one of self-improvement through self-empowerment, meaning these people look to the government primarily for its role in keeping the playing field reasonably level. The rich, in contrast, look to the government primarily to protect them (and their wealth) from the demands of the poor, while the poor look to the government for protection from their very circumstances. What we're missing right now in globalization is that sense of a worldwide middle-class ideology that says, "We're the hardworking members of this global community and this is what we think would be a fair deal." Invariably, too many experts today describe the world as a superelite sitting high above the bottom billion, reducing everything to the extremes of haves versus have-nots. We have no global leaders of note speaking to the global middle right now, just narrow-minded populist leaders echoing the hopes and fears of their own "middle" back home, typically promising them refuge from the storm when they should be linking those hopes and fears to what Jeffrey Sachs dubs globalization's emerging "common wealth" overwhelmingly found in the global middle class.

So in relatively open democracies, globalization tends to trigger the self-examining question "*What* does it mean to be an [American]?" more than "*Who* gets to be an [American]?" By and large, democracies assume the individual's right to choose his family/networks/citizenship, so questions about globalization are less nationalistic in tenor and more individualistic—less "How is globalization changing [America]?" and more "How's it working out for you?"

The short answer for anybody, whether in a democracy or not, depends primarily on the freedom to network with others. Globalization's mix of stable behemoths surrounded by innovative tykes is clearly reflected on the level of individual workers. More people work in small firms than in big ones, and an increasing share of workers assume the role of free agents within the economy, either formally or informally. At first, it seemed like only those who worked for larger firms were in danger of having their jobs outsourced, but increasingly free agents realize they're in much the same boat, especially since free markets, in their capacity for innovation, tend to outsource most jobs "to the past," as international business consultant David Rothkopf observes. So the real shift in risk here seems to be from the collective (whether it's a country, a culture, or a company) to the individual in the sense that globalization takes what was once a given, your occupation (often inherited from your parent), and says in effect, "You don't own it, because virtually everybody else on this planet can do it, and anybody can add new technologies or services that consign it to the dustbin of economic history." So even among the freest agents in this world, there's no success unless you're willing to regularly adapt to changing circumstances. Globalization is all about networks, and networks allow for workarounds. Workarounds are the essence of resilience—rerendering rules on the fly. So being good at globalization means being able to adjust your rules (as a person, company, military, country) in response to environmental change. Simply put, globalization demands we all evolve faster.

I work for a start-up technology/consulting firm based in . . . uh, pockets spread all over the planet. My boss is based in Philadelphia and I live in Indianapolis. Our third top executive hails from Florida. Our technology center is located in Pennsylvania but our operations center is in northern Virginia. We create a new local office wherever in the world our partnerships take us (so far, Kurdish Iraq, Dubai, and Turkey). I work full-time for the company, but I also write weekly for a newspaper chain based in Ohio and periodically for a magazine based in New York while serving as a visiting scholar for a think tank in Tennessee. The guy who edits my books lives in Manhattan, but my book agent is based in Massachusetts. The lady who manages my speaking career lives in New Jersey, and the fellow who designs all my PowerPoint presentations is located in South Carolina, not too far from my blog's webmaster. I talk to all these people quite regularly, but meet most of them face-to-face quite rarely. Depending on what I'm doing at any one time, I can call myself a senior managing director, blogger, author, journalist, columnist, public speaker, business developer, consultant, visiting scholar, military analyst, or grand strategist. I'm both self-employed and work for a formal company (actually, a cluster of them, all related to one another). I was born and reared in Wisconsin but went to Massachusetts for grad school. My wife was born in Indiana and grew up in Ohio. I was raised Catholic and she was the daughter of a Congregational minister. We've lived together in nine homes spread across five states, with two kids born in Virginia, one in Rhode Island, and the most recent "insourced" from China. I have no idea what I'll be doing ten years from now or where I'll be doing it or with whom. I'm just certain that I'll be forced to adapt my career and home life to new circumstances beyond my control. I feel at once superempowered by American-style capitalism and its progeny—modern globalization—and constantly put at risk by its stunningly rapid evolutions. After all, I began my professional life, in 1990, as a Soviet expert, only to see that job immediately outsourced to history. When my kids ask me if they can grow up to be just like me, I tell them, "I have no idea if that will be possible, but you can come work for me, assuming you can transform yourself into whatever I'm doing at that time."

If that's my constantly-on-the-make life as an entrepreneur in the most competitive economy in the world, then you have to believe globalization is a stunningly revolutionary force across the rest of the planet, where, quite frankly, the vast majority of cultures simply aren't built for that speed of change. In most places in this world, rules are not only *not* made to be broken, they're not made to be changed, either. But rules do change in response to network growth, because networks empower individuals. In globalization, networks are the equivalent of Luther's reformation: They take a distant, mediated relationship and make it a direct connection, empowering each individual node. If you have a question to ask "God" today, you just get him on your phone's Web browser and ping Google or Wikipedia.

This individual-empowerment-through-networks takes many forms.

Regions that were "media-dark" ten years ago now feature networks that connect potential consumers to producers the world over. But that connectivity empowers in both directions: Big firms access the bottom of the pyramid, but those lowly consumers can—and will—turn into vigilantes against those same firms if their expectations are not met. And no, that's not just a matter of poor people in developing markets bringing big old multinationals to their knees. Sometimes it's angry American consumers becoming a revolutionary force within "Communist" China, forcing levels of transparency and product liability that the ruling party elite had no intention of granting as part of this transaction. Another time it's a rogue trader who ends up costing his French employer, one of the world's largest and most respected banks, roughly $7 billion in bogus investments, triggering much the same demands from angry shareholders.

Twenty years ago, official development aid represented the biggest financial flow to developing markets from developed ones. Across the 1990s, it was rapidly overtaken by foreign direct investment flows, which in turn seem to have been rapidly overtaken, thanks to a stunning uptick in global people migrations, by remittances sent home by guest workers and recent emigrants. Just across my short professional career, globalization has gone from having governments controlling the biggest Core-to-Gap financial flows, to having corporations trigger more, to having individuals send roughly as much as the other two combined! Befitting the frontier nature of this age, the American firm Western Union, which began life extending the reach of telegraphs across our Western frontier in the mid–nineteenth century, recently reinvented itself as the world's number-one network handler of remittance payments, controlling roughly one-seventh of the flow.

As a kid who came of age in the early 1970s, I found it was revolutionary enough to see the president of the United States brought down by the reporting of the *Washington Post*. Nowadays, powerful leaders are dislodged—seemingly overnight—by packs of bloggers who can uncover the truth with a speed that's almost godlike. This same blogosphere, and the "Net-roots" political communities it nurtures, can likewise increasingly propel candidates into office, help newcomer politicians smash all previous records for political fundraising (typically tapping large armies of ordinary citizens for small donations over the Web), and then police these same politicians with a vehemence bordering on an angry mob once they take office and—God forbid!—somehow do not measure up to expectations.

And these dynamics are hardly limited to open societies. Globalization's many communication networks are helping to shine a light on human rights abuses the world over. Yes, there are still plenty of places where abuses go unchallenged but almost no places where they go unnoticed.

A good example of this struggle can be found in China, where the so-called Great Firewall, created and monitored by the government, keeps more than 200 million Internet users under a form of "mouse arrest." Unless these users go to the effort of using proxy servers or encrypting their traffic through virtual private networks, they're essentially experiencing a walled-in-garden version of the Internet—a virtual Matrix. The purpose of such a control system is not to prevent any or all leakage, so it's not that hard to get around. The real goal, as journalist James Fallows argues, is simply to make such workarounds so difficult and/or so costly that your average Chinese simply gives up and thus remains satisfied with his Matrix-like version of the Internet, fundamentally ignorant of how these virtual walls separate his online experience from that of the real world out there. In effect, the Chinese Communist Party is trying to do the same thing in cyberspace that it's long done on broadcast networks: insulate its people from any significant criticism of its ruling brand.

But here's why that doesn't work over the long haul: The walled-in approach is just fine for much of your first generation of users of any new technology—consider the rise and fall of America Online. At first, most people don't want maximum freedom, just easy access, so they accept packages that are relatively restrictive. The problem that emerges over time is threefold: (1) as people get used to the service, and their sense of entitlement grows, they tend to get mad when they bump up against artificial limits; (2) as people use the service more and more in a business sense, they want maximum capacity to grow their client base as well as protect it, so the early restrictions that were tolerable when the associated business services represented only a small portion of the company's earnings become unbearable when that share grows; and (3) as soon as your first generation of users grows up wholly in that environment, expect them to start pushing your boundaries simply because their baseline expectations are so much higher than those of the initial generation of users. The Chinese Communist Party's problem with the Internet is a microcosm of every authoritarian government's problem with globalization: Once you let it in, you face an independent source of rising expectations that you can only control by disconnecting it all together. In a peer-to-peer world, there's nothing more powerful than peer pressure. Globalization is thus a virtual Helsinki Accords for everyone who logs on—especially celebrities (God love 'em) with a cause.

Harry Emerson Fosdick, the early-twentieth-century American clergyman, once said, "Democracy is based upon the conviction that there are extraordinary possibilities in ordinary people." The American System–cum–globalization is based on the same premise: The sum creativity of all these ordinary people vastly outweighs the dangers posed by all this shared vulnerability. To live in a modern world is to rely on the trustworthiness of strangers to a stunning degree, and much of that faith comes in knowing that people are empowered to do what's necessary and right. What the Old Core West finds so scary about globalization is not superempowerment per se but the potential bad effects of its uneven distribution.

Collectively, the West is a high-trust networked commonwealth. Compared with the rest of the global economy, it remains a somewhat walled-in garden, but one that's recently found itself abutting a huge chunk of humanity encased in relatively low-trust environments—rising New Core pillars and the frighteningly untrustworthy Gap regions of the world. In the case of many authoritarian regimes, neither these governments nor the United States trusts these newly superempowered individuals to do the right thing, as each might define it. So we're both basically bumping into the walls of this Matrix, shocked to discover what's going on beyond what we've long assumed were the absolute limits of our trusted universe. We're stunned to discover the lack of safety regulations and human rights *outside, over there,* and the average Chinese or Iranian is stunned to discover the lack of information restrictions *outside, over here,* including our seemingly limitless supply of pornography.

To be superempowered is to be superconnected, and to be superconnected is often to be superstunned at how others get by in this world, especially since new forms of connectivity have been exploited, throughout recorded history, first and foremost by nefarious elements.

THE AMERICAN SYSTEM PERTURBED: THE RISE OF GLOBAL GUERRILLAS

The American System began as a continental network, then became hemispheric around the start of the twentieth century, then made its true bid to globalize after WWII, becoming—in effect—transoceanic. After the Cold War's collapse we began to recognize this American-inspired globalization as truly global in scope, if not yet universal in its enforcement of rules: The Core's increasingly dense networks function all right, but the Gap's more brittle networks are still characterized by great uncertainty regarding the lack of transparent rules and the persistence of mass violence. In short, you know what to expect across the Core, but you're never quite sure inside the Gap. Even breakdowns inside the Core have their own protocols, but inside the Gap, situations can unravel to the point where networks crumble and simply disappear for long stretches, maybe never to return. That's why China's investment in African infrastructure is so stunning: Often it resurrects roads and railroads and networks that nobody has used in decades, basically since the colonial powers left. The same can be said of America's security efforts there through AFRICOM: old colonial forts rebuilt because the networks they protect are being revived.

In this way, the spread of the American System–cum–globalization widens our pool of enemies while also making it more shallow: While emerging powers are increasingly integrated economically and great-power war remains off the table thanks to nuclear weapons, every pirate and smuggler and druggie and transnational terrorist/criminal now registers on our radar. By spreading our networks so, we now have to care about a host of small players who live like parasites on these systems—as they have for ages. For all the same reasons we link up with other economies and powers to manage these global networks, these parasites do the same. Hence, the notion emerges that all insurgencies are part of a global insurgency and all security responses to the same should be viewed as part and parcel of a global counterinsurgency. Security experts will often try to sell you these notions as new and radical, but you have to remember this: This fight against modernity by the jihadists is a problem of our success, not of our failure. We have to combat radical elements of Islam and other bad actors just as we fought all such characters in our own West more than a century ago. We just tamed all our out-of-control "badlands" a long time ago. Now we're forced to do the same for the planet as a whole. Why? Again, those 3 billion new capitalists force the issue: We make money off one another and improve one another's lives, and they need a lot more resources to pull off their rise, so our money is tied to their money and their money is tied to the Gap more and more. To secure our money, our networks, and our global economy, we must help them do the same for their own. Connectivity is the gift that keeps on giving . . . and empowering . . . and demanding.

Thus the global economy's rapid expansion forces both the West and emerging markets to radically increase the resilience of all these new networks, especially those extending into regions still largely disconnected from globalization's deep embrace, such as Africa and the Middle East. Very bad actors capable of very bad things tend to congregate in these thinly connected regions. Using guerrilla-style tactics, they can not only frustrate our efforts at postwar reconstruction in Afghanistan and Iraq, but also bring their weapons of "system disruption" eventually to the very networks and infrastructure that fuel globalization's advance. The 9/11 attacks previewed this new form of system-focused warfare, and since that fateful day the U.S. military and government have struggled mightily to construct new operational approaches to tame and ultimately marginalize transnational terrorism.

What we have lacked most in this agonizingly slow adjustment is a good description of our enemy's emerging tactics—in short, a "red team"

exposé of our own system vulnerabilities. One of the first experts to attempt to scale that mountain was former Air Force special operations officer and terrorism expert John Robb, whose 2007 book, *Brave New War,*
deserves both significant attention and vigorous debate, in large part because it makes the provocative case that global guerrillas using "open-
source warfare" can defeat nation-states in the same way that Wikipedia
has eclipsed the *Encyclopaedia Britannica*—the innovative mind of the
many outweighs the dated knowledge of the few.

In an open-source world where research on, and development of, new
technologies has become nearly as accessible as the Internet itself, conflicts are increasingly decided by which side learns the fastest. The same
Internet that allows your teenager to share his or her latest video exploits
with the world also enables what Robb calls the "bazaar of violence,"
where bleeding-edge tactics are rapidly disseminated among globalization's many extremist opponents. Global guerrillas are cheap and plentiful. By contrast, we field the few, the proud, and the incredibly expensive.
The guerrillas change battlefield tactics daily. Until quite recently, our
lumbering Leviathan developed new military doctrine every other decade or so. We wrap our efforts in great secrecy, but they swap their
tradecraft over the Web, with every jihadist-wannabe on the planet down-
loading hints from Hezbollah.

Analogizing the Iraq insurgency to the 1930s Spanish Civil War, which
debuted many tactics later employed in World War II, Robb argues that
we're glimpsing the future of terrorism designed to weaken states on globalization's fringes and keep them in perpetual failure. Robb believes
these same tactics, properly developed, can bring advanced economies to
their knees. But even at their most ambitious, John Robb's twenty-first-
century "global guerrillas" don't aspire to defeat our militaries or topple
our governments, but merely to bankrupt both, hollowing out the West's
institutions to the point where Osama bin Laden's vision of future—make
that, *feudal*—order carries the day across the Islamic world. Robb warns,
"This is the first time in modern history that a nonstate group has the
ability to fight a global war and win." If that assertion strikes you as a tad
sci-fi, then you need to take a hard look at your thoroughly networked
existence, says Robb, and contemplate the myriad choke points and

soft underbellies and general brittleness we've baked into all our infra-structure—both hard and soft.

Here's where Robb's thesis stalls, in my opinion, because it's one thing to keep a weak state in failure, but quite another thing to sow systemic chaos in advanced economies. After all, these societies advanced precisely by mastering such network complexity in the first place, typically in re-sponse to disasters and scandals that regularly perturbed their systems and thus exposed vulnerabilities. Thankfully, transnational terrorism re-mains a fringe activity with virtually no impact on the global economy's performance, which has remained at near-record levels since 2001. By contrast, the cumulative impact of system perturbations caused by man-made and natural disasters in recent years has been far more substantial, and arguably far more beneficial in triggering new rule sets designed to prevent future disruptions.

But here is where Robb's warnings are dead-on: Our global connec-tivity races ahead of our ability to manage all its vulnerabilities. In effect, our rules haven't kept pace, and those gaps and bottlenecks become obvi-ous targets for our enemies in this long war. "Hollowing out" advanced states may be a tall order, but applying just enough system disruption to torpedo an emerging market gets a whole lot easier. Think about how much simpler it would be to generate a true financial panic in China than, say, the United States. Authoritarian China may be more crudely robust in handling shocks to its less developed infrastructure, but it has nowhere near our capacity for processing financial crises through regulating/intervening state entities, agile capital markets, a responsive insurance in-dustry, or a federally insured banking sector—to name a few of our Ameri-can institutions recently tested yet again. As for a far less robust but resource-rich Nigeria, there a small band of insurgents can easily generate overnight upward of a billion-dollar loss to the nation's oil industry. Thus the weaker the state, the more damaging the bill and the easier it is for terrorists to create cascading network failures. The workarounds simply don't yet exist.

Those failures inside the Gap can matter a tremendous amount to the Core as a whole, because, as statistician Nassim Taleb argues in his book *The Black Swan: The Impact of the Highly Improbable*, globalization's rapid

spread creates a worldwide network environment that is "increasingly recursive," meaning more feedback loops and thus more potential for snow-
balling dynamics that are highly unpredictable but trigger planetwide,
winner-take-all effects. History, Taleb reminds us, "does not crawl, it
jumps." While our tendency is to throw up some new Maginot Line of
fortifications every time we get beat from one direction, all those globalization networks, and all the workarounds they enable, truly work in both
directions: Bad effects can work around our defenses just as easily as
our responses can work around the bad effects. If that sounds like a race
of sorts, it is, but to imagine that terrorists are the only players on the
"dark side" is incorrect. The most powerfully disruptive forces in our
networks tend to be our own carelessness in operations and design. Our
"stupid networks" truly limit the impact of nefarious bad actors (i.e., they
get lost in the noise of day-to-day failures), as globalization's vast expansion means, in Taleb's words, that "the sources of Black Swans [highly
improbable but high-impact events] today have multiplied beyond
measurability."

"The pull of the sensational," as Taleb puts it, means our attention is
typically focused on purposeful bad actors, like terrorists and criminals
who opt, as Robb says, to focus their activities in the world of "black globalization," or the globalized version of any nation's informal economy.
For the same reason a nation can never quite get rid of criminal markets,
the global economy will always feature some portion of black globalization. That such nefarious activities have ballooned in the last couple of
decades is no surprise; the same thing always happens whenever frontiers
are rapidly expanded. Indeed, that's why we called it the "wild" American
West. The trick for the Core's great powers is to increase coordination
among themselves in dealing with the Gap's many sources of black globalization. How hard should this be? Not that hard. The Core's rising resource requirements alone will force an immense amount of effort in
improving the efficiency of globalization's networks. That will decrease
the black operations considerably. Moreover, as global warming changes
food production patterns, the planet as a whole will be forced into even
more transregional food trade, the requirements for which will force an
even higher level of efficiency because of perishability and health con-

cerns. Beyond all that, there's simply globalization's flat-world dynamic that pushes all global corporations toward making their networks as lean and efficient as possible in order to keep costs down.

So yes, it's easy to overemphasize the threat of transnational terrorism even as it is a wonderful prompt to do a lot of things we should be pursuing anyway. The truth is, "al Qaeda central," as terrorism expert Marc Sageman points out, is no longer the global control element it once was. As we now head into an era of predominantly "freelance" terrorism, we should be careful not to ascribe more coherence to our enemies than truly exists. The Middle East and Islam in general *are* joining globalization, which will only intensify the actions of radical jihadists in the short term even as their importance within the Islamic world already fades with time (e.g., less popular support for terrorism, more Islamist groups pursuing peaceful change). The *only* reason Islamic radicalism went global was that the threat these extremists faced was globalization itself. We can buy into al Qaeda's propaganda that if America does A, B, and C, then this conflict is over, but the conflict was never really about us. We can get tagged—correctly—for being the progenitor of the global economy, and for playing globalization's bodyguard, but at the end of the day it is globalization itself that will end the jihadists' dreams of a back-to-the-future, pre-economic paradise where "righteous" men can be men and women will remain in their "natural" place. Against that enemy, these bad actors have no more chance than the Lakota guerrilla leader Crazy Horse had against the American System once gold and other mineral resources were found in *them thar hills.*

Having said that, it is unwise to underestimate the fear factor generated by transnational terrorism. Every system needs a bogeyman to force efficiencies and upgrades, and I say, better for globalization that Robb's global guerrillas perform that role than to have economic nationalists make globalization itself the "great evil of our day." Transnational terrorists and other criminal elements are the quintessential "short sellers" in globalization's networks market: They seek out choke points and vulnerabilities and inefficiencies and exploit them for varieties of gain—monetary being the least impressive and damaging. To the extent we want to disintermediate these bad actors from this admittedly useful function (assuming we avoid Maginot Line/Berlin Wall responses), we need to harness globalization's flat-world dynamics in the form of useful enforcers, or entities that trigger the same upgrades in security that bad actors sometimes do, but do so preemptively and pervasively and persistently, without the pain. Insurance companies always come to mind in this regard, but so too does any globally integrated enterprise (e.g., Toyota, Wal-Mart) that pushes its feeder nodes (producer/buyer chains) toward more efficient operations.

Thus, globalization needs many more watchdogs, and since watchdogs are typically posted *after* scandals erupt, America and the rest of the Core need to learn how to welcome such crises and scandals for what they represent—a chance to make all these networks work better. Just as in the American System, it's not a matter of avoiding scandal per se, but rather of processing scandals as rapidly as possible. As the French Enlightenment philosopher René Descartes once put it, "Each problem that I solved became a rule which served afterwards to solve other problems."

In globalization, this is the most valuable asset one can accumulate: good rules leading to good reputation.

THE NEW RULES: FROM "KNOW YOUR CUSTOMER" TO "KNOW YOUR SUPPLY CHAIN"

In the history of globalization's rapid expansion in the last quarter of the twentieth century, two events stand out most. The first is Deng Xiaoping's decision to begin marketizing China's economy across the 1980s. The second is the contemporaneous decisions by Ronald Reagan and Margaret Thatcher to launch a wave of deregulation that, along with advances in information technology, laid the groundwork for the globalization of financial markets across the 1990s. The sum of these changes turbocharged globalization's advance by radically increasing the velocity, volume, variety, and visibility of market transactions, or in Nayan Chanda's terminology, the "four V's" of "modern interconnectedness." Naturally, bad actors jumped on that bandwagon, and after 9/11 we saw the empire strike back in the form of new and more stringent rules regarding all those transactions.

All of a sudden, thanks to the Bush administration's USA Patriot Act, it wasn't enough to say your bank processed all these money flows according to the old rules. Now banks were told that they needed to know exactly what kind of customers they were serving. That's a pretty easy progression to understand when we're talking about something as fungible and symbolic and uniform as money, but inevitably that logic must be extended into globalization's supply chains—meaning, soon it won't be enough just to know with whom you're dealing; you'll want verification of every ingredient in every product. In short, the global economy will soon be forced to account for every aspect in its supply chains just as if they were police departments handling evidence for a court trial.

While some of this coming network transparency will be triggered by a growing concern over carbon footprints and the general notion of improved energy efficiency, product liability and the potential for disease and poisoning outbreaks (both accidental and purposeful) will be a bigger driver, especially as global warming forces hyperconnectivity and hyperdependency for all sorts of nations on the global economy's food and water trade networks. It won't be enough to say, "I can verify all these ingredients were put together correctly." Increasingly, assemblers will be forced to verify the purity of their ingredients going all the way up the supply chain. Just as a modern automobile tends to be built with parts from all over the world, so, too, do modern foodstuffs, drugs, and all sorts of consumables with the potential to inflict harm on consumers.

The global food trade is a particular worry, because it combines loose international regulatory regimes with a highly fragmented production network. Yes, such a network is highly susceptible to terrorist attack, but again, quite frankly, that threat pales in comparison to what human mistakes and greed cost us every year in tainted products. The temptation, of course, is for the Old Core's populations to demand "Made in [home country]" products, but since nobody is interested in dramatically raising the prices of food and drugs any more than necessary (indeed, global demand does that quite nicely), that impulse tends to dissipate as a rule (although persistently high oil prices can cut back a certain amount of globalization's assembly traffic). Plus, in truth, it's the supplying countries, like China, where the public typically faces the worst liabilities, meaning, if you think tainted Chinese products can hurt us now and then, they tend to ruin Chinese lives on a far more consistent basis.

Moreover, while it's tempting to view a surge in global scandals as evidence that globalization's network chains are out of control—even *beyond* control—we have to view these crises as positive evidence that a more "recursive environment," as Taleb likes to describe globalization, is actually a more robust and therefore resilient environment. Each new feedback loop, however achieved ("vigilante consumers," blogging muckrakers, etc.), increases the "what we know" pool while decreasing the "what we don't know" universe. Granted, as the complexity and density of these networks increase, the "what we don't know" universe will always tend to overshadow the known universe, but that just means that the dynamic management of rules becomes far more important. In effect, we need rules that are so smart that they can sense, think, and respond on their own (more on that in a bit).

One might think that this is an unprecedented global threat. Of course, all you have to do is go back to that great first "counterfeit nation" of the global economy—nineteenth-century *caveat emptor* America, full of criminals, scam artists, snake-oil salesmen, and the like—to realize that today's China isn't globalization's first nation of outlaws but merely the latest in a long line that includes several current Core stalwarts like Japan and South Korea. The difference this time around, though, is significant. Back in the early days of globalization, the vast majority of food consumed was grown locally. That won't be the case on a planet where global warming will shift regional food production patterns, largely through drought. It's not just that the Gap will get a lot drier, and thus have a harder time than it already does in feeding itself. All those New Core economies, where the bulk of the burgeoning global middle class will emerge, will likewise find themselves unable to meet the demands of their populations for food—less in volume than in quality.

When our pediatric dentist told me a few years back that our adopted Chinese daughter was going to prematurely lose her top front baby teeth, it occurred to me that Wisconsin's dairy industry was facing a long boom. A leap of logic, perhaps, but let this native "cheesehead" connect the dots on this stunning global-demand shift.

My wife and I adopted Vonne Mei when she was nine months old, by which time the fate of her baby teeth had been sealed by eighteen months of the diet in her native province of Jiangxi, part of China's vast interior

rural landscape. Being a "persona au gratin," I was struck by the dearth of
dairy in Jiangxi cuisine. There were poultry, pork, and vegetables galore,
but few milk products and virtually no cheese. Butter seemed a luxury
item. Think back to that childhood admonition: Drink your milk so you'll
have strong bones and good teeth! Well, Vonne Mei's choppers turned
out as brittle, as you might imagine, given that low-calcium diet. By the
time we first noticed the large brownish areas on her front teeth, thinking
they were plaque, it was too late. Our relatively high-sugar diet had destroyed what thin enamel our little Mei Mei possessed. Ten crowns and
many procedures later, her top front four teeth were gone. Naturally,
Vonne Mei's diet is much improved here in the States, where calcium-
rich dairy products abound. X-rays indicate that her permanent teeth will
not suffer the same weaknesses. By adopting Mei Mei, our family radically
elevated her up the global income chain, meaning she escapes certain
medical liabilities associated with poor diet and picks up different ones
associated with a rich diet, with the net effect being a longer, healthier—
and somewhat "taller"—life.

Now consider India and China rapidly growing their economies, with
upward of 2.5 billion people upgrading their diet as a result. For example,
China's per capita income has doubled in recent years, and Beijing's leaders pledge to double it again over the next generation. As someone who
has seen his own personal income rise like that over a similar time frame,
let me say that I eat a lot better today than I did as a starving college student, not just more food but food of much higher quality. Invariably, Chinese and Indians are doing exactly the same, with the net effect being a
huge increase in global demand for dairy products. The average Chinese
consumed 11 pounds of dairy products per year a decade ago, but that
number jumped to 51 pounds by 2006. Americans, by contrast, consume
an average of 181 pounds of milk products a year, or the equivalent of 21
gallons. When a big chunk of humanity decides to quintuple its milk consumption over a decade, that triggers a profound global market shock. A
2007 *New York Times* article even went so far as to declare milk "the new
oil," noting that global milk prices had doubled since 2005, leading to "reports of cows being stolen on Wisconsin dairy farms." So much for the
feared "cheddar curtain"!

Now, here's the trick on accommodating all that new demand. Unlike oil, dairy products are perishable, so dairy markets—like "all politics"—tend to be local. As the *Times* piece noted, "only about 7 percent of all the milk produced globally is traded across borders." But with much greater Chinese and Indian demand coming online in the next decade or so, something's got to give. Having worked on a dairy farm in my youth and lived for years with a nursing wife, let me present one inescapable fact about creating milk: It takes one heckuva lot of water. For the average dairy cow to produce nine gallons of milk a day, it needs to drink eighteen gallons of fresh, clean water, something booming China does not possess in abundance. China is already a top global milk producer and the world's largest importer. With water tables dropping precipitously throughout the country, thanks to China's prodigious use in both industry and agriculture, there's little hope that the country can keep up with its booming dairy requirements, especially when you factor in the resource competition from the expanding domestic beef industry. China's meat consumption has increased by more than 50 percent since 1995, higher than that of any other emerging market.

The upshot for my birth state, otherwise known as America's Dairyland, is that global milk prices increasingly surpass our subsidized domestic prices, meaning American farmers could dramatically increase exports without government support, something the dairy industry managed to do in New Zealand a while back. New Zealand, the "Saudi Arabia of milk," exports dairy products to China like crazy. For the world's major agricultural exporters as a whole, such trade expansion would only reemphasize that, as globalization's advance triggers local resource constraints, nations are forced into greater economic interdependence—otherwise known as comparative advantage. Think about that whenever politicians propose turning America's heartland into one giant ethanol plant as part of some quixotic quest for energy independence.

Globalization is going to need all the future farmers it can get. By 2030, world food production is predicted to rise by a whopping fifty percent, and hardly just in the low-end foodstuffs. That means we'll need to continue and dramatically speed up our current "green revolution" through biotechnology, yet another issue where America will find itself more in line with rising New Core pillars (e.g., China, India, Brazil, Argentina, Chile, Australia, and South Africa) than with Old Core Europe and Japan.

Not only does this emerging global reality provide hope that the Old Core will soon abandon its ruinous agricultural subsidies, thus freeing the WTO's Doha Development Round currently held hostage to them, it'll also force the Old Core economies (including America) to both upgrade their current systems of food inspection and export them to other states in a bid to globalize such transparency. Again, given the high stakes involved (i.e., tainted food can close an overseas market permanently to your products), it won't be enough to sample every *nth* portion. No, you'll see the rise of pervasive and persistent scanning throughout the supply chain.

That may strike you as an implausibly expensive goal, but only because you're thinking about this in terms of running every item past a choke point of scanners when the future of nanotechnology suggests a far different path. Nanosensors (atomic- and molecular-sized) can be clustered in the thousands on a tiny tag-emitter slapped onto every wrapped or boxed agricultural product (or sprinkled throughout bulk supplies only to be removed later in processing). The emitter only needs to be strong enough to signal the next one over, which then signals the next one over again, and so on, until larger sensors, placed along the supply chain, pick up the distress call. In short, we don't need to run everything past some sensor; in the future we'll simply embed nanosensors throughout the process. I'm not talking science fiction here; I've seen plenty of these nanosensors in my status as visiting strategist at Oak Ridge National Laboratory in eastern Tennessee. Australian cattlemen already do a simple version of this with their beef, using sensors to track every cow from birth to death in this manner.

Such biometric or genetic-mapping technologies represent the future of supply-chain management, including the processing of travelers whom we must always suspect of passing disease in this day and age. So don't be surprised if these nanosensors are embedded through jetliners in coming years, triggering all sorts of new protocols, because the future of all such safety regimes is to move away from spot checks, like those in airport security lines, and toward environments with ubiquitous sensing. In this manner, what America should be doing right now is giving away such technology to any less wealthy nation that connects up to us on any level, making that a key component of future aid programs. By generating such "external improvements" for our trade partners, we heighten our own security while buttressing their ability to "fast-pass" their products and people into our system.

This would be the best kind of connecting aid, one that extends the transparency of our networks (think our national security community wouldn't be interested in that?) while making sensor-dark portions of the global economy less opaque. As our sensor networks expand, driven largely by our own fears of what all this connectivity can do to us, less of the world will be able to remain off-grid and therefore attractive to transnational bad actors who prefer anonymity the vast majority of the time. This is swamp-draining of the best sort: increasing our nation's safety while bolstering its economic efficiency and therefore competitiveness. I say, don't be frightened or dismayed when Wal-Mart starts hiring its own small army of intelligence officers. Instead, weave them and their growing capabilities into your system.

In an age when "worldsourcing" replaces outsourcing, all these know-your-chain rule sets are both inevitable and good. As Don Tapscott and Anthony Williams argue in their book *Wikinomics: How Mass Collaboration Changes Everything*, smart global firms are abandoning the multinational corporate model completely and turning themselves into systems integrators of entire production and buyer and even R&D chains. In moving in this direction, we see companies exhibiting the same sort of system-administrator approach long seen in the world of information technology, but now employing it upon the larger universe of the global economy, thanks to the rise of service-oriented architectural thinking: Anything that can be netted will be netted, and so services and even entire companies can be reconfigured *around* networks instead of networks merely being adapted to their existing structures. The principles of "wikinomics" are the same ones I've been preaching across these "realignment" chapters: Be open (connect!), treat peers as equals, and don't force hierarchies (no primacy please!); share both technology and workloads (like those sensor nets I just described), and act globally whenever possible (i.e., make globalization *truly* global!).

Good grand strategy goes with the major flows of the age. It exploits the technologies that *must* appear instead of waiting on ones (like effective strategic missile defense) that may never appear. It tries to get in front of major resource and money flows, sensing that is where the future infrastructure will be built and thus where future sensor nets must go. It utilizes the undeniable forces of the era to effect its desired ends (e.g., ubiquitous sensing to drain the swamp), instead of asking local governments to leapfrog into capabilities not easily transferred, like democracy. At its heart, good grand strategy is both economically deterministic and technologically opportunistic.

THE NEW NORMAL:
IN SEARCH OF NEW DETERRENCE

As someone who works with national security agencies and the military to figure out what their roles need to be in this age of rising connectivity, I can readily attest to the following dynamic: This community tends to bump into some new aspect of America's rising interdependency with the global economy and then will immediately—and rather reflexively—declare the protection of that network a "national security requirement." Since the community is already overburdened by ongoing operations and has a tendency to completely discount any private-sector efforts to protect such chains, this requirement is also immediately dubbed an "unfunded mandate," meaning it would be nice to do but we don't have enough resources. Public-private partnerships are pursued, mostly just conversations about the shared vulnerabilities ("Both you, the military, and we, this sector, rely on these networks!"), and in the end a certain amount of faith is extended in each direction, with the national security community hoping the private sector will do its part to keep these networks safe and the private sector assuming the military will show up and help out if some serious system perturbation erupts down the road. The rest, as the professional fearmongers say, is "pure chaos"!

But in truth, the two sides usually respond to such crises completely differently, so cooperation is hard to come by. The private sector responds to system disruptions by further decentralizing the networks—more workarounds equals more resilience. The national security community, however, does just the opposite: more centralization ("Get me a czar!"). The private sector wants a flexible rule set, able to change with circumstances, and the government favors a fixed, clear rule set, subject to periodic review. The private sector seeks to adapt itself to regular disruptions, the government seeks to deter them altogether. The private sector lives in a world of constant network breakdowns and break-ins (high-probability and low-impact events), while the government focuses on preventing low-probability and high-impact events. The private sector views globalization as being all about security—very non-zero-sum. The national security community still views globalization as being all about complicating defense—a very zero-sum dynamic. By and large, these two communities speak very different languages; I base this statement on my years of experience in each, with the private sector having left the Cold War completely behind, and the national security community still largely trapped in the Cold War mindset. All you have to do is check their respective views on China to verify this.

The search for "Deterrence 2.0," as one U.S. Strategic Command 2008 workshop report (to which I contributed) on the subject put it, "is as much an emerging phenomenon as it is a sought-after method for dealing with both state and non-state actors in an increasingly interconnected world." By admitting this, the report's authors simply acknowledged that we're still in the learning phase regarding globalization's dense connectivity. We're not sure what constitutes effective trust or realistic deterrence, or why some networks are inherently resilient while others are more brittle. We have a crude sense of firewalls, both technological and cultural. We search for the sensational scenarios even as we know that what we really seek is to understand the "dogs that did not bark"—the blasé outcomes that no one remembers because they weren't considered truly disruptive. We want to fathom danger when what really matters is the mundane.

Because the Cold War's defining conflict scenario was so binary (nuclear war happens or it does not), the national security community has a hard time translating concepts of deterrence into the globalization era: The interconnectedness of everything makes most threats of retaliation seem counterproductive—every response feeling like we're cutting off our nose to spite our face (not a great competition with nihilists who have no expectation of winning, and whose reward is heaven). We seek to confuse and disinform terrorist groups online or to shame them within their real-world communities, and generally endeavor to make our response pattern highly unpredictable ("You just never know where we'll be, do you?"). But all these responses seem so asymmetrical: our top-down planners against their bottom-up searchers, to recall William Easterly's terminology. They capitalize on the "wisdom of crowds," while we pool expert opinion. As someone who has worked with the intelligence community for years, I can't help thinking that it is better off joining that which it cannot beat.

James Surowiecki, author of *The Wisdom of Crowds*, says the collective mind outperforms individual expertise when the following conditions are met: (1) there is a diversity of opinion in the pool; (2) there is independence among participants (no bandwagoning through implicit hierarchies); (3) the group is decentralized; and (4) there is some mechanism to aggregate opinions efficiently. When you hear those requirements, the first examples that may come to mind are gambling pools. But you could describe Wikipedia in much the same way. Indeed, it comes closer to the concept of a "central intelligence agency" than our own CIA—in its infinite secrecy—does. Ground truth, or the shared understanding of what's actually happening in any unfolding event, is the most powerful source of deterrence ("We know exactly what you're up to!"), and to be achieved, it must be assembled from a vast array of characters, none of whom retain control over their inputs. This is the essential problem of information sharing within the intelligence community (IC): ORCON, or "originator-controlled" information. When every participant in the discussion decides what others "need to know," pretty much everyone ends up being treated like a mushroom (the IC joke being "You're kept in the dark and fed a lot of shit"). The IC has most everything it needs to become a wise crowd: diversity (not a lot, but enough), independence (all agencies completely distrust one another), and decentralization (despite the creation of a director of national intelligence, each agency still largely goes it own way). What has been lacking up to now is a mechanism for aggregating opinion, because that mechanism requires the death of ORCON. The good news here is that the IC is currently in the process of creating several such aggregating venues (e.g., blogs, social networks, an Intellipedia modeled on Wikipedia) that mirror much of what you and I currently enjoy on the Web today. My recent favorite nongovernmental offering is Wikileaks, which basically serves as a wormhole between the two communities—the secret and the unclassified. The Wikileaks motto—"We protect you and get your disclosure out to the world"—marks it as the Radio Free Europe of the surveillance age.

After we have flattened our intelligence community in this way, which will be incredibly helpful, the next step in improving our situational awareness is to connect our collective intelligence to on-the-ground reporting in countries of interest. Here, the blogging phenomenon provides a rich harvest (something I've spent some time over the years preaching to the IC). Not surprisingly, most of the countries we worry about are those that have half embraced globalization: allowing broadband connectivity while trying to control for content. China and Iran are two good examples. Naturally, both have vast and thriving blogging communities (funny how that works!) that remind me, quite frankly, of our own military's burgeoning online community. A few years back, many regular soldiers and officers who were fed up with the pace of change in training began their own discussion groups to swap tradecraft in much the same way that Robb's global guerrillas do, their lack of secrecy based on the notion that they weren't discussing anything the terrorists and insurgents didn't already know! Over time, the U.S. Army and Marine Corps have become smart to invite many of these online forums inside the "wire" of accepted military Internet traffic—yet another example of established behemoths buying up innovative start-ups.

If working their hearts and minds online is one strategy, and matching their decentralization is another, a third strategy for dealing with what Ori Brafman and Rod Beckstrom call "starfish" organizations (as in, regenerative) is to force centralization upon them. They dub this the "cow approach," in honor of the U.S. Government's tactic in the American West of giving nomadic Native American tribes (in one celebrated case, the Apache) cattle to force them into a more sedentary lifestyle, where rewards became less symbolic and more material. In short, when people have less, honor matters more, so attacking that social structure basically amounts to bribing them "down" to our level. What would constitute "cattle" today? Given the overwhelming demographic skew inside many Gap regions toward restless youth, I can't think of anything better than MTV and iPods and cell phones for the connectivity, but—most important—decent-paying jobs for the lifestyle tie-down, because jobs allow young men to marry and start families. In a traditional society struggling to retain cultural coherence, nothing matters more for reducing the pool of idle young males.

A final concept begging for consideration as strategic deterrence in the globalization age is simply the well-attuned public. When everybody in American society, for example, practices good security behavior, almost all of which corresponds to "neighborhood watch" best practices, you've just added an additional 300 million–plus sense-think-and-respond human sensors across your network, boosting your resilience infinitely. As the columnist Brad Todd noted, the 9/11 hijackers aboard United flight 93 had their months of planning foiled spontaneously by ordinary citizens who, through real-time networking, cracked their enemies' code and mounted an effective response within minutes. In short, we have no shortage of "white hats" ready to man battle stations and fight back on a 24/7/365 basis. Today's globalization, as über-blogger Glenn Reynolds argues, provides the network connections that allow any ordinary citizen the same breadth of knowledge and (virtual) experience as only elites once enjoyed in the past. Tapping into that broadband capability only makes sense in a world where every "swinging mouse" can make a difference.

Add all these ideas up and you quickly come to the conclusion that deterrence today is no longer about holding our enemies' assets at risk. Globalization's advance actively reformats our enemies' most prized assets—their culture and community. You might think that reprehensible. I consider it God's work in a world where we can't all afford to go our own way any longer and still leave behind a planet our children will enjoy. If that means my culture's got to change a lot to accommodate yours, then so be it, but the reverse will also be true. Let's have no illusions here: Globalization is the ultimate remix, doing on a global scale what American culture has been doing here for over two centuries—blending the best and discarding the rest. What that inevitable outcome tells us is that real deterrence in this age must be based in transmitting that context and making clear its inevitability. The only way to combat exclusionary, collective identities is to offer globalization's glorious hi-low mix of universal identity coupled with maximum individual freedom—the very essence of being American. And no, that's not implying that everybody on the planet ends up looking and acting more like us than themselves. As Americans constitute a mere one-twentieth of the world's population, that's an unlikely outcome. I'm just pointing out that, as the population furthest along in this globalization experiment (have we not been accepting all comers to our completely synthetic culture for over two centuries?), we'll just be among those most comfortable with the outcome.

Real deterrence in this day and age will remain focused on resilience, not the threat of disproportionate punishment. It will remain focused on this message: *Anything you can do, I can counter faster; I can absorb anything better than you.* America is often derided for its lack of cultural and historical awareness, its attention-deficit disorder. In truth, this is one of our greatest strengths—our sheer speed in adaptation. No power should ever want to engage America in a race to shift paradigms. We cannot be shell-shocked or demoralized by change. *We simply live for it.*

THE GLOBAL ACCELERANT:
THE GREAT GLOBALIZATION BUILD-OUT

I can't overemphasize what a world-turned-upside-down change has occurred in infrastructure development in emerging and developing economies thanks to globalization. Starting with the "big push" heyday of Western foreign aid in the 1950s, the vast majority of infrastructure building in the so-called Third World was directed by Western public entities using public funds. It was a supply-push function: Depending on how "rich" the West felt, that's how much was available. Today the situation is overwhelmingly reversed, as the majority of infrastructure building in emerging and developing economies can be described as a demand-pull function: Asian companies—from west to east—creating the necessary physical connectivity to access developing economies' raw materials and markets, while back home their governments and national flagship companies engage in massive build-outs of road, railroad, airport, educational, manufacturing, research and development, and power generation and distribution systems. After decades of hand-wringing by the West over "Who is going to save the world's poor?" we find ourselves largely standing on the sidelines while Asians step up to save themselves and the rest of the Gap.

Will Asians do any better in connecting these Gap regions to globalization in a sustainable fashion? They have three things going for them right now. First, they've got the cash, thanks to trade imbalances with the West over goods or energy. We know that historically globalization tends to expand when the global economy is flush with money. Second, they're demographically incentivized, whether we're talking East Asians facing a growing population of elders or West Asians trying to accommodate youth bulges as they head into working age. Third, they're doing it out of greed and ambition instead of empathy and guilt, and, no offense, but I'll take Asian greed over Western guilt any day.

Some sense of the scope involved here:

Overall, emerging markets are expected to build over $20 trillion of infrastructure over the next decade, according to recent calculations by the Wall Street firm Morgan Stanley.

China is the clear global demand center when it comes to infrastructure-building, accounting for over 40 percent of that stunning total. Right now they're deep into a road-building spree that recalls America's construction of its interstate system starting in the 1950s. By 2020, China will have roughly the same amount of freeways—about 50,000 miles—and it will have pulled off this feat in roughly half the time it took America. In its efforts to construct the "new socialist countryside" (really, just a desperate attempt to keep the interior poor from falling too far behind the booming coast), Beijing plans to increase road networks there by almost 50 percent in the next few years alone. As China now crams 25 percent of the world's rail traffic on just 6 percent of the world's track length, it is looking to embark on the biggest railway expansion the world has seen since the nineteenth century, adding 60 percent more track in a dozen years. Air travel has skyrocketed since 1985, increasing more than twenty-five-fold, leading to plans for ninety-seven new major airports by 2020. Seaport capacity will likewise grow dramatically, almost doubling by 2020. You want to know why U.S. export of construction equipment is booming? This is why.

In the emerging great powers of the New Core—Russia, China, India, and Brazil—there is also a new assertiveness on the part of their multinational corporations. It is not just the buying up of ailing Western companies that attracts attention, but also the desire to go "downstream" in ways that outsiders just didn't do in the past. I mean, it's one thing for the UK's National Grid to buy up electrical grids on America's northeast coast, but quite another for Russia's Gazprom to move aggressively into retail natural-gas markets in Europe on top of its already extensive network of pipelines. Historically, it has always been a matter of Western energy companies going over there, getting the stuff, and marketing it back here. Now we're seeing national energy companies from over there bringing their own stuff over here and marketing it directly. To some, that is awfully scary, highlighting the West's dependency on foreign energy sources, but to me, it's a natural and welcome business instinct on the part of these outside firms, indicating they seek the same sort of vertical integration in their industries that Western firms have long achieved. If you want stakeholders, you've got to give them legitimate stakes.

What's fascinating this time around with the oil boom is that the Middle East is *not* sending all its money west and asking us what they should invest in. This time around, the Middle East is either investing its profits locally or sending them east to both tap into and encourage the sort of infrastructure build-out that will further cement (no pun intended) energy ties east-east—as in, the Middle East to East Asia. This is yet another reason why it is unsustainable for America to have a grand strategy in which we play sole Leviathan to the Persian Gulf: It is just not our oil and they—meaning both "Easts"—simply won't pay for it. The Gulf Cooperation Council countries, including Saudi Arabia, are expected to pocket as much as $3 trillion between 2005 and 2020. About half of that money is expected to stay at home for infrastructural development of all sorts aimed at providing jobs to young people (true draining-the-swamp work), about a quarter ($750 billion) is expected to be invested in the larger Middle East/North Africa (MENA) region, and the remainder will probably go into sovereign wealth funds of the sort that buy equity in Wall Street firms—at bargain-basement prices—during periods of turbulence while simultaneously availing themselves of good investment opportunities in the East. The good news for the West is simply the overwhelming scope of the profits: A good portion inevitably comes our way simply because we've got the biggest and best financial markets to handle that sort of flow (for now, at least).

Here's how I wrap this all up in terms of Western companies thinking ahead to growth opportunities.

First, you've got to get in on this huge infrastructural build-out going on in Asia. There's just too much money to be made in all this construction and the associated business.

Second, it you're not there, you can't participate in the roll-up season that must inevitably occur. By "roll-up season," I mean a long period of intensive mergers and acquisitions (M&A) to create the infrastructure behemoths that will make all this expansion happen. Simply put, the world doesn't currently have corporations big enough to handle all this work efficiently, but inevitably those behemoths will arise through M&A, creating global "trusts" that dominate markets in the same way that such giants once ruled in late-nineteenth-century America. No, they won't be as easy to whittle down to more acceptable size on the basis of national legislation, because many of these firms will arrive on the scene with the firm backing of their national governments. But I would expect them to submit to a progressively "downward" evolution in the direction of Palmisano's "globally integrated enterprise," or a firm that sources, develops, manufactures, and markets locally. In other words, I'd expect these behemoths to shed their nationalistic flavor over time and become truly global brands largely detached from cultural moorings—like a Toyota.

Remember, good globalizers, whether they're companies or religions, must leave behind their original cultural context. For example, Hollywood markets increasingly internationalized films, because roughly half its box office registers overseas. Commensurately, when a Bollywood (Indian) entertainment giant steps up to finance American film director Steven Spielberg's future creative freedom, it's also looking to create a marketing beachhead for its major stars. So again, count on greed to make the necessary changes to firms, such that we're not looking at a future where great powers clash through their corporate giants. Where protectionism is likely to rear its ugly head, though, will be when Eastern firms start gobbling up Western ones, a process we've already witnessed in several industries. But we'd simply better get used to the idea that most mergers will feature an Asian name, either fore or aft. So if you think DaimlerChrysler was shocking, better fasten your seat belt.

Third, Western companies want to be there simply to partake in the stunning amount of new R&D that will necessarily accompany all this infrastructural development. Since we're often talking harsher environments with more fragile ecosystems, plus a lot of regions that will be harder hit by global warming, the ingenuity required to pull this off will be immense—and highly profitable for multiple sales elsewhere.

That gets me to the final reason. By jumping in, not only will you get smarter, you'll learn how to sell to that fabled "bottom of the pyramid" of the global working class that will present the opportunity for highest corporate returns in coming decades. You'll learn how to sell to people who don't have a lot of money but do have a lot of value expectations, or basically the market Wal-Mart has mastered back here in the States and aims to conquer globally. I know, I know. It's fantastic to think our global economy's future growth is dependent on a lot of poor people becoming both innovative and greedy at the same time, but hey! That's how these United States were built. So sit on the sidelines at your own risk.

Some caveats before I move on:

First, there are clearly new opportunities in this environment for international financial institutions such as the International Monetary Fund and the World Bank. Both have suffered an existential crisis recently—namely, they're just not sure what their role is anymore in this transforming global economy. Here's my two cents: Having watched the U.S. Federal Reserve basically redefine its role—thanks to the subprime crisis—from mere protector of American banks to rescuer of America's financial markets, I suspect the IMF will continue its 1990s evolution in that direction, but with a greater focus on threshold economies, or those near-emerging markets where a financial panic can overnight kill a healthy progression from Gap to Core status. I think the global economy has evolved to the point of interdependency where the Functioning Core's economies can look out for one another, leaving the IMF to move "down" the development chain. As for the World Bank, I foresee a greater focus on financing postconflict and postdisaster recoveries in fragile states than on classic Western foreign aid. The World Bank is simply losing its relevance in peacetime development inside the Gap, and therefore should likewise move into more needier areas. In sum, I'd like to see the IMF focus on preventive interventions in New Core and Gap countries on the economic upswing and the World Bank focus on postincident interventions in Gap countries on the downswing. In both instances, we're talking about institutions "playing down" from their original purposes, but as globalization expands and matures, that's how I'd update Bretton Woods.

Second, as globalization's great infrastructural build-out unfolds, shifting over time from the New Core East to the Gap as a whole, we're clearly going to see a major increase in the role of nuclear power. Africa, home to about one-fifth of the world's uranium, wants to move aggressively in this direction. The West and Russia, fearful of proliferation of nuclear weapons–grade uranium, push to create a Core-dominated consortium that will oversee the entire fuel-enrichment cycle for any country willing to outsource that process, in effect asking Gap countries to assume an energy-dependency relationship. Several proposals are on the table, and while there is a chance of competing rule sets fighting it out over time (e.g., competing U.S. and Russian systems), the odds are that the Core will come to some agreement that Gap countries find acceptable. But the clear upshot of all this will be that far more nuclear material will move along globalization's networks, only emphasizing the worldwide need for better real-time, pervasive monitoring systems. So again, a shift from Cold War deterrence to globalization-era transparency seems inevitable.

Finally, it is ironic that much of the antiglobalization sentiment is centered in the Functioning Core's most advanced economies, especially America and Europe. In effect, we're the rich in the global economy who essentially look for protection from its poor and their "unfair cheap labor." This unfortunate sentiment creates strange bedfellows, for as economist Paul Collier notes, "Rich-country protectionism masquerades in alliance with antiglobalization romantics and third world crooks." Since I count al

Qaeda and most other radical extremists in that mix of "antiglobalization romantics and third world crooks" (i.e., they promise retreats into the past and avail themselves of black globalization to finance their activities), this kind of thinking works decidedly against serious grand strategy designed to make sure America prevails in a long-war context, primarily because it is defeatist: When the global economy that America put in place gets too competitive for our comfort, we threaten withdrawal and/or demand self-serving renegotiation of the rules. My point is this: With globalization's great infrastructural build-out well under way, the West has essentially lost control of the global dialogue over rules. From here on out, there's no dictating, just negotiations.

Like the other caveats named above, this too is a price of our success in replicating the American System on a global scale. If we want to regain some measure of national control over globalization's rapid expansion, then we'll have to get far better at working its seams and frontiers. We'll have to get better at reconnecting postconflict and postdisaster states to the global economy, catching them at the moment of network connection that we purposefully engineer in a manner consistent with our preferred rules. For if we don't, I guarantee you, others will. That's why the cry of "no more Iraqs!" is so on-target: America either gets better at playing the "second half" or we'll find ourselves shut out from the ground zero of new rule-making in the system—the generation of new markets in previously off-grid locations (remember, that's how we once began). While America's economic interests in these locations may seem marginal at first glance, our political-military interests are anything but. Because if we don't push for good connectivity of the sort that extends the Core's transparency inside the Gap instead of simply exposing the Core to the Gap's worst "exports" (i.e., disease, terror, drugs, crime), the frontier-taming activities of many New Core countries like China may well end up creating more system instability than system integration.

THE INESCAPABLE REALIGNMENT:
REENGINEERING DEVELOPMENT (IN-A-BOX™)

In this section I want to explain how I think America needs to improve its overall approach regarding postconflict, postdisaster and—best of all—prefailure, prebankruptcy situations inside the Gap. While I think the U.S. government has a big role to play in this, I don't think governments build economies or markets, but rather that businesses do. I also don't think we can expect to create sustainable economies inside the Gap using a combination of military personnel plus aid/relief workers, neither of whom know, quite frankly, much of anything about enabling entrepreneurship. They're both supply-push public-sector providers, and globalization has entered an age of demand-pull private-sector builders, so if I'm going to describe the missing link in America's "second half" equation, I'm naturally going to address private-sector contributors first and foremost.

The small company I work for, Enterra Solutions, has done significant work figuring out how to make America better at rapidly reconnecting Gap economies to globalization after a crisis. Since early 2007, Enterra has been doing work in Kurdish northern Iraq that is qualitatively different from reconstruction work attempted before: We don't focus on getting old businesses up and running. We expect the Iraqis to do that on their own, or to start up new ones based on what they want to produce and sell. Instead, we focus on generating the baseline network connectivity required for Iraqis to actually conduct business transactions with the outside world, meaning a focus on telecoms, banking, business and investment exchanges, utilities, and border security. Enterra's initial work in Iraq is a proof of concept for something we call Development-in-a-Box, meaning, once templated here (e.g., how do you bring a local telecom immediately up to global connectivity standards?), we plan to sell such upgrades as a repeatable solution throughout the Gap, partnering with some of the world's largest systems integrators, utilities providers, dealerbrokers, logistical firms, and the like.

First, some background on how this came about.

In late 2004, when I decided to write a sequel to *The Pentagon's New Map*, it basically cost me my job at the Naval War College. Not a bad move for either side, as it was time for me to move on to bigger and better opportunities. I simply felt that more of the answers regarding the things I care most about would be found in the private sector than in the public sector, so I was open to moving in that direction. Luckily for me, I was immediately approached by a serial entrepreneur named Stephen De-

Angelis. DeAngelis, a China scholar in college at the same time I was studying Russia in the early 1980s, took a far different route following his undergraduate degree. While I went on to grad school and then the national security community, DeAngelis bypassed further education to jump right into the business world, cutting his teeth in mergers and acquisitions at a major retail bank in the late 1980s. Over time, that led him to a variety of opportunities, including working for economic development in the U.S Virgin Islands after Hurricane Hugo, acquiring and operating a specialty paint company in the Caribbean for an institutional investor, conducting a lot of foreign direct investment reconnaissance efforts in China long before the crowds showed up, and eventually starting his own Internet-based technology firm (exiting before the 2000 tech crash). After 9/11, DeAngelis, a native New Yorker, decided he was going to take his own time and money to think through the following problem set: If 9/11 could happen because America couldn't adequately "connect the dots," or spot the emerging pattern of events in time to foil the plot, then what would a private-sector company have to create to fill this void in terms of a new class of products, technology, or services? In other words, how would it make America more resilient? His vision eventually grew to include how to make businesses more resilient in the age of globalization.

When we met in the spring of 2005, I wanted to lead a revolution in thinking within the national security community regarding war and peace, spreading my personal vision that "shrinking the Gap" should be America's grand strategy of the future, and DeAngelis *merely* wanted to fix America's public-sector connect-the-dots problem while forging a new enterprise management philosophy for its private sector, making our companies more competitive and resilient. I viewed globalization's spread primarily in terms of rules—as in, connectivity drives code, and code enables peace. DeAngelis saw things similarly but from a different angle: He believed the complexity involved in running companies and governments was skyrocketing, thanks to globalization's mix of ballooning transaction rates, new regulatory requirements, and increased security threats, and so the only way companies and governments could master that rising complexity was to create and spread the technological means by which rules can be dynamically managed.

Let me unpack that notion a bit.

In a simpler world, when your company or government bumped into some new phenomenon, you simply took out your three-ring binder of rules and looked up the steps you were supposed to take in this situation. If it was completely unprecedented, you called up the chain of command until you reached some level where responsible parties could articulate new rules. Upon receiving them, you'd insert them into your three-ring binder and proceed as instructed, and over time those new rules would be extended throughout the rest of your company or government agency as required. It was a relatively slow process that could be automated in some places, but the new rule sets tended to come in bunches and at best sporadically, with the "man in the loop" driving the process.

Add modern information technology and network connectivity to this dynamic and everything speeds up dramatically, including a lot more automation of rules and far more rapid responses to new phenomena. A good example of this involves computer viruses spreading across the Internet. That's a collective problem not feasibly solved company by company, so we collectively outsource that function to specialized companies that provide rapid-fire "patches" as soon as viruses are diagnosed. Symantec's Norton antivirus line of products provides this sort of service.

But here's the code that DeAngelis started cracking with his new start-up, Enterra Solutions, back in the summer of 2003: Because the operations of private firms and government agencies were becoming so IT-intensive, it was getting harder to segregate what were becoming increasingly overlapping universes of rules. The systems-integration rules (i.e., How do these databases talk to one another?) were overlapping with the performance-metric rules (i.e., How do we define our company's preferred operational standards?), and they in turn were collectively overlapping with security rules (both physical and cyber) and compliance rules (i.e., Is everything we're doing in compliance with all the relevant local, state, federal, and international laws?). Historically, a company would have four sets of outside contractors help with these issue areas: systems integrators, management consultancies, security companies, and accounting firms. The problem was, whenever a rule was changed in one domain, it usually had significant impact on other domains, but those interrelationships weren't being properly addressed by the traditional stovepiped approach. As DeAngelis foresaw, companies and governments would need to move beyond mere automation of rules to something better: new technologies and architectural approaches by which rules are "baked" into information systems and made updatable on a real-time basis, allowing the system of rules as a whole to be rerendered on the fly as circumstances warranted. This is the first practical step toward integrating—in a systemic fashion—dynamically rendered logic with technology to create autonomic computing. Think about that for a second. Any complex organism, like a human for example, runs on countless rules that must be autonomically applied in response to outside stimuli, leaving the leadership (like your brain) to focus on the big decisions. So say one night as you're walking along a street, something pops up in the dark and scares you. Your body will make thousands of decisions on its own to respond to that perceived threat (e.g., speeding blood flow, tensing muscles, widening eyes, breathing faster), leaving your brain with only the big question: Fight or flight? Well, Enterra's goal of dynamically managing rules for complex organizations is basically the same: making autonomic all the basic decisions (e.g., which streetlights to turn green to evacuate the city) so that top decision-makers can focus on the big calls.

The key technology DeAngelis invented involved taking written rules and turning them into living, breathing code that could act intelligently within your company's or government agency's information systems to sense, think, and respond to changing circumstances—in other words, rules *smart enough to rule themselves.*

What Enterra does is take large bundles of rules, like the USA Patriot Act or a major metropolitan area's contingency plans for a disaster, and turn them into software code and mathematical algorithms.

Enterra's code and algorithms take the process a step further by making them "genetic," meaning they can respond to outside stimuli and rerender—or basically rewrite—themselves in reply. So if I'm following the genetic algorithm for "bake a cake," and I decide to substitute margarine for butter in the middle of the process, Enterra's "recipe" would sense that change and recalibrate the rest of the ingredients to account for it. But it wouldn't stop there, for if I'm baking that cake within a resilient architec-

ture, my "bake a cake" genetic algorithm would know enough to contact
all of the other relevant algorithms in the process to negotiate further
changes. For example, my recipe might talk with the stove, deciding on a
different temperature and cooking time. If I'm a commercial baker, it
would contact the wrapping machinery, negotiating slight differences in
packaging and labeling, including a change in price. My genetic recipe
could also contact the shipping segment, mandating changes in schedules
and refrigeration on the trucks. Farther down the line, my recipe would
contact retailers themselves, instructing them to plan on different de-
livery timing, different shelf prices and shelf life, and God only knows
what else.

That all sounds great, but how does that vision link to national
security?

Well, say I'm a saboteur targeting this baking company and my real
goal today is to insert poison into thousands of loaves of bread, creating
terror and panic in the community and destroying the company's reputation. This is where my genetic algorithms really come in handy, because if
they're set to sense for bad ingredients (as well as good), they can alert the
rest of the process to perform a variety of relevant responses. Perhaps the
system lets me, the terrorist infiltrator, believe I'm actually succeeding
when all my actions are being thwarted elsewhere in the system, meaning
the system is spoofing me. Perhaps that allows the system to track my further activities, automatically linking its investigation to other security
measures throughout the company, including alerting law-enforcement
agencies. You get the idea. The same basic approach could apply to a nuclear power plant or the information systems of a global bank.

This approach toward dynamically managing rules in complex rule-
set environments has virtually unlimited applications: It can be used
within the intelligence community to foster effective information-
sharing, managing the need-to-know rule sets on a case-by-case, minute-
by-minute basis; it can be used to manage the complex traffic patterns of
a major port, allowing the scanning of cargo on a real-time, sense-think-
respond basis, not just flipping on a red light when a sensor picks up
something but also deciding the next several thousand simultaneous steps
that need to be taken with regard to that container, the port, the sur-

rounding region, and so forth; and it can be used to help emerging economies upgrade their connectivity interfaces with the outside world, making
their links more transparent and trusted to both themselves and the
higher-trust environments to which they're connecting.

Which leads us back to Development-in-a-Box.

I joined Enterra Solutions in the summer of 2005, and while Steve
DeAngelis and I spent much of our time spreading our ideas of how
all companies and government agencies need to embrace this next-
generation capacity to dynamically manage complex rule-set environments, both of us became intrigued with the notion that if we could
make, say, a major U.S. port truly resilient in this fashion, as Enterra is
doing today with the port of Philadelphia, why couldn't we market a
slightly simplified version of our approach for similar entities in emerging
and developing economies that would allow them to connect to ours in a
fashion that America would find acceptable while extending our networks of transparency and boosting local development as a by-product?
Well, that's one of the ideas we started calling Development-in-a-Box.
Instead of trying to fix a broken economy from the bottom up, why not
let the immediate focus be on "external improvements" that dramatically
upgrade that economy's connectivity with the global economy and *on
that basis* make the local situation more attractive to foreign direct
investors?

Imagine that I, the United States, am a developer of a housing subdivision called the global economy. You, a developing country, want to build
a home in my subdivision and I want you in there as well. So what do I
provide you with to make that happen? I give you an entire slew of connectivity, prepackaged and preapproved to global standards: I tell you
how you're going to build your house in rough outline: things like "Your
windows need to be *this* size" and "Your electrical wiring must be installed
according to *that* standard." I'm going to tell you about all the pipes that
will go into your house, like the telephone "pipe," or the cable TV "pipe,"
or the electrical and water and sewer connections. I won't give any options on these standards, because they've all already been decided upon
by the global community. If you want to connect to the Internet, it's
called TCP/IP—no negotiation. My goal as a subdivision developer is to
combine all this connectivity and regulations in as simple a package as

possible, providing it to you at the lowest cost possible, because, over time, my global economy will make more money by selling you all those services year-in and year-out than I would make by keeping you off the grid. So yes, it's a package deal that's designed to get you hooked up to the world as quickly and comprehensively as possible.

As the subdivision developer, what I shouldn't be in the business of doing is this: I shouldn't be telling you which draperies to buy, or what food to cook, or what God to worship, or which TV channels to watch, or—in general—how to run your family. What goes on inside your house should be largely yours to decide. Of course, if you and your family want to be successful in this subdivision over time, I'm pretty sure you'll pick up on the clues regarding how best to do that, but I won't be in the business of mandating the particulars.

Development-in-a-Box is *globalization connectivity with the rules baked in*. It's no good to raise an economy or a working population to international standards unless you supply the basic connectivity necessary to act on those global standards. Otherwise, as Paul Collier notes, all you trigger is a brain drain. But it's equally useless to provide the connectivity without the accompanying global standards or rules, because that just means you're trying to link low-trust environments with higher-trust ones without realistically accounting for the differences. For example, many sub-Saharan economies do not adhere to the International Standards Organization's best-practices regimes, such as the ISO 9000 series governing production and manufacturing industries. Development-in-a-Box is, in many ways, a starter kit for moving an economy toward ISO 9000 accreditation or for achieving C. K. Prahalad's goal of "transaction governance capacity." In a growing worldwide market for "sovereignty services," Development-in-a-Box allows governments in developing economies to outsource the creation of their civilian infrastructure.

Let me explain that concept of sovereignty services, because it's a key one.

With American combat troops now slated to depart Iraq by 2011, our intervention moves into its final phase, with the crucial goal being the expansion of economic opportunity for ordinary citizens. Our—and Iraq's—success here will determine the likelihood of our military's return down the road under less favorable circumstances. Much is made of Iraq's seem-

ing unwillingness to spend its oil profits on infrastructure, the assumption
being that Baghdad is milking American taxpayers. Let me offer another
explanation: Iraq lacks sufficient "counterparty" capacity to negotiate,
conclude, and manage the necessary deals with the outside world. Any
market for services or goods requires counterparties of roughly equal capacity: Player A wants to sell and B wants to buy, and both possess all the
necessary skills to pull off that transaction. It takes two to tango—and sign
a contract.

When international business looks at oil-rich Iraq today, it sees plenty
of opportunity. What it doesn't see in many instances, despite rising security, are sufficient local counterparties—both private and public—to make
the necessary deals happen. Such skills were hoarded under Saddam Hussein by the top political leadership to maintain state control of the economy. Iraq is hardly unique in this deficit. It characterizes a lot of poor
economies struggling to connect to the global economic grid. They just
don't have sufficient personnel, venues, and associated rule sets for striking deals and then executing them. It generally takes a generation to grow
such "soft" infrastructure because it's a people-driven process in which
experience is accumulated and best practices are identified.

Americans take this capacity for granted, because it's so woven into
our communities: the chamber of commerce, the local land-titling office,
and the realtors and lawyers eager to deal. Drop a businessperson armed
with ambition and vision into your average American community, and he
or she will soon be approached by a small network of locals ready to facilitate the identification of appropriate counterparties. All economically vi-
brant communities possess this informal network.

When a country lacks such deal-making infrastructure, it's essentially
a low-trust environment, meaning most deals are managed by family or
clan-defined businesses. These networks are inherently limited in size:
Blood ties define the known, trusted universe. These traditional networks
may suffice when economic activity is modest or within a classic sustenance economy in which everybody's just getting by, but they're insuffi-
cient when globalization knocks on the door. Globalization is knocking
down a lot of doors right now, as the rising East's seemingly unquenchable thirst for energy and commodities propels all manner of infrastructure investment in emerging and underdeveloped economies alike. That

push, however, reveals just how many immature economies out there lack those institutional and informal counterparty capacities. Do Eastern companies take advantage of this deficiency? You bet. The so-called China model sees Chinese companies employing a lot of bribery to win preferred access.

How do we fight that model so that emerging markets aren't trapped into playing down to China's lower standard? We have to help these developing economies rapidly insource (or import) the requisite counterparty capacity. When the fictional Jed Clampett, a "poor mountaineer," struck "black gold" and suddenly amassed a fortune, he instinctively recognized his own lack of deal-making skills and quickly outsourced that function to his new Beverly Hills banker, Mr. Drysdale, who in turn represented the Clampett family as its competent counterparty in deals with outside entities seeking advantage. When a state does that, as the House of Saud did almost eight decades ago by creating the Arabian American Oil Co., or Aramco, it's essentially buying time to develop its own counterparty capability. Once that capacity emerged over generations, the Saudis progressively bought out their foreign partners, taking complete control of the company.

As globalization knits together high-trust economies with low-trust ones, a market emerges wherein private entities—typically in partnership with local public ones—temporarily provide an emerging market with sufficient counterparty capacity to jump-start desired connectivity with the global economy. Steve DeAngelis and I call that market the "sovereignty services space." We think the Core as a whole needs to compete in that space to facilitate rapid integration of Gap economies, not just leaving the China model (or the Hezbollah model, or the Hamas model, or . . .) as the suboptimal default mode. As such, we foresee a big, initial part of the Development-in-a-Box process consisting of filling in the sovereignty services space (more in a bit on how DeAngelis is pioneering this now in Kurdish Iraq).

Some pundits have commented that the name Development-in-a-Box is a bit too flippant—that it trivializes the difficulties involved in fostering development and that it doesn't reflect the fact that each nation's situation is unique. We don't ignore such criticism, but since the centerpiece of the approach is adapting internationally recognized standards and best practices to local conditions to jump-start development, and improve lives in the bargain, we couldn't find another name that emphasized both development and standardization. Countries are welcomed as full, contributing members of the global economy when they can be trusted by the rest of the Core. Trust must be earned, but there are shortcuts that can help garner trust when there is no prior history. Those shortcuts are contained in the standards and best practices used by the Core. It makes no sense for each emerging market country to have to reinvent these standards and practices. They can be imported as in-the-box solutions and, where necessary, adapted to local conditions (like financial instruments adapted to account for certain Koranic prohibitions).

This approach doesn't intend to step on the toes of those already engaged in relief and development. They are providing valuable work and their heroic efforts must continue. Development-in-a-Box, though, offers them a way to better coordinate their efforts with others in a larger community of practice, building on lessons learned in the past. The beauty of communities of practice is that they are voluntary groups, so organizations can opt in or out as their interests coincide with those of others. Because it's a leaderless community, no organization need fear that joining the community of practice means that it is buying into someone else's agenda. What keeps the group together is goodwill and shared objectives. Communities of practice also help refine the approach by sharing new lessons learned. They form the critical feedback loop that makes any process sustainable and valuable. If this language sounds in tune with all networking philosophies so far examined in this chapter, that's by design. Steve and I have no intention of reinventing any wheels here.

Development-in-a-Box is not a humanitarian-assistance program, although traditional development programs often lay the foundations upon which subsequent development efforts build. Development-in-a-Box also doesn't ignore the special knowledge of those working locally; it provides a framework in which such knowledge can be more usefully applied. It doesn't try to impose an outside solution on an emerging economy, but it helps reduce the number of roadblocks that could otherwise slow economic progress. Most important, Development-in-a-Box helps set in place the trust framework necessary to attract foreign direct investment—the key to achieving sustainable economic growth.

Supporting this effort is a public information campaign that attempts to educate the population about critical components of economic development. Let me give you a glimpse of how these pieces fit together in a notional emerging market country that is ready to take the next step forward: The country has stabilized and its expatriate citizens begin returning or start investing in the country. Buildings start to go up, other infrastructure investments begin to emerge, but key economic pieces are missing. Some low-price consumer products begin to appear, such as fast food and toiletries. Mobile phone service was one of the first utilities to gain purchase in the new economy, but it was not accompanied by a high-speed, broadband network that is essential for economic trade. The country wants to take the next step, but there is no reason that it has to reinvent how to develop and install the necessary infrastructure. For broadband service, for example, it can adopt standards and practices, such as those used in Asia and Europe, to ensure that once it is up and running, it is world-class. This system is essential to ensure that international business transactions can take place.

Business deals also require a national banking system to process these transactions and handle foreign direct investment. People simply can't run around the country carrying satchels full of unconvertible hard currency. Banking transactions are also necessary to handle e-commerce, collect taxes, and ensure that payrolls are efficiently handled. For example, more than 1,400 business processes exist that are core and common to every global retail bank. Globalization has rapidly created these as standards and best practices to which all banks subscribe, so there's no need for the country to stumble through a mistake-ridden, learn-as-you-go process when such a system can be put in place without the local government having to conceive of it.

Local businesses that have no history or expertise in connecting with the global economy need a way to ensure their products meet world standards. They need a way to market their products and support customers once contracts have been signed. To meet their needs, business support offices and business-to-business exchanges can be created to meet local requirements, but using accepted standards and practices. Job training and mentoring programs can be established using the best techniques currently available.

For proving these concepts, Iraq was a pretty daunting environment. We initially weren't eager to get involved in a situation so highly politicized, thinking we'd instead give it a try in some less in-the-news West African economy. But when the Pentagon offered Enterra the opportunity to hit the ground running in the relatively stable Kurdish north, it seemed like a reasonable risk to endure for getting a chance to prove the idea. DeAngelis operated from a forward operating center in Erbil, the capital of Kurdistan, and this is what quickly ensued: First, he identified a need to sell Iraqi products around the world; however, there were problems with doing this in Iraq. Buyers from around the world would not be willing to get on a plane and fly to Kurdish Iraq, much less southern Iraq, to inspect factories, place orders, and pay for the goods and services in cash. To solve the problem, Enterra created two solution-as-services offerings (i.e., customized technology plus services): (1) a multilingual business-to-business and business-to-customer e-commerce exchange, and (2) an international call center. Sensing the business opportunity, we decided to invest the capital to build both while proposing a services contract to the Pentagon to support former state-owned Iraqi businesses. Once that contract was in place, DeAngelis began pounding the pavement in northern Iraq, signing up commercial entities. But our ambitions went beyond mere systems integration. The trading exchange markets Iraqi products both for Internet-based sales to customers and for trading on major worldwide exchanges, while an associated products portal, also created by Enterra, offers secure credit card and vendor services in English, Arabic, and Kurdish. Naturally, both venues immediately boosted sales for Iraqi manufacturers and suppliers and started attracting foreign direct investment—connectivity leading to transparency leading to opportunity.

Enterra then won a grant from the Pentagon to operate the locally based call center, which pushed us into a partnership with a local Kurdish telecom. To move the goods sold over the e-commerce exchange, Enterra made an alliance with a Kuwaiti logistical firm—one of the biggest, most trusted players in the region. To create the basic banking connectivity to support these transactions, Enterra allied itself with a Lebanese bank, a well-respected firm with great experience at bringing frontier economies online. Distribution centers are being established in Erbil, as well as in Jordan and Philadelphia, to create a trusted chain of logistics from Iraq to the United States. Again, we figured that nobody was going to Iraq to buy two dozen leather jackets, but retail stores would buy the same from a distribution center based in Philly.

Finally, in yet another DeAngelis brainstorm, Enterra proposed and created the Kurdish Business Center, an investment-processing conduit currently coheadquartered in Erbil and Washington, D.C., with regional offices in capital market locations such as Dubai and Abu Dhabi. These offices structure the investment deals triggered by a network of business relationships developed and integrated by Enterra, to include the Kurdish government's cluster of trusted companies, the U.S. government's roster of companies coming to Iraq on trade missions, and Enterra's own global contacts.

All this deal-making connectivity was great, but here's where De-Angelis spotted, in that sovereignty services space just mentioned, the Kurdish Regional Government's (KRG) compelling need to rapidly develop a baseline, in-country, counterparty capacity to interact with outside entities eager to develop its oil industry and build its infrastructure. Part of that capacity is being developed via the Kurdish Business Center, but to facilitate the more complex oil-for-infrastructure deals wanted by the Kurds, DeAngelis boldly proposed a twenty-first-century version of the Saudi Aramco model, which Enterra continues to pioneer with the KRG as this book went to print.

Where does this Development-in-a-Box process go next in Iraq? Clearly, our goal, shared by the Pentagon, is to replicate this model in southern Iraq, where we'll need to employ the same charismatic selling capacity that DeAngelis displayed up north. And this is a key takeaway: establishing the personal trust factor here is paramount. Executing investment deals is a skill any experienced international company possesses, but playing the honest broker on the behalf of Iraq's Kurds, Sunni, and Shia is far more complex—the "everything else" of effective nation-building that America must master in both public- (i.e., hearts and minds) and private-sector (stomachs and wallets) venues. When we invite a developing economy to rapidly attach itself to globalization's myriad networks, we're asking for a lot of trust, or faith that we won't screw it over and leave it permanently disadvantaged. In many instances, the locals will get only one good bite at the apple—the initial-contact connectivity. Get it right and you've expanded the Core. Get it wrong and you've simply destabilized a portion of the Gap all over again.

Again, Development-in-a-Box is not a model of extending the Core's nation-building responsibilities but of curtailing them by speeding up any fragile economy's integration into the global economic grid. What Enterra received in funding from the Pentagon helped jump-start the process by credentializing us with the Kurds, but beyond that, all the subsequent funding came directly from the Kurdistan Regional Government and the infrastructure providers (both hard and soft) that quickly joined in. Make no mistake, we're not interested in proving out an infrastructural development model for an emerging market that sees everybody involved lose money. Markets rule, just as they do everywhere else. We assume there will be winners and losers, but that there's no faster way to develop a stable middle class. In the end, the key thing about Enterra's Development-in-a-Box process is that it is triggering network connectivity between Iraq and the global economy that simply wasn't happening under coalition efforts up to that point. We don't believe America can mandate *how* Iraqis respond to that opportunity, just that America *owes* them that opportunity.

My point in explaining all this: With relatively few resources, and armed with nothing more than a new business-oriented vision that emphasized connectivity-building on a regional basis *over* far more difficult efforts at political reconciliation at the national level, a small business such as Enterra effectively turbocharged Kurdish Iraq's economic boom. And it was done by providing a simple but standards-based approach for linking external infrastructure providers to Kurdish Iraq's government and existing businesses, promising each side the opportunity to get these network connections right from the start. And when that happened, the paradigm shifted radically from "quagmire" to "virgin market."

In short, if we want America to field a robust SysAdmin force to deal with failed or recovering states, we need to create institutions that tap into a suitably wide array of players. We've got to get our private sector to *want* to fund the SysAdmin function for the myriad market opportunities that stabilization creates.

THE BETTER NORMAL: THE RISE OF
THE SYSADMIN-INDUSTRIAL COMPLEX

In March 2008, a collection of over fifty retired senior U.S. military leaders banded together in an avowed political movement designed to pressure Congress into rethinking the way America organizes its approach to postconflict and postdisaster situations overseas. Their demands? They wanted U.S. foreign aid overhauled and expanded, and "a corps of civilian workers trained and deployed to work directly with the military and help build education, transportation, economic and political systems in troubled countries." In the words of one member, General Anthony Zinni, former head of Central Command, "We desperately need civilian partners who have the same robust capabilities that we have." And if we don't make such adjustments? As respected defense analyst Chet Richards then noted:

> Our defense establishment has suffered some 4,000 fatal casualties, forced the Army into offering enlistment bonuses of $40,000 to raw recruits, begun a program of buying armored jeeps that cost a million dollars each, and run up a generational spending obligation. We did all this not while engaging some worthy foe armed with tanks, missiles and aircraft similar to ours, nor while contending with massed armies of skilled troops on fields of battle. No, we incurred these costs while trying to suppress resistance to our occupations of Iraq and Afghanistan, resistance by lightly armed civilians and poorly equipped militias.

As one of my blog readers, historyguy99, wrote: "Drop the mention of tanks, missiles, etc., and change the location to North America, and this could be a conversation that the British military would be having about the American rebels in 1780."

America's window for realigning its grand strategy to the security challenges presented by modern globalization is shorter than we think. The key players in this process are staring us in the face—everywhere we send our troops across the Gap. They're the frontier integrators of this age, and they hail overwhelmingly from Asia. In our search for an ideological comfort zone, we retreat to the kinetics of "shock and awe," primacy, and unilateralism, and the West with its "league of democracies." We go with what we know and surround ourselves with allies who look exactly like us, hoping we'll find cohesion in our uniformity. *All these things worked in the past and they must work again now!*

But the truth is that none of these things represents our best choices today. We can't win this struggle with guns. We can't win it by ourselves or with the small fraction of humanity we call the West. We can't win it with a focus on just terrorism and democracy. We can't secure this most fantastic victory—a truly global liberal trade order—by demanding states leapfrog from their sheltered, disconnected past into an immediate present that matches *our* level of globalization connectivity, *our* level of free markets, and *our* level of political pluralism—*all at once.* We need to bring them into this globalization universe at a pace their cultures can withstand, employing development models closer to their current realities, fielding allies they can relate to and agents of change who address their most immediate concerns for security and economic opportunity.

America has all these resources in abundance, and our logical grand-strategic goals all resonate with the rising powers of this age. History continues to bless our global leadership, but only when we find the courage to adapt ourselves to changing circumstances. We are today beset by too many leaders who view the world in terms of political ideologies, buying into the propaganda and rhetoric of merely our most obvious enemies, when economic transformation triggers all the violence and instability and environmental ruin of our day. We lead a global revolution that we do not even recognize, so intimidated are we by our own success.

But there are tectonic shifts underfoot, years in the making. Our military leadership understands this need to change, even if our political leadership doesn't. Most important, our business leadership—even in the defense sector—is moving rapidly in this new direction.

In the winter of 2004, I keynoted a conclave of Lockheed Martin's top 500 global executives in Phoenix, Arizona. Lockheed Martin is the biggest defense firm in the world, and aims to hold on to that number-one slot. What I told Lockheed's assembled leaders then was that if the company hoped to remain on top of its industry, it would have to move its focus progressively from the "first half" that is war to the "second half" that is beyond war, including all the stabilization and infrastructure-building activities associated with bringing new economies online with globalization. I told them that remaining America's number-one *defense* contractor wasn't enough to ensure it had the technology and means to provide for America's future needs; it would have to aim higher, becoming the world's biggest security contractor, adept at simultaneously serving both the top and bottom of globalization's pyramid.

Lockheed took this admonition to heart, and three years later, after much soul-searching, bought Pacific Architects and Engineers, a longtime contractor to the U.S. State Department. Indeed, you could describe PA&E as basically State's version of Kellogg Brown & Root, the longtime full-service contractor to the Pentagon. Lockheed's purchase was a shot across the bow of the entire U.S. defense industry, signaling its historic decision to focus more on serving the U.S. military's ballooning postwar portfolio. Within a generation, I predict Lockheed will evolve from being primarily a U.S. defense firm to operating as a global security contractor whose systems-integration work spans all manner of crucial network flows. In other words, Lockheed will see its future less in supplying the Leviathan a small number of superexpensive platforms and weapons and more in building up America's SysAdmin capabilities for network security and market integration.

When Lockheed Martin executives sought to convince PA&E's leadership that their two companies were destined to share a combined future, they provided them with copies of my first book, *The Pentagon's New Map*, telling them to read it in order to understand their motivations. When Lockheed held its first management retreat in the spring of 2007 to officially welcome PA&E's senior executives to the fold, it brought me in as the sole outside speaker, and all of PA&E's leaders were given a copy of my second book, *Blueprint for Action*. In introducing me to the gathering, Lockheed executive Michael Dignam, who would eventually become PA&E's new boss, told the crowd that they were to become serious agents of change within the world's largest defense firm, teaching it how it needed to adapt to this new world of opportunity. A year later, as the massive Lockheed division (Information Systems & Global Services) that houses PA&E held its first postacquisition summit, I was again brought in to make a speech. IS&GS is a new consolidated division of Lockheed that brings together all the information service contracts the company holds throughout the world. It already represents roughly a quarter of Lockheed's portfolio, and in the future will constitute Lockheed's primary profit engine.

I don't kid myself that I alone somehow convinced the world's largest defense firm to shift gears. Lockheed is a notoriously conservative corporation. It does not adapt itself to fads, nor does it lightly reconsider its relationship with its number-one client—the U.S. military. When Lockheed buys PA&E, it is nothing more than the usual dynamic of the established behemoth snatching up the innovative smaller firm, adding the seemingly exotic skills of the new company to its own, but, in doing so, indicating that it knows which way the wind blows in the global security environment. My books and speeches are simply a reflection of that reality, a useful articulation of the way ahead. When readers and audience members ask me whether or not people in Washington are listening to me, I tell them that, as far as the "iron triangle" of the military-industrial complex is concerned, I work the military first, industry second, and Congress last.

You can't argue with operation experience as it builds up—along with the casualties. That operation experience demands a response from industry. Needs must be addressed. As those industry responses pile up, budgets must shift, and here's where Congress can either lead or obstruct, because the military has no choice but to execute and industry has no desire but to provide. It is Congress and the executive branch that must either meet those emerging requirements or tell the American people why they cannot. And if, in that explanation, we hear that different security priorities must prevail, then Americans must ask Washington why its employment of military force around the world *does not match its implied grand strategy.* Because when the Bush administration's Millennium Challenge Corporation says, "The private sector is our exit strategy," that strikes me as a pretty big hint of where victory lies.

I view efforts like Development-in-a-Box as a crucial bridge between America and rising economic powers: We fear their economic penetration of the Gap will result in bad or weak regimes, while they fear our efforts to improve regimes inside the Gap will shut them out of economic opportunities. Development-in-a-Box provides a neutral engagement space, within which each side's concerns can be addressed. We want connectivity according to standards that promote certainty and security, something nobody argues against. In this way, we recast our foreign aid to account for advances we make inside the Core regarding system resiliency, as anything that improves the resiliency of our networks there can be applied to even greater positive effect inside the Gap. Moreover, what we learn from such applications inside the Gap will assuredly improve our understanding of our own resiliency inside the Core—the pyramid's bottom and top truly networked with each other.

Here's a good example of how this can work, courtesy of one far-sighted U.S. Navy admiral.

One of the main problems in counterterrorism today is that there are so many people and vehicles and so much data and material moving through globalization's myriad networks that it seems virtually impossible to track it all effectively. Nowhere has this problem been more acute than on the high seas, which is how most commerce moves around this dirty globe. In 2006, Admiral Harry Ulrich, then commander of U.S./NATO Naval Forces Europe, decided to do something about it. He had no money and virtually no resources to pull it off, but his dream was to apply the same system we currently use in air-traffic control to sea traffic. Worldwide, aircraft are transparent, because they're all required to carry an "identification friend or foe" beacon that allows them to be tracked leaving and entering airports by aircraft-traffic-control systems and monitored between airports by sensors distributed across a global network. Trip the wire that defines "suspicious activity" and somebody's fighter aircraft will soon be on your tail. NATO routinely launches several fighters a week to identify unknown aircraft.

No such pervasive system currently exists globally for maritime traffic. If a ship any bigger than a small freighter is flagged by a nation belonging to the International Maritime Organization, it carries an ID beacon similar to that carried by aircraft. But without a shared monitoring network, that's like tracking only selected commercial jets part of the time and giving everyone else a pass. So Admiral Ulrich, upon taking command in Naples, Italy, asked a simple question: "If we can do that in the air, why can't we do it on the sea?" He made a point of pioneering his sea-traffic-control effort first inside the Mediterranean, where NATO's southern naval forces have been historically concentrated, but his real target was Africa. Africa's littoral waters are the most ungoverned maritime space in the world. Smuggling, drug running, human trafficking, illegal immigration, illegal fishing, environmental degradation, oil theft, and piracy—you name it, it's all there in abundance. Ulrich wanted somebody to govern that ungoverned space, and he knew the U.S. Navy couldn't do it alone, much less bring Africa's meager coast-guard-like navies up to snuff so they could do it on their own. So he quickly came to the conclusion that he'd need to create a network of assets—both public and private—to manage that space; thus his decision to model his monitoring system on international air-traffic control.

Taking his cues from that global consortium, Ulrich began stitching together a network of shore-based sensors ringing the Mediterranean, and then began his initial monitoring by having his naval command tap into an existing IMO Automated Identification System, transforming NATO's ability to track ship traffic in the Med. Almost overnight, NATO went from tracking dozens of ships on the Med to thousands of craft, and instead of getting the data sometimes as long as 72 hours late, now the contacts were being tracked within one to five minutes—all within 50 feet on the earth's surface. When the classic big-firm systems integrators told Ulrich it would be cost-prohibitive to pull it off, the admiral turned to the Volpe Center in Cambridge, Massachusetts, a Department of Transportation research center. Instead of hundreds of millions, Ulrich's initial network cost $900,000. The shore-based receivers are small, roughly the size of a radar dish you might find on a pleasure craft. Most can be attached to tall buildings or existing cell towers along the coast.

The strength of the system is obviously a function of its reach: The more countries join, the larger the shared operational picture. By the time Ulrich retired at the end of 2007, he had enlisted thirty-two countries throughout the Mediterranean and the North Atlantic, along the west coast of Africa, around the Black Sea, and in the Pacific. Today, the network continues to spread around the planet.

This is where the SysAdmin function kicks in, cleverly blending private-sector and public-sector elements: With Ulrich's system in place, local police, coast guards, and border patrols catch all the bad guys for NATO, saving an American military response. As Harry told me for an article I wrote about his work in a fall 2007 issue of *Esquire*, "I don't do defense; I do security. When you talk defense, you talk containment and mutually assured destruction. When you talk security, you talk collaboration and networking. This is the future." The current chairman of the Joint Chiefs of Staff, Admiral Mike Mullen, has long posited the notion of a "thousand-ship navy" that's really a global SysAdmin force consisting of the U.S. Navy and Coast Guard, plus navies and coast guards the world over. This navy would be able to police the entirety of the world's oceans, but *only* if it was augmented with the sort of sensor network that Admiral Ulrich pioneered. Whom do you get to pay for all this effort? Think about insurance companies interested in reducing liability, as well as global corporations looking for fast-pass entry into ports. Then think about linking these highly sensored ports to these sensor-laden ships to all those sensor-tagged containers and boxes and individually wrapped products—all of them networked for maximum transparency. Then think about packaging all that up and delivering that capability to developing or damaged countries eager to join the global economy, and that's what we call Development-in-a-Box—an essential building block for a global SysAdmin-industrial complex.

Harry, by the way, is now an executive vice president at Enterra Solutions—no coincidence, that. When you come across great ideas, you don't get jealous and you don't get defensive. You immediately bring them—and the person behind them—into your network and keep building. The admiral's legacy program, known officially as the Maritime Safety and Security Information System, is the crown jewel of the U.S. Department of Transportation's ongoing collaboration with the U.S. Navy and Coast Guard, known as the Global Maritime Domain Awareness program. Collectively, that effort earned the Volpe Center a prestigious "Innovations in American Government" award in 2008 from Harvard University's Kennedy School of Government's Ash Institute for Democratic Governance and Innovation.

What, then, does victory look like for the SysAdmin-industrial complex? One of my favorite examples is an advertisement I keep coming across in the back pages of *The Economist* and the *Wall Street Journal.* Its message is disarmingly simple: "Invest in Macedonia."

"Macedonia?" you might ask. Isn't that one of those lousy Balkan countries we fought in a while back? The answer is, sort of. Of the six independent states to emerge from the ruins of Yugoslavia, Macedonia is arguably the least well known internationally, in large part because it escaped mass bloodshed following its quiet departure in 1991. Having joined the UN in 1993, Macedonia seeks future membership in both NATO and the European Union, which named it a "candidate country" a few years ago. Roughly the size of Vermont and landlocked amid Albania, Greece, Bulgaria, and Serbia, Macedonia offers little beyond its location as a major transportation corridor between larger economic players. To that end, Macedonia, with the help of the U.S. Agency for International Development, made itself the first all-broadband wireless country of its size in the world. The name of that USAID program, "Macedonia Connects," is wonderfully symbolic of this small country's dogged determination to join the global economy. So when I first came across those "Invest in Macedonia" ads, I couldn't help but think to myself that this is what victory would look like in places like Iraq and Afghanistan—*their* victory, not ours.

The ad, appropriately enough, is one big sales job. Describing itself as the "new business heaven in Europe," the unspoken come-on seems to be, "If you can't afford Croatia anymore, try us instead!" As for investor benefit packages, which the ad declares "will be approved within 10 business days," try these on for size: no corporate tax for ten years; 5 percent individual income tax for five years; free connections to gas, electricity, sewer, and water; and concessionary land leases "for up to 75 years." All that for joining a free economic zone with "immediate access to main international airport, railroad and vital road corridors." As an international businessman who focuses on infrastructure development, let me tell you, that sort of offer gets my attention, along with the fact that the World Bank's "Doing Business 2008" report named Macedonia the fourth-best reforming economy in the world (China was ninth). What I like about the ad is how shamelessly Macedonia sells its existing connectivity to attract even more: free economic zone, transportation hubs, and free-trade agreements encompassing 650 million consumers. Toss in cheap labor and nationwide Wi-Fi, and you've got yourself a country just itching to be "exploited."

And that's what I think victory will look like for your average failed state in the years ahead: getting yourself off the front page of the *New York Times* and into the business advertising section of the *Wall Street Journal*. Now, you might choose to interpret this dynamic as globalization's army of multinational corporations swooping in to enslave people to meet the insatiable demands of the capitalist world order. But if that's your take, I'd advise you to consider the alternative: that bottom billion falling ever further behind, with much of the Gap integrated into China's updated version of imperial Japan's "Co-Prosperity Sphere." That would not make a safer world, or one that's environmentally sustainable—judging by what China has already accomplished at home. It wouldn't be a more just world either, but one in which a good third of humanity would continue to live in scary neighborhoods threatened by nasty dictatorships and the even nastier failed states they tend to leave behind once they collapse. Extreme deprivation breeds extreme ideologies the world over. No culture is immune. But every country can be inoculated, and the vaccine is called economic connectivity.

America needs to create a SysAdmin-industrial complex that's just as hungry for preconflict and postconflict/postdisaster opportunities as our long-standing military-industrial complex is for big war. If all you do is build hammers, then the entire world starts to look like nails.

You want a different world? Build a different toolkit.

Eight

———◼◆◼———

THE STRATEGIC REALIGNMENT
Resurrecting the Progressive Agenda

The fundamental premise of this book has been that America must dramatically realign its own post-9/11 trajectory with that of the world at large—a world undergoing deep transformation. This comprehensive realignment requires a new understanding of the world and our role in its evolution. Such understanding is found in the realm of grand strategy. When it comes to crafting grand strategy in the era of modern globalization, this is what I believe.

1. To be plausible, grand strategic vision must combine a clear-eyed view of today's reality with a broad capture of the dominant trends shaping the long-term environment, meaning no sharp detours— much less U-turns—in history's advance.

2. Grand strategy does not seek to change human nature (which got us to this point quite nicely) but to placate it, thereby ensuring the portability of its strategic concepts (the *dos* and *don'ts*) among minds from different backgrounds, cultures, and ages.

3. Grand strategic thinking always keeps the U.S. government's role in proper perspective, because globalization comes with rules but not a ruler.

4. Grand strategic analysis starts with security, which is always 100 percent of your problem until it's reasonably achieved, because then it's at most 10 percent of your ultimate solution.

5. Grand strategy is not clairvoyance; it does not seek to predict future events, but rather to contextualize them in a confident, opportunistic worldview.

6. Because we live in a time of pervasive and persistent revolutions, the grand strategist is neither surprised nor dismayed when the awesome force of globalization's tectonic shifts elicits vociferous or even violent friction from locals.

7. Grand strategy purposefully aspires to be proactive, not merely protecting itself from failure but also exploiting avenues of success as they are revealed.

8. So grand strategists do not entertain, much less succumb to, single-point-failure doomsaying, because systematic thinking about the future means you're not "for" or "against" issues like peak oil or global warming or resource scarcity but instead accept the implied dynamics of the change that has been triggered and factor them in accordingly.

9. The grand strategist is therefore interested more in direction than in degree of change, recognizing that politics lags dramatically behind economics and that security lags dramatically behind connectivity.

10. Grand strategy isn't about keeping it a "fair fight"; the grand strategist desires as many allies as possible and as few enemies

as possible, and so he's interested in *everything* and *anything* that brings adherents to his cause while sapping his enemy's numbers.

This chapter is about that "everything and anything" that either wins hearts and minds—or at least disarms them. Everything we've examined up to now suggests that globalization's expansion plays into our hands. Now let's factor in those trends where mitigation will be the order of the day, rather than exploitation, for therein lies—as far as America is concerned—the most challenging realignment of all.

THE UNDENIABLE TRAJECTORY: THE DEVIL WE KNEW

Nothing retraditionalizes a culture as quickly as crisis, especially crisis triggered by violent contact with outsiders. When that happens, ancient legends are dutifully resurrected—as in, *This is how we dealt with such monsters before!* America in 2001 was ripe for just such a retraditionaliza-tion, having just gone through the single biggest influx of immigrants our country has ever absorbed in one decade. According to the American cus-tom, as long as the economy hummed, all this change was taken in stride, but once the tech crash of 2000 segued into the corporate scandals of 2001, all the usual elements were in place for a nativist backlash: stagnat-ing incomes, fears of the country being overrun by the latest version of "those people," and a sense that America had lost its competitive edge—witness "good" jobs being "shipped overseas." When terrorists struck on 9/11, the Statue of Liberty was recast overnight from a welcoming sym-bol for immigrants to the poster child for homeland security. Suddenly, Americans no longer owned the future but scrambled to prevent it. We've been scrambling ever since.

Cultural critic Susan Faludi's 2007 book *The Terror Dream* paints a fascinating portrait of our social response to 9/11 and the wars since spawned. It is at once accurate, somewhat overtaken by events, and yet highly predictive of the road ahead in this long war against violent ex-tremism. Faludi observes that America reflexively retraditionalized itself following 9/11's shock. We retreated into our past or, specifically, the 1950s childhood of our Boomer leadership—comfort food spiced with familiar fears. Self-absorbed individualism was out, nurturing families back in. Wimpy male icons were dumped for he-men, especially soldiers and firefighters (make that fire*men*!). There were immediate predictions of marriage and baby booms. Security moms suddenly ruled the political landscape and body-snatching aliens once again threatened our streets ("Is that man wearing a turban?"). Our political leaders likewise indulged. Square-jawed, tough-talking Donald Rumsfeld instantly morphed into a craggy babe magnet, and George W. Bush embraced his inner cowboy by donning a military flight suit and routinely giving out salutes. More predictably, hawkish pundits gleefully blamed feminism for making America too pacific, too Oprah-ish, too emasculated. In his polemic *The Enemy at Home*, conservative Dinesh D'Souza even went so far as to suggest that America should rein in its provocative young women, lest their sexuality and outspokenness invite future attacks from Islamic fundamentalists. It was American mirror-imaging at its best: If our 1950s superconformity kept those Soviets from turning red-blooded Americans into socialist automatons, then a retraditionalized post-9/11 America would likewise protect us from those Muslim fundamentalists. Smells like teen spirit to me!

Delving deeper into the American psyche, Faludi also notes that after 9/11 our media started resurrecting appropriately frightening archetypes, chief among them being the rescue of the vulnerable maiden snatched from the frontier homestead by savages. The classic movie that immediately springs to mind here is John Ford's *The Searchers*, starring iconic John Wayne as the former Confederate soldier who spends years tracking down a young niece held captive by bloodthirsty Indians who "ruined" her; he almost dispatches her in an "honor killing" at the end before coming to his senses. This simple narrative is a staple of American literature, beginning with James Fenimore Cooper's *Last of the Mohicans*, and its tale of hostage-taking "savages" is no myth. One of my Barnett ancestors suffered this strange fate in western Pennsylvania in the late 1700s. But these frontier attacks were less frequent than popularly portrayed. Most wagon trains traveling the nineteenth-century Oregon Trail reported no violence from Native Americans, finding them instead quite helpful. That era's dime novels told a different story, as did later Hollywood films. Abduction and rape were not the biggest threats pioneer women faced. That would be disease. Nor were they weaklings who needed constant male protection. Life was simply too hard and demanded too much from them.

But when you read Faludi's chapter on Army soldier Jessica Lynch, it gets hard to deny that the post-9/11 myth-manufacturing got way out of hand. The lurid storylines of torture and rape by "Saddam's beasts" simply weren't true, and neither were the cartoonish portrayals of Lynch as either female Rambo or hapless hostage. Lynch handled the ordeal with admirable skill, despite all the media misrepresentation. The real hero was lost in the intense media blitz surrounding Lynch's rather staged rescue from an Iraqi hospital, where—by the way—she received great care by local doctors. That hero, according to Lynch herself, was fellow soldier and good friend Lori Piestewa, a Native American who acted with uncommon bravery when their unit was attacked in March 2003. Piestewa was the first Native American woman to die in combat while *serving in* the U.S. military. A prominent peak in the Phoenix mountains—which I climbed with my children a year later—today bears her name.

As Faludi concedes, much of this retraditionalization phenomenon associated with the trauma of 9/11 has faded with time. There were no marriage or baby booms, and reports of the death of irony were greatly exaggerated. With Nancy Pelosi taking over leadership of the U.S. House of Representatives and Senator Hillary Clinton nearly becoming America's first female major-party nominee for president, plus Alaska governor Sarah Palin's star turn as John McCain's running mate, it gets hard to argue that the role of women in our society has suffered any damage whatsoever as a result.

In the end, American citizens do more than merely shop to marginalize extremists: We simply realize that we like being our modern selves *more* than we fear *their* attacks on our modernity. Just like our enemies, we decide that we're not going to have our lives dramatically altered by this latest iteration of globalization's *Kulturkampf* (and no, it won't be the last). Instead, with our typical focus on self-help and self-improvement, we largely shelve our original, Oprah-like instincts to explain ourselves better to the world, and instead set about that most insulting of American practices: We began deconstructing the "Islamic threat" in our mass media, making the "disturbing" subject a sort of national obsession (also very Oprah-like). Within five years, we had processed this learning to the point where humor became an appropriate weapon, the surest sign being the network sitcoms that began the process of demystifying Islamic ways—to wit, the Canadian Broadcasting Corporation's *Little Mosque on the Prairie* and the CW network's *Aliens in America*. As always, given our uniquely synthetic mash-up of culture, we ultimately choose to view Muslims as being more like us than dissimilar, our Judeo-Christian identity being increasingly expanded to a Judeo-Christian-Islamic identity that recognizes all such religions as "children of Abraham."

I know, we really are Borg-like in that manner—just like the globalization we spawned. But putting us on some nationwide "war footing" is hardly the answer, either. By casting this struggle as an all-out war of survival, requiring such mobilization, we'd be guilty of buying into the radical fundamentalists' ideology that claims (1) they speak for all of Islam, and (2) this is truly a clash between civilizations instead of one *within* a single civilization. Thus making the conflict symmetrical would amount to elevating al Qaeda to the status of a legitimate international actor, which it is not, being unable and/or unwilling to seek such political credentials. In the end, their resistance really is futile, so why pretend otherwise?

The attacks of 9/11 were a classic case of "chosen trauma": We *chose* to become deeply attached to these events. In America's "thirty years' war" with radical Islam since 1979, as historian Michael Oren puts it, we did not let similarly tragic events absorb our attention in the same way. Yes, we can all now say that Bush-Cheney lied to us about Iraq and that without such trickery America never would have gone to such lengths to transform the Arab world. But let's be honest here: Americans were collectively more than open to this vision of taking care of the "frontier savages" problem once and for all. Indeed, we have a long history of being moved to such high retribution. For Americans, the cry "Remember the [*chosen trauma*]!" has always been aimed at triggering immediate action, and not merely remembrance of some tragic shame we all share. As frontier settlers, Americans are natural problem-solvers: Once society identifies the danger, the posse is rounded up and direct action taken.

Here's where Faludi's larger point about America naturally dipping into the metaphors of its frontier-age past makes sense when you consider our age of rapid economic globalization. When the global economy expands today, it naturally moves into the most traditional, off-grid cultures left to be found on this planet, disrupting patriarchal social structures and predictably eliciting violent fundamentalist backlashes. We "contaminate" the Arab world, for example, much in the same way that American settlers once spread "white contamination" among Native Americans in the trans-Mississippi West in yet another fearful dream of civilizational destruction featuring gold of a different color. As back then, today both sides in this perceived clash of civilizations see their destiny commanded by scriptures: They "cleanse" themselves of our contamination as we push them to recognize that all men—and their faiths—are equal, with everything else going at market prices. Sitting Bull, Crazy Horse, and Geronimo are now replaced by equally compelling and charismatic figures, the badlands shifted to the wondrously harmonic Federally Administered Tribal Areas of northwest Pakistan. As before, the invaders ponder infinite spaces, while the locals assume infinite time. In the resulting conflict, both perceptions will ultimately be proven wrong—yet again. And the ultimate cause will be the same: a vast sucking sound from the East. Nothing invades like insatiability.

Just as in our wars of today, America's wars against the Western Indian tribes were enormously expensive and cost a significant number of lives. There was a constant sense of frustration and the spiraling of conflict into chaos. Corners were frequently turned, only to see America suffer new humiliating reversals that led—as always—to more crushing reprisals. It was a long war featuring stubborn insurgencies that dragged on for decades. The U.S. Cavalry and the Sioux, for example, fought for thirty-five years. And yes, the conflict became more messianic the further it extended, as warriors who recognized that their cultures were being destroyed through assimilation adopted apocalyptic religious visions out of sheer desperation. Where more than a century ago some radical believers dreamed that a warrior dance (the Ghost Dance) might bring on a new world of the past, today we face those who dream that the perfectly calibrated terrorist strike will usher in their vision of a seventh-century pre-economic paradise. It is as sad and conclusive as a dying man's last breath.

This isn't about winning. The outcome of this thirty years' war was decided by Deng Xiaoping the year it began: 1979. Our strategic realignment here is about managing the loss of identity—both theirs and ours. As this convergence of civilizations unfolds, the Arab world will lose its unique distance from the rest of humanity and America will eventually lose its place as humanity's revolutionary force without equal, our success in assimilating their collective identity into this American System–cum– globalization signaling yet another stage in its maturation beyond our control. In the end, then, both sides lose their devil.

Remember, the Union lost its Northern identity even as it defeated and assimilated the Confederacy. It lost it in the trans-Mississippi West, yielding to a new Western identity that commands America's imagination to this day. The same fate befalls us now, in this moment of our nation's unprecedented historical success. The American "world order" that emerged from the Cold War's end wasn't "new." It was a century in the gestation and five decades in the making, the fall of the Berlin Wall merely marking our global coming-out party that was the 1990s. It was also overwhelmingly economic in nature, which is why our national security leadership, so ingrained with the delusion that they controlled all that was crucial in international affairs (otherwise known as the realists/ neocons' soda-straw view of reality, for truly here the two camps suffer the same strategic myopia), had virtually no idea how to manage its fur- ther advance—until 9/11 interceded and revealed a world they once again recognized as their own.

Unfortunately for them but fortunately for the rest of humanity, the seed subsequently planted by Bush-Cheney—and the fearful story that they wished to tell—has found no lasting purchase.

THE AMERICAN SYSTEM PERTURBED: KATRINA AND THE GORE COUNTERNARRATIVE

Hurricane Katrina served as a narrative tipping point for multiple sto- rylines in America's ongoing grand strategy of shaping a post-9/11 world. First, it effectively erased what remained of Iraqi expectations for an ele- vating reconstruction of their economy by their American occupiers. If they had, as General David Petraeus told me, a "man on the moon" belief regarding American capabilities up to that point (i.e., they assumed we could do anything after that enormous technological feat), then Washington's Katrina response completely sealed their pessimism. Indeed, many Iraqi leaders plausibly feared an immediate redirection of American attention from their country to the homeland. The American public's perception of the Bush administration likewise took a dive from which the president never recovered. Now it was clear, just as it was to the Iraqis, that the American government lacked the wherewithal to manage such complex humanitarian disasters both abroad and at home. Third, by signaling with great force President Bush's emerging lame-duck status, Katrina ushered in the earliest postpresidency seen since Richard Nixon faced impeachment and ultimately resigned twenty months into his second term. And Bush's diminished presidency had significant international repercussions. Suddenly, allies were openly challenging our leadership, rising powers began ignoring the same, and a rogue's gallery of tinhorn dictators started back-talking the United States in every forum imaginable. It was open season on American credibility, no matter what the subject.

Katrina itself served as a microcosm of the Iraq response, with Louisiana's local and state governments playing their own incompetent occupational authority and the Bush administration displaying all the same situational awareness and speed that it previously brought to Iraq—meaning virtually none. According to former General Electric CEO Jack Welch, the federal response to Katrina featured all the classically bad management stages, moving slowly from denial to containment, then shamemongering with blood-on-the-floor heads rolling, and *finally* a concentrated push to fix real problems. As in Iraq, interagency coordination within the federal government was confused and weak, with nobody really seeming in charge of the situation until Army Lieutenant General Russell Honoré took command of Joint Task Force Katrina two days after New Orleans was devastated by the storm surge. It wasn't until deep into the first week of September 2005, however, that law and order was reestablished in New Orleans (and yes, Blackwater gunmen were involved), where looting and violence had been substantial (although hardly as chaotic as initially reported).

The overall impact of Katrina was a national humiliation. Over 1,800 people had been killed and approximately 378,000 were displaced from

New Orleans alone, creating one of the largest internal diasporas in American history! U.S. oil production from the Gulf of Mexico was shut down for a substantial period, and America received government donations from all over the world. Mexican troops, providing emergency aid, operated on American soil for the first time since 1846. Naturally, many pundits began comparing Katrina-the-poststorm-response to Iraq-the-postwar-response, arguing that America's incompetence in Iraq had tied down troops—specifically the National Guard—that should have been available back home. But the real crux of the matter wasn't available resources so much as the "last resort" mentality of the federal government: Much like the immediate postwar situation in Iraq, the Bush administration displayed a strange operational detachment from the proceedings until the resulting instability grew out of control.

Fortunately, this was not the case among the U.S. private sector, whose immediate logistical response to Katrina significantly outperformed that of governments at all levels. Wal-Mart's network prowess was in awesome display, along with other bottom-of-the-pyramid sellers who recognized that the do-it-yourself demand for recovery would be substantial. Erik Prince's Blackwater Worldwide firm mounted its own impromptu relief response on the spot, winning enough emergency contracts from various players to convince him to begin a new line of products and services aimed at domestic disaster operations. When you place Blackwater's experience in Iraq on security alongside its humanitarian supply response in New Orleans, then Prince's ambition for mounting a private-army peacekeeping response to the Darfur situation becomes more understandable. In effect, he spots an unmet demand for outsourced sovereignty services at the bottom of globalization's pyramid and aims to meet it. Just because failed states fail to attract public-sector responses doesn't mean they cannot elicit private-sector ones.

But the aspect of Katrina that caught most Americans' imagination was the theme of environmental collapse, right out of Jared Diamond's bestselling book of the same name. As soon as urban planners began arguing that New Orleans would never return to its previous population because it simply could not support so many people on such a fragile environmental base, Katrina became a touchstone in public debates about unsustainable environmental policies in a world increasingly marked by global warming. To many, Katrina quickly became a symbol of everything wrong with America's overall approach to this issue—yet another "inconvenient truth" not yet confronted.

Enter Al Gore, the perfect vessel for a counternarrative to President Bush's "global war on terror." The presidential vote-winner, denied his victory in 2000, Gore represents the perfectly plausible historical alternative—the political road not taken. Gore was a longtime environmentalist, and his subsequent embrace of a Paul Revere–like role in warning the planet about the oncoming effects of global warming represents much more than just his personal search for a politically meaningful role after his 2000 election loss. In many ways, Gore's message promises an entire generation of Americans unhappy with Bush's "global war" that a suitably transcendent grand strategy is there for the taking. Rather than dealing with our failures in places like Baghdad and New Orleans (or worse, our nonresponses in places like Darfur), and refashioning our national security establishment to manage such inevitable future challenges, Gore's message promises more familiar dynamics: a planet-threatening foe against which the proper response consists more of an internal decades-long rebalancing than an immediate external exposure to danger. Rather than facing up to the unsavory challenges of shrinking the Gap, global warming allows us to justify pulling back from a chaotic world and addressing its "ultimate" challenge through new technology (always an American favorite) and do-it-yourself sacrifice on an individual level. In short, if American "empire" gets you down, why not register your disapproval, don your global-warming hair shirt, and display your asceticism as a political statement?

Of course, this states the dichotomy too starkly, but you can see the inherent temptation in replacing an unpopular global narrative with one more compellingly familiar in its Cold War logic (e.g., "saving the planet from man's recklessness"). As always, ending today's crisis is as easy as naming tomorrow's scarier crisis. Humans crave life-focusing crises. As globalization creates inescapable complexity (e.g., terror *plus* global warming *plus* financial meltdowns *plus* energy shortages), it is nice to have one big boulder to push up that hill every day, no matter how Sisyphean the task (in fact, the more outlandish the better). We're naturally resilient creatures, and self-sacrifice is embedded in our evolutionary code. When Al Gore wins the Nobel Peace Prize in 2007, it tells me that the world wants a different organizing principle to animate American grand strategy. The world's worry list goes far beyond America's preoccupation with its postwar occupations of Afghanistan and Iraq and the nuclear newborns North Korea and Iran. Every intervention mustn't be hardwired to the threat of transnational terrorism and nukes. Today's globalization is simultaneously far too expansive in its reach and far too immature in its rule sets to be captured by our now discredited storyline of defeating terrorism and thus making the world safe for democracy (echoing Wilson's post-WWI dreams for a politically engineered peace that ignored the economic underpinnings). Again, in historical terms, we are arguing over the bell curve's sloping shoulders while ignoring the huge territory in between.

Given that it has been my living to systemically examine the future, you'd think it would be easy for me to get excited about global warming, but it hasn't been. Let me tell you why. Right up to 9/11, I directed a Naval War College research project that involved partnering with the Wall Street brokerage firm Cantor Fitzgerald—the very same firm that lost six hundred–plus workers that fateful day. As part of this project on globalization's future, we held an "economic security exercise," or scenario-driven war game, to explore the profound environmental issues arising from Asia's rapid development. This war game followed two previous ones on the questions of Asia's rising energy requirements and need for foreign direct investment to fund its stunning infrastructural build-out. If the energy game represented the "motive," and the FDI event explored the "opportunity," then the third exercise exploring the resulting environmental damage captured the "crime."

The exercise centered on the notion that Asia's increasing production of CO_2 would become a major political issue in the collective fight to address global warming. Indeed, the primary reason the United States didn't ratify the Kyoto Treaty was that it left rising India and China out of its global equation. Cantor Fitzgerald had successfully pioneered financial markets to take advantage of, and further enable, the cap-and-trade regime imposed on acid rain emissions by the 1990 Clean Air Act. So in this war game, held atop World Trade Center One in June 2001, the firm was clearly interested in promoting similar market mechanisms for Asia on CO_2, having recently created a subsidiary (CantorCO$_2$e) for just such purposes. In designing the war game, however, I didn't want to stack the deck so obviously in favor of the global-warming scenario. As participants were drawn from Wall Street, the U.S. government, the energy industry, and environmental organizations (including the head of the Intergovernmental Panel on Climate Change, Rajendra Pachauri, who along with the IPCC shared the 2007 Nobel Peace Prize with Gore), I thought it would be interesting to force them to rank a list of competing environmental dangers in order of perceived priority—a bang-for-the-buck hierarchy. In a world of limited resources, I wanted them to tell me where they'd put their next dollar to fix things.

So I had the group play *Survivor* by "voting off the island" one danger each successive round following a discussion of some measure of environmental degradation. As the selected measures focused attention on global warming, I was nonetheless surprised to find that it was the first issue voted off, along with acid rain. Next dispatched were deforestation/species loss and hazardous substances, followed by population pressures/loss of arable land. The runner-up ended up being marine habitat destruction (e.g., fisheries), while the hands-down winner was lack of clean water. Now, one can immediately counter that if humanity deals with global warming effectively, then water issues would likewise improve. Our question, however, was all about timing and priority: for example, how much effort should be made to cut global warming x percent by 2100, versus more immediately addressing all the lives shortened by lack of access to clean water?

Three years later, Danish economist Bjørn Lomborg employed the same thought exercise in his Copenhagen Consensus project, which utilized the combined talents of several Nobel Prize–winning experts. When forced to rank solutions, they too chose to prioritize certain near-term goals (e.g., clean water, malnutrition, debilitating diseases) over the longer-term challenge of slowing global warming. Lomborg later repeated the exercise with a collection of political leaders drawn from all over the world and got the same result. Ditto when he assembled youth representatives from across the planet.

But having said all that, I think so many Americans want to embrace global warming as the preeminent global challenge of our age because it beats the heck out of the alternatives currently offered. I would love to see humanity focus on a "blue revolution" to address looming water shortages linked to global warming, but I know full well that the war on terror and clash of civilizations are current front-runners for crisis of the age among national security experts, and when push comes to shove with the big-war crowd on the subject of defense acquisitions, I fully expect it to mount a full-court press on the subject of resource wars with those new Gap "colonialists"—the Chinese. So how to hijack this myopic strategic dialogue? Replace it with a bigger, more attractive one and, by doing so, deescalate the harmful rhetoric vis-à-vis Islam while systematically delegitimizing al Qaeda's self-declared importance as that religion's lead resistance to globalization's advance. So if forced to choose, I'd also go with global warming right now, because we'll do less damage to both our world and ourselves by myopically focusing on that crisis versus terrorism or radical Islam or China's latest submarine.

And to me, that's pretty sad, because it means that the only way we can talk ourselves out of overhyping the global terror threat is to break its current lock on our attention with an even more hyped presentation on global warming, right down to retired military officers warning us that global warming will be the source of much of the world's future conflicts, a notion that—conveniently enough—quickly gets us back to resource wars. Over time, it's easy to imagine the painfully skewed Bush narrative being replaced with an equally skewed Gore counternarrative: Where Bush focused on the extremes of terror and democracy, Gore's vision promises an equally extreme mix of resource wars on the lower end of Maslow's hierarchy of needs, and postindustrial clean living on the higher end. Meanwhile, in both cases, globalization's huge emerging middle is ignored or—worse—is thwarted in its reasonable ambitions.

China and India, for example, can't afford either extreme, making the implied dichotomy unrealistic: Neither can wage long-term conventional wars to fence off the world's resources. They can neither spare the resources nor anger their financial partners in the West. They're already simply too connected to globalization to try and carve out resource empires that feed their growth while killing their market connectivity. Such fantastic dreams died with the Soviet bloc's mini-me global economy in

1989. Once you connect to globalization, all resource constraints become collective problems. That's the fundamental subversion of global conflict foisted upon great powers by the American System–cum–globalization: Our liberal international trade order denies such partitioning strategies by rendering moot all such attempts at segmented autarky. Simply put, you can't become interdependent economically and then hold apart some aspect—be it energy or military power—as essentially autarkic. If it didn't work for the Bush neocons on security, then it will hardly work for China on raw materials. Still, expect a lot of security experts to keep feeding you this strategic nonsense in the years ahead.

Then there's the bigger argument offered by Lomborg in his brilliant little 2007 book, *Cool It*. Like Lomborg, I see no reason to debate whether the world is getting warmer or whether human activity is causing such change. Both points seem reasonably well established by the global scientific community. The real question is whether or not we need to elevate global warming to the status of the greatest crisis of our age. Gore's counternarrative explicitly promises to deliver meaning to individual lives, much as Bush's terror narrative did for some. But much like Bush's narrow narrative, Gore's narrative demands we act to prevent a negative future rather than enable a better one. As Lomborg argues, our ultimate goal shouldn't be the reduction of greenhouse gases or global warming per se, "but to improve the quality of life and the environment" for future generations. Rather than explore—quite self-centeredly, I would add— the aesthetics of asceticism in the rich West to avoid imagined future resource wars among great powers, why not ask that emerging global middle class how the global economy can best meet its needs and expectations for a better life? Why not center globalization's ideology in that massive middle instead of on the extreme have/have-not margins? Those rising New Core economies will eventually account for the large majority of CO_2 emissions come the year 2100. If the West's fundamental offer to these emerging economies is to curtail their growth potential as a way of avoiding future resource wars, then we will end up doing nothing more than guaranteeing that such conflicts occur. If the choice falls between progress *plus* war versus nonprogress *plus* internal instability, expect these powers to choose the former every time. After all, that's the story of the West in a nutshell.

Human history, as Lomborg points out, says we do better when it gets warmer and that we do worse when it gets colder. It also tells us that it's far easier (and cheaper) to cool people in hot climes than keep them warm in cold ones. Setting aside the fantastic scenarios of resource wars among great powers whose economic interdependence is already advanced and will deepen further over rising food requirements, we're looking at life getting much worse in major portions of the Gap but not much more complicated in the Core as a whole. By 2100, average personal incomes in the Old Core West should rise sixfold, just as they did in each of the previous two centuries. Meanwhile, the United Nations projects that individual incomes across the emerging economies of the New Core East and South, along with those of the Gap in aggregate, should rise roughly twice as fast, or twelvefold. That means the average poor person on the planet should enjoy an income in 2100 that equates to $27,000 today. What we know from human history is that mass violence in developing economies tends to disappear once you get per capita income above $3,000. We also know that as incomes rise to the $5,000–$10,000 range, societies tend to take better care of their environment and move toward political pluralism. Indeed, as Fareed Zakaria argues, democracies, once they get above that range, become "immortal," meaning they never slide back toward authoritarianism. Sadly, the only sheer limit we can cite in such an income trajectory is the limit of personal happiness, which by all measures seems to top out at roughly $20,000 per capita.

You can say that all such "optimistic" projections are logically held captive to the "unprecedented" challenges presented by global warming, but I would argue that it's the other way around, and that the challenges presented by global warming are not that unprecedented. Major urban areas, as Lomborg notes, have already weathered in the last century temperature increases similar to those projected for this one, and guess what? More inhabitants still die from the cold than from the heat! Whether you're talking rising sea levels or more volatile weather or more difficulty in growing food or more invasive spreading of disease, in each instance these challenges are better addressed through rising incomes than, as Lomborg puts it, turning the "CO_2 knob" down as far as possible. Deaths from natural disasters are strongly related to economic development but only weakly related to a changing climate, as are deaths from infectious diseases. The same is true for water shortages and food shortages. Rising wealth insulates people from environmental dangers quite effectively. Where sea levels rise and land is dear, money is found to manage that process. Where rising sea levels meet an impoverished population, there you will definitely see increased flooding. But in that instance, should our response focus on holding back that tide, in the manner of King Canute? Or should it focus on raising income levels and accepting that such a goal means carbon emissions will be near impossible to stabilize anytime soon?

Lomborg sums up his measured position this way:

> Global warming is happening; the consequences are important and mostly negative. It will cause more heat deaths, an increase in sea level, possibly more intense hurricanes, and more flooding. It will give rise to more malaria, starvation, and poverty. It is therefore not surprising that a vast array of environmental organizations, pundits, and world leaders have concluded that we must act to fix global warming. The problem with this analysis is that it overlooks a simple but important fact. Cutting CO_2—even substantially—will not matter much for the problems on this list. From polar bears to water scarcity . . . we can do relatively little with climate policies and a lot more with social policies.

The tendency right now to blame everything on global warming is grand strategic escapism at its worst. My favorite recent example was the horrors of Darfur, which some international opinion leaders blamed on global warming. Such logic allowed us to argue, in effect, "Let's not intervene militarily when we can swap out all our inefficient lightbulbs back home and chant 'Genocide Olympics' during the Beijing Games, thus fulfilling our duty as citizens of the world!" What sounds more responsible, I ask: buying the T-shirt or paying Blackwater to actually do something? Because shaming China into impoverishing Sudan further is unlikely to get us the outcome we seek. So please, spare me the transference of guilt from do-nothing America to do-something China. If you really want to shame China into more action, outperform it on the ground instead of out-talking it in the United Nations.

America stands on the verge of locking in its international liberal trade order through the successful integration of rising economic pillars in the East and South, whose recent accession shifted our American System–cum–globalization from its past narrow global minority into an overwhelming majority status worldwide. There is no good reason to sabotage the emergence of a truly global middle class by having America's grand strategy fixate excessively in the near term on extreme definitions of either transnational terrorism or global warming, two dangers logically framed as chronic long-term threats destined to be managed and mitigated by long-term responses. By meeting the demands of that emerging global middle class, we set in motion the evolution of worldwide democracy that invariably develops in response to rising income levels, which in turn will sufficiently empower nations to mitigate effectively the challenges posed by the twenty-first century. Moreover, by embracing the global competitiveness forced upon all by this liberal trade order, humans will continue their natural journey "down" the carbon-emissions chain (i.e., from wood to coal to oil to natural gas), moving now toward hydrogen. But as always, those answers will arise largely in response to the most immediate pain felt across the system—for instance, high energy prices. In environmental terms, that means the New Core East and South, with their typically more "dirty" industries and skyrocketing consumption rates, will play the same tipping-point role on future solutions as they now play on emerging problems.

Our goal must continue to be the effective integration of these emerging powers into the corridors of decision-making power within globalization's expanding Core. If global warming forces a new Core-wide dialogue on technology and development, then Al Gore will have served his grand-strategic purpose: replacing a divisive American grand strategic focus with a unifying one. The problem for now is that global warming, being logically located somewhat far down the list of immediate global challenges, provides the aging West and especially tiring America the dangerous opportunity to short-circuit that integration effort in the name of a superseding crusade for humanity's future. Thus, in our haste to rid ourselves of one unsustainable and divisive grand strategy, we might immediately transform global warming into its painfully similar replacement. Rather than fantasize about future resource wars in an attempt to obviate this challenge, much as we fantasize about energy autarky to rid us of the troublesome Middle East, the crucial challenge we face today is to continue trusting in this global system of our creation. We came to these crossroads before—at home—and we fashioned a "new deal" to make the emerging middle class our political center of gravity while addressing the environmental limits of our rapid economic development. This is no time to go wobbly or grow vindictive or to gin up even scarier bogeymen.

THE NEW RULES: FROM "UNITED WE STAND" TO DEMOGRAPHIC DEMAGOGUERY

Some observers increasingly preach the notion that a global economy no longer so dominated by America represents a post-American age, when in truth it represents our greatest achievement: the extension of our very American-style liberal trade order. Do not fall under the spell of this most subtle fearmongering, because it encourages accommodation through defeatism when the world needs our self-confident leadership now more than ever. That the rest of the planet doesn't immediately ape our mature embrace of the political, economic, and social implications of that order need not blind us to our continuing role as global revolutionaries, for again, our own achievements in all those categories were long in the making. In effect, by expanding our American System–cum–globalization so rapidly around the planet in recent years, we've simply exposed ourselves, in an inverted fashion, to a far greater universe of "stationary states" whose populations have, for all practical purposes, virtually emigrated to our now globalized "land of opportunity." As a result, we now find ourselves, for the first time in this grand strategic process, adjusting more to globalization than globalization adjusts to us.

That naturally scares us, but it shouldn't. Politics will always lag behind economics. It has throughout our nation's history and it does so today. But that doesn't mean we should—in our immediate fears—attempt to remake the Gap militarily when our globalization source code does that with a frightening speed all its own. If, in our patience, we choose to recognize our younger economic and—especially—political selves in these rising powers that now appear to offer us challenge, we'll effectively migrate the planet down a path that enables states collectively to mitigate dangers like terrorism and global warming in the short run, while forcing societies toward sustainable development choices that ultimately conquer these threats over the long haul. That strategic vision cannot be described on the margins of globalization's bell curve but only in its vast middle. Thus, the global narrative we seek must be one that links America's middle-class ideology to globalization's emerging middle class, for it is there that the expanding Core as a whole will ultimately stand united.

America simply cannot obtain a quorum for such global change either at home, amid our own beleaguered middle class, or abroad in a demographically moribund West. We are forced by our success in spreading our American System–cum–globalization to cast our nets further. Adjusting to that success is the primary task of American grand strategy today, not cowering in fear from globalization's competitive landscape or the political immaturity of its rising powers. That's like the father fearing the son for his strength while condemning him for his lack of wisdom, when we should exploit the former to trigger the latter's emergence. That's why, whenever I hear an American politician proclaim the need to strengthen the Western alliance, I know that leader proposes to steer by our historical wake instead of crafting a forward-looking grand strategy. Recapturing past glory is not recapturing our youth but denying our parentage of this world we inhabit so uneasily today.

Our most immediate challenge right now is avoiding the temptation to define our own middle-class security in terms of walls that shut out "unfair" competition, when we should recognize globalization's open frontiers for the same opportunity they've always presented Americans: the chance to redefine ourselves. For example, the global economy, in its rapid growth, can no longer subsist on a single reserve currency—the dollar. More balance and flexibility are required beyond the sort of once-every-decade Plaza Accord–style agreements to shift the dollar's value in tectonic trajectories. We fear that brave new world as much as we did when Nixon took us off the gold standard in 1971; we worry that the world won't respect—and possibly fear—us as it once did. But here's the deal: We lured *them* into this liberal trade order and *they're* doing the best they can with it right now, many of them scaling production chains at rates that defy historical predictions. Our job is the same as it's always been: stay out in front in terms of innovation and entrepreneurship, recognizing the need for new rule sets as they appear. American history serves as guide: When our stock market crashed in 1929, we responded with new regulatory institutions. Now we face that task on a global level.

On the more personal level, Americans should remain grateful that we're still a fertile nation, one that continues to attract both high-skilled and low-skilled labor. We are unlike Europe or Japan in that our synthetic culture allows for assimilation, meaning we'll manage our aging population in a manner unique in the world. By 2025, rapidly aging Europe and Japan will be shrinking in size while we're still adding almost 3 million people a year. We'll sport the highest growth rate among developed countries, as well as one of the lowest median ages. We'll also be the only sizable developed country where the kids still outnumber the elders. As demographer Nicholas Eberstadt argues, "Such trends might reinforce U.S. international prominence—even though the divergence in demographic profiles between the United States and other developed countries may also portend an era of diminishing affinities between the United States and its historical Western allies."

That's just one of the many demographic hints staring us in the face regarding future allies. In a world of economic frontier integration, the regions that simultaneously "rise" and export labor are the natural network-builders and infrastructure-builders. Europe played this role in the seventeenth through the nineteenth centuries; now Asia does the same. Between them, China and India have placed over 50 million workers abroad, with Indians in America emerging as the new Jews: disproportionately well educated, well paid, and increasingly well connected politically. As for East Asians in America, well, there the stereotypes are already well established—the super-students who crush all competition. Yes, in the short term there will be spy scandals and fear factors associated with foreign corporate takeovers, but if demography is destiny, then alliances are allocated accordingly.

Yet there is such cultural angst in America regarding the "loss" of Europe and so much fuss generated by our aging Boomer leaders regarding the need to "save" or "resurrect" or "repair" the transatlantic relationship, when truth be told, "grandpa" is coming along for the ride no matter who's sitting in the front seat with us. Europe, with its postreligious identity (lest it be once again fused with nationalism and lead to civil wars), is desperately scared by the challenges of assimilating an Islamic underclass that performs the so-called 3D jobs—dirty, dangerous, and difficult. Unlike America's similarly employed Hispanics, who present themselves in the familiar spiritual garb of Catholicism, Europe's Muslims resurrect fears there of an invading horde determined to subvert democracy just as the pooled European identity seems perfected. In reality, these ambitious immigrants (if they weren't, they would have stayed home) will naturally avail themselves—if properly incentivized—of democracy's many avenues of redress to press their economic and political demands. Sure, today's political fires will often be lit by street protests, but that is how political movements are often birthed. Europe's challenge is to facilitate either the rise of new political parties that represent these immigrants' needs directly or the incorporation of their agendas within existing ones, a process already begun in France, where in the 2007 elections immigrant minorities ran for parliamentary seats in record numbers.

For every frightened pundit (see Mark Steyn's *America Alone*) who sees his European heritage disappearing in a tide of Islam, there's a next-generation globalist (see Parag Khanna's *The Second World*) who sees the EU effectively rebranding itself and ambitiously integrating new frontiers both eastward and southward in coming decades. Some will argue that Europe can incorporate only more Europeans, stretching that definition to Russia's doorstep but denying Turkey, but since Western Europe's plunging birthrates have already spread eastward with stunning speed, a southward integration strategy is inevitable, meaning Europe's cultural center of gravity will once again center on the Mediterranean—hardly the end of the world as we know it. In fact, Spain's recent "open border" policy, resulting in a population that's roughly one-quarter (!) foreign-born (most just south across the sea), demonstrates the sort of shocking therapy that invariably all European countries will be forced to adopt in order to stop their aging populations from turning their economies into globalization's stagnant backwaters.

None of this will be easy, and if America is any example, the aging West will veer between periods of openness and retrenchment, with economic stagnation triggering the former and political violence the latter.

Every wave of new immigrants in America, going all the way back to the early seventeenth century, has fought to close the door behind it—yesterday's "niggers" invariably become tomorrow's Know-Nothings. My own Irish ancestors provide a perfect example in this regard, triggering in their early-nineteenth-century bow wave the rise of public education in America (lest those "filthy" Papists spread their undemocratic ways), only to become, by the end of that same century, nativists of the worst sort determined to stop the flood of East Europeans! But in the end, it's all about assimilation and political inclusiveness; otherwise a ghettoized underclass results, like France's Muslims today. You can say the problem is immigration or religious difference, but rising incomes tend to close all cultural gaps—meaning economic achievement drives political accommodation rather than the other way around. That's not to say that France can't effectively cycle new Muslim immigrants through *les cités*, because it does to a certain extent, but rather that these inner-city ghettos will present a constant political sore until they are properly mobilized in a political sense.

Again, the American System proves to be modern globalization's first and still best example of the way ahead. Between 1978 and 2002, the percentage of foreign-born Americans doubled from 6 percent to 12 percent, even as our five-year average unemployment rate dropped. Why no great social unrest? Among immigrants, median family incomes rose by roughly $10,000 for every decade they remained in the country. The same financial experiments that triggered the subprime crisis likewise made it easier for immigrant Hispanics in America to buy homes, so don't toss out all of those debt-spreading financial instruments just yet, because the potential long-term political losses may end up being even more profound than the temporary economic hit. Obviously, if you want stakeholders in either your American System or globalization as a whole, then you need to give them the opportunity to create stakes (and as global risk management goes, this is pennies on the dollar compared with military interventions). Hispanics are expected to make up 40 percent of first-time home buyers in America over the next two decades. As for cultural assimilation, it proceeds apace. Only 40 percent of Mexican immigrants go to college, but nearly two-thirds of the second-generation Mexican-Americans do. By the third generation, three-quarters speak nothing but English. One out of four first-generation Hispanic immigrants intermarry with whites, but one-third of American-born Hispanics do the same.

But if none of that assuages your fears, let the following speak to your greed. Immigrant Latinos open new businesses at a rate three times the national norm. They're also replenishing the ranks of American farm labor *just* as our agricultural business hits an inflection point in response to the global economy's skyrocketing demand for food. If you're a Boomer heading into retirement, you need immigrants to do well economically, because their rising incomes are going to replenish your retirement coffers, not to mention allow you to sell your house. Since the end of the Cold War, 80 percent of population growth in this country has come in the form of African-American and Hispanic-American kids, yet they're not getting the same schooling as their white counterparts. This isn't about closing our borders to make sure America's middle class doesn't disappear, this is about keeping our borders open to make sure we have a middle class several decades down the road. The challenges we face today—as we did in post–Civil War America—are the same ones the Core faces with the New Core's emerging economies as well as the Gap's developing economies and failed states: We are forced to recognize that tomorrow's global middle class will rise from their frontier ranks. The nativists are absolutely correct: Our culture is on the line. But the culture that matters most here is our economic culture—our ability to nurture entrepreneurship. The rest will be a mashed-up social remix that only our children will find readily recognizable.

The temptation to reach for shortcuts here, again, is profound. To insist you only want highly educated immigrants ignores the demographics, but clearly every advanced economy is scrambling for top technological and management talent, so there's plenty of logic in offering special packages. Hell, if serving in our military gets you instant citizenship, then a Ph.D. in one of our universities (even in their satellite facilities abroad) might make an equally utilitarian golden ticket. As for the longer-term fear that we'll be overrun with impoverished immigrants, history says otherwise. As Michael Barone points out, America's East Coast was awash with Puerto Rican immigrants in the 1960s, fueled in large part because of increasingly cheap connectivity (especially airfares), but that flow tapered off once Puerto Rico's per capita income rose to about one-third of America's. At that point, the purchasing-power differential washed out and Puerto Ricans, on average, preferred staying home. In the more distant past, the same dynamics could be spotted in the flows of immigrants from Europe and Asia: Once their economies grew enough, the flow diminished spectacularly. So the answer isn't building a bigger wall along our southern border, where more Hispanics die each year trying to cross than did East Germans scaling over or tunneling under the Berlin Wall across its entire history. Rather, it's about raising income levels in Latin America through further trade and economic integration, a strategic goal congressional Democrats casually trashed last year in their treatment of Colombia's proposed free-trade agreement. To that end, an America that isn't fifteen to twenty states bigger by 2050 is missing the boat—and simply inviting more boat people.

That's where the growing European Union truly outperforms the United States today: Those populations that it grows weary of beating back are ultimately asked to join. That the EU can add stars while our flag remains fixed at fifty is a sad reflection of our continued Cold War tendency to favor the status quo over system expansion, and to presume our world order is defined in political-military terms instead of economic liberty. Mexico has provided us with numerous new states in the past and it should do so in the future. The economic merger was forged with NAFTA; we simply refuse to admit the logic of complete acquisition. Would the price be too steep? If you want to keep the "old" America from becoming too Hispanic, you'd better think about extending the "new" America farther southward, because global warming is going to exacerbate the northward flow beyond past expectations of sustainability, so we either pay soon or pay later.

America's absorption of its Western frontiers constituted the most troubling and transformative period of our history. Even as we conceived our "manifest destiny," our acquisition was largely defensive—as in, better us than *them*. Eventually, we'll be forced into a similarly aggressive mindset regarding the courting of an emerging global middle class: We'll come to believe that if our ideology doesn't reign supreme, its survival will be put at risk—along with the American System itself. For now, we have the luxury of viewing this struggle with the relatively weak forces of antiglobalization, currently embodied by radical Islam, as a war of discipline. But it remains so only because globalization's frontline "settlers" today are primarily Asians. Over time, their success in developing a world-spanning middle class will present us with a rule-set clash of truly global proportions—unless we shape and ultimately conquer that ideological space *first*. In this regard, we have to stop playing China's "useful idiot" and start making it our own, more self-aware partner. This is what the next generation of warfare will be all about: achieving nonkinetic victories by steering other nations' ambitions.

Our historical moment of declaring such victories America's and America's alone has passed. Our global economic model of integration, now firmly in place, requires no such braggadocio on our part. Let China, as it slowly forges an Asian union in coming years, pretend it is reinventing our wheel, just as Europeans do today, because, in the end, our model of states uniting in multinational security, economic, and political union will kill state-on-state war there, just as it did in Europe, marking America as the most pacifying force in human history.

THE NEW NORMAL: APOCALYPSE SOON

Both pre- and postmillennialism have thrived in America's competitive religious landscape over the past two-plus centuries, with the majority view tending toward the latter perspective. In postmillennialism, human progress contributes to the realization of God's ultimate design, meaning the "end times" come *after* we make this Earth worthy of God's return. In premillennialism, God's return starts the global renovation for real. Premillennialism is escapism at its spiritual core: "I can't stand/change this evil world and so I wait for God's intervention to accomplish this for me." Postmillennialism captures the Protestant work ethic most commonly associated with American-style capitalism: "God wants me to live long and prosper, remaking this world in his/my image." When times are good, the sort of death-wish fantasies of premillennialism tend to remain on the fringes of society. When times are uncertain, certainty is sought in such notions, making premillennialism the spiritual foodstuff of losers— "We're not worthy!"

Secular versions of premillennialism abound in my profession of strategic planning, because they represent the ultimate trump card: "All these issues pale compared with the coming disaster in [X]!" They're a show-stopping, discussion-ending "last word" that brooks no opposition. If you cannot see the "undeniable logic" of the argument, then you are described as "brainwashed" or "deluded" by conventional wisdom on the subject. As somebody who argues for grand strategy, I am constantly bombarded by readers who want me to alter my entire vision on the basis of the last short-term crisis or the looming "train wreck," as though my strategy assumed a linear projection with nary a setback! It is very hard to argue with such thinking, because these advocates' faith in the primacy of whatever element they've decided to focus upon is usually unshakable. Often the strongest proponents of such doom-and-gloom are longtime experts in the field who, at the end of their lives, seem transfixed with some profound internal guilt that their careers constituted one big lie. If they worked nuclear weapons all their lives, then they suffer a conversion in their later years, becoming convinced that nuclear weapons constitute the greatest threat facing mankind, and so on. Such conversions are not uncommon in the military realm; some of the biggest "peaceniks" I know are retired flag officers. They're like lapsed Catholics. You don't want to start arguing with them unless you've got the rest of the day to pursue the conversation.

That such logic is commonplace in America's foreign policy debates today signals nothing more than our inability to congregate around a grand strategy upon which a strong majority of us can agree. Being in a transitional period of profound rule-set adjustment, where we're trying to take what was the West's security/economic order and suddenly spread it across a much larger swath of humanity, the marketplace of ideas concerning grand strategy is both deeply unsettled and highly competitive. Americans are uncomfortable about recognizing today's globalization as our historical progeny; we expected it to be so much tidier in its expression. In effect, those who believed that dispatching the Soviet threat was enough to achieve a sort of postmillennialist global paradise, a "new world order" marking the "end of history," are disappointed to sense that our nation's burden is far from complete. To these souls, an argument for making globalization truly global is often interpreted as "perpetual global war." They feel like they already gave at the office that was the Cold War, and now they want their peace dividend pronto. In waiting almost two decades now, witnessing the United States' being drawn militarily into numerous Gap environments, many Americans find their patience simply tapped; thus the shift to premillennialist escapism. "If you, the national security establishment, cannot deliver," they say, "then we'll uncover some inescapable truth that makes all this effort meaningless!"

A famous TV commercial from my youth featured a harried housewife who, when confronted with a messy, chaotic home life, cried out, "Calgon, take me away!" With this simple incantation, our housewife found herself magically whisked away to a steaming bubble bath that made everything better—a sort of domestic premillennialism on call. In ancient Greece, playwrights tied off convoluted scripts with a similarly satisfying plot twist known as the *deus ex machina*, or literally, "god from a machine." Want a tidy ending? The god lowered from the rafters announced one. Many would-be grand strategists now struggle mightily to provide America with a quick exit from this long war against the global jihadist insurgency. The Cold War taught us that dedicated foes take decades to defeat, and yet Americans just naturally want to come home. If we created this globalization, then apparently it has betrayed us, generating too much complexity, too much conflict, and too many challengers. Given our love of technology, it's no surprise that science, our modern god-machine, is viewed as our most likely salvation and/or curse: The right new gizmo renders this entire fight unnecessary, or some looming disaster makes it entirely pointless. The desperate search befits modern America: We prefer rapid-fire problem-solving to the long, hard slog of nation-building. This backlash has already begun within the U.S. military: In an almost Orwellian twist, many officers argue we must abandon all pretense of optimizing the force for small wars, because our opponents will trump us with big-war capabilities, even though history clearly proves that if you want to take on the Americans and win, asymmetrical warfare is the way to go. As such, arguments for a rededication to a Leviathan-only force amounts to a "Calgon, take me away!" request in national security terms.

Outside those ranks, other *deus ex machina* are proposed. A good example is the theory of "peak oil." This controversial prediction stems from a provable observation: For any known oil field, production naturally peaks, and then it subsequently declines as it nears depletion. Technology seeks to maximize capture, but since any reserve is—in geological terms—nonrenewable, the total yield is both finite and calculable. Some oil analysts employ this observation to extrapolate a global oil peak, declaring we've already passed the point of no return. The problem with this theory is twofold: (1) it's based on existing known reserves when so much of the Gap hasn't been adequately surveyed, and (2) it discounts unconventional sources of oil, such as tar sands and oil shale, as well as nonoil sources for transportation energy. Cambridge Energy Research Associates, a highly respected industry authority, estimates that if unconventional sources are added into the mix, our planet's currently known oil reserves are actually three times larger than that predicted by peak oil, suggesting that alleged doomsday is decades off—Asia's skyrocketing requirements notwithstanding. The logic here is market-derived: Persistently higher prices drive new exploration and boost R&D in both energy extraction and the technology of transportation. That means we'll go deeper and farther to access new reserves while extracting better yields from both existing and future fields as we upgrade our automotive fleet.

We won't leave the oil age because we've run out of oil, any more than we stopped using whale oil because we ran out of whales. Instead, humanity moves progressively "down" the carbon chain for the sheer reason that each step we take brings us higher efficiency and less environmental damage—a veritable win-win. That market logic unfolds far too slowly for peak oil advocates, who daily decry our global economy's "looming collapse"—the real target of the theory. Their prescription brings us to the second great *deus ex machina* of our times: a Manhattan Project–like crash program to "get us off our oil addiction!" This call dovetails nicely with the "Let's beggar those nasty Muslims" camp that claims we fund both sides of this war. Impatient with the Middle East's glacial embrace of democracy, this wedge strategy seeks to force local regimes into rapid political change by severing their current, fairly narrow connectivity with the global economy—the Big Bang yields to the slow strangle. Toss in global climate change, today's *deus ex machina* without peer, and soon you're convinced there's no reason for us to remain in the Middle East whatsoever. Compared with rising sea levels, terrorism just doesn't rank. Probably the strongest recent such "call to arms" comes

in Thomas Friedman's latest bestseller, *Hot, Flat, and Crowded*, where he declares, in response to this cluster of challenges, the need for "nation-building in America"—italics and exclamation points *included*!

Don't get me wrong. Humanity is destined to move beyond oil and seriously address global warming. I'm just not willing to kneel before any god-machine for an excuse slip from this long war. If all we want is the Core's access to Persian Gulf oil, Osama bin Laden poses little threat. His goal is civilizational apartheid, not economic isolation per se. And if the region lacked oil or even Islam, the real problem would remain: traditional cultures poorly adapting themselves to globalization's creeping embrace, primarily because its gender-neutral networks empower women disproportionately to men. That's not our fault or Israel's, but rather an inherent weakness of Arab culture, exacerbated by particular interpretations of Islamic faith, which—by the way—imposes no such apparent limitations on emerging Muslim economies in Asia. All god-machines aside, it's tempting to abandon the fight against violent extremism in the Middle East, but a problem shelved is not solved.

The underlying reality on oil is more complex than simply noting global supplies are concentrated in unstable areas, which, of course, is absolutely true. The Core used up most of its oil a long time ago, forcing the global economy's narrow embrace of several Gap regions—most significantly the Persian Gulf. Because the global economy's demand was relatively light during the Cold War, it wasn't until its radical expansion to include those 3 billion new capitalists that we entered into this period of dangerously tight production capacity, meaning no matter how big our global oil reserves are, our current worldwide oil industry infrastructure is dangerously close to being maxed out in its capacity to extract, refine, and deliver oil around the planet.

With oil stuck well above the $100-a-barrel mark for much of last year, there's little surprise that we're once again inundated by calls for more regulation of so-called super-major oil companies (e.g., Exxon-Mobil, BP, Royal Dutch Shell, Chevron) and an end to our military presence in the Persian Gulf, in addition to the usual demand for a Manhattan Project on alternative energy. The assumptions are that America's energy demand drives prices, the super-majors determine supply, and instability in the Middle East explains recent spikes. So if this is all our doing, then

it can all be our undoing as well! Would that Washington were so eminently in control of global energy markets. The big driver on oil prices
today is rising Asia's increasing demand. At the Cold War's end, Asia
accounted for 10 percent of global oil demand. Today it gobbles up double that share. Before 2025, Asia will become the oil market's global demand center, dislodging North America. So as I've noted before, it's
basically *our* blood and *their* oil, and not surprisingly, when Americans are
confronted with that strategic reality, we want out—and fast!

A second big driver is that many key producers are themselves becoming significant consumers, shriveling their capacity for exports. Indonesia became a net importer years ago, while Mexico, a crucial supplier
for the United States, heads down the same path unless it soon opens up
its national oil company to foreign direct investment. Meanwhile, strong-
man Hugo Chávez diminishes Venezuela's future export capacity by scar-
ing off investors and—in essence—eating his seed corn: funneling today's
windfall profits into socialist programs designed to buttress his popular
standing. His latest scheme involves Venezuela's national oil company using its logistical networks to import foodstuffs currently in short supply.
Fire-breathing Mahmoud Ahmadinejad has pursued a similarly short-
sighted course in Iran to predictable outcomes. In general, all the big producers are seeing their oil consumption skyrocket far above global growth,
with Saudi Arabia, Russia, and Norway leading the way. So while rising
Asia demands a lot more oil, the biggest sources have trouble boosting
production.

What can the super-major oil companies do about any of this? Not as
much as you think. Increasingly, it's the home team national oil companies, or NOCs, that control the bulk of reserves. Today, these state-owned
firms directly manage 40 percent of the world's production. Because the
NOCs own roughly 90 percent of known reserves, any increase in production naturally favors their increased control over the industry. By
2030, NOCs are expected to control as much as three-quarters of global
production, meaning ExxonMobil, BP, and others will be squeezed out of
new big projects as national oil companies grow rich enough to finance
these on their own. Already, a significant chunk of the super-majors' current production is locked into sharing agreements that favor the national

oil companies as prices rise. As the national oil companies grab more control over future production, the super-majors face more restricted access
to existing oil fields, pushing them toward increasingly complex ventures
to discover new supplies: tougher geology, deeper seabeds, harsher arctic
environments, and thicker oil. Those tougher conditions drive up production costs just as a worldwide shortage of rigs and workers emerges. Toss
in years of underinvesting by everybody in refining capacity, and this situation won't be remedied anytime soon, even as a global recession de-
presses demand temporarily.

Do continuing violence and threats in the Middle East add a sur-
charge on top of all this? Sure, although the real problem comes in chronic
instability or rogue regimes keeping certain countries essentially off-line
from comprehensive exploration, something the national oil companies
increasingly accomplish even in stable nations, so stability's unlikely to
improve the situation over the long term. When the NOCs let in Western
super-majors and their world-class technology, these outsiders tend to
discover significant amounts of new reserves (just watch Iraq today). Plus,
the super-majors' technology for extracting oil from existing fields continues to improve. Historically, for every three barrels of oil found, classic
lift technology extracts only one, leaving two in the ground. New technology improves the yield, meaning we get more of those other two barrels
out of the ground. When Chevron, for example, applied its high-pressure
steam technology to an aging Indonesia field a few years back, the yield
went from 65,000 barrels a day to over 200,000. So if oil is priced high
enough, the extra effort to boost yields and seek out more isolated sources,
like in the increasingly ice-free Arctic Circle, makes more sense—oil production being a function of price and technology.

How about trusting in OPEC's ability to boost production sufficiently
to cover rising global demand? That's where it gets tricky, because OPEC's
national oil companies are incentivized to discourage outside competition
and refuse foreign investments, so more and more of the global economy's
future is being tied to Gap economies that feature low levels of transparency, increasing everyone's sense of risk further. Beyond that, growing international concern over global warming, combined with Asia's ballooning
car fleet and associated air pollution, casts a long-term shadow over the

oil industry. Simply put, it's hard to imagine Asia quadrupling (or worse) its automobiles over the next two decades and surviving the resulting environmental degradation, even if it could import enough oil.

For the increasingly squeezed super-majors, it doesn't make sense to stick out their necks on long-term investments to grow supply-side infrastructure. Instead, watch them invariably warm up to new vehicle drive technologies that major automakers pursue in their greed to stay on top. As for national oil companies, expect them to invest in just enough production capacity to keep prices from rising too far above $100 a barrel but not enough to drive them significantly below that mark—if they can help it.

In sum, crude prices will remain relatively high for the long run as everybody involved squeezes out maximum profits across the final decades of oil's supremacy. As for what comes next, watch Asia, because America's strictly in the backseat on this tumultuous ride. The world took over a century to field its first billion cars, but the second billion will arrive in roughly three decades' time—thanks to rising Asia. If just China and India approximate Japan's current rate of car saturation (roughly one-half that of the United States), then we're looking at a rough doubling of global oil demand in our lifetimes, something that's hard to imagine no matter what level of technology and investment is employed, especially since much of that effort will go into replacing the declining output of existing oil fields.

Here's where we reach a fork in the road of *deus ex machina* outcomes. Some experts will point to China's fixation on "equity oil," meaning Beijing wants to own the barrel in the ground and all the infrastructure between that field and its domestic market, and state that we're inevitably slated to wage wars with China over dwindling oil supplies. Again, that logic tends to break down when you realize how intertwined our economy is already with China's. Other experts take a more optimistic tack: Asia's skyrocketing transportation requirements allow it to skip a generation in car technology and move rapidly toward hydrogen fuel-cell cars, with the migration running like this: gas-electric hybrids to ultra-light-chassis gas-electric hybrids to fuel-cell/gas ultralight hybrids to pure fuel-cell ultralights (got that?). As automotive visionary Amory Lovins puts it, "Once hydrogen is introduced, the complete elimination of oil use is inevitable; the only question is how fast." Lovins notes that most shifts "down" the carbon chain (e.g., wood to coal) took about fifty years to unfold, with the previous mainstay decreasing dramatically but hardly disappearing altogether. If the world effectively began the oil-to-hydrogen shift in transportation when the first gas-electric cars hit American roads a few years back, then long before 2050, Asia's rising transportation requirements should be more than enough to complete the transition. Lovins thinks it will happen in roughly half that time, or by 2030. Of course, that will be too slow for the hard-core peak-oil types and far too slow for those who cast global warming as the global crisis of our age, but as I've learned long ago with the doom-and-gloom crowd, there's simply no pleasing them with such market-driven analysis. Instead, only government-sponsored Manhattan Projects will do.

A more plausible fly-in-the-ointment argument posits that China's stunning economic trajectory, combined with its weak environmental regulation at home, inevitably slates it for a near-term ecological "collapse" in the vein of Jared Diamond's famous book (which, by the way, has a long chapter on China's numerous environmental woes). Moreover, to the extent China exports those bad practices to all those Gap resource providers that it progressively integrates into its supply chains, Beijing's monomaniacal push for global economic power may end up taking a good chunk of the global ecosystem with it when it finally does collapse into complete environmental chaos. But here again, we find ourselves on somewhat familiar ground. As noted Chinese expert Elizabeth Economy argues:

> A century ago, the United States was grappling with many of the same problems that currently confront China: rapid deforestation in the midwestern states, water scarcity in the west, soil erosion and dust storms in the nation's heartland, and loss of fish and wildlife. These challenges sparked a number of grand-scale public and private initiatives to conserve the land, water and forest resources, as well as the biodiversity of the country.

The big difference with China today, as Economy notes, is the scale of environmental degradation, for China's trying to pull off a trajectory like late-nineteenth-century America but with a current population that's more than ten times larger than ours was back then. Trying to make that growth happen for roughly one out of every five humans concentrated on a landmass roughly the same size as our own is unimaginably hard. But that's one of the many reasons why I don't see China picking fights with the United States. It will simply need our help—meaning our investments and our technology—too much in coming decades. As it is, the Chinese Communist Party is running an "enormous gamble," in Economy's words, by encouraging the rise of grassroots nongovernmental organizations (still often government-sponsored) focused on protecting the environment. By making protection of the environment a social cause, the Party exposes itself to outside judgment, from both its people and the world, in the same way that the Soviet Union exposed itself during détente on the subject of human rights—the Helsinki Accords. In many ways, Economy's analysis suggests that the United States and the rest of the West should engage China in an OSCE-like, Northern Hemispheric dialogue on shared environmental concerns, so as to further encourage both Beijing's use of domestic environmental NGOs and its importation of Western environmental technologies. In general, Economy finds, China responds well to such multilateral forums so long as access to new technology is facilitated.

Our grand strategic goal here should be to create as many avenues of dialogue between China and the outside world as possible so that when the environmental disasters do start piling up, as I believe they will, China won't respond in a knee-jerk, authoritarian fashion out of the fear that anything less aggressive will make it seem weak in the eyes of the outside world. We all want China to move in the direction of political pluralism. The question is, what is the best route, meaning one that the Chinese Communist Party finds both acceptable (i.e., regime-enhancing) and necessary (i.e., regime-protecting)? Lead with political autonomy for Tibet or Xinjiang's Uighers and Beijing will throw up as many walls as necessary to protect itself from outside pressure, thus curtailing its integration into the global economy. Lead with environmental issues that speak to China's continued political stability *and* growing competitiveness in the global economy, and we'll plant the seeds for political liberty not only for such minorities but for the Chinese people as a whole. Fast enough for

Tibet's supporters in the West? Probably not. But our grand strategy cannot be simply a summation of the desires of our domestic pressure groups, as Henry Kissinger has frequently lamented.

Already, we can see a serious "green awakening" throughout much of China, from the grassroots NGOs right up to the seniormost leadership. This awakening will only push Beijing harder in its quest to cannibalize its high-polluting state-run sector in the direction of its far less corrupt and less polluting private sector, meaning it will incentivize China to speed up its transformation from a centrally planned economy to a market-based one more in the mold of the United States. Again, for those strategists intent on finding a path for increased conflict between the United States and China over resources, the future is not bright. As a recent World Bank study pointed out, the fastest-growing cities in China are those that feature the best climate for foreign investment, the lowest pollution, the lowest quotient of state-run enterprises, and the least amount of corruption. China is progressively remaking itself in much the same manner as America did during its own Progressive Era, turning Mao's revolutionary war strategy on its head: The "golden cities" are expanding and thus attracting the rural poor in an unprecedented internal migration.

None of these arguments are designed to make light of the incredible challenges humanity faces in the decades ahead. Instead, my goal here was simply to suggest how we might collectively untie some of the Gordian knots often cited by the doom-and-gloom crowd. The fact that the American System–cum–globalization is only beginning to tackle the challenge of continued economic growth in a resource-constrained environment—meaning we're now asking the bulk of humanity to grow in a far more intensive manner than we Westerners did in the past—doesn't mean we've crossed the Rubicon into some premillennialist nightmare of never-ending global crisis. A good example? When the first oil shocks struck in the 1970s, the world responded by depressing and holding steady its total oil use for roughly a decade: In 1979 the world used approximately 65 million barrels of oil a day, and that amount was not surpassed until 1989. Meanwhile, the global economy grew dramatically across the decade—the beginning of the "long boom" that continued until 2008. Think we can't wring out more efficiencies today, given all the computing power we've amassed in the past three decades? Or all the advances in material sciences and nanotechnology and biotech? Experts will tell you that more than two-thirds of all energy used in the world today is wasted, meaning lost when fuels are burned and heat escapes or when electricity is transmitted along wires. Lovins himself likes to point out that less than one percent of the fuel energy consumed in today's automobiles actually ends up moving the car's occupants forward. None of these inefficiencies require "god machines" for their reduction, just the same sort of innovation that got humanity to this point in the first place.

And the best news is, now we've got 3 billion new brains all working the same puzzles.

THE GLOBAL ACCELERANT:
THE GREATEST AWAKENING

While America's recent premillennialist bent has unfortunately mirror-imaged that of our radical Islamic enemies, the rest of the planet—outside of Europe—has hit a spiritual inflection point of a different sort, one that should seem distantly familiar to us. Per our postmillennialist expectations ("We won the Cold War, didn't we?"), this global religious awakening can seem quite intimidating ("Doesn't the 'end of history' now put us all past this irrational stuff?"), as if Sisyphus needs to start pushing that boulder up the hill again. But in reality, it's time to start chasing that rock as it rolls down the far side. This sort of religious awakening does not represent sheer resistance, or friction in response to globalization's rapid advance. Rather, it reflects a blossoming coping mechanism: people reaching for spiritual handholds amid all this tremendous social and economic change.

What it portends is this: People want an independent code of behavior to help them navigate all this new connectivity and the individual opportunities it affords. As they scale up from mere sustenance to serious consumption, they're looking for guidelines for a life well led. Religion is the natural supplier here, but if left to its own devices, especially under conditions of political authoritarianism, it can just as easily justify alternative forms of dictatorship—for example, theocracy (religious law substituted for civil code). As soon as people glom onto religion as an all-purpose guide to the good life, it gets really hard to recognize alternative paths to happiness, thus short-circuiting the possibility of political pluralism. Accepting alternative political viewpoints is easy in a society where God's law is separated from man's law, but where God's law is held supreme, extending reciprocity ("Your view should be considered equally to my own") gets stunningly hard, because applying the Golden Rule within a religion is far easier than applying it *among* religions. In the latter case, asking those from another faith to respect your right to worship God as you see fit because you're willing to offer the same to them can *still* be interpreted as an abject rejection of their faith. Worse, they may not be able to distinguish between their spiritual logic of "one path to happiness" and the desirability of many paths in the political realm. For some people, heaven *can't* wait, as there's simply no spiritual corollary to economic credit. It's cash-and-carry all the time.

All of the world's major religions were formed during the Malthusian era of human economics, or basically before the Industrial Revolutions of the nineteenth century permeated societies, freeing people from a just-getting-by paradigm to the question "How do I deal with abundance?" When it's all about survival, the code tends to be very strict, but when the possibility of abundance rears its attractive head, then people are given a choice: "Do I adapt the ancient code to this economic trajectory or do I reject its premise as evil—a force of improper liberation?" In general, the rising wealth is easy enough to justify in spiritual terms: "God wants me to live long and prosper." It's just that once the demographic logic is disrupted ("Go forth and multiply"), then long-held strictures regarding marriage, family, sex, homosexuality, and so on are suddenly put in jeopardy. Almost like the foreign aid or oil curse, the abundance curse provides individuals with their own source of funding, independent from the collective: "I simply don't need the family to build and retain wealth, so such bonds matter to me less." Worse, abundance allows for "chosen families," replacing the previous iron logic of "given families." Unhappy with your family circumstances? Then upgrade just the way you switch jobs.

This is where globalization's economic connectivity becomes immediately revolutionary in the social realm, unleashing a sense of personal freedom that is stunning—even perverse by historical standards. The upside, of course, is the commensurate unleashing of personal creativity. Genius isn't made, it's *allowed*. Progress thrives off such genius, thus creating the virtuous cycle by which more freedom is granted and made reciprocal throughout society (the Golden Rule) because the collective sees the utility: a rising standard of living. Once society enters this realm, the logic of unfolding political pluralism is easily obtained: "We need to lock in these personal freedoms and continuously upgrade them to maximize the resulting economic progress"—a logic arguably first cracked by the Dutch in the early 1600s. At that point, God's law has nearly lost all control of the situation. It is clearly outperformed by man's law, so the only choice left is postmillennialism—as in, "We must continue perfecting this progress to the point of achieving heaven here on earth." At that point, the technocrats take over and science declares God dead (see the Netherlands today, where churches are abandoned by the hundreds).

Of course, as society divides between economic winners and losers, the temptation for the latter is the exact opposite: premillennialism that rationalizes their subpar performance and promises their deliverance from these unacceptable circumstances. Pursued in a peaceful, fundamentalist manner, this presents no problem: For example, the Amish carve out separate lives and their collective desire is accommodated within conditions of political pluralism. But on a global scale, such as that presented by globalization's rapid advance, the fundamentalist impulse is often conflated with the logic of political liberation: "I seek such protection at the level of a state." And if the state standing in the way of this desire can be accused of spiritual infidelity, either because it encourages decadence through modernizing economic connectivity (either widely or just among the hypocritical elite) or suppresses the same while simultaneously repressing God's law (i.e., the secular autocrat), then it is logically tarred as the "local devil" backed up by the "distant devil" of modernizing globalization. That globalization flows naturally from the American System model, and is frequently defended by that nation's military force. By this logic, the ultimate root of all evil/destabilizing liberation is the United States itself, whose orgy of individualism stands as a frightening harbinger of mongrelized evolution to come unless righteous resistance is mounted.

Under conditions of great disconnectedness (my definition of the

Gap), economic losers do tend to outnumber greatly the economic winners, so the choices faced by people seeking out a firm rule set for such a
not-so-good life are these: (1) live with the status quo of relative deprivation (hard in a world of connecting mass media, because you can see how
the other half lives) that often features either uncaring autocrats or failed
governments; (2) seek connectivity and try to catch up (i.e., deal with the
"devil," since alternative routes have all been discredited), accepting that,
on an individual basis, this may require temporary or complete emigra-
tion from the homeland; or (3) seek firm disconnectedness in order to
achieve the spiritual ideal, which requires clear rejection of this evil connectivity and its barren promises. Once the last route is chosen, it's typically "in for a penny, in for a pound," because the only way to ensure the
proper and lasting level of insulation from a decadent outside world is to
enforce it throughout the country in question, or, in the case of the radical
Salafis, throughout the entirety of the Islamic world.

So this is why we live in such revolutionary times, even though, in an
economic sense, history really has "ended." It is precisely because there's
little debate over the utility of connecting to the global economy that so
much social tumult is being created right now. That tumult, whether positive (i.e., increasing abundance) or negative (those left behind), fuels the
instinctive reach for more spirituality. Abundance can trigger either accepting evangelical responses ("I've found God, and you must too!") or
rejectionist/rationalizing fundamentalism ("This is evil and we must distance ourselves from it!"), whereas deprivation tends to promote fundamentalism in general, because a stricter moral code is required for survival
in hard times and its separatist message dovetails nicely with the already
poor or narrow connectivity with the outside world. Both types of responses are easily located in all major religions, so any one religion per se
(e.g., Islam) is hardly the problem. Rather, it's either the lack of abundance-
providing connectivity or the inability of that society, when experiencing
new abundance through rising connectivity, to sequence itself from its
Malthusian mindset ("This is how we survive") to what comes next ("How
do we handle prosperity?").

What I'm trying to get across here is that religion will always be the
most important bridge in this transition, either sabotaging it completely
or facilitating it and thus suffering separation from society's public sphere,

which becomes increasingly filled with economic relationships that, over time, generate a superstructure of political institutions designed to protect and further nurture that economic activity. Religion, then, retreats into the private sphere. In certain societies, like Europe, this retreat signals the pervasive secularization of the public sphere. But in highly entrepreneurial societies, like our own, it's possible and even highly desirable to see strong competition develop in that private sphere among a multiplicity of religious faiths. Religion, at its core, has always been a demand function, meaning it has been adapted to the needs of the people *in their time.* In the precapitalist Malthusian era of survivalist economics, such adaptation was glacial because the conditions—and thus the needs of the people—were largely unchanging (i.e., the same religious rule set worked for centuries on end). But once the Industrial Revolution ushered in the age of abundance, people's conditions and thus spiritual needs changed with stunning speed. The bourgeoisie needed a bourgeois God.

Again, these United States provide the historical example for what must come next, or—indeed—what is already unfolding: What we perceive to be a clash of civilizations today is merely the recognition among religions of the new competitive spiritual landscape afforded by globalization (to succeed as a religion today, you must globalize your faith, thus purging its local cultural content), as well as continuing violent competition within and among major religions inside the Gap (a blast from the Core's all-too-bloody past). None of this should come as a surprise to us, especially the reality that the most violently competitive wings within Islam represent its most rejectionist strains. After all, our continent was initially settled by such rejectionist-minded Puritans, or those seeking a "purer" expression of faith, and it was their religious awakening, the first such "great awakening" in our history in the mid–eighteenth century, that animated our revolutionary push for independence from our more corrupt European brethren. That such thinking constituted a very thin veneer covering issues of economic freedom is equally unsurprising, because remember the argument here: Religion is a coping mechanism whose importance rises during periods of economic change (upward or down) because it justifies the new rule sets required for success or survival.

America's Second Great Awakening at the beginning of the nineteenth century provides further clues to religion's utility in frontier integration, because it "burned hottest on the southern and western frontiers,"
according to religious historian Stephen Prothero. As a result, he notes,
"by the end of the 1830s America's religious landscape had assumed its
current shape. The population had been rapidly Christianized, but Christianity itself had become extraordinarily diverse. Evangelicalism had sup-
planted Puritanism as the dominant religious impulse, thanks in no small
measure to the willingness of evangelicals to mix the ways and means of
revivalism with those of republicanism."

By that, Prothero means that evangelical brands of Christianity (e.g.,
Methodists, Baptists) exploited the era's trend toward disestablishing
state religions (prominent in New England) and the rise of public, or
"common," schooling (a fear-threat reaction to the rising influx of the Roman Catholic Irish). As such, nondenominational Protestantism became
the reigning religious impulse, an expansive trend that, over time, has left
Americans both highly religious and religiously illiterate, meaning we
have a lot of faith but we're increasingly fuzzy on the details (both historical and in terms of rules). This is the essential compromise religion makes
in the post-Malthusian era of economic abundance: more adherence to
less specificity, or a rationalizing function that allows us to navigate an increasingly complex world while retaining a spiritual bond with a God
that is, itself, subject to a division of labor—namely, the triune deity that
is simultaneously immanent, distant, and transcendent (or, in my Catholic
faith: the Holy Spirit, God the Father, and Jesus the Messiah, respectively). In this quintessential American adaptation, Christianity was made
a full-service faith for a diverse society undergoing rapid economic development. No matter what brand you required, the suddenly competitive
marketplace of religion could meet your needs—witness the megachurch
phenomenon headlined by spiritual superstars Rick Warren and Joel
Osteen. In this sense, Prothero argues, a nation of immigrants logically
begets a "nation of religions," with our First Amendment forcing such
competition by denying any faith supremacy and granting all freedom of
operation.

Religions in America compete not only with one another but with the state and the private sector, providing a profound continuing impulse for a progressive agenda of change. This dynamic was clearly seen throughout the nineteenth century, beginning with the abolition movement, the suffragist movement, the entirety of the Progressive Era's agenda for positive social change (e.g., labor conditions, government corruption, social welfare of impoverished women and children, medical care and sanitation, universal education, care of the environment), and the temperance movement. It should come as no surprise to us that highly evangelical forms of Islam excel best in similar socioeconomic conditions across the Gap today by providing many of these same social services, or that they're perceived by secular autocrats as constituting a political threat by pointing out the inadequacy of existing government services. Nor should we be surprised to see evangelical forms of all faiths succeed in spreading their gospel throughout rising New Core economies such as Brazil or China. By definition, such emerging markets logically supply the world's most zealous missionaries (the frontier, as always, provides the best Bible-thumpers), not only to developing economies but to developed ones as well. A good New Core country to track in this regard is South Korea, arguably the most dynamic force—on a per capita basis—in international missionary work. In today's world, the flow of missionaries reverses that of the colonialist age: now moving from East to West and increasingly from the Gap to the Core.

As our era features globalization's rapid and unprecedented advance, it will logically also feature the greatest single religious awakening the world has ever seen. Religion will become eminently more important because economic conditions will change more dramatically in coming years and decades than at any other time in human history. Hardly the clash of civilizations, this upsurge will reflect the efforts of societies to adapt themselves to an era of widespread abundance. Many regimes undergoing rapid growth trajectories will seek to wrap themselves in the mantle of nationalism, which provides some coherence with regard to the outside world but unfortunately does little to temper rising internal demand for progressive social and political change. Indeed, nationalism tends to increase such demand by encouraging the public to—in effect—call the government's bluff by saying, "If our country is as powerful internationally as you claim, then we deserve better service at home!" Already we see this social impulse growing dramatically in China, as the Communist Party's proud promotion of the nation's impending superpower status is generating more calls for responsive government (especially on the environment), not to mention more religious freedom and regional autonomy. Beijing's 2008 Summer Olympic games were a textbook example in this regard, as was the preceding Sichuan earthquake. You may spot only the government's response (repression) and decry it, but I note its rising requirements and welcome the struggle.

But again, this is why I don't advocate an aggressive targeting by the West of such emerging powers regarding their political evolution. I say, let their own ambitions, along with their rising spiritualism, drive this process. By trying to substitute what should be an internal, demand-pull function ("We want more rights!") with an external, supply-push function ("We demand you give your people more rights!"), we're triggering a fear-threat reaction at a time of rising nationalism—a counterproductive approach that promotes downstream military confrontation and/or rivalry. As always, American grand strategy should exploit globalization's momentum in any country and not seek to stem its powerful tides. Rather than quell the natural rise in nationalism, America should meet popular demands by shaping international opportunities for such emerging powers to succeed in positive (meaning, connecting) international interventions—both military and financial. While I'm not interested in encouraging any emerging powers to move in the direction of a Leviathan-like capacity, our "give" in this instance is to promote China's many successes in the SysAdmin function, accepting the notion that our successful grand strategy in this era requires not only a division of labor but a division of credit. My definition of success in next-generation warfare is to make our allies desire our collective victory more than we do; thus they must receive more immediate benefit than we do.

To this end, America should push China to model its state-building inside the Gap on its own current development trajectory at home: increasing privatization, decreasing the reach of state power, and an increase in transnational connections, including nongovernmental organizations. Because of China's fixation on achieving secure access to raw materials and energy, it prefers to deal with, and support, authoritarian regimes that possess firm control over their natural resources. The irony here is rich: What China actually pursues at home is the state-building model in favor right now, or one that favors the spread of globalization and—commensurately—religious awakening/radicalism. While America favors the spread of globalization, it tries, with great futility, to stop the accompanying spread of religious radicalism. On that score, China and the United States are one in their penchant for relying on secular autocrats, even though such leaders typically increase their populations' demand for religious/political radicalism, which, over time, often gets exported in the Core's direction.

Now we begin to see the outlines of our sequencing challenge: Economic connectivity, done well, triggers movement toward abundance; that secularizing dynamic naturally triggers religious awakening and even radicalism, as well as rising nationalism; to exploit the progressive political impulses of that awakening, a religious marketplace must be encouraged but not demanded, because asking for tolerance of other faiths amid all this change is a risky business, but until it's achieved, all progress toward democracy is more likely to result in illiberal outcomes rather than true political pluralism. So if economic globalization drives the onset of this sequence (arguably too fast for comfort), and political pluralism is the desired long-term outcome, then the question becomes, How to navigate the highly charged middle sequence?

Based on the American experience, there seem to be two answers: (1) encourage nondenominationalism among the major sects of a country's dominant religion or among the competing religions; or (2) allow the religion in question to maintain its social model of separatism while subjugating itself to the secular state. The first example pertains to the evolution of Protestantism in America, while the latter speaks more to the effective nonevolution of Catholicism in America and the relatively recent emergence of socially conservative evangelical Protestantism. In both cases, believers accept the "two kingdoms" thesis, meaning both heaven and hell can wait on life here on Earth. In the latter situations, believers likewise accept the fact that there is a significant chasm between God's law, which governs their personal behavior, and man's law, which allows society more latitude in behavior. The continuing controversy over abortion is a good example. In this hybrid, a certain fundamentalism is internalized, allowing the believer to pursue life on his or her own terms within a wider, more secular world.

As French Islamic expert Olivier Roy argues, Islam faces very similar challenges, both in the West and within globalization as a whole. A Muslim female, for example, who lives in the West may well feel the need to signal her spiritual distance by wearing a burkha or merely a veil, not unlike a Christian wearing a cross. In a strictly secular society, such religious displays in the public sphere can be interpreted as a challenge to social cohesion and national identity (in "competitive" America, it can be more easily dismissed as religious pride or even spiritual advertising). For the firmly secular society, the question then becomes, Is it better to pursue multiculturalism and risk separatism or is it necessary to pursue assimilation, accepting the friction that may ensue? In a traditional country, or one whose identity is coincident with nationality (e.g., a Germany based on Germans, a France based on the French), there's no easy answer to that one, because multiculturalism equates to postculturalism. So when it gets hard to be a Frenchman in France, what exactly has France become? Plus, the more multicultural your society becomes, the more religious it's likely to become, because in the absence of shared cultural identity, people will cling more closely to religious identity. Elevate this dynamic up to the level of nation-states operating within globalization and the same logic holds.

In many ways, multiculturalism is simply globalization inverted (or with "training wheels," I'm tempted to add), meaning imported *inside* a country. That's why immigrant-based countries like the United States, Canada, Australia, and New Zealand feature more abstract definitions of national character—less *who you are* than *how you act*. Religious identity flourishes in such environments because it speaks to the *how you act* paradigm ("I am a Catholic because I act this way. My ethnic background is irrelevant"). Again, America represents the leading edge of the globalization experience in this regard, because of its highly competitive marketplace for religion, marked by the fact that many Americans switch religions with ease across their lifetimes (confession: I have twice, my wife has three times, and only one of our kids has kept the same faith his entire life—to date). The kind of religiosity prevalent in America today speaks to this "greatest awakening" that the planet as a whole now experiences with globalization's advance. According to Roy, it is (1) highly individual-istic, featuring a very direct connection to God; (2) highly mobile, mean-ing conversions are common; (3) weakly institutional, so low trust in churches per se; (4) anti-intellectual, so theologians are typically ignored; and (5) highly communitarian by choice instead of heritage. In short, it is a connecting mechanism by which individuals, challenged by complexity, seek out those of their own kind, meaning people who want to live by the same rule sets or code—the walled garden as refuge.

So again we see that globalization is defined fundamentally by the spread of rules—across networks, throughout markets, and even spiritu-ally among individuals. National governments remain the main purveyors and codifiers of these rules, but they face many competitors, thanks to globalization—religions chief among them. The competition we see emerging among world religions does not constitute a clash of civiliza-tions, because religions, including Islam, by globalizing themselves, de-tached from cultural moorings a long time ago. Much like major urban areas have long played the role of laboratories on global warming, so too did America—as globalization's original superstate start-up—on the sub-ject of religious competition. I'm not saying that America was the first great battlefield of competing religions. That sort of conflict had existed for many centuries before we showed up. I'm saying that America has forged a unique success story in fostering religious competition within a multinational union structure—in effect, previewing all the dynamics we witness today in globalization. As always, it's not the individual rules that make America unique, but the combination of rules and our capacity over time to popularize them globally.

This is why Americans should not fear this global era of rising religios-ity; we should neither regret our unprecedented success in extending our American System–cum–globalization around the planet nor recoil from our innate sense of continuing responsibility for this, our ideological prog-eny. We have not opened Pandora's Box here. In our typically revolution-ary manner, we've enabled the rest of humanity to subjugate religion to its own purposes. No longer merely a refuge from deprivation and suffer-ing, thanks to globalization, religion now serves primarily as an escape from too much freedom. A central tenet of American grand strategy *must* involve our owning up to this unique political heritage and understanding its importance for the world today. If we cannot explain this concept of religious freedom to the world, then we do not know *who we are*. Worse, we will not be able to forge the essential compromises that must come next.

THE INESCAPABLE REALIGNMENT: RESURRECTING THE PROGRESSIVE AGENDA

Despite Americans' current angst about globalization and the challenges it presents, what we face over the next couple of generations are problems of more success—not failure. By introducing, codifying, and protecting our international liberal trade order across the decades of the Cold War, America not only set in motion Europe's recovery from its disastrous great-power wars (WWI, WWII), but also expanded the global economy to encompass effectively more than four-fifths of the world's population. By doing so, America has made possible the global correction of the so-called Great Divergence that began in 1800, an unprecedented historical period in which the West's income grew twelvefold over two centuries while the rest of the planet's income dropped by half. The Great Convergence of income and consumption that this century will witness will change everything in global affairs yet again. The projected twelve-fold increase in income for the New Core and Gap will effectively eclipse the have/have-not divide by generating globalization's first truly dominant middle class—for the first time in human history.

This is America's gift to the world: the chance for a global middle class to finally escape the sort of Malthusian growth limits that the advanced West left behind in the nineteenth century. Our success in spreading our international liberal trade order is without parallel in human history. At its height, the European colonial world order encompassed a mere third of the earth's surface; our globalization model encompasses virtually all of it. What that means is this: Long before the end of this century we will see the bulk of the planet move into the same sort of middle-class lifestyle (not to be automatically confused with consumption) that America has known over the past half-century-plus. The Euro-

pean colonial-era globalization simply does not compare with what
America has achieved in the past several decades. The European colonial
order created no widespread wealth and no global middle class, and came
nowhere near encompassing the bulk of the planet's geography or population. If globalization signifies America's "empire," then it's the first empire
in history ever to enrich those integrated.

But here's the trick: As long as man stayed Malthusian in his economic orientation, meaning population growth worked against income
growth in a zero-sum struggle, anything that decreased population was a
"virtue," as economist Gregory Clark argues in his 2007 book *A Farewell
to Alms.* So for the world in general prior to 1800, war was good, violence
was good, and so were bad sanitation, infanticide, income inequality, epidemics, and harvest failures. All these "virtues" made the surviving population richer. That all changed with the Industrial Revolution, whereupon
man's wealth and income growth were no longer tethered to the organic
world but instead were vastly expanded by his growing mastery over the
inorganic world. At that point, for the advancing West at least, past "virtues" were slowly but surely turned into vices. With abundance came the
extension of life and the ability for wealthier people to have more children and leave them with more resources upon death, extending their
demographic dominance further. That meant *some* (i.e., the West) got to
"go forth and prosper" and *still* enjoy the added benefits of raised income.
Over time, the ancient impulse to propagate dissipated in the ever
wealthier West, so fewer people got to enjoy more wealth while the rest
of the planet stayed largely stuck in the planet's Malthusian past.

Here is where America's still revolutionary impact upon the world is
clearly seen: By expanding the liberal international trade order of our
American System–cum–globalization, we now elevate—over the next
several decades—the vast bulk of the rest of the world's population out of
the Malthusian resource equation and into a planetary age of abundance.
By 2020, the global middle class should expand from just under one-third
of the world's population to just over half, with much of that increase
found in China (the world's biggest middle class by 2025) and India (a
tenfold increase in a generation's time). The problem is that, culturally
speaking, much of this newly and soon-to-be-elevated chunk of world

population remains wedded to the "virtues" of their not-so-distant Malthusian past. A good example? The West's world of security now tries to incorporate New Core powers (e.g., Russia, India, China) with decidedly nineteenth-century views of great-power politics, along with a Gap whose style of mass violence remains as primordial as ever—with great local pride in the obvious (to them at least) "virtue." Thus, numerous profound social shifts will occur as we successfully extend globalization around the planet, consolidating vast levels of new connectivity and suddenly elevating entire societies from sustenance to abundance, often turning their definitions of vice and virtue on their heads.

It's therefore important for us to recognize this long list of historical "inversions," where something long held to be "white" is, in the course of integration with the global economy, now held to be "black" ("Hey, buddy! I'm just growing poppies here like we always have. What you do with it is your *business!*"). It's important because it helps us understand our continuing revolutionary impact on global society while tempering our demand—on top of all this tumultuous change—for near-instant political adjustment toward a form of democracy we recognize as familiar. This great consolidation of globalization in coming decades will yield a global society likely to resemble America's own at the end of the nineteenth century, featuring a dominant middle-class ideology that regards the "hardworking" folk that make this planet work as virtuous, and regards the "special interests," both rich and poor, that exist on the margins as full of vice to be corrected. It will also yield the equivalent of a global progressive era (meaning new rules galore) that will necessarily outpace the version the West experienced, with serious leapfrogging not merely in technology choices but likewise in social norms (which will struggle to keep pace with all the technological advances—especially in biology).

As such, the next forty years are likely to be among the most tumultuous the world has ever seen, even as they will undoubtedly be among the most peaceful. Many experts naturally reach for late-nineteenth-century imperial histories to imagine what lies ahead (e.g., empires and colonial wars), but I think more value is found in examining late-nineteenth-century American domestic history, in which a vast collection of regional economies was rapidly and radically stitched together into a far more unified, integrated, efficient whole. In that process of network and production integration, which by no means was approximated in Europe's relatively crude colonial global economic order, huge inefficiencies were wrung out of the system. Likewise, all that networking exposed the population as a whole to new levels of communicable danger: disease, poor sanitation, bad food handling, environmental damage, and criminality of all sorts. As a result, vast domains of economic, social, and political life needed to be cleaned up, or essentially elevated to new minimum standards so as to avoid the transmission of destabilizing elements (e.g., epidemics, labor unrest, environmental catastrophes, radical ideologies). So rather than look for who's playing the Kaiser's Germany this time versus Victorian-era Britain, we instead need to be looking out for rising non-state actors, including leaders of state, who will aspire to the same roles once played within the American System by Booker T. Washington, Upton Sinclair, Theodore Roosevelt, and others. Indeed, the past decade's list of Nobel Peace Prize winners suggests we're just hitting our stride in this regard: cleaning up land mines (1997), medical work in remote areas (1999), the rights of women and children (2003), environmentalism in Africa (2004), nuclear energy (2005), micro-lending (2006), and global climate change (2007). In short, we're heading into an era of great individual leaders, great organizations, and great change—but not great-power war.

The following is my best list of the many shifts I see the world enduring over the next couple of decades, all of which will figure as global tipping points in shaping an international progressive agenda focused on cleaning up globalization's many dark corners.

The Consumption Shift

Right now the advanced Old Core West consumes resources and produces waste at a level approximately 32 times higher than the rest of the world. As that rest of the world catches up dramatically on income over this century, there's simply no way our consumption pattern can be emulated. Indeed, the only way that rising middle-class demand can be accommodated is for the West to reduce its resource footprint, which many Americans might assume requires we live according to a lower standard of living, when—in truth—it does not. As Jared Diamond points out, "living standards are not tightly coupled to consumption rates." Mobility is a good example: The global middle class will want increased mobility over time, but that doesn't mean we need to extend America's current rather wasteful gas-combustion vehicle pattern to the rest of the planet, nor that shifting off that model in America will make us any less mobile. But here's where the consumption shift is twofold: Not only do the New Core and the Gap need to rapidly abandon the Malthusian "virtues" of their near-past, the Old Core has to abandon its Industrial Era disregard for organic limits to growth as well. Both shifts require a lot of political will, which simply hasn't kept pace, on a global basis, with globalization's rapid expansion. So, as Jeffrey Sachs argues, "the paradox of a unified global economy and divided global political society poses the single greatest threat to the planet because it makes impossible the cooperation needed to address the remaining challenges," a condition he dubs "globalization without trust." Thus the first item we can add to our progressive agenda is to clean up the impression that sustainable development is just a concept for the New Core and the Gap, when it will apply in equal measure to the Old Core West in coming years.

The Food and Water Shift

In the global oil industry, there is Saudi Arabia and everybody else. But when it comes to agriculture, it turns out that North America is the OPEC of global grain. So if the world's got us over a barrel on energy, then we've got the world over a breadbasket. Moreover, while global climate change will progressively diminish OPEC's importance as we're forced to improve transportation technologies, it will only strengthen NAFTA's role as the world's preeminent food exporter.

Here's the lay of the land when it comes to the global grain trade. There are four net exporting regions: North America exports 105 million metric tons, followed by the former Soviet Union at 21, South America at 18, and Australia/New Zealand at 9. So when it comes to spare capacity, North America accounts for a whopping 68 percent of the world's movable feast, dominating global grain markets as we once dominated the cotton trade. The net importing regions are as follows: North Africa and the Middle East import 58 million metric tons, followed by Asia at 47 million tons, sub-Saharan Africa at 17, and Europe at 12. You want to talk "addicted" to foreign food? The Middle East imports just over three-quarters of its total food supply! Compare this with a North America that imports half that percentage.

Now add in the impact of global climate change and what do we foresee? Basically, the tech-rich regions that are net food exporters today will do as well as they do now or better, while the regions that are currently forced into importing will do decidedly worse—save Europe. On average, the farther you are from the equator, the less negative—and potentially more positive—will be the agricultural impact of global warming. This is why farmers in the Dakotas are presently tilling fields that have lain fallow for decades. It's also why land speculators are having a field day in Russia, Ukraine, and Kazakhstan, where roughly an entire Idaho-sized chunk of arable land awaits exploitation, and where current yields are less than half of America's far more advanced agricultural system. It is also why the Chinese government (with Saudi Arabia right on its heels) has launched a not-very-secret plan to buy up arable land around the world, believing—rather naïvely—that in some future global food crunch, it will somehow siphon off precious grains from foreign lands with nobody noticing. Good luck with that transparent strategy, because during the 2008 price shock, many of the world's major producing nations suddenly slapped restrictions on crop exports—including China! Why such extreme measures? In industrialized nations, food eats up only about one-tenth to one-fifth of a household's spending, but in developing countries, that share can rise to as high as four-fifths. So if you think it's tough to be poor in fragile states today, global warming and continued population growth will make it a lot harder—absent globalization's successful expansion into these poorly developed and weakly connected markets.

A lot of things account for recently skyrocketing food prices: bad harvests, immoral Western trade barriers, the rising price of energy, the diversion of croplands to biofuel production, and increasing demand from rising economic pillars like India and China. None of these factors can be easily curtailed. Indeed, several of them increasingly feed on one another.

But here's where it gets interesting for global food networks: Today, only a small fraction of worldwide grain production is traded globally— for example, only 7 percent of rice and 12 percent of corn. Looking ahead a couple of decades, we're likely to see those percentages rise dramatically, making the global food trade network as important as—arguably far more important than—today's global energy trade network, which it will come to resemble in that much of its major supply sources will be located distant from its rising sources of demand.

The Transportation Shift

As Iain Carson and Vijay Vaitheeswaran argue in *Zoom: The Global Race to Fuel the Car of the Future*, "Oil is the problem; cars are the solution." Neither Big Auto nor Big Oil has been interested in seeing America pay an honest price for gasoline these past few decades, so our sense of entitlement has ballooned while our apparent—but not real—threshold of economic pain has lowered. The result? We're suffused right now with all sorts of "Calgon, take me away!" proposals to leapfrog the U.S. car fleet into a post-oil future. The problem is, even with our rising fears about global warming and an unstable Middle East, our vehicle-heavy lifestyle makes it hard for us to muster the political will necessary to force a rapid shift. So where will this shift come first? Asia, partly from its desire to dominate global manufacturing in this industry, but more so in response to its declining air quality as the region's vehicle fleet skyrockets. Because China will soon become both a global demand center and a global production center for cars and trucks, we're already seeing the world's major auto manufacturers scramble to make Asia their future global center of R&D. This might seem like a huge loss to American industry, but you have to remember that automobiles began in Old Core Europe in the nineteenth century, came of age in twentieth-century America, and so logically are transformed by twenty-first-century Asia's rise—an evolution mirroring globalization's expansion. In the end, the progressive agenda that drives the transformation of transportation in this century will center on cleaning up Asia's air quality.

The Energy Shift

Despite the current focus on global climate change and the push to reduce CO_2 emissions, in my mind the big "going-green" shift of the next couple of decades will be more about reducing energy costs than about pollution per se. Because of the overall rising global energy demand, we're unlikely to lower carbon emissions worldwide for quite some time. But because the Old Core West has already exported much of its dirtiest and most energy-intensive industries to the New Core East, the main route for lower energy usage in the West will be through cost-savings efforts designed to improve our economic competitiveness. In the East, fears of energy dependence and lost profit margins will do more to generate greater efficiencies than local pollution, although that will be a close race. In general, the two big shifts in energy will concern the movement to a far more distributed model of power generation, and the shift from coal and natural gas generation of electricity to nuclear generation. If there is a place for heightened East–West cooperation across the Core, this is it, because both of these shifts can easily be held up by fears of proliferating nuclear technologies. So one of the key items on a global progressive agenda must be a Core-wide rule set for creating and operating a closed nuclear fuel enrichment cycle that allows the rapid spread of nuclear power generation of electricity across the planet.

The Security Shift

With global logistical networks coming to define globalization's essential functioning more and more, our planet's definition of crisis will continue shifting from a past focus on kinetics leading to human deaths (classic violence and war) to a future focus on nonkinetics leading to business discontinuities, which is just a fancy way of saying, *Stuff isn't moving and so business can't be conducted*. Right now, we tend to view the movement of energy (i.e., oil) as the most important logistical network, but faster than you can anticipate, the movement of food and water will come to be seen as more strategic and therefore requiring more scrutiny (i.e., sensor-based transparency to ensure purity). So another item for our global progressive agenda would be to create a Food and Drug Administration for the planet as a whole (we currently have the UN's World Health Organization, but that is human-health-oriented versus product-safety-oriented), including a worldwide scanning capacity to ensure that unapproved biological materials are not transported. If the nineteenth century's Industrial Revolution brought us chemical weapons (WWI), and the twentieth century's focus on physics yielded nuclear weapons, then the twenty-first century is logically the age of biological weapons/

terrorism. So a focus on biological security dovetails nicely with the growing hyperdependence on food and water traffic that the planet will experience as a result of rising incomes and climate change, in addition to the rising climate volatility (i.e., higher frequency of natural disasters) caused by the latter.

The Communications Shift

One of the reasons I continue to eschew "strategic communications" as a weapon to win hearts and minds is that the concept is rooted in the broadcast era of communications, when the planet collectively stands on the verge of a huge expansion in peer-to-peer communications that's likely to radically alter the way we process information in general, communicate with one another, and conduct business and political dialogue— at least judging by my kids! The first billion users of Internet and wireless technologies were already plugged into the global economy as they adapted their lives to these innovations, so a lot of broadcast-era methodologies could simply be imported into these new realms, because the vast bulk of the users would accept their supply-push logic. But as the world elevates rapidly from that first billion to the second and third billions, we're talking about a vast new sea of players in globalization's previously underserved New Core and Gap markets. This large bottom of the pyramid is likely to rewrite the rules for business, social, and political (see Obama, Barack) uses of communications networks, shifting to a pronounced demand-pull function. Because the providers best able to meet those demands will probably be local players, the West should expect the East and South to force a lot of market change here, for example forcing us to make free things that we've always charged for or charging for things that we've always thought should be free. The key goal for America will be adaptability to the rising "nomadism" made possible by all this connectivity, because being connectable everywhere means a lot of people will be able to live and work anywhere. Americans tend to view the Web, for example, as something over which we retain ultimate control, when in coming years and decades, we're likely to be scrambling—as much as any other nation—to make sure our population is as plugged in as it needs to be. If there's one area where I see more government discretionary spending in coming years, it's in ensuring that Americans have the cheapest, fastest, and most reliable communications networks in the world. Referencing the security shift noted above, communications continuity is likely to become the primary definition of a "secure" America.

The Religious Shift

The rise in religiosity worldwide in conjunction with globalization's advance—and subsequent enablement of the economics of abundance—is going to trigger a global shift toward more social conservatism combined with more social activism. I see an immediate future where a lot of religious and secular transnational groups come together increasingly to "battle the evil of X." In that regard, the Bush administration's Office of Faith-Based and Community Initiatives within the White House should survive Bush's presidency, for it is a harbinger of things to come, meaning more explicit coordination between governments and religious charities. The spread of globalization turbocharges the more general long-term historical trend of risk-shifting from the collective to the individual, and so, just as religious groups were instrumental in rescuing and protecting the weak in the early days of the Industrial Revolution, they'll likewise be early and powerful entrants into this field on a global basis in coming years, in conjunction with their secular counterparts. In combination, these groups make for a formidable global missionary function. But again, that's no surprise for an age of rapid and extensive frontier integration.

The Urbanization Shift

The planet as a whole has just reached majority urban status, meaning most of the world's future social problems—and hence progressive agenda—will be more urban than rural in nature. This affords humanity a lot of opportunity, because if we can link up the world's major coastal cities in next-generation networks for communications, travel, logistics, sensing, and so on, then we've effectively captured roughly half of humanity and the vast majority of the world's network traffic. Moreover, major coastal cities can serve as laboratories for curing globalization's many ills, including rising sea levels, air pollution, traffic and people congestion, caring for the elderly, and ethnic tension. This is essentially the historic role New York City has played throughout American history, generating the "first" of too many urban innovations to recount. So a key progressive agenda item would seem to be encouraging growing cooperation and coordination among the world's biggest cities.

The Feminization Shift

The more globalization spreads industrialization (reducing the brute-strength advantage of men and the agricultural chores of women) and gender-neutral networks in general, the more women are empowered relative to men, meaning the twenty-first century is likely to witness a huge uptick in women's issues globally. This emerging market trend will dovetail nicely with the feminization of certain key professions, such as law and medicine, in advanced economies. Such trends are crucial and must be encouraged, because if globalization encourages a risk shift by gender, then it's clearly women who end up shouldering more risk over time (e.g., more divorces, more out-of-wedlock pregnancies, more every-bad-thing-you-can-name).

The Demographic Shift

Because globalization in general favors the aging of populations through industrialization and urbanization, the rising importance of elder issues will constitute *the* long-term trend for the twenty-first century—especially as life-lengthening biological advances kick in. On the other hand, the rapid expansion of the global economy has connected a lot of youth-dominated countries to those rapidly aging, postindustrial powers of the West, setting up the first half of the twenty-first century for a significant amount of age tension between an elder Core and a very young Gap. There is no Progressive Era corollary to this phenomenon. At best we can cite a certain similarity between the youth-connecting role played by rock 'n' roll during the Cold War and hip-hop in the current globalization era. As such, to the extent that Core governments seek to implement strategic communications in the direction of the Gap's restless youth, they would do well to partner themselves with the main private-sector purveyors of youth mass media content and the online communities where much of this social behavior is now conducted. Of course, the Middle East's current youth bulge cannot be socialized away as a source of instability, it can only be integrated as a new cheap pool of labor in the global economy. To the extent the governments of the Middle East are successful in migrating that youth bulge into gainful private-sector employment, their ability to communicate effectively with this newly empowered and relatively well-networked (compared with their parents) cohort will go a long way in deciding how stable the region is in coming decades. So while I might not advocate a direct U.S. government strategic communications program aimed at this population, I could certainly see the Core as a whole being highly interested in helping local governments get better in such communications on their own.

The Health Shift

As the Gap middle ages and the Core's elder population balloons, the world as a whole is set to see a huge explosion in medical burden costs. This could be a source of great political instability, as futurologist Robert J. Shapiro argues, when "people seek treatments that neither they nor their governments can afford." America has long suffered the dynamic by which more generous state health care and welfare programs draw in destitute populations from neighboring states. We are likely to see such "medical refugees" swell in numbers in coming years. Approached in a bottom-of-the-pyramid manner, such rising global demand can be effectively processed as a growing business opportunity, meaning, for example, that India doesn't just offer cheap medical alternatives to Westerners but begins to market such services "downward" to developing economies, as Brazil and India have already done in the manner of cheap generic drugs. In the same way that regional hospitals are developed in America to service populations that otherwise would be forced to travel long distances, the Core's future foreign aid efforts should focus on generating similar medical pillars in Gap regions. In general, then, the progressive agenda item here involves pushing reasonably priced capabilities down the economic pyramid in order to stem unsustainable people flows. As the current migration of American seniors into Central American countries demonstrates, people will move to access more affordable medical care environments. Another progressive agenda item would be to stem the "downshifting" of negative health behaviors from advanced economies to emerging and developing ones. A classic example here is smoking. I would expect to see worldwide health campaigns on the part of Old Core countries to reduce such emerging burdens in New Core and Gap nations.

The Market Shift

The essential economic shift of coming decades will be toward what Amory Lovins and his colleagues at the Rocky Mountain Institute have dubbed "natural capitalism." By this they mean industrial-era business models are simply updated to take into account the limits of inorganic and organic resources on the planet—in effect, finally pricing them correctly. They see four strategies as paramount: (1) a radical increase in the efficient use of natural resources; (2) biomimicry to reduce waste (basically copycatting nature's form of biodegradation); (3) shifting from a "goods and purchases" model of transactions to one that emphasizes "services and flows," meaning business seeks to create closed-loop cycles with nature that are sustainable instead of draining, so goods and purchases are more intimately linked by price to their natural resource-base components; and (4) the encouragement of private- and public-sector investment in natural resources ("natural capital"). In many ways, the progressive agenda here revolves around reducing the "industrial metabolism" of national economies and the global economy as a whole. Historically, once nations achieve a certain level of development, they begin to think along these preservation lines, the result being an effort to set aside natural resources for future generations while exporting the dirtiest and most resource-consuming industries to other markets. Lovins et al.'s argument is simply that the planet as a whole has reached a development tipping point where exporting such problems abroad is no longer a sustainable option.

The Governance Shift

The political scientist Francis Fukuyama divides governments along two axes: the scope of their power and the strength of their power. In this manner, we can describe the governance ideal as strong states with limited scope. While state-building in failed states is relatively straightforward, meaning you're trying to extend both scope and power, the real trick comes in maturing the political systems of emerging markets, where governments are often characterized by too much ambition on scope and not enough strength in their institutions—in other words, they try to do too much with too little. For most of the go-go nineties, when globalization was rapidly extending itself, the reformist notion held that the best way to fix such bad governments was by improving their policies (e.g., the Washington Consensus). The new emerging consensus focuses more on the strength of political institutions (rule of law) than on their particular policies, so more focus on good design than—at first—optimal functioning. As a concept, rule of law has long remained rather fuzzy, with some experts offering a "thin" definition of certain basic good laws (e.g., contracts, property rights) that must be put in place, and others offering a more "thick" definition of an overall culture of respect for legality. What's important about this growing academic debate is this: We're beginning to see the rise of a global dialogue on government best practices when it comes to income growth creation. Because the global economy has expanded to include such a wide variety of players now, we're starting to enjoy the ability to compare and contrast government policies in the same way that businesses have long done with one another in any sector. The growing diversity of capitalism is becoming one of its global strengths, meaning there's a growing competition among governments. As such, one of the key components of a global progressive agenda should be further collective research and dialogue on exactly what constitutes good rule of law, a concept—unlike democracy—that enjoys widespread global endorsement because of its focus on efficiency.

One crucial caveat here: America's ability to influence this global debate is slowly diminishing. First, there's the sheer competition from the EU's courts as they confront the complex issues of integration and harmonization of the legal systems of member states. As these courts grow in their constitutional sophistication, their rulings represent an alternative to American courts. Second, U.S. courts have suffered a serious loss of international credibility owing to America's overly aggressive prosecution of our "global war on terror," especially in the realm of human rights, leading to, for example, European court decisions' being increasingly cited by Canadian and Australian courts in preference to our own. Third, the increasingly conservative nature of the U.S. Supreme Court results in its growing unwillingness to consider the rulings of foreign judicial systems, reflecting a dangerously isolating hubris. These are, in aggregate, highly disturbing trends that portend a serious decline in America's ability to export legal rule sets—a power we have enjoyed for decades. America's global leadership in the legal realm, especially in the matter of good governance, will be especially important as the world heads into an inevitable period of heightened regulation—reversing a three-decade trend of Western-led global deregulation—as globalization matures in the years ahead. This loss of influence is made all the worse by America's ongoing financial crisis, which calls into serious question our long commitment to, and preaching of, limited government interference in economic affairs. In sum, just when the world is looking for innovative thinking on global risk management on the part of governments, our voice, and the great experience it represents in terms of our states-uniting and economies-integrating model, may be increasingly ignored.

The Class Shift

The fundamental political challenge we face today is that the biggest economic change going on right now is the rise of a global middle class, and because much of that emerging middle class is found within the confines of this era's rising economic pillars, too many of America's politicians are framing this dynamic more in terms of a nation-state challenge ("How do we counteract China?" "How do we respond to authoritarian capitalism?") than in terms of a global economic opportunity ("How do we forge a global middle-class identity favorable to our grand strategy of extending our liberal international trade order?"). When the American System was its own model of globalization, the United States was blessed by the likes of Alexander Hamilton, Abraham Lincoln, and Theodore Roosevelt, three seminal leaders obsessed with shaping America so as to make it possible for the average man to succeed, their assumption being that good citizens start as economic stakeholders seriously interested in the country's continued success. The toughest questions we face now are: How do we get such leaders not just for America but for the global economy as a whole? Can they be one and the same, or has America grown too distant from its progeny, globalization, for our leaders to play that role anymore?

Obviously, I believe the United States *hasn't* grown so temporally or ideologically distant from its American System–cum–globalization to still display such farsighted global leadership, otherwise I wouldn't have written this book. Still, I will confess that I find the current uncertainty surrounding those questions to constitute the single biggest wild card I can come up with regarding future global scenarios. That's not to say that I can't imagine future "black swans" (read: Wall Street) that shift our perspectives suddenly and with great force, but rather that I remain confident that if such a grand strategic connection can be maintained between our citizens' definition of a "good" America and a "good" globalization, there's nothing out there that we can't handle with aplomb.

We're not staring at some American decline or "post-American" global future, but the universalization of a dream begun centuries ago when the first colonists reached these shores: the creation of a new model of living that would superempower all who partake of its challenges and responsibilities. Since that time we have gone forth and multiplied this model beyond all expectations: pacifying our hemisphere, then stopping Europe's ceaseless wars, and then quieting a turbulent Asia. Then, at the apogee of our model's success and attractiveness, we suffered a blow to our national psyche that we've spent seven long years trying to repair. We discovered that, just like every past era, this one brings enemies to our American System–cum–globalization's advance. In fear and anger, we alienated old friends and turned away potential new ones with our frantic behavior, damaging our status as a world leader to such an extent that we ourselves begin to doubt in our own capacity to fill such a role in coming years. Maybe, we wonder, globalization has grown beyond us and doesn't need us anymore. Maybe now's the time we should look out for #1 (or maybe #2 or #3?) and do whatever it takes to succeed on this hot, flat, and crowded (oh, my!) world.

Or maybe we just close this global deal over the next couple of decades.

THE BETTER NORMAL: THE GREAT COMPROMISE

I will keep this last section short and sweet, by "walking the dog" through the previous chapters.

Our economic compromise is as follows: We asked *you*, the New Core East and South, to join this international liberal trade order so long restricted to just the Old Core West. Having done so, overwhelmingly on our terms (even if you were too smart to buy our fast-forwarding argument known as the Washington Consensus), our *quid pro quo* seems obvious enough: We need to do whatever it takes to meet your demand for a middle-class lifestyle within this global economy. So no, we won't be cutting your legs out from under you on global warming, nor will we make unreasonable demands that you support us as much on the kinetics of this long war as you logically should on the follow-up state-building and market creation and infrastructure networking. As far as posses go, our rules will be *come as you are* and *come when you can*, because we're no longer under any illusions about which half is harder—the war or the postwar.

Our diplomatic compromise is a bit trickier: If you connect your population in a broadband fashion to the global economy and its many networks, we'll allow you to pursue control over content. If you can't handle the MTV right away, or the pornography, or the "challenging" depictions of personal liberty that Western societies routinely produce, we'll help you exercise some equivalent of "parental controls" over the flow. While we may find such censorship offensive from the standpoint of our mature democracies, we're not too ignorant of our own history to realize that we didn't reach this level of—if you'll pardon the term—sophistication overnight, so we certainly shouldn't expect you to accept such wide-open content as the initial requirement for aspiring to such global connectivity. We're confident, based on our experience, that you'll come to open up your controls over time, but we respect your need to go slow at first. While we believe that all people want the same basic things out of life, we recognize that life is a journey each of us—either individually or collectively—must take at a pace of our choosing. That's an essential freedom we recognize too. As long as you give your people the essential choice of stay-or-go on the basis of this new connectivity, how you regulate its flow internally should remain your political decision and yours alone.

On security, our offer is a simple one: In this increasingly connected world, dangers know no boundaries, so we're done with trying to firewall ourselves off from scary things and have come to understand that our homeland is only as secure as every other homeland to which it is connected. Along these lines, experience has taught us that certain minimal rule sets must be obeyed by any and all who interact with us economically and socially. If you accept this minimal rule set, then we'll promise to document all our kills in defense of these proposed global rules. If either the rules or our execution come under question, we'll listen to your complaints, realizing that our role as global Leviathan does not excuse us from responding to the demands of globalization's stakeholders, to include civilized compensation for all losses incurred. We don't pretend such efforts repay all sacrifices endured; we simply believe in demonstrating that all lives have value. In sum, we won't use force unless certain conditions are clearly met, and when we do, we'll offer complete transparency regarding its employment—as in, *every round fired.*

Moving on to globalization's vast array of networks: If you allow us to enter your networks, achieving the transparency we think is necessary to keep our people safe, we will grant you "fast-pass" access to our networks—without bias. If you can't afford such network connections, we will endeavor to provide them to you at the lowest possible cost you can bear. We recognize your fears of falling behind as globalization surges forward, and we want to make clear from the start that we want you to become as connected as you can currently manage.

Finally, on the most personal questions of identity: If you can find your way to allowing freedom of religion in your country, we will do our best to reciprocate regarding any demands you may have for cultural separatism. While we don't believe that such separatism is good or healthy, because it tends to prejudge the talents and ambitions of those we fear are trapped within its walls, we believe in voluntary associations—even those that *won't have us as members.* But we know this: Humanity's paths to happiness are as varied as the human condition. While some of us may applaud your achievement of a strict social rule set in this regard, none of us will countenance your unreasonable desire to impose those strict rules unwillingly on others. If you can accept that while your definition of God's law may be forever, humanity's need for rule of law is persistent, then we're willing to let you carve out an enclave within our global society.

America doesn't pretend to have all the answers regarding this historical integration process we now call globalization. We do, however, want you to recognize that we inhabit the longest-running experiment of states and nationalities and religions uniting in the common cause of individual freedom, collective security, and economic prosperity. We understand that our model does not constitute the universe of possibilities even as we seek to universalize those possibilities.

Coda

———◆◆◆———

THE FUTURE
PERFECT TENSE

The future does have a way of happening.

As much as man is inclined to believe that his end time is *the* end time, it is not. And it has been thus since the beginning of time. Further to that, our present would have been as implausible to our forebears as the events and innovations of the next decades would be to us today. But while the future is inexorable, many of the twenty-first century's most important outcomes will be determined largely by the choices we make over the next dozen years.

Despite today's boom market in dark futures, the realignments in America's grand strategy presented here *will* unfold—the unleashed needs of the many overwhelming the long-held prerogatives of the few. We have finally moved the world, in Woodrow Wilson's terms, to "our way of thinking" on the economics. Now comes the harder part, but also the best part: extending that understanding to its full political implications. Such perfection, as most Americans will recognize, remains a distant objective—even for us. But as complex sculptures go, we have removed the vast majority of the stone that does not belong. Now comes the finishing work.

Richard Nixon believed that nations aspiring to great power needed to possess great ideas. To Nixon, without great ideas, great powers ceased to be great. And that simple maxim is the reason America's faith in itself is so crucial to the planet right now. What the rising great powers of our age present in terms of great ideas are merely successful catch-up development (e.g., the China model) or integration (e.g., the EU) strategies—basically, how best to engage the liberal international trade order of America's creation. As such, they represent a powerful idea to those nations across the Gap that struggle to find policy handholds amid globalization's frighteningly rapid and tumultuous churn. They say, "This is how you connect and keep your political order from crumbling under all the accompanying social and economic change." In an age of frontier integration, that might seem like enough grand strategic direction for the planet as a whole, but it is not, because all that vision sets in motion is a worldwide acceleration of all the trends that currently set so much of humanity on edge, wondering what comes next and "How can we keep this all going without everything spinning out of control?"

The great ideas that define great powers in coming years will center on the cluster of global challenges explored across the previous chapters, because once the EU, China, India, Russia, and others move past the "Yes, we can!" stage of their current historical trajectories, they will soon find themselves running into the "Now what?" questions. To the extent that America fails to realign itself to this changed global landscape, we will do worse than simply deny ourselves effective alliance with fellow great powers, we will predetermine their "great ideas" by default, first and foremost being containment of a "reckless" America that seems hopelessly alienated from the global order it set in motion. The longer we indulge ourselves in this regard, the more uncertainty we will create, because none of these great powers will aspire to fill that global leadership void, fearing such a strategic tack would draw America's retaliatory response. Instead, we'll see more of what Russia just did in the Caucasus: opportunistically working the strategic margins, ostensibly to mark spheres of influence but ultimately to enhance market domination. Indeed, the world's rising great powers will instinctively seek to exploit such a void only to hedge against one of two possibilities: America's progressive withdrawal from the world, or its mindless emulation of their own limited, getting-our-house-in-order strategies.

Rather, as we see the world's regions move, each at its best speed, toward some version of "states uniting," America needs to be thinking through and enunciating some global vision of "great powers uniting" as a natural precursor to regions uniting. I don't want to suggest a political primacy here. But if no vision is articulated by the world system's largest and most important actor, then what we're going to see is a lot of regionally idiosyncratic rule-building leading to—at best—a lot of policy jerry-rigging among competing networked commonwealths (each centered on a great power), or—at worst—a lot of policy firewalling among the same designed to protect each from the threat of cascading failures. In sum, we will collectively suffer an estrangement between a globalization process that promotes an open, service-oriented architecture and a regionalized political integration process that demands the preservation of policy autonomy.

In a networked global economy such as the one America has set in motion, there really can't be any "go your own way" regions. Yes, just like in America, we can and should encourage policy experimentation on shared problems, letting the best rule sets win out. As I've made clear throughout this book, I expect America to learn plenty from other great powers in the coming years, as you can never have enough Californias out there probing the rule-set horizon. What we can't have are regions that proclaim, "*Your* rules simply don't work here," as the Soviet bloc once claimed and radical Islam claims today. The critical-mass reality we now face in our successful expansion of a liberal international trade order just doesn't allow for significant opting-out, for we have hit the inflection point on globalization that our Founding Fathers once reached in their revolution, when Benjamin Franklin observed, "We must, indeed, all hang together, or most assuredly we shall all hang separately."

So here's the practical challenge as I see it: America has gone so long since the last period when we had to rethink the world and how it works that we've basically lost the grand-strategy skill set. Worse, this is the first time in our nation's history when our trajectory of success has led to such a clustering of rising great powers that our instinct for continued leadership could easily be overwhelmed by fears of competitive disadvantage—that is, we're left holding the bag on global security while all our competitors catch up. The realist school would tell us to cut back on our leadership in global security to get our own economic and social house in order for the inevitable great-power conflicts to come, when, of course, doing so will most assuredly trigger a lot of fear-threat reaction on the part of those same rising great powers, thus making the outcome as "inevitable" as the realists claim—a self-fulfilling prophecy if ever there was one. So here's where our faith in this world system of our creation comes most into play. We need enough confidence in our model of economic-development-forcing-political-pluralism that we don't abandon our bodyguard role in protecting globalization's continued advance and subsequent network consolidation. If we can't muster that confidence, we'll be unable to lead the shift from defense to security that must occur amid all this worldwide infrastructure/network construction, the result being a world afraid of the inevitable "chaos" that ensues. At that point, we'd be looking at an end-of-the-repeating-cycle, Matrix-like collapse and globalization reboot, an outcome that answers the prayers of only the survivalists among us, who've long preached a return to such primitive, localized communitarianism.

Naturally, I'd like to think that America's decades of effort in creating and spreading this international liberal trade order will end up accomplishing more than simply triggering the Great-Depression-after-next outcome that so many doom-and-gloomers anticipate with glee. This is where our need for a new generation of grand strategists becomes acute. Karl Marx believed that any great thinker's ability to see beyond his own era was inherently limited, a notion he himself proved. That's true because any generation, as it heads into old age, tends to view both itself and its accomplishments as unique and unrepeatable: The Greatest Generation frets that the Boomers have trashed the world order they created, and the Boomers assume the Millennials won't have a clue about what needs to come next. In reality, of course, the Boomers, through their technological and business innovations, dramatically capitalized on the Greatest Generation's Cold War victory to extend globalization's reach far beyond its limited Western base. In so doing, the Boomers have set in motion an age that will demand far greater political and strategic imagination from their Millennial progeny than they themselves ever mustered from their modestly talented cohort of political leaders.

The good news is, of course, that America's up-and-coming Millennials will be able to draw from a global talent pool, a wellspring their predecessors could never have dreamed of tapping, in large part because, as I noted above, those rising great powers were too busy getting their own houses in order. By the time the Millennials become *the* major political force in America in the 2020s, they will be facing similarly talented and intrinsically networked knowledge elites spread across a global network of great powers never before seen in history. Each major global region will enjoy the unprecedented situation of having multiple great powers in place at the same time (for example, an Asia with a powerful China *and* Japan *and* India *and* Korea *and* . . .), in addition to having multiple great-power-dominated regions all simultaneously rising at the same time. In sum, our children will enjoy an era of unprecedented global wealth employed to address unprecedented global challenges.

Which brings me to H. G. Wells and his vision of the future. This book took as its guiding inspiration Wells's minor classic from 1933, *The Shape of Things to Come.* In this novel, whose narrative extends from the 1930s into the start of the twenty-second century, Wells presents the historical projections of Philip Raven, a League of Nations official who, having "read" a future history in his dreams, bequeaths the recorded manuscript to Wells after his death. It is a startling book that posits that mankind's perfection will be realized only in response to the near-destruction of modern civilization through war and pestilence. It was not in Wells's nature to assume the worst as a precursor to the best. But from his historical perspective, in a year when Adolf Hitler's Nazi movement swept into power in a prostrate Germany, Wells clearly felt his projection of a future perfected could follow no other path.

I interpret the future differently. Armageddon is popular in the marketplace, and it would have been easier to threaten you with all manner of frightening scenarios to obtain your buy-in to the grand strategy laid out here, but it wouldn't have been very American to do so. Instead, this book has been about creating a very different future—and a very different sense of the possible—through acts of great will and strategic imagination in the present. Because unlike that of the vast majority of this world, American identity has never been one of shared suffering, but of challenges embraced and opportunities exploited. As an experiment without borders, much less conclusion, America has always leaned forward, living the world's future while shaping its present.

The American System blossomed into an international liberal trade order, which in turn gave birth to the globalization we enjoy today. These are the United States' most powerful acts of creation. This world-transforming legacy created the twenty-first-century environment, one marked by more pervasive poverty reduction, wealth creation, technological advance, and—most important—stabilizing peace *than any previous era in human history*. That legacy is worth preserving, defending, and expanding to its ultimate heights—a globalization made truly global. I have asked you to consider a globalization-centric American grand strategy for this century, believing it to be the most logical and courageous choice we can yet make as a people. But as our own history as a nation clearly shows, such courage is familiar to us. Indeed, it defines who we are.

It is just such courage that remains this country's—and the world's—most precious and inexhaustible resource. Treat it with great care in the tumultuous years ahead.

Acknowledgments

———◆———

This book began with a statement that I often make in the dozens of presentations I deliver annually around the globe: America is the source code for today's globalization. For roughly a decade now, I've put that phrase out there—completely unpacked, expecting the audience to grasp it whole with the same comprehension that I feel intrinsically after contemplating it from a wide variety of angles across my career. When Robert Kagan wrote his brilliant history of America's early decades, *Dangerous Nation*, I realized I needed to explore that concept in some detail if I was going to accomplish what I set out to do in this book—namely, to connect Americans to this globalization process that so many of us now fear. Once that bond was properly recognized, I knew I could place the Bush-Cheney period in historical context, in turn allowing me to argue for the realignments in American grand strategy that my advisory work—with governments and militaries and corporations around the world these past four years—had convinced me were necessary for our nation's future success in this long war against violent extremism amid globalization's rapid expansion.

I drew on a large network of thinkers and practitioners—beyond the many wonderful authors cited already—to bring this volume to fruition.

First, let me thank my colleagues at Enterra Solutions for the amazing journey of discovery afforded by our start-up's rather meteoric rise. It is most gratifying to participate in the real-world applications of so many of my ideas, especially seeing them merge and further develop with those of my partner, Steve DeAngelis, an inventor of towering intellect and unparalleled skill in translating complex ideas into pragmatic solutions. Steve is, in the words of one director of our board, a "functioning genius." Without Steve's inventive mind and all the career opportunities it has afforded me, I don't think this book would have happened. Steve is also a very dear friend.

Next, I need to thank my part-time manager and full-time business developer, Jennifer Wang Posda. Like Steve, Jenn has become a primary mentor over the past few years, so much so that it's hard for me to imagine my arriving at this point in my career without her strategic guidance. Simply put, I couldn't serve as Enterra's senior managing director without her collaboration on a daily basis, and without that vantage point, this book would not have been written. Like Steve, Jenn is a beloved member of my chosen family.

A third chosen sibling is Mark Warren, the editor whose vision has guided my writing for more than half a decade now. What advances I've made as an author over the years are owed substantially to his tutelage. Collaborating with Mark is a pure joy. Besides being my favorite reason for writing, Mark is arguably the best thing that's ever happened to my career—the undeniable inflection point from which all connectivity now flows.

As with my previous two books, my literary agent, Jennifer Gates of Zachary Shuster Harmsworth, played a seminal role in defining this volume's approach to the reader, as did my publisher, the legendary Neil Nyren of G. P. Putnam's Sons. Their guidance made all the difference in the world. My mind is given to all manner of experiments, but Jenn and Neil found a way to locate the right expression consistently across this lengthy production process. It is my great privilege to continue working with both of them.

My webmaster and research assistant, Sean Meade, has been a hugely stabilizing influence on not just my frantic schedule but my entire work over the past three years. Sean has elevated my game by allowing me to concentrate my energies where they can be best applied. He is my Drucker-in-a-Box.

Three readers advised me on the manuscript as I produced it—all of them fellow bloggers. My thanks to Dan Abbott, Mark Safranski, and Michael Lotus for their efforts. Collectively, they constituted a vital emotional and intellectual crutch when I needed one most, filling in for my late brother-in-law, Steve, to whom this book is dedicated.

My weblog has remained my primary workspace, along with my weekly column for Scripps Howard News Service and my periodic articles in *Esquire*. Among the many bloggers, readers, and frequent commentators who deserve my special thanks for connecting me to so many sources over the past few years are: 54th Bn CEF, 77grampa77, a517dogg, Al Alborn, Alicescheshirecat, Allen, Andrew in Baghdad, Andrew Sullivan, Andy Shelley, andyinsdca, ansmeister, antonymous, Arherring, Art Hutchinson, Baltimoron, bdunbar, Benjamin, Bill C, Bill Millan, Bill Nagle, bill s, blairistic, boqueronman, Brad B., Brandon Winter, Brent Grace, Brian, Brian H, Brian Rhea, BrotherCaine, Bruce Sterling, Cadet Echo Boomer, Caitlyn, Cbiggs, Chad, Chap, Charles Ganske, Charles Sheehan-Miles, Chicago Boyz, China Law Blog, Chirol, Chris Albon, Chris Janiec, Christofer Hoff, Christopher Plummer, Chuck Butcher, CitSAR, Constantina, Consul-At-Arms, Critt Jarvis, Cuffy Meigs, Curtis Gale Weeks, Curzon, cyberdyver, Czechbikr, D Blair, Dan, Dan Hare, dan tdaxp, Dave Dilegge, Dave Goldberg, David Hallowell, David Stewart, David Sutton, Desiree Fox, DHM, dipaolom, drsteph, Eddie Beaver, EJDUBYA, Elmer Humes, emjayinc, Ethan Zuckerman, Fabius Maximus, farhad, felixdzerzhinsky, Fipps, Francisco, Frank Hecker, Galrahn, Gerry, Gilbert Garza, Gunnar Peterson, Hansrudolf Suter, historyguy99, hof1991, Hugh, Information Dissemination, Iskendar, jake, Jarrod Myrick, Javaid Akhtar, JBAndrsn, Jeff J., Jeremiah, Jeremy A, jerseyrefugee, Jesse, JFRiley, Jim Keenan, Jimmy J., Jimmy the Dhimmi, Joe Blizzard, Joe Canepa, Joe Crawford, Joel Helgeson, John of Argghhh!, John Robb, JohnShreffler, Joshua Foust, JTM, jwbarton, Keith, Keith_Indy, Kevin in Dallas, kilngoddess, Kim McD, Lance, Larry Dunbar, Larry Y, Lexington Green, Louis Heberlein, lrb, Major B, Manny, Marcus Vitruvius, Mark in Texas, Matt R., Matthew Garcia, Michael, Michael SteelWolf, Michael Tanji, michael75we,

Michal Shapiro, MountainRunner, Mystery Meat, Nate Edwards, Nathan Machula, Noah Shachtman, nykrindc, outback71, Outside the Beltway, PamC, PeteJ, Peter Kay, phil, Phil Windley, Pilgrim, Prescottrjp, Purpleslog, Ray Kimball, Robert L, Robert Langland, sailordude, Sergio, Seth, Shane Deichman, shloky, Sopwith, SR, Steve Barrera, Steve Knott, Steven, Stuart Abrams, Sturt, subadei, taka2k7, TCG, Ted O'Connor, TEJ, thaddeusphoenix, The Globalizer, Tim Lerew, Tim Roth, TM Lutas, Todd McLauchlin, Tom Mull, Tyler Durden of CENTCOM, Valdis, Vinay Gupta, VoteWithTroops.com, Wiggins, William R. Cumming, Wiredman, Younghusband, and zenpundit.

My continued gratitude to my PowerPoint maven, Bradd Hayes. I love live theater, and Bradd is my director.

Fellow authors and colleagues I must single out for their help and advice at various times over the past few years include: Frank Akers, Andrew Barnett, Colleen Barnett, Jerome Barnett, Gennaro Buonocore, Hoyt Canady, Robert Clark, Geoff Davis, Paul Davis, Lu Dehong, Kent Franklin, Randy Fullhart, Hank Gaffney, David Granger, Peter Griffin, Steffany Hedenkamp, Tim Heffernan, Carl Hunt, Larry Kudlow, Alan Lowe, Denise McAuliffe, Jack McElroy, Steve McKnight, Vonne Meussling, Robert Moeller, Timothy Moon, Siobhan O'Connor, Steve Oppenheim, John Phillips, Eric Prince, Chet Richards, Don Rippert, Gary Roughhead, Michael Sfraga, Mark Sharpe, Nolan Sklute, Matt Smith-Meck, Yu Tiejun, Harry Ulrich, Ding Wei, Jessica Weigmann, Robert Wright, Zhang Yue, Yan Xuetong, and Andrew Zolli.

Finally, a huge thanks to my spouse, Vonne, who not only held down the family fort during this long effort but likewise evaluated and chose most of the historical sources I used in the book. She taught me a lot about America in the process, reminding me why I fell in love with her in the first place.

Glossary

---

asymmetrical warfare A conflict between two foes of vastly different capabilities. After the Red Army dissolved in the 1990s, the U.S. military knew it was basically unbeatable, especially in a straight-up fight. But that meant that much smaller opponents would seek to negate its strengths by exploiting its weaknesses, by being clever and "dirty" in combat. On 9/11, America got a real dose of what asymmetrical warfare is going to be like in the twenty-first century.

Big Bang refers to the strategy (alas, seldom articulated) of the Bush administration to trigger widespread political, social, economic, and ultimately security change in the Middle East through the initial spark caused by the toppling of Saddam Hussein's regime in Iraq and the hoped-for emergence of a truly market-based, democratic Arab state. Thus, the Big Bang aimed primarily for a demonstration effect, but likewise was also a direct, in-your-face attempt by the Bush administration to shake things up in the stagnant Middle East, where decades of diplomacy and military crisis response by outside forces (primarily the United States) had accomplished basically nothing. The implied threat of the Big Bang was "We're not leaving the region until the region truly joins the global economy in a broadband fashion, leading to political pluralism domestically." The Big

Bang was a bold strategic move by Bush, one that I supported. All terrorism is local, so either deal with that or resort to firewalling America off from the outside world.

connectivity The enormous changes being brought on by the information revolution, including the emerging financial, technological, and logistical architecture of the global economy (i.e., the movement of money, services accompanied by content, and people and materials). During the boom times of the 1990s, many thought that advances in communications such as the Internet and mobile phones would trump all, erasing the business cycle, erasing national borders, erasing the very utility of the state in managing a global security order that seemed more virtual than real, but 9/11 proved differently. That connectivity, while a profoundly transforming force, could not by itself maintain global security, primarily because a substantial rise in connectivity between any nation and the outside world typically leads to a host of tumultuous reactions, including heightened nationalism and religiosity.

Department of Everything Else A Back-to-the-Future proposal (first offered in *Blueprint for Action*) to return to the past structure when the Army was the Department of War and the Navy was the "Department of Peace" (especially business continuity). This department would fill the gap between the current Departments of Defense and State, engaging in unconventional pursuits such as nation-building, disaster relief, and counterinsurgency. In many ways, it could be a virtual department, bringing together various resources from the government, nongovernmental organization, and business sectors, along with foreign governments and the linchpin SysAdmin force. Compare the virtual department with the way movie companies work, coming together to make a film, then dissolving. Such a virtual department would work an Iraq one way and a Sudan very differently. In contrast with the Department of Homeland Security, our first and greatest strategic error in the long war on terror, the Department of Everything Else would realize that our American networks are only as secure as every network they are connected to. Such a department would feature many more civilian and older, wiser roles when compared with the current Defense Department.

disconnectedness In this century, it is disconnectedness that defines danger. Disconnectedness allows bad actors to flourish by keeping entire societies detached from the global community and under their dictatorial control, or in the case of failed states, it allows dangerous transnational actors to exploit the resulting chaos to their own dangerous ends. Eradicating disconnectedness is the defining security task of our age, as well as a supreme moral cause in the cases of those who suffer it against their will. Just as important, however, by expanding the connectivity of globalization, we increase peace and prosperity planet-wide.

frontier integration Globalization has entered into an extended period of frontier integration—as in economic and network integration of previously off-grid or poorly connected societies. The historical example par excellence is the settling and taming of the American West after the Civil War. The chief activities are infrastructure building, the extension of social networks and rule of law, state building, the generation of permanent and pervasive security, the squelching of insurgencies and criminal mafias, and the formal marketization of existing and new economic activities—to include both "exploiting" the labor of and selling to the so-called bottom-of-the-pyramid population. America's frontier integration was continental-sized, involving millions. Today's project targets the globe's entire Gap, involving billions in so-called emerging or frontier economies. It also involves the impoverished rural regions of New Core pillars such as China and India. In general, neither Americans nor Europeans will lead this frontier integration effort. We price out too high. Instead, the frontier integrators of the age will be mostly Asians, who know better how to jump-start development in these harsher environments. America's role can be to mentor and enable the integrators, helping especially on security, or we can sit the whole thing out and hope for the best in terms of resulting political outcomes.

Functioning Core Those parts of the world that are actively integrating their national economies into a global economy and that adhere to globalization's emerging security rule set. The Functioning Core at present consists of North America, Europe both "old" and "new," Russia, Japan and South Korea, China (although the interior far less so), India (in a pockmarked sense), Australia and New Zealand, South Africa, and the ABCs of South America (Argentina, Brazil, and Chile). That is roughly 4 billion out of a global population of more than 6 billion. The Functioning Core can be subdivided into the Old Core, anchored by America, Europe, and Japan; and the New Core, whose leading pillars are China, India, Brazil, and Russia. There is no substantial threat of intra-Core war among these great powers. However, there remain competing rule sets regarding what constitutes proper Core interventions inside the Gap, as recently indicated by Russia's contested intervention in Georgia's ongoing civil strife.

globalization The worldwide integration and increasing flows of trade, capital, ideas, and people. Until 9/11, the U.S. government tended to identify globalization primarily as an economic rule set, but thanks to the long war against violent extremism, we now understand that it likewise demands the clear enunciation and enforcement of a security rule set as well.

grand strategy As far as a world power like America is concerned, a grand strategy involves first imagining some future world order within which our nation's standing, prosperity, and security are significantly enhanced, and then plotting and maintaining a course to that desired end while employing—to the fullest extent possible—all elements of our nation's power toward generating those conditions. Naturally, such grand goals typically take decades to achieve, thus the importance of having a continuous supply of grand thinkers able to maintain strategic focus.

Leviathan The U.S. military's warfighting capacity and the high-performance combat troops, weapon systems, aircraft, armor, and ships associated with all-out war against traditionally defined opponents (i.e., other great-power militaries). This is the force America created to defend the West against the Soviet threat, now transformed from its industrial-era roots to its information-age capacity for high-speed, high-lethality, and high-precision major combat operations. The Leviathan force is without peer in the world today, and—as such—frequently finds itself fighting shorter and easier wars. This "overmatch" means, however, that current and future enemies in the long war on violent extremism will largely seek to avoid triggering the Leviathan's employment, preferring to wage asymmetrical war against the United States, focusing on its economic interests and citizenry. The Leviathan rules the "first half" of war, but it is often ill suited, by design and temperament, to the "second half" of peace, to include postconflict stabilization-and-reconstruction operations and counterinsurgency campaigns. It is thus counterposed to the System Administrators force.

Non-Integrated Gap Regions of the world that are largely disconnected from the global economy and the rule sets that define its stability. Today, the Non-Integrated Gap is made up of the Caribbean Rim, Andean South America, virtually all of Africa, the Caucasus, Central Asia, the Middle East, and most of the Southeast Asian littoral. These regions constitute globalization's "ozone hole," where connectivity remains thin or absent in far too many cases. Of course, each region contains some countries that are very Core-like in their attributes (just as there are Gap-like pockets throughout the Core defined primarily by poverty), but these are like mansions in an otherwise seedy neighborhood, and as such are trapped by these larger Gap-defining circumstances.

rule set A collection of rules (both formal and informal) that delineates how some activity normally unfolds. *The Pentagon's New Map* explores the new rule sets concerning conflict and violence in international affairs— or under what conditions governments decide it makes sense to switch from the rule set that defines peace to the rule set that defines war. The events of 9/11 shocked the Pentagon and the rest of the world into the realization that we needed a new rule set concerning war and peace, one that replaces the old rule set that governed America's Cold War with the Soviet Union. The book explained how the new rule set will actually work in the years ahead, not just from America's perspective but from an international one.

rule-set reset When a crisis triggers your realization that your world is woefully lacking certain types of rules, you start making up those new rules with a vengeance (e.g., the Patriot Act and the doctrine of preemption following 9/11). Such a rule-set reset can be a very good thing. But it can also be a very dangerous time, because in your rush to fill in all the rule-set gaps, your cure may end up being worse than your disease. The world is currently engaged in such a reset concerning international financial flows, in response to America's subprime crisis.

System Administrators (SysAdmin) The "second half" blended force that wages the peace after the Leviathan force has successfully waged war. Therefore, it is a force optimized for such categories of operations as "stability and support operations" (SASO), postconflict stabilization and reconstruction operations, "humanitarian assistance/disaster relief" (HA/DR), and any and all operations associated with low-intensity conflict (LIC), counterinsurgency operations (COIN), and small-scale crisis response. Beyond such military-intensive activities, the SysAdmin force likewise provides civil security with its police component, as well as civilian personnel with expertise in rebuilding networks, infrastructure, and social and political institutions. While the core security and logistical capabilities are derived from uniformed military components, the SysAdmin force is fundamentally envisioned as a standing capacity for interagency (i.e., among various U.S. federal agencies) and international collaboration in nation-building, meaning that both the SysAdmin force and function end up being more civilian than uniform in composition, more government-wide than just Defense Department, more rest-of-the-world than just the United States, and more private-sector-invested than public-sector-funded.

system perturbation A system-level definition of crisis and instability in the age of globalization; a new ordering principle that has already begun to transform the military and U.S. security policy; also a particular event that forces a country or region to rethink everything. The terrorist attacks of 9/11 served as the first great "existence proof" for this concept, but there have been and will be others over time. Some are purposeful, like the Bush administration's Big Bang strategy of fomenting political change in the Middle East, but others will be accidents, like the Asian tsunamis of December 2004, or America's recent financial crises.

Notes

―― ◼◂◾▸◼ ――

v. A lonely sail . . . peace!

Translation from "From the Ends to the Beginning: A Bilingual Anthology of Russian Verse," found online at max.mmlc.northwestern.edu/~mdenner/Demo/texts/sail .html.

PREFACE: THE SHAPE OF THINGS TO COME

1. Neither accident nor providence, this "flat world" . . . states uniting.

See Thomas L. Friedman, *The World Is Flat: A Brief History of the Twenty-first Century,* expanded edition (New York: Penguin, 2006).

CHAPTER 1. THE SEVEN DEADLY SINS OF BUSH-CHENEY

6. Having triggered this global counterreaction . . . autocracies (read, Russia and China).

The classic expression of this view is found in Robert Kagan, *The Return of History and the End of Dreams* (New York: Alfred A. Knopf, 2008).

6. This would be a double mistake . . . logically more willing to defend it.

Oddly enough, the classic expression of this view is found in a slightly younger Robert Kagan, *Of Paradise and Power: America and Europe in the New World Order* (New York: Alfred A. Knopf, 2003). What a difference a second Bush administration makes!

But First, the Virtues Worth Citing

8. In the grand sweep of history . . . "stakeholder" in global security—Zoellick's term.

"Deputy Secretary Zoellick Statement on Conclusion of the Second U.S.-China Senior Dialogue," December 8, 2005, found online at www.state.gov/r/pa/prs/ps/2005/57822 .htm.

11. This wave of disintegrating integration is beyond . . . will endure across this century.

This phrase comes from Clyde V. Prestowitz, *Three Billion New Capitalists: The Great Shift of Wealth and Power to the East* (New York: Basic Books, 2005).

11. As Fareed Zakaria notes . . . and thriving the region is *despite* Iraq's violence.

Fareed Zakaria, *The Post-American World* (New York: W.W. Norton, 2008), p. 8.

Now for the Sins
Lust, Leading to the Quest for Primacy
12. The Bush administration's allegedly secret plan . . . Paul Wolfowitz.
     The initial version of the "Defense Planning Guidance for the 1994–99 fiscal years" was
     leaked to the *New York Times* on March 7, 1992: "U.S. Strategy Plan Calls for Insuring
     No Rivals Develop," by Patrick E. Tyler, *New York Times*, March 8, 1992.
12. At the time, I can tell you, few . . . America's "unipolar moment" of the early 1990s.
     Krauthammer first used this term in his Henry M. Jackson Memorial Lecture delivered
     in Washington, D.C., September 18, 1990. This lecture was later adapted into an arti-
     cle: Charles Krauthammer, "The Unipolar Moment," *Foreign Affairs*, "America and the
     World" issue, 1990/91, vol. 70, no. 1.
13. But after 9/11 forced a strategic redirect . . . declaration of a "global war on terror."
     In the 1970s, the Central Intelligence Agency commissioned a "Team B" of outside ex-
     perts to compete analytically with the CIA's "Team A" on describing the nature of the
     Soviet threat.
15. To remain "fit" . . . grand strategy needs to attract more allies than it repulses.
     On Boyd's life and influence, read Robert Coram, *Boyd: The Fighter Pilot Who Changed
     the Art of War* (New York: Little, Brown, 2002); on this specific point, see Chet Rich-
     ards, "Grand Strategy," found online at www.d-n-i.net/fcs/boyd_grand_strategy.htm,
     and Mark Safranski, editor, *The John Boyd Roundtable: Debating Science, Strategy, and
     War* (Ann Arbor, MI: Nimble Books, 2008), which contains a foreword by yours truly
     on Boyd's impact upon the field.

Anger, Leading to the Demonization of Enemies
18. In *Fiasco* . . . personnel that sum up this danger.
     Thomas E. Ricks, *Fiasco: The American Military Adventure in Iraq* (New York: Penguin
     Books, 2007), pp. 290–91.

Greed, Leading to the Concentration of War Powers
19. As Charlie Savage notes . . . "just as those powers had come under fierce assault."
     Charlie Savage, *Takeover: The Return of the Imperial Presidency and the Subversion of
     American Democracy* (New York: Little, Brown, 2007), p. 26.
19. In subsequent years, Cheney . . . the president of the United States to do his job."
     Cheney made these comments to Cokie Roberts on ABC's *This Week* in early 2002; see
     Savage, *Takeover*, pp. 26 and 75.
20. There is no surer sign of this . . . grand strategists in the collective public mind.
     See Michael Cavna, "Comedians of Clout: In a Funny Way, Satirical Takes Can Color
     Perceptions of the Presidential Contenders," *Washington Post*, June 12, 2008; and
     Michiko Kakutani, "Is Jon Stewart the Most Trusted Man in America?" *New York Times*,
     August 15, 2008.

Pride, Leading to Avoidable Postwar Failures
21. Already in print are numerous . . . jihadists from abroad, soft partition).
     Besides Ricks, the two best accounts are found in Rajiv Chandrasekaran, *Imperial Life
     in the Emerald City: Inside Iraq's Green Zone* (New York: Vintage Books, 2007); and
     George Packer, *The Assassins' Gate: America in Iraq* (New York: Farrar, Straus & Gir-
     oux, 2005).
21. In his 2008 political memoir . . . Rice's personal management style.
     Douglas J. Feith, *War and Decision: Inside the Pentagon at the Dawn of the War on Terror-
     ism* (New York: Harper, 2008), pp. 249–50.
22. The main beneficiary of such confusion . . . stabilizing Iraq in the early postwar months).
     For the most damning portrait of Cheney, see Scott McClellan, *What Happened: Inside*

the Bush White House and Washington's Culture of Deception (New York: Public Affairs, 2008); on the mobilization of message "force multipliers," see David Barstow, "Behind TV Analysts, Pentagon's Hidden Hand: Courting Ex-Officers Tied to Military Contractors," *New York Times*, April 20, 2008.

23. Some, like onetime neoconservative . . . at the end of the Cold War.
See Francis Fukuyama, "After Neoconservatism," *New York Times Magazine*, February 19, 2006; and his opening chapter, "Nation-Building and the Failure of Institutional Memory," in Fukuyama, ed., *Nation-Building: Beyond Afghanistan and Iraq* (Baltimore: Johns Hopkins University Press, 2006), pp. 1–16.

23. Other examples cited . . . coordinated efforts with Northern Alliance forces.
See Ricks, *Fiasco*, Part One—"Containment"; and Larry Diamond, "What Went Wrong and Right in Iraq," in Fukuyama, ed., *Nation-Building*, pp. 173–75.

23. Nor should we be surprised that the most prominent Shia . . . decision-making.
See Ricks, *Fiasco*, pp. 56–57; and Aram Roston, *The Man Who Pushed America to War: The Extraordinary Life, Adventures, and Obsessions of Ahmed Chalabi* (New York: Nation Books, 2008).

23. As Thomas Ricks observes . . . was tear down the goalposts at halftime in the game."
Ricks, *Fiasco*, p. 145.

23. The White House would deny . . . "If you break it, you own it").
Cited in Bob Woodward, *Plan of Attack* (New York: Simon & Schuster, 2004), p. 150.

24. So Rumsfeld was right . . . Army you might want or wish to have at a later time."
See "Troops Put Thorny Questions to Rumsfeld: Defense Chief Speaks to Iraq-bound Soldiers in Kuwait," CNN.com, December 9, 2004, found online at www.cnn.com/2004/WORLD/meast/12/08/rumsfeld.troops/.

Envy, Leading to the Misguided Redirect on Iran
25. As Vali Nasr argues . . . completely predictable.
See Vali Nasr, *The Shia Revival: How Conflicts Within Islam Will Shape the Future* (New York: W. W. Norton, 2006), chaps. 7–9.

25. Much as Turkey has . . . liberation from Saddam Hussein's dictatorship.
Cited in Andrew Purvis, "Istanbul's Economic Tension," *Time*, May 1, 2008.

Sloth, Leading to the U.S. Military Finally Asserting Command
28. For a presidency devoted to expanding . . . Petraeus's longtime mentor.
See Bob Woodward, *The War Within: A Secret White House History, 2006–2008* (New York: Simon & Schuster, 2008), pp. 129–46, 276–82, 296–99, and 331–33.

28. After Petraeus's historic testimony . . . *President of the United States.*
Quoted in Woodward, *The War Within*, p. 392.

30. Together, these two "monks of war" . . . published formally in December 2006.
Thomas P. M. Barnett, "The Monks of War," *Esquire*, March 2006, found online at www.esquire.com/features/articles/2006/060426_mfe_March_06_Generals_1.html.

30. For as Sarah Sewall, a Harvard human rights experts . . . fundamentally at odds."
The U.S. Army/Marine Corps, Counterinsurgency Field Manual (Chicago: University of Chicago Press, 2007), p. xxxix.

Gluttony, Leading to Strategic Overhang Cynically Foisted upon the Next President
31. U.S. defense spending as a percentage . . . hovering in the 4.3–4.4 percent range.
These data are compiled from the "Truth and Politics" website page ("Relative Size of US Military Spending, 1940–2003") found online at www.truthandpolitics.org/military-relative-size.php#gdp-graph.

31. Yes, the American military has spread itself out . . . to about thirty or so foreign states.
This calculation was supplied by Henry H. Gaffney, Director of the Strategy and Con-

cepts Group in the Center for Strategic Studies at the Center for Naval Analyses, Alexandria, Virginia; it is buttressed by Tim Kane, "Global U.S. Troop Deployment, 1950–2003" (Washington, DC: Heritage Foundation Center for Data Analysis Report #04–11, 27 October 2004), found online at www.heritage.org/Research/National Security/cda04–11.cfm.

31. Finally, consider this measure of individual burden . . . one out of every 800 Americans. In 1968, roughly one million Americans served abroad in uniform, out of a total population of approximately 200 million. Today, somewhat less than 400,000 troops are stationed abroad, out of a national population of over 300 million. For details, see Kane, "Global U.S. Troop Deployment, 1950–2003."

CHAPTER 2. A TWELVE-STEP RECOVERY PROGRAM
FOR AMERICAN GRAND STRATEGY

36. A world that rapidly doubles . . . to ensure either outcome than America.
The global middle class is currently estimated in the 25–30 percent range and is expected to increase to the 50–55 percent range over the next 10 to 15 years; see Moises Naim, "Can the World Afford a Middle Class? Yes, But It Will Be Awfully Expensive," *Foreign Policy*, March–April 2008.

37. In the best tradition of self-help programs . . . back to where we once belonged.

THE TWELVE STEPS OF ALCOHOLICS ANONYMOUS
1. We admitted we were powerless over alcohol—that our lives had become unmanageable.
2. Came to believe that a Power greater than ourselves could restore us to sanity.
3. Made a decision to turn our will and our lives over to the care of God as we understood Him.
4. Made a searching and fearless moral inventory of ourselves.
5. Admitted to God, to ourselves and to another human being the exact nature of our wrongs.
6. Were entirely ready to have God remove all these defects of character.
7. Humbly asked Him to remove our shortcomings.
8. Made a list of all persons we had harmed, and became willing to make amends to them all.
9. Made direct amends to such people wherever possible, except when to do so would injure them or others.
10. Continued to take personal inventory and when we were wrong promptly admitted it.
11. Sought through prayer and meditation to improve our conscious contact with God, as we understood Him, praying only for knowledge of His will for us and the power to carry that out.
12. Having had a spiritual awakening as the result of these steps, we tried to carry this message to alcoholics, and to practice these principles in all our affairs.

"A Brief Guide to Alcoholics Anonymous," Alcoholics Anonymous World Services, Inc., 1972, found online at www.aa.org/en_pdfs/p-42_abriefguidetoaa.pdf.

1. Admit that we Americans are powerless over globalization
38. So we Americans need . . . at suitably discounted prices.
See Thomas L. Friedman, *Hot, Flat, and Crowded: Why We Need a Green Revolution— And How It Can Renew America* (New York: Farrar, Straus and Giroux, 2008).

2. Come to believe that only a bipartisanship . . . restore sanity to America's foreign affairs.

39. As Ronald Brownstein notes . . . in those first decades of modern America.

See Ronald Brownstein, *The Second Civil War: How Extreme Partisanship Has Paralyzed Washington and Polarized America* (New York: Penguin Press, 2007), pp. 27–56 ("The Age of Partisan Armies").

39. As the country moved deeper . . . the longest such period in American history.

See Brownstein, *Second Civil War,* pp. 57–91 ("The Age of Bargaining").

39. That age of bargaining yielded . . . subsequent rise of the "Reagan Republicans."

See Brownstein, *Second Civil War,* pp. 93–136 ("The Age of Transition").

39. Since that time we've seen . . . commands a serious majority.

See Brownstein, *Second Civil War,* pp. 137–74 ("The Rise of Hyperpartisanship").

40. Morris Massey, an expert on conflict . . . we discover a world larger than ourselves.

Massey's work appears to exist only on tape; see Morris Massey, *What You Are Is Where You Were When,* Program 1 of The Massey Triad, found online at www.enterprise media.com/product/00121/massey_triad.html.

3. Make the decision to coordinate all elements . . . that we have collectively defined.

43. While it is technically . . . a third pillar alongside diplomacy and defense."

See Lael Brainard and Patrick Cronin, Codirectors, *Brookings–CSIS Task Force: Transforming Foreign Assistance for the 21st Century,* "Executive Recommendations," found online at www.brookings.edu/~/media/Files/rc/articles/2006/fall_foreign_assistance _reform_brainard/fall_foreign_assistance_reform_brainard.pdf.

43. With a current portfolio . . . WWII to have a modest foreign policy agenda.

On this, see Lael Brainard, "A Unified Framework for U.S. Foreign Assistance" (pp. 1–32) and "Organizing U.S. Foreign Assistance to Meet Twenty-first Century Challenges" (pp. 33–66) in Brainard, ed., *Security by Other Means: Foreign Assistance, Global Poverty, and American Leadership* (Washington, DC: Brookings Institution Press, 2007).

44. Seeing them as such, I'm less interested in "supersizing" State . . . cabinet department.

I was one of several dozen experts who testified to the HELP (Helping to Enhance the Livelihood of People Around the Globe) Commission; see their report, "Beyond Assistance: The HELP Commission Report on Foreign Assistance Reform," December 2007, found online at www.helpcommission.gov/portals/0/Beyond%20Assistance_HELP _Commission_Report.pdf.

45. When almost 90 percent of your officers say . . . and platforms third.

See the polling data in "The U.S. Military Index," *Foreign Policy,* March–April 2008, found online at ww.foreignpolicy.com/story/cms.php?story_id=4198.

45. And when over 90 percent of your casualties . . . in treasure—and blood.

A good source of casualties by month is provided by GlobalSecurity.org and found online at www.globalsecurity.org/military/ops/iraq_casualties.htm.

46. Now, as the real push comes to shove . . . for these purposes the whole time?

On this sad state of affairs, see David Morgan and Kristin Roberts, "U.S. Seeks Bigger Role Assisting Pakistani Forces," Reuters, February 6, 2008.

4. Make a searching and fearless moral inventory of the "global war on terror."

46. Most crucial is that al Qaeda's brutal tactics . . . support throughout the Islamic world.

See Pew Global Attitudes Project polling on this trend, located online at pewglobal.org/.

47. According to experts who track such trends . . . will be far more religious than the last.

See Laurie Goodstein, "More Religion, but Not the Old-Time Kind," *New York Times,* January 9, 2005.

48. The opposite of war isn't peace, it's creation.

A line from Jonathan Larson's 1996 Broadway musical, *Rent*, specifically from the song "La Vie Boheme."

49. Foreign direct investment flows to the Middle East . . . quadrupled since 2000.
    See Roula Khalaf, "Boomtime in Lands of Oil and Money: The Rise in the Oil Price Is Driving Investment Growth," *Financial Times*, November 20, 2007.

50. That demographic . . . Middle East will "middle-age" over the next quarter-century.
    See Graham Fuller's paper, "The Youth Crisis in Middle Eastern Society" (Clinton, MI: Institute for Social Policy and Understanding, 2004).

51. And we'd better . . . time is on our side—but not forever.
    See Richard Jackson and Neil Howe, *The Graying of the Great Powers: Demography and Geopolitics in the 21st Century* (Washington, DC: Center for Strategic and International Studies, 2008), pp. 133–41.

51. The same goes for Islamic youth . . . infuriate their parents.
    Cathy Lynn Grossman, "Tension Between Sunnis, Shiites Emerging in USA," *USA Today*, September 25, 2007.

51. Turkey's the "lead goose" in this formation . . . within the framework of modern life.
    See Christopher Dickey and Owen Matthews, "The New Face of Islam: A Critique of Radicalism Is Building Within the Heart of the Muslim World," *Newsweek*, June 9, 2008.

52. History says that as long as your population . . . democratic political systems.
    On this point, see Richard P. Cincotta, "How Democracies Grow Up: Countries with Too Many Young People May Not Have a Fighting Chance at Freedom," *Foreign Policy*, March–April 2008.

5. Admit to the world and to ourselves the exact nature of our mistakes in Iraq and Afghanistan.

54. What did that legacy cost us?
    See Global Security.org for casualty data, found online at www.globalsecurity.org/military/ops/iraq_casualties.htm.

6. We are entirely ready to work with the international community . . . wartime injustice.

57. America's relationship with the ICC . . . render us exempt from its prosecution.
    On this subject, see the Coalition for the International Criminal Court, "US Bilateral Immunity or So-called 'Article 98' Agreements," *Global Policy Forum*, April 18, 2003, found online at www.globalpolicy.org/intljustice/icc/2003/0606usbilaterals.htm.

57. Good example: The ICC has indicted Sudanese . . . ethnic cleansing in Darfur.
    See Romesh Ratnesar, "The Don Quixote of Darfur," *Time*, November 12, 2007.

8. Make a list of all the great powers . . . become willing to make concessions to them all.

60. Vice President Dick Cheney stated that the long war . . . administrations to come."
    See "Interview of the Vice President by Richard Wolffe, *Newsweek* Magazine," Office of the Vice President, January 28, 2007, found online at www.whitehouse.gov/news/releases/2007/01/20070128.html.

62. Right now there's nothing in the Middle East . . . James Baker, argued, there should be.
    See James A. Baker III and Lee H. Hamilton, *The Iraq Study Group Report: The Way Forward—A New Approach* (New York: Vintage, 2006), pp. 58–64.

9. Make direct overtures to violent nonstate actors . . . would damage existing alliances.

This section began as an unclassified report that I authored for U.S. Strategic Command in January 2008 as part of its ongoing study of violent nonstate actors.

10. Continue to review our goal of accelerated democratization . . . promptly admit it.

67. Princeton economist Alan Krueger . . . more likely to turn to terrorist tactics."

Alan B. Krueger, *What Makes a Terrorist: Economics and the Roots of Terrorism* (Princeton, NJ: Princeton University Press, 2007), p. 7.

67. But since almost 90 percent of attacks occur . . . killed by lightning than by al Qaeda.

See Krueger, *Terrorist*, p. 71; and John Muller, "A False Sense of Insecurity?: How Does the Risk of Terrorism Measure Up Against Everyday Dangers?" *Regulation*, Fall 2004.

68. Indeed, numerous studies today note . . . the greater that country's civil liberties.

The top quarter of countries, according to size of the middle class, is over 90 percent democratic, whereas the bottom quarter is less than 50 percent; see William Easterly, *The White Man's Burden: Why the West's Efforts to Aid the Rest Have Done So Much Ill and So Little Good* (New York: Penguin Press, 2006), pp. 124–25.

68. If you attempt to short-circuit . . . radical extremists prevail.

On this point, see Fareed Zakaria, *The Future of Freedom: Illiberal Democracy at Home and Abroad* (New York: W. W. Norton, 2003).

CHAPTER 3. THE AMERICAN TRAJECTORY:
OF GREAT MEN AND GREAT POWERS

74. In fact, its parliament was the first in history . . . violent attacks against its commerce.

Several British Members of Parliament reminded me of this fact when I delivered a presentation there in the fall of 2004.

74. Less than 2 percent of our country's population . . . patricians selecting one of their own.

The best estimate is somewhat less than 1.3 percent, or less than 40,000 popular votes cast out of a total American population of roughly 3 million; see the Wikipedia entry online at en.wikipedia.org/wiki/United_States_presidential_election,_1789.

74. During that election . . . to vote in the presidential race.

Those six states that allowed for popular or partly popular election of electors were Kentucky, Maryland, North Carolina, Rhode Island, Tennessee, and Virginia; see the Wikipedia entry online at en.wikipedia.org/wiki/United_States_presidential_election %2C_1800.

75. This one-party rule, subsequently dubbed . . . president ran unopposed.

James Monroe in 1820; see the Wikipedia entry online at en.wikipedia.org/wiki/United_States_presidential_election%2C_1820.

75. Finally, a whopping forty-eight years after . . . citizens vote directly for electors.

Of the twenty-six states, only Delaware and South Carolina had their legislatures pick the electors. In Maryland, Maine, New York, and Tennessee, most electors were selected by popular election. In the other twenty states, all electors were popularly elected. See the Wikipedia entry online at en.wikipedia.org/wiki/1828_election.

75. Naturally, he was another war hero . . . the equivalent of a "third term."

On Andrew Jackson, see Daniel Walker Howe, *What Hath God Wrought: The Transformation of America, 1815–1848* (New York: Oxford University Press, 2007), pp. 328–66.

The American System, Proposed and Imposed

80. As Walter Russell Mead correctly notes . . . which states must observe and protect."

Walter Russell Mead, *God and Gold: Britain, America, and the Making of the Modern World* (New York: Alfred A. Knopf, 2007), p. 4.

81. In a time of "great upheaval" that historian . . . ambitious reforms in Imperial Russia.

See Jay Winik, *The Great Upheaval: America and the Birth of the Modern World, 1788–1800* (New York: HarperCollins, 2007), pp. xi–xx.

81. As Winik describes our infancy . . . agreements, charters and covenants."

Winik, *Great Upheaval*, p. 55.

82. Meanwhile, our ships came under such . . . ransom for cargo and personnel captured.
That figure comes from Michael B. Oren, *Power, Faith, and Fantasy: America in the Middle East, 1776 to the Present* (New York: W.W. Norton, 2007), p. 38.

82. Despite its internal divisions and inherent weakness . . . "sport of European politics."
Quoted in Winik, *Great Upheaval*, p. 54.

82. As Robert Kagan writes in *Dangerous Nation* . . . their political influence with them."
Robert Kagan, *Dangerous Nation: America's Place in the World from Its Earliest Days to the Dawn of the Twentieth Century* (New York: Alfred A. Knopf, 2006), p. 76. This is the most interesting history of America that I have ever read. It inspired me to write Chapter 3 of this book.

82. As Kagan notes, by imposing "one set of values . . . *will now be valued and traded.*
Kagan, *Dangerous Nation*, p. 85.

83. As such, George Washington's retiring admonition . . . those same European powers.
On this point see Kagan's brilliant analysis in *Dangerous Nation*, pp. 112–25.

84. Intimidated by the loss of Britain's protection . . . establishing an inland empire.
Kagan, *Dangerous Nation*, pp. 53–54 and 126–29.

84. Indeed, Washington himself foresaw . . . inimical to the long-term health of the nation.
Doris Kearns Goodwin, *Team of Rivals: The Political Genius of Abraham Lincoln* (New York: Simon & Schuster, 2005), p. 357.

85. Later, as cotton became king . . . today's OPEC could never dream of achieving in oil.
In 1850, America accounted for 68 percent of world cotton production; see Howe, *What Hath God Wrought*, p. 128.

86. As biographer Ron Chernow writes . . . piracy of British trade secrets."
Ron Chernow, *Alexander Hamilton* (New York: Penguin Press, 2004), pp. 371–72.

86. But even more crucial than such initial . . . markets into a single unified whole."
Chernow, *Alexander Hamilton*, p. 378.

87. Chernow calls him "a messenger from a future that we now inhabit."
Chernow, *Alexander Hamilton*, p. 6.

87. As Winik notes: "Hamilton's fingerprints . . . remarkably, that is not an exhaustive list."
Winik, *Great Upheaval*, p. 479.

87. A committed Jefferson Republican . . . to "become real and true Americans."
Maurice G. Baxter, *Henry Clay and the American System* (Lexington, KY: University Press of Kentucky, 2004), p. 57.

88. It is argued by some historians . . . the Civil War itself might have been averted.
On this, see Howe, *What Hath God Wrought*, p. 690.

88. Clay's primary scheme to implement . . . basis for funding roads and canals.
Baxter, *Henry Clay*, p. 33.

88. An unrepentant economic nationalist . . . in effect, *external* improvements.
The term "external improvements" comes from Howe, *What Hath God Wrought*, p. 360.

88. Still, much as Hamilton pushed Jefferson . . . surpassed until the late 1850s.
See Howe's chart on "Federal Government Expenses for Internal Improvements, 1789–1858" in *What Hath God Wrought*, p. 361.

88. Jackson, as historian Daniel Walker Howe . . . the town eight years later on a train.
Howe, *What Hath God Wrought*, p. 563.

88. Howe argues that Clay expanded Hamilton's . . . domination of the global economy.
Howe, *What Hath God Wrought*, pp. 270–71.

89. This was Hamilton's ambition . . . protect herself, both at home and abroad."
Kagan, *Dangerous Nation*, p. 37.

The American System, Tested and Transformed

90. For all practical purposes . . . until Andrew Jackson . . . rode into power in 1828.
Howe, *What Hath God Wrought*, p. 210.

90. As Howe writes: "Our own age finds . . . the years between 1815 and 1848."
Howe, *What Hath God Wrought*, p. 4.

90. It is surprising that the word "nationalism" . . . into a nationwide market economy."
Howe, *What Hath God Wrought*, p. 116.

91. The canal also catapulted . . . map of the United States and put itself at the center."
Howe, *What Hath God Wrought*, p. 120.

92. Jackson's age likewise saw plenty of social . . . viewed as essentially nonwhite.
On this point, see Stephen Prothero, *Religious Literacy: What Every American Needs to Know—and Doesn't* (New York: Harper One, 2007), pp. 70–71.

92. The incoming Irish were . . . the Great Potato Famine of the 1840s.
Howe, *What Hath God Wrought*, p. 825.

92. America's Second Awakening in religious fervor . . . promised lands of the Middle East.
See Howe, *What Hath God Wrought*, p. 165; and Oren, *Power, Faith, and Fantasy*, pp. 80–97.

92. Quincy Adams, by the way . . . unwanted association with the abominable practice.
See Howe, *What Hath God Wrought*, p. 610.

92. As Robert Kagan argues, the South . . . the North's free-labor civilization."
Kagan, *Dangerous Nation*, p. 212.

93. As the South increasingly dreamed of erecting . . . biggest slave state yet—Texas.
On "tropical empire," see Kagan, *Dangerous Nation*, pp. 234–45.

93. By the time the Fugitive Slave Act of 1850 . . . an emerging global antislavery crusade.
Kagan, *Dangerous Nation*, pp. 210–18.

94. Lincoln and Seward, Kagan notes . . . and a strong federal bank."
Kagan, *Dangerous Nation*, p. 258.

94. Lincoln himself, who idolized fellow . . . with the construction of the Erie Canal.
The quote regarding Clay comes from Carl Sandburg, *Abraham Lincoln: The Prairie Years and the War Years* (New York: Harcourt, Brace, 1954), p. 105. On the "Illinois System," see Howe, *What Hath God Wrought*, p. 569; and Goodwin, *Team of Rivals*, p. 92.

94. Lincoln believed deeply in the essential equation . . . "elevate the condition of men."
Goodwin, *Team of Rivals*, p. 90.

94. In this manner, historian Doris Kearns Goodwin . . . undisputed giant.
Goodwin, *Team of Rivals*, p. 28.

95. Lincoln wisely tempered . . . Britain and France from intervening in the war."
Goodwin, *Team of Rivals*, pp. 342 and 364.

95. But Lincoln, Goodwin writes . . . easily maneuvered into supporting the South."
Goodwin, *Team of Rivals*, p. 468.

97. Perhaps the most important bill was the Homestead . . . plough to unbroken soil."
Sandburg, *Abraham Lincoln*, p. 300.

97. As a wartime measure . . . normal agricultural workforce was otherwise employed.
See Sandburg, *Abraham Lincoln*, p. 300.

97. One out of every sixteen of those people settled on farms through the Homestead Act.
See Hernando de Soto, "Citadels of Dead Capital: What the Third World Must Learn from U.S. history," *Reason*, May 2001, found online at www.reason.com/news/show/28018.html.

97. According to the U.S. Archives . . . of all U.S. lands—passed into the hands of individuals."
U.S. Archives, "Teaching with Documents: The Homestead Act of 1862," found online at www.archives.gov/education/lessons/homestead-act/.

97. The rest of Lincoln's legislative agenda . . . to be permanently instituted in 1913).
On this, see Sandburg, *Abraham Lincoln*, p. 383; Goodwin, *Team of Rivals*, pp. 460–61; and Heather Cox Richardson, *West from Appomattox: The Reconstruction of America After the Civil War* (New Haven, CT: Yale University Press, 2007), pp. 24–25.

98. In Richardson's view . . . both rich and poor—that inhabited society's margins.
    Cox Richardson, *West from Appomattox*, p. 1.
98. Its erosion—both perceived and real . . . what Fareed Zakaria calls the "rise of the rest."
    Zakaria, *Post-American World*, pp. 1–2.

The American System Matured, Then Extrapolated
101. If you view the American Civil War . . . opening to America in the early 1970s.
    Kagan, *Dangerous Nation*, p. 265.
103. Railroad companies dominated the economic . . . other way around in the West).
    On these phenomena, see Cox Richardson, *West from Appomattox*, p. 208.
103. In the metaphors Thomas Friedman uses . . . production and international commerce.
    Thomas L. Friedman, *The Lexus and the Olive Tree* (New York: Random House, 1999).
103. As historian Edmund Morris notes . . . cities of salt and cloth and corn and copper."
    Edmund Morris, *Theodore Rex* (New York: Modern Library, 2001), pp. 28–29.
103. Consider this account from Morris . . . under the efficient glare of Edison light bulbs."
    Morris, *Theodore Rex*, pp. 20–21.
104. If Americans today fear that China . . . and settle Britain's national debt in the bargain."
    Morris, *Theodore Rex*, p. 21.
104. But before America could display . . . latter decades of the nineteenth century.
    Kagan, *Dangerous Nation*, p. 65.
105. After the Civil War . . . never met their companies' owners face-to-face.
    See Cox Richardson, *West from Appomattox*, p. 93.
105. Before the Civil War, public corporations . . . private ambition was enough.
    See Cox Richardson, *West from Appomattox*, p. 131.
105. Despite the incredible rise of disposable income . . . in our nation's history.
    See Cox Richardson, *West from Appomattox*, pp. 189–92. The inequality of income analysis comes from Benjamin Friedman, *The Moral Consequences of Economic Growth* (New Haven, CT: Yale University Press, 2005), p. 112.
105. In the 1880s, it was common for one-quarter . . . Only half made it to the age of five.
    See Cox Richardson, *West from Appomattox*, pp. 97–98.
105. Not surprisingly, hard times amid apparent plenty . . . extended into the mid-1890s.
    See Friedman, *Moral Consequences of Economic Growth*, pp. 120–24.
106. When TR was sworn into office . . . experienced individual ever to serve as president.
    See Edmund Morris, *The Rise of Theodore Roosevelt* (New York: Modern Library, 2001), pp. xi–xxiv. Morris's prologue is the hands-down best preface to a biography that I have ever read—a real masterpiece in miniature. What follows naturally relies heavily on Morris's brilliant two-volume biography (the second being titled *Theodore Rex*).
107. Despite his reputation as a "cowboy" . . . across his seven-plus years as president.
    A point made by Morris, *Rise of Theodore Roosevelt*, p. xvi.
108. Following Frederick Jackson Turner's notion . . . would be authoritarianism.
    On the "stationary state," see Morris, *Rise of Theodore Roosevelt*, pp. 478–84.
108. The defensive impulse was external . . . waste spaces are being settled and seeded."
    Quoted in Morris, *Rise of Theodore Roosevelt*, p. 481.
108. That "new and dark power" . . . the trusts and combinations of the imperial age.
    Quoted in Morris, *Theodore Rex*, p. 27.
108. When a younger Teddy declared . . . made available to all *Americans*—north and south.
    Quoted in Morris, *Rise of Theodore Roosevelt*, p. 473.
109. It's interesting to note . . . popularized the term "Middle East").
    Oren, *Power, Faith, and Fantasy*, p. 307.
109. Mahan's notion of sea commerce "pressure points" . . . most of the Cold War.
    On Mahan, I suggest the "Introduction" by Antony Preston in Alfred Thayer Mahan,

The Influence of Sea Power upon History, 1660–1805 (New York: Gallery Books, 1980), pp. 6–11.

109. By progressively extending . . . keeping sea lanes open for everyone's trade.
For an excellent history of how the Dutch ceded that role to the British, who in turn ceded it to the Americans, see Mead, *God and Gold*, pp. 85–101.

109. America consumes about one-tenth of the Persian Gulf's oil; the rest goes elsewhere.
See data from the U.S. Department of Energy's *International Energy Outlook 2006* report (the 2007 report did not include a chart on global oil trade), found online at www.eia.doe.gov/oiaf/archive/ieo06/pdf/tbl4.pdf.

110. As he himself declared, "I could not ask a finer . . . for my administrations."
Quoted in Morris, *Theodore Rex*, p. 549.

110. Roosevelt was a depressed, volatile . . . "the most dangerous man of the age."
Quoted in Morris, *Rise of Theodore Roosevelt*, p. xv.

110. Plus, quite frankly, given his seven years . . . that makes for effective diplomacy."
Quoted in Morris, *Rise of Theodore Roosevelt*, p. xvi.

110. I don't pretend that Roosevelt was anything . . . adjudicators that kept the game fair.
Quoted in William H. Harbaugh, "About Theodore Roosevelt, Modern American Poetry website: www.english.uiuc.edu/maps/poets/a_f/espada/roosevelt_life.htm.

A Global American System, an American Century

2. Figure out your actual economic leverage going in and make it clear in negotiations.

118. It would, as Wilson confided to an aide, "force them to our way of thinking."
Kendrick A. Clements, *Woodrow Wilson: World Statesman* (Chicago: Ivan R. Dee, 1999), p. 185.

119. As historian Kendrick Clements notes . . . than its leaders imagined."
Clements, *Woodrow Wilson*, p. 201.

119. Lend-Lease was designed, as historian . . . in yet another costly European world war.
Elizabeth Borgwardt, *A New Deal for the World: America's Vision for Human Rights* (Cambridge, MA: Belknap Press, 2005), p. 100.

119. Robert Skidelsky, British biographer . . . America did right through WWI.
Robert Skidelsky, *John Maynard Keynes: A Biography*, vol. 3: *Fighting for Freedom, 1937–1946* (New York: Viking, 2000), p. 100; cited in Borgwardt, *New Deal for the World*, p. 101.

119. As President Calvin Coolidge coldly replied . . . "We hired them the money, didn't we?"
Robert Skidelsky, *John Maynard Keynes, 1883–1946: Economist, Philosopher, Statesman* (New York: Penguin Books, 2005), p. 320.

3. Build your domestic constituency from the start and keep it bipartisan.

120. Wilson, whose 1885 scholarly book . . . the highly partisan nature of that age.
Clements, *Woodrow Wilson*, p. 14.

120. It also reflected Wilson's personality . . . limit their number to an absolute minimum.
On these points, see Clements, *Woodrow Wilson*, pp. 147 and 186; and Brownstein, *Second Civil War*, pp. 44–45.

121. As Clements argues, "He wanted to be remembered . . . that structure needed to be.
Clements, *Woodrow Wilson*, p. 197.

121. As Walter Lippmann, a future influential . . . viewed it as the "great loot of the war."
Quoted in Oren, *Power, Faith, and Fantasy*, p. 377; see also pp. 376–87.

122. Senator Arthur Vandenberg . . . opponent in the Senate, Henry Cabot Lodge.
A point made by Borgwardt, *New Deal for the World*, p. 161.

4. Be realistic about what you can achieve by intervening.

123. Wilson's first-term effort to conclude . . . more such interventions in the future.
Quoted in Clements, *Woodrow Wilson*, p. 126; see also pp. 124–27 and 144–46.

123. In FDR's final address to Congress . . . and expect the world to survive again."
     Quoted in David McCullough, *Truman* (New York: Simon & Schuster, 1992), p. 337.
123. For FDR, leveraging the Soviet Union's manpower . . . war among all participants).
     For details, see the casualties graphic at the Wikipedia entry for World War II, found
     online at en.wikipedia.org/wiki/Image:World_War_II_Casualties2.svg.
124. Despite his lack of foreign policy experience . . . and launching the Berlin Airlift.
     Quoted in McCullough, *Truman*, p. 452.

5. No political solutions for economic problems.
125. In this amazingly prescient book . . . with one another and the larger world outside.
     On the question of German anger over the peace settlement, see John Maynard Keynes,
     The Economic Consequences of the Peace (New York: BiblioBazaar, 2007), pp. 133–34,
     154–55, and 165–67.
125. In short, "Europe before the war" . . . and great havoc inflicted upon global order.
     On this, see Keynes, *Economic Consequences of the Peace*, pp. 15–24.
126. In less than thirty pages of text . . . *sine qua non* of a stable peace.
     On this, see Keynes, *Economic Consequences of the Peace*, pp. 155–83.
126. Wendell Willkie, Republican nominee . . . house built upon sand."
     Cited in Borgwardt, *New Deal for the World, p. 96.*

6. State your positive goals as early as possible.
127. Once into the fight, however, Wilson . . . the freedom of nations can make them."
     For the complete text of the speech, delivered April 2, 1917, find it online at www
     .firstworldwar.com/source/usawardeclaration.htm.
128. As Elizabeth Borgwardt argues . . . a modern declaration of *individual* independence.
     For quotes and overall analysis of the Atlantic Charter's historical importance, see
     Borgwardt, *New Deal for the World*, pp. 4–21.

7. Plan for the postwar right from the start.
129. Almost purposefully playing behind the curve . . . of the American Protective League.
     Quoted in Clements, *Woodrow Wilson*, p. 159.
129. Having made virtually no prewar attempt . . . new standard of "100% Americanism."
     See Clements, *Woodrow Wilson*, pp. 173–75.
130. His Pulitzer Prize–winning 1970 autobiography . . . "present at the creation."
     Dean Acheson, *Present at the Creation: My Years in the State Department* (New York:
     W.W. Norton, 1987).

8. Recognize that your recent experiences determine your usable skills.
131. The Great Depression, of course . . . the "economic laboratory of the world."
     See Skidelsky, *John Maynard Keynes*, pp. 506–7.
131. Paramount in their thinking . . . "one overriding aim: to do better than last time."
     Skidelsky, *John Maynard Keynes*, p. 669.
131. As policymakers on both sides . . . chosen withdrawal after the last world war.
     Skidelsky, *John Maynard Keynes*, p. 669.
132. Sensing that FDR did not have long to live . . . "the Missouri Compromise."
     Cited in McCullough, *Truman*, p. 320.
132. Even FDR admitted as late as July 1944, "I hardly know Truman."
     Quoted in McCullough, *Truman*, p. 292.
132. But here are the two key connections . . . postwar economic and security order.
     Quoted in McCullough, *Truman*, p. 219.
132. When stunned by his new responsibilities . . . his first day after being sworn in.
     Quoted in McCullough, *Truman*, p. 353.

132. As journalist Allen Drury noted . . . this first time, ask them to come to him."
Quoted in McCullough, *Truman*, p. 353.
132. This single request, coming in the highly charged . . . House minority leader.
Quoted in McCullough, *Truman*, pp. 468–69.
133. As McCullough writes of his subsequent inauguration . . . prosperity and power."
McCullough, *Truman*, p. 733.
133. McCullough notes of his inaugural address . . . 'people all over the world.' "
McCullough, *Truman*, pp. 729–31.
133. The *Washington Post* headline said it all: . . . and Abraham Lincoln!
Cited in McCullough, *Truman*, p. 731.

9. Once the war is won, the only alternative to withdrawal or domination is transformation.
133. After achieving decisive victory in war . . . other states within the order."
John G. Ikenberry, *After Victory: Institutions, Strategic Restraint and the Rebuilding of Order After Major Wars* (Princeton, NJ: Princeton University Press, 2001), p. 4; cited in Borgwardt, *New Deal for the World*, p. 15.
133. Woodrow Wilson knew, as Franklin Roosevelt . . . he sought to end that system.
Quoted in Oren, *Power, Faith, and Fantasy*, p. 456.
134. His replacement . . . "normalcy," withdrawing America from world power.
See Brownstein, *Second Civil War*, pp. 46–47.

11. Expect a challenge to your best-laid plans.
136. By making clear to the Soviets what behavior . . . starting with Truman's second term.
Acheson, *Present at the Creation*, p. 727.

12. Selling grand strategy is one thing, executing it is quite another.
138. As Acheson himself put it in his memoirs . . . amid the smoke and confusion of battle."
Acheson, *Present at the Creation*, p. 727.
138. Also, like any good grand strategist, Kennan . . . the hand of time a chance to work."
George F. Kennan, *Memoirs, 1925–1950* (Boston: Little, Brown, 1967), p. 364; see his chapter on the "X" article, pp. 354–67.
139. Here, the narrow orthodoxy of Nitze's . . . "loss" of China to Communism; and so on.
Quoted in Walter Isaacson and Evan Thomas, *The Wise Men: Six Friends and the World They Made* (New York: Simon & Schuster, 1997), p. 395.

13. If you want to make it stick, then the boys are never coming home.
140. What largely defined America's status . . . about 300,000 troops in Europe at all times.
For details, see Kane, "Global U.S. Troop Deployment, 1950–2003.

14. Nukes killed great-power war.
143. Gallup polls at the time indicated . . . would run for and win the presidency in 1952.
See McCullough, *Truman*, p. 848.

The Global American System Becomes Globalization
144. The market's "hidden hand" . . . dismember losers on a continuing basis.
On this, see James Surowiecki, *The Wisdom of Crowds: Why the Many Are Smarter Than the Few and How Collective Wisdom Shapes Business, Economies, Societies, and Nations* (New York: Doubleday, 2004).
145. We also allowed ourselves, as Kennan himself . . . "allies" in many instances.
Kennan, *Memoirs, 1925–1950*, p. 322.

148. In this instance, as eminent Soviet . . . their infamous wall the previous year.
    See Adam B. Ulam, *Expansion and Coexistence: Soviet Foreign Policy 1917–1973* (New
    York: Praeger Publishers, 1974), pp. 667–77; and Ulam, *Understanding the Cold War: A
    Historian's Personal Reflections* (Charlottesville, VA: Leopolis Press, 2000), p. 112.

149. By agreeing for the first time ever to limit . . . as Ulam states, "was finished."
    Ulam, *Understanding the Cold War*, p. 152.

150. Read the White House memoirs of both Nixon . . . America off the gold standard.
    Richard Nixon, *RN: The Memoirs of Richard Nixon* (New York: Simon & Schuster,
    1990); Henry Kissinger, *White House Years* (Boston: Little, Brown, 1979).

150. Nixon was intent from the start . . . and then under Johnson to the Vietnam war."
    Nixon, *Memoirs of Richard Nixon*, p. 343.

151. Like Nixon, Kissinger was wholly unsatisfied . . . assumes to have perfect vision."
    Kissinger, *White House Years*, p. 522.

151. Not given, as he put it . . . "sentimental conciliation" to "liturgical belligerence."
    Kissinger, *White House Years*, pp. 120 and 123.

151. With Nixon, he would establish concreteness . . . as the principles for engagement.
    Kissinger, *White House Years*, pp. 128–29.

151. Linkage, in Nixon's mind, was most important . . . compartmentalize areas of concern."
    Nixon, *Memoirs of Richard Nixon*, p. 346.

151. But as Kissinger points out . . . would be arranged by the superpowers alone.
    Kissinger, *White House Years*, p. 57.

151. In the piece he stated that America . . . cherish its hates and threaten its neighbors."
    See Richard Nixon, "Asia After Viet Nam," in Hamilton Fish Armstrong, ed., *Fifty Years
    of Foreign Affairs* (New York: Praeger Publishers, 1972), p. 395. The message was re-
    ceived, notes Margaret MacMillan, as Mao instructed Zhou to read the article; see her
    Nixon and Mao: The Week That Changed the World (New York: Random House, 2007),
    p. 166.

151. He put it more expansively . . . live in angry isolation."
    Find the entire address online at www.yale.edu/lawweb/avalon/presiden/inaug/
    nixon1.htm.

152. Once Nixon publicly announced . . . accomplished in Moscow than in Peking."
    Kissinger, *White House Years*, p. 766.

152. As Brezhnev later quipped, Nixon went . . . but to Moscow to do business."
    Kissinger, *White House Years*, p. 836.

152. Through the Helsinki Accords . . . "within as well as across national borders."
    Borgwardt, *New Deal for the World*, p. 6; see also her chapter "Forgotten Legacies of the
    Atlantic Charter," pp. 250–84.

152. As historian John Lewis Gaddis argues . . . with Moscow's official sanction.
    John Lewis Gaddis, *The Cold War: A New History* (New York: Penguin, 2006),
    pp. 204–7.

154. In that sense, as Ulam noted, SDI was a wonderful psychological weapon.
    See Ulam, *Understanding the Cold War*, pp. 242–43.

155. In his idealism, Gorbachev mistook . . . somebody they "could do business with."
    On this, see Nicholas Wapshott, *Ronald Reagan and Margaret Thatcher: A Political Mar-
    riage* (New York: Sentinel, 2007), pp. 226–50.

157. But of course that was a wildly . . . *The Return of History and the End of Dreams.*
    See Kagan, *Return of History*, pp. 3–10.

CHAPTER 4. THE ECONOMIC REALIGNMENT:
RACING TO THE BOTTOM OF THE PYRAMID

161. If our fifty members . . . Republic (VT) and Uzbekistan (WY).
    This listing comes from a map ("US States Renamed for Countries with Similar
    GDPs") created by The York Group International; it can be found online (with

neat annotation) at the Strange Maps site (strangemaps.wordpress.com/2007/06/10/131-us-states-renamed-for-countries-with-similar-gdps/).

The Undeniable Trajectory: Deng Chose Wisely

165. Deng's dream for China in 1979 . . . by the middle of the twenty-first century."
Michael E. Marti, *China and the Legacy of Deng Xiaoping: From Communist Revolution to Capitalist Evolution* (Washington, DC: Brassey's, 2002), p. xiii.

166. Deng's ultimate dream, as Marti notes . . . a Chinese system for an Asian union.
Marti, *Deng Xiaoping*, p. 3.

166. As Marti writes: "With a weak Russia . . . must be pushed to the limit."
Marti, *Deng Xiaoping*, p. 153.

167. But China is also nowhere near becoming . . . and remain a single-party state.
For the most dark view, see James Mann, *The China Fantasy: How Our Leaders Explain Away Chinese Repression* (New York: Viking, 2007).

The American System Perturbed: 3 Billion New Capitalists Register Their Demand

169. That's how Wal-Mart, the single biggest . . . export market), keeps its prices so low.
Burton G. Malkiel and Patricia A. Taylor, *From Wall Street to the Great Wall: How Investors Can Profit from China's Booming Economy* (New York: W. W. Norton, 2008), p. 254.

169. Now, thanks to significant flows . . . great majority of China's hardware IT exports.
See Malkiel and Taylor, *Wall Street to the Great Wall*, pp. 248–49.

170. China's explosive economic growth . . . suck in resources from all over the world.
For a good overview of this phenomenon, along with its long-term environmental impact, see Jared Diamond, *Collapse: How Societies Choose to Fail or Succeed* (New York: Viking, 2005), pp. 358–77. See also Edward McBride, "China's Quest for Resources: A Ravenous Dragon; China's Hunger for Natural Resources Has Set Off a Global Commodity Boom," *The Economist*, March 13, 2008.

170. As a longtime China-watcher, James Kynge . . . possess the natural resources of one.
James Kynge, *China Shakes the World: A Titan's Rise and Troubled Future—and the Challenge for America* (Boston: Houghton Mifflin, 2006), p. 133.

170. Take, for instance, China's relationship . . . Hezbollah as it faces Israeli forces.
For a sense of how such technology flows begin, see Parag Khanna, *Second World: Empires and Influence in the New Global Order* (New York: Random House, 2008), p. 208.

171. When bad things happen . . . you should fear, because it needs that oil.
See Anita Powell, "Ethiopian Rebels Kill 74 in Oil Attack," Associated Press, April 24, 2007.

171. You know that Thomas Friedman . . . America funding both sides of the "war on terror"?
See Thomas L. Friedman, "No Mullah Left Behind," *New York Times*, February 13, 2005.

172. According to longtime observer Edward Luce . . . like driving an unlicensed taxi.
Edward Luce, *In Spite of the Gods: The Strange Rise of Modern India* (New York: Doubleday, 2007), p. 47.

173. Shanghai already has twice as many skyscrapers . . . and plans another thousand.
See David Barboza, "China Builds Its Dreams and Some Fear a Bubble," *New York Times*, October 18, 2005.

173. There's also a sexual revolution . . . *Father Knows Best* to *Sex and the City*.
For examples, see "China Discovers Hot Sheets Motels," Newsmax.com, March 2, 2008, found online at www.newsmax.com/international/chinas_sexual_revolution/2008/03/02/77153.html; and Maureen Fan, "Too Much Information?: A Radio Advice Program Tests China's Taboo on Talking Sex," *Washington Post*, September 11, 2006.

173. As the writer and political scientist Ian Bremmer says . . . all those camera phones!
Ian Bremmer, *The J Curve: A New Way to Understand Why Nations Rise and Fall* (New York: Simon & Schuster, 2006), p. 18.

173. In terms of corruption, Beijing remains . . . nineteenth century, and that's not good.
For the best analysis of how corruption limits further economic development in China, see Minxin Pei, *China's Trapped Transition: The Limits of Developmental Autocracy* (Cambridge, MA: Harvard University Press, 2006).

173. Citizens are simply growing angrier . . . downtown Shanghai to the suburbs.
For example, see Howard W. French, "Shanghai Rail-Line Plan Fuels Middle-Class Protest," *New York Times*, January 27, 2008.

174. The Sichuan earthquake of 2008 . . . Communist Party scrambled to accommodate.
For example, see Andrew Jacobs, "Parents' Grief Turns to Rage at Chinese Officials," *New York Times*, May 28, 2008; and the *New York Times* online slide show found at www.nytimes.com/slide show/2008/05/28/world/20080528QUAKE_6.html.

174. A couple of decades ago, China's courts . . . more than 5 million cases a year.
Cited in Mure Dickie, "A Potential Threat to Stability?: The Government Has Created Popular Expectations Without Fulfilling Them," *Financial Times*, November 8, 2005.

174. Corruption already consumes upward . . . China's gross domestic product.
An OECD report estimate, cited in James Kynge, *China Shakes the World*, p. 201.

174. The 2008 Beijing Olympics was . . . they had sold to foreign broadcasters.
See Peter Burrows, "Why China Is Finally Tackling Video Piracy: Beijing Wants to Prove It Can Protect the Lucrative Broadcasting Rights for the Summer Games," *Business-Week*, June 9, 2008.

174. As sociologist Juan Enriquez writes . . . so many people out of poverty as quickly."
Juan Enriquez, *The Untied States of America: Polarization, Fracturing, and Our Future* (New York: Crown Publishers, 2005), p. 67.

The New Rules: China Breaks the Mold or Merely Recasts It?

175. As business academics William Baumol . . . four types of capitalism operating today.
See William J. Baumol, Robert E. Litan, and Carl J. Schramm, *Good Capitalism, Bad Capitalism, and the Economics of Growth and Prosperity* (New Haven, CT: Yale University Press, 2007), pp. 60–92.

176. In their book, Baumol et al. argue . . . once their innovations mature.
See Baumol et al., *Good Capitalism, Bad Capitalism*, pp. 85–92.

176. Thus, China's strategy seems clear . . . one-third of China's gross domestic product today.
Baumol et al., *Good Capitalism, Bad Capitalism*, p. 165.

177. This strategy of "incremental change . . . entrepreneurial small firms.
Baumol et al., *Good Capitalism, Bad Capitalism*, p. 165.

177. As Fareed Zakaria notes in *The Post-American* . . . that the country has defied this trend."
Zakaria, *Post-American World*, pp. 100–101.

The New Normal: Defaulting to the Beijing Consensus

177. Neo-Marxists have long argued . . . budget deficits over the course of the Cold War.
A classic recent historical account in this vein can be found in Giovanni Arrighi, *Adam Smith in Beijing: Lineages of the Twenty-first Century* (New York: Verso, 2007); see especially Part II: "Tracking Global Turbulence" and Part III: "Hegemony Unraveling" (pp. 99–274). To read it is to visit another universe of economic interpretation.

181. This is especially true for China . . . all those workers coming into the mix.
By 2030, China will have 400 million senior citizens, according to Chinese government estimates cited in Sheng-Wei Wang, *China's Ascendancy: An Opportunity or a Threat?*

What Every American Should Know About China (Washington, DC: International Publishing House for China's Culture, 2007), p. 269. As for the job-creation estimate in the Middle East/North Africa, I attended a Jordanian FDI conference at the Dead Sea in February 2008, where that number was repeated by speakers more times than I can remember, indicating that—true or not—that's the expectation among business and political leaders.

183. Not surprisingly . . . and, in particular, al Qaeda's brutality.
See "Global Opinion Trends 2002–2007: A Rising Tide Lifts Mood in the Developing World; Sharp Decline in Support for Suicide Bombing in Muslim Countries (47-Nation Pew Global Attitudes Survey)" at the Pew Global Attitudes Project site, found online at pewglobal.org/reports/pdf/257.pdf. The general rule is, the poorer the country, the more positively globalization polls.

183. The World Bank recently recalculated the . . . 40 percent smaller than we imagined.
On this, see Walter Russell Mead, "The Great Fall of China: Revised GDP Calculations Show That Beijing Isn't the Giant We Thought It Was," *Los Angeles Times*, December 30, 2007.

184. The so-called Washington Consensus of the 1990s . . . emulate our success of that era.
On this, see George Lodge and Craig Wilson, *A Corporate Solution to Global Poverty: How Multinationals Can Help the Poor and Invigorate Their Own Legitimacy* (Princeton, NJ: Princeton University Pres, 2006), pp. 37–38 and 122–25.

185. In many ways, then, the so-called Beijing Consensus . . . "consultative" approach.
On this, see Joshua Kurlantzick, *Charm Offensive: How China's Soft Power Is Transforming the World* (New Haven, CT: Yale University Press, 2007), pp. 1–12 and 56–58.

185. Some globalization experts, such as Parag Khanna . . . consensus-style rule.
Khanna, *Second World*, pp. xvi–xviii.

The Global Accelerant: Rushing to Settle Frontiers

187. Europe, or more to the point . . . the United States, Australia, and New Zealand.
On the Dutch influence in early America, a fantastically entertaining history can be found in Russell Shorto, *The Island at the Center of the World: The Epic Story of Dutch Manhattan and the Forgotten Colony That Shaped America* (New York: Random House, 2005). During my last trip (June 2008) consulting with the national security elements of the Dutch government, I was given the book as a gift—and perhaps a none-too-subtle hint that I need to increase my appreciation for the Netherlands' role in creating American "exceptionalism" (especially on religious tolerance)!

187. In these sparsely populated . . . indigenous populations to assimilation or death.
On the original iteration of globalization, see Tim Blanning, *The Pursuit of Glory: Europe 1648–1815* (New York: Viking, 2007).

189. Looking back over the spread of modern capitalism . . . lagging India by example.
On the Anglosphere concept, see James C. Bennett, *The Anglosphere Challenge: Why the English-Speaking Nations Will Lead the Way in the Twenty-first Century* (Lanham, MD: Rowman & Littlefield Publishers, 2004).

189. There are roughly 300 FTAs in the world today . . . negotiating upward of 30 FTAs.
Cited in the editorial "Trading Without America," *Wall Street Journal*, August 7, 2007.

190. By most calculations, China has . . . any nation has ever aged in human history.
Again, see Wang, *China's Ascendancy*, p. 269.

190. Toyota and Honda were forced . . . that source local, build local, and sell local.
Samuel Palmisano, "Multinationals Have Been Superseded," *Financial Times*, June 12, 2006.

191. If you tell me that Asian religious . . . let's facilitate that process the best we can.
See Rob Moll, "Missions Incredible: South Korea Sends More Missionaries Than Any Country but the U.S.: And It Won't Be Long Before It's Number One," *Christianity*

Today, March 1, 2006, found online at www.christianitytoday.com/ct/2006/march/ 16.28.html.

191. If you tell me Chinese farmers . . . homesteaders once helped trigger in America.
See "Landless Chinese Farmers Migrate to Africa in Search of Agricultural Op-portunities," *BioPact*, December 2, 2007, found online at biopact.com/2007/12/ landless-chinese-farmers-migrate-to.html.

191. Finally, if you tell me the global economy . . . globalization's networks faster.
See Sarah Childress, "Investors Go to Treacherous Places Seeking Returns: Funds Pour Money into Zimbabwe on the Theory Mugabe Can't Rule Forever, Nation Will Re-bound," *Wall Street Journal*, November 17–18, 2007; Joanna Chung, "Investors in Push into Africa: Commodities Boom Flags Growth Potential; Private Capital Flows Triple Since 2003," *Financial Times*, November 19, 2007; and Joanna Chung, "Investors' En-thusiasm Grows for the New Frontiers," *Financial Times*, November 20, 2007.

191. So can greed save Africa, as one *BusinessWeek* story asked a while back?
Roben Farzad, "Can Greed Save Africa: Fearless Investing Is Succeeding Where Aid Often Hasn't," *BusinessWeek*, December 10, 2007.

192. Economist Paul Collier, for example . . . more than periodic "profit-taking" exercises.
Paul Collier, *The Bottom Billion: Why the Poorest Countries Are Failing and What Can Be Done About It* (New York: Oxford University Press, 2007), pp. 99–123.

192. As far as where to direct . . . that specifically targets those issues is most warranted.
See Jeffrey D. Sachs, *The End of Poverty: Economic Possibilities for Our Time* (New York: Penguin Press, 2005), pp. 188–209.

193. Longtime aid expert William Easterly . . . difficult choices up to Africans themselves.
William Easterly, *The White Man's Burden: Why the West's Efforts to Aid the Rest Have Done So Much Ill and So Little Good* (New York: Penguin Press, 2006), pp. 249–58; on aid "vouchers," see his point on pp. 376–79.

193. As Francis Fukuyama has argued . . . *attract foreign direct investment.*
Francis Fukuyama, speech to annual Society for International Development confer-ence (Washington, DC, chapter), February 6, 2007.

193. As Easterly notes, China once had all the same . . . efforts to shape events there.
Easterly, *White Man's Burden*, pp. 351–55.

193. Deng, as Easterly describes him, was a natural "searcher" instead of a "planner."
On the difference, see Easterly, *White Man's Burden*, pp. 3–7.

193. As Deng's famous maxim put it . . . the cat is black or white, as long as it catches mice."
Wang renders the same saying as "Black cat, white cat, all that matters is that it catches mice"; see *China's Ascendancy*, p. 45.

193. The simplest definition of good government . . . pothole fixed in front of your house.
Easterly, *White Man's Burden*, p. 173.

194. So if we look at Jeffrey Sachs's list . . . (e.g., property and contract laws).
They are human capital, business capital, infrastructure, natural capital, and public in-stitutional capital; see Sachs, *End of Poverty*, p. 244.

194. Let the business capital (including the 40 percent . . . P2P programs like Kiva.
The 40 percent estimate comes from Collier, *Bottom Billion*, p. 92. On the attractive-ness of P2P models, see Easterly, *White Man's Burden*, pp. 376–77.

194. Easterly calls this phenomenon . . . but it's a truism for any frontier environment.
See Easterly, *White Man's Burden*, pp. 81–82.

194. This is the so-called bamboo network.
See Easterly, *White Man's Burden*, p. 83.

195. Most Western businessmen . . . never known the premarket system.
I got this idea from Fred Laurenzo, who sits on the board of Enterra Solutions LLC and has conducted business overseas, but particularly in China. I first used the concept in "The Chinese Are Our Friends: . . . Despite Everything You Hear from the Fearmongers

at the Pentagon. Don't Listen to Them. The Sino-American Partnership Will Define the Twenty-first Century," *Esquire*, November 2005, found online at www.esquire.com/features/essay/ESQ0207CHINA.

195. Economist George Ayittey makes similar arguments . . . clarity and objectivity."
George B. N. Ayittey, *Africa Unchained: The Blueprint for Africa's Future* (New York: Palgrave MacMillan, 2005), pp. xix–xx.

The Inescapable Realignment: Remapping Fake States

196. Easterly's research on artificial states . . . with squiggly natural borders.
Easterly, *White Man's Burden*, pp. 290–93.

197. Collier says that fifty-eight countries . . . those recent globalizers.
See Collier for the basic characteristics of the bottom billion, in *Bottom Billion*, pp. 3–13 and 79–96. Collier does not identify his fifty-eight states. Of the bottom billion, Collier says 73 percent have recently suffered a civil war, 29 percent are resource-deprived, 30 percent are landlocked and resource-deprived and have bad neighbors, and 76 percent have suffered long periods of bad government.

197. Only one percent of the Functioning Core's . . . simply don't become countries."
Collier, *Bottom Billion*, p. 57.

197. As the former director of research for the World Bank puts it . . . they are falling apart."
Collier, *Bottom Billion*, p. x.

197. As Easterly pointed out in his magnificent book . . . literacy, and clean water.
Easterly, *White Man's Burden*, pp. 292–93.

198. According to Easterly's research . . . some colonial master took a ruler to a map.
See Alberto Alesina, William Easterly, and Janina Matuszeski, "Artificial States," National Bureau of Economic Research Working Paper 12328, found online at www.nber.org/papers/w12328.

199. If applied prophylactically . . . marines courageously proved in Sierra Leone in 1999.
On this story, see "British Marines Leave Sierra Leone," BBC News "On This Day," June 15, 2000, found online at news.bbc.co.uk/onthisday/hi/dates/stories/june/15/newsid_2512000/2512669.stm.

The Better Normal: Racing to the Bottom of the Pyramid

202. Prahalad's description . . . fascinating on many levels.
C. K. Prahalad, *The Fortune at the Bottom of the Pyramid: Eradicating Poverty Through Profits* (Upper Saddle River, NJ: Wharton School Publishing, 2005).

202. First, he alerts us to the growing reality . . . thanks to globalization's advance.
See Prahalad, *Bottom of the Pyramid*, pp. 3–12.

202. Second, Prahalad reminds us that . . . couldn't afford your standard large purchase.
See Prahalad, *Bottom of the Pyramid*, pp. 65–66; the Singer example comes from the talk I attended several years back.

202. How to get the product in front of "media-dark" . . . traveling salesman.
See Prahalad, *Bottom of the Pyramid*, pp. 12–13.

202. Third and most important to American grand strategy . . . democracy inside the Gap.
See Prahalad, *Bottom of the Pyramid*, pp. 109–12.

202. By tapping into this "latent market . . . by the state.
See Prahalad, *Bottom of the Pyramid*, pp. 77–98; the quote comes from p. 5.

203. The bottom of the pyramid . . . the essence of the economic frontier setting.
Prahalad, *Bottom of the Pyramid*, p. 54.

203. One example Prahalad cites in his book . . . create cheap but highly absorbent diapers.
Prahalad, *Bottom of the Pyramid*, pp. 48–49.

204. As Prahalad sums up: "Innovation in bottom . . . pyramid markets is increasingly critical."
Prahalad, *Bottom of the Pyramid*, pp. 27–28.

204. We will add about one billion people . . . percentage share of the world population.
See Naim, "Can the World Afford a Middle Class?"
205. According to a new World Bank . . . markets, i.e., the West.
See Harry G. Broadman, *Africa's Silk Road: China and India's New Economic Frontier* (Washington, DC: World Bank, 2007), pp. 1–40.
206. Yes, in the grand scheme . . . far more than resources."
Broadman, *Africa's Silk Road*, p. 2.
206. China and India have become . . . overlapping free-trade areas.
Broadman, *Africa's Silk Road*, pp. 177-83.
206. World trade has more than tripled . . . globalization's rapid advance around the planet.
Lodge and Wilson, *Corporate Solution to Global Poverty*, pp. 12–13.

CHAPTER 5. THE DIPLOMATIC REALIGNMENT: REBRANDING THE TEAM OF RIVALS

208. Its *why* must be inculcated in . . . which levers of power to pull—and when.
I spend a lot of time studying why some ideals succeed while others do not. Some great books in this regard include Peter F. Drucker, *The Essential Drucker: The Best of Sixty Years of Peter Drucker's Essential Writings on Management* (New York: HarperCollins, 2001); Chip Heath and Dan Heath, *Made to Stick: Why Some Ideas Survive and Others Die* (New York: Random House, 2007); Frans Johansson, *The Medici Effect: What Elephants & Epidemics Can Teach Us About Innovation* (Cambridge, MA: Harvard Business School Press, 2006); John Kao, *Jamming: The Art and Discipline of Business Creativity* (New York: Harper Business, 1996); and Peter Schwartz, *The Art of the Long View: Planning for the Future in an Uncertain World* (New York: Doubleday, 1991).
209. As Parag Khanna argues . . . connectivity) has been effectively erased.
Khanna, *Second World*, pp. xix–xxiii.

The Undeniable Trajectory: The "Global War on Terror"
210. If we admit that we cannot kill them faster . . . demand for personal liberty.
Bremmer, *J Curve*, p. 272.
213. Our intelligence community's November 2007 estimate . . . building the "bullets."
"National Intelligence Estimate: Iran: Nuclear Intentions and Capabilities," Office of the Director of National Intelligence, November 2007, available online at www.dni .gov/press_releases/20071203_release.pdf.

The American System Perturbed: The Big Bang Launched
216. According to two former National Security Council . . . possible rapprochement.
On this story, see John H. Richardson, "The Secret History of the Impending War with Iran That the White House Doesn't Want You to Know," *Esquire*, November 2007.
217. From a December 2001 memo stating . . . We won't try to build on it."
Quoted in Richardson, "Secret History of the Impending War with Iran."
217. Ironically enough, thanks to our poorly run . . . favoring American firms.
On this, see Jim Michaels, "Foreign Firms Investing in Iraq: U.S. Companies Slow to Make the Move," *USA Today*, June 17, 2008; and "Iraq Signs $3 Billion Oil Deal with China," *CNN*, August 30, 2008, found online at edition.cnn.com/2008/BUSINESS/ 08/30/iraq.china.oil.deal/.
218. This is not a fantastic scenario . . . perceptions of Iran remain hopelessly outdated.
Nasr, *Revival*, pp. 21–29 and 227–54.
219. As Beijing did then, Tehran now shows . . . Persian Gulf, Central and South Asia).
On this, see MacMillan, *Nixon and Mao*, and Stephen Kinzer, "A New Partner in the Mideast," *Boston Globe*, March 14, 2008.

219. Second, despite the obvious control . . . allowed to retire or even continue political life.
On this, see Ali Gheissari and Vali Nasr, *Democracy in Iran: History and the Quest for Liberty* (New York: Oxford University Press, 2006).

The New Rules: From Indispensable Superpower to Insolvent Leviathan
220. Madeleine Albright, secretary of state to Bill Clinton . . . "the indispensable nation."
As Albright stated, "If we have to use force, it is because we are America! We are the indispensable nation. We stand tall. We see further into the future"; see "Secretary of State Madeleine K. Albright Interview on NBC-TV *The Today Show* with Matt Lauer," February 19, 1998, as released by the Office of the Spokesman, U.S. Department of State.
220. Where Clinton tried to do too little . . . need the world's support to succeed."
Richard N. Haass, *The Opportunity: America's Moment to Alter History's Course* (New York: Public Affairs, 2005), pp. ix–x and 27.
221. Part of the problem was the Bush administration's desire . . . to be an additional crisis.
Haass, *Opportunity*, pp. 3–8.
221. The dream, of course, is of energy independence . . . goal that makes zero sense.
On this, see Robert Bryce, *Gusher of Lies: The Dangerous Delusions of Energy Independence* (New York: Public Affairs, 2008).
222. Wish away enough reasons for Western . . . Middle East into Central Africa.
One of the most interesting such counterfactual examinations is found in Graham Fuller, "A World Without Islam," *Foreign Policy*, January 2008.
222. As Ian Bremmer wisely . . . playing field available to them: insurgency and terror."
Bremmer, *J Curve*, p. 276; see also pp. 270–77.
223. This is a Cold War storyline . . . hermetically sealed off from one another.
On this, see Michael T. Klare, *Rising Power and Shrinking Planet: The New Geopolitics of Energy* (New York: Metropolitan Books, 2008); but note that even here, Klare, a longtime proponent of this conflict paradigm, sees little choice but for America and China to cooperate on energy in the future (p. 249).
223. Right now, the United States . . . China's dependence continues to grow rapidly.
See U.S. Department of Energy, *International Energy Outlook 2006*, found online at www.eia.doe.gov/oiaf/archive/ieo06/pdf/tbl4.pdf.
224. The strategic horizon . . . operational concepts, through the next 20 years."
Find the report online at www.globalsecurity.org/military/library/report/2008/2008-prc-military-power04.htm.

The New Normal: America the Contained
226. The White House, thus challenged . . . opposition to military strikes on Iran.
See Thomas P. M. Barnett, "The Man Between War and Peace," *Esquire*, March 2008, found online at www.esquire.com/features/fox-fallon.
229. As Gustavo de las Casas . . . focus their energies on bettering their countries."
Gustavo de las Casas, "Is Nationalism Good for You?," *Foreign Policy*, March–April 2008.
229. There, as longtime observer Dmitri Trenin . . . expanding NATO/EU).
Dmitri Trenin, "Russia Redefines Itself and Its Relations with the West," *Washington Quarterly*, Spring 2007, p. 95.
229. As Trenin puts it, Russian leaders . . . separated primarily by the power they wield.
Trenin, "Russia Redefines Itself and Its Relations with the West," pp. 96–97.
230. As such, we make an easy target . . . in Russia than in most European nations.
On this observation, I am indebted to Lilia Shevtsova, senior associate (Moscow Office), Carnegie Endowment for International Peace; see her *Russia—Lost in Transition: The Yeltsin and Putin Legacies* (Washington, DC: Carnegie Endowment for International Peace, 2007).

The Global Accelerant: Soft-Power Balancing

233. This is the essential forecast of Parag Khanna . . . networks managing Asia and the rest.
See Khanna, *Second World*, pp. ix–xxvii and 321–41.
234. If so, Joshua Kurlantzick's recent book *Charm Offensive* . . . tools to implement that strategy."
Kurlantzick, *Charm Offensive*, p. xi.
235. The self-limiting aspect of this process . . . business interests and expatriates abroad.
"With great power comes great responsibility" was made famous in the origin of Spider-Man: Stan Lee, *Amazing Fantasy* #15 (New York: Marvel Comics, August 1962).
235. The downside is, as Kurlantzick points out . . . regulatory standards in general.
Kurlantzick, *Charm Offensive*, pp. 148–75.
235. Naturally, as Kurlantzick points out, the local backlash . . . just beginning.
Kurlantzick, *Charm Offensive*, pp. 197–225.

The Inescapable Realignment: Rebranding a Team of Rivals

238. When Doris Kearns Goodwin described . . . can also be impressive political resources."
Goodwin, *Team of Rivals*, p. xvii.
239. Again, some will say we must stick with . . . America see the world differently.
See Kagan, *Return of History*, pp. 53–80. The "previous claim" is found in his 2003 book, *Of Paradise and Power.*
239. But frankly, we'll be waiting for those Godots forever.
Samuel Beckett, *Waiting for Godot: A Tragicomedy in Two Acts* (New York: Grove Press 1954).
240. Nayan Chanda's history of globalization . . . private security corporations.
Nayan Chanda, *Bound Together: How Traders, Preachers, Adventurers, and Warriors Shaped Globalization* (New Haven, CT: Yale University Press, 2007).
240. Whether it's an Indian industrialist who wants to build . . . will not be denied.
On the car, see "The One-Lakh Car: A 'People's Car' from India; Tata Motors Reveals a Dirt-Cheap Model," *The Economist*, January 10, 2008.
241. As economist Adam Lerrick . . . these latest lenders "rogue creditors."
See Adam Lerrick, "World Bank Weary: Private Lenders Channel 300 Times More Capital to Developing Nations," *Wall Street Journal*, October 19, 2007.
241. As *Financial Times* bureau chief Edward Luce writes . . . superpower status."
Luce, *In Spite of the Gods*, p. 7.
241. A while back I had the opportunity to have dinner . . . risen to world-power status.
The documentary series was titled "The Rise of Great Nations." It was aired in 2006–7. As Fareed Zakaria notes, "The episodes on the United States, for example, deal extensively with Theodore and Franklin Roosevelt's programs to regulate and tame capitalism"; see *Post-American World*, p. 107.
242. Yes, many American national security . . . "hedge our bets" in the meantime.
A classic example of this thinking can be found in Michael J. Mazarr, "The Folly of 'Asymmetric War,'" *Washington Quarterly*, Summer 2008.
243. As one Army War College professor . . . has argued, "One NATO is not enough."
Joseph Núñez, "One NATO Is Not Enough," *New York Times*, January 27, 2007.
243. But here's the main reason . . . discipline, not survival.
I got this distinction from Shelby Steele, "Obama Is Right on Iran," *Wall Street Journal*, November 26, 2007.

The Better Normal: The Service-Oriented Alliance

245. Service-oriented architecture . . . software packages and hardwired applications.
This is a huge and evolving subject. For two easy-entry approaches, see the Wikipedia

entry on SOA, found online at en.wikipedia.org/wiki/Service-oriented_architecture; and a great op-ed by Don J. Rippert, "The Building Blocks of a Simpler Future Are in Place," *Financial Times*, May 10, 2006.

247. Again, some readers will bristle at such language . . . a fantastic sum total to this vision. See Joseph E. Stiglitz and Linda J. Bilme, *The Three Trillion Dollar War: The True Cost of the Iraq Conflict* (New York: W.W. Norton, 2008).

250. And no, accepting this pathway . . . "post-American world," in Fareed Zakaria's analysis. See Zakaria, *Post-American World.*

251. Of his cabinet filled with past . . . "They will be just as likely to eat each other up." Quoted in Sandburg, *Abraham Lincoln*, p. 216.

CHAPTER 6. THE SECURITY REALIGNMENT:
REDISCOVERING DIPLOMACY, DEFENSE, AND DEVELOPMENT

253. Listen to Marine Corps general James Mattis . . . it was Spain, right? Well, Iraq is ours." Barnett, "Monks of War."

The Undeniable Trajectory: The Miseducation of Colin Powell

254. As he put it . . . realization of your political objectives, whatever they might be." Kennan, *Memoirs, 1925–1950*, p. 309.

255. The American military's fix . . . "A war is a war is a war," and let it go at that. The phrase comes from Harry G. Summers Jr., "A War Is a War Is a War," in Loren B. Thompson, ed., *Low Intensity Conflict* (Lexington, MA: Rowman & Littlefield, 1989), pp. 27–49. Summers, of course, wrote the Vietnam classic that defined this viewpoint for the Powell generation: Harry G. Summers Jr., *On Strategy: A Critical Analysis of the Vietnam War* (Novato, CA: Dell, 1984).

256. Suddenly, the military was back in frontier mode—back in "Injun country." On this, see Robert D. Kaplan, *Imperial Grunts: The American Military on the Ground* (New York: Random House, 2005), pp. 3–15.

257. Dissenting voices were quelled or cowed . . . he was not a grand strategist." Karen DeYoung, *Soldier: The Life of Colin Powell* (New York: Alfred A. Knopf, 2006), p. 163 (where Powell dismisses the idea that he needs a "view of the world" to function as Secretary of State), p. 194 (for his fears of repeating Vietnam), and p. 519 (for the DeYoung description).

258. Of Vietnam, Colin Powell had once said that . . . by their country's leaders." Quoted in DeYoung, *Soldier*, p. 91.

The American System Perturbed: The Lost Year in Iraq

259. The CPA was also guilty of operating . . . sobriquet of "Versailles on the Tigris." See Chandrasekaran, *Imperial Life*, pp. 9–28.

259. Back in Washington, the Pentagon's senior . . . "Inquiry" group during World War I. On this, see especially DeYoung, *Soldier*, pp. 458–62, where the author writes (461–62): "The Pentagon's civilian leadership—with energetic support from the vice president's office—restricted participation by Powell's Mideast experts in the Office of Reconstruction and Humanitarian Assistance (ORHA), set up by Defense Undersecretary Douglas Feith in February to manage civilian administration in postwar Iraq."

259. Under Rumsfeld, the Pentagon . . . detailed in their planning. But they weren't. On the exercises and poor postwar planning, see Ricks, *Fiasco*, pp. 72–81. Douglas Feith counters that perception in his book, *War and Decision*, detailing the Pentagon's plans (pp. 360–90) and dismissing the Future of Iraq project report's utility by saying it only "produced concept papers" (pp. 375–76). The problem with that defense is that Feith's own attempts to produce detailed planning struck most participants as PowerPoint slides and nothing else. Decrying "Rumsfeld's amateurish approach to war planning" (Ricks's

words), retired Army commander Andrew Bacevich said, "To imagine that PowerPoint slides can substitute for such means [detailed plans] is really the height of arrogance." Ricks says further, "It was like telling an automobile mechanic to use a manufacturer's glossy sales brochure to figure out how to repair an engine," see pp. 75–76.

259. As Thomas Ricks states . . . cost and difficulty of occupying the country."
Ricks, *Fiasco*, p. 4.

260. While Rumsfeld's "transformed" force toppled . . . length of time (a matter of weeks).
These are all Pentagon official estimates supplied by the Office of the Secretary of Defense.

260. Part of the invasion force's success . . . "cakewalk" was both accurate and irrelevant.
The infamous "cakewalk" statement was offered by Kenneth Adelman in his op-ed "Cakewalk in Iraq," *Washington Post*, February 13, 2002.

260. As Thomas Ricks argues . . . transformed force "didn't kill the enemy—it bypassed him."
Ricks, *Fiasco*, p. 127.

260. Because the U.S. military focused . . . "seemed to fall asleep at the wheel."
Ricks, *Fiasco*, p. 133.

261. As one soldier who fought in Operation Iraqi Freedom . . . to be doing some of that."
Fredric Smoler, "History and War: An Interview with Eliot Cohen," AmericanHeritage. com, found online at www.americanheritage.com/articles/web/20070312-eliot-cohen-military-theory-iraq-vietnam-antietam-guerrilla-warfare-nation-building-winston-churchill-military-history-condoleezza-rice.shtml.

261. In the Bosnian peacekeeping . . . occupying force within four months of "victory"!
See Ricks, *Fiasco*, pp. 96–106.

261. Such plans constituted a complete rejection . . . about 14 per 1,000 by the end of 2006.
I base these calculations on data provided by James T. Quinlivan, "Burden of Victory: The Painful Arithmetic of Stability Operations," *Rand Review*, Summer 2003, found online at www.rand.org/publications/randreview/issues/summer2003/burden.html. For more history, see John J. McGrath, *Boots on the Ground: Troop Density in Contingency Operations* (Fort Leavenworth, KS: Combat Studies Institute Press Occasional Paper 16, 2006).

261. Ironically, when U.S. forces surged . . . the form of private-sector contractors (182,000).
Cited in "Privatizing the War," *Time*, October 22, 2007.

262. Adding to the overall sloppiness . . . put it, "whatever could be outsourced was."
Chandrasekaran, *Emerald City*, p. 14.

262. Some of these wounds the U.S. military . . . allowing relatively open borders.
The list comes from Table 1–1: Successful and unsuccessful counterinsurgency operational practices, found on p. 51 of *Counterinsurgency Field Manual*.

264. In the end . . . eliminated the potential costs of coming clean.
See Woodward, *The War Within*, p. 71.

The New Rules: From the "Monks of War," a New COIN of the Realm

For background on this section, see my "Monks of War," *Esquire*, March 2005, found online at www.esquire.com/features/ESQ0306MONKS_214. Most of what follows was based on extensive interviews with several dozen senior military and civilian leaders starting in early 2005 (when I began research for a cover story on Secretary of Defense Donald Rumsfeld, "Old Man in a Hurry," July 2005) and extending through the spring of 2006.

265. Prior to World War I, the U.S. Army . . . smaller companies (100 to 200 soldiers).
For more details, see Bill Yenne, *Indian Wars: The Campaign for the American West* (Yardley, PA: Westholme, 2006); and Robert Wooster, "The Frontier Army and the Occupation of the West, 1865–1900," in *Armed Diplomacy: Two Centuries of American Campaigning* (Fort Leavenworth, KS: Combat Studies Institute Press, August 5–7, 2003), pp. 65–76.

266. As General Mattis likes to say, "Success is a poor teacher."
Quoted in Barnett, "Monks of War."

268. The timing of the piece . . . Army/Marine Corps *Counterinsurgency Field Manual*.
The U.S. Army/Marine Corps Counterinsurgency Field Manual (Chicago: University of Chicago Press, 2007).

268. So the sum total of these changes . . . counterinsurgency done right.
John A. Nagl, *Counterinsurgency Lessons from Malaya and Vietnam: Learning to Eat Soup with a Knife* (Chicago: University of Chicago Press, 2005).

268. To no one's surprise, Nagl ended up . . . weapons for counterinsurgents do not shoot").
Counterinsurgency Field Manual, pp. 47–51.

269. Now the long war was reformatting . . . in the early twentieth century.
The best recent source on this period is Max Boot, *The Savage Wars of Peace: Small Wars and the Rise of American Power* (New York: Basic Books, 2002). The historical learning curve culminates in the publication of the United States Marine Corps's *Small Wars Manual* (Manhattan, KS: Sunflower University Press, 2004).

269. As such, the new counterinsurgency . . . or at least understand what it's up against."
Counterinsurgency Field Manual, p. xxi.

The New Normal: The Long (Post)war

271. As historian Max Boot argued . . . of broken states in the manner of a social worker.
Max Boot, *The Savage Wars of Peace: Small Wars and the Rise of American Power* (New York: Basic Books, 2002), pp. 336–41.

271. Having said that, history tells us that most insurgencies fail . . . sufficient autonomy.
See Donald Stoker, "Insurgencies Rarely Win—and Iraq Won't Be Any Different (Maybe)," *Foreign Policy*, January 2007, found online at www.foreignpolicy.com/story/cms.php?story_id=3689.

271. As Sewall argues in her introduction . . . can yield success more rapidly and efficiently."
Counterinsurgency Field Manual, p. xxviii.

272. In this way, as Sewall notes . . . to the Geneva Conventions in this long (post)war.
Counterinsurgency Field Manual, pp. xxxiii–xxxv.

272. The dangers of "doctrinal miscegenation," as Sewall puts it, are real.
Counterinsurgency Field Manual, pp. xxii–xxiv.

273. Sarah Sewall declares that COIN . . . "favors peace over justice."
Counterinsurgency Field Manual, p. xxxix.

274. On the first point, consider this excerpt . . . clerks more in demand than riflemen."
David Galula, *Counterinsurgency Warfare: Theory and Practice* (New York: Frederick A. Praeger, 2005), p. 94.

274. As Galula avers wryly, "There is room . . . in conventional fights whenever possible).
Galula, *Counterinsurgency*, p. 96.

275. As for the logic of designating some . . . strike the American public as "compelling."
Counterinsurgency Field Manual, pp. xxxi and xl.

275. The Navy elevates humanitarian . . . unable to fill its own quota of personnel in Iraq.
On the Navy, see Lieutenant Commander David K. Richardson, USN, Major Lane V. Packwood, ID National Guard, and Daniel E. Aldana, "A Great White Fleet for the 21st Century," *U.S. Naval Institute Proceedings*, January 2008. On the Army, see Michael R. Gordon, "After Hard-Won Lessons, Army Doctrine Revised," *New York Times*, February 8, 2008. On the Marines, see Harold C. Hutchinson, "Landing Ships Outmaneuver Terrorists," *Strategy Page*, June 22, 2007, found online at www.strategypage.com/htmw/htmph/articles/20070622.aspx. On the Air Force, see Greg Jaffe, "To Fight Terrorists, Air Force Seeks a Bomb with Less Bang: It Cuts Collateral Damage by Using a Metal Powder Instead of Flying Shrapnel; Destroying the Blast Gauges," *Wall Street Journal*,

April 6, 2006. On the CRC, see Robin Wright, "Civilian Response Corps Gains Ground," *Washington Post*, February 15, 2008.

275. Meanwhile the burden of duty gets heavier . . . describes difficult postwar operations. *Counterinsurgency Field Manual*, p. xxxi; the original colorful phrase comes from John J. Yeosock, "What We Should Have Done Different," Part II of *In the Wake of the Storm: Gulf War Commanders Discuss Desert Storm* (Wheaton, IL: Cantigny First Division Foundation, 2000), p. 25.

275. Twenty-something Army and Marine captains . . . and feature seven-day workweeks. See Michael Kamber, "Sovereigns of All They're Assigned, Captains Have Many Missions to Oversee: Pressures Beset 'Fixers' of Iraq," *New York Times*, March 21, 2008; and Elizabeth Rubin, "Battle Company Is Out There," *New York Times Magazine*, February 24, 2008.

The Global Accelerant: The Privatization of American Foreign Policy

277. The Indian agency system . . . portions of its operations to religious charities. On this, see the article "Indian Agency System," at the Access Genealogy website, found online at www.accessgenealogy.com/native/tribes/history/agency_system.htm; and Yenne, *Indian Wars*, pp. 223–307.

277. For the U.S. Army, the Indian Wars . . . Geronimo in the American Southwest. On this subject in general, I found the best overall history to be Yenne, *Indian Wars*.

278. As Max Boot observes . . . similar experience back home in the Indian Wars. Boot, *Savage Wars*, p. 127.

278. Kellogg Brown & Root—whose previous incarnation . . . of the mid-1990s. See Robert Young Pelton, *Licensed to Kill: Hired Guns in the War on Terror* (New York: Crown Publishers, 2006), pp. 100–3.

278. Having achieved its initial fame by guarding . . . as one Blackwater executive puts it). See Pelton, *Licensed to Kill*, pp. 2–4, 36–41, and 284–87.

279. You'll also see the U.S. military letting its first LOGCAP . . . facilities overseas to KBR. See Pelton, *Licensed to Kill*, pp. 100–6 and 119–21.

279. By the time we reached the year 2000 . . . representing another 4 to 5 percent. For data, see Allison Stanger and Omnivore (graphic design firm), "Foreign Policy, Privatized," *New York Times*, October 5, 2008. See also Allison Stanger, *Empire of the Willing: Why Outsourcing Is the Future of American Foreign Policy—and Why We Have to Get It Right* (New York: Basic Books, 2009).

279. Moreover, as Galula noted, insurgencies tend . . . fluid in their ability to change tactics. Galula, *Counterinsurgency*, pp. 11–13.

280. While it's true that during the Cold War . . . catch up in economic development. See the 2008 estimate provided by Morgan Stanley, as reported in "Building BRICs of Growth: Record Spending on Infrastructure Will Help to Sustain Rapid Growth in Emerging Economies," *The Economist*, June 7, 2008. The estimate projects the following totals: $9.3T China, $2.8T India, $2.2T Russia, $1.1T Brazil, $2.4T other Asia, $0.9T Middle East, and $3.1T other.

The Inescapable Realignment: Reblending Diplomacy, Defense, and Development

281. President George W. Bush's 2002 National Security Strategy . . . preemptive war. "The National Security Strategy of the United States of America" (September 2007), found online at www.whitehouse.gov/nsc/nssall.html.

281. Taking that high-level cue . . . either the Afghanistan or the Iraq occupation. For an example, see Walid Maalouf, "Presentation, Before the US-Japan Cultural Program, USAID Visitor Center, August 26, 2004, found online at www.usaid.gov/about_usaid/presidential_initiative/diplomacy/sp082604.html.

281. Based on my interviews locally for a 2007 *Esquire* story . . . across the Horn of Africa.

This story was published as "The Americans Have Landed," *Esquire*, July 2007. It can be found online at www.esquire.com/features/africacommand0707.

281. General James Mattis had been arguing . . . popular support for an insurgency.
See the Mattis PowerPoint slide in the *Counterinsurgency Field Manual*, p. 149.

281. The COIN field manual, in arguing for an 80/20 blend . . . 80 percent political.
The COIN posits five essential "lines of operation": combat operations/civil security operations, host-nation security force development, providing essential services to the population, governance, and economic development. Thus only one of the five lines of operation is logically described as kinetic (combat operations/civil security operations). See the *Counterinsurgency Field Manual*, p. 156. See also the section on Mao (pp. 11–13).

281. As such, throughout the Iraq and Afghanistan occupations . . . each other seamlessly.
Again, the most important work in this regard is found in the Center for Strategic Studies and International Security/Brookings Institution joint task force, which produced the *Transforming Foreign Assistance for the 21st Century* report. Prominent security experts who've also proposed something similar (despite the titles imposed on their articles) include Robert Kaplan ("Send in the State Department," *New York Times*, February 21, 2006), and Max Boot ("Diplomacy for the Real World: Without Changes, the State Department Isn't Ready to Meet Today's Challenges," *Los Angeles Times*, February 22, 2006).

281. While most nongovernmental voices . . . style of operations found acceptable.
Again, this is basically the route taken by the HELP Commission in their *Beyond Assistance* report.

282. By most historians' judgment . . . counterinsurgency and in state-building.
See Boot, *Savage Wars*, pp. 99–128; and Robert D. Ramsey III, *Savage Wars of Peace: Case Studies of Pacification in the Philippines, 1900–1902* (Fort Leavenworth, KS: Combat Studies Institute Press Occasional Paper 24, 2007); and Lawrence A. Yates, *The U.S. Military's Experience in Stability Operations, 1789–2005* (Fort Leavenworth, KS: Combat Studies Institute Press Occasional Paper 15, 2006).

282. But here's where the "rise of the rest," as Zakaria calls it . . . to our advantage.
Zakaria, *Post-American World*, pp. 1–5.

283. The *Counterinsurgency Field Manual* . . . in any coordinated COIN campaign.
Counterinsurgency Field Manual, p. 63; the fourteen are State, USAID, CIA, Justice, DEA, Treasury, Homeland Security, Energy, Agriculture, Commerce, Transportation, Coast Guard, FBI, and Customs.

283. Legendary baseball manager Casey Stengel . . . from the guys who are undecided."
Listed at "Casey Stengel, The Official Site," found online at www.caseystengel.com/quotes_by.htm.

283. This is what Secretary . . . conventional wars to come—great-power wars.
Robert M. Gates, "Remarks to the Heritage Foundation," Colorado Springs, CO (May 13, 2008) available online at www.defenselink.mil/speeches/speech.aspx?speechid=1240.

283. Colonel John Nagl . . . mentoring and building up militaries in failed states.
See John Nagl, "A Battalion's Worth of Good Ideas," *New York Times*, April 2, 2008.

284. Interestingly enough, the "direct action" . . . of this growing responsibility.
See Sean D. Naylor, "Support Grows for Standing Up an Unconventional Warfare Command," *Armed Forces Journal*, November 2007.

284. Our troops in the field . . . defense budget that is higher than it has ever been!
For an example of how bad this was in Iraq, see John Files, "Reimbursement Program for Troops Stalls: Rules for Repaying Soldiers for Equipment Remain Unfinished After a Year," *New York Times*, October 3, 2005; and Major Paul Cucuzzella, USA, "Soldiers May be Reimbursed for Protective Gear: There Is No Need Anymore for Soldiers to

Purchase Protective Equipment on Their Own," ArmyStudyGuide.com, January 13, 2006, found online at www.armystudyguide.com/content/news/Top_Military_News/ soldiers-may-be-reimburse.shtml.

284. Run through the list of insurgent tactics in the COIN . . . sabotage, and seizure. *Counterinsurgency Field Manual*, pp. 115–17.

285. The harsh truth, as Barrett Tillman argues . . . aerial vehicles for real-time surveillance. Barrett Tillman, *What We Need: Extravagance and Shortages in America's Military* (St. Paul, MN: Zenith Press, 2007), pp. 17–218.

The Better Normal: The Command-After-Next
This section owes much to reporting I did in eastern Africa in the spring of 2007 for the *Esquire* article "The Americans Have Landed" (July 2007), found online at www .esquire.com/features/africacommand0707.

286. The recent rise of the Salafist Group for Preaching . . . confirm that judgment. For an example of its spread, see Michael Slackman, "In Algeria, a Tug of War for Young Minds," *New York Times*, June 23, 2008.

286. The task force did register one immediate big hit . . . right out of the movie *Syriana*. See Philip Smucker, "The Intrigue Behind the Drone Strike: Yemeni Official Says US Lacks Discretion as Antiterror Partner," *Christian Science Monitor*, November 12, 2002.

287. It will "reduce the future battlespace" that America . . . intention nor desire to own. "Reduce the battlespace" is the motto of Combined Joint Task Force–Horn of Africa.

289. This is an unprecedented development . . . operations in both Afghanistan and Iraq. For an example of the blowback, see Gordon Lubold, "Pentagon Scales Back AFRI- COM Ambitions," *Christian Science Monitor*, May 16, 2008.

289. To that end, SOUTHCOM already moves . . . commander structure of AFRICOM. An internal Southern Command briefing of early 2008 proposed a "new model" similar to that of Joint Interagency Task Force–South in Key West, but also replicated the AF- RICOM split deputy commander model, with the civilian to be a Department of State official.

289. That sort of vertical knowledge . . . is Colonel John Boyd's famous "OODA loop"). See Coram, *Boyd*, pp. 327–44.

289. But according to the new Army-Marine COIN . . . built up—not a loop to be rushed. *Counterinsurgency Field Manual*, p. 144.

290. Across the entirety of the Cold War . . . it has accumulated almost four dozen more. Find the list of sixty-three operations (as of June 2008) online at www.un.org/Depts/ dpko/list/list.pdf.

292. Eventually, Congress would grow so frustrated . . . conversation with this entity. As of September 2008, Congress was already expressing its frustration with AFRI- COM's proposed blend of diplomatic, defense, and developmental aid assets, threaten- ing to cut the command's budget deeply if the Secretary of Defense could not offer a better rationale for the command's structure, indicating a desire on the part of Con- gress to demilitarize the entity somewhat—not a bad instinct; see "Questions About Military's Role in Africa Spur Steep Africom Cuts," *Inside the Navy*, September 15, 2008.

CHAPTER 7. THE NETWORK REALIGNMENT:
THE RISE OF THE SYSADMIN-INDUSTRIAL COMPLEX

294. Vint Cerf, a universally acknowledged . . . uses it, and anybody can add services to it." Quoted in Tapscott and Williams, *Wikinomics*, pp. 273–74.

The Undeniable Trajectory: Superempower Me!

295. That's why, of all nations on this planet . . . we represent their most natural home. See Friedman, *Lexus and the Olive Tree*, pp. 29–42.

295. All politics begins with this question: Are man's paths to happiness singular or infinite?
Professor Stanley Hoffman's question to me during my oral examination (comprehensive) at Harvard University's Government Department in the spring of 1987. It is still burned into my memory!

296. For now, the reality is that globalization creates . . . inside too many "stationary states."
"Unreasonable men" comes from the writing of George Bernard Shaw; source is Wikiquote entry for Shaw, found online at en.wikiquote.org/wiki/George_Bernard_Shaw.

296. Invariably, too many experts today describe the world . . . haves versus have-nots.
On this point, see David Rothkopf, *Superclass: The Global Power Elite and the World They Are Making* (New York: Farrar, Straus & Giroux, 2008), especially his list of eight ways to know you're a member of the superclass, pp. 289–91.

296. We have no global leaders of note . . . overwhelmingly found in the global middle class.
Jeffrey D. Sachs, *Common Wealth: Economics for a Crowded Planet* (New York: Penguin Press, 2008).

297. More people work in small firms . . . the economy, either formally or informally.
On this see Daniel Pink, *Free Agent Nation: The Future of Working for Yourself* (New York: Warner Business, 2002).

297. At first, it seemed like only those who worked . . . David Rothkopf observes.
Quoted in Friedman, *The World Is Flat*, p. 278.

299. But that connectivity empowers in both directions . . . expectations are not met.
On this see Jena McGregor, "Consumer Vigilantes: Memo to Corporate America: Hell Now Hath No Fury Like a Customer Scorned," *BusinessWeek*, March 3, 2008.

299. Another time it's a rogue trader who . . . demands from angry shareholders.
See Doreen Carvajal and Caroline Brothers, " 'Rogue Trader' Is Remembered as Mr. Average: Unassuming Suspect in a $7 Billion Loss," *New York Times*, January 26, 2008.

299. Twenty years ago, official development . . . as much as the other two combined!
One recent estimate put official development aid at $106 billion for 2006, foreign direct investment at $167 billion, and remittances at $301 billion; see James Mehring and Laurel Daunis-Allen, "Robust Global Trade: A Virtuous Circle," *BusinessWeek*, November 12, 2007.

299. Befitting the frontier nature of this age . . . controlling roughly one-seventh of the flow.
See Jason DeParle, "A Western Union Empire Moves Migrant Cash Home," *New York Times*, November 22, 2007.

300. This same blogosphere . . . somehow do not measure up to expectations.
On this, see Brownstein, *Second Civil War*, pp. 327–38; Glenn Reynolds, *An Army of Davids: How Markets and Technology Empower Ordinary People to Beat Big Media, Big Government and Other Goliaths* (Nashville: Thomas Nelson, 2006), pp. 89–114; and Dan Gillmor, *We the Media: Grassroots Journalism by the People, for the People* (Sebastopol, CA: O'Reilly, 2004).

300. The real goal, as journalist James Fallows argues . . . from that of the real world out there.
James Fallows, " 'The Connection Has Been Reset': China's Great Firewall Is Crude, Slapdash, and Surprisingly Easy to Breach. Here's Why It's So Effective Anyway," *Atlantic Monthly*, March 2008.

301. Harry Emerson Fosdick, the early-twentieth-century . . . ordinary people."
Found online at en.wikiquote.org/wiki/Harry_Emerson_Fosdick.

301. Collectively, the West is a high-trust networked commonwealth.
This concept comes from Bennett, *Anglosphere Challenge*, pp. 39–40.

The American System Perturbed: The Rise of Global Guerrillas

303. By spreading our networks . . . parasites on these systems—as they have for ages.
On this subject, see Misha Glenny, *McMafia: A Journey Through the Global Criminal Underworld* (New York: Alfred A. Knopf, 2008), especially the chapter on China, pp. 313–41.

304. One of the first experts to attempt . . . many outweighs the dated knowledge of the few.
John Robb, *Brave New War: The Next Stage of Terrorism and the End of Globalization* (Hoboken, NJ: John Wiley & Sons, 2007), pp. 67–129.

304. The same Internet that allows . . . globalization's many extremist opponents.
Robb, *Brave New War*, pp. 117–19.

304. Analogizing the Iraq insurgency to the 1930s Spanish Civil War . . . perpetual failure.
Robb, *Brave New War*, pp. 47–49.

304. Robb warns, "This is the first time in modern history . . . fight a global war and win."
Robb, *Brave New War*, p. 19.

305. As for a far less robust but resource-rich Nigeria . . . the nation's oil industry.
For an example, see Steven Mufson, "Nigeria's Oil Morass: Shell Takes $716 Million Charge After Attacks," *Washington Post*, February 1, 2008.

305. Those failures inside the Gap . . . but trigger planetwide, winner-take-all effects.
Nassim Nicholas Taleb, *The Black Swan: The Impact of the Highly Improbable* (New York: Random House, 2007), pp. xxi–xxii.

306. History, Taleb reminds us, "does not crawl, it jumps."
Taleb, *Black Swan*, p. 10.

306. Our "stupid networks" . . . today have multiplied beyond measurability."
The concept of "stupid networks" comes from David Isenberg, "The Rise of the Stupid Network," *Computer Telephony*, August 1997, found online at isen.com/stupid.html; Taleb, *The Black Swan*, p. 61.

306. "The pull of the sensational," as Taleb puts it . . . any nation's informal economy.
Taleb, *The Black Swan*, pp. 79–80; and Robb, *Brave New War*, pp. 148–51.

307. The truth is, "al Qaeda central," as terrorism . . . global control element it once was.
See Marc Sageman, "The Next Generation of Terror," *Foreign Policy*, March–April 2008.

307. We can buy into al Qaeda's propaganda . . . but the conflict was never really about us.
The classic in this genre is Michael Scheuer, *Imperial Hubris: Why the West Is Losing the War on Terror* (Dulles, VA: Potomac Books, 2004).

307. Transnational terrorists and other criminal . . . least impressive and damaging.
As James Surowiecki, author of *The Wisdom of Crowds*, argues (p. 228), "Short selling isn't one of the great commercial evils of the day. The lack of short selling is."

308. As the French Enlightenment . . . served afterwards to solve other problems."
René Descartes, *Le Discours de la Méthode*, Part II (1637), as found at Wikiquote: en.wikiquote.org/wiki/Ren%C3%A9_Descartes.

The New Rules: From "Know Your Customer" to "Know Your Supply Chain"

308. The sum of these changes . . . the "four V's" of "modern interconnectedness."
Chanda, *Bound Together*, pp. 94 and 253.

310. Of course, all you have to do is go back . . . Core stalwarts like Japan and South Korea.
On this, see Stephen Mihm, *A Nation of Counterfeiters: Capitalists, Con Men, and the Making of the United States* (Cambridge, MA: Harvard University Press, 2007).

311. The average Chinese consumed 11 pounds of dairy . . . or the equivalent of 21 gallons.
See Chi-Chu Tschang, "Got Milk?," *BusinessWeek*, December 10, 2007.

311. A 2007 *New York Times* article . . . milk produced globally is traded across borders."
Wayne Arnold, "A Thirst for Milk Bred by New Wealth Sends Prices Soaring," *New York Times*, September 4, 2007.

312. China's meat consumption . . . higher than that of any other emerging market.
See "A Meatier Diet," *BusinessWeek*, November 6, 2007.

312. The upshot . . . "Saudi Arabia of milk," exports dairy products to China like crazy.
See Wayne Arnold, "Cultivating a Business: In New Zealand, Farmers Who Lost Subsidies Fine-Tune Their Trade," *New York Times*, August 2, 2007; and Patrick Barta, "'Saudi Arabia of Milk' Hits Production Limits: New Zealand Dairy Thirsts for Capital, a Big Issue in Food," *Wall Street Journal*, May 8, 2008.

312. By 2030, world food production is predicted to rise . . . just in the low-end foodstuffs.
Cited in "U.N.: 50 Percent More Food Needed by 2030; Global Summit Aims to Tackle Skyrocketing Prices Sparking Unrest," Associated Press, June 3, 2008.

313. Australian cattlemen already . . . track every cow from birth to death in this manner.
See Steve Stecklow, "U.S. Falls Behind in Tracking Cattle to Control Disease: USDA Plans Voluntary System After Cattlemen Divide on Making One Mandatory; Mad-Cow Mysteries," *Wall Street Journal*, June 21, 2006.

314. I say, don't be frightened or dismayed when Wal-Mart . . . into your system.
See Marcus Kabel, "Wal-Mart Recruits Intelligence Officers," Associated Press, April 24, 2008.

314. As Don Tapscott and Anthony Williams . . . production and buyer and even R&D chains.
Tapscott and Williams, *Wikinomics*, pp. 59–62.

314. The principles of "wikinomics" . . . (i.e., make globalization *truly* global!).
Tapscott and Williams, *Wikinomics*, pp. 20–30.

The New Normal: In Search of New Deterrence

316. The search for "Deterrence 2.0," as one . . . increasingly interconnected world."
Carl W. Hunt, "Promoting and Protecting US Interests in the Cyber World: Violent (and Non-Violent) Non-state Actors—Workshop Summary," Institute for Defense Analyses, January 9–10, 2008.

317. But all these responses seem so asymmetrical . . . William Easterly's terminology.
Easterly, *White Man's Burden*, pp. 3–7.

317. James Surowiecki, author of *The Wisdom of Crowds* . . . opinions efficiently.
Surowiecki, *Wisdom of Crowds*, p. 10.

318. My recent favorite nongovernmental . . . the secret and the unclassified.
See wikileaks.org/.

318. If working their hearts and minds online . . . less symbolic and more material.
Ori Brafman and Rod A. Beckstrom, *The Starfish and the Spider: The Unstoppable Power of Leaderless Organizations* (New York: Portfolio, 2006), p. 136.

319. As the columnist Brad Todd noted . . . an effective response within minutes.
Brad Todd, "109 Minutes," found online on westernphalanx.blogspot.com/2005/07/109-minutes.html; cited in Reynolds, *Army of Davids*, p. 69.

319. Today's globalization, as über-blogger Glenn Reynolds . . . once enjoyed in the past.
See Reynolds, *Army of Davids*, p. 139.

The Global Accelerant: The Great Globalization Build-out

321. Overall, emerging markets are expected . . . for over 40 percent of that stunning total.
See "Building BRICs of growth," *The Economist*, June 5, 2008.

321. By 2020, China will have roughly the same . . . almost doubling by 2020.
See "China's Infrastructure Splurge: Rushing On by Road, Rail and Air: China's Race to Build Roads, Railways and Airports Speeds Ahead," *The Economist*, February 16, 2008.

322. I mean, it's one thing for the UK's National Grid . . . extensive network of pipelines.
See "A Bear at the Throat: The European Union Is Belatedly Grasping the Riskiness of Its Dependence on Russian Gas, but It Is Disunited and Short of Ideas for How to Reduce It," *The Economist*, April 14, 2008; and Guy Chazan, "Gazprom Drills Deeper into Europe: U.K. Becomes Foothold in Entry to Consumer Market; Mistrust Lingers," *Wall Street Journal*, January 28, 2008.

322. The Gulf Cooperation Council countries . . . investment opportunities in the East.
See Khalaf, "Boomtime in Lands of Oil and Money."

323. For example, Hollywood markets . . . roughly half its box office registers overseas.
See Nic Hopkins, "Foreign Box Offices Contribute Most to Hollywood's Coffers," *The Times of London*, March 16, 2005.

323. Commensurately, when a Bollywood (Indian) . . . beachhead for its major stars.

See Eric Bellman, "Bollywood Dreams Benefit Both Parties: Deal for Dreamworks, a New Market Awaits; Passport for India Stars," *Wall Street Journal*, June 19, 2008.

325. Africa, home to about one-fifth of the world's uranium . . . in this direction.
   See Natalie Obiko Pearson, "African Nations Pin Power Hopes on Nuclear Energy: Western Interests Help Spur the Push to Develop Plants," *Wall Street Journal*, November 13, 2007.

325. This unfortunate sentiment creates strange bedfellows . . . third world crooks."
   Collier, *Bottom Billion*, p. 187.

The Inescapable Realignment: Reengineering Development (in-a-Box™)

332. I joined Enterra Solutions . . . and boosting local development as a by-product?
   For a generic, early description of this sort of port capabilities, see Brian Mockenhaupt, "The Age of Resilience: Or, How I Learned to Stop Worrying and Love Global Threats. Welcome to the Institute for Advanced Technologies in Global Resilience," *Esquire*, December 2006, where Stephen DeAngelis was named to the "Best and Brightest" list as an "inventor."

333. Otherwise, as Paul Collier notes, all you trigger is a brain drain.
   Collier, *Bottom Billion*, p. 112.

333. Development-in-a-Box is, in many ways . . . goal of "transaction governance capacity."
   See Prahalad, *Bottom of the Pyramid*, pp. 77–78.

337. For example, more than 1,400 . . . core and common to every global retail bank.
   This is according to one of the world's largest consultancies, Accenture, which, of course, has service products for each of those 1,400 processes.

338. For proving these concepts, Iraq was a pretty daunting environment.
   For some early coverage on our work there, see Linda Loyd, "Enterra Solutions Provides Technology to Iraq," *Philadelphia Inquirer*, March 7, 2008, found online at www.philly.com/philly/business/homepage/20080307_Enterra_Solutions_provides_technology_to_Iraq.html.

The Better Normal: The Rise of the SysAdmin-Industrial Complex

341. In March 2008, a collection of over fifty retired . . . capabilities that we have."
   See Dale Eisman, "Analysts Call for 'Soft Power' Tactics in Future Conflicts," *Virginian-Pilot*, March 19, 2008.

341. As respected defense analyst Chet Richards . . . poorly equipped militias."
   See Eisman, "Analysts Call for 'Soft Power' Tactics in Future Conflicts."

341. As one of my blog readers . . . be having about the American rebels in 1780."
   Found online at www.thomaspmbarnett.com/weblog/2008/03/long_war_soft_power.html#comment–453830.

343. Lockheed's purchase was a shot across the bow . . . manner of crucial network flows.
   See August Cole, "Lockheed Looks Beyond Weapons: Contractor Targets Growth with Services in Strife-Torn Areas," *Wall Street Journal*, September 24, 2007.

344. Because when the Bush administration's . . . pretty big hint of where victory lies."
   See John Hewko, "Mobilizing Aid for Trade," Latin America Panel, WTO General Council meeting, November 20, 2007.

347. As Harry told me for an article I wrote . . . This is the future."
   Thomas P. M. Barnett, "No. 40: Sea-Traffic Control," *Esquire*, October 2007, found online at www.esquire.com/features/esquire–100/seatraffic1007.

347. Then think about packaging all that up . . . SysAdmin-industrial Complex.
   I am indebted to Dan Abbott of tdaxp.com for mashing up my SysAdmin concept with the military-industrial complex to produce the idea of the SysAdmin-industrial complex.

347. Collectively, that effort . . . Ash Institute for Democratic Governance and Innovation.

See the institute's award website found online at ashinstitute.harvard.edu/corporate_site/innovations.

347. One of my favorite examples is an advertisement . . . simple: "Invest in Macedonia." Find it online at www.investinmacedonia.com/.

349. But if that's your take . . . updated version of imperial Japan's "Co-Prosperity Sphere." For a glimpse, see Khanna, *Second World*, pp. 278–91.

CHAPTER 8. THE STRATEGIC REALIGNMENT: RESURRECTING THE PROGRESSIVE AGENDA

The Undeniable Trajectory: The Devil We Knew

352. Cultural critic Susan Faludi's 2007 book . . . too Oprah-ish, too emasculated. See Susan Faludi, *The Terror Dream: Fear and Fantasy in Post–9/11 America* (New York: Metropolitan Books, 2007), pp. 1–88 and 116–64.

353. In his polemic *The Enemy at Home* . . . attacks from Islamic fundamentalists. Dinesh D'Souza, *The Enemy at Home: The Cultural Left and Its Responsibility for 9/11* (New York: Doubleday, 2007).

353. Delving deeper into the American psyche . . . hostage-taking "savages," is no myth. See Faludi, *The Terror Dream*, pp. 199–216 and 241–86.

354. But when you read Faludi's . . . die in combat while *serving in* the U.S. military. Faludi, *The Terror Dream*, pp. 165–95.

354. As Faludi concedes, much of this retraditionalization . . . irony were greatly exaggerated. Faludi, *The Terror Dream*, pp. 142–64 and 287–96.

354. Within five years, we had processed . . . the CW network's *Aliens in America*. See Christopher Mason, "Little Sensitivity Lesson on the Prairie: A Canadian Sitcom Pokes Fun at Muslim Stereotypes," *New York Times*, January 16, 2007; and Bill Keveney, "*Aliens* Shows Its Serious Side: Muslim Character Seen as Positive Influence," *USA Today*, October 1, 2007.

355. As always, given our uniquely synthetic . . . such religions as "children of Abraham." See Prothero, *Religious Literacy*, p. 155.

355. The attacks of 9/11 were a classic case of "chosen trauma" . . . these events. On this concept, my thanks to Richard Landes, Boston University.

356. We "contaminate" the Arab world . . . while the locals assume infinite time. On this subject, see director Ric Burns's fantastic documentary, *The Way West: How the West Was Lost & Won, 1845–1893* (1995), and Margaret Walsh, *The American West: Visions and Revisions* (Cambridge: Cambridge University Press, 2005).

356. Just as in our wars of today, America's . . . seventh-century pre-economic paradise. See Yenne, *Indian Wars*, pp. 109–299.

The American System Perturbed: Katrina and the Gore Counternarrative

357. If they had, as General David Petraeus told me . . . completely sealed their pessimism. December 8, 2005, interview for Barnett, "Monks of War."

358. According to former General Electric CEO Jack Welch . . . push to fix real problems. Jack Welch, "The Five Stages of Crisis-Management: After Katrina—and a Hurricane of Debate—a Well-Worn Pattern Emerges," *Wall Street Journal*, September 14, 2005.

358. Over 1,800 people had been killed . . . government donations from all over the world. See Blaine Harden and Shankar Vedantam, "Many Displaced by Katrina Turn to Relatives for Shelter," *Washington Post*, September 8, 2005; Savage, *Takeover*, pp. 262–63, and 317–18; and Rick Jervis, "New Orleans May Have Hit a Plateau," *USA Today*, August 4, 2008.

359. Mexican troops, providing emergency aid . . . for the first time since 1846. See "Mexican Troops Aid Katrina Efforts," Associated Press, September 8, 2005.

359. Wal-Mart's network prowess was . . . demand for recovery would be substantial.
    See Colby Bosh, "In Wal-Mart We Trust," *National Post*, March 28, 2008; and Del
    Jones, "Next Time: Companies Are Pleased with Their Responses to Hurricane
    Katrina, but the Disaster Has Some Re-examining Their Plans," *USA Today*, Octo-
    ber 4, 2005.

359. Erik Prince's Blackwater . . . services aimed at domestic disaster operations.
    June 2, 2006 interview with Erik Prince, Moyock, North Carolina.

359. But the aspect of Katrina . . . Diamond's bestselling book of the same name.
    For Diamond's own postmortem, see Beata Mostafavi, "Pulitzer Prize–Winning Author,
    Jared Diamond, Has Warning for America During His Speech at Mott Community
    College in Flint," *Flint Journal*, April 18, 2008.

360. Enter Al Gore, the perfect vessel . . . to President Bush's "global war on terror."
    See Al Gore, *An Inconvenient Truth* (New York: Rodale Books, 2006).

361. As part of this project on globalization's future . . . arising from Asia's rapid development.
    Find the planning document and results of this exercise on my website: www
    .thomaspmbarnett.com/projects/newrulesset/nrs_index.html

362. Three years later, Danish economist Bjørn Lomborg . . . Nobel Prize–winning experts.
    See Bjørn Lomborg, editor, *Global Crises, Global Solutions* (New York: Cambridge Uni-
    versity Press, 2004), pp. 1–9.

362. Lomborg later repeated the exercise . . . youth representatives from across the planet.
    See Bjørn Lomborg, *Cool It: The Skeptical Environmentalist's Guide to Global Warming*
    (New York: Alfred A. Knopf, 2007), pp. 44–46.

363. I would love to see humanity focus . . . Gap "colonialists"—the Chinese.
    My thanks to Matthew Garcia, NASA, for the "blue revolution" concept. On the Chi-
    nese, see "The New Colonialists: China's Hunger for Natural Resources Is Causing
    More Problems at Home Than Abroad," *The Economist*, March 15, 2008.

364. As Lomborg argues . . . of life and the environment" for future generations.
    Lomborg, *Cool It*, p. 9.

365. Human history . . . in hot climes than keep them warm in cold ones.
    Lomborg, *Cool It*, pp. 13–19.

365. By 2100, average personal incomes . . . that equates to $27,000 today.
    Lomborg, *Cool It*, pp. 47–48.

365. What we know from human history . . . you get per capita income above $3,000.
    Barnett, *Pentagon's New Map*, p. 239.

365. We also know that as incomes rise . . . and move toward political pluralism.
    See Yale University's Environmental Performance Index, found online at
    epi.yale.edu/Home.

365. Indeed, as Fareed Zakaria argues, democracies . . . slide back toward authoritarianism.
    Zakaria, *Future of Freedom*, p. 70.

365. Sadly, the only sheer limit we can cite . . . seems to top out at roughly $20,000 per capita.
    Gregory Clark, *A Farewell to Alms: A Brief Economic History of the World* (Princeton, NJ:
    Princeton University Press, 2007), p. 375.

365. Major urban areas, as Lomborg notes . . . still die from the cold than from the heat!
    Lomborg, *Cool It*, pp. 20–21.

365. Whether you're talking rising sea levels . . . "CO_2 knob" down as far as possible.
    Lomborg, *Cool It*, p. 41.

366. Lomborg sums up . . . with climate policies and a lot more with social policies."
    Lomborg, *Cool It*, p. 113.

366. My favorite recent example was the horrors of Darfur . . . blamed on global warming.
    See Ban Ki Moon (United Nations Secretary-General), "A Climate Culprit in Darfur,"
    Washington Post, June 16, 2007.

The New Rules: From "United We Stand" to Demographic Demagoguery

370. By 2025, rapidly aging Europe . . . the United States and its historical Western allies."
See Nicholas Eberstadt, "America the Fertile," *Washington Post*, May 6, 2007.

370. Between them, China and India have placed . . . well connected politically.
See Chanda, *Bound Together*, p. 169.

371. Europe's challenge is to facilitate . . . ran for parliamentary seats in record numbers.
See Molly Moore, "New French Political Cry: Liberté, Egalité, Diversité: Minorities Run for Parliament in Record Numbers," *Washington Post*, June 10, 2007.

371. For every frightened pundit (see Mark Steyn's . . . and southward in coming decades.
See Mark Steyn, *America Alone: The End of the World as We Know It* (Washington, DC: Regnery, 2006); and Khanna, *Second World*, pp. 3–9, 36–46, and 60–61.

371. Some will argue that Europe . . . hardly the end of the world as we know it.
See Elisabeth Rosenthal, "European Union's Plunging Birthrates Spread Eastward," *New York Times*, September 4, 2006.

371. In fact, Spain's recent "open border" . . . globalization's stagnant backwaters.
See "Spain: Immigrants Welcome; How Spain's Open-Border Policy Is Driving an Economic and Social Revival," *BusinessWeek*, May 21, 2007.

372. Between 1978 and 2002 . . . for every decade they remained in the country.
See "French Lessons: How to Create a Muslim Underclass," *Wall Street Journal*, November 11, 2005.

372. The same financial . . . home buyers in America over the next two decades.
See Haya El Nasser, "Analysis Finds Boom in Hispanics' Home Buying: Low Interest Rates, Flexible Loan Rules Contribute to Spike," *USA Today*, May 11, 2006.

372. Only 40 percent of Mexican immigrants . . . Hispanics do the same.
See "Of Meat, Mexicans and Social Mobility: Among the Very Poor, the American Dream Is Alive and Well," *The Economist*, June 17, 2006; and Linda Chavez, "The Great Assimilation Machine," *Wall Street Journal*, June 5, 2007.

373. Immigrant Latinos open new businesses at a rate three times the national norm.
"Of Meat, Mexicans and Social Mobility," *The Economist*.

373. They're also replenishing the ranks . . . economy's skyrocketing demand for food.
See Frederick Kunkle, "The Changing Face of Farm Labor: Frederick Dairy Reflects Growing Importance of Latino Immigrants," *Washington Post*, September 15, 2005.

373. If you're a Boomer heading . . . same schooling as their white counterparts.
See Miriam Jordan, "Boomers' Good Life Tied to Better Life for Immigrants," *Wall Street Journal*, May 7, 2007.

373. Hell, if serving in our military gets you . . . equally utilitarian golden ticket.
See Thomas L. Friedman, "Laughing and Crying," *New York Times*, May 23, 2007.

373. As Michael Barone points out . . . the flow diminished spectacularly.
Michael Barone, "The Newest Americans," *Wall Street Journal*, April 11, 2006.

374. So the answer isn't building a bigger wall . . . Berlin Wall across its entire history.
See Chanda, *Bound Together*, p. 213.

The New Normal: Apocalypse Soon

377. A good example is the theory of "peak oil."
The article that started it all is M. K. Hubbert, "Nuclear Energy and the Fossil Fuels," presented before the Spring Meeting of the Southern District, American Petroleum Institute, Plaza Hotel, San Antonio, Texas, March 7–9, 1956.

378. Cambridge Energy Research Associates . . . requirements notwithstanding.
See Cambridge Energy Resource Associates, "Why the 'Peak Oil' Theory Falls Down—Myths, Legends, and the Future of Oil Resources," November 10, 2006, found online at cera.ecnext.com/coms2/summary_0236-821_ITM.

378. Probably the strongest recent . . . America"—italics and exclamation points *included*!
Friedman, *Hot, Flat, and Crowded*, p. 9.

380. At the Cold War's end, Asia . . . global demand center, dislodging North America.
See data from the U.S. Department of Energy's *International Energy Outlook 2006* report (the 2007 report did not include a chart on global oil trade), found online at www.eia.doe.gov/oiaf/archive/ieo06/pdf/tbl4.pdf.

380. Indonesia became a net importer . . . oil company to foreign direct investment.
See Peter Millard and David Luhnow, "Crunch Time for Mexican Oil: Political Will Lacking for Production Overhaul as Output Tumbles," *Wall Street Journal*, February 15, 2008.

380. His latest scheme involves Venezuela's . . . import foodstuffs currently in short supply.
See Simon Romero, "Venezuela's Gas Prices Remain Low, but the Political Costs May Be Rising," *Wall Street Journal*, October 30, 2007.

380. Because the NOCs own roughly 90 percent . . . to finance these on their own.
See Guy Chazan and Russell Gold, "Big Oil's Not-So-Big Growth Plans: With New Reserves Harder to Snag, Western Firms Could Opt for Smaller Role," *Wall Street Journal*, January 31, 2008.

381. When Chevron . . . went from 65,000 barrels a day to over 200,000.
Jad Mouawad, "Oil Innovations Pump New Life into Old Wells," *New York Times*, March 5, 2008.

382. Simply put, it's hard to imagine Asia quadrupling . . . even if it could import enough oil.
See Gordon Fairclough and Shai Oster, "As China's Auto Market Booms, Leaders Clash over Heavy Toll: Vehicles Foul Air, Jam Streets but Plump Local Coffers; Restrictions Remain Few," *Wall Street Journal*, June 13, 2006.

382. The world took over a century to field its first billion cars . . . existing oil fields.
Iain Carson and Vijay V. Vaitheeswaran, *Zoom: The Global Race to Fuel the Car of the Future* (New York: Twelve, 2007), p. 197.

382. Other experts take a more optimistic tack . . . fuel-cell ultralights (got that?).
Amory Lovins et al., *Winning the Oil Endgame: Innovation for Profits, Jobs, and Security* (Snowmass, CO: Rocky Mountain Institute, 2007), p. 241.

382. As automotive visionary . . . oil use is inevitable; the only question is how fast."
Lovins et al., *Winning the Oil Endgame*, p. 228.

383. Lovins notes that most shifts "down" . . . but hardly disappearing altogether.
Lovins et al., *Winning the Oil Endgame*, p. 229.

383. Lovins thinks it will happen in roughly half that time, or by 2030.
Lovins et al., *Winning the Oil Endgame*, p. 229.

383. As noted Chinese expert Elizabeth Economy . . . the biodiversity of the country."
Elizabeth C. Economy, *The River Runs Black: The Environmental Challenge to China's Future* (Ithaca, NY: Cornell University Press, 2004), p. 28.

384. As it is, the Chinese Communist Party . . . focused on protecting the environment.
Economy, *River Runs Black*, p. 130.

384. In general, Economy finds . . . so long as access to new technology is facilitated.
Economy, *River Runs Black*, p. 16.

385. Already, we can see a serious "green awakening" . . . seniormost leadership.
See "Visions of Ecopolis: China Has Ambitious Plans to Build a Model 'Eco-City' Near Shanghai. How Green Will It Be?" *The Economist*, September 23, 2006; Jane Spencer, "How Weak Pollution Controls May Be Causing a Drag on China's Economic Growth," *Wall Street Journal*, October 2, 2006; Ariana Eunjung Cha, "In China, a Green Awakening: City Clamps Down on the Polluting Factories That Built Its Economy," *Washington Post*, October 6, 2007; and Jen Phillips, "China's Green Movement," *Mother Jones*, December 11, 2007.

385. As a recent World Bank study pointed out . . . the least amount of corruption.
See David Dollar, "China's Golden Cities," *Newsweek*, July 10, 2006.

385. When the first oil shocks struck in the 1970s . . . was not surpassed until 1989.
See the chart, Lovins et al., *Winning the Oil Endgame*, p. 15.

386. Lovins himself likes to point out . . . moving the car's occupants forward.
Cited in Carson and Vaitheeswaran, *Zoom*, p. 37.

The Global Accelerant: The Greatest Awakening

387. Worse, abundance allows for "chosen families" . . . iron logic of "given families."
See Dough Muder, "Red Family, Blue Family," February 2005, found online at www
.gurus.com/dougdeb/politics/209.html.
390. Religion, at its core . . . to the needs of the people *in their time*.
For a fascinating exploration of this function in early Christianity, see Daniel H. Abbott, *Revolutionary Strategies in Early Christianity* (Ann Arbor, MI: Nimble Books LLC,
2008).
391. America's Second Great Awakening . . . revivalism with those of republicanism."
Prothero, *Religious Literacy*, pp. 89–90.
391. By that, Prothero means that evangelical . . . influx of the Roman Catholic Irish).
Prothero, *Religious Literacy*, p. 70.
391. This is the essential compromise . . . and Jesus the Messiah, respectively).
See Mark Lilla, *The Stillborn God: Religion, Politics and the Modern West* (New York: Alfred A. Knopf, 2007), p. 30.
391. In this sense, Prothero argues . . . supremacy and granting all freedom of operation.
Prothero, *Religious Literacy*, p. 25.
392. A good New Core country . . . and increasingly from the Gap to the Core.
See Kevin Sullivan, "Foreign Missionaries Find Fertile Ground in Europe: Singaporean
Pastor Fires Up Staid Danes," *Washington Post*, June 11, 2007; and Leslie Hook, "Further Fervor: Missionaries Go from East to West," *Wall Street Journal*, August 3, 2007.
395. As French Islamic expert Olivier Roy . . . within globalization as a whole.
Olivier Roy (translated by George Holoch), *Secularism Confronts Islam* (New York:
Columbia University Press, 2007), pp. vii–xiii and 73–77.
395. Again, America represents the leading edge . . . same faith his entire life—to date).
See Michelle Boorsteing and Jacqueline L. Salmon, "In Major Poll, U.S. Religious Identity Appears Very Slippery," *Washington Post*, February 26, 2008.
396. According to Roy, it is . . . and (5) highly communitarian by choice instead of
heritage.
Roy, *Secularism Confronts Islam*, p. 69.

The Inescapable Realignment: Resurrecting the Progressive Agenda

397. By doing so, America has made possible . . . for the first time in human history.
See Clark, *Farewell to Alms*, pp. 1–16.
398. But here's the trick: As long as man stayed Malthusian . . . *A Farewell to Alms*.
Clark, *Farewell to Alms*, pp. 19–39.
398. By 2020, the global middle class should . . . (a tenfold increase in a generation's time).
See Naim, "Can the World Afford a Middle Class?"
400. In that process of network . . . wrung out of the system.
In many ways, this is the "green revolution" that Thomas Friedman now craves for the
United States in its global leadership role in this worldwide era of frontier integration;
see his *Hot, Flat, and Crowded*, pp. 170–99.

The consumption shift

400. Right now the advanced Old Core West . . . 32 times higher than the rest of the
world.
See Jared Diamond, "What's Your Consumption Factor?" *New York Times*, January 2, 2007.
400. As Jared Diamond . . . "living standards are not tightly coupled to consumption rates."
Diamond, "What's Your Consumption Factor?"

401. So, as Jeffrey Sachs argues . . . a condition he dubs "globalization without trust."
     Sachs, *Common Wealth*, p. 7.

The food and water shift
401. Here's the lay of the land when it comes . . . sub-Saharan Africa at 17, and Europe
     at 12.
     See Anthony Faiola, "The Economics of Hunger: A Brutal Convergence of Events Has
     Hit an Unprepared Global Market," *Washington Post*, April 27, 2008.
401. The Middle East imports just over three-quarters . . . imports half that percentage.
     See Anthony Faiola, "In Mauritania, Every Meal Becomes a Sacrifice," *Washington Post*,
     April 28, 2008.
402. Basically, the tech-rich regions that are net . . . will do decidedly worse—save Europe.
     See Lomborg, *Cool It* (New York: Alfred A. Knopf, 2007), pp. 103–5.
402. This is why farmers in the Dakotas . . . advanced agricultural system.
     See John W. Miller, "In Ukraine, Mavericks Gamble on Scarce Land," *Wall Street Jour-
     nal*, May 12, 2008, and Andrew E. Kramer, "Russia's Lazy Collective Farms Are a Hot
     Capitalist Property," *New York Times*, August 31, 2008.
402. It is also why the Chinese government . . . foreign lands with nobody noticing.
     See Jamil Anderlini, "Beijing Looks at Foreign Fields in Push to Guarantee Food Sup-
     plies: China Losing Its Ability to Be Self-Sufficient," *Financial Times*, May 9, 2008; and
     Meena Janardhan, "Gulf Eyes Oil-for-Food Pacts," *Asian Times*, June 20, 2008.
402. Good luck with that transparent strategy . . . can rise to as high as four-fifths.
     See Faiola, "Economics of Hunger" and "Every Meal Becomes a Sacrifice."
402. Today, only a small fraction of worldwide . . . 7 percent of rice and 12 percent of corn.
     See Faiola, "Economics of Hunger."

The transportation shift
403. As Iain Carson and Vijay V. Vaitheeswaran . . . threshold of economic pain has
     lowered.
     Carson and Vaitheeswaran, *Zoom*, pp. 1 and 10.
403. Because China will soon become . . . to make Asia their future global center of R&D.
     See Gordon Fairclough, "Bill Ford Jr.: For Auto Makers, China Is the New Frontier,"
     Wall Street Journal, October 27, 2006; Keith Bradsher, "China's Automakers,
     With Beijing's Prodding, Show Alternative-Fuel Cars: An Unexpected Array of
     Hybrids as Well as Hydrogen Power," *New York Times*, April 21, 2007; Amy Chozick,
     "Japan's Auto Giants Steer Toward China: Toyota, Nissan, Honda Refocus Their
     Efforts as U.S. Demand Slows," *Wall Street Journal*, May 16, 2007; Fairclough, "China
     Is Becoming Chrysler's Test Track for Growth," *Wall Street Journal*, August 20, 2007;
     and Rebecca Blumenstein, "GM to Invest in Green Technology in China: Move
     Shows How Important Nation Is to the Auto Industry," *Wall Street Journal*, Octo-
     ber 30, 2007.

The energy shift
404. So one of the key items . . . generation of electricity across the planet.
     For a nonideological take on nuclear power's future promise, see Gwyneth Cravens,
     Power to Save the World: The Truth About Nuclear Energy (New York: Alfred A. Knopf,
     2007).

The communications shift
405. The first billion users of Internet and wireless . . . New Core and Gap markets.
     On this, see Michael S. Malone, "Taking On the World," *Wall Street Journal*,
     April 5–6, 2008.

405. The key goal for America . . . lot of people will be able to live and work anywhere.
      On this, see Andreas Kluth, "Nomads: A Special Report on Mobile Telecoms," *The Economist*, April 12, 2008.

The urbanization shift
406. The planet as a whole has just reached . . . vast majority of the world's network traffic.
      On this, see Amy Meyers Jaffe, "The Coastal-Cities Phenomenon," *Esquire*, October 2006.

The feminization shift
407. This emerging market trend . . . in advanced economies.
      Chart: "Balancing the Scales of Justice: More Women Are Attending U.S. Law Schools," *USA Today*, June 27, 2008.

The health shift
408. This could be a source of great political . . . they nor their governments can afford."
      Robert J. Shapiro, *Futurecast: How Superpowers, Populations, and Globalization Will Change the Way You Live and Work* (New York: St. Martin's Press, 2008), pp. 247–66.

The market shift
409. They see four strategies as paramount . . . in natural resources ("natural capital").
      See Paul Hawken, Amory Lovins, and L. Hunter Lovins, *Natural Capitalism: Creating the Next Industrial Revolution* (Boston: Little, Brown, 1999), pp. 1–21.

The governance shift
409. The political scientist Francis Fukuyama divides . . . the strength of their power.
      Francis Fukuyama, *State-Building: Governance and World Order in the 21st Century* (Ithaca, NY: Cornell University Press, 2004), pp. 15–16.
410. The new emerging consensus . . . overall culture of respect for legality.
      See "Order in the Jungle: The Rule of Law Has Become a Big Idea in Economics. But It Has Had Its Difficulties," *The Economist*, March 15, 2008.
410. One crucial caveat here . . . to influence this global debate is slowly diminishing.
      See Adam Liptak, "U.S. Court, a Longtime Beacon, Is Now Guiding Fewer Nations," *New York Times*, September 18, 2008.

The Better Normal: The Great Compromise
414. If you accept this minimal rule set . . . in defense of these proposed global rules.
      My thanks to Jerome E. Barnett for this concept.
414. In sum, we won't use force unless . . . employment—as in, *every round fired*.
      For an example of what this must ultimately resemble down the road, see Al Baker, "11 Years of Police Gunfire, in Painstaking Detail," *New York Times*, May 8, 2008.

CODA: THE FUTURE PERFECT TENSE
417. Richard Nixon believed that nations aspiring to great power . . . great ideas.
      Nixon said this to Kissinger in a phone conversation on May 11, 1969, according to David S. Patterson, editor, *Foreign Relations, 1969–1976: Volume I, Foundations of Foreign Policy, 1969–1972* (Washington, DC: Government Printing Office, 2003), p. 142; cited in MacMillan, *Nixon and Mao*, p. 10.
419. The critical-mass reality . . . most assuredly we shall all hang separately."
      Attributed to Franklin at the signing of the Declaration of Independence.
420. Karl Marx believed that . . . a notion he himself proved.
      As Marx argued in the preface to his 1859 book, *A Contribution to the Critique of Politi-*

cal Economy, "The mode of production of material life conditions the general process of social, political and intellectual life," and thus "It is not the consciousness of men that determines their existence, but their social existence that determines their consciousness"; find the preface online at www.marxists.org/archive/marx/works/1859/critique-pol-economy/preface.htm.

421. Which brings me to . . . *The Shape of Things to Come.*
    H. G. Wells, *The Shape of Things to Come* (New York: Penguin Books, 2005).

Index